Clerical

Peter L. Agnew

Professor of Business Education and
Vice President for Business Affairs
New York University

James R. Meehan

Professor of Business Education and
Dean of Administration
Hunter College
of the City University of New York

William R. Pasewark

Head, Business Education Department
Texas Technological College

Office Practice

Fourth Edition

published by South-Western Publishing Company
Cincinnati • Chicago • Burlingame, Calif. • Dallas • New Rochelle, N.Y.

Preface

Office practice and procedures are constantly chang-
ing. In this fourth edition of CLERICAL OFFICE PRACTICE, an attempt
has been made to update all the materials presented in the previous edition and
to bring into proper focus the training of the prospective clerical worker for
initial employment in the modern office.

With automation frequently in the foreground regard-
ing office work, it is essential that any book on clerical office practice take
cognizance of the fact that automation is part of the business world and yet
recognize that a number of clerical procedures have not been automated, at least
not in the medium- or small-size concerns; and that vast numbers of young
people will be employed in the foreseeable future at office tasks that require skill
in the operation and understanding of currently used procedures.

Students of CLERICAL OFFICE PRACTICE should be prepared for immediate employment. This means that they must master certain office procedures and techniques while at the same time they review the understandings and skills previously learned. All of these must be carefully melded with the proper development of skills that are most likely to help a young person succeed on the job.

In addition to preparing students for clerical employment, this textbook endeavors to qualify prospective office workers for promotion to more responsible positions.

In preparing this edition of CLERICAL OFFICE PRACTICE, the authors have made every effort to retain the valuable features of the previous edition and yet freshen up the content by providing a carefully refined and improved presentation of the basic subject matter. The content is based on continued study and research in the field of clerical office practice and has taken into consideration state and city courses of study that are available in this field.

The "you" approach has been emphasized throughout this edition. Every effort has been made to have the material personalized and well within the range of the student taking this course. Materials in the book have been updated with special emphasis on the phases of office work that have been changing. These include changes that have been brought about in various types of office machines, especially in the field of adding, calculating, and reproduction; and, of course, the many changes that are taking place due to the introduction of data processing equipment. The materials in the textbook have been organized into short, teachable assignments arranged in logical sequence. These units have, however, been designed so that they are flexible and enable the teacher to start at any point in the book. The material at the end of each part has been carefully restudied and includes:

a. Study Questions — A series of questions that should be easily answered by the student who has carefully studied the text material.

b. What Do You Think? — Thought-provoking questions that should lead to stimulating discussions.

c. Your Personal Qualities — Case problems designed to improve personal qualities and work habits.

d. How's Your English? — Exercises that provide much-needed review of the language arts.

e. Office Work — Practical office projects for which special forms are not necessarily needed.

f. Office Work Assignments — Exercises that present the student with typical office situations. Although not necessary for the completion of these work assignments, stationery and business forms that provide for realistic practice are available in a correlated workbook, which has also been carefully updated.

The authors are indebted to numerous businessmen, secretaries, teachers, and students whose suggestions have contributed to the improvement of this book. We especially want to express our appreciation to Lois Corbeil, A. B. Dick Company; Leta J. Stroben, Shaw-Walker Company; Rosemary Houlihan, New York Telephone Company; Philip Pepe, Remington Rand Division of the Sperry Rand Corporation; L. Millard Collins, International Business Machines Corporation; Margaret O'Shea Kane and Mary Emily Little, Hunter College; Isabelle A. Krey, Bronx Community College; Frances M. Alagna, John E. Clewis, Ronald Coster, Ray F. Smith, Jr., and Joseph P. Whiteside, New York University; Julio Torres, Lawrence Wakefield, Inc.; Nadine Golladay Simmons, Public Information Supervisor, American Telephone and Telegraph Company; Dr. Wayne J. Holman, Jr., Robert Gamgort, and William F. O'Brien, Johnson & Johnson; and E. Dolores Kilchenstein, Texas Technological College.

PLA/JRM/WRP

Contents

Unit 1. The Office Worker

Unit 2. Business Forms

Unit 3. Purchasing and Selling

Unit 4. Inventory and the Stock Room

Unit 5. Processing Data

Unit 6. Mail and Telegrams

Unit 7. The Telephone

Unit 8. The Receptionist

UNIT 1 | The Office Worker

PART 1

Your Career as an Office Worker

Who is the first person you meet when you enter a business office? The receptionist. Who is the first person you speak to on the telephone? Usually, the switchboard operator. Who looks up that bill about which you are inquiring, the order you sent in last week, the contract to which you are referring? The file clerk. When a report has been carefully composed and edited, it is written in final form by the typist. The messenger may be the difference between that report's getting to the president's desk early enough for him to give it his attention that day or not. The giant data processing machines await the information which the tabulating machine operator feeds into the computer before it can produce the answers by which management can function. Even the simple supplies — letterheads, envelopes, carbon paper, ribbons, duplicating paper — without which that office would stop short are inventoried and kept constant by the storekeeper. No business can run smoothly without the services of the office workers. Is it any wonder that they are in great demand?

The Business Office. The office is the nerve center of any business. Here the long-range policies of the board of directors and the officers of the firm are formulated and, based upon these policies, the day-to-day operations of the business are directed. Here the records of business are installed, maintained, and filed so that all information required for efficient management is readily available. All business firms, even the smallest ones, must keep more and better records than ever before if they are to arrive at correct decisions and survive in this era of intense competition. In addition, an ever-increasing number of records and reports must be submitted periodically to governmental agencies at all levels to comply with their regulations.

The office is also the communications center of any business. Here written communications in a great variety of forms which include letters, order forms, memorandums, and telegrams are received, recorded, processed, filed, and dispatched. Oral communications, mainly in the form of telephone calls, are constantly being received and placed during regular business hours. The figures of business, in the form of handwritten and typewritten reports, orders and vouchers, receipts and payments, punched cards and paper tape, and in many other forms, move through the office where they are verified, classified, calculated, recorded, and summarized.

Job Opportunities. At the present time slightly more than 11 million men and women, or one of every seven employed persons, work in an office. The number of employment opportunities for office workers is exceeded only by the number in the production phase of industry. The United States Department of Labor forecasts that there will be a total labor force of 90 million in 1970 and that one of every three employed persons will be a woman. By that time it is estimated that 20 percent of the entire labor force will be office workers. In other words, one of every five employed persons will then be engaged in office work.

The Large Office. The job opportunities for office workers in the larger offices cover a very wide range of interests and abilities. The current *Clerical Job Evaluation* guide of the Administrative Management Society, an international office management organization, lists 32 typical office positions available in large offices. The positions are listed in five major areas of office work:

    I. Accounting and Related Areas
        A. Account-Classification Clerk
        B. Accounting Clerk
        C. Billing Checker or Invoice Checker
        D. Senior Bookkeeper
        E. Junior Bookkeeper
        F. Cashier or Teller
        G. Cost Clerk
        H. Invoice Audit Clerk
        I. Payroll Clerk
        J. Audit Clerk

    II. Business Machine Operations
        A. Accounting Machine Operator
        B. Calculating Machine Operator
        C. Duplicating Machine Operator
        D. Key-Punch Operator
        E. Tabulating Machine Operator

    III. General Clerical Area
        A. Senior General Clerk
        B. Intermediate General Clerk
        C. Junior General Clerk
        D. Beginning General Clerk

IV. Office Services Area
    A. File Clerk
    B. Mail Clerk
    C. Messenger
    D. Receptionist
    E. Storekeeper
    F. Telephone Operator

V. Stenographic Area
    A. Clerk-Typist
    B. Secretary
    C. Stenographer
    D. Tabular Typist
    E. Transcribing Machine Operator
    F. Typist
    G. Teletype Operator

Approximately 50 percent of all office positions are classified as clerical positions; the highest single percentage, one in every seven office positions, is held by a general clerk. The tasks of general clerks become highly specialized in large offices, although they all tend to work with business records, reports, and files and use telephones, typewriters, and desk calculators. A high percentage of clerical positions in large offices are also held by file clerks, clerk-typists, accounting clerks, and mail clerks.

The Small Office. The inexperienced office worker often chooses to begin in a small, one-girl office in her neighborhood. All duties fall to her. She is a combination receptionist, typist, bookkeeper, and file clerk — the typical "girl Friday." She may place orders for merchandise, prepare sales invoices, keep the checkbook, and perform several other office tasks in the course of a single week. If two people are employed in an office, they tend to divide the stenographic and clerical tasks. One usually takes dictation, transcribes letters, types business papers, files the correspondence, and performs other stenographic duties, while the other keeps the records and accounts, handles the receipts and payments, and performs other related accounting and clerical tasks.

The average firm employs seven office workers, and all seven perform many different office tasks. As a prospective employee, you will be best equipped to enter the typical office if you possess a wide range of office knowledges and skills. Thus, you will be able to perform the duties that can reasonably be expected of an office worker starting on his or her first job.

Clerical Duties. It would be a long list that included every duty and responsibility of the general clerical worker or the specialized clerical worker. The payroll clerk, for example, has many highly specialized duties and responsibilities within a single phase of the entire office operation.

Keeping records

The clerical worker in a small office may keep the routine records of the business.

You would need a crystal ball to predict precisely what kind of office job you will obtain as your initial position or what your exact duties will be on that job. Consequently, the wisest course for you to follow is to become broadly acquainted with a wide variety of knowledges and skills. These should be of greatest value on your first job. These duties and responsibilities, these knowledges and skills divide themselves into the 12 major areas that are discussed in the following paragraphs:

1) Preparing business forms — both handwritten and typewritten
2) Processing purchase and sales records
3) Maintaining stock inventories and related records
4) Processing data for computers
5) Handling the mail
6) Using telegraphic services
7) Using the telephone
8) Meeting business callers
9) Filing and retrieving records
10) Reproducing business papers
11) Typing business papers
12) Keeping financial records

(1) Preparing Business Forms. When you buy a paperback dictionary to improve your vocabulary or a plant to decorate your desk, some form of sales slip is filled out. When you receive your salary check, a series of business forms has been completed. Almost every operation in a business depends upon some type of business form. You and all office employees will work with business forms. Each of these forms has a specific name and a specific purpose. When merchandise is bought, a purchase order is made out; when it is paid for, additional forms are made out to record the completed transaction. When an automobile is made, numerous forms are used along every step of its manufacture. When it is sold, additional forms are filled out and registered with the state motor vehicle bureau. Forms are needed to record and transmit the information and instructions required for business transactions in all kinds of enterprises, from small, local establishments to large, nationally known corporations. They are usually classified according to their use, such as purchase orders, sales invoices, personnel forms, and W-2 forms (tax withholding statements).

What part will you, the office worker, have in handling business forms? Of course, how much or how little you do with business forms will depend on the size of the office and the type of work in which your employer is engaged. As a clerical office worker, you may fill out a handwritten form occasionally, or you may mark sense columns on a punched card with a graphite pencil, but you will probably spend much more time at a typewriter completing printed forms. You may also use an adding machine or a desk calculator to add the columns or multiply the listed items. You may spend considerable time copying descriptive information and compiling statistical data from business forms, and you will surely be expected to check, sort, and file forms. An understanding of the purposes of all the parts of a form and of the basic principles of form design is essential if you are to work most effectively with the forms.

(2) Processing Purchase and Sales Records. Purchasing is a key operation in any business organization. It requires a thorough knowledge of where hundreds of needed high-quality items can be bought at the best price under prevailing marketing conditions. The purchasing operations and the related paper work depend, to a very large extent, upon the volume of buying. The operations are handled by separate purchasing and receiving departments in large organizations, by purchasing and receiving clerks in smaller organizations. The purchasing procedure must be carefully planned, completely executed in every detail, and adequately supervised because it must be coordinated with all related operations if the firm is to operate efficiently.

The purchase order of one firm becomes the sales order of another. The quality of the products or services offered for sale, the effectiveness of

The invoice audit clerk

You may check invoices in the accounts payable department.

the marketing of the products or services, and the efficiency of the sales force all have a bearing upon the ultimate success or failure of a business organization. The sales force, in turn, must have the complete support and cooperation of the sales office if it is to compete effectively for the sales dollar. As in the purchasing division, the degree of specialization in sales operations and forms depends to a large extent upon volume. At first the sales operations which may involve hundreds of products, voluminous records, and specially designed forms may appear to be very complicated. Basically, however, the operations fall into a rather simple and orderly sequence — a sales order is received and approved for credit, the merchandise is withdrawn from stock, packed and shipped, and the customer is billed. As a prospective office employee, you should be aware of both the purchasing and sales procedures in modern business offices.

(3) Maintaining Stock Inventories and Related Records. The receiving and control of stock offers initial employment opportunities to many young men. They become responsible for keeping accurate records

of the receipt of the stock and for its physical movement to the assigned storage areas on shelves or racks or in boxes or bins. The commodities may be kept in the receiving department, in a separate stock room, or in a warehouse, depending upon the size and scope of the operation. Most stockroom employees are required to assist in the maintenance of a perpetual inventory as they receive or issue the various commodities. If a perpetual inventory is maintained, a stocked item is automatically reordered when the supply on hand has been reduced to a predetermined level. The effective operation of the control prevents shortages from occurring and tends to reduce to a minimum the amount of emergency ordering.

As a knowledgeable office worker, you must be aware not only of the entire receiving procedure but also of the various shippers' guidebooks which can be used to find the best method of shipping each commodity. You should also know how to complete the different shipping forms associated with each of the major shipping services. Because speed of delivery has become a very important element in modern shipping service, you should know when it would be most advantageous to ship by air parcel post, air express, air freight, or railway express.

(4) Processing Data. When you are employed as an office worker, your social security contributions, income tax withholdings, and health insurance premiums will probably be processed with a modern data processing system. You should have a clear understanding of the basic operations of the major mechanical data processing systems because they now handle about one third of all office paper work. All data processing systems use one or more of the common languages — punched cards, perforated paper tapes, and magnetic tapes — to capture or record data before feeding it into the computer for processing. An input machine with a numeric or an alphabetic keyboard, or a combination of both keyboards, which can be operated by an accurate touch typist, is used to convert these data written on the source document (purchase requisition, sales invoice, timecard, etc.) into the common language of the punched cards or tapes. After the data have been converted, they must be verified to guarantee absolute accuracy. They then become a permanent record which can be read by other machines that compare, store, compute, and otherwise process the data at high speeds.

You should make every effort to study the role of computer systems in modern offices because almost every office has some contact with data-processed records. After you have had some experience with a data-processing system, you may be called upon to help decide what work could be done most efficiently in the office with typewriters, desk calculators, and other office machines, and what work should be sent to the company's computer center for processing.

(5) Handling the Mail. Handling the incoming mail is not a quick, easy job. It may be your first duty each morning, and it demands serious attention. Time stamping and dating, underlining, annotating (which entails checking and researching), and sorting must be accomplished rapidly so that the mail is on the administrator's desk as promptly as possible.

Throughout the day and particularly at the end of the day, office workers are processing forms and preparing business correspondence for the outgoing mail. In some offices, mail is picked up frequently during the day; in other offices, particularly the smaller ones, a single office worker is responsible for seeing that mail is actually placed in the mailbox.

This activity requires that an office worker have a complete knowledge of mail handling and post office regulations. In many instances, it involves the responsibility for making decisions, such as determining whether a letter should go regular mail, airmail, or special delivery.

(6) Using Telegraphic Services. As an alert office worker, you should know that a telegram is the most rapid means of *written* communication. It can be transmitted from coast to coast and delivered in a few minutes. A telegram usually conveys a sense of urgency; therefore, it commands more attention than a letter and often causes the recipient to act promptly. You will be expected to know about the three different types of telegraphic service: full-rate telegrams, day letters, and night letters. You should also be familiar with the rules for counting words and figures so that you can compose the least costly messages which, at the same time, are accurate and clearly understood. You should be aware of the methods of filing messages with the telegraph offices. The four traditional methods are: over the counter at the Western Union office; over the telephone; by using call boxes and messenger service; and tie line service, a system of direct wires between the office of the patron and the office of the telegraph company. Four more recent developments for the extensive use of telegraph service are:

a) Facsimile service — the transmission of handwritten or type-written messages from a business office on a *Desk-Fax*, a small facsimile sending and receiving machine.
b) Teleprinter service — a specially installed telegraph machine with a teletypewriter-like keyboard called a teleprinter.
c) Telex service — a two-way teleprinter service linking the major cities in the United States.
d) Private wire systems — for telegraph users with a large volume of communications who require private telegraph systems of their own.

You should also know that the telegraph money order is one of the quickest and safest ways to forward money in an emergency.

Using the telephone

You may use the telephone to make appointments. When you use the telephone, you represent your employer and your firm to the business world.

Underwood & Underwood

(7) Using the Telephone. Again and again the telephone rings, for the telephone is used extensively in the conduct of any business, and its use is increasing. One of your principal duties as an office worker will be to answer the telephone and to provide the caller with the information he needs or to transfer the call to a co-worker. Frequently you will be able to screen and handle incoming calls without bringing your co-worker into the conversation at all. At other times, of course, an incoming call will be transferred immediately to a co-worker or an administrator.

Not only will you be expected to answer your incoming calls, but you may have to place outgoing calls of all types: local, long distance, and occasionally, overseas calls. To place calls properly you must be able to use the alphabetic telephone directories effectively, and you should maintain a personal telephone directory of frequently called local and out-of-town telephone numbers. In addition, you will be expected to use many of the other telephone services properly. These include the *push-button telephone*, the *Call Director* console, and the *Card Dialer*.

When you realize that in some offices a great deal of an office worker's time is spent in handling matters by telephone, you will understand the importance of telephone courtesy, proper dialing, and many other telephone techniques. They are an integral part of the job.

(8) Meeting Callers. Keep that smile! Always be gracious and courteous! Any caller may be the most important one to your firm! No matter how pressing the task at hand, the office worker puts it aside and gives her wholehearted attention to the caller. When a member of the office staff acts as a receptionist, she represents the firm to all who call at the office.

Perhaps no other phase of your office work will be more demanding than the reception of callers. You will be expected to meet all types of people easily, to get information from them without annoying them, and to decide quickly whether they should be admitted to an inner office. If callers are to be turned away, they must be treated with a deftness that will tend to retain their goodwill. Those who have appointments should be made welcome; and if they must wait while some other caller is conferring with the executive they wish to see, they should be made as comfortable and as much at ease as is possible. Skillful handling of callers is high on the scale of the most important duties of an office worker. It is one that you must master if you hope to become a successful member of the office staff.

(9) Filing and Retrieving Records. Files are kept so that business papers and records can be found easily. Several times a day you may be asked for papers and records that are wanted immediately. In each case you must be able to locate the paper in question and give it to your supervisor immediately. In order to do this, you must know the essentials of records management: filing rules, filing systems, and how best to handle different kinds of records. You will be expected to know how to keep track of records and papers removed from the files, how long to keep papers and records in an active file, and when to transfer them to storage or to destroy them.

(10) Reproducing Business Papers. One rule which wise office workers always follow is "Never make just one copy of anything!" In all offices, an original and one or more copies are made of all letters, business forms, and other papers prepared in the office. Extra copies are usually made by using carbon paper; but copying machines are frequently used.

The type of duplicating equipment selected to reproduce materials depends, to a very large extent, upon the number of copies needed and upon their ultimate distribution. If a single, exact copy of a letter, business form, drawing, illustration, or printed page is required, a photographic reproduction can be made with a copying machine in less than a minute. Copying machines are used for producing a limited number of copies of a document because the process is relatively slow and expensive. For the reproduction of interoffice communications, such as reports and announcements, in quantities ranging from 15 to 300 copies, fluid duplicators are used extensively. Copies of letters, notices, and reports of all kinds, in quantities ranging from fewer than a hundred to several thousand, can be run off inexpensively on the stencil duplicator. The offset machine is an ideal duplicator for producing large quantities of superior quality copy at high speed — ranging from 4,500 to 8,000 copies in a single hour.

If you are an efficient typist, you will be expected to type and photocopy most of your own materials. You will also be expected to prepare master copy for the duplicators: to type master sets for the fluid-process machine, stencils for the mimeograph, and paper or metal master plates for the offset duplicator. The actual amount of running off of copy that you will be required to do will depend upon the size of the office where you are employed. If you are employed in a small office, you may be asked to operate both the fluid duplicator and the stencil duplicator, and possibly, a desk-size offset duplicator. If you are employed in a large office, your master sets and stencils will be duplicated and collated by the duplicating department.

(11) Typing Business Papers. Who is responsible for much of the preparation of typewritten material so necessary to any business operation? To answer this question, let's drop in on a number of different types of offices. In a prominent advertising firm, a typist is preparing material for a news release. Some of the copy has been typed in rough by somebody else, and some of the information was sought out from the files and from different executives in the firm. In a small accounting firm, a typist is preparing tax forms from longhand. Next he prepares some monthly statements from the firm's records; finally he types some postcards. Our next stop is the local television studio. The clerk-typist is quickly revising a script from a rough draft. It must be ready for an afternoon rehearsal. Our last stop is at a chemical concern in which the typist has on her desk four or five texts and several technical magazines. She is using these to bring her employer's speech up to date for him by adding some additional quotes from newer articles and indicating the source of quoted material. She had to make a special trip to the library for those texts. The final draft of the speech is to be completed in time for her employer to review it before leaving next week for the convention in Denver at which he is the main speaker. After that, he may want her to prepare it for publication in one of the technical magazines.

All young people who aspire to be good office workers should be fast, accurate typists. They should be able to type a letter in an attractive style, to address the envelope that goes with the letter, to type from rough drafts, and to type any number of the many business forms that are in

Typing business forms

You may type any number of the many business forms prepared daily in the office.

everyday use in virtually all business offices. Prospective office workers should take pride in the quality and the quantity of typewritten matter that they can produce.

(12) Keeping Financial Records. When more stamps are needed, it would be embarrassing, indeed, for you to have to run to your supervisor to ask him for the money for their purchase. Provision is made for this type of expense by giving some member of the office staff control of the petty cash fund. When you need taxi fare to go to the airport to meet an important customer and to bring him to the office, you should take the money from the petty cash fund. All expenditures, however small, must be carefully listed in a periodic report that you should prepare for your supervisor. This is a simple, but an essential, form of financial record keeping.

Some other types of financial record keeping which you, the office worker, will be expected to do for your employer are the keeping of records of cash payments received and the issuance of receipts, the keeping of records involved in the maintenance of a business checking account, and the preparing and submitting of vouchers to reimburse your employer for his business expenses.

Federal and state income taxes are important items for every executive today, and you may be asked to help in assembling material and preparing data for your employer's income tax reports and schedules. This will require keeping records pertaining to the dividends, interest, and other income he has received during the year as well as his deductible expenses. The latter include such items as his health insurance premiums for the year, his donations to recognized charitable and educational institutions, and his business entertainment expenses.

Training. Now that you have covered the basic duties of an office worker, consider what training is needed to obtain a position. Think of this training in terms of three steps. The first step is basic skill. You will have to acquire the ability to turn out acceptable typewritten office materials at a production rate that will justify your employment. You will also need a thorough knowledge of basic office operations and a mastery of the fundamentals of English. The second step is the acquisition of the knowledges and understandings which we have just discussed in the 12 major duties of the clerical office worker. The third step is the development of the business personality without which you cannot succeed. If you do not develop the personality traits that enable you to operate efficiently on the job and help you to work well with others, no amount of skill or knowledge will permit you to succeed. Personality development is the key factor in your future advancement.

REWARDS OF OFFICE POSITIONS

Salaries. Salaries vary in different parts of the country and at different times, depending upon business conditions, the cost of living, and the available supply of trained office workers. The salary offered is frequently determined by the ability and experience required for the position; therefore, senior bookkeepers are among the highest paid office employees. In 1965, their average salaries were slightly above $120 a week, according to the annual survey of office salary rates conducted by the Administrative Management Society. At that time the average weekly salary paid to all office workers in the different areas of the United States was $85. The salaries paid to senior general clerks, payroll clerks, and senior tabulating machine operators were above the national average; the salaries of typist-clerks, file clerks, and junior general clerks were below it.

For many years the average salaries of all office workers have consistently moved upward at rates varying from two to three percent each year. In addition, fringe benefits, which amount to from 15 to 20 percent of their salaries, are granted to almost all office employees. They include such benefits as a company-shared pension plan, group life insurance, hospitalization, surgical benefits, and sickness benefits insurance.

Working Conditions. In general, the office is a very pleasant place in which to work. The tendency is to improve the immediate surroundings and working conditions of office workers by installing modern office furniture, coordinated carpeting and draperies, fluorescent lighting, and air conditioning. Many of your associations with your co-workers will prove to be enriching and pleasant. In fact, most office employees participate in some of the many company-sponsored activities. You may be interested in becoming a member of a bowling team, a theater group, or a photography club. Perhaps you may wish to join your co-workers on a weekend ski trip or a chartered vacation flight.

The basic workweek ranges from 35 to 40 hours; however, the 40-hour week is still the standard in the majority of offices in the United States. It is slightly shorter in most Canadian offices. Almost all firms pay their office employees overtime for hours worked beyond the basic workweek. Over half of the companies in the United States grant eight paid holidays; Canadian firms grant an average of nine. Most firms give a paid vacation of one week after six months of employment to their new office workers and two weeks after a year of service. Longer vacations are usually given to employees with many years of service to the company.

Prospects for the Future. First of all, it is hoped that you will continue to grow professionally in the future, that you will seize every opportunity to improve yourself after you have obtained your first office job. If your firm should offer an in-service training program that may qualify you for a better position, by all means take it. If your employer should be willing to pay part or all of your tuition for courses taken in the evening division of a business or technical school or a junior or senior college, make the most of this opportunity to further your education. The reading of books and periodicals in your field will also keep you abreast of changes and developments, and perhaps give you ideas for improving your work habits.

Second, it is hoped that in the foreseeable future other office positions in addition to the Certified Professional Accountant (CPA) and the Certified Shorthand Reporter (CSR) will be considered as professional positions. The National Secretaries Association, a professional organization of experienced secretaries, is working toward that goal. Upon successful completion of a standard twelve-hour examination, a secretary is granted the privilege of using the letters "CPS" after her name. The examination covers a wide variety of topics including human relations and personal adjustment, business law, secretarial accounting, economics, business organization and management, English usage, secretarial office practice, and stenography and typewriting. Professional organizations have been formed to improve the professional standing of office workers engaged in records management, office administration, systems management, and data processing. After you have met the admissions requirements in your field of interest, you should join a professional organization. Membership in a professional group and association with other people who share your interests will be enjoyable. In addition, it will extend your opportunities for attaining higher-level positions at higher salaries and will give you wider recognition in the business world.

Study Questions

1. Approximately how many men and women are now engaged in office work? What percentage of the labor force do they represent?
2. What are the five major areas of office work?
3. What percentage of office workers are classified as general clerks?
4. How many office workers does the average business firm employ?
5. What are some of the modern telephone services that an office worker should be able to use?
6. Under what circumstances would you suggest the sending of a telegram?
7. What general duties would an office worker perform when she acts as a receptionist?
8. Suggest times when you would recommend the photocopying, rather than the typing or duplicating, of business papers.
9. What are some of the business papers, other than letters, that are usually typed by an office worker?
10. What are the three common languages of data processing systems?
11. Why should an office worker have a complete knowledge of handling mail?
12. What is the meaning of the initials CPA? of the initials CSR?

What Do You Think?

1. As a public service, the Advertising Council has publicized this statement: "BOY. Drop out of school now, and that's what they'll call you all your working life." Do you agree with the statement, or do you think that it is too severe? Be prepared to discuss your viewpoint in class.
2. A lack of experience has often prevented a well-trained office worker from getting a job in keeping with his or her training. How can a young man use his first position as a messenger to insure his advancement? How can a young lady use her first position as a clerk-typist to insure her advancement?
3. Prepare a list of the skills that you think are most important for an office worker in the order of their importance. Be prepared to present your list to the class and to justify the order in which you have listed the skills.
4. Businessmen frequently speak of an office worker's "telephone personality." Discuss the elements that would contribute to a favorable telephone personality for an office worker.
5. Office workers are in such great demand that anyone not satisfied with his or her progress can move elsewhere readily. Discuss the advantages and the disadvantages of changing jobs frequently.

Your Personal Qualities

Alfred Watson has been employed in the payroll department since he was graduated from high school 14 months ago. One of his principal duties is to assist with the preparation of two weekly cash payrolls: one is for the cafeteria workers and one is for the custodial staff. In September, his supervisor calls him into his office to tell him that the firm has decided to put all payrolls on a computer which is scheduled for delivery sometime next summer. Alfred is assured that he will not lose his job when the computer is installed. However, the supervisor tells Alfred that the firm would like him to take a two-semester course in data processing at a nearby community college on Tuesday and Thursday evenings. Furthermore, the firm will pay Alfred's entire tuition for both semesters. Unfortunately, the data processing course conflicts with the firm's Thursday night bowling league. During the past year, Alfred brought his bowling average up to a respectable 160 and has won a place as a regular member of the business office team.

Question: Assume that you are one of Alfred's co-workers and that he comes to you for help in resolving the conflict. What advice would you give him?

 How's Your English?

Read the paragraph on nouns in Appendix A; list the nouns in the section on page 14 entitled *Prospects for the Future.* Indicate which are common nouns, which are proper nouns, and which are collective nouns.

 Office Work

Assume that your teacher has invited some former students who are now employed as clerical office workers to address the class on their present duties and responsibilities. In anticipation of this visit, prepare a list of questions about clerical office work that you would like to have answered by the visitors after their talks, provided the answers have not already been given.

Office Work Assignments

1: Duties of Clerical Office Workers

Locate one or more persons in your neighborhood who are now employed as clerical office workers and ask them about their jobs. Obtain the following information:

a. Exact title of position.
b. The major duties performed.
c. Special duties performed.
d. Workweek and overtime policy.
e. Approximate starting salary and fringe benefits.
f. Promotional opportunities.
g. Training in school that was most beneficial.
h. Additional training that might have been beneficial.
i. Helpful suggestions for an inexperienced clerical office worker.

Prepare typewritten reports on your interviews and be prepared to discuss them in class. If you are using the workbook correlated with this textbook, you will find an interview form provided for you.

UNIT 1 | The Office Worker

PART 2:

Your Personal Qualities

The presence or absence of desirable personal qualities and character traits determines the degree of an office worker's success. You can develop an excellent personality that will bring you outstanding success in your work. The secret is to start now to acquire and refine those traits that win the respect and admiration of employers and co-workers.

"Yes, she is the best typist, the best calculating machine operator, the most efficient girl in the office, but I have to ask the personnel department to place her somewhere else. She just doesn't get along. She just isn't happy here!" Don't let this happen to you! Assess your personal qualities and character traits today so that you can develop a personality that will spell success in your work. You, too, can win the respect and admiration of your employers and co-workers. Your success in your beginning office position, your advancement to a better position, and your happiness in your work depend on the degree to which you possess the personal qualities and traits classified under these three major headings:

Your Image	Your Relationship with Others	Your Efficiency on the Job
Dress	Cooperativeness	Initiative
Makeup and Hairstyle	Tact	Mental Alertness and
Neatness and Cleanliness	Social Attitude	Memory
Facial Expression	Courtesy and Manners	Punctuality
Health	Common Sense	Organization
Poise	Trustworthiness	Dependability
Posture and Gait	Loyalty	Production Ability
Voice and Speech		

Your personality is a blend of all these factors, many of which you already possess to some degree. Your personality is your total impression on others.

The office worker dresses the part

This office worker is wearing a conservative business suit in appropriate colors with matching accessories. Her hair is arranged simply, and her hands are carefully manicured. She uses make-up with caution.

Underwood & Underwood

Take a good look at yourself in terms of these qualities; evaluate yourself objectively; plan for a self-improvement program that will continue throughout your professional career.

YOUR IMAGE

Personal Appearance. From your personal appearance, people gain their first impressions of you; and on the basis of it, they frequently judge you before you have an opportunity to speak. The importance of good appearance in getting a job and holding it cannot be overestimated.

In his guidebook which is recommended for your reading, *How to Have Model Beauty, Poise, and Personality*, John Robert Powers, one of the foremost charm experts, gives the following reasons for the success of the Powers Girl, reasons that may well be applied to office workers:

> She is not just a model, she is a *personality*. She has learned to develop her own individual charms — not fashion herself on someone else's pattern. She is a natural girl who looks like herself. Good health, good sense and good taste are the basic ingredients of her good looks. She makes the most of her natural endowments. She does not distort her face with careless or exaggerated makeup; she does not distort her body with awkward movements; she does not distort her charm with affected mannerisms. She is poised because she has confidence without conceit.[1]

Dress. Good personal appearance includes the proper selection and care of clothes. The well-dressed girl has a good style sense without becoming a slave to high fashion. Learn to select those fashions that are

---

[1]Powers, *How to Have Model Beauty, Poise, and Personality* (Englewood Cliffs, New Jersey: Prentice-Hall, Inc., 1960), p. xiii.

right for you. The clothes that you choose to be part of your office wardrobe should be attractive, interesting, appropriate, and neat.

Considering your own coloring and figure, choose designs that enhance your most attractive features. Line, shape, color, and texture are all very important in choosing becoming outfits. Remember also that it is often easier to be well-dressed with a few well-chosen clothes of excellent quality than with a wide variety of poorly made garments.

Although dark shades of the neutral colors are usually more appropriate for office wear, you do not want to look drab or monotonous. Spark your basic colors with interesting accents. If you are not too sure of your own taste, the following chart of successful color combinations by Genevieve Antoine Dariaux,[2] former directress of the Nina Ricci salon in Paris, may prove helpful.

COLOR COMBINATIONS

Pale Basic Color for Suit or Dress	Secondary Color for Accessories: Gloves, shoes, handbag, and hat
White	Black and all the dark and bright shades
Pale beige	Black, browns, reds, greens
Pale gray	Browns, dark greens, dark gray, red
Sky blue	Browns, dark greens, raspberry, purple, beige, dark gray
Pink	Beige, purple, navy, gray
Pale yellow	Black, navy, brown, gray
Mauve	Plum, brown, navy
Pale green	Dark green, red
Dark Basic Color for Suit or Dress	**Secondary Color for Accessories: Gloves, shoes, handbag, and hat**
Black	Beige, white, toast; clear shades, but not pastels such as sky blue or pink (with exception of pale yellow, but only for a hat with black shoes, bag, and gloves)
Brown	White, beige, black, orange-red, orange, dark green
Dark gray	Beige, black, all the pale and bright colors
Navy blue	White, lemon yellow, turquoise, raspberry, bright green, mauve
Dark green	Sky blue, white, beige, bright red, pale yellow
Plum	Sky blue
Dark red	Black, sky blue, beige

The accessories you wear with a suit or dress — gloves, shoes, handbag, and hat — are important elements of your appearance. A modestly priced dress or suit can enhance its value when it is worn with an elegant hat, bag, gloves, and shoes, while a costly ensemble can lose much

---

[2]Dariaux, "The Sensible Woman's Guide to Elegance," *Redbook Magazine* (March, 1964), pp. 110–111.

of its prestige if it is worn with carelessly selected accessories. To your gloves, bag, and shoes should be added a hat, and it ought to be against the law to have all four of these accessories in the same color as your ensemble.[3]

Recently a beginning office worker was interviewed for a higher position in the clerical field. She wore her most flattering dress which was perfect in color but the wrong style for office work; it would have been all right for evening wear. Of course, she didn't get the promotion. The interviewer assumed that she was very immature in her judgment. So, no longer may you think only of yourself in selecting your wardrobe; you must also consider what is appropriate for the office. Suits, basic dresses, skirts with fresh-looking blouses are some styles that are acceptable for office wear. Another point that you cannot neglect is the matter of fit. Proper fit is essential to good appearance, but you should avoid the dress that is too tight and the skirt that does not allow you to walk gracefully or to sit with ease. Thus, the wardrobe you select should enable you to look the part of a professional employee. Start out with good basic clothes. Wear a variety of accessories to give the impression of different costumes.

Choosing your wardrobe is one thing, but maintaining it is another. Your apparel must always look fresh, crisp, and new; therefore, you should select fabrics that retain their shape, are easy to care for, and resist wrinkles. Taking care of your wardrobe demands a great deal of time and planning. Try to plan your various daily outfits for the entire week. Be sure that when you take that last look in a full-length mirror before leaving for the office each day not a wrinkle can be seen, not a thing is wrong with your attire. Your shoes, your stockings, your gloves, and your hat should have that well-cared-for neatness that adds to every office worker's grooming.

Makeup and Hairstyle. Is your makeup showing? Then your skill in applying it is not proficient. There is no question about it — office workers, in general, should wear cosmetics. You must learn to apply them deftly so that you do not have a heavy masked look but rather a dewy fresh look. This takes practice and knowledge of the correct coloring to use.

You have probably been experimenting with different hairstyles; but now, with an office position near at hand, some of your concepts of hairstyling must change. Extremes must be avoided. Short hair or hair styled into a chignon are the types most popular because they are the easiest to manage and the neatest.

Neatness and Cleanliness. A glowing appearance demands care about such things as the condition of your hair, your face, and your hands. Hair that is clean, healthy looking, and attractively styled is an asset to any office employee. Eye makeup should be used with extreme caution — the

---

[3]*Ibid.*, p. 67.

theatrical appearance is considered out of place in an office. Well-groomed hands help to make a favorable impression on other people, but poorly cared for hands and nails give an immediate suggestion of a general lack of cleanliness that detracts seriously from your appearance and efficiency. A pleasant smile is a tremendous asset; therefore, you should brush your teeth often and visit your dentist regularly. A daily bath plus a deodorant and a faint scent of perfume give you confidence in your appearance and add assurance to your manner.

Health. Your success in your business occupation depends to a very great extent upon the condition of your health. Good health should be your constant goal and, if it is possessed, should be preserved. Though there are exceptions, the average person can keep himself in a state of good health by eating the proper food and getting a reasonable amount of exercise, plenty of fresh air, and adequate sleep. Plan your weekly activities so that you get enough sleep each night, have time for exercise and recreation, and eat well-balanced meals. Good health will contribute to better performance of your job — it will also give you that complexion you covet.

Poise. Poise is a reflection of inner confidence. It is a combination of self-control, self-confidence, and the ability to adapt oneself to different situations without any apparent distress or disturbance. A well-poised person is always at ease with others. She readily adapts herself to new people by showing a genuine interest in them and their problems. She acts naturally without exhibiting any annoying mannerisms; she carries on a conversation with self-confidence; and she never loses her temper.

It will take time for you to develop poise. You can start by *looking* poised; then you will begin to *feel* poised. The next time someone interrupts you at your work, instead of showing annoyance, try to smile. This is your first step in developing poise. Others will soon respond to your graciousness if you permit nothing to ruffle your disposition. You will quickly learn to accept the pressure of work without panicking. Your self-control should be such that you never show irritation, anger, nervousness, or tenseness, no matter how provoking the situation is.

Posture and Gait. Whether you're sitting, standing, or walking, good posture is a very important element in the total impression you create. It is also a contributing factor to your general health because it helps maintain the proper functioning of the vital organs of your body. To acquire and retain good posture, remember to stand tall, to sit tall, and to breathe deeply. When you stand, hold your head erect, keep your chin in, keep your shoulders even, and hold your abdomen flat. When you sit, keep your spine flat against the chair back and your knees close together with one foot slightly ahead of the other. Your feet should be near the chair to

The well-dressed office worker

This young man is wearing appropriate office dress. His grooming is immaculate.

create a better appearance and to assist you in rising. To sit and rise gracefully from a chair or to walk smoothly in high or medium heels demands practice and conscious effort. Take the time to study yourself in front of a full-length mirror to see just how you look when you stand erect, when you walk into a room, and when you sit at a typewriter. During business hours try not to allow your body to slump into the shape of a question mark — it will detract so much from the smartness of your appearance.

Voice and Speech. As an office worker, you will be expected to have a good command of the English language and a reasonable vocabulary. With careful reading from selected literature, you can improve your vocabulary. In your conversation, try to avoid the common grammatical errors of colloquial speech and the provincial pronunciation of words.

The quality of your voice is an important part of your personality. It should be pleasant, not shrill or rasping. A loud voice is always irritating — people prefer to listen to a soft voice. If, on the other hand, your voice is so weak that you are constantly asked to repeat what you have said, it can be almost as annoying. Too many beginning office workers have high-pitched voices. Deliberately try to lower the pitch of your voice, use breath for resonance, and you will develop a well-modulated yet forceful style of speaking that will be pleasant to your listeners.

BUSINESS WEAR FOR MEN

First impressions count! Forget the old saying — that you can't tell a book by its cover — because people do judge you on the basis of their first impression. And most of these first impressions center on your appearance. It does not always follow that the well-dressed man always succeeds in business, but the connection between dress and success is too strong to be ignored. Good appearance does attract favorable attention; furthermore, when you *look* your best, you *do* your best.

The American Institute of Men's and Boys' Wear asserts that:

Dressing right is simply dressing appropriately, choosing proper apparel to fit occasions and circumstances. Surely, you wouldn't expect to see a loud sportcoat at an important conference, or brightly colored socks detracting from a conservative business suit. It's the attention he gives to small details that marks the dressed-right man.

What to Wear When. The foundation of any wardrobe is the suit. On it you build your selection of shoes, hats, accessories, furnishings, outerwear, and so on. The proper color combinations are as important as the proper selection of a suit. The basic color guides for masculine business dress are outlined in the "What to Wear with What" color selector chart on the next page.

Good Grooming. Men's clothing should be appropriate, neat, and clean; but the most important ingredient in dressing right is good grooming. Without it, the most expensive garments will look shoddy. Here are twelve general rules to follow if you wish to dress well for business:

1) *Wear shirts, ties, handkerchiefs, and hose that work with each other* toward a more attractive, complete picture, rather than a shirt and a tie that seem to be at war with each other.
2) *Favor colors that favor you.* For example, blue-gray and gray tones are right for the man whose hair is turning gray.
3) *Avoid extremes.* Even though a certain style may be the rage, it may not necessarily suit you.
4) *Avoid tight-fitting garments*, particularly if you're on the portly side.
5) *Avoid that unkempt look* of pockets bulging with pencils and papers.
6) *Avoid frayed shirt collars and soiled cuffs.* Change your linen every day.
7) *Keep your handkerchiefs clean and neat.*
8) *When a suit needs a cleaning, have it done.* Don't economize at the expense of your appearance.
9) *Keep your fingernails neat and trim.*
10) *Shave every day* and pay regular visits to your barber.
11) *Keep your shoes polished.*
12) *Shower every day* and use a deodorant.

WHAT TO WEAR WITH WHAT .⁴. .

Your Color Selector for Business Wear

(This dress-up selector offers two alternative color schemes. If you elect to use color scheme No. 1, follow No. 1 all the way down — from top to bottom — and the same applies to color scheme No. 2.)

SUIT	GREY	BLUE	BROWN
SHIRT Solid or Stripe	1. Blue 2. Off White / Yellow	1. Blue 2. Off White	1. Tan 2. Off White
TIE	1. Red /Navy 2. Black /Gold	1. Red /Gold 2. Blue /Yellow	1. Brown /Red 2. Brown /Yellow
SOCKS	1. Navy or Gray 2. Black	1. 2. } Navy	1. 2. } Brown
SHOES	1. Cordovan 2. Black	1. Black 2. Cordovan	1. 2. } Brown or Cordovan
POCKET SQUARE OR SCARF	1. Blue 2. Black /Gold	1. Red /Gold 2. Yellow	1. Red 2. Yellow
HAT	1. Medium Gray 2. Black	1. Gray 2. Brown	1. Brown 2. Green
OUTERCOAT	1. Gray or Black 2. Black or Covert	1. Gray 2. Tan	1. 2. } Brown, Tan or Charcoal
GLOVES	1. 2. } Gray Suede or Black Capeskin	1. 2. } Gray Fabric or Brown Cape or Mocha	1. Brown Cape 2. Natural Pigskin
JEWELRY	1. Silver Finish 2. Gold Finish	1. Silver Finish 2. Gold Finish	1. 2. } Gold Finish
BELT	1. Cordovan 2. Black	1. Black 2. Cordovan	1. 2. } Brown or Cordovan

RELATIONSHIP WITH OTHERS

Cooperativeness. That office functions best where an atmosphere of real friendliness and cooperation exists among employees. Office workers should be helpful, giving each other whatever information is

---

⁴American Institute of Men's and Boys' Wear, Inc.

needed and doing promptly the things that are asked of them so that all the work of the firm will progress smoothly. You should give careful consideration to all the people encountered in the office and make a genuine effort to get along well with all of them. This may mean overlooking a number of traits that are not entirely desirable in a co-worker; it may mean making diplomatic suggestions to improve the whole office situation; and it certainly means adjusting your own reactions. A sympathetic understanding of others and of their opinions is essential in bringing about harmony. If you can keep an office staff working together happily, you will be one of the most valued employees in the firm.

Tact. Frequently, you may be asked to get others to do things. Under such circumstances, you must, above all, avoid being "bossy" or domineering. If it is advisable that instructions be in writing, they should be embodied in a courteous, clearly worded statement that contains all the essential facts. If instructions are to be given orally, either personally or over the telephone, you should never fail to be courteous and at the same time certain that the other person clearly understands exactly what is to be done. A firm, polite approach is the best attitude.

Social Attitude. You, as a new office employee, will have to make proper social adjustments if you are to enjoy a successful business career. There are no hard-and-fast rules for making these adjustments. In every office, as in every situation where people work together, there is a degree of friction and a certain amount of office gossip. You should not become identified with particular factions or cliques, nor should you create or convey office gossip. If you are uncertain as to a course of action, ask your immediate supervisor for advice.

A natural sense of humor is a great asset. It can often relieve a tense situation or the monotony of a tedious assignment. A forced or misplaced sense of humor, however, only detracts from one's personality.

Courtesy and Manners. Courtesy costs nothing, yet it pays the greatest dividends. Most people are well acquainted with the common rules of etiquette, but too frequently these common rules are the ones that are neglected. A friendly "Good morning," a gracious "Thank you," and a courteous answer are a few ways to show consideration for others.

A person who commits a breach of courtesy should apologize promptly and sincerely. A genuine effort to be thoughtful and considerate of others at all times is the best way to avoid offending. There are a number of personal habits that may or may not actually annoy others but are considered to be poor form. Such things as combing one's hair, applying makeup, filing and cleaning fingernails, and adjusting clothing are all necessary. They should be taken care of in private — not in the office.

The office worker is trustworthy

She devotes all her business hours to business matters. She is loyal to her employer and her firm. She considers all business documents and business conversations confidential.

Common Sense. The executive was thinking of something else at the moment, and he called a conference for January 1 without remembering that it was a legal holiday. His assistant sent out the notice of the conference, and her employer was irate because she had shown such lack of common sense. Be on your toes to catch such errors.

Be sure, too, to take a hint that your employer may give you. Most businessmen dislike making pointed remarks, but frequently they will drop hints about the condition of the office, the appearance of the office worker, or personal habits that may be somewhat offensive.

Most of these remarks should be unnecessary. They usually will be unnecessary for you if you continually strive to do your utmost to keep your working area and yourself neat and orderly, and if at all times you are refined.

Like all other employees, however, you may at times slacken your pace and drop below par. Then come the hints, suggestions, and sometimes outright statements about such matters. Be wise enough to take a hint; adjust that which is offending before it leads to further complications.

Trustworthiness. During office hours, your time should be spent in taking care of regular business duties and not in attending to personal affairs. It can hardly be considered ethical for you to spend working time in writing personal letters, receiving and making personal telephone calls, entertaining personal callers, or reading books. Moreover, friends should be discouraged from calling at the office in person or on the telephone, except in unusual instances, and from addressing personal mail to you at the office. You are hired to be in the office to take care of the company business; attend to your personal affairs at another time.

Taking care of personal affairs during business hours makes for improper use of the time for which the business is paying. This kind of conduct also involves improper use of equipment paid for by the company which should at all times be available for company business. Needless to say, no employee has any right to charge personal telephone calls to the company or to use company stationery and company stamps for personal letters. Such practices constitute dishonesty.

Loyalty. You should at all times be loyal to your employer by refraining from doing anything or saying anything that later may cause embarrassment. All office workers handle confidential material. Through conversations, conferences, and filing, the clerical office worker becomes intimately acquainted with many items that under no circumstances should be discussed outside of, or even in other parts of, the office. This information is definitely private, and it must not be divulged accidentally or otherwise, even to intimate friends.

EFFICIENCY ON THE JOB

Initiative. As you become more and more accustomed to your position, you will be able to anticipate many of the things that should be done; you should then proceed to do them without any specific instructions. A good worker anticipates and makes whatever preparations are necessary; a mediocre or poor worker has to be told exactly what to do.

Mental Alertness and Memory. A good measure of an intelligent business worker is his ability to understand, judge, and follow either oral or written instructions. Of equal importance is his ability to select the more important things from the lesser.

There are many times when certain special instructions will be given to you. It is of prime importance that those instructions be clearly understood. Naturally, you should not waste the time of your employer by asking for unnecessary explanations. If instructions are hurriedly or not too clearly given, it is far better for you to ask for clarification than to proceed to do the wrong thing.

Your memory cannot and should not be depended upon to carry too many details connected with office work. Avoid the possibility of forgetting by making notes of at least the important details of the instructions.

The notes help you to know exactly what is to be done when the time comes for doing it.

Punctuality and Reliability. Your responsibility is to be at your desk during regular business hours. Once these hours have been established, the smooth running of the office depends to an important degree upon their strict observance. Insofar as possible, avoid being away from your desk during regular business hours. During your absence, your employer may want to give you instructions about a matter of some urgency, or he may require your assistance in assembling correspondence and other materials for an important appointment or a pending conference. He will depend upon you to be at your desk to meet callers, to answer the telephone, and to take care of your regular duties.

Dependability. An employer has every right to expect you to be at work on time in the morning, to lunch within the allotted time, not to prolong the coffee break, and to work honestly until closing time. You should always tell the truth; never tell deliberate falsehoods, part truths, or even evade the point. You should be scrupulously honest and sincere.

Your work must be of such caliber that your employer knows he can depend upon you to complete a job correctly. Once he has given you instructions, he ought to be able to feel that you will carry them out.

Production Ability. In any office, you will be expected to have a high rate of production. You will be expected to turn out materials at high speed and with complete accuracy. In order to maintain a high production rate, you should be able to arrange your time to allow for uninterrupted periods of work. You must be willing and ready to learn new ways of doing things that will save time and energy. You must always be on your toes to take new courses, to obtain refresher training, to keep abreast of new techniques in order to maintain your status as a valuable employee.

More than this, you must want to give the best possible service to your employer, to make the best possible use of your time, and to do a little more than is expected of you. It is a poor policy to put things off. It is a wise policy to get things done as soon as possible. Use every minute of your time wisely.

 Study Questions

1. What are the traits or qualities that make up a pleasing business personality?

2. Why is good grooming so impor-

tant for an office worker?

3. What rules would you follow to become well groomed for business?

4. What are some of the personal

factors to be taken into consideration when selecting a business wardrobe?
5. How can poor health impair an office worker's opportunities for advancement?
6. How is good posture acquired and maintained?
7. Suggest some of the hazards of conveying office gossip.
8. How should gentle hints about offending office situations be treated by an office worker?
9. If an office worker does not understand the directions for completing a job, what should he do?
10. Why should an office worker be loyal to his employer?
11. How does an office worker's punctuality and reliability affect the operation of his or her employer's office?
12. Suggest ways of maintaining a high rate of production on the job.

What Do You Think?

1. "Since the office worker is relatively well paid and receives many more fringe benefits than the industrial worker, his or her employer has every right to expect loyal and ethical service and a high rate of production." Discuss this statement from the viewpoint of the (a) employer, and (b) office worker.
2. Studies of dismissed office workers show that more employees are discharged because of poor character traits than for a lack of specific skills. Why do you think this is true?

3. Discuss this statement by John Robert Powers, the beauty expert: "In my opinion, *poor posture is woman's Number One Beauty Enemy!*"

4. If you were the office assistant to a key executive of a firm, how would you avoid being officious in dealing with his subordinates?

5. Discuss what you consider to be the best ways of getting along with your co-workers during your first week on the job.

Your Personal Qualities

The following inventory is a checklist, arranged in descending order, of the personal qualities and traits of an office worker. Study the entire list carefully before you start to rate yourself. Indicate your own rating on a separate sheet of paper by listing the general categories ("Personal Appearance," etc.) and the qualities ("Taste in Dress," etc.). For each quality write the description that most nearly fits you. (Save your self-evaluation for use in the exercises in *Office Work* which follow.)

After you have completed your self-evaluation, let a friend or classmate evaluate you and compare both ratings.

A. Personal Appearance

1. *Taste in Dress*
   Almost always clothed in good taste
   Usually dresses in good taste
   Dresses acceptably
   Occasionally dresses inappropriately
   Frequently dresses carelessly

2. *Cleanliness and Neatness*
   Always noticeably tidy, neat, and clean
   Usually neat and clean
   Generally conforms in cleanliness and neatness
   Sometimes negligent
   Sometimes offensive

3. *Health*
   Practically never absent for illness
   Adequate health
   Occasionally absent for illness
   Affects amount of work produced
   Impairs appearance and greatly reduces production of work

4. *Stamina*
   Unusual energy, almost tireless
   Usually energetic and vigorous
   Sustains effort fairly well without loss of efficiency
   Tires rather easily on some types of work
   Tires very easily on all types of work

5. *Poise*
   Self-assured and unusually well poised
   Usually well poised
   Occasionally loses poise
   Either frequently embarrassed or too bold
   Either very timid and shy or too aggressive

6. *Posture*
   Excellent posture, giving fine appearance when standing, sitting, or walking
   Usually good posture, giving good appearance
   Ordinary posture
   Usually poor posture, detracting from appearance
   Posture always poor, detracting greatly from appearance and health

B. Personality

7. *Tact*
   Exceptionally tactful and diplomatic
   More tactful than average
   Ordinary tact
   Tendency to say or do the wrong thing
   Frequently abrupt and tactless

8. *Voice and Speech*
   Good diction and an exceptionally clear and pleasant voice
   Few weaknesses in enunciation and diction
   Average voice and speech
   Weak voice and occasional errors in speech
   Irritating voice and frequent errors in speech

9. *Social Attitude*
   Active contributor and harmonious worker in all groups
   Generally works well with others
   Reasonably considerate of others, having little or no difficulty
   Seldom shows consideration for others
   Desires to be alone, hostile with others

10. *Initiative*
    Assumes responsibility and gets cooperation from others
    Often does things on own initiative with moderate success
    Does some things with little or no direction
    Shows some initiative, but often offends others
    Never shows any initiative

11. *Expression*
    Clear and effective expression
    Expression usually good
    Average expression
    Some difficulty in expression
    Expression poor and inadequate

12. *Manners*
    Manners invariably reflect a natural ease, grace, and refinement
    Manners good, attract friends
    Reasonably well-mannered
    Sometimes impolite and disrespectful
    Often ill-mannered, crude, and offensive

C. Mental Alertness

13. *Oral or Written Instructions*
    Grasps instructions instantly and unerringly
    Usually understands difficult instructions
    Follows ordinary instructions well
    Often misunderstands ordinary instructions
    Generally misses or forgets oral and written instructions

14. *Judgment*
    Good judgment upon most occasions
    Judgment reasonably accurate
    Fair judgment with ordinary problems
    Tendency to make errors in judgment
    Frequently makes errors in judgment, poor judgment

15. *Sense of Values*
    Uncanny insight in distinguishing the important from the unimportant
    Reasonably successful with conflicting values
    Distinguishes between usual values
    Occasionally confuses the important with the unimportant
    Places too much emphasis upon the unimportant

16. *Speed of Mental Reaction*
    Very seldom is at a loss for a thought
    Usually a quick thinker
    Thinks with average speed
    Sometimes slow in mental reactions
    Noticeably slow in understanding and thinking

D. Dependability

17. *Punctuality*
    Always punctual and prompt in keeping both appointments and work assignments
    Seldom tardy, prompt in completing work assignments
    Often tardy, but prompt in completing work assignments
    Often tardy, a bit slow in completing work assignments
    Habitually tardy, very slow in completing work assignments

18. *Persistence*
    Exceedingly persistent in completing every assignment
    Seldom discouraged with difficult tasks
    Persistent to an average degree
    Leaves many difficult tasks unfinished
    Easily deterred and needs constant encouragement to finish an assignment

19. *Ambition*
    Sees each job as a new challenge
    Enjoys satisfaction of finished work
    Works steadily, but only under supervision
    Requires some prodding
    Lacks evidence of ambition

20. *Loyalty*
    Considers business with deep possessive pride — can be trusted with strictly confidential matters
    Works faithfully and is interested in the success of the business
    Works steadily until closing time, but has little interest in the success of the business
    Loyalty to the business sometimes questionable
    Has little or no interest in the business

E. Production Ability

21. *Volume of Work*
    Exceptionally large output, steady worker
    Above average output, seldom stops work
    Average output
    Below average output, often wastes time
    Very much below average in output, constantly wastes time

22. *Quality of Work*
    Very high, nearly always free of fault or error
    Above average, usually free of fault or error
    Average, usually free of serious error
    Often unacceptable because of errors
    Usually unacceptable because of serious errors

23. *Organization of Work*
    Exceptionally orderly and systematic
    Above average in orderliness and systematic work
    Average orderliness and systematic work habits
    Disorderly and unsystematic to some extent
    Almost no organizational ability

24. *Teamwork*
    Always cooperates
    Above average in cooperation
    Average in cooperation
    Sometimes fails to cooperate
    Usually uncooperative

25. *Resourcefulness*
    Very resourceful, meets every challenge
    Above average in resourcefulness, faces problems honestly and solves most of them
    Average in resourcefulness, solves average problems
    Easily discouraged
    Generally admits failure with average problems

How's Your English?

After studying the section on pronouns in Appendix A, read the opening paragraphs of Part 2 beginning with the italicized paragraph and reading up to the heading "Your Image." Then list on a separate sheet of paper the pronouns and their antecedents. Indicate which pronouns are personal and which are relative.

Office Work

Review your rating on the personality inventory which you completed in *Your Personal Qualities.* Study the individual ratings on each quality. Select one item on which you gave yourself a low rating, and write a plan or outline for action you can undertake during the next few weeks to improve your rating.

Office Work Assignments

2: Personal Data

Your teacher will probably want to have a considerable amount of information about you just as an employer would want information about a new employee.

Write a statement about your background, including part-time and full-time employment, if any, and the schools you have attended, including a list of the business courses you have taken in this or other schools.

If you are using the workbook correlated with this textbook, fill in the form provided in the workbook for this problem.

As you have not had work on employment problems yet, you may want to take a "sneak preview" of that part of the course by reading the last unit in the textbook before you fill in the form.

UNIT 2 | Business Forms

PART 1:

Handwriting and Lettering

Many business forms must be completed with pen or pencil rather than by a typewriter. Forms are frequently prepared at the point of origin when typewriters or other mechanical printing devices are not available. Examples are the completion of a sales slip when taking an order from a customer, lettering the address on a large package, and taking an important telephone message.

To avoid confusion and possible embarrassment resulting from illegible handwriting and lettering, every office worker must cultivate the ability to write and letter legibly. These abilities will be useful to you in business and personal-life activities.

HANDWRITING

Legible handwriting is essential even in this age of office automation. Many office records are prepared in handwritten form. These records may include sales slips, bank checks and deposit slips, application blanks, tax returns, and countless other business papers. The original documents, from which many typewritten and card-punched records and reports are prepared, are generally handwritten. Therefore, you should strive to develop neat, legible handwriting. It is an important asset for all office workers. It may even mean the difference between being employed and being passed over when you are requested to fill out an application blank or when you answer a want ad requesting that you "reply in your own handwriting."

Poor handwriting is the source of many costly errors. A single department store in Detroit revealed that 20,000 sales slips representing about $165,000 in purchases were held up in the audit department each year because of poor writing — usually too hastily scribbled. The Handwriting Institute estimates that "illegible penmanship costs United States businessmen approximately a million dollars a *week* in scrambled orders,

33

lost time, missent deliveries, clerical mistakes, and other forms of inefficiency."[1] Furthermore, poor handwriting consumes the valuable time of everyone who reads it — not only once — but each time someone tries to read it. Some business firms are now insisting that employees print names and addresses to insure legibility and thereby eliminate costly errors and wasted time.

Principal Causes of Poor Handwriting. Four principal causes for poor handwriting are given in the pamphlet "How to Improve Your Handwriting."[2] They are excessive speed, sloppy posture, poor paper position, and indifferent attitude.

Excessive Speed. Much poor handwriting can be traced to excessive writing speed. Most of us make the mistake of trying to write as fast as we think. It will not work. Twenty-five words a minute is just about the top speed at which most people can write legibly in longhand. However, the mind runs as much as ten to twelve times faster, at rates of 250 to 300 words a minute. Too often you may write in a rapid scrawl to save time, but it may later take all the time you "saved" to figure out what you wrote.

Sloppy Posture. Sloppy posture produces sloppy writing. Many writers ignore the fact that good posture is essential for good writing. If you slouch or teeter on the edge of your chair, your writing will reflect it.

Poor Position of Paper. When your paper is at an awkward angle, writing will be at an awkward slant. Many of us try to write without first positioning our paper in a comfortable way so that we can write legibly. Writing on paper at various angles will produce different slants even if you use the same hand and wrist position.

Indifferent Attitude. If you are not concerned about the legibility of your handwriting, your handwriting will not improve. If you take the attitude that *your* handwriting is not the concern of your fellow workers who will have to read it from time to time, it will not improve. You should not assume that it is too late to improve your handwriting or that no one else cares about it.

Improving Your Handwriting. Like all other skills, good handwriting cannot be retained long without conscientious practice. At one time you probably had training in penmanship, but you may have become careless and lost some of this valuable business skill. If you are to keep

---

[1]Robert O'Brien, "The Moving Finger Writes — But Who Can Read It?" *Saturday Review of Literature* (July 18, 1959), p. 8.
[2]Veterans Administration, *How to Improve Your Handwriting*, VA Pamphlet 03-2 (Washington: U.S. Government Printing Office), pp. 12–13.

readable records, you must have legible handwriting. This part of the unit reacquaints you with the basic principles and practices associated with good handwriting and provides a review of the procedures to be followed to develop and retain good handwriting.

a b c d e f g h i j k l m n o p q r s t u v w x y z

A B C D E F G H I J K L M N O P Q R S T U V W X Y Z

Business-style handwriting

Rating Your Handwriting. How does your handwriting rate according to the basic principles of legibility? To find out, write, in your usual manner, the preceding paragraph. Now check the following points:

Uniformity

Do all strokes have the same slant?
Are all *a*'s identical? all *n*'s? *u*'s?
Do all strokes rest on a straight line?
Is the size of the letters uniform?

Readability

Choose words at random in the paragraph. Can you read them?
Can every letter be discerned when the word is spelled backward?
Are letters formed properly?
Is every *a*, *g*, and *d* closed?
Is every *e*, *l*, and *f* open?
Does every *r*, *l*, and *i* begin with a curved upstroke?
Is every *t*, *i*, and *d* written without a loop?
Is every capital letter clearly formed?

Spacing

Is the space between letters in the word ample and similar?
Is the space between words ample and similar?
Is the space between lines ample and similar?

Figures. You know that you will write figures in your office, perhaps every day — a telephone number, a price, an address, or a stock quotation. Most office workers write figures each day, sometimes writing very little else. It is important, therefore, that the figures you write be well-formed, legible symbols that can be read by the executive for whom you work, your co-workers, and yourself.

1 2 3 4 5 6 7 8 9 0

Write the figures *1 2 3 4 5 6 7 8 9 0*. Now check your figures to see if they meet the standards for writing numbers as suggested by the Handwriting Institute:

1) Do numbers *1, 4, 5, 7,* and *9* have straight strokes which have the same slant as the straight strokes in your writing?
2) Are numbers *6, 8, 9,* and *0* closed?
3) Did you make all figures except *4* and *5* with one stroke?
4) Are your numbers the same height as the letter "t"?

If you can answer "yes" to all these questions, your writing is legible and clear, and you won't be an office worker whose handwriting errors will cause business losses.

Figures in Columns. You will find that many figures are placed in columns. Money columns in accounting forms are ruled so that a separate space is provided for each figure. The figures you write in columnar work must be written small enough so that each will fit easily in the space provided. When you write figures without column rulings, you should be sure to write figures of like digits directly below one another so that they can be added or subtracted accurately.

The illustration below shows an acceptable style of handwriting for a columnar record.

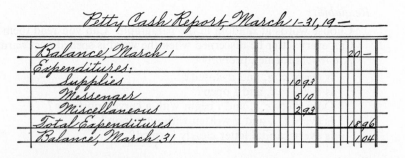

The Handwriting Clinic. If you can't give yourself a good rating on handwriting, check the faults in your technique. Thus, you will be conducting your own handwriting clinic.

Posture

Sit erect.
Lean forward from the waist.
Keep both arms (including the elbows) on the desk.
Keep feet flat on the floor and put some weight on them.

Hand Position. The Handwriting Institute offers the following suggestions for keeping your hand from tiring as you write:

Hold the pencil or pen about an inch above the point, between the thumb (which should be slightly bent) and the side of the middle finger, near the base of the fingernail. Keep your palm down and your wrist flat.
Tip the pencil or pen toward the shoulder of your writing arm.
Try not to turn the hand too far to the side — it will require too much finger movement.
Write with a flowing, free motion of both arm and fingers.

Speed of Writing. Finally, your writing speed has an influence upon the quality of your writing. If you write at too fast a rate, your letters will be carelessly formed; and if you write too slowly, the lines will waver. If you write with excessive speed, it will affect the exactness, alignment, and evenness of your strokes. Remember, if you are writing longhand, write it to be read. Keep your writing speed at the rate at which you can write effortlessly letters that are discernible.

LETTERING

Business firms frequently specify that certain information requested on their business forms, usually names and addresses, be lettered or typed to insure legibility. A common fault of office workers who have had no instruction in lettering is to mix capital and lower-case letters. This results in a hodgepodge of printing that is both unattractive and difficult to read.

The ability to letter well, like any other business skill, comes only with correct and diligent practice. Lyon[3] offers three suggestions to follow while practicing to improve your business printing:

1) Use simple letter forms.
2) Use well-rounded letters. They look better than skimpy ones.
3) Use vertical letters. They are easier to print uniformly than slanted letters.

---

[3]L. H. Lyon, *Applied Penmanship* (2d ed.; Cincinnati: South-Western Publishing Co., 1960), p. 89.

You will probably not be called upon to do any fancy lettering in business; therefore, you should use only capital letters. Furthermore, the lower-case letters, unless they are made very carefully, are much more likely to be illegible. Capital letters, illustrated below, may be lettered in uniform height or in large and small letters:

ABCDEFGHIJKLM
NOPQRSTUVWXYZ

The study of the lower-case forms is justified, however, if for no other reason than to avoid using them incorrectly.

a b c d e f g h i j k l m n
o p q r s t u v w x y (y) z

The two examples below illustrate a confusion of capital and lower-case letter forms.

MeRCHANDise
FuRniture

In *Merchandise*, we have two lower-case *e*'s and a lower-case *i* used with capital letter forms in the rest of the word. In the second illustration, the two *R*'s are capital letter forms; the remaining letters in the body of the word are lower-case forms. Be on guard against making similar mistakes.

Your pen is held in a slightly different manner for lettering than it is for writing.

The pen should rest slightly above the base of the forefinger. The index finger itself, from its tip to the second joint, should rest along the pen. This position gives you the control needed for making the short, quick strokes with which printed letters are formed.

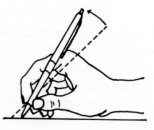

Study Questions

1. Why is handwriting important in this age of office automation?
2. What are the four principal causes of poor handwriting?
3. Give the principal items in a handwriting rating scale.

4. What standards must good handwritten figures meet?

5. Suggest guides to consider when writing figures in columns.

6. For good writing posture, what should be the position of the arm and of the hand?

7. What determines one's best handwriting speed?

8. What type of letters are recommended for lettering in business?

What Do You Think?

1. It is often said that a person who types well does not need to write well in longhand. What is your opinion of this point of view?

2. Describe handwriting that you believe to be suitable for office work.

3. What measures can anyone take to improve his handwriting?

4. In what types of office work is handwriting important?

5. Why do some business firms prefer lettered forms to handwritten forms?

6. What type of information is usually lettered on a business form?

Your Personal Qualities

James Eastland, an automobile insurance policyholder, has written to Frank Curry, the branch manager, to report that his claim for damages of $150 has not been settled despite the fact that it had been filed and approved by Mr. Curry over six months ago.

After weeks of checking, it is discovered that Mr. Eastland's claim, which was originally numbered 5,092, was recopied and misfiled as claim number 8,692 because the figure 5 had looked so much like an 8, and the poorly formed 0 looked like a 6.

Question: What suggestions would you make to Mr. Eastland about his writing?

How's Your English?

Read the section on verbs in Appendix A; then, on a separate sheet of paper, type each verb from the following sentences and classify it.

For the following sentences, type each verb and indicate whether it is transitive or intransitive:

1. In order to work at top efficiency, the typist must have the desk and its contents in perfect order.

2. A typist should understand the corrections on rough copy well enough to know what changes must be made and what changes should not be made in the copy without asking for any clarification.

For the following sentences, type each verb and indicate whether it is active or passive:

3. Many typists prefer to keep the top of the desk clear except for the work being handled.

4. Reports are usually edited by most typists before they begin the actual typing.

For the following sentences, type each participle and indicate whether it is present, past, or perfect:

5. Receiving a new delivery of mail, the typist takes care of rush items first.

6. By using carbon paper, the typist easily is able to make as many as six copies of a report.

7. Carbon paper, used because it is inexpensive and convenient, enables management to know exactly what was written in a letter or on a business form.

Office Work

1. In your very best handwriting, write a paragraph telling which one of the three principles of legibility you consider the most important. Give your reason.

2. Analyze the suggestions given in regard to the writing of letters and figures. List the six suggestions that you consider most important.

3. Copy a paragraph of 100 words from this book in your best handwriting, and evaluate the quality of your handwriting.

4. Write a column of at least 50 figures in which you write each figure from 1 to 0 at least three times. Judge the quality of your work using the checklist presented in this part.

Office Work Assignments

3: Application for Federal Employment

Obtain an *Application for Federal Employment*, Standard Form 57, from your regional office of the United States Civil Service Commission. (You may wish to consult Unit 14, Part 4, for a preview of civil service employment.) Assume that you are applying for a position, and complete the form in your best lettering, following these directions:

A. *Letter* all the required information in the proper spaces.

B. Depending upon your interests and qualifications, answer Question 1 by applying for *one* of the following positions:

Kind of Position	Starting Annual Salary
GS-2 Clerk-Typist	$3,925
GS-3 Stenographer-Typist	4,269
GS-4 Accounting Clerk	4,776

C. In Part A of Item 17: AVAILABILITY INFORMATION, list the starting annual salary for the position for which you are applying as the lowest salary you will accept.

D. Letter the full names and the correct addresses and occupations of your three references.

E. *Sign*, do not letter, your name in the space following "*Signature of applicant.*"

UNIT 2 | Business Forms

PART 2:

Typewriting

No skill is in greater demand for office employment than the ability to type accurately at a satisfactory rate of speed. A study of the job descriptions of 29 standard office titles listed by the Administrative Management Society showed that proficiency in typewriting is required to hold at least one half of all office positions. Naturally, the amount of typing varies from job to job. Clerical typists and machine transcriptionists use machines almost all of the time; however, only half of the tasks performed by general clerks require typewriting skills. Other office workers use typewriters occasionally. For example, file clerks usually type folder labels, and receptionists often use typewriters in their spare time to address envelopes and to insert fill-in information on form letters.

If you are employed as a typist, you will be asked to type requisitions, orders, invoices, and other standard business forms. These forms contain far more numbers than the letters and related correspondence typed by secretarial office workers; consequently, your ability to type numbers accurately on forms — in appropriate spaces, in boxes, and in ruled columns — will be almost as essential as your ability to type from alphabetic copy.

Typing on Other Office Machines. Your skill in touch typewriting need not be limited to the typewriter — it can be applied to the operation of a great variety of other office machines. Every descriptive office machine — every machine on which words are written — is equipped with an alphabetic keyboard like that on the standard typewriter. A mastery of touch typewriting is therefore required in order to operate the written-communication machines in sending telegrams and teletyped messages and perforating words on paper tape for wire transmission. Touch typewriting is also essential to record names, addresses, and other descriptive information on the alphabetic keyboards of billing, bookkeeping, and card-punch machines. Typing skill, combined with a very high degree of accuracy, is needed to transfer words from the input machine into the memory unit of all electronic computers.

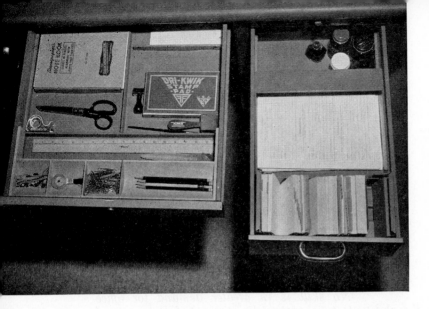

Desk drawer arrangement

The arrangement of materials in the center drawer and the first, or top, drawer indicate orderliness and efficiency.

Shaw-Walker Co.

Organization of Work. One of the "musts" in your position as an office worker is planning the day's work. Everyone has a certain amount of daily routine work that must be done so that the work of other employees will not be retarded. The more important the position, the more desirable it is that work be planned to fit easily into the office routine. A memorandum pad kept within easy reach will assist you greatly in planning the day and will be a constant reminder of the duties to be performed. A list of duties that must be performed regularly may well be prepared and checked daily or weekly to be certain that they have been completed. You may want to use three headings in listing the things to be done: *Immediately, Later,* and *When Time Permits.*

Work Habits. Whether you use an electric or a manual typewriter, you should develop good work habits at the typewriter to utilize to the fullest your ability to type accurately at high speed. You will produce more copy with less fatigue if you make good posture a habit, and if you arrange your materials efficiently. The copy from which you type should be placed in the very best light so that it can be read easily with little or no eyestrain. Your eraser and erasing shield should have a fixed location on your desk. You should also use the functional parts of your typewriter efficiently to increase your typing output. These functional parts include the margin stops, the margin-release key, the tabular mechanism, the line-space lever, the variable line-space lever, the ratchet release or automatic line finder, and the paper-release lever.

The Typist's Desk. In order for you to work at top efficiency, your desk and its contents must be in perfect order. Many typists prefer keeping the top of the desk clear except for the work being handled. This necessitates perfect organization of materials — filing at the beginning of each day papers from the previous day, rerouting papers to other departments, even disposing of advertising or other materials of no value to your employer.

Effective arrangement of supplies differs according to the physical arrangement of the office. It is always helpful for you to have certain types of supplies in the desk:

Center Drawer — This is the ideal place for the frequently used supplies such as sharpened pencils (black and red), pens, erasers and erasing shields, paper clips, rubber bands, staples, transparent tape, thumbtacks, ruler, scissors, and a letter opener. Most center drawers are equipped with dividers so that you can make up compartments for the various supplies (see illustration on page 42).

The First Drawer — The first or top drawer might contain manila file folders to aid in the organization of work. Such folders can be labeled (a) material to be filed; (b) work in process; (c) work for slack periods. Separation of materials in this way enables you to keep the top of the desk cleared for action, yet permits an orderly arrangement of working papers. A tickler file, a 5″ x 3″ card file of frequently referred to names, may also be kept here.

The Second Drawer — The second or middle drawer is usually the stationery drawer. It has some partitions to separate letterhead stationery, onionskin, carbon paper, and bond paper for second sheets and reports. Many businesses use different sizes of letterhead paper for letters of varying lengths. Envelopes of various sizes are also kept in the stationery drawer.

The Third Drawer — The third or bottom drawer is ordinarily used for the typist's personal belongings.

Care of Your Typewriter. You will turn out neater work, and your typewriter will last longer if you take proper care of your machine. The manufacturers of typewriters offer the following recommendations for the care of your machine:

1) Prevent eraser grit and dust from accumulating in the type basket by NEVER erasing over the type basket. ALWAYS move the carriage to one side before erasing.

2) Dust the machine every day. Use a dry-bristle brush to clean out eraser grit and dust. After spreading a cloth or cleansing tissue in front of the type to protect your clothing, *brush away from mechanism and toward you.*

3) Clean the keys by using a tapping motion with the ends of the bristles of your type-cleaning brush and finish the cleaning by

wiping the type faces with a clean, dry cloth. Another way to clean the type is by rolling a type-cleaning cushion sheet into the machine. Set the ribbon in the stencil-cutting position, and type the alphabet in capital and lower-case letters until the imprint of each key is clean and sharp.

You can also clean the keys by rolling a type-cleaning putty back and forth over the keys until all the ink sludge has been removed. Still another way is by using a cleaning fluid. If you use a cleaning fluid, moisten a cloth *slightly*, and dab the type faces lightly. *Avoid excessive use of any cleaning fluid.*

4) Clean the platen, feed rolls, and bail rolls periodically with a platen cleaner to assure proper feeding of the paper and to prevent feed-roll or bail-roll markings on the typed copy. Apply the cleaner with a dauber or a cloth.

5) Use oil sparingly. Oil only the carriage rail, and that only lightly. Oil used indiscriminately may come in contact with the rubber parts of your machine and cause a great deal of damage.

Typing. Typewritten material should be intelligently and carefully planned in order to make a favorable impression. A lack of consideration for proper placement of material may be entirely responsible for destroying the effectiveness of your work. For this reason, careful attention must be given to margins, headings, centering, proper use and placement of punctuation marks, underscoring of phrases or passages, and corrections.

You will be given a complete understanding of how to do all these things in later units in this book.

Duplicate Copies. Management frequently needs to know exactly what was written in a letter or on a business form, such as an invoice or a statement. For this reason, duplicate copies of business letters and of most business forms are made and filed. Remember the admonition in Part 1 of Unit 1 — make a carbon copy of everything. In many instances, you will be instructed to make more than one copy.

When only a few copies other than the original are required, carbon paper is used because it is inexpensive and convenient and also because the copies may be written either by hand or on the typewriter. When more than a few copies are desired, some type of duplicating device is used. Duplicating devices are discussed in Unit 10.

The quality of carbon copies depends upon a number of factors — the quality of the carbon paper, the manner of using it, the kind of typewriter used (manual or electric), the kind of type (pica or elite), and the quality or weight of the stationery. The number of copies desired determines the weight of carbon paper to be used. When only one copy is to be made, heavy carbon paper is satisfactory. You will probably follow the lead of most transcribers, however, and use medium-weight carbon paper. You will find it serviceable for up to three or four copies. If five or more carbon copies are to be made, it is wise to use lightweight carbon paper.

A soft-finish carbon paper should be used if the typist's touch is very light. Most typists use medium-finish carbon paper for regular work, and hard-finish carbon paper when copies up to eight or ten are required. Elite type requires a harder carbon finish than pica type for the same number of copies.

Most firms use black carbon, but some prefer colors. Occasionally, when more than one copy is regularly prepared on white paper, a different colored carbon is used for each copy so that the copies can be distinguished from each other.

Use of Carbon Paper. To insert the carbon pack in the typewriter, the typist should use the paper-release lever, slip the pack into the machine with the shiny side of the carbon facing forward, snap the paper-release lever into position, and twirl the cylinder knob to bring the paper into writing position. For the insertion of a thick carbon pack, place the flap of a long envelope over the top of the pack and remove the envelope after the pack has been turned to the position for typing.

When more than two carbons are used, it is easier to insert the carbons separately. To do this:

1) Arrange letterhead and onionskin papers and slip them behind the platen, making sure they are firmly anchored.
2) Flip the pack forward over the front of the typewriter.
3) Turn the last sheet of onionskin back and insert a piece of carbon, shiny-side upward, repeating this until all carbons have been inserted.
4) Turn the cylinder knob, bringing the papers into typing position.

This system of insertion provides for the easy removal of all carbons after typing, for they will extend beyond the bottom edge of the papers.

Carbon paper with guide numbers on the right side is also available. The numbers serve to indicate the exact number of vertical lines remaining on the page.

Before starting a job, you should find out how many carbon copies are needed. Check the number carefully so that you will not have to retype the material for additional copies. The number of legible carbons you can produce is dependent upon the typewriter you use, the weight of the paper, and the weight of the carbon paper. Carbon paper varies from an extra light weight of No. 3 to a very heavy weight of No. 14. The more copies wanted, the lighter the weight of the paper and the carbon paper you will use, as shown by the following table:

Number of Carbons That Can Be Made with Different Stationery

Paper	No. of Copies (Manual Typewriter)	Weight of Carbon Paper	No. of Copies (Electric Typewriter)	Weight of Carbon Paper
16 lb. Bond	3–4	#8	5–7	#5
20 lb. Bond	2–3	#8	4–5	#5
Onionskin	8–10	#4	12–14	#3

Hints on Handling Carbon Paper.

1) Assembled sheets should never be squeezed together too tightly. A thumbprint or fingernail scratch on a sheet of carbon paper may spoil the appearance of the carbon copy.

2) Handle the carbon paper carefully so that the carbon is not transferred to your fingers. Keep your fingers free of carbon so that carbon smudges will not be transferred to the original and the carbon copies.

3) Never use more than a natural touch in typing, or the carbon paper and original copy will be damaged.

4) If the typewriter feed rolls make unsightly marks, adjust the feed rolls and turn the paper up more slowly, or use carbon paper with a harder finish.

5) To make many carbon copies, use thin carbon paper and thin paper, or the last several carbon copies will be blurred, smudgy, and illegible.

6) Never use a wrinkled sheet of carbon paper because it will cause a carbon smudge to appear on the duplicate copy.

7) Always keep carbon paper in a flat folder or box away from dust, moisture, and heat.

8) When several sheets of paper and carbon are being used in an assembly, clip the sheets of paper and carbon together at the top after they have been inserted in the machine. This prevents the copies, especially the last ones, from being wound around the platen of the typewriter.

9) By inserting the carbon after inserting the letterhead and onionskin, you can easily remove all the sheets of carbon from the pack without smudging by holding the very top of the letterhead and onionskin (no carbon paper reaches the very top line of the pack) while you pull all the carbon sheets by the small amount that protrudes from the bottom of the pack.

Proofreading. Remember, it is not an error if you find it and correct it! Every typist makes an error once in a while. You must be the one to find it, however, not your employer. Whether the error is a typing error or one in fact, figure, name, or common sense, you must train yourself to be on the alert to see it. The only way to do this is to proofread each and every sheet before removing it from your typewriter, no matter how rushed you

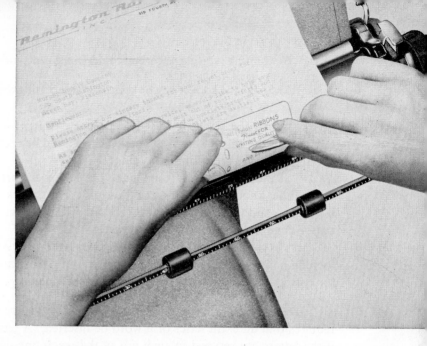

Erasing

Move the carriage to the side before erasing so that the filings do not fall into the mechanism. Use a shield to protect copy that is not to be erased.

are. If there is an error, it will take a mere matter of minutes to correct it while it is in the typewriter.

Erasures and Corrections. Even the most proficient typist will make an occasional error, but a careful proofreader will always find it, and a careful typist will always correct the error so that it is not obviously an erasure. Strikeovers give your work an untidy, careless appearance and, therefore, should never appear in the work of a typist who strives for perfection.

Good Procedure for Erasing. It is usually easier to erase if the line in which the error occurs is raised a few spaces in the typewriter. This should be done with the cylinder knob. Here is a good erasing procedure to follow:

1) Slide the carriage to the right or left to prevent erasure particles from falling into the machine.
2) Insert a solid metal or plastic shield or a piece of heavy cardboard directly behind the original. Make certain that it is placed between the original and the first carbon. This protects the carbon copies from smudges.
3) Place a plastic or metal shield with cutouts over the material to be erased. Use of the cutout shield enables you to erase a single letter of single-spaced copy without smearing adjoining letters or adjacent lines.
4) Erase in a circular movement for more than one letter; use up and down motions for one letter.
5) Transfer the solid shield to behind the first carbon copy and erase that copy, using the cutout shield.

6) Continue erasing *all* carbon copies in the pack, moving from front to back of the pack.
7) Strike the correct key or keys lightly, repeating the stroking until the desired shading is achieved.

When the paper is raised to permit erasing, the sheets may slip a bit. After the erasure has been made, care should be exercised in checking the alignment before resuming typing.

If the correction is to be made on the lower portion of the paper, the cylinder knob is turned toward the typist. The papers will then be rolled backward, and the correction can be made without having the papers slip out of alignment or out of the typewriter.

A typist should be alert to discover better ways to provide clean-looking copy. The newly patented correction papers are especially good for corrections on originals. Instructions are included on the package.

Crowding and Spreading. Sometimes the correction of an error requires that an extra letter or a word be inserted. A letter may be added if the letters are retyped in such a way that each one occupies less space than it did formerly. On a manual typewriter, this is done by striking the first letter, then holding the backspacer down slightly and striking the second letter, and continuing this operation until the complete word has been typed. With an electric typewriter, move the carriage back slightly with your hand instead of holding down the backspacer. This manipulation requires skill that may be acquired only through practice.

At other times the correction of an error requires that a letter be omitted. A letter may be omitted without spoiling the appearance of the page if the remaining letters are typed in such a way that each one occupies more space than it did formerly. On manual typewriters, this is done by striking the first letter, striking the space bar, then depressing the back-spacer slightly (on electric typewriters, move the carriage with your hand instead of holding down the backspacer) and holding it in that position while striking the second letter, continuing this operation until the complete word has been typed.

You will find the ability to crowd and spread letters of inestimable help in turning out acceptable work without retyping whole pages.

Electric Typewriters. At your desk you may have either an electric or a manual typewriter. At different times, however, you may be asked to operate both types of machines to produce various kinds of work.

You will produce more attractive material in a shorter time and with considerably less effort when you use an electric typewriter. A feather touch on each key, requiring only two ounces of energy, activates and completes each stroke. Since the pressure on all the keys is uniform, the finished copy shows an attractive, even stroking. You can adjust the pressure from very light for single copies to very heavy for multiple copies.

Most electric typewriters have a number of automatic features — keys and bars that continue to operate for as long as depressed. They include the automatic carriage return key, the automatic underscoring key for underlining and making horizontal lines, the automatic backspace key, and the automatic space bar, which continues to space across the paper as long as it is held down. Some manufacturers have added the numeral "one" and the exclamation point to their keyboards; others have changed the location of the quotation marks and the apostrophe.

Electric typewriters are particularly suited for the typing of stencils and other duplicating masters because of the uniformity of pressure on all keys. They are also well suited for the production of multiple copies. As many as 14 copies can be typed at one time with the proper grade of carbon and onionskin paper.

Justifying the Right Margin. Some executives prefer to have their reports prepared in such a way that both the right and left margins are even. The process is known as *justifying*. It gives your typewritten copy the professional look of newspaper and magazine columns. To justify copy on a manual typewriter:

1) Set the margins for the exact column width desired and type each line of copy the full column width, filling in each unused space at the end with a diagonal.
2) Pencil in a check mark to indicate where you will insert each extra space within the line. Try not to use an extra space after the first word in a line or to isolate a short word with an extra space on each side.
3) Retype the copy, inserting the extra spaces.

```
              Rough Copy

The process is known as justifying.
It gives the√typewritten√copy the//
professional look of√newspaper and/
magazine columns.


            Justified Copy

The process is known as justifying.
It gives the   typewritten   copy the
professional look of  newspaper and
magazine columns.
```

Some electric typewriters are equipped with "proportional spacing" to justify the right margin. The material must be typed twice. The first copy is a rough draft typed with a two-unit space bar within the desired margin limits. The typist then:

1) Notes how many units must be increased or decreased in each typed line.
2) Places a check mark between words where units are to be increased.
3) Places a diagonal between words where units are to be decreased.
4) Retypes the copy, adding or subtracting a space where necessary by using the 2- or 3-unit *space bar* or the 1-unit *backspace key*.

Study Questions

1. Proficiency in typewriting is needed by what proportion of office workers?

2. Why should the office worker be proficient in the typing of numbers?

3. In addition to typewriters, what office machines have typewriter-like keyboards?

4. Why are good work habits essential to typing accurately at high speeds?

5. For top efficiency, how must the typist's desk be kept?

6. What are the key points in the care of a typewriter?

7. Why are duplicate copies of letters necessary?

8. What are the differences among the various types of carbon paper? When is each type used?

9. What cautions should be observed in handling carbon paper?

10. When is the proofreading of typewritten material done?

11. How is an erasure best made on the original and on carbon copies?

12. How may an extra letter or word be inserted in typewritten material?

13. For what are electric typewriters especially suited?

14. How does a typist justify the right margin on a manual typewriter? on an electric typewriter equipped with proportional spacing?

What Do You Think?

1. What advantages are there in knowing how to type well when applying for a beginning position in business? What are the disadvantages in not knowing how?

2. What advantages does an office worker who does his work in an organized fashion have over the worker who does his work in a haphazard fashion?

3. If the typist believes that the typewriter ribbons and carbon paper that are supplied to the office are responsible for poor originals and carbon copies, should she give that information to the executive for whom she types or to the person who buys those supplies?

4. Why should the typist be held responsible for the care of the machine?

Your Personal Qualities

Miss Joan Albert does typing for four junior executives in the sales office. All of them, except Mr. Dean, are completely satisfied with her work. He demands that each letter or report be typed absolutely perfect. If there is the slightest error in her work, he makes a large "X" through the letter with his pen.

Miss Albert spends anywhere from a half hour to a full hour each day retyping the work for Mr. Dean, letters and reports that could be corrected in less than a minute were it not for the "X" marks. She finds that she must work after hours almost every day to get out the work for the other three executives.

Question: If you were Miss Albert, what would you do to improve this work situation?

How's Your English?

Read about agreement of verb and subject in Appendix A. Then on a separate sheet of paper complete each of the following sentences, choosing the proper verb. Following each sentence indicate in as few words as possible the reason for your choice.

1. Dictating and transcribing machines (is, are) used extensively to record and transcribe dictation in business offices where there (is, are) a relatively heavy volume of correspondence.

2. The handling of correspondence (is, are) facilitated by the use of dictating and transcribing machines.

3. Either you (is, are) to use the dictating machine or I (am, are).

4. Neither the tape nor the belt (is, are) usable on a home-style record player.

5. The outstanding advantage of dictating machines (is, are) that a stenographer need not be present during the dictation.

6. The combination dictation and transcription model (is, are) used by only one person at a time — the dictator or the transcriber.

7. The Dictaphone and the Voicewriter (are, is) widely used machines.

8. The general manager, as well as his assistant, (is, are) making plans to tour the plant.

9. Each record and disc (is, are) to be transcribed promptly.

10. The dictator and not the machine (are, is) usually at fault.

11. The board of directors of this corporation (want, wants) meetings recorded on tape.

Office Work

1. Prepare a list of items that a typist needs to keep in the desk, and indicate which items should be in each of four drawers. Include in your list any personal items that a typist should keep in the desk.

2. List the steps one would follow for erasing an error on several copies. Be prepared to demonstrate the procedure before the class.

3. One of the newly employed typists is having more than the usual amount of difficulty with carbon copies: (a) smudges on carbon copies, (b) realigning after making erasures, and (c) cutting certain letters and punctuation marks through the original copy. Briefly outline the steps you would take to help her overcome her difficulties.

UNIT 2 | Business Forms

PART 3:

Business Forms Design

When you buy that lamp for your desk or your employer's desk, a sales slip is filled out. When you receive your monthly check, another form is completed. Almost every operation in a business depends upon some type of business form. You and all office employees will work with business forms. Each of these forms should have a specific name and a specific purpose. When merchandise is bought, a purchase order is made out; when a sale is made, many forms are made out to record the complete transaction. When an automobile is made, numerous forms are used along every step of its manufacture. Forms are needed to record and transmit the information and instructions required for business transactions in all kinds of enterprises. They are usually classified according to their use, such as purchase forms, sales forms, correspondence forms, accounting forms, or personnel forms.

What part will you have in handling business forms? How much or how little you do with business forms will depend on the size of the office and the type of work in which your employer is engaged. As an office worker, you will probably fill out handwritten forms occasionally, but you will probably spend much more time preparing completely typewritten forms. You may also use a calculating machine with the typewriter to complete forms containing a series of computations. You may spend considerable time copying descriptive information and compiling statistical data from business forms, and surely you will be expected to check, sort, and file forms. An understanding of the purposes of all the parts of a form and of the basic principles of form design is essential if you are to work most effectively with the forms.

Purpose of Business Forms. Forms are used extensively in business to eliminate the necessity of repeating and rewriting information that is the same on each of a number of records. Forms also arrange information so it can be read easily and filed accurately.

Each section of a business form should serve a specific purpose. The heading shows that the form is a genuine document issued by a business firm. A statement, for example, should be prepared on a firm's statement form to prove that the request for payment is authentic. The printed name of the form will indicate its purpose: a purchase order (authority to buy); an invoice (bill of sale); and a statement (a request for payment).

Column headings on a form indicate what is to be done. For example, if an earnings record shows the gross earnings of each employee in one column and the payroll deductions in the following columns, you would be expected to subtract the deductions from the gross earnings and record the difference in the *net earnings* column for each employee. You would also be expected to add all columns and record the totals in the spaces provided at the bottom of the earnings record.

The printed information on a form — the firm name, address, telephone number, payment terms, shipping conditions — eliminates the need for recopying this information on every document. For efficient handling, the most important information on the form, whether it be the name, invoice number, amount, or due date, should be printed where it can be read easily and filed accurately.

Form Design. You may not only work with business forms but may also be requested to make suggestions or to design a new form. Business forms to be filled in on typewriters and other office machines should be designed to take advantage of the spacing and tabular mechanisms of the machines. For example, if a form is to be filled in on a typewriter, the horizontal lines should be one sixth or one third of an inch apart to permit continuous single- or double-space typewriting and make it unnecessary to use the variable line spacer. Insofar as possible, horizontal and vertical lines should not be used on business forms, especially lines for names and addresses and the traditional vertical line to separate dollars and cents in the amount columns. These lines merely add to the time spent in setting up the proper tab stops or in typing on lines. The name and address are usually typed within a specific area on the form to permit the use of a window envelope. To illustrate:

Right	**Wrong**
S	S
O .	O _____
L .	L _____
D .	D _____
T ·	T _____
O	O _____

Forms should be printed so that as many lines as possible start at an aligned left margin and at all tabular stops:

	Marginal Stop v	*Tabular Stop* v
Right	Consigned to Destination Route	Order No. Invoice No. Invoice Date

Marginal and Tabular Stops Not Feasible

Wrong	Consigned to_____ Destination _____ Route_____	Order No._____ Invoice No._____ Invoice Date_____

To minimize tabulating, spacing for boxed information should be aligned with spacing for columns, as in this example:

Marginal Stop v   *Tab Stops* v v   *Tab Stops* v v

Date Entered	Ship Via	Salesman	Cust. No.	Dept. No.
May 23, 19--	Truck	JCT	3149	B-31

Quantity Ordered	Quantity Shipped	Description		Unit Price	Amount
148	148	Radios, 77K3180		4.25	629.00
50	50	Radios, 77K3240		6.53	326.50

Ample space should be allowed at the top, bottom, and sides of the forms to permit binding, perforating, and stapling.

Study Questions

1. What will determine how much or how little you will be concerned with business forms?

2. For efficient handling, where should the most important information on a form be placed?

3. What is the purpose of business forms?

4. Why is form design so important to the office worker? How is it related to the use of the typewriter?

What Do You Think?

1. What is the typist's responsibility for encouraging a firm to design its invoices and requisitions to take advantage of the spacing and tabular mechanisms of the machines?

2. How can forms design increase the profits of a company?

Your Personal Qualities

Miss Mary Young, receptionist and assistant for Dr. Allan Brooks, a very prominent dentist, types and mails out the monthly bills.

Unfortunately, the bills are rarely mailed out before the tenth of each month. If the statements were mailed out earlier, payments would be made sooner.

Miss Young feels that she could get out the statements earlier if she were permitted to use a new form. The present form contains horizontal lines for the name and address of each patient, but the lines do not agree with the vertical spacing on the typewriter, and the variable line spacer must be used to move from one line to another.

Questions: 1. If you were Miss Young, what recommendation would you make for redesigning the statement?

2. How would you convince the dentist of the value of a change in statement form?

How's Your English?

Read the information on adjectives in Appendix A; then on a separate sheet of paper type each adjective from the following sentences and classify it.

Example: Business forms are necessary in most types of businesses.

business   descriptive adjective
most   definitive adjective

1. Office workers must understand the purpose of all forms they process.
2. Every section of a business form should serve a specific purpose.
3. Efficient employees seek ways to improve company forms.
4. Horizontal lines should not be used in forms.
5. Align blank spaces on a form so tabulator stops can be used to save maximum time when typing.

Office Work

1. Make a collection of business forms that have been received at home or that you can procure from your friends who work in offices. Be prepared to discuss their use with the class.

2. Redesign one or more of the forms collected for Exercise 1, and give reasons for the changes you recommend.

UNIT 3 | Purchasing and Selling

PART 1:

Purchasing

Purchasing and receiving goods are important operations in business enterprises. In large organizations these operations are handled by separate departments; in smaller organizations, by purchasing and receiving clerks. Whether the buying is done through a department head, by a purchasing agent, or by a purchasing clerk, the aim is the same — to secure for the firm the needed material and equipment of the desired quality at the most reasonable price. The reputation of the seller for honest dealing and prompt delivery is an important factor to be considered in deciding where major purchases should be made.

The whole purchasing procedure is a very well-planned office routine in which each step is determined by the work that precedes it. All purchasing falls into the following orderly sequence: requesting the goods needed, obtaining quotations on the cost of the goods needed, preparing a purchase order, checking the incoming shipment, and adjusting any damage or claim.

Purchase Requisition. Most of the work of the purchasing department revolves around the purchase order. Before the purchase order can be made out, however, the purchasing agent must be told what goods, supplies, equipment, or services are needed and the approximate date on which they will be required. The *purchase requisition* is the form used to inform the purchasing agent or some other authorized buyer for the firm what specific items should be purchased.

You will find that the purchase requisition requires such information as the current date, the date the goods are needed, and a detailed description of the goods requested, which includes the trade name, catalog number, quantity to be ordered, and the price of each item, if it is known. It may also indicate the name and address of a firm from which the goods may be purchased. All this information you must ascertain before completing this form.

Requisition No.:	10113	142C-1	PURCHASE REQUISITION

Requisition No.: 10113   142C-1   PURCHASE REQUISITION

Date Issued: June 25, 19--

Date Required: July 25, 19--

Deliver To: Assembly Department

Location: Basement

Job. No.: 584-31

Electronic
RESEARCH CO.
32 FOSTER ROAD
LONG BEACH, CALIFORNIA 90805

Approved By: L.M.C.

Quantity	Description
35	Spring assembly #622
200	Bearings #230
70	Heavy duty relay 50V #272
490	Screw set #478

Purchase requisition

As a rule, you would prepare two copies of a purchase requisition. You would send the original copy to the purchasing agent and keep the duplicate in your files. Before forwarding the purchase requisition to the purchasing agent, you should have it signed by the head of your department or the executive for whom you work. If you are employed by a large organization, you may be required to prepare additional copies of each purchase requisition so that they may be available for the auditing department or other departments.

In some instances, approval by some other officer of the firm, in addition to the purchasing agent, is necessary before the requisition can be acted upon. This is particularly true when new equipment or out-of-the-ordinary items are being requested.

Request for Quotation.   When your requisition reaches the purchasing department, a quotation file is consulted. Almost all purchasing departments maintain such a file which they consult to determine whether a recent price for the item or items in question is on file and what firm or firms submitted such a price. The quotation file is usually a file of 6″ x 4″ cards on which essential information about quotations is entered as it is received. If a recent quotation for goods that you requisitioned is available, the goods will probably be ordered immediately. If a recent price is not available, it is customary to send a *request for quotation* to some or all of the business organizations that sell the product requested. The purchasing

```
          ┌                              ┐
          │  BYRON JACKSON & COMPANY     │
 TO       │  4998 Michigan Avenue        │
          │  Chicago, Illinois  60614    │
          └                              ┘
```

Electronic RESEARCH CO.

32 FOSTER ROAD
LONG BEACH, CALIFORNIA 90805

ORDER NO. 05202

SHIP VIA Railway Express

DATE June 27, 19--

TERMS 2/10 net 30

QUANTITY	CAT. NO.	DESCRIPTION	PRICE	TOTAL
35	622	Spring assembly	14.35 ea.	502.25
200	230	Bearings	3.35 ea.	670.00
70	272	Heavy duty relay 50V	7.50 ea.	525.00
490	478	Screw set	.03 ea.	14.70
				1,711.95

Purchase order

agent determines which business would be likely to sell the commodity by referring to his own catalog file, to *Thomas' Register of American Manufacturers*, or to a similar general purchasing directory.

The request for quotation carries the name of the firm making the request, the current date, a description of the item, the quantity to be purchased, and the desired delivery date. The form is sometimes marked in large letters "THIS IS NOT AN ORDER!"

Purchase Order. The goods that you requisitioned may be ordered in a number of ways: by writing an order letter, by sending a telegram, by making a telephone call, by giving an order to a salesman, by filling out and mailing an order blank that is included as part of a catalog, or by filling out a *purchase order* that has been especially designed for the purpose. As a general rule, firms prefer to use purchase orders which they mail to the persons or firms from which they order goods (the vendors). If the goods are urgently needed, they are usually ordered by telephone or telegraph, but a purchase order to cover the transaction is prepared and mailed to the vendor as a confirmation of the order.

The printed purchase order, of which four or more duplicate copies are usually prepared, bears the name, address, and telephone number of the firm issuing the order, and usually provides space for the date of issue, date required or delivery schedule, the name and address of the vendor, the purchase order number, the requisition number, the quantity and unit, the description of the material, the price and amount, and the shipping instructions. The four duplicate copies, after they are signed by the purchasing agent, are usually distributed in this manner:

Original........................To vendor
First carbon copy...............Filed in purchasing department
Second carbon copy.............To accounting department or accounts payable department
Third carbon copy..............To department where requisition originated
Fourth carbon copy.............To receiving department

Receiving Record. When goods you requisitioned arrive, the receiving clerk checks the goods received against the copy of the purchase order. In some instances, he checks by taking a physical count of the items received. If the check of the goods actually received does not agree with the quantities listed on the purchase order, the discrepancies are brought to the attention of the seller.

The receiving department fills out a *receiving record* when goods are received. This record ordinarily carries such information as the name of the firm from which the material was received, the date of receipt, the packing slip or box number, method of shipment, cost of transportation, purchase order number, quantity or the number of items received, and such other descriptive information as may be necessary, including catalog numbers, parts numbers, net weight, delivery instructions, and condition of shipment.

Four or more copies of the receiving record are usually prepared, depending upon the size of the organization, and are routed in this manner:

Original........................To purchasing department
First carbon copy...............To accounts payable department
Second carbon copy.............Filed in receiving department
Third carbon copy..............To stock room

The purchasing department uses its copy to check against the purchase orders. Many firms follow a practice of transferring the items from the receiving record to the back of the purchase order on file in the purchasing department. This is particularly important when only part of an order is delivered at one time. The receiving records are usually filed in the purchasing department alphabetically by vendors' names for a limited period of time and then destroyed. Rarely are they kept more than six months; frequently they are kept for only one month.

Purchase Invoice. When the vendor ships the merchandise you requisitioned, he usually mails an invoice to your firm's buyer on the same day. The invoice is known to the vendor as a *sales invoice* and to the buyer,

Invoice	376621		Byron Jackson & Company			
Telephone MElrose 1-9072			4998 Michigan Avenue • Chicago, Illinois 60614			

Sold To	Electronic Research Co. 32 Foster Road Long Beach, Calif. 90805		Date	July 6, 19—		
			Our Order No.	20337		
			Your Order No.	05202		
Terms	2/10 net 30		Shipped By	Railway Express		

Quantity	Description	Cat. No.	Unit Price	Amount
35	Spring assembly	622	14.35 each	502.25
200	Bearings	230	3.35 each	670.00
70	Heavy duty relay 50V	272	7.50 each	525.00
490	Screw set	478	.03 each	14.70
				1,711.95

Checked By	16			Salesman	Johnson

Purchase invoice

your firm, as a *purchase invoice*. An invoice usually includes the current date, the name and address of the vendor, the name and address of the purchaser, the invoice number, the purchaser's order number, the terms of payment, the method of shipment, the quantity of each item, a description of each item, the unit price, the extensions, and the total. It may also show trade discounts and other deductions allowed the purchaser.

Incoming purchase invoices are usually handled by the purchasing department. As a rule only one copy is received, although some firms request additional copies. A clerk in the purchasing department checks the purchase invoices against the terms and conditions of the purchase order to be sure that they agree, especially in regard to quantity and price. If they agree, the date and the amount of the invoice are entered on the reverse side of the purchasing department's copy of the purchase order. If and when the invoice is approved by the purchasing department, it is stamped "approved," initialed by the proper authority, and then sent to the accounts payable department.

Request for Credit. If the purchase order and the purchase invoice do not agree, the discrepancy is called to the attention of the purchasing agent. He either approves the difference or, if the discrepancy is in the nature of an overcharge, writes the vendor for a credit memorandum to cover the discrepancy. Some firms have a special form called a *request for credit* that they use in such a situation. This same form is used when goods are returned because they are not satisfactory or when there is a return of containers or other articles on which credits or rebates are owing to the purchaser.

So, the original requisition which you sent to the purchasing department or clerk has been filled, after going through the purchasing procedure, and the goods presumably arrive in your office on the date you requested. All that you had to do was to fill out the requisition; the purchasing department did the rest.

Follow-up. You may often find it necessary to write to a firm from which goods have been ordered requesting it to speed shipment. Orders are often placed with firms that are doing a considerable amount of business, and as a result it is necessary to find out when goods will be delivered. Follow-up may be necessary only occasionally in most businesses, but may occur more frequently in certain lines of business.

As a rule, purchase orders carry a definite date when the goods should be shipped or delivered. A follow-up file should be maintained in which duplicates of the purchase orders are placed according to the dates on which delivery is expected. If the goods have not been delivered by the established date, the purchasing department usually sends a follow-up to the vendor to determine why shipment has been delayed. In some lines of business, late delivery may make the merchandise worthless, and in such instances, the purchaser may cancel the order if a written request for immediate delivery is not acted upon at once.

A follow-up is either an individually dictated letter or a form letter, depending upon the circumstances. Sometimes telegraph messages are used; in very urgent cases, you might place a long-distance telephone call to expedite delivery.

Catalog File. All purchasing departments receive a large number of catalogs. Because these catalogs vary so widely in size, they must be stored in bookcases and file cabinets. The catalogs that can be stored on end like books are placed together on a bookshelf or in bookcases. The catalogs that are more like pamphlets are often placed in open-back files, which are themselves placed on shelves or in bookcases; and the catalogs that are really announcements containing only a few pages are placed in folders and filed in regular file cabinets. Each section of this file is assigned a letter so that the section that contains the book-like catalogs might be section "A"; the section containing the pamphlet-like catalogs, section "B"; and the section containing the thin announcements, section "C."

The catalogs within a section are also assigned a number, these numbers being assigned in the order in which the catalogs are received. When a new catalog is received to replace an old one, the old catalog is discarded and the new one assigned the number that the old one had. When a catalog is received that does *not* replace an old one, it is assigned the next unused number.

Two card indexes are usually maintained in connection with the catalog file. One index shows the names and addresses of the firms that issued the catalogs. The other shows the names of commodities in the catalogs, listing for each commodity the names of the firms selling that product together with the section letter and number that have been assigned to their catalogs. Maintaining this catalog file and its indexes may be your responsibility upon employment in a purchasing office.

Interviewing Salesmen. In a small organization, the telephone operator might greet the salesmen; but in a larger organization where the purchasing department has its own office or suite of offices, a person employed in that department might have this responsibility.

Salesmen call for a number of reasons — to introduce a new or lower-priced product, to discuss a change in price, to take up problems that concern the use of their products or services in the plant, to secure a larger portion of business, to negotiate a contract for purchases of materials or supplies, or to answer a request for them to call.

Regardless of the reason for a salesman's call, whether it be by telephone or in person, it is most important that he be well received and interviewed promptly, courteously, and intelligently. It is true that salesmen are interested in selling and therefore may not be of as great interest to the business as are prospective customers. However, it is definitely wise to follow the policy that those who have a legitimate reason for calling should be well received. This will create the best type of relationship between buyer and seller. Furthermore, from representatives of other organizations many excellent ideas may be obtained relating to such things as different or new materials, new machines or devices, and new ways of performing certain operations.

One of the most important duties of employees in the purchasing department is talking with these businessmen; and the most important duty of the clerk who receives them is to see that they are treated with businesslike courtesy and that the interview is scheduled as satisfactorily as possible. Unit 8 covers the activities of a receptionist in detail.

Study Questions

1. What are the principal steps in the purchasing routine?
2. In a large business, how is a *purchase requisition* used?

3. What is the value of a *request for quotation*? What information does this form show?
4. What is a *purchase order*?

5. How does the *receiving record* protect the purchaser from shortages?

6. What information is shown on a *purchase invoice*?

7. What is the purpose of a *request for credit* form?

8. In what ways may a follow-up of a purchase order be made?

9. Describe the plan usually used for cross-indexing the catalog file.

10. Why should you be courteous to salesmen seeking to visit the purchasing department?

What Do You Think?

1. Why is the purchasing activity important in any company?

2. Would the purchasing department of a bank be as important as the purchasing department of a manufacturing concern? Why or why not?

3. Should a new employee in a purchasing department offer to set up a system and file the catalogs if there is no logical system being used?

Your Personal Qualities

Bob Matthew, a clerk in the buying office, types and mails out the firm's purchase orders. Unfortunately, he is always behind in his work, and the purchase orders are delayed from four to seven days.

Bob feels that he could get out the orders earlier if he were permitted to use a new form. The present form contains horizontal lines for *Destination, Route, Order No., Date, Terms,* etc., but the lines do not agree with the vertical spacing on the typewriter. The spacing for the boxed information at the top of the purchase order does not agree with the spacing for the columns.

Questions: 1. If you were Bob, what recommendations would you make for redesigning the purchase order?

2. How would you convince your employer of the value of a change in the purchase order form?

How's Your English?

Read the section on adverbs in Appendix A, and type on a separate sheet of paper the correct sentences in the following groups:

1. a. The typist was very pleased.
   b. The typist was very much pleased.

2. a. The instructions were of no value to nobody.
   b. The instructions were of no value to anybody.

3. a. She arranges letters nice.
   b. She arranges letters nicely.

4. a. This style of letter is very nice.
   b. This style of letter is real nice.

5. How are you?
   a. I am good.
   b. I am well.

6. a. The typist had to much to do.
   b. The typist had too much to do.

Office Work

Using the form design suggestions on pages 53–55, draw up the following business forms:

1. Purchase Requisition
2. Purchase Order
3. Sales Invoice

Office Work Assignments

4: Requisitions

Prepare the following requisitions in duplicate. If suitable requisition forms are not available, prepare the requisitions in the form of memorandums.

1. Requisition No. 101 from the purchasing department for the personnel department; Advise Mr. James on delivery; Date Issued (today's date); Date Required (20 days later); Approved by Michael Henry; Requested by Florence Field.

1 Executive Desk, 78″ x 38″, Style 15001, Custom Finish. Price: $177.40

1 Executive Chair, Style C-198, Top Grain Leather. Price: $92.55

2. Requisition No. 102 from the purchasing department for the statistical department; Advise John Andrews on delivery; Date Issued (today's date); Date Required (45 days later); Approved by Michael Henry; Requested by Harry Brown.

2 Calculating Machine Desks, 60″ x 30″, Style 15027-R, Metal, Gray and Olive Green Finish. Price: $103.65 each.

2 Fully automatic Bryan Calculators, 10 bank, Model STW-10. Price: $825.00 each.

5: Purchase Orders

1. If you do not have a blank purchase order, type one according to the style illustrated on page 59.

Purchase Order No. 2274 from:

MELROSE CORPORATION
7600 Talman Avenue
Melrose Park, Illinois 60161

to:

Gordon Brothers
1200 State Street
Chicago, Illinois 60605

Deliver to:

Melrose Park, Illinois

Date: December 20, 19--; Requisition No. 3961; Terms 2/10, net 30 days

Ship Via: ICRR; F.O.B. Point: Chicago

4 Legal-Size Filing Cabinets, List price $84.50 each

8 Letter-Size Filing Cabinets, List price $75.50 each

6 Adjustable Posture Chairs, List price $42.50 each

2. Type Purchase Order No. 2278 from:

MELROSE CORPORATION
7600 Talman Avenue
Melrose Park, Illinois 60161

to:

Allied Office Machine Co.
1230 Wabash Avenue
Chicago, Illinois 60605

Deliver to:

Melrose Park, Illinois

Date: December 22, 19--; Requisition No. 3971; Terms 2/10, net 30 days

Ship Via: ICRR; F.O.B. Point: Chicago

6 Manual National Type-writers, 11″ carriage, pica type. List price: $195.00 each

2 Electric National Type-writers, 12″ carriage, Canterbury type. List price: $325.00 each

1 Dayton Printing Calculator, Model #96. List price: $655.00

6: Invoices

If blank business forms are not available for this and the following problems, use plain paper, and type the information that is ordinarily printed on such forms as shown in the illustrations on page 61.

Type invoices in duplicate for the following sales by the National Furniture Company, 1440 Jefferson Avenue, Forest Hills, New York 12068, on December 3, 19--, terms 2/10, net 30 days. The quantities and unit prices are given; you are to make all extensions and ascertain the totals.

1. The Howard Supply Co., 426 Edwards Road, Trenton, New Jersey 08603:

9 Four-Drawer Filing Cabinets, Standard Finish, Style #1805. Price: $85.10 each

15 Counter-Height (3-drawer) Filing Cabinets, Standard Finish, Style #1855. Price: $64.25 each

84 Frames for Pendaflex File Folders Style #812. Price: $1.35 each

2. The Kramer Publishing Co., 684 Carter Street, Unionville, Connecticut 06805:

8 Bookcases, open, 52 3/8″ × 37 1/2″ × 15″, Style #1597, Grained Finish. Price: $43.55 each

2 Single Pedestal Desks, 60″ × 30″, Style 15021-S1, Custom Finish. Price: $114.75 each

28 Desk Trays, Letter Size, Style #032. Price: $2.05 each

2 Office Chairs, Side Arm Chairs, Style #198, Custom Finish. Price: $50.95 each

UNIT 3 | Purchasing and Selling

PART 2:

Selling

Recording the data directly connected with the sale of merchandise or services is one of the key operations of any business enterprise. The sales forms on which the data are recorded vary with the size and type of business, but all firms use a sales order or order-invoice form. Department stores and other retail stores also use "layaway" order forms, installment order forms, and sales books. Almost all sales organizations use sales summary forms, sales analysis forms, and call reports.

As an office worker, you should understand the sales procedures followed by modern business firms and the purpose of each of the standard sales forms because much of your activity may deal with sales. If you are employed in a sales department or by a small firm, you may be expected to prepare and process sales forms.

Sales Order Forms. What happened to the purchase order prepared by your purchasing department when it was received by the vendor? First, a sales order form was prepared. A *sales order* form is used by most firms to record the sale of merchandise. It provides space for the name and address of the customer, the customer's order number, the seller's invoice number, the terms of payment, the shipping instructions, the number of items, a description of each item, and the unit price. The sales order usually lists any special instructions or conditions and the trade discounts allowed.

The number of copies of a sales order varies with the requirements of different business enterprises, but they are usually distributed as follows:

Original......................Filed in sales or order department

First carbon copy...............To billing department

Second carbon copy.............To stockkeeping department to take items from stock

Third carbon copy...............To shipping department

Fourth carbon copy.............To customer to acknowledge order

Fifth carbon copy...............To statistical department
Sixth carbon copy...............To salesman who placed or gets
                                   credit for the order

Credit Approval. When the order is received without an accompanying payment in full, it must be approved by the credit department before the merchandise can be packed and shipped. In some firms, the credit approval is obtained before the sales order form is prepared. In other firms, the sales order is prepared first and then the credit department is asked to indicate its approval or disapproval. The credit department may approve the shipment of the goods on the terms your firm suggested for the goods ordered; but for some concerns with poor credit reputations, it may decide that the goods should be shipped C.O.D. When the latter procedure is recommended, and the terms are different from the credit terms suggested by the buyer, it is often necessary to write to the customer tactfully informing him of the situation and asking him whether the goods should be shipped under the vendor's terms.

Billing. When the order is shipped to your firm, the bill or invoice is mailed. This vital operation of a business enterprise is commonly known as *billing*, but in some firms is called *invoicing*. After the sales order has been approved by the credit department, and after the stock room, shipping department, and other affected departments have been informed of the order, the invoice is prepared.

An invoice shows a complete listing of the goods shipped, including the following information about each item: the quantity, unit, description, price, and the extension (multiplication of the quantity by the unit price). It also carries the firm's name, the customer's name and address, the shipping destination, the method of shipping, the customer's order number, the firm's invoice number, the total amount of the invoice, and the terms of payment.

The copies of an invoice are usually distributed as follows:

Original........................To customer
First carbon copy...............To accounting department for
                                   accounts receivable
Second carbon copy.............To filing department for alpha-
                                   betic filing by customer's name
Third carbon copy..............To filing department for nu-
                                   meric filing by customer's in-
                                   voice number
Fourth carbon copy.............To sales department

Preparing the Invoice. Every well-organized business enterprise establishes a definite procedure for preparing invoices. This procedure may differ with the number of invoices prepared by each concern. A small number of invoices may be prepared on typewriters, a greater number on special billing machines, and a very large volume of invoices with integrated data processing equipment.

Most invoices prepared on billing machines or integrated data processing equipment are typed on continuous multiple forms with interleaved one-time carbon paper.

Most wholesale and manufacturing concerns mail an invoice on the day that the goods are shipped. Retail stores usually issue a sales slip at the time the goods are sold and send the customer at the end of the month, or sometime during the month, a statement listing all the items that have appeared on the sales slips, or merely enclosing a copy of the sales slips and listing the amount of each slip and a total due.

Cycle Billing. Your firm may not receive all bills at the end of the month. Some companies may bill you on the fourteenth; others, on the twenty-first. This procedure is called *cycle billing*. Many department stores and several public utilities, including telephone companies and gas and electric companies, have divided their lists of customers and send out bills on different dates in the month, rather than send out all bills at the end of the month. This makes it possible for the billing departments to work steadily, to avoid peak loads, and to send out bills when they are completed. Some companies divide their customer lists alphabetically; others, by districts, geographic locations, or sales territories.

Punched-Card Bills. More and more companies are using punched cards for monthly bills. This procedure not only reduces the cost of postage, but also saves the cost of envelopes and the stuffing of each bill into an envelope. It also permits the returned bills to be sorted and tabulated mechanically with punched-card machines. If the punched-card bills are sent in envelopes, however, they are usually enclosed in window envelopes to eliminate the time-consuming envelope addressing process.

Calculating and Checking Invoices. All invoices should be checked for accuracy before they are mailed to the customers. The checking should be done by someone other than the person who actually prepared the invoice. The extensions can be checked with a desk calculator or by checking the items against precomputed tables. A *precomputed table* is one that lists the items that might be sold and in other columns the prices charged for the various units, such as a dozen, a gross, or a case.

Credit Memorandum. It is inevitable that some customers will return merchandise for one reason or another. Your firm, too, may return merchandise delivered too late to be of value, merchandise of the wrong

		No. 722		

Credit Memorandum

Byron Jackson & Company

4998 Michigan Avenue • Chicago, Illinois 60614
Telephone MElrose 1-9072

No. 722

Date July 23, 19--

To Electronic Research Co.
32 Foster Road
Long Beach, California 90805

YOUR ACCOUNT HAS BEEN CREDITED FOR:

Quantity	Description	Cat. No.	Unit Price	Amount
6	Heavy duty relay 50V	272	7.50 ea	45.00

Credit memorandum

kind, style, or color, or merchandise received in a damaged condition. There may be other reasons why customers do not wish to keep the goods. In most instances, after the customer informs the seller of the situation, the customer will be instructed to return the merchandise. In some cases, it may be more advantageous to make a special allowance to the customer to cover the loss if he keeps the merchandise.

When merchandise is returned or when an allowance is granted to a customer, a *credit memorandum* is issued. This credit memorandum is very much like an invoice and carries about the same information that appears on an invoice. At least two copies are made: one for the customer to whom the credit memorandum is issued, and the other copy for the accounting department to be used in crediting the customer's account for the amount of the returned goods or of the allowance. Frequently, additional copies are prepared: one copy for the receiving department to indicate the goods to be returned, and one copy for the sales department as a record of sales returns and allowances. All business organizations endeavor to keep sales returns and allowances at a minimum.

Statements. At regular intervals, usually monthly, the accounting department sends each customer a *statement* of his account. The statement shows the amount the customer owed at the beginning of the month, the charges and payments made during the month, and the balance the customer owes at the end of the month. An illustration of a statement is shown on page 71.

Date		July 31, 19--		Statement of Account

Byron Jackson & Company

4998 Michigan Avenue • Chicago, Illinois 60614
Telephone MElrose 1-9072

To: Electronic Research Co.
32 Foster Road
Long Beach, Calif. 90805

Date	Items	Debits	Credits	Balance Due
July 1	Balance			850.21
July 6	Our invoice #376621	1,711.95		
July 9	Check		850.21	
July 22	Credit #722		45.00	1,666.95

Statement

Statements are usually prepared on bookkeeping machines, punched-card tabulating machines, and other data processing equipment, depending upon the size of the business. Although the preparation of the statements is the responsibility of the accounting department in all but small businesses, it is sometimes necessary for the office employees in other departments to assist in the preparation of statements, particularly during peak periods.

It may be that your position will be in the sales office, and you will have more to do with the sales procedure described than just completing a requisition form. Your knowledge and understanding of these key operations of purchasing and selling, in any case, will enable you to be a more capable assistant and partner to your supervisor in any business.

Wholesale Selling. In addition to the office duties for selling already described, many special types of clerical work are involved in the activities of the sales department of a company that supplies materials to manufacturers, of a manufacturer who sells to wholesalers, and of a wholesaler who sells to retailers. These responsibilities include the preparation of lists of prospective customers, the maintenance of prospect files, and the analysis of sales data.

Prospect Lists. Obviously, a small firm intending to sell most of its products locally has a different problem in preparing a list of prospective customers from the one a nationally known business has in marketing a product in almost every community in the country. A candymaker who plans to market his product in local and nearby communities could prepare a list of prospects by referring to the classified section of the telephone directories of the area. A firm that plans to distribute its product to retail stores nationally would obtain a list of the retail outlets that might buy its product.

Naturally, firms use different means for making up a list of prospects. Some firms develop their list of prospects by salesmen's contacts; others make up a list by advertising in newspapers and magazines, requesting customers to respond. Clerks then transfer to the prospect list or to prospect cards the names of those individuals or firms appearing on the advertising coupons sent in.

Prospect File. The prospect file is usually a card file, frequently a visible-card file, arranged alphabetically or geographically. Each card shows the name and address of the prospect, the product or products in which the prospect is most likely to be interested, and has space to indicate the last date on which the prospect was contacted by mail or telephone and his response. The card may also indicate when the next contact should be made.

In some firms, the salesmen decide when a prospect should be contacted, but in other firms a standard period is established so that each customer is contacted at more or less regular intervals. Clerks are frequently employed to prepare the card and to transfer the information to it from various reports. One of your office routines might be to set indicators or signals on the cards to draw attention to the time when the next contact is to be made.

Analyses of Sales Data. A clerk or group of clerks is usually assigned the responsibility of preparing sales analyses to give the sales manager, the salesmen, and others in the organization who might be interested in this type of information a picture of sales activities over given periods of time. Sales may be classified according to individual commodities or groups of commodities, by departments, or by territories.

If the number of items is large, the necessary computations may be made by machine. One type of bookkeeping machine permits the distribution of items into many different classifications. The operator presses a key for each extension on each invoice and then presses another key for the type of commodity. The totals indicate the amount of each product sold in the period for which the analysis is made.

If the number of different items sold and the volume of business are large enough, another group of machines of the card-punch data processing variety may be used. With this type of machine, a card is punched for each extension and the cards are separated on a sorting machine according to products. The cards are then processed on an analysis machine that lists the amounts and shows the totals. More and more of this type of work is being done automatically with the use of integrated data processing equipment.

Retail Selling. A number of the special office tasks in a retail sales department are similar to those in a wholesale sales department. For example, a retail store may prepare a prospect list or maintain a prospect file. In addition, however, the employee in a retail sales department may have such duties as preparing price tags that use code numbers or figures for cost prices, checking the sales slips or tickets that are prepared by the sales clerks, and preparing summaries of sales.

Price Tags. In many retail stores, a price tag is attached to every item in stock. The tag indicates the selling price and, frequently, the cost price of the item. The cost price is usually placed on the tag in code so that people in the organization can tell what the item cost is but the customer cannot. Some words are generally used to represent the code. It can be any set of words containing ten different letters. For example, a sales tag showing "twe" on an article would indicate that the article cost $4.15 if the code were:

WHITE CLOUD
1 2345 67890

Sales Slips. The information that the sales slips carry depends largely upon what the firm desires. Ordinarily, they include the name and address of the customer; the name and address of the firm selling the goods; a place to indicate whether the sale is cash, C.O.D., or charge; and a list of the items sold and the prices of those items. The sales slips are totaled by the salesclerk, who retains one copy to send to the office later. The other copy is given to the customer with the merchandise or, if the purchase is to be delivered, is enclosed in the package containing the merchandise.

When the sales slips are received in the office, they are checked for accuracy. Frequently, adding or calculating machines are used in this work to check computations.

Sales Summaries. At the close of the day's work, the salesclerk is expected to prepare a summary of the day's sales. The sales are usually classified as cash, C.O.D., or charge. As a rule, a three-column summary sheet is furnished so that the sales may be easily classified and totaled. This record is also checked for accuracy by someone in the office.

In most stores, especially those that sell more than one type of commodity, sales are further analyzed by departments. This analysis is completed in the office. It is usually accomplished by taking the summary sheets that are submitted by the salesclerks and adding the totals by departments. In this way, a total of the sales of each department is prepared each day, and a summary report is made for the interested individuals in the firm. One copy of this summary of sales is usually kept in a chronological file so that the sales for a particular period may be found easily and compared with the sales of other periods. The daily summaries are totaled to obtain weekly, monthly, and yearly summaries.

Study Questions

1. Why should an office worker understand the sales procedure?
2. How is a *sales order* form used?
3. What is the purpose of credit approval?
4. What is *cycle billing*?
5. What are the advantages of using a punched-card bill?
6. How may accuracy be insured in preparing customers' bills?

7. What is a *precomputed table*?
8. When is a *credit memorandum* issued and how is it used?
9. What information is shown on a *statement*?
10. How are prospect lists developed?
11. Why are sales analyses prepared?
12. Why is a code desirable in listing cost prices on price tags?

What Do You Think?

1. Why have so many forms and reports been developed to cover the activities of the selling function of a business?
2. As a new florist in town, what steps would you take in developing a prospect file?

3. What agencies in your community might be of special help in developing prospect lists?

4. Do you think that the purchasing and sales departments are equally important in a business?

Your Personal Qualities

Clark Miller is employed in the sales division of Lippincott and Company. One of his duties is to compile sales records for all the salesmen in the northwest area of the United States. Mr. Kendrick, a salesman in the state of Washington, is consistently late in submitting his reports. As a consequence, Clark must work many hours overtime in completing his monthly report, as he must wait until all reports are in before he begins his computations. Mr. Lippincott has recently announced that no compensation is to be made for overtime work.

Question: What should Clark do about this situation?

How's Your English?

Read about prepositions and conjunctions in Appendix A and type a list of correct prepositions or conjunctions for the following sentences:

1. The clerk went (into, in) the manager's office only to learn that he was (in, into) the mail room.

2. A typist must choose (between, among) three possible salutations.

3. Seldom (if, or) ever should you fail to check computations.

4. She types (as, like) you do.

5. You will not type good figure work (without, unless) you practice it.

Office Work

Prepare a prospect list of ten firms in your community which should be contacted for advertising in your school newspaper. Include the prospects' company names and addresses and the names of the owners or other persons for the advertising manager to contact.

Office Work Assignments

7: Credit Memorandums

Type credit memorandums in duplicate for the following credits allowed customers on January 14, by the Modern Furniture Company, Coral Gables, Florida 33926:

1. Mr. J. B. Young, 1462 Alhambra Circle, Coral Gables, Florida 33926:

1 Captain's Chair $55.00
1 Night Table $39.50

2. Mrs. Ellen Baker, 3714 Ponce de Leon Boulevard, Coral Gables, Florida 33926:

2 Arm Chairs at $99.50 each
1 End Table $35.00

8: Statements of Account

Type monthly statements of account in duplicate to be sent to the following customers of Haines and Williams, wholesale grocers, Knoxville, Tennessee 37903, May 1, 19--:

1. Robert L. Wilkins, 2580 Moorman Avenue, Knoxville, Tennessee 37905:

Date	Code	Division	Charges	Credits
April 1	C-111	83	142.80	
6	C-113	83	129.65	
10	R-201	90		142.80
15	R-212	90		4.95
21	C-119	83	18.50	

2. Anthony M. Upshaw, 501 Klotter Street, Athens, Tennessee 37303:

Date	Code	Division	Charges	Credits
April 15	C-151	83	39.20	
26	R-171	90		39.20
28	C-155	83	14.95	

9: Handwritten Statements

Some business organizations make a practice of having their monthly statements handwritten. In your best handwriting, with ink, make the two statements below to be mailed by a dry cleaner. If you do not have blank statement paper, draw up your own in the style of the one shown on page 71. (The abbreviation "pr" means "pressed," and "dc" means "dry cleaned.")

1. April 30, 19--. Mr. Frank L. Porton, 32 Washington Place, Freeland, New York.

Mar 31	4 suits, pr	3.00
Apr 5	1 suit, pr	.75
7	1 suit, pr	.75
8	2 suits, dc	3.00
	3 suits, pr	2.25
	1 quilted robe, dc	2.00
	1 suit, pr	.75
Apr 12	1 suit, dc	2.00
21	1 tux, dc	2.00

	1 suit, dc	1.50
	1 jacket, pr	.50
	2 pants, pr	.70
	1 suit, pr	.75
28	2 jackets, dc	2.00
	2 suits, pr	1.50

2. December 31, 19--. Mr. Frank L. Porton, 32 Washington Place, Freeland, New York.

Dec 1	4 suits, pr	3.00
5	1 topper, dc	1.50
10	2 suits, pr	1.50
	2 chair, 3 cushion covers, dc	6.00
11	2 suits, altered	19.00
12	2 suits, pr	1.50
15	1 dress, dc	3.00
	2 black velvet dresses, dc	6.00
	1 red velvet dress, dc	3.00
17	2 suits, pr	1.50
21	2 suits, pr	1.50
24	1 suit, pr	.75

UNIT 4 | Inventory and the Stock Room

PART 1:

Goods Received and on Hand

The receiving department of a business firm offers fine opportunities for initial employment to young men. If you are employed in this type of office work, you will be responsible for receiving and checking all shipments coming into the company The parcel post packages will be delivered at regular intervals during the day by mailmen; the air and railway express packages will be delivered by expressmen. You will also receive shipments from truckmen who deliver merchandise shipped initially by air freight and by local and long-distance truck. If the railroads maintain pickup and delivery service, truckmen will also deliver railroad freight shipments. If this service is not maintained, you will receive an arrival notice from the railroad when goods reach the local terminal. In such cases, the firm will send its trucks or employ a local truckman to pick up the shipments.

Transportation Charges on Goods Received. The transportation charges for many items are prepaid, but in other instances goods are shipped collect. In some firms, collect charges are paid in cash when the goods are delivered; in other cases, arrangements have been made with the carrier to send a bill for such charges at the end of the month. If a package is received C.O.D., the amount due is paid in cash or by check according to the amount due and the willingness of the carrier to accept a check.

Record of Goods Received. As the clerk responsible for receiving goods, you will find it necessary to keep a careful record of all incoming shipments in the order in which they are received. Such a record, known as a "record of goods received" or a "goods received record," must include the name and the address of the vendor (the seller of the goods), the number of pieces in the shipment, the weight of the shipment, the purchase order number, material, lot, or batch number, and your name as the employee who received the goods. It must also indicate the name of the carrier, the amount of the transportation charges, and whether the goods were sent prepaid or collect. If the shipment was sent collect, such a record should show whether the charges were paid in cash at the time of delivery or if a bill for them is to be submitted later by the carrier.

Checking Goods Received. After you accept a shipment, you must unpack the goods, inspect them, count them, and check against the copy of the purchase order, which you should ordinarily have on file. You should be sure that the correct number of items has been received and that the items meet fully the specifications set forth in the purchase order. As a result of increased government regulatory controls, all food and drug items must be identified by batch or lot number. As the receiving clerk, you should fill out a *goods received slip* or *goods received report* when goods are received.

Goods Received Slip. In many firms, when the goods in a shipment have been counted and checked, the receiving clerk is required to prepare a special form called a "goods received slip" or a "goods received report." This form ordinarily carries such information as the name of the firm from which the material was received, the date, the packing slip or box number, how shipped, cost of transportation, purchase order number, quantity or the number of items, and such other descriptive information as may be necessary, including catalog numbers, parts numbers, net weight, delivery instructions, and condition of shipment.

Three or more copies of this receiving report are usually made, depending upon the size of the organization and the number of departments that may need copies of the report. Copies usually go to the purchasing agent, the stock clerk, and the bookkeeper.

The purchasing department uses its copy to check against the purchase orders. In many firms the information on the items is transferred from the goods received slip to the back of the purchase order on file in the purchasing department. This is particularly important when only part of an order is delivered at one time. For example, a mail-order house may order fifty cases of shoes from a manufacturer, and the manufacturer may ship the shoes to the mail-order house in five- or ten-case lots. Each time a shipment is received it is necessary for the receiving department of the mail-order house to make out a goods received slip, and each time, the purchasing department enters the items received on the back of its copy of the purchase order. In this way, deducting the shipment received from the amount of the original purchase will indicate the balance of the order yet to be received.

Goods received reports are usually filed in the purchasing department alphabetically by the vendors' names for a limited period of time and then destroyed. The length of time that a report is retained depends on the nature of the business. Frequently they are kept for only one month, rarely more than six months.

Disposition of Goods Received. If a shipment of goods that has been received is not completely satisfactory, that shipment is usually set aside while an executive takes the matter up with the vendor and makes arrangements either for a satisfactory adjustment or for the return of the goods. If the goods are to be returned, they must be repacked and shipped to the vendor, usually by the same means by which they arrived. If the goods are satisfactory on arrival or if a satisfactory adjustment has been made about those that were not, the goods are sent to the individual or department that requisitioned them.

If the goods were ordered by the stock room, they will be sent by the receiving clerk to the stock room where the stock clerk will check them against his copy of the purchase requisition, put them in the proper place in the stock room, and make an entry on the stock record card.

Purchases Invoices. These have been described in Part 1 of Unit 3. When a firm ships merchandise, it usually mails an invoice on the same day. See the illustration of an invoice on page 61.

Incoming purchase invoices are usually handled by the purchasing department. As a rule, only one copy is received, although some firms request additional copies.

A clerk in the purchasing department checks the purchase invoice against the terms and conditions of the purchase order to be sure that they agree, especially in regard to quantity and price. If they check, the date and the amount of the invoice are entered on the reverse side of the purchasing department's copy of the purchase order. If and when the invoice is approved by the purchasing department, it is stamped "approved," initialed by the proper authority, and then sent to the bookkeeper or the accounting department.

In firms where more than one copy of the purchase invoice is required and received, one copy is retained by the purchasing agent, who files it for a short time and then destroys it.

Request for Credit. If the purchase order and the invoice do not agree, you call the discrepancy to the attention of the purchasing agent. He either approves the difference or, if the discrepancy is in the nature of an overcharge, writes the vendor for a credit memorandum to cover it. Some firms have a special form called a *request for credit* that they use in such a situation. This same form is used when goods are returned because they are not satisfactory or when articles such as empty bottles or other containers are returned on which credits or rebates are due.

Stockkeeping. Almost all businesses, small and large, find it advisable to establish one or more stock rooms where goods are kept between the time that those goods are received and the time they are sold or used in the operation of the business. A clerk, known as a *stock clerk*, is usually charged with the responsibility of operating the stock room. If you were working in this type of job, you would receive the goods from the receiving clerk and, after checking them, store them neatly on shelves, in bins, or in some other fashion in the stock room. You usually would be required to keep a running or perpetual inventory of all the goods in the stock room so that you could know at anytime just how much of each kind of goods was in stock. When goods were requisitioned by properly authorized persons, you would deliver them; when the supply of any item began to get low, you would request the buyer to purchase more.

Stock Requisitions. When various people or departments in a business want goods from the stock room, it is usually necessary for them to prepare a stock requisition, have it signed by the department head or by another person with the authority to do so, and present it to the stock clerk. As the stock clerk, you would deliver the goods so requisitioned and have the person who accepted them sign for them. Ordinarily, two copies of such a requisition are prepared — one kept by the person or department that prepared it and the other kept by the stock room. In some firms, no requisition form is used. Instead, the person desiring goods merely telephones or goes to the stock room for them; and when the goods are delivered, he merely signs a receipt, which is kept by the stock clerk.

Perpetual Inventory. In order that you may know exactly what is on hand at all times, you will usually maintain a special inventory record. This record is generally a series of cards kept in a file, one card for every type of goods in stock. On each card is a column in which to record items when they come into the stock room, another column in which to record items when they go out, and a third column in which to record the number of items on hand. A fourth column may also be provided to record the fact that a certain number of items has been ordered. Also on the card are spaces for the name of the article, the place where it is stored, the maximum and the minimum numbers that should ever be on hand, and the point below which stock should not be allowed to drop before a new supply is ordered. You should keep this stock card up to date at all times so that it will always show the amount on hand. This amount should be checked for accuracy from time to time by making an actual physical count of the materials on hand.

Bin Tags. As a supplement to the stock record card, many firms also have the stock clerk keep a bin tag at each bin or shelf. On this tag

ARTICLE BALL-POINT PENS, BLACK								LOCATION	

								AISLE	BIN
UNIT Dozen	STOCK NO. 253	PRICE $1.57	MAXIMUM 144	MINIMUM 48	REORDER POINT 96			C	11

ORDERED			STOCK						
DATE	ORD. NO.	QUANTITY	DATE	REQ. NO.	ISSUED	RECEIVED	ORDER NO.	BALANCE	
			6/1/--					108	
			6/3	57	12			96	
6/3/--	147	96	6/7	63	26			70	
			6/10	68	29			41	
			6/13			96	147	137	

Perpetual inventory record card

you record the number of articles added to the supply or taken from it and the number of articles on hand.

Physical Inventory. From time to time, at least once a year, an actual count of goods on hand is made. This is called taking a physical inventory. This type of inventory is usually taken by at least two clerks working together; one counts the articles and calls out the name and number on hand, while the other records this information on a printed or duplicated inventory sheet. When the actual count of all goods on hand has been completed, the same clerks, or others, fill in the cost of each article, multiply the cost by the number of articles on hand, and add all of these extensions to determine the total. The accuracy of the calculations is then usually checked by still another clerk.

Inventory Records and Data Processing. In larger firms, integrated data processing equipment is increasingly being introduced. Under this system, the machines automatically update the inventory and thus eliminate the need for hand-kept records.

As a further development of automation, some companies have redesigned their entire shipping room so that articles to be shipped are automatically selected from the bins in which they are stored, assembled on a continuous-belt arrangement, and on these belts delivered direct to the truck body where men stack them in the proper order for delivery. In such a system the order clerk prepares the original document, which later

	INVENTORY		May 31	19--			PAGE 4

SHEET NO. 4 DEPARTMENT Accounting PRICED BY Eric Anderson
CALLED BY Robert Walker LOCATION 4th Floor EXTENDED BY Helen Richards
ENTERED BY Roger Dunn EXAMINED BY E. Carson

CHECK	QUANTITY	DESCRIPTION	UNIT	PRICE	EXTENSION
	5	Paper, Analysis, 6-Column	Ream	4.59	22 95
	3	Ball-Point Pencils, Medium, No. 10	Gross	6.75	20 25
	4	Typewriter Pads	Each	0.59	2 36

Physical inventory sheet

becomes directly or indirectly the input instrument which causes this automatic device to function. By a special system of numbering, orders are arranged so that those going to a particular district will be automatically delivered to the truck body that is to carry them. A further refinement of the system makes it possible for the last items to be delivered on the delivery route to be placed in the front of the truck body and the first to be delivered at the back so that the deliveryman will have everything arranged properly when he leaves the plant to start distributing the orders.

Inventory Control. Whether records are kept by hand or by machine, inventory control is vitally important. Basically this means that just enough stock is kept on hand to meet the needs of the business. Understocking may mean the loss of customers. Overstocking may seriously reduce profit. Some companies make the following errors:

1) They keep obsolete items on hand long after they should have been disposed of.
2) They buy too much, often because they have been offered a good price for buying in quantities.
3) They stock too many products — many that sell infrequently.
4) They fail to relate buying and inventory to the rate of sale. This is especially true of seasonal merchandise.
5) They fail to keep the rapidity of turnover as high as possible.

Study Questions

1. Why is it desirable that a careful record be kept of all incoming shipments?

2. How is the receiving clerk held responsible for the accuracy of quantity and condition of goods received?

3. What disposition is made of an unsatisfactory shipment of goods?
4. When is a request for credit used?
5. What are the duties of the stock clerk?
6. Name the business forms with which the stock clerk most frequently works.
7. What information is usually contained in a stock requisition?
8. What is a perpetual inventory?

9. How is a bin tag used?
10. When and how is a physical inventory taken?
11. How does data processing change inventory record keeping?
12. Describe the operation of an automated shipping room.
13. Suggest five ways to prevent overstocking of merchandise.

What Do You Think?

1. What would be the advantages for a young man entering initial employment as a receiving clerk or as a stock clerk?
2. Is it always desirable for a business organization to keep stock records?

Your Personal Qualities

Paul and Allen are good friends who work in a receiving room. They are responsible for keeping accurate records of all merchandise which arrives and certain shipments which leave the firm. Paul is very conscientious about his work and carefully records each shipment he handles. He observes that Allen is careless about the records. Allen's usual comment is, "They'll never know the difference." On two occasions, their supervisor has told the boys that they will have to be more careful in their record keeping or risk losing their jobs. The supervisor assumes that both boys have been guilty of keeping poor records.

Questions: 1. What do you think of Allen's attitude?

2. What courses of action are open to Paul?

How's Your English?

Read the information on prepositions and conjunctions in Appendix A. Type each sentence below, choosing the preposition or conjunction which you believe is correct.

1. The executive went (in, into) the mail room to see if a letter he needed had been received.

2. The typist must choose (between, among) two positions for the subject line of a letter.

3. The typist should be careful (and, to) type the special lines of a letter correctly.

4. You will not type attractive letters (without, unless) you plan carefully.

5. Neither the clerk-typist (or, nor) the executive knew the address of the new company.

6. A good office worker does not become angry (with, at) her employer.

7. Seldom (if, or) ever should the letter be signed for the employer.

8. The new typist is attempting to produce attractive letters (like, as) the secretary does.

9. The address on the envelope should be (like, as) the address in the letter.

10. (Between, Among) the salutations are some that are more formal than others.

Office Work

With a few of your classmates, visit some local organizations and study their receiving and stockkeeping procedures. Collect copies of forms they use and prepare a written report in which you describe the procedures you saw in operation, and tell how the forms are used. Also be prepared to make an oral report to the class.

Office Work Assignments

10: Perpetual Inventory

In this problem, you will keep the perpetual inventory records for four items in the stock room. Use the illustration on page 81 as a guide.

Open a stock record form dated June 1 for each of the four items using the following information:

a. Stock No. 990; typewriter ribbons; Unit each; Price $0.84; maximum supply 48; minimum supply 12; reorder point 36; Location — Aisle G, Bin 10; beginning balance, June 1, 19—, 36.

b. Stock No. 135; steno pads; Unit each; Price $0.12; maximum supply 180; minimum supply 36; reorder point 144; Location — Aisle F, Bin 9; beginning balance 50.

c. Stock No. 118; ruled white pads, 8 1/2 x 11; Unit dozen; Price $1.13; maximum supply 27; minimum supply 3; reorder point 24; Location — Aisle L, Bin 20; beginning balance 27.

d. Stock No. 540; mimeograph paper, white, 8 1/2 x 11; Unit ream; Price $0.64; maximum supply 125; minimum supply 25; reorder point 100; Location — Aisle B, Bin 4; beginning balance 110.

Record on the stock record forms the following transactions:

June 1. Ordered 36 typewriter ribbons No. 990, order No. 2031.

June 2. Issued 2 dozen ruled white pads No. 118, requisition No. 129.

June 3. Issued 12 steno pads No. 135, requisition No. 138.

June 4. Issued 9 reams of mimeograph paper No. 540, requisition No. 140.

June 4. Issued 14 typewriter ribbons No. 990, requisition No. 152.

June 6. Ordered 144 steno pads No. 135, order No. 2036.

June 6. Issued 10 typewriter ribbons No. 990, requisition No. 162.

June 7. Issued 12 reams of mimeograph paper No. 540, requisition No. 163.

June 8. Ordered 100 reams of mimeograph paper No. 540, order No. 2040.

June 10. Issued 2 steno pads No. 135, requisition No. 197.

June 10. Received order No. 2031 for 36 typewriter ribbons No. 990.

June 10. Issued 18 typewriter ribbons No. 990, requisition No. 210.

June 11. Ordered 24 dozen ruled white pads No. 118, order No. 2042.

June 11. Issued 10 dozen ruled white pads No. 118, requisition No. 213.

June 13. Ordered 36 typewriter ribbons No. 990, order No. 2043.

June 13. Issued 15 reams of mimeograph paper No. 540, requisition No. 223.

June 15. Issued 16 typewriter ribbons No. 990, requisition No. 224.

June 17. Issued 20 reams of mimeograph paper No. 540, requisition No. 225.

June 18. Received order No. 2036 for 144 steno pads No. 135.

June 18. Issued 12 dozen ruled white pads No. 118, requisition No. 261.

June 20. Received order No. 2042 for 24 dozen ruled white pads No. 118.

June 20. Issued 30 reams of mimeograph paper No. 540, requisition No. 262.

June 22. Issued 2 typewriter ribbons No. 990, requisition No. 264.

June 22. Received order No. 2043 for 36 typewriter ribbons No. 990.

June 25. Issued 24 steno pads No. 135, requisition No. 296.

June 27. Issued 17 typewriter ribbons No. 990, requisition No. 301.

June 27. Ordered 36 typewriter ribbons No. 990, order No. 2051.

June 28. Issued 7 dozen ruled white pads No. 118, requisition No. 310.

June 29. Issued 15 steno pads No. 135, requisition No. 313.

June 29. Received order No. 2040 for 100 reams of mimeograph paper No. 540.

June 29. Issued 10 typewriter ribbons No. 990, requisition No. 325.

June 29. Issued 13 typewriter ribbons No. 990, requisition No. 332.

June 30. Received order No. 2051 for 36 typewriter ribbons No. 990.

The balances on hand on June 30 for these four items, as determined by a physical count, are as follows:

Typewriter ribbons No. 990..   44
Steno pads No. 135......... 141
Ruled white pads No. 118....   20
Mimeograph paper No. 540.. 124

If the balances on your records do not agree with these figures, check your work carefully to locate your errors.

11: Physical Inventory

Handwrite a physical inventory sheet, similar to the one on page 82, for the Office Department, Location 3d Floor, as of June 30, 19—. At the top of the sheet indicate that this is page 1, Sheet No. 1. The inventory was *Called by* Alfred Hooper, *Entered by* James Cotton, and *Priced by* Jon Russell. It is *Extended by* you (write in your own name) and is to be *Examined by* your teacher (write in your teacher's name).

The quantity, description, unit, and cost per unit of merchandise are given on the next page. Complete the physical inventory sheet by computing and entering the extensions and totaling the extension column.

QUANTITY	DESCRIPTION	UNIT	PRICE
5	Stamp Pads, Assorted	Pad	.28
45	Steno Pads	Pad	.09
10	Typewriter Pads	Each	.59
100	Telephone Message Pads	Each	.12
150	Yellow Pads (Legal size)	Each	.09
125	White Pads (Letter size)	Each	.08
10	Ditto Paper, Process B, 8 1/2 x 11	Ream	.79
15	Ditto Paper, Process B, 8 1/2 x 14	Ream	1.02
30	Mimeograph Paper, 8 1/2 x 11 Substance 16	Ream	.64
20	Mimeograph Paper, 8 1/2 x 15 Substance 16	Ream	.90
20	Mimeograph Paper, 8 1/2 x 11 Substance 20	Ream	.80
10	Onion Skin Paper, 8 1/2 x 11	Ream	1.69
12	Analysis Paper, 12-Column	Ream	5.18
5	Bond Paper, Old Hampshire, 8 1/2 x 11	Ream	3.85
6	Bond Paper, Plover, 8 1/2 x 11	Ream	1.75

UNIT 4 | Inventory and the Stock Room

PART 2:

Goods Shipped

"What's the best way to send that package?" *may be the query put to you by your employer. It may be a large package of advertising materials or samples, or a small personal parcel. Your employer may be more interested in the speed with which it is delivered than the cost of delivery. Whatever the case may be, you may have to be familiar with the types of shipping services available over land, in the air, and on the waterways.*

Every business firm uses a number of different shipping services to distribute commodities. As an alert and intelligent office worker, you should be thoroughly familiar with the relative advantages of each service. You may encounter them in your regular office duties, or you might become a clerk in the shipping department. There you would be called upon to prepare the necessary forms for freight and express shipments for which trains, planes, ships, or trucks may be used. You may be asked to prepare the forms for tracing a shipment or for filing a claim for goods damaged in transit.

Recent Developments in Shipping. The shipping of goods in the United States and Canada has undergone many rapid changes in the past few years. Competition between trucks and trains is increasing, and now shipping by air is becoming widespread, especially to distant and isolated areas. As a result of the increased competition, all three types of carriers are being designed for larger capacity, greater speed, and greater economy of operation. Combinations of truck/rail and truck/ship services are now becoming widespread.

Recent developments in packaging have also aided in the shipping process. Lightweight, disposable paper containers are being used in place of heavy wood crating. In addition, shipping docks are being furnished with automatic equipment which uses high-speed assorter-conveyor belts to handle packages of all sizes. Railroad terminal yards are also being equipped with automatic switching equipment and closed-circuit TV to save time and money.

Methods of Shipping. Commodities may be shipped to various points by parcel post, by railway express and railway freight, truck, bus, ship, air express and air freight, or by a combination of two or more of these services. All of these services have their own peculiar advantages: some are less expensive than others; some offer a higher degree of safety; some offer faster delivery; and some are much more convenient for the shipper, for the consignee, or for both. The relative values of each of these services should be known to the shipper so that he may select the best and the most suitable shipping service.

Shipping Guides. Where can you look for the information you and your employer need about shipping? Various guidebooks are printed to assist in selecting the method of shipment that is best for each shipment. Guides which are widely used in business offices and which you will find helpful include:

United States Official Postal Manual, Chapter I, Domestic, published by the United States Post Office Department. This guide gives complete information about all classes of mail. A list of the post offices in the United States is arranged alphabetically by towns and cities under each state. The unit number is given for each town or city, and from this unit number you can determine the parcel-post zone in which the town or city is located.

United States Official Postal Manual, Chapter II, International Postal Service, published by the United States Post Office Department. Information similar to that appearing in the domestic edition of the *United States Official Postal Manual* is contained in this chapter. The information applies only to shipments to foreign countries.

Express and Parcel Post Comparative Rate Guide, published by the Express Audit Company, Providence, Rhode Island. A complete list of all express stations, arranged alphabetically by towns and cities in the states, is given in this guide. As is indicated by the name, the comparative charges between express and parcel post shipments to any express station are shown in this guide. If there is no express office in a town or city, the nearest office is given in parentheses after the name of that town or city.

Parcel Post and Express Guide, published by the Parcel Post and Express Guide Company, with offices in various cities. A special guide is published for each large city. A comparison of parcel post and express rates between the particular city and any other town or city in the United

States is given. The towns and cities are arranged alphabetically under the states.

Leonard's Guide, published by G. R. Leonard & Company, Inc., New York. This guide contains rates and routings for freight, express, and parcel post. The cities are arranged alphabetically under the states. Information concerning Canadian and foreign parcel post is also contained in this guide. Different editions of this guide are issued for different sections of the country.

Bullinger's Postal and Shipper's Guide for the United States, Canada, and Newfoundland, published by Bullinger's Guides, Inc., New York. This guide is useful in planning the routings of shipments.

Parcel Post. Also referred to as fourth-class mail, parcel post is a method of transporting goods that is used most extensively when relatively small items are to be shipped to widely scattered places. Some details of parcel post service are discussed in connection with the classes of mail in Unit 6, Part 2.

Parcel post shipments are handled by the United States Post Office Department. To be classified as parcel post or, in Post Office terminology, fourth-class mail, a package must weigh 16 ounces or over. In order to limit possibility of competition with express services, the upper limits for weight and size of parcel post shipments are now determined by the class of post office handling the mail. You can mail from one first-class post office (a post office in a well-populated area where express service is also available) to another parcels not over 40 pounds in weight if you are sending them to the local, first, or second postal zones, or not over 20 pounds if you are mailing them to the third through the eighth postal zones. The size limit of parcels mailed between first-class post offices is 72 inches in length and girth combined. In measuring a parcel, the greatest distance in a straight line between the ends is taken as the length, while the distance around the parcel at its thickest part is taken as its girth. Thus a package 40 inches in length and 10 inches high and 8 inches wide would measure:

$$40 + \underset{18}{[10 + 8]} + \underset{18}{[10 + 8]} = 76 \text{ inches}$$

It could not be mailed parcel post. Parcels mailed at, or addressed for delivery to, any second-, third-, or fourth-class post office or military post office have a weight limit of 70 pounds and a size limit of 100 inches in length and girth combined.

Air Parcel Post. When speed is an important element, you will probably send the parcel by air. The delivery time can be greatly reduced

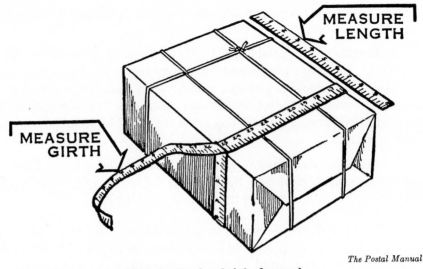

Measuring length and girth of a parcel

by using air parcel post. The rates are considerably higher than for ordinary parcel post. Increasingly, air parcel post is being used to carry merchandise to distant and isolated areas. This is especially true for Hawaii and Alaska and other areas where surface travel is necessarily slow. Packages shipped by air may weigh up to 70 pounds, but are limited to 100 inches in length and girth.

Railway Express. Your telephone call to the nearest REA Express office will bring an express pickup truck to your door to pick up packages of all kinds and sizes. This is a very convenient way to ship. Express traffic is expedited by movement on fast passenger trains, and delivery is made direct to the consignee if he is located in a city or town. The merchandise may be sent with shipping charges prepaid, C.O.D., or paid-in-part.

REA Express (formerly the Railway Express Agency, Inc.) maintains offices in all centers of population in the United States and Puerto Rico. The cost of shipping depends upon the weight of the shipment and the distance it must travel to reach its destination. First-class rates are assessed on all kinds of merchandise and nonperishable articles, while foodstuffs move at second-class rates, approximately three fourths of the first-class rate. Express rates include free insurance on shipments valued up to $50 and weighing 100 pounds or less. Reduced commodity rates are also available for shipments of certain commodities.

Air Express. You will find the newest and swiftest method of commercial transportation, air express, of great value not only for its speed but for its convenience to you in picking up the package for delivery. This

Loading air freight

American Airlines

service now includes shipping by air to all parts of the United States (domestic air express) and to most foreign countries (international air express).

Air express shipments, in addition to speed of transportation, receive special pickup service at points of origin and quick delivery to the airports throughout the country. Almost all types of commodities, including machine parts, perishable foods, printed matter, and cut flowers are moved by air express. Domestic shipments weighing up to 200 pounds with a value of not more than $25,000 may be sent prepaid or C.O.D. Information about specific domestic air express shipments may be obtained by referring to the *Official Air Express Guide*, or by telephoning the local REA Express office.

For international air express shipments, merchandise may be routed domestically by air or by railway express and then transferred to overseas planes for rapid shipment to foreign countries. The local REA Express office will supply the charges for specific international air express shipments as well as the documents required and the limits of weight, size, and value.

Bus Express. Most bus lines throughout the country offer package express service. This is a particularly useful service when destination points are located where there is no airport and speed of delivery is important.

Many points receive same-day delivery; many, within a few hours, faster even than air service. Frequent and direct bus trips between cities and the fact that terminals are almost always located in the center of the business districts account for the speed of handling and delivery. Packages are insurable, but they are limited to 100 pounds in weight and 24″ x 24″ x 45″ in size. Door-to-bus pickup and delivery is available at extra charge.

Truck Transportation. Another shipping service which your employer may use is truck transportation. In the early stages of automotive transportation, trucks were used only for the delivery of local shipments, but today truck lines regularly make long hauls from one part of the country to another. In addition to trucks carrying different items in a single truckload, there are many specialized trucks that carry single commodities such as milk, gasoline, new cars, sand, and gravel in truckload quantities.

Local. For local transportation, the truck undoubtedly is the best type of transportation available. Arrangements can easily be made with a trucking company to make regular calls at a place of business to pick up packages and to deliver them locally.

Long-Distance. Truck transportation service has been extended to long-distance hauls. The merchandise is picked up by a local truck at the door of the shipper and transferred at a clearing depot to trucks that are routed to various destinations. Some long-distance truck firms offer overnight service to insure the prompt delivery of goods. Both full truck-load and less than truckload shipments are handled.

Speed. The time element is extremely important to manufacturers and merchants who want their merchandise to reach the market as soon as possible. This is particularly true if the merchandise is perishable or if it is of a seasonable type. Truck transportation is usually able to provide this rush service.

Combination with Rail Service. Some railroads have organized truck lines which they use to supplement their rail service. By combining truck and railroad transportation in this way, railroad companies have been able to render service to towns and districts that are not on the regular railroad lines. In some instances, unprofitable local railroad lines have been discontinued, and trucks are used in their stead to transport merchandise to and from the more important railroad lines.

The railroads are also offering a service called "piggyback" to trucking firms for long-distance hauls. Loaded truck trailers may be driven to the railroad depot in one city, the trailers detached from the trucks and placed on railroad flatcars, usually two trailers on a single flatcar, and moved to another city by rail. There are several different types of piggyback

Piggyback service

This semitrailer carrying car accommodates two large truck trailers. Trailers are easily switched by the driver. The transfer is made in about four minutes.

New York Central System

service available depending on the needs of the shipper. There is now a trend toward trucks carrying huge removable containers which may be transferred from truck to flatcar by crane or some other lift. These sealed containers may be handled many times without the usual danger of pilferage or damage during transit.

United Parcel Service is a private trucking company specializing in small shipments. It is similar to parcel post, yet it can be more economical and flexible. It will handle packages up to 108 inches in length and girth combined. Weight restrictions are up to 50 pounds per package or 100 pounds per shipment. The service territory is currently limited, but it is hoped that national rights will be obtained. U.P.S. furnishes a shipping guide entitled "Information Guide for U.P.S. Customers."

Freight Service and Rates. For shipping bulky articles and commodities for which the speed of delivery is not vitally important, your employer will generally use freight service. The cost of shipping by freight is lower than the cost of shipping by truck.

Uniform freight rates are set by a classification committee of the Interstate Commerce Commission. Rates are divided into two groups — class rates and commodity rates. Class rates apply to articles that are grouped into general categories. Commodity rates are based on volume of specific commodities and are usually lower than the class rates between the same points.

Another factor affecting rates is quantity. Carload shipments have one rate, and *less-than-carload-lot* (*L.C.L.*) shipments have a higher rate.

Routing the Freight. The routing of a freight shipment involves careful selection of the railroad lines over which a shipment should travel. If your employer is one of the many small shippers who know little or nothing about railroad routes, he will turn over the problem of routing his goods to the railroad company to which he delivers the shipment. Proper routing will usually speed the service and may reduce the charges.

(Uniform Domestic Straight Bill of Lading, adopted by Carriers in Official, Southern, Western and Illinois Classification territories, March 15, 1922, as amended August 1, 1930.)

THIS MEMORANDUM is an acknowledgment that a Bill of Lading has been issued and is not the Original Bill of Lading, nor a copy or duplicate, covering the property named herein, and is intended solely for filing or record.

Shipper's No._____

CLEVELAND, CINCINNATI, CHICAGO & ST. LOUIS RY. Company Agent's No._____

RECEIVED, subject to the classifications and tariffs in effect on the date of the receipt by the carrier of the property described in the Original Bill of Lading.

FROM E. D. Carter

at Cleveland, Ohio, Sept. 30, 19___

(Mail or street address of consignee—For purposes of notification only.)

295 Lincoln Avenue

B. M. Jenkins

(Uniform Domestic Straight Bill of Lading, adopted by Carriers in Official, Southern, Western and Illinois Classification territories, March 15, 1922, as amended August 1, 1930.)

THIS SHIPPING ORDER must be legibly filled in, in Ink, in Indelible Pencil, or in Carbon, and retained by the Agent.

Shipper's No._____

CLEVELAND, CINCINNATI, CHICAGO & ST. LOUIS RY. Company Agent's No._____

RECEIVE, subject to the classifications and tariffs in effect on the date of the issue of this Shipping Order,

FROM E. D. Carter

at Cleveland, Ohio, Sept. 30, 19___

(Mail or street address of consignee—For purposes of notification only.)

295 Lincoln Avenue

B. M. Jenkins

(Uniform Domestic Straight Bill of Lading, adopted by Carriers in Official, Southern, Western and Illinois Classification territories, March 15, 1922, as amended August 1, 1930.)

UNIFORM STRAIGHT BILL OF LADING--ORIGINAL--NOT NEGOTIABLE Shipper's No._____

CLEVELAND, CINCINNATI, CHICAGO & ST. LOUIS RY. Company Agent's No._____

RECEIVED, subject to the classifications and tariffs in effect on the date of the issue of this Bill of Lading,

FROM E. D. Carter

at Cleveland, Ohio, Sept. 30, 19___

(Mail or street address of consignee—For purposes of notification only.)

295 Lincoln Avenue

Consigned to B. M. Jenkins

Destination Cincinnati State of Ohio County of Hamilton

Route Your Line

Delivering Carrier Car Initial Car No.

No. Packages	Description of Articles, Special Marks and Exceptions	*WEIGHT (Subject to Correction)	Class or Rate	Check Column
1	Upright Piano	825#		

Subject to Section 7 of conditions, if this shipment is to be delivered to the consignee without recourse on the consignor, the consignor shall sign the following statement:
The carrier shall not make delivery of this shipment without payment of freight and all other lawful charges.

(Signature of Consignor)

If charges are to be prepaid, write or stamp here, "To be Prepaid."

Received $_____
to apply in prepayment of the charges on the property described hereon.

Agent or Cashier

Per_____
(The signature here acknowledges only the amount prepaid.)

Charges Advanced: $_____

*If the shipment moves between two ports by a carrier by water, the law requires that the bill of lading shall state whether it is "carrier's or shipper's weight." Note—Where the rate is dependent on value, shippers are required to state specifically in writing the agreed or declared value of the property. The agreed or declared value of the property is hereby specifically stated by the shipper to be not exceeding _____ per _____

E. D. Carter Shipper, Per D. O. C._____ Agent, Per_____

Permanent post-office address of shipper 849 Baxter Avenue, Cleveland, Ohio

Bills of lading

Waybill. This form is prepared by the railroad company to indicate the route over which the freight will travel. A waybill is made out for each freight shipment giving the shipping instructions, a description of the goods, its weight and destination. It also serves as an accounting form in determining the amount of freight charges that accrue to the various railroads on which the freight is carried. Waybills are also used with truck and air cargo shipments.

Bill of Lading. The bill of lading is the principal document used in freight shipments. It includes such information as the name of the consignee, his address, the name of the transportation company, the name of the shipper, the route of the shipment, the car number, the freight item, and the weight of the shipment.

There are two forms of the bill of lading — one known as a *straight* bill of lading, and other known as the *order* bill of lading. The number of copies of the bill of lading varies depending on the shipment or carrier's usage. A minimum of three copies is always prepared.

Straight Bill of Lading. The straight bill of lading is used if the goods are consigned to the person or firm to whom the goods are sold. If this form is used, the copies are distributed as follows:

1) The *original copy* is attached to the invoice and mailed to the customer after it has been signed by both the shipper and the freight agent. The original copy serves to identify the consignee as the person having the right to receive the merchandise upon its arrival.
2) The second copy, known as the *shipping order*, is filed by the railroad company at the point where the shipment originates.
3) The third copy, known as the *memorandum copy*, is kept in the files of the company shipping the goods.

Order Bill of Lading. The order bill of lading is used if goods, for some reason or other, are not to be shipped or consigned directly to the company that is ultimately to receive them. Most commonly, the order bill of lading is used if the goods are to be paid for by the customer before he is permitted to obtain them from the transportation company. In such a case, the shipper attaches a sight draft to the original bill of lading and forwards both to the bank of the customer. The bank will then call the customer or inform him that it has a bill of lading with a sight draft attached that the customer must pay if he desires to accept the merchandise. After the customer has paid the sight draft, the bank will indorse the order bill of lading to him. He may then take the properly indorsed copy of the order bill of lading to the freight depot and obtain his merchandise.

C.O.D. freight shipments are also sent on a straight bill of lading. In this case, the railroad collects the value of the goods from the consignee and sends the remittance to the consignor.

Claim for Loss. You will make a claim on the transportation company for a total or a partial loss if a shipment is not delivered, if it is totally or partially destroyed, or if it is delivered in a damaged condition. Claims for loss are presented by either the consignor or the consignee, depending upon ownership. If the claim is for damaged goods, the items involved should be held until the claim is settled because the shipping company will want to investigate these damage claims.

Overcharge. Overcharges in freight bills result from errors in weighing, in classification, in rate, in extension, or in the collection from the consignee of charges that were prepaid by the consignor. Claims for overcharge are filed by the person or business that originally paid the freight bill.

Store-Door Delivery. Practically all railroads have adopted the policy of store-door delivery. If a railroad company has store-door delivery, it engages or owns a fleet of trucks to collect merchandise and transport it to and from its terminals. Many businesses like this service because it eliminates trucking that otherwise would have to be paid for as a separate item. The railroads generally make an allowance to shippers and consignees who prefer to do their own hauling to and from the freight station.

Shipping by Water. Shipping by water is also used widely, and your employer may use this means of transporting his goods. The amount of freight carried on inland waterways has increased greatly in recent years. The principal waterways are the Great Lakes and the Ohio and Mississippi rivers. The St. Lawrence Seaway has linked the Great Lakes with the Atlantic Ocean, thereby permitting ocean-going steamships to carry cargoes directly to and from the major Great Lakes ports.

Transportation along our inland waterways is much slower than transportation by truck or railroad. For this reason, water transportation is used chiefly for bulky, heavy merchandise for which speed of delivery is not so important as a low freight rate. Shipping by water is especially favored for shipment of iron ore, coal, oil, and other items shipped in bulk, but it is by no means limited to such goods.

Shipping from our coastal ports, such as Boston, New Orleans, and San Francisco, is classified as coastwise, intercoastal, and deepwater shipping. A *coastwise line* is one that transports merchandise between coastal ports such as Boston, New York, and Philadelphia. An *intercoastal line* goes through the Panama Canal between the East Coast and the West Coast. *Deepwater shipping* involves overseas shipments.

Akin to "piggyback" shipment by rail is "fishyback" shipment by boat. Loaded truck trailers are driven to the docks or delivered by "piggyback" and transferred to ships. As is the case in truck and rail shipment services, there is an increased tendency in shipping by water toward trucks carrying removable containers so that the container without the truck or trailer wheels is loaded by crane aboard ship. This is especially desirable in shipments by water because considerable space aboard ship can be saved when the wheels of the truck or trailer and the accompanying chassis are left ashore. This service covers shipping between the major Eastern, Gulf, and Western ports. By coordinating shipments to the sailing schedule, low-cost transportation can be obtained with reasonable transit times. Shipments of less than truckload or truckload can be handled.

Loading cargo

This view of the Port of New York is typical of an average day in the world's greatest harbor.

The Port of New York Authority

Manifests. If your employer exports materials, the United States government requires that he file an official shipper's manifest that shows in detail the amount and the value of the goods being exported. This manifest forms the basis for freight accounting on the part of the steamship company in much the same way as does the waybill for railroads. A manifest also serves as a means of cargo identification in case a shipment is searched or detained for some reason. It is also a routing document.

Lighterage. If goods are shipped to a port and are to be delivered to a ship in the harbor, a lighterage service is required. This service includes delivery of merchandise from the end of the railroad line to the ship on which it will be transported. In case such lighterage is necessary, the car containing the merchandise is shunted to the lighterage dock, and the contents are unloaded from the car into a lighter or barge. The barge is then towed by a tugboat to the side of a ship and the contents are placed aboard.

Tramp Steamers. If your employer has bulky materials to be shipped overseas and is not too concerned with speed, he may make use of the services of tramp steamers. Tramp steamers are independent vessels that are dispatched to different ports at times when shipping conditions are favorable and shippers are not concerned primarily with regularity of sailing or directness of route. The commodities transported by tramp steamer are usually bulky and often low in value in proportion to bulk. Coal, iron ore, building materials, grain, lumber, and the like are the kinds of commodities most frequently carried. The tramp steamer is ordinarily a vessel of moderate size, of average speed, and built for maximum economy and freight capacity. Many of them carry a few passengers.

Liners. When your employer sends materials overseas at specified times for specific dates of arrival, he will be more interested in using the services of the liners. Liners are vessels that operate over definite routes and according to a fixed and regular schedule of sailing. Liners handle passenger traffic, ocean-going mail, and express and freight shipments. Some liners, of course, are primarily passenger-service ships; others are principally freight steamers that also carry passengers. The freight carried by liners is characteristically less bulky than that carried by tramp steamers, for it consists mainly of packaged freight — freight put up in boxes, barrels, crates, and other receptacles or packages. Vessels that are used in liner service vary greatly in size, speed, and equipment. Some of the ordinary freighters differ little, if at all, from the better tramp steamers. But liners, especially passenger-carrying vessels, are generally larger, faster, and more elegantly equipped than are tramp steamers. Liner service calls for extensive terminal facilities, and these may be owned or controlled by individual lines or by the cities that the liners serve.

Shipping Terms and Abbreviations. There are certain common shipping terms and abbreviations that should be in the vocabulary of every office worker who deals with the shipment of goods. Some of the most important ones are explained in the following paragraphs. Other abbreviations commonly used in connection with the shipping of goods are included in the following list:

avoir., avdp., or av.	avoirdupois weight
bbl.	barrel, barrels
bds.	bundles
bgs.	bags
B/L or b. l.	bill of lading
bls.	bales
bu.	bushel, bushels
bx.	box, boxes
CIF or CFI.	cost, insurance, and freight
ctge.	cartage
cwt.	hundredweight (100 lbs.)
frt.	freight
hhd.	hogshead
pk.	peck
RR.	railroad
Ry.	railway
S/D-B/L.	sight draft with bill of lading attached
shpt.	shipment
stge.	storage

```
via..............................by way of
W /B or WB.......................waybill
whf..............................wharf
```

C.O.D. This abbreviation means *collect on delivery* or *cash on delivery*. When goods are sent C.O.D., the amount to be collected is the cost of the commodity itself; the amount may include the transportation charges. C.O.D. shipments may be sent by all of the methods listed in the paragraph on "Methods of Shipping."

The term C.O.D. should be distinguished from the term *collect*. The latter term refers to the transportation charges only. When a shipment is sent collect, the transportation charges are paid by the consignee. When the shipment is sent prepaid, the shipper pays the transportation charges. In the case of prepaid shipments, the amount of the transportation charges may be added to the invoice and thus finally be paid by the consignee, even though they were first paid for by the shipper.

F.O.B. (or f.o.b.). The meaning of this abbreviation is *free on board*. It is used with an address to indicate the point to which the freight is paid by the shipper. For example, if you bought goods from a Detroit firm to be delivered in New York with the terms *f.o.b. New York*, the transportation charges to New York would be paid by the shipper. If these goods were sold *f.o.b. Detroit*, the shipper would deliver them to the receiving depot in Detroit, and you would be responsible for the transportation costs from Detroit to your place of business. The f.o.b. point determines the point at which the ownership of the goods is transferred.

L.C.L. This abbreviation means *less-than-carload lot*. Goods purchased in relatively small quantities may be shipped by L.C.L. freight. The freight rates for goods shipped in less-than-carload lots are higher than for those shipped in carload lots.

Marking. Whether the goods are to be shipped by freight, express, parcel post, or some other way, it is essential to the prompt movement and proper delivery of shipments that the goods be marked correctly. The careful labeling of less-than-carload shipments is particularly necessary, because they may be handled many times. A correct marking of the goods being shipped will prevent confusion at transfer points.

The rules of the carriers require that the shipper shall mark plainly, legibly, and durably each and every package, bundle, and piece of a less-than-carload shipment. If the shipment occupies a full car, no marking is required on each individual package.

In marking shipments, the following rules should be observed in order to insure the proper delivery by the carriers:

1) The consignee's name, address, and bill of lading destination should be shown.
2) The name and address of the shipper should be preceded by the word *From*. This explanation is of great assistance to both the shipper and the carrier if the shipment goes astray, is unclaimed, or is refused by the consignee.
3) When goods are consigned to a place not located on the line of a carrier, the packages should be marked with the name of the station where the consignee will accept the goods.
4) If the shipment is to be made by order bill of lading, the words *to order* should be shown on each package.
5) Packages containing articles easily broken should be marked *Fragile* or *Handle with Care*. Packages containing merchandise that is perishable, such as fruit, should be marked *Perishable*.
6) Marking should be made by brush, stencil, crayon, or rubber stamp. If lettered by hand, a good clear style of lettering should be used. Labels or paper tags should be prepared on a typewriter and fastened securely to the packages. Metal tags should be fastened by wire.
7) All previous marks on the wrappings should be obliterated.

Packaging. Just as the marking of a package must be proper to insure timely and correct delivery, the same applies to packaging. It is the responsibility of the shipper to package properly the item for shipment. The method of shipping used and the distance to be traveled will be determining factors in packaging. The decision on a damage claim is often decided on the basis of how well the goods have been packaged.

Tracing. It may be necessary to trace a shipment if delivery has been unexplainably delayed. All carriers in all modes of transportation provide tracing services. Information required to trace a shipment is:

1) Shipper's name and address
2) Name and address of consignee
3) Shipping date
4) Quantity involved
5) Bill of lading number
6) Routing used

Study Questions

1. Why should most office workers understand shipping terms and matters pertaining to the shipment of merchandise?
2. What are some of the recent developments in shipping services?
3. What methods may be used for shipping goods?
4. What shipping guides are commonly used in business offices?
5. When would one use parcel post service? air parcel post service?
6. Upon what does the cost of shipping by railway express depend?

7. What are the advantages of air express?

8. Why is shipping by truck often desirable for both long-distance and local transportation?

9. What are some of the advantages of railroad-operated truck lines that supplement rail service?

10. What is "piggyback" service?

11. Give information regarding United Parcel Service.

12. How do rates for carload and less-than-carload shipments differ?

13. What is meant by routing a freight shipment?

14. For what purpose is a waybill prepared?

15. What information does the bill of lading include?

16. How does a straight bill of lading differ from an order bill of lading in use?

17. What is store-door delivery?

18. What is lighterage?

19. What is coastwise shipping? intercoastal shipping? deepwater shipping?

20. What is a manifest?

21. What are tramp steamers? What types of commodities are commonly transported by them?

22. What are liners?

23. How does the freight carried by liners differ from that commonly carried by tramp steamers?

24. What is the meaning of the abbreviation *C.O.D.*? How does it differ from the term *collect*?

25. When is tracing necessary, and what information is required by the carrier?

What Do You Think?

1. Assume that you have been asked to determine what method should be used in sending a rather large shipment. How would you proceed to find the agencies in your community that might handle this shipment for you? What information about the shipment would you need to know before you make a decision as to how the merchandise should be shipped?

2. When would each of the following shipping services be the best one to use? Consider such factors as speed, cost, and dependability. Be specific in your answers; give such information as the kind of merchandise being shipped and the names of the cities involved.

a. Freight (railroad) **e.** Air express
b. Railway express **f.** Air parcel post
c. Parcel post **g.** Water
d. Truck

Your Personal Qualities

Mr. Howard, the executive of a New York firm by whom Elizabeth Rowen is employed, asked her to send a small package of merchandise manufactured by the firm to a friend in Honolulu.

Two weeks later an airmail letter was received asking about the package, indicating that it had not been received.

Investigation showed that Miss Rowen had delayed sending it because she said she did not have time to wrap it. She felt that it was not her job to wrap and ship packages anyway. When she finally did have it ready, she sent it by ordinary parcel post.

Questions: 1. Did Miss Rowen display the proper attitude?

2. Did she ship the package by the best method?

3. What action should Mr. Howard now take?

How's Your English?

Read about prepositions and conjunctions in Appendix A and type a correct list of prepositions or conjunctions for the following sentences:
1. Dorothy went (into, in) the filing room to place the folder of correspondence (in, into) the file.
2. Agreement (between, among) so many people is difficult to attain.
3. Mistakes on invoices should not occur very frequently (if, or) ever.
4. She is always on time, (as, like) a good employee should be.
5. One cannot achieve success in life (without, unless) he strives toward definite goals.

Office Work

1. Make a study of the various services available in your community for the transportation of goods, and be prepared to report your findings orally to the class and in writing to your teacher. Along with your report, submit all the printed material you are able to gather that is descriptive of these services.
2. By what transportation service would you ship the following packages from your local community?
  a. A 2-pound package of ordinary merchandise to New York.
  b. A manuscript weighing 9 pounds to Chicago.
  c. Several cases of canned goods to New Orleans.
  d. A 25-pound package of luncheon meats to a town 10 miles away.
  e. A factory machine weighing 2 tons to a town 400 miles away.
  f. A machine part weighing about 100 pounds that is needed as soon as possible in San Francisco.

Office Work Assignments

12: Straight Bill of Lading and Notice of Shipment

The Wakefield Publishing Company, 181 West Fourth Street, New York, New York 10014, is shipping to The Brown Book Shop, 1014 Market Street, Babylon, New York 11703, Suffolk County, 10 cartons of textbooks. The cartons weigh 100 pounds, 125 pounds, 50 pounds, 75 pounds, 117 pounds, 150 pounds, 141 pounds, 60 pounds, 115 pounds, and 132 pounds, respectively. The shipment is being sent over the Long Island Railroad. The shipper's number is 32537.

  a. Make out only the original copy of the straight bill of lading.

  b. Write to The Brown Book Shop saying that the goods are being shipped and that they will be delivered within the next few days. Call special attention to the enclosed bill of lading.

UNIT 5 | Processing Data

PART 1:

Business Arithmetic —
Fundamental Processes

Even in this day of the electronic computer, the ability to use the fundamental arithmetical processes is a prerequisite for office positions. You will learn that employers frequently require prospective office employees to take clerical aptitude tests. These usually contain one or more sections involving arithmetical skills. So many office tasks require the use of numbers that speed *and* accuracy *in addition, subtraction, multiplication, and division are indispensable for even the beginning clerical positions.*

While most routine clerical tasks involve only simple arithmetical computations, others require careful analysis and the ability to select an arithmetical procedure that will solve the problem. Because absolute accuracy *is required in the solution of clerical problems involving numbers, every prospective clerk must have instruction in business arithmetic. This instruction must include practice in determining "what to do" as well as in "how to do."*

Work Habits. Very early in your arithmetical instruction, you should recognize the need for developing good work habits. These begin with acquiring the ability to sustain your attention and to concentrate exclusively on the problem you are trying to solve or the clerical task you are endeavoring to complete. Also, you should form the habit of withholding a decision on "what to do" until you have studied the problem carefully.

As a first step in determining "what to do," you should analyze the problem. The analysis should provide the answers to five questions:

1) What facts are available?
2) How are they related to each other?
3) What are the possible solutions?
4) Which solution is best suited to the problem?
5) How can the accuracy of the solution be verified?

For example, you are asked to make out a bill for 175 chairs at $12 each. In solving this problem, you answer the five questions as follows:

1. *Question:* What are the facts?

   Answer: The sale of 175 chairs at $12 each.

2. *Question:* How are the facts related to each other?

   Answer: The quantity is in units, and the price is in units of one chair.

3. *Question:* What are the possible solutions or methods of determining the total price?

   Answer: **a.** Find the total price by multiplying 175 (the number of chairs) by $12 (the price per chair).
   b. Find the total price by multiplying $12 (the price per chair) by 175 (the number of chairs).

4. *Question:* Which solution is best suited to the problem?

   Answer: Solution **a** is best suited to the problem because it requires the simplest computations. It is easier, faster, and more accurate to multiply 175 by 12 than it is to multiply 12 by 175.

175	12
a. $\times$ 12	**b.** $\times$175
350	60
175	84
	12
$2100	$2100

   That multiplying 12 by 175 would be cumbersome is evident in the computation in **b** above. It is not so simple as the computation in Solution **a**; it requires more work and it provides more chance for error.

5. *Question:* How may the accuracy of the solution be verified?

   Answer: The accuracy of the solution may be verified by reversing the operation in Solution **a**, thus performing the operation shown in **b**. A less desirable way of verifying the answer is to repeat the original operation, for one may commit the same mistakes he may have made in the original attempt to solve the problem.

You should extend good work habits to the problem of "how to do it." You must be careful and methodical in solving problems involving arithmetical computations. Even in the simplest situations, you will find carelessness causes many costly errors. Crowded, illegible writing is one of the major causes of errors. The improper placement of a figure or a decimal point in the preparation of payrolls, financial reports, invoices, or sales slips may result in mistakes that may be very embarrassing to you. Always take a few minutes to verify your computations before submitting their solutions. The habit of "taking another look" pays off in accurate results.

Fundamental Processes. In the course of a day's work, you may have to use the four fundamental processes of arithmetic many times.

Addition is needed in finding totals of columns in payrolls, inventory sheets, statistical reports, accounts, deposit slips, sales slips, and many other business forms. Of course, adding machines are available in offices for the adding of very long columns of figures. If an adding machine is not handy, you may be able to add short columns of figures more quickly without an adding machine than to take the time to go to a machine. It is necessary that each office worker learn how to add rapidly and accurately.

Speed in addition is the result of two abilities. These are the mastery of the basic addition facts and the ability to add a column of figures by using combinations of two or more figures. For example, in adding the following columns of figures, you can increase your speed by picking out combinations as shown below:

a.		b.		c.		d.	
4	10	4	4	5	9	6	14
6	+	1	+	4	+	1	+
5	10	9	10	3	10	7	10
5	+	7	+	7	+	8	+
8	10	7	7	4	8	2	14
2	+	8	+	4	+	5	+
9	10	2	10	9	12	9	15
1	+	6	+	3	+	3	
7	10	3	9	7	11	7	
3		5	+	4	+	5	
		5	10	8	12		
50				4		53	
		50					
				62			

In adding column **b**, think of 4 plus 10 equals 14, plus 7 equals 21, plus 10 equals 31, plus 9 equals 40, plus 10 equals 50. In adding the figures in columns **c** and **d**, you can almost double your speed by developing the habit of adding by groups instead of by individual items.

You will use subtraction to determine the amount due from a customer when a discount is allowed, when a credit allowance is granted, or when a partial payment is made. You will also use subtraction when you prepare a payroll. Deductions for income taxes, social security, insurance, pensions, or union dues are examples of some of the items that are subtracted from employees' gross earnings.

Subtraction by Addition. Addition is used to prove the accuracy of subtraction or to provide a shortcut to subtraction. For example: in subtracting $1.25 from $12.70, an office worker mentally reasons that 25¢ from 70¢ leaves 45¢ because 25¢ plus 45¢ equals 70¢. He completes the subtraction by reasoning that $1 from $12 leaves $11. He then verifies the accuracy of the answer, $11.45, by adding $11.45, the remainder, to $1.25, the subtrahend, to get $12.70, the minuend.

This process of subtracting by adding is used effectively by sales-clerks in making change. Assume that a sale of $2.42 is paid for with a five-dollar bill. In making change, the salesclerk counts the change by adding each coin or bill to the amount of the sales as he gives them to the customer: "Two dollars and forty-two cents; (3 pennies) two forty-five; (nickel) two fifty; (half-dollar) three dollars; (two $1 bills) five dollars."

Addition is also used effectively to facilitate rapid mental subtraction. You should be able to achieve both accuracy and speed in subtraction by using this shortcut method. The minuend (the top number) is rounded off so that it becomes a multiple of 10. The amount needed to round off the minuend is also added to the subtrahend (the bottom number). For example:

$$96 + 4 \ (100) \qquad\qquad \$1.98 + 2 \ (\$2.00)$$
$$-29 + 4 \ (\ 33) \qquad\qquad -.29 + 2 \ (-.31)$$

$$\underline{} \qquad \underline{} \qquad\qquad \underline{} \qquad \underline{}$$

$$? \qquad 67 \qquad\qquad\qquad ? \qquad \$1.69$$

Shortcuts in Multiplication. Multiplication is needed to obtain the cost of items appearing on sales tickets, invoices, inventory sheets, statistical reports, sales reports, and the amount of sales taxes on them. It is also needed to compute gross earnings and the amount of the deductions that appear on payrolls. Computing discounts, insurance costs, depreciation charges, income taxes, interest charges, and dividends are examples of other arithmetical problems in which multiplication is used by the office worker.

Because multiplication is used extensively in solving practical business problems, every office worker should be familiar with the short-cuts in multiplication. Squaring a two-digit number ending in five such as 35 may be performed as follows:

$$35 \quad \text{(a)} \ 5 \times 5 = 25$$
$$35 \quad \text{(b)} \ 3 + 1 = 4, 4 \times 3 = 12$$

$$\overline{}$$

1225 (c) Product

(a) Multiply 5×5, and write the answer [25] as the two extreme right digits of the product (answer).
(b) Add "1" to one of the tens digits [$3 + 1 = 4$], and multiply the result by the other tens digit.
(c) Write the answer for (b) [12] to the left of the answer for (a) [25] to complete the product.

When the multiplier is 10, 100, or 1,000, add one, two, or three zeros to the multiplicand, depending upon the number of zeros following the figure in the multiplier.

Example: How much is $861 × 100? ($86,100 × 1)
Answer: $86,100

If the multiplier ends with one or more zeros that are preceded by a number other than the figure 1, a similar procedure is followed.

Example: How much is $52 × 20? ($520 × 2)
Answer: $1,040

Example: How much is $173 × 300? ($17,300 × 3)
Answer: $51,900

When the multiplicand involves sums of dollars and cents or other decimal items, the decimal point is moved one place to the right for every cipher in the multiplier.

Example: How much would 10 files listed at $23.75 each cost?
Answer: $237.50

When the multiplier is 1¢ or a multiple of 1¢, the decimal in the multiplicand is moved *two places to the left.* The product is then mentally multiplied by the multiple of 1 (such as 4, if the multiplier is 4¢) to get the answer.

Example: How much is 175 × 1¢?   *Example:* How much is 53 × 4¢?
Answer: $1.75   *Answer:* $.53 × 4 = $2.12

When the multiplier is 10¢ or a multiple of 10¢, the decimal point in the multiplicand is moved *one place to the left.* The product is then multiplied by the multiple of 10¢ (such as 3, if the multiplier is 30¢) to get the answer.

Example: How much is 147 × 10¢?   *Example:* How much is 250 × 40¢?
Answer: $14.70   *Answer:* $25.00 × 4 = $100

Fractions. A part of a whole number may be expressed either as a common fraction or as a decimal fraction. A common fraction consists of a numerator (the top number) and a denominator (the bottom number). A decimal fraction is also a part of a whole number, but only the numerator is expressed in figures; the denominator is represented by a period called a decimal point. The denominator in a decimal fraction, though not written, is "1" followed by a "0" for every figure in the decimal. The common fraction 32/100 is expressed as .32 in decimal fraction form.

Decimals are read as if they were written as common fractions; that is, .25 is read as "twenty-five hundredths"; .3 as "three tenths"; and .184 as "one hundred eighty-four thousandths." You use the word "and" between a whole number and the decimal fraction to denote the place of the decimal point. In proofreading you read the word "point" instead of the word "and." The number "3.75" is read as "three point seven five."

Decimal Equivalents of Fractions. Quantities expressed in fractions can be added, subtracted, multiplied, and divided readily and quickly by changing fractions to their decimal equivalents. To do this, you must learn the decimal equivalents of the fractions most commonly used in business. These are:

1/2 is equivalent to .5			1/3 is equivalent to .33333		
1/4 "	"	" .25	2/3 "	"	" .66667
3/4 "	"	" .75	1/6 "	"	" .16667
1/5 "	"	" .2	5/6 "	"	" .83333
2/5 "	"	" .4	1/12 "	"	" .08333
3/5 "	"	" .6	5/12 "	"	" .41667
4/5 "	"	" .8	7/12 "	"	" .58333
1/8 "	"	" .125	11/12 "	"	" .91667
3/8 "	"	" .375	1/15 "	"	" .06667
5/8 "	"	" .625	1/16 "	"	" .0625
7/8 "	"	" .875			

A salesclerk preparing an inventory for a dry goods store may find five bolts of muslin on hand measuring 25 1/2 yards, 30 1/4 yards, 20 3/8 yards, 10 3/4 yards, and 26 1/8 yards. These measurements can be added as follows:

```
25 1/2 yds.  =   25.5
30 1/4  "    =   30.25
20 3/8  "    =   20.375
10 3/4  "    =   10.75
26 1/8  "    =   26.125
             _____
     Total      113.000 yds.
```

To determine the number of yards left in a bolt of material which originally measured 37 1/4 yds. from which pieces measuring 5 1/8 yds., 4 3/4 yds., 2 1/2 yds., and 7 3/8 yds. were sold, a salesclerk would do the following:

1) Add the yardage sold:

```
 5 1/8 yds.  =   5.125
 4 3/4  "    =   4.75
 2 1/2  "    =   2.5
 7 3/8  "    =   7.375
             _____
     Total   =  19.750 or 19 3/4 yds. sold.
```

2) Subtract yardage sold from 37 1/4 yds.:

$$37 \ 1/4 \text{ yds.} = 37.25 \text{ yds. on hand}$$
$$19 \ 3/4 \text{ yds.} = 19.75 \text{ yds. sold}$$

17.50 or 17 1/2 yds. left

Changing common fractions to their decimal equivalents can be used effectively in multiplying and dividing mixed numbers.

Example: $145 \ 3/4 \times 23 \ 1/2 = 145.75$

$$\times 23.5$$

72875
43725
29150

3425.125 or 3425 1/8

Example: $175 \ 7/8 \div 1/2 = .5)175.875 = 5.)1758.75$

351.75 or 351 3/4

Aliquot Parts.   A number that is contained in another number without a remainder is an *aliquot* part of the second number. Some of the aliquot parts of 100 are 10 (1/10); 20 (1/5); 25 (1/4); 33 1/3 (1/3); and 50 (1/2). Most numbers have aliquot parts, but the aliquot parts of 100, or one dollar, and its fractions are the ones most extensively used in business calculations.

You will find that knowledge of the aliquot parts of $1 may be used advantageously in computing sales tickets, sales invoices, payrolls, installment sales, discounts, and commissions. For instance, when the price of an item is an aliquot part of a dollar, the quantity is multiplied by the fractional equivalent rather than by the price itself.

Example: What is the cost of 120 yards of cheesecloth at 12 1/2 cents a yard?

Because 12 1/2 cents is 1/8 of a dollar, a dollar will buy 8 yards of cloth. Divide the number of yards, 120, by 8 to obtain the answer, $15. Were the price 37 1/2 cents a yard, or 3/8 of a dollar, the answer given above would be $45 ($15 × 3).

Multiplication by using aliquot parts is very important, for it permits you to do rather difficult problems mentally. In the example below, note how easily the salaries for those employees who are paid by the hour at an aliquot-part-of-a-dollar rate may be found. In some cases, the total number of hours worked may be considered an aliquot part of 100 hours.

Employee	Total Hours	Wage Per Hour	Mental Calculations	Total Earnings
Adams	40	$1.87 1/2	$40 + $35 (40 hrs. × $7/8)	$75.00
Dougherty	35	1.80	$35 + $28 (35 hrs. × $4/5)	63.00
Hoffman	40	1.75	$40 + $30 (40 hrs. × $3/4)	70.00

Checking Answers. You will always find it desirable to check the correctness of a solution. Proving the answer to a problem in which the fundamental processes have been used is done as follows:

1) Addition — if columns of figures are added from top to bottom, the second time add the columns from bottom to top.
2) Multiplication — remultiply, reversing the original multiplicand and multiplier.
3) Subtraction — add the difference to the subtrahend to see that the total equals the minuend.
4) Division — multiply the quotient by the divisor and add the remainder. The result should equal the dividend.

Frequently, the time needed to prove an answer may be saved if the clerk merely estimates the reasonableness of an answer. Obviously, incorrect answers can be quickly discovered, and in some instances estimating the answer may give some clue to the method of solution.

Example: Add $8.21, $9.56, $4.98, $1.23, $0.87

> *Estimate:* Round off each amount to be added to nearest whole number. $8 + 10 + 5 + 1 + 1 = \$25$
>
> *Exact Answer:* $24.85

Example: Multiply $205.32 by 94

> *Estimate:* $\$200 \times 100 = \$20,000$
>
> *Exact Answer:* $19,300.08

Example: What is 49% of $1,754.32?

> *Estimate:* Round off 49% to 50%, or 1/2, and $1,754.32 to $1,700. 1/2 of $1,700 = $850
>
> *Exact Answer:* $859.62

The most frequent error made in dealing with decimals is the inaccurate placement of the decimal point, particularly in multiplication and division. Estimating the answer before solving the problem is the best way of avoiding this type of error.

Terms and Signs. Often abbreviations are used in business forms and reports to indicate various weights, measurements, and other details. Frequently, the abbreviations indicate a necessary calculation before the problem can be solved.

One must know the meaning of an abbreviation and the manner in which it is to be interpreted. The letter "T" represents a ton, which is 2,000 pounds (lbs.), and is the unit in which coal is sold. A thorough knowledge of the tables of weights and measurements will prove worthwhile in certain types of jobs. The following are a few common abbreviations and symbols:

56°	56 degrees
7″	7 inches or 7 seconds
5′	5 feet or 5 minutes
16 oz.	16 ounces (a pound)
C	100 items
M	1,000 items
doz.	dozen (12 items)
qr.	quire (24 items)
gr.	gross (144 items)
rm.	ream (480 pieces)
pc.	piece
cwt.	hundredweight or 100 pounds

Study Questions

1. Why is a knowledge of arithmetic still necessary in an era of electronic computing?

2. How do good work habits help an office worker to perform his duties more effectively?

3. Name the five steps followed in analyzing an arithmetic problem.

4. What are the four fundamental processes of arithmetic?

5. Name several business forms that require the use of addition.

6. How can a person increase his speed in addition?

7. List several office tasks that require the use of subtraction.

8. Name three multiplication shortcuts.

9. What is a common fraction?

10. How does a decimal fraction differ from a common fraction?

11. How are decimals read?

12. Why should an office worker know the decimal equivalents of the fractions most commonly used in business?

13. Explain how a knowledge of aliquot parts is useful in preparing invoices and payrolls.

14. What is the most frequent error made in computing with decimals?

15. What are the meanings of the following signs and terms: ″, qr., M, C, pc., cwt., °?

What Do You Think?

1. Are calculating machines a substitute for a thorough knowledge of the fundamental arithmetical processes? Give reasons for your answer.

2. In what manner can shortcut methods of multiplication be used advantageously in business? Illustrate by describing some conditions under which these methods would be used.

3. Amounts involving fractions can be added, subtracted, multiplied, and divided without learning about least common denominators, changing mixed numbers to improper fractions, or raising or reducing fractions. How is this done? Describe in detail.

4. Is it easier to multiply using decimal fractions or common fractions? Give the reason for your answer.

5. Why should all computations be checked for accuracy? Tell how you would check the accuracy of your answers for addition, subtraction, multiplication, and division problems.

6. A clerk once stated, "If I could estimate the answer to the problem, I would know how to do the problem." Illustrate what the clerk had in mind.

Your Personal Qualities

John Alvey is newly employed as a clerk in the purchasing department of a large company. One of his specific duties is checking the extensions on purchase orders after they have been prepared by the typists. He has been severely reprimanded for allowing purchase orders with errors to be sent out of the office. His answer is that the computations were correct when they went to the typists; therefore, the typists should be fired if they cannot type. Besides, he says, he is too busy to recheck all the purchase orders. His supervisor has noted that John does check some of the purchase orders but does them very slowly.

Questions: 1. What appears to be the difficulty in this situation?
2. What are the possible remedies?

How's Your English?

Read about the use of the comma in Appendix B. Rewrite the following:
1. Mr. Holbrook who is now in Europe will send you a cable soon.
2. Generally speaking a telegram will receive more attention than a letter.
3. An ancient developmental typewriter was the only machine available.
4. Miss Elder my secretary should be here presently.
5. You may therefore draw this conclusion.

Office Work

1. Add the numbers in each column from the top down, using combinations of ten whenever possible. Record the answers on a sheet of paper. Verify the accuracy of your answer by adding the columns of numbers a second time, adding from the bottom up.

a.	b.	c.	d.	e.
1	.41	1.23	15.62	580.46
9	.69	1.11	52.25	329.34
5	.54	8.76	43.23	201.30
5	.56	1.23	65.43	432.13
8	.82	2.22	35.50	267.85
2	.28	7.65	10.17	411.12
6	.67	1.23	86.21	384.31
4	.43	3.33	11.66	120.29
7	.46	6.54	13.23	606.50
3	.64	1.23	75.41	123.46
2	.81	4.24	14.27	867.53
8	.29	5.43	21.42	120.11
4	.52	9.89	19.28	287.34
6	.58	1.21	91.82	823.76

2. Add the numbers in each column from top to bottom using combinations of two or three figures whenever possible. Record the answers on a sheet of paper. Verify the accuracy of your answer by adding the columns of numbers a second time, adding from the bottom up.

a.	b.	c.	d.	e.
7	87	376	29.38	579.40
3	31	294	81.29	65.32
1	55	681	43.50	9.67
5	37	527	16.48	.85
4	89	456	23.42	436.81
6	75	794	55.24	21.23
2	42	532	86.28	352.54
8	86	967	17.24	46.83
1	79	658	72.19	287.65
4	48	369	35.42	51.24
5	63	123	27.26	8.70
9	99	254	10.00	524.97
3	75	683	69.81	37.82
5	32	765	18.95	716.76

3. In each of the following problems, you are given the amount of the sale and the amount of money received from the customer. You are to indicate the exact method of making change by following the method described on pages 105 and 106.

	Amount of Sale	Money Received
a.	$ .95	$ 1.00
b.	4.98	5.00
c.	5.00	10.00
d.	2.50	5.00
e.	1.25	2.00
f.	18.71	20.00
g.	4.42	5.00
h.	.13	1.00
i.	6.84	10.00
j.	46.50	50.00

4. Supply the answers to the following problems by using the shortcut methods described on pages 106–107:

a. 4.38 × 10	g. 5.08 × 100
b. 7.28 × 100	h. 3.4 × 1,000
c. 4.58 × 1,000	i. 200 × 16
d. .595 × 10	j. 38 × 500
e. 9.85 × 1,000	k. 300 × 95
f. 5.3 × 10	l. 2,000 × 56

5. Supply the answers to the following problems by multiplying by multiples of 10 or 10¢:

a. 10 × 75¢	g. 41 × 30¢
b. 35 × 10¢	h. 93 × 40¢
c. 82 × 10¢	i. 55 × 30¢
d. 10 × 93¢	j. 70 × 45¢
e. 20 × 48¢	k. 22 × 40¢
f. 60 × 35¢	l. 115 × 30¢

6. Find the cost of the following items by using the shortcuts described on pages 106–107:

a. 200 articles   @ $ 9.00 per C.
b. 1,200 pounds @ $ 3.50 per cwt.
c. 1,500 articles @ $ 7.00 per M.
d. 4,000 pounds @ $25.00 per T.
e. 150 articles   @ $12.00 per C.

7. Convert the decimals in Column 1 into common fractions; convert the common fractions in Column 2 into decimals.

Column 1	Column 2
a. .25	a. 3/4
b. .12 1/2	b. 5/8
c. .33 1/3	c. 1/5
d. .6	d. 2/3
e. .87 1/2	e. 2/5
f. .1	f. 5/6
g. .16 2/3	g. 4/5
h. .5	h. 1/15
i. .08 1/3	i. 3/10
j. .37 1/2	j. 1/16

8. Calculate the total earnings for each of the following employees:

Employee	Total Hours	Wage Per Hr.
a. J. A. Bird	40	$1.87 1/2
b. F. A. Bush	36	1.83 1/3
c. M. J. Carleton	36	2.33 1/3
d. Frank Harris	32	1.87 1/2
e. Noah Oliver	40	2.80
f. Meredith Parry	36	1.75
g. John Price	36	2.16 2/3
h. W. C. Scott	40	2.12 1/2
i. Leonard B. Shafer	30	2.83 1/3
j. Walter K. Young	25	4.76

9. For each word in Column 1, give the correct abbreviation. For each abbreviation in Column 2, give the word represented by the abbreviation. Indicate whether or not the abbreviations stand for plurals as well as singulars. Refer to Appendix D.

Column 1	Column 2
a. pint	a. qt.
b. peck	b. gal.
c. square	c. bbl.
d. piece	d. cu.
e. thousand	e. rm.
f. dozen	f. lb.
g. ounces	g. cwt.
h. inches	h. mi.
i. feet	i. inv.
j. yards	j. T

Office Work Assignments

13: Invoice with One Arithmetical Computation

If blank forms are not available for this and the following problem, use plain paper, and type the information that is ordinarily printed on such forms as shown in the illustration on page 61.

Type the following invoice in duplicate for the Terrace Biscuit Company, 217 Seventh Avenue, Springdale, New York 14135. The quantities and unit prices are given; you are to make all extensions and ascertain the totals:

Wakefield Food Store, 39 Main Street, Wakefield, New Jersey 07602; Shipped Via *Our truck;* today's date; No. 100.

Quantity	Description	Price	Amount
2	Animal Crackers	.83	
2	Chocolate Snaps	.87	
4	Chocolate Chip Cookies	1.20	
8	Fig Newtons	1.09	
4	Fruit Biscuits	1.20	
2	Marshmallow Cookies	.87	
2	Sugar Wafers	.86	
10	Tea Biscuits	.77	
2	Milk Crackers	.92	
3	Saltines	1.05	
2	Pretzel Sticks	.83	
4	Peanut Cookies	.38	
2	Macaroon Cookies	2.52	
2	Graham Crackers	.91	

14: Invoice with Double Arithmetical Computation

Type the following invoice in duplicate for the Cooper Candy Company, 34 American Avenue, Ridgewood, New Jersey 07448. The quantities and unit prices are given; you are to make all extensions and ascertain the totals:

Wakefield Food Store, 39 Main Street, Wakefield, New Jersey 07602; Salesman R. M. Staff; Today's date; Shipping Order No. 8; Shipped Via *Truck.*

Quantity	Pack		Description	Unit Price	Amount
2	16	Bxs. ea.	Marshmallows	.40	
4	12	"	Wintergreen Wafers	.45	
10	16	"	Buttercups	.48	
5	1	"	Milk Chocolate Bars	1.44	
3	12	"	Molasses Bars	.64	
12	12	"	Lemon Drops	.64	
3	16	"	Sugared Almonds	.64	
5	12	"	Chocolate Buds	.64	
6	8	"	Molasses Chips	.64	
2	12	"	Jelly Beans	.60	
1	16	"	Licorice Shoestrings	.40	

UNIT 5 | Processing Data

PART 2:

Percentage and Discount

Percentages and discounts are used frequently in business. Well-prepared office workers must know how to calculate percentages and discounts rapidly and accurately.

Meaning of Percentage. Percentage means "on or by the hundred." It is used to express the fractional relationship that exists between two or more numbers. The number with which another number is compared is said to contain 100 parts. The other number may be smaller, the same, or bigger. The difference between them is easier to understand when you express it as a part of 100. For example: A sales tag that reads "100% Wool" or "All Wool" can be expressed diagrammatically in the following manner:

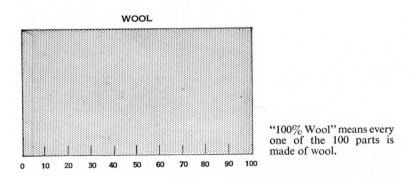

WOOL

0 10 20 30 40 50 60 70 80 90 100

"100% Wool" means every one of the 100 parts is made of wool.

A sales tag that reads "80% Wool, 20% Rayon" indicates that a large proportion of the material is made of wool. The relationship between 80% and 20% can be expressed diagrammatically in the following manner:

115

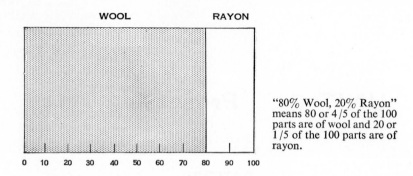

"80% Wool, 20% Rayon" means 80 or 4/5 of the 100 parts are of wool and 20 or 1/5 of the 100 parts are of rayon.

A sales tag that reads "70% Wool, 20% Rayon, 10% Nylon" indicates that the material contains more wool than either rayon or nylon. You can illustrate the relationship as follows:

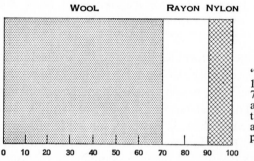

"70% Wool, 20% Rayon, 10% Nylon," means that 70 or 7/10 of the 100 parts are of wool, 20 or 2/10 of the 100 parts are of rayon, and 10 or 1/10 of the 100 parts are of nylon.

You will find that percentage is just as helpful in understanding the relationship that exists between prices and quantities as it is in understanding the relationship between materials of which wearing apparel is made. For example, take the relationship of 364 to 489. When it is found that 364 is 74.4% of 489, the relationship is easier to understand. The smaller figure is almost 75%, or 3/4, of the larger figure. You can express this relationship as follows:

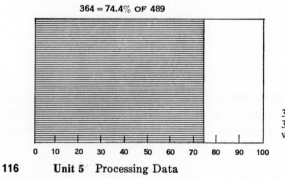

364 equals 74.4, or about 3/4 of the 100 parts into which 489 is divided.

Ways of Expressing Fractional Relationships. As an office worker, you should be familiar with the procedure followed to change percentages to decimals and to fractions. The percent sign (%) always represents 100 or two decimal places. To change a percentage to a decimal, drop the percent sign and move the decimal point two places to the left.

Examples: 48% = .48
               125% = 1.25
           12 1/2% = .125
            10.5% = .105

To change a percentage to a fraction, drop the percent sign (%) and write 100 as the denominator; the number in the percentage becomes the numerator. Reduce the fraction to its lowest terms.

Examples: 5% = 5/100 = 1/20
              15% = 15/100 = 3/20
             125% = 125/100 = 1 1/4

If the percentage contains a fraction (3 3/4), change the percentage to a decimal and then change the decimal to a fraction. Reduce the fraction to its lowest terms.

Examples: 3 3/4% = .0375 = 375/10000 = 15/400 = 3/80
            4 1/2% = .045 = 45/1000 = 9/200
           15 1/4% = .1525 = 1525/10000 = 61/400

Finding the Percentage, the Base, and the Rate. To find the percentage, multiply the base by the rate. In most instances, drop the percent sign of a figure and substitute the decimal point.

Examples: What is 44 percent of $1,560?
                 $1,560 (base)
              × .44 (rate)
              _____

                6240
                6240
              _____

              $686.40 (percentage)

To find the base when the percentage and the rate are known, divide the percentage by the rate expressed as a whole number, and multiply the answer by 100.

Example: One salesman sent in $4,387 in orders, which represented 46% of the sales made during the week. What were the total sales?

        46% = $4,387
         1% = $ 95.36956 (1/46 of $4,387)
       100% = $9,536.96 ($95.36956 × 100)

To find the rate, divide the percentage by the base and express the answer as a percent.

Example: A real estate broker earned a commission of $632.50 on a $12,650 sale. What was his rate of commission?

$632.50 (percentage) ÷ $12,650 (base) = .05 or 5% rate

Percent of Increase and Decrease. When you wish to show the percent of increase or decrease in figures for similar items for different periods of time, use the following method:

Example: What is the amount of the increase and the percent of increase of sales from 1967 to 1968 if the sales for 1967 were $450,000, while those for 1968 were $684,000?

$684,000 (1968) — $450,000 (1967) = $234,000 (amount of increase)
$234,000 ÷ $450,000 = .52 or 52% increase

Had the sales in 1968 been $300,000 and the sales in 1967, $450,000, the percent of decrease would be found as follows:

$450,000 (1967) — $300,000 (1968) = $150,000 (amount of decrease)
$150,000 ÷ $450,000 = .3333 or 33.3% decrease

Rounding Off Percentages and Estimating Answers. When it is necessary to express percentages in a predetermined number of decimal places, you should carry out the computation to *one more place* than is required. Then round off the percentage by dropping the last figure at the right. If the figure to be dropped is 5 or more, add *one* to the preceding figure; if it is less, merely drop it and change nothing.

Example: Find the percentage of increase of this year's sales of $6,264 over last year's sales of $5,837. Carry the percentage to two decimal places.

$6,264 (this year's sales)
−5,837 (last year's sales)
_____

$ 427 (amount of increase)
427 ÷ 5,837 = .07315 = 7.315% or 7.32%

The improper placement of a decimal point or an absurd answer caused by a gross computation error can be detected by estimating the answer. You can do this by rounding out amounts to simple numbers that can be multiplied or divided mentally.

Examples: 48.5 × 6.15 = 298.275 (exact answer)
Rounded off to: 50 × 6 = 300 (estimated answer)
(An answer of 29.8275 would obviously indicate a misplacement of the decimal point.)

$416.75 ÷ 49 = $8.5005 (exact answer)
Rounded off to: 400 ÷ 50 = 8 (estimated answer)
(An answer of $18.5005 would indicate an obvious gross computation error.)

Using Percents in Reports. Most businesses make reports in which comparisons between certain items are calculated on a percent basis. Comparable percents in a statistical report are easily understood and are an accurate method of presenting such items as sales, expenses, and profit or loss. A glance at the important facts presented in this manner indicates the trend of business conditions.

The report given below shows comparative sales made by several departments in a retail store. A report of this type shows the significant relationship between departments, the sales for a similar period of two years, and the general trend of the sales in the business.

Depart-ment	Total Sales Last Year	Total Sales This Year	Increase or Decrease	Percent of Increase or Decrease
A	$3,486.12	$3,805.00	$ 318.88	9.1%
B	4,680.00	6,283.86	1,603.86	34.2
C	3,265.15	4,186.23	921.08	28.2
D	1,384.21	1,243.57	− 140.64	−10.1

The relationship of the sales in the various departments to the total sales is often shown. Observe the illustration given below with the same figures used in the illustration above. This is called prorating the 100 percent. You will find the kind of table given below quite widely used in the preparation of operations reports — that is, reports showing the cost of running a business.

Depart-ment	Total Sales Last Year	Percent of Total Sales	Total Sales This Year	Percent of Total Sales
A	$ 3,486.12	27.2%	$ 3,805.00	24.5%
B	4,680.00	36.5	6,283.86	40.5
C	3,265.15	25.5	4,186.23	27.0
D	1,384.21	10.8	1,243.57	8.0
Totals	$12,815.48	100.0%	$15,518.66	100.0%

Markup. To stay in business, a company must charge more for an article than it costs. The difference between the selling price and the cost is called *markup* or *gross profit*. The amount of the markup or gross profit must cover operating expenses, such as salaries, rent, taxes, and advertising expenses, as well as a reasonable profit. The markup varies with the type of merchandise sold. It is usually between 25% and 50% of the cost.

When the markup is based on the cost, you determine the selling price by multiplying the cost by the percent of markup.

Example: What is the selling price of an article that costs $15 if the markup is 40%?

$15 × .40 = $6 Markup
$15 + $6 = $21 Selling Price

When the markup is based on the selling price, the formula for calculating the selling price is based on the assumption that the selling price equals 100%. Because the selling price (100%) includes the markup as well as the cost, subtracting the percent of markup will give the cost in percent. The selling price is found by dividing the cost in dollars by the cost in percent and moving the decimal point two places to the right.

Example: If the cost of an article is $6 and the markup is 40% of the selling price, what is the selling price?

100% Selling Price in percent   60% = $6
−40% Markup in percent   1% = 10¢ ($6 ÷ 60)
                         100% = $10 Selling Price
60% Cost in percent

Markdown. In order to stimulate sales, dispose of obsolete goods, or meet or beat competitive prices, selling prices are frequently marked down. The amount of the markdown is the difference between the old marked price and the new selling price.

Example: An article selling for $50 is marked down for clearance to $40. Find the amount of the markdown.

$50 Marked Price (original selling price)
−40 Selling Price (new selling price)
────
$10 Markdown

To find the rate of markdown, divide the amount of the markdown by the old selling price.

Example: A store advertises a dress for $30.75 which formerly sold for $37.50. Find the rate of markdown.

$37.50 Marked Price (original selling price)
−30.75 Selling Price (marked down price)
──────
$ 6.75 Markdown
$6.75 ÷ $37.50 = .18 or 18% (rate of markdown)

Percentage of Profit and Loss. To determine the percent of profit or loss on an article, divide the profit or the loss by the selling price.

Example: Find the rate of profit on a hat that costs $6.75 which was sold for $9.

$9.00 Selling Price
−6.75 Cost
_____
$2.25 Profit
$2.25 ÷ $9 = .25 or 25% Profit

To find the amount of the profit or loss when the rate is given, multiply the selling price by the rate of profit or loss.

Example: Find the profit on a sewing machine that sells for $162 on which a profit of 23% is realized.

$162 × .23 = $37.26 Profit

To find the selling price when the amount of the profit and the rate of the profit are given, divide the profit by the rate, and multiply by 100.

Example: Find the selling price of a book on which a profit of $2 represents a 25% gain.

25% = $2
1% = 8¢ (1/25 of $2)
100% = $8 ($.08 × 100)

Sometimes a businessman wants to know the rate of profit or loss on a sale in terms of the cost of an article as well as on the selling price. To obtain the percent of profit or loss based on the cost of an article, divide the profit by the cost.

Example: Find the rate of profit on a refrigerator that costs $375 and sells for $525.

$525 Selling Price
−375 Cost
_____
$150 Profit
$150 ÷ $375 = .40 or 40% of the *Cost*

Shortcuts. When the rate of profit or loss on the cost is known, the rate of profit based on the selling price can be determined without dividing the profit by the selling price. The shortcut method is based on the common fraction equivalent of the percent of profit or loss. Thus, in the problem on the refrigerator, a profit of 40% is equal to 2/5 of the cost (40% = 40/100, which can be reduced to 2/5). To find the percent of profit on the selling price, *add* the numerator, 2, to the denominator, 5, to get the new denominator of the fraction of profit based on the selling price. *The numerator remains the same.* The profit of 2/5 based on the cost is equal to 2/7 based on the selling price (2 + 5 = 7, the denominator of the new fraction).

Example: $500 Selling Price

−400 Cost
___
$100 Profit

$100 divided by $400 (Cost) = 25% Profit or 1/4 of *Cost*

1 + 4 = 5 or 1/5 or 20% of the *Selling Price*

Proof: $400 (Cost) × .25 = $100 Profit

$500 (Selling Price) × .20 = $100 Profit

To get the percent of profit based on the *cost* when the percent of profit on the *selling price* is known, *subtract* the numerator from the denominator to get the denominator of the new fraction based on the cost. *The numerator remains the same.*

Example: $1000 Selling Price

−600 Cost
___
$ 400 Profit

$400 ÷ $1000 = 40% or 2/5 of the *Selling Price*

5 − 2 or 2/3 or 66 2/3% of the *Cost*

Proof: $1000 (Selling Price) × .40 = $400 Profit

$600 (Cost) × .66 2/3 = $400 Profit

Chain Trade Discounts. Two processes may be used to arrive at the net amount of an invoice with a series of discounts known as *chain trade discounts.* Either procedure is satisfactory; but, as you will observe, one process is easier than the other. In both instances, the answer is carried out three decimal places.

Example: What would be the net amount of an invoice on a quotation of 60 chairs at $3.75 each, less 20%, 10%, and 5%?

Step 1

$3.75 Gross cost

×.20 Rate of first discount
___
$.7500 First discount

$3.75 Gross cost

−.75 First discount
___
$3.00 Cost after first discount

Step 2

$3.00 Gross cost after first discount

×.10 Rate of second discount
___
$.3000 Second discount

$3.00 Gross cost after first discount

−.30 Second discount
___
$2.70 Cost after second discount

Step 3

$2.70 Gross cost after second discount

×.05 Rate of third discount
___
$.1350 Third discount

$2.700 Gross cost after second discount

−.135 Third discount
___
$2.565 Net cost

Step 4

$2.565 Net cost

×60 Chairs
___
$153.900 Net amount of invoice

Another procedure is indicated by the following example:

$100\% - 20\% = 80\%$		Net after first discount
10% of $80\% = 8\%$		Second discount
$80\% - 8\% = 72\%$		Net after second discount
5% of $72\% = 3.6\%$		Third discount
$72\% - 3.6\% = 68.4\%$		Net after third discount (percent of invoice to be paid)
$\$3.75 \times .684 = \$2.565$		Gross cost
$\$2.565 \times 60 = \$153.90$		Net amount of invoice

Cash Discount. To encourage prompt payment of a bill or an invoice, many businesses grant a discount for a cash payment or for prompt payment within a certain time. Such a rate is usually stated on the invoice, for example, as 2/10, n/30. These terms mean that 2 percent may be deducted if the bill is paid within 10 days, but the bill must be paid in full within 30 days. To determine the discount, multiply the amount of the invoice by the rate. To find the net amount due, subtract the discount from the total of the invoice or bill.

When a calculating machine is used, the process is frequently shortened by subtracting the discount rate from 100 percent mentally, and by multiplying the total of the invoice by the percent that has to be paid.

Example: What is the net on an invoice of $683.14 with terms of 5/10, n/30?

Solution A

$683.14	List price	$683.140	List price
$\times$ .05	Discount rate	$ 34.157	Discount
$ 34.1570	Amount of discount	$648.983	Net amount of invoice

Solution B

100%	List price	$683.14 List price
−5%	Discount	$\times$.95 Net rate
95%	Net price	$648.98 Net amount of invoice

Study Questions

1. What is the meaning of the word *percentage?*

2. Name three ways of expressing fractional relationships.

3. How is a percentage changed to a decimal?

4. Give two ways of changing percentages to fractions.

5. What is the formula for finding a percentage of a number?

6. How do you find the *base* when the *percentage* as a whole number and the *rate* as a percent are known?

7. How do you find the *rate* expressed as a percent of the *base* when the *percentage* as a whole number and the *base* are known?

8. What is meant by "rounding off" a percent?

9. Why is it wise to estimate the answer to a problem involving percentage?

10. Why are many business reports which show a comparison between items expressed in percentages?

11. Why is markup necessary? How is the markup determined?

12. When do businessmen use markdowns?

13. What is the formula for computing the *rate* of markdown?

14. Describe two processes that may be used to arrive at the *net amount* of an invoice showing a series of discounts.

15. Explain the purpose of a cash discount and how the seller and the buyer benefit through prompt payment of invoices.

What Do You Think?

1. How is quantity buying stimulated by the use of chain discounts?

2. How do percentages in financial or statistical reports help a business executive to formulate or change merchandising policies?

3. Should percent of profit or loss be based on *cost* or *selling price*? Why?

4. Is it good business to borrow at 6% per annum in order to take advantage of a cash discount of 2% for cash payment within 10 days?

Your Personal Qualities

Your company sells on terms of 2/10, n/30 from the date of the invoice. The latest Pinson Company invoice for $130.50 is dated January 3. Their check is dated January 15 for $127.89. This means Pinson Company took the cash discount, but they paid after the ten-day discount period. On the last four invoices Pinson took the discount after the discount period expired.

Question: What should you do?

How's Your English?

Read about the use of the apostrophe in Appendix B, and insert apostrophes in appropriate places in the following:

1. Dont call too late because I cant wait too long.

2. The 1890s are referred to as the Gay Nineties.

3. The 2s and 9s are typed too lightly.

4. Mr. Grants manuscript is ready.

5. The committees report is still in rough draft, but Ill have it typed by tomorrow.

6. The mens report has been typed in final form, but the womens report wont be ready until next week.

7. Ross typing is excellent, but Lawrences work is poor.

8. We have our printing done at Jones and Williams print shop.

9. Marys leaving at the end of the week.

10. Typing Xs over incorrect work is permissible in preparing rough drafts.

Office Work

1. Find the *amount* of commission to be paid each of the following salesmen:

Salesman	Weekly Sales	Rate of Commission
a. John White	$ 940	5%
b. James Carey	1,215	4%
c. Vincent Wright	2,506	3 1/2%
d. Alfred Reed	3,675	6%
e. Raymond Farr	6,125	2%
f. Joseph Dee	7,345	4%

2. Find the *rate* of commission paid to each of the following salesmen:

Salesman	Weekly Sales	Commission
a. John Spears	$ 6,750	$337.50
b. Ronald Jones	8,135	488.10
c. William Wilson	8,576	257.28
d. Allan Furchak	10,150	406.00
e. Claude Hammer	3,750	93.75
f. Carmen DeRosa	6,180	200.85

3. Find the *amount* of the weekly sales of each of the following salesmen:

Salesman	Commission	Rate
a. Walter Johnson	$242.50	5%
b. Simon Lee	429.30	6%
c. Art Johns	325.00	4%
d. Ford Wright	183.34	2%
e. Alex O'Donnell	184.26	3%
f. Sal Maggio	974.80	8%

4. In each of the following sales, determine the *amount* and the *rate* of profit based on the selling price:

Selling Price	Cost
a. $ 750.25	$ 450.25
b. 375.00	300.00
c. 1,750.00	1,050.00
d. 2,250.00	1,500.00
e. 7,458.50	5,220.95
f. 9,411.00	5,176.05

5. Follow the examples on pages 117–118 in calculating the amount of the missing item in each of the following problems:

	Base	Rate	Percentage
a.	$ 3,021.00	56%	?
b.	896.00	?	562.08
c.	?	13%	97.50
d.	10,940.00	?	875.20
e.	98.50	19%	?
f.	?	28%	682.12
g.	1,750.50	?	735.21

6. Calculate the *difference* in total sales for each department for the two periods listed; then calculate the *percent* of increase or decrease. An example is given on page 118.

Department	Total Sales Last Year	Total Sales This Year
Children's	$5,609.17	$6,090.82
Furniture	9,032.50	7,650.18
Housewares	876.94	842.10
Ladies' Ready-to-Wear	4,702.19	5,910.16
Men's	4,816.48	6,032.97
Toy	2,839.60	2,756.13

7. Find the *percent* of total sales for the periods listed for each department. Refer to pages 118–119.

Department	Total Sales June 1967	Total Sales June 1968
Children's	$5,609.17	$6,090.82
Furniture	9,032.50	7,650.18
Housewares	876.94	842.10
Ladies' Ready-to-Wear	4,702.19	5,910.16
Men's	4,816.48	6,032.97
Toy	2,839.60	2,756.13

8. In each of the following problems, determine the *amounts* of the selling price and the markup. An example is given on page 120.

	Cost	Percent of Markup
a.	$12.55	15%
b.	9.00	25%
c.	26.30	30%
d.	16.00	60%
e.	34.25	15%
f.	8.35	25%
g.	46.50	60%

9. Determine the *net cost* for each of the following items. Use either of the procedures explained starting on page 122.

	Catalog Price	Discount Rates
a.	$37.00	20%, 10%, 5%
b.	25.00	10%
c.	5.50	10%, 5%
d.	4.00	20%, 10%
e.	1.10	5%
f.	4.50	20%, 10%, 5%
g.	10.00	10%, 5%

10. Determine the *net amount* paid on each of the following invoices, assuming that the cash discount is taken in each case:

Amount of Invoice	Terms
a. $ 3.10	1/10, n/30
b. 93.58	3/10, n/30
c. 150.00	2/20, n/90
d. 265.13	2/15, n/30
e. 1,902.17	3/10, n/30
f. 652.10	3/15, n/60
g. 872.98	2/10, n/30
h. 16.48	2/10, n/30
i. 2,009.68	2/20, n/90

Office Work Assignments

15: Invoice with Special Discount

Type the following invoice in duplicate for Roland and Sons, Main and Grover Streets, Newark, New Jersey 07113. The quantities and unit prices are given. You are to make all extensions and ascertain the totals.

Wakefield Food Stores, 39 Main Street, Wakefield, New Jersey 07602; Invoice Date (today's date); Invoice No. 865; Via Truck; Sold by A. J. Baker; 5% special discount on all soups.

Quantity	Description	List Price	Amount
25	Ketchup	5.80	
10	Chicken Noodle Soup	3.94	
5	Cream of Mushroom Soup	5.24	
50	Pork and Beans	3.89	
3	Mustard	2.00	
10	Cooked Spaghetti	3.90	
3	Apple Jelly	2.10	
15	Cream of Tomato Soup	3.94	
10	Sweet Relish	1.95	
5	Clam Chowder	3.70	
2	Chile con Carne	8.40	
10	Vegetable Soup	3.06	
2	Vinegar	2.50	
3	Blackberry Jelly	3.45	
10	Chicken with Rice Soup	3.94	

16: Invoice with Price Quoted per Unit

Type the following invoice in duplicate for the Wakefield Paper Supply Company, 383–389 Crown Street, Wakefield, New Jersey 07602. The quantities and unit prices are given. Make all extensions and ascertain the totals.

Wakefield Food Store, 39 Main Street, Wakefield, New Jersey 07602; today's date; No. 1364; salesman Mr. C. Mullins.

Quantity	Pack	Description	Price	Total
6,000 sheets	14 × 14	Lumaphane Paper	.0388M	
10,000 sheets	16 × 16	Lumaphane Paper	.0388M	
6 cartons	500	12 oz. Paper Salad Tubs	20.50M	
10 cartons	500	16 oz. Paper Salad Tubs	22.90M	
2 cartons	2,500	Printed Lids (Potato Salad)	8.67M	
5 cartons	1,000	8 oz. Salad Tubs	17.90M	

17: Invoice with Fractions

As this type of invoice is usually completed without a typewriter, use a pencil to list the quantity, list price, and the extension.

Write the following invoice in duplicate for Stevens Farm Products, Inc., 407 Grant Avenue, Wakefield, New Jersey 07602. The quantities and unit prices are given. Make all extensions and ascertain the totals.

Wakefield Food Store, 39 Main Street, Wakefield, New Jersey 07602; today's date.

Quantity	Description	Price	Total
96	Butter	.78 1/2	
24	Yogurt	.14	
48	Margarine	.31 1/2	
35	Mayonnaise	.25	
	Cheeses		
104	Cottage	.14	
48	Pot	.21	
50 1/2	Swiss	.74	
5	Muenster	.67	
67	Edam	.70	
	Cheese Spreads		
23	Pimento	2.38	
7	Chive	2.00	
5	Old English	2.00	
	Frozen Fruits		
33	Berries	.45	
	Salads		
55	Potato	.33	
60	Cole Slaw	.31	

18: Invoice with Multiplication of Two Fractions

As this type of invoice is usually completed without a typewriter, use a pencil to list the product, weight, price, and the extension.

Write the invoice in duplicate for Better Meats, Inc., 25–26 Standard Avenue, Wakefield, New Jersey 07602. The quantities and unit prices are given. Make all extensions and ascertain the totals.

Wakefield Food Store, 39 Main Street, Wakefield, New Jersey 07602; today's date.

Product	Weight	Price	Amount
Boiled Ham	77 3/4	1.01 1/2	
Sliced Ham	34 1/2	.83 1/4	
Salt Pork	12	.33 1/4	
Lard	45	.27 1/2	
Bologna	28 1/2	.47	
Sliced Bacon	30	.85 1/2	
Luncheon Meat	25	.55 1/2	
Liverwurst	10 1/2	.49	
Olive Loaf	58 1/4	.77	
Salami	17 1/2	.69 1/2	

UNIT 5 | Processing Data

PART 3:

Adding Machines
and Calculators

As a member of the office staff, you may be called upon to do such things as prepare and verify the accuracy of bills, invoices, accounts, inventories, payrolls, purchase and sales summaries, purchase and sales analyses, cost analyses, expense distribution statements, tax reports, budgets, production reports, and cash receipts and disbursements summaries. Preparation and verification of these business papers and reports involve a considerable amount of figure work that can be done more easily and accurately with the aid of an office machine. An adding machine or a desk calculator will be of valuable assistance to you in preparing reports. You will not only save time in completing the required computations when you use a machine, but you will also have the assurance that the figures which you incorporate in the reports are accurate.

The two main groups of adding and calculating machines are listing and nonlisting office machines.

Listing Machines. You may have a listing machine on your desk which prints on a roll of paper tape all amounts added, subtracted, multiplied, or divided. The printed answers to all computations are followed by special symbols to indicate whether they are subtotals, totals, remainders, or credit balances. The printed tapes will enable you to check the amounts computed in the machine with the original amounts on the checks, sales slips, invoices, timecards, or other business forms from which they were taken. Three types of listing machines are used extensively: full-keyboard adding machines, ten-key adding machines, and printing calculators.

Full-Keyboard Listing Machines. Let's look at the illustration of a full-keyboard listing machine on page 130. A full-keyboard adding machine may have anywhere from five to twenty columns of keys ranging in ascending order from 1 to 9. You will see that there are no 0-keys on the

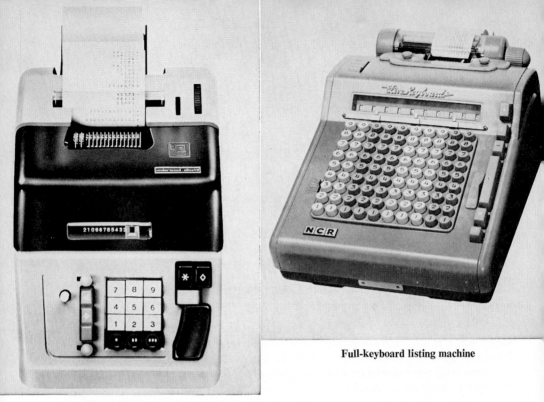

Ten-key listing machine

Full-keyboard listing machine

keyboard; ciphers are printed automatically. How would you enter $50.60?
You would depress the 5 key in the *fourth* column from the right of the
keyboard, the 6 key in the *second* column from the right, and the motor bar
to add and print the amount 50.60. The machines are used primarily for
addition and subtraction. It is possible, however, to multiply by using
repeated addition; a table of reciprocals of the divisors may be used to
solve division problems.

Most adding machines of this type are equipped with a credit
balance key which permits the credit balance to be directly recorded on
the tape when the amounts subtracted are greater than the amounts added.
For instance, a credit balance would be printed when the total credits on a
statement are found to exceed the total of the charges, or when a checking
account is overdrawn (when the withdrawals exceed the deposits).

Ten-Key Listing Machines. Adding and listing machines with ten-
figure keyboards are used more extensively than machines with full keyboards. As the name implies, a ten-key machine has only ten figure keys
on the keyboard. Amounts are entered on the keyboard and printed on the
paper tape in the order in which they are read. Each figure key, including
the 0 or cipher key, is depressed separately. For example, to list $50.60
you would depress the 5, 0, 6, and 0 keys and then depress the motor bar.

Because the machine has only ten figure keys, all within easy reach, you will be able to enter amounts on the keyboard without looking at the keys after a few hours of instruction. Touch operation will increase your production rate and greatly reduce your chances of omitting amounts or transposing figures in an amount.

Ten-key listing machines, like the full-keyboard machines, are used primarily for addition and subtraction. Repeated addition is used to multiply amounts, and a table of reciprocals is used for division.

Printing Calculators. If your work demands much multiplication and division, you will want to use a printing calculator. The printing calculator is used extensively as an all-purpose calculator. It is preferred by some office workers, particularly accountants, because the tapes can be forwarded with the source material from which the computations were made. All printing calculators have ten-figure keyboards and, like the other ten-key machines, can be operated by touch. However, they represent a further development in the operation of listing machines because both multiplication and division problems can be solved directly on the machine without the use of either repeated addition or a table of reciprocals. For example, in order to multiply $18.36 by 24 on an Olivetti printing calculator, you would:

Figures on Tape

A. Clear the machine.....................
B. Strike the figures 1 8 3 6 on the keyboard
C. Depress the multiplier (×) key..........
D. Strike the figures 2 4 on the keyboard...
E. Depress the multiplication (=) key. ....
F. The answer is automatically printed on the tape. Record the answer as $440.64.

```
              T
    1 8 3 6  x <
        2 4   =
    4 4 0 6 4  T
```

To divide $145.00 by 12:

A. Clear the machine....................
B. Strike the figures 1 4 5 0 0 on the keyboard.
C. Depress the addition (+) key..........
D. Strike the figures 1 2 on the keyboard...
E. Depress the divide (÷) key............
F. The answer is automatically printed on the tape. Record the answer as $12.08 and disregard the remainder of 4.

```
              T
    1 4 5 0 0  +
        1 2    ÷
    1 2 0 8    T
        4      T
```

The larger models have two separate registers, permitting amounts to be calculated in one register and accumulated in the other. For example, all the separate items in an invoice can be extended (multiplication of each

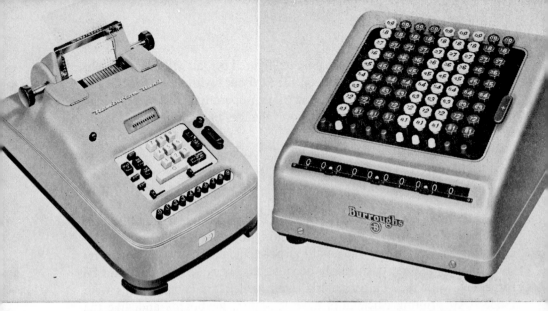

Printing calculator   Key-driven calculator

quantity by the price) in one register, and the total of the entire invoice can
be immediately obtained from the other register.

Nonlisting Machines. The nonlisting office machines, key-driven
calculators and rotary calculators, are usually referred to as desk calculators. It is possible to perform all four arithmetic processes — addition,
subtraction, multiplication, and division — on both the key-driven and
the rotary calculators, but the operating processes are performed differently
on the two types of machines.

Key-Driven Calculators. Machines in this category are called key-
driven calculators because the depression of a key actually operates the
mechanism of the machine. As the keys are depressed, the results are
registered in the answer dials located directly below the figure columns on
the keyboard. For example, if 3 5 0 and 2 4 5 are added at the right of the
keyboard, the total, or 595, is immediately shown in the answer dials
below.

Key-driven calculators are especially suited for the rapid addition
and multiplication of numbers with fewer than five digits. A two-finger
touch system, in which no key above 5 is depressed, is usually used to add.
The index and middle fingers of both hands are used on all the figure keys
to multiply amounts. The machines are widely used in business to multiply
and add invoices, to compute payrolls, and to verify the accuracy of the
addition and multiplication in business forms and business reports. The
small figures on the keytops, which are the machine complements of the

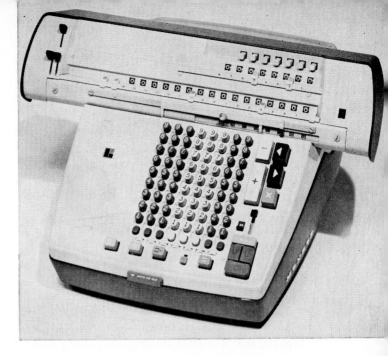

Automatic rotary calculator

large figures on the keytops, are used when solving problems in subtraction and division.

Rotary Calculators. Three different types of rotary calculators are available: fully automatic models which multiply and divide automatically, semiautomatic models which divide automatically, and hand-operated models on which all operations are performed manually. The hand-operated models have been almost completely replaced in business offices by the electrically operated fully automatic and semiautomatic models.

Addition and subtraction are simple operations on rotary calculators — an amount is depressed on the keyboard, and it is added or subtracted by depressing either the plus bar or the minus bar.

Rotary calculators are particularly suited for multiplication and division of numbers with five digits or more and for computing answers to four or more decimal places. Tabulator keys and decimal markers on the keyboard and in the answer dials should be used as guides in multiplication and division and in recording amounts with decimals.

Rotary calculators are used to solve all types of business problems, actuarial problems, and engineering problems, and to compute square root, cube root, and other statistics.

Electronic Calculators. These calculators perform the four fundamental arithmetical processes. Numbers are struck on the keyboard and are then transferred to one of the four visible registers. There is also

Electronic calculator

a fifth register used for storage. A cathode-ray tube displays the contents of the four registers on a television-like screen. Since there are no moving parts, the calculator is completely silent and very fast.

Study Questions

1. Under what circumstances might you use adding and calculating machines?
2. What are the advantages of using a listing machine?
3. When is a full-keyboard listing machine most useful?
4. For what type of work is a ten-key listing machine particularly valuable?
5. What is one of the chief advantages of a ten-key listing machine?
6. What is the chief difference between an ordinary ten-key listing machine and a printing calculator?
7. Why are key-driven calculators so named?
8. In what type of work is a key-driven calculator most efficient?
9. When are rotary calculators most commonly used?
10. What are three types of rotary calculators?
11. What are the features of the electronic calculator?

What Do You Think?

1. What are some of the types of errors that might be made when using an adding or calculating machine?
2. Is it better to check items against the listings on an adding machine tape or to run a second tape?
3. In what types of businesses would you recommend that the company acquire a ten-key machine rather than a full-keyboard machine? a full-keyboard machine rather than a ten-key machine?

4. What types of computations can be done more efficiently on a key-driven calculator than on a rotary calculator?

Your Personal Qualities

The hand-operated, full-keyboard listing machine used by all employees in the uptown branch of the Capital Finance Company is beyond repair. It has been decided to buy a new machine instead of having the old machine completely overhauled. A listing machine is needed because a tape listing all of the amounts must accompany all checks that are sent to the main office.

Two of the older employees prefer a full-keyboard listing machine similar to the model that is to be traded in. Two of the younger employees who are acquainted with the touch system of the ten-key listing machine prefer that type over the full-keyboard type. Both machines cost approximately the same amount.

Questions: 1. What machine should be bought? Why?

2. What are some of the implications of your decision?

How's Your English?

Read about the use of the parentheses and the dash in Appendix B. Then rewrite the following, using correct punctuation:

1. A contract for employment was written that included 1 the annual salary 2 the number of years the contract was to run 3 the amount of expenses to be allowed and 4 the ways in which the contract could be terminated by either party. The salary indicated was to be nine thousand $9000 dollars a year.

2. In this report the figures see exhibit B speak for themselves.

3. After reading the report the man said he was not interested his wife doesnt want to move.

4. Mr A of our company and Mr W of the competition both checked the proof on their joint statement.

5. Rough drafts finished manuscripts and proofs these are the things you work with in getting out a booklet.

Office Work

1. Visit one or more offices in your community to find out what adding and calculating machines are being used. Also find out what kinds of jobs are being done on the machines. If possible, procure some of the business forms that are used in connection with these jobs. Prepare a typewritten report on your visit, attaching the forms collected. Be prepared to make an oral presentation to the class.

2. Write to one or more manufacturers of adding and calculating machines asking for literature on their machines. Use this material for a bulletin-board display.

Office Work Assignments

If adding or calculating machines are available, find the answers for the following problems. If you are using the workbook correlated with the text, record your answers in the blanks provided for that purpose.

19: Computing Increases and Decreases

Ascertain the amount of the increase or the decrease in each of the following items. Indicate an increase by a plus sign after the amount, a decrease by a minus sign after the amount.

		Last Year	This Year
a.	Sales	$66,875.42	$72,492.80
b.	Returned Sales	1,034.90	882.45
c.	Purchases	58,145.25	59,671.38
d.	Returned Purchases	782.31	645.90
e.	Freight In	581.45	596.71
f.	Sales Salaries	7,580.00	7,800.00
g.	Delivery Expense	1,694.40	1,725.75
h.	Advertising Expense	972.95	887.40
i.	Depreciation	385.50	412.75
j.	Office Salaries	5,675.00	5,750.00
k.	Rent	2,400.00	2,500.00
l.	Miscellaneous Expense	429.87	356.12

20: Computing Sales Report

Complete the following weekly sales report by adding vertically each column in the report. Verify the accuracy of your addition by adding horizontally.

A B C Department Store
Weekly Sales Report
For the Week Ending September 7, 19--

Merchandise	Fisher	Adams	Reid	White	Total
Sweaters	$ 81.50	$ 89.75	$ 90.10	$ 75.15	_____
Shirts, work	79.94	78.43	87.15	92.25	_____
Shirts, dress	97.85	99.87	92.14	86.75	_____
Ties	86.86	44.10	34.75	28.80	_____
Bow Ties	15.35	12.66	17.25	11.05	_____
Hats	86.75	31.50	92.25	21.75	_____
Gloves	24.17	38.48	41.66	18.27	_____
Scarfs	51.01	45.73	70.84	91.01	_____
Slacks	67.32	45.68	49.62	96.78	_____
Coveralls	31.54	63.43	80.19	86.20	_____
Work Gloves	20.19	24.25	11.70	12.30	_____
Umbrellas	23.10	42.00	24.30	14.70	_____
Caps	10.79	20.84	318.21	37.50	_____
Jackets	89.10	78.14	64.30	96.78	_____
Top Coats	95.00	85.00	98.00	92.00	_____
Overcoats	176.59	358.35	91.79	192.93	_____
Suits	438.48	276.96	145.65	258.90	_____
Sport Coats	141.13	128.21	137.50	50.14	_____
Totals	_____	_____	_____	_____	_____

21: Computing Extensions

Make the extensions in the following invoice lists:

a.

87 yds.	Woolen	$1.95 per yd.	_____
67 yds.	Worsted	2.07 per yd.	_____
39 yds.	Cotton Print	.58 per yd.	_____
67 yds.	Washable Woolen	2.15 per yd.	_____
		Total	_____

b.

47 yds.	Gingham	$ .89 per yd.	_____
92 yds.	Cotton Plaid	1.19 per yd.	_____
32 yds.	Cotton Check	.97 per yd.	_____
47 yds.	Cotton Print	.62 per yd.	_____
		Total	_____

c.

86 yds.	Wool Flannel	$4.50 per yd.	_____
172 yds.	Leather	4.62 per yd.	_____
95 yds.	Tweed	4.75 per yd.	_____
39 yds.	Plaid	4.82 per yd.	_____
		Total	_____

d.

45 yds.	Rayon Tweed	$ .92 per yd.	_____
173 yds.	Orlon Check	1.05 per yd.	_____
76 yds.	Rayon Check	.95 per yd.	_____
149 yds.	Cotton Plaid	.82 per yd.	_____
		Total	_____

22: Computing Averages

Find the average sale per customer by dividing the amount of sales for each department by the number of customers. Round the answer to the nearest cent.

Dept.	Amount of Sales	No. of Customers
A-100	$ 8,623.74	920
A-101	17,620.93	345
A-102	9,842.65	587
A-103	4,368.69	1769
B-200	17,579.64	112
B-201	8,496.71	39
B-202	4,392.70	724
C-300	9,658.21	1563
C-301	5,291.16	435
C-302	6,789.42	673
C-303	7,432.36	360
C-350	2,293.50	162
D-400	4,456.62	133
D-401	1,975.30	59
D-402	1,727.13	694

23: Computing Payroll

Ascertain the total hours worked and the total weekly wages for each employee on the following payroll time sheet:

PAYROLL TIME SHEET

Employee No.	Mon.	Tues.	Wed.	Thurs.	Fri.	Wages Per Hour
1	8	8	4	8	8	$4.90
2	8	6 1/2	..	4	8	3.20
3	5 1/2	8	8	8	8	2.25
4	8	8	8	8	8	1.85
5	8	8	8	..	8	1.60
6	8	8	5 1/2	8	8	1.70
7	8	6	8	8	8	2.10
8	8	8	8	8	7 1/2	1.80
9	..	4	6	8	8	1.60
10	8	8	8	8	8	2.60
11	8	8	8	6 1/2	8	1.65
12	8	8	8	8	8	2.40
13	8	7	8	8	5	1.80
14	8	8	8	8	8	2.90
15	8	8	7	8	8	2.50

UNIT 5 | Processing Data

PART 4:

Automation

Your social security contributions, your income tax deductions, and your life insurance premiums are probably processed with the use of an ultramodern data processing system. These machines have been installed in modern business offices to handle the ever-increasing volume of paper work: to prepare payrolls, to process orders, to maintain inventories, and to perform other routine and repetitive tasks. It is estimated that about one third of all paper work is now processed with the help of a data processing system. You will frequently work with processed records when you are employed in an office, and you should have a clear understanding of the basic operation of data processing systems.

All data processing systems use one or more of the common storage media — punched cards, perforated paper tapes, magnetic tapes — to transfer information from one machine to another automatically. There are three different types of data processing systems:

1) Punched-card accounting systems
2) Integrated data processing (IDP) systems
3) Electronic data processing (EDP) systems

PUNCHED-CARD ACCOUNTING SYSTEMS

The leading manufacturers of punched-card machines are the International Business Machines Corporation (IBM) and the Remington Rand Division of the Sperry Rand Corporation. The IBM machines use a standard card which has 80 vertical columns; the Remington Rand machines, a standard card containing 90 columns. Each column in a card will accommodate a punched hole (or holes) to represent a single number or letter. Information to be processed through the machines must be punched in the cards according to a standard arrangement. Consequently, columns on the cards are grouped and reserved for the recording of specific facts about each business transaction. After a card has been punched and

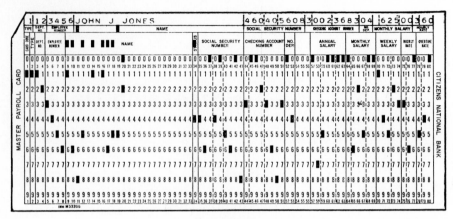

Punched card

verified, it becomes a permanent record. It can be read by machines that transcribe, calculate, or otherwise process the data at high speed.

Both IBM and Remington Rand use four basic machines in the punched-card accounting process: (1) key punch, (2) verifier, (3) sorter, and (4) tabulator. What part does each machine play in processing data?

Card Keypunching. Card punching is the basic method of transferring original information into punched cards. The key-punch operator reads the original document and depresses keys that punch holes in the cards. These holes represent data from the original document. The machine feeds, positions, and ejects each card automatically. The operator's primary concern is to strike the proper keys in the correct sequence.

Three types of keyboards are available for card punching: *numeric, alphabetic,* and a *combination of numeric and alphabetic keyboards.* A three-finger touch system should be used on the numeric keyboard to strike the figure keys with a high degree of speed and accuracy. The first vertical row of keys (12, 1, 4, and 7) should be struck with the index finger, the second row of keys (X, 2, 5, and 8) with the middle finger, and the third row (0, 3, 6, and 9) with the ring finger. The alphabetic keyboards are very similar to the standard typewriter keyboards and can be operated by any accurate touch typist.

The combination keyboard is the most widely used of the three keyboards. It has the best features of a typewriter and a numeric key punch. The usual row of numeric keys on a typewriter has been eliminated; instead, a group of dual-purpose keys at the right are used to punch both numbers and letters. For example, when the keyboard is in an alphabetic shift, the letters U, J, and M are struck with the index finger of the right hand; when the keyboard is in a numeric shift, the same keys are struck to punch the numbers 1, 4, and 7.

A key-punch machine

This is a combination machine which features both numeric and alphabetic punching.

Card Verifying. Since accuracy is so essential, card verifying is necessary to check original keypunching. A different operator usually verifies the original punching by striking the keys of a verifier while reading from the same source of information used to punch the cards. The verifying machine compares the key struck with the hole already punched in the column on the card. A difference causes the machine to stop, indicating a discrepancy between the two operations. A notch in the upper right edge of the card indicates that it has been keypunched and verified correctly. A notch directly above a column signifies that the punching of that column is in error.

Card Sorting. Imagine sorting from 800 to 1000 cards a minute with complete accuracy! This is one of the outstanding advantages of the punched-card accounting system. After the punched cards have been verified, they are sorted in a numeric or alphabetic order according to the information that has been punched in them. Payroll cards, for example, may be sorted alphabetically according to the last and given names of the employees or numerically according to their timecard numbers.

If cards were to be arranged in numeric order from 1 to 999, they would be passed through the sorting machine three times. They would be sorted first in the last, or units, column of the punched numbers, then in the tens column, and finally in the hundreds column.

Card Collating. Sometimes the information to be processed is contained on two or more sets of punched cards. After these cards have

Sorting machine

This machine automatically arranges punched cards in numeric or alphabetic sequence according to classifications punched in the cards.

been sorted numerically and alphabetically, they are run through a collator The collator interfiles punched cards so that those pertaining to a given invoice or a particular customer are arranged in a predetermined order.

Tabulating. After the cards have been sorted, they are fed through a tabulator to transcribe and print automatically the information punched in the cards. The tabulator will print names and other descriptive information from a group of cards, add or subtract punched amounts, and print totals and grand totals. It will also print totals and grand totals only, without listing either the descriptive information or the separate amounts punched in the individual cards. Tabulating machines operate at speeds ranging from 100 to 150 cards per minute, depending upon the type of machine used.

INTEGRATED DATA PROCESSING

Now let's look at the second type of data processing. Integrated data processing, or IDP as it is called, is a system of machine control based on the ability of office machines to transfer information to other machines automatically. Punched paper tape, the "common storage media" of IDP, serves as the medium for automatically transferring data from one machine to another. The *Flexowriter*, an automatic writing machine, is a key instrument in the system. As information is typed on it, a punched paper tape is produced simultaneously. Other machines in the system

Programatic Flexowriter

can read the tape and produce typed invoices and other business papers from it at the rate of 100 words per minute.

Operation of an IDP System. The following steps are taken in processing a typical order through the office machines in the *Friden Flexowriter* integrated data processing system:

1) A single "hard copy" (typewriter copy) of the entire order is typed on the *Flexowriter* so that the accuracy of the order can be checked before it is transmitted. If the order is from a regular customer, the heading need not be typed. His name, address, and other pertinent data can be automatically typed from a prepunched tape kept in the master tape file.

2) As the order is typed, a complete tape is produced. It operates on the principle of the player piano roll — as the piano roll translates holes into music, the *Flexowriter* tape translates the punched information to machines which are able to read and transmit the information. Some *Flexowriters* produce edge-punched cards instead of tapes. They perform the same function as the tape, but because they are kept in files, the cards are more convenient to handle.

3) The *Computyper* takes the tape from the *Flexowriter* and adds, subtracts, or multiplies the figures in the order. It also produces a complete summary tape and a by-product tape for tabulating.

4) The summary tape is fed into a *Teletypewriter* which creates an eleven-part invoice and automatically and instantaneously transmits by wire shipping instructions to the various plants or warehouses.

5) At the receiving end, a four-part shipping form is also simultaneously created to serve as shipping information.

Advantages of IDP. An integrated data processing system is fast and accurate because:

1) All the information in an order — heading, descriptions of items, quantities, prices, shipping instructions, and so forth — is typed only once in the entire process. The taped copy of the order is used to reproduce the information on the forms sent to the customer, the accounts receivable department, the shipping department, and other affected departments.
2) The tapes can be transmitted by wire quickly from widely separated branch offices to main offices, warehouses, and plants where the necessary business forms can be automatically reproduced.
3) The automatically reproduced information is accurate and therefore much more dependable than manually retyped information.

ELECTRONIC DATA PROCESSING

The third type of data processing in which you will be interested is electronic data processing, or EDP. This term is used to describe the most advanced development in data processing — the processing of records with electronic systems. An EDP system requires very careful programming — the entering of a complete set of instructions for each step in a procedure — before any of the data can be stored or processed. The person who prepares the set of instructions, or program, is called a programmer. He must be thoroughly familiar with all phases of the actual business application to be processed (computing monthly interest on all types of bank loans, for example) and with the specific functions of all the related machines used in the procedure.

A typical electronic data processing system utilizes three groups of linked devices or machines to perform the related steps in an operation. The IBM 360 and 1401 installations are widely used for business applications and include:

1) *Input* devices which are used to enter instructions and transaction data into the storage section of the system. The information to be placed in the computer may be recorded on punched cards, paper tape, or magnetic tape.
2) *Central processing* unit that includes
   a. The *storage* section which stores transaction data, instructions, tables, intermediate results, final results, historical data, summary files, master records, and any information that can be advantageously stored within the computer. Four types of magnetic storage are used: drums, cores, tapes, and disks.
   b. The *process* section which manipulates the data. Computing — addition, subtraction, multiplication, and division — is performed here. So, also, are made comparisons on which logical decisions are based. In short, the work is done here.

CONTROL STORAGE INPUT/OUTPUT CONTROL

IBM

OUTPUT

OUTPUT

STORAGE

PROCESSOR

INPUT/OUTPUT

An electronic data processing system

    c. The *control* section which could be called the nerve center of the data processing system. It receives each instruction of the program and analyzes it to determine the operation to be performed. The movement of data into or out of storage is supervised by the control section. It controls the execution of the operation, monitors and supervises the flow of data within the system, and notifies the operator when his attention is required.

  3) The *output* devices, which are used to take the results of the processing out of the system. The output devices usually reproduce information on punched cards or in printed form on wide continuous forms.

Glossary of Data Processing Terms. Remington Rand, manufacturers of the *Univac* data processing systems, uses the following terms to describe the functions of its basic equipment:

    CARD PUNCHING is the primary conversion of source data into punched cards.

    COLLATING is the process of interfiling two decks of cards in numerical sequence.

    COMPARING is the automatic checking of cards on a match or nonmatch basis.

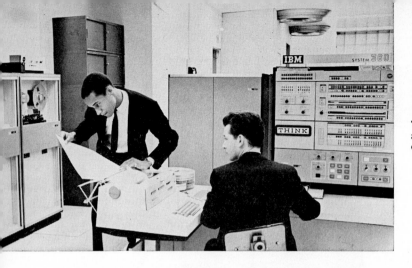

COMPUTING entails the arithmetical processes of addition, subtraction, multiplication, and division and the ability to make comparisons and logical decisions based upon a predetermined program or the results of previous operations.

ELECTRONIC DATA PROCESSING combines the automatic functions of transmitting, receiving, storing, sorting, collating, computing data, and converting the final results into usable form as printed output.

INTERPRETING consists of sensing alphabetic or numerical data punched in a card and printing it on the same card.

PRINTING is the automatic transcription in numerical and alphabetic characters of information recorded in punched cards.

REPRODUCING is the function of punching a new set or file of cards from an original set.

SEGREGATING is the process of pulling or separating individual cards from a group.

SORTING is the automatic arrangement of cards in any predetermined numerical or alphabetic sequence of the punched data.

SUMMARY PUNCHING is the punching of specific group information contained in numerous detail cards into one card.

TAG CONVERTING is the automatic reproduction of information from perforated price tags to punched cards.

TAPE PERFORATING is the recording of data in paper tape by means of punched holes.

TAPE PROCESSING includes the functions of recording, transcribing, transmitting, receiving, and converting data recorded in perforated paper tape.

VERIFYING is the process of checking punched data to prove that it has been transcribed correctly.

Study Questions

1. What are some of the common types of jobs done on modern data processing systems?

2. Name three types of data processing systems.

3. What are the four basic machines in a punched-card system and for what is each used?

4. How is a *Flexowriter* used?

5. What are the major steps in the IDP system in which a *Flexowriter* is used?

6. Give two advantages of IDP.

7. Explain the special features of electronic data processing.

8. In what ways may the office worker become involved in data processing systems?

What Do You Think?

1. Why are business firms changing to data processing systems?

2. What is the effect of electronic data processing on office employment?

Your Personal Qualities

Miss Mildred Wright is now employed as a statistical typist by the Allied Insurance Company. An electronic data processing system is to be installed, and much of the statistical data will be produced by the equipment.

Miss Wright is asked if she would care to attend a key-punch school maintained by the manufacturer for one week to master the numeric keyboard of the key-punch machine. She is told that, while she may continue as a statistical typist, her chances for advancement are relatively slim. On the other hand, if she becomes an efficient operator of the key-punch machine, her chances of becoming a supervisor are very good.

Question: Should Miss Wright continue as a statistical typist, or should she accept the offer to retrain on a key-punch machine?

How's Your English?

Read about quotation marks and parentheses with other marks of punctuation in Appendix B, and then punctuate the following:

1. William she said is the first name of the president of our club

2. The title is Mrs. the woman is married

3. Did you see the picture entitled A Comparison of IDP and EDP Systems

4. Punched-card accounting systems use key-punch machines not Flexowriters Flexowriters are used in IDP systems see discussion on pages 139–143

5. When I found the advertisement of a man saying apply the brake filed under applications I was astonished

Office Work

1. With others in the class, form a committee to visit one of the local offices where a data processing system has been installed. Prepare a list of questions that you want to ask and things you will want to observe before you go. Be prepared to discuss this list with the class and then refine it. While visiting the office collect as many related forms as you can, along with getting answers to your questions. Prepare a typed report of your visit, and be prepared to make an oral report to the class.

2. The principal of your school desires to relieve your teachers of the routine clerical tasks that take up so much of their time. The paper work he wishes to eliminate consists of:

   a. Preparing alphabetic lists of names and addresses of students — sometimes in duplicate and triplicate.

   b. Posting marks, test scores, personality ratings, etc., to permanent record cards.

   c. Preparing student class lists.

   d. Preparing class schedules for students and teachers.

   e. Posting marks to report cards — distributing and collecting them.

   f. Preparing statements of student attendance and tardiness.

Which data processing system should be recommended and why?

3. One of your local businesses that employs over 300 clerks wishes to install a data processing system. A survey of its clerical work reveals that:

   a. It keeps a book inventory of merchandise on hand.

   b. It processes 500 orders daily. Copies of these orders have to be mailed out to its branch warehouses located in the principal cities of 15 different states.

   c. It uses desk calculators to compute the amount of each bill mailed to its customers.

   d. It has a billing department that prepares copies of bills to be used within the office and to be sent to its customers.

Which data processing system should be recommended and why?

4. The Acme Manufacturing Company employs more than 25,000 persons in its plants and offices. It wishes to modernize its payroll department. At present it employs 25 persons on a full-time basis and 50 on a part-time basis to prepare its weekly payrolls. Would the firm be well advised to consider an electronic data processing system? Why?

UNIT 6 | Mail and Telegrams

PART 1:

Incoming Mail

One of your first duties, and one of your most interesting ones as an office worker, will be to handle the daily mail. You can be of invaluable assistance when you learn to process the mail efficiently. The system of handling mail depends, to a great extent, upon the size and the type of business in which you are employed. In a small office you will be expected to open, read, and sort all incoming mail, except that marked "Personal" or "Confidential"; mail so marked should be delivered unopened. In a large office the incoming mail is opened, sorted, and distributed by the mailing department, where the handling of both incoming and outgoing mail is mechanized and systematic. You should attempt to be informed about the efficient procedures used in a mailing department even though the volume of mail you will handle in your own office may be much smaller.

Opening the Mail. When the volume of incoming mail is very large, the letters are opened in the mailing department with an automatic envelope opener. It trims a narrow strip off one edge of each envelope. The amount taken off is so small that there is little risk that the contents will be mutilated. In order to reduce the chances of cutting the contents, the envelopes may be jogged on the table before they are placed in the opener so that the contents will fall away from the edge that is to be trimmed.

If you are to open the mail in your office, use a hand-operated letter opener or a paper knife, depending upon the amount of incoming mail received each day. To open an envelope with a paper knife, place it face down on the desk and run the knife under the flap. If you should cut a letter or an enclosure as you are opening an envelope, use transparent mending tape to put it together again.

After you have opened a number of envelopes, remove the letters and other enclosures carefully. Some concerns will require you to inspect each letter and its enclosures as soon as they are removed and to attach the

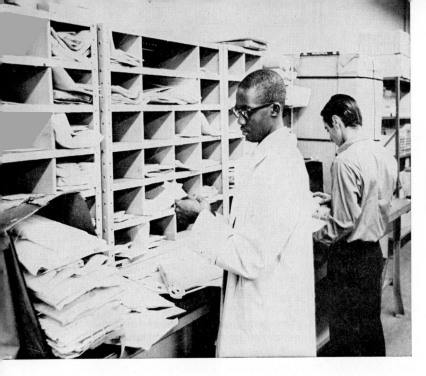

Sorting mail

In a large office, the incoming mail must be sorted before it can be distributed.

enclosures to the letter. If an enclosure is missing, you should note the omission on the margin of the letter. You may be expected to make out a special memorandum and keep it on file if the missing enclosure is a check, a money order, cash, or stamps.

Keep the envelopes until you have examined each letter for the signature and the address. If either is missing, attach the envelope to the letter. Sometimes a check is received with no other means of identification except the envelope in which it was mailed. If the date of the letter is at variance with the postmark, keep the envelope. Sometimes the envelope of an important document is stapled to the document because the date of mailing may prove to be of some importance. If, after you have discarded the envelope, you notice that the return address is not printed or typed on a letter, you may be able to find it in a telephone directory, a city directory, or in the correspondence files. Once in a while, you may make an error by opening a personal letter. If this happens, place the letter back in the envelope and write on the outside "Sorry — opened by mistake," and add your initials. Don't let this happen too frequently, however. Personal mail should remain personal, so deliver it to the executive's desk unopened.

Dating, Sorting, and Distributing Mail. After you have checked the incoming mail for enclosures, return addresses, and signatures, stamp it with the date and time. You can do this with a clock-dating device or a rubber stamp. The dating and timing of mail tend to increase the general efficiency of the concern by fixing the responsibility for promptness in answering correspondence.

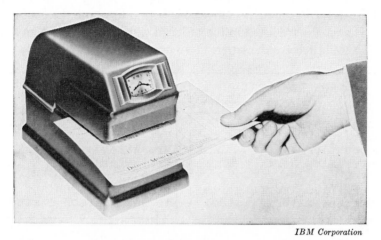

Time stamp

This time stamp prints the year, month, day, hour, and minute of receipt and dispatch of letters, telegrams, and other documents.

In the mailing room the mail is sorted by departments. A sorting tray, with a separate compartment for each department, is usually used for this purpose. After the mail has been sorted, it is delivered by a mail clerk or a messenger. Ordinarily, mail is distributed several times a day; usually the first mail of the day is the heaviest.

When the mail reaches an executive's office, his secretary may put aside the letters that can be answered or handled without being referred to the executive. She will give them her attention when she has some free time. This type of mail includes the communications that can be answered with form letters, circulars, advertisements, and routine reports.

Special-delivery letters and registered mail are usually not delivered to the firm along with regular mail. They should be handled promptly upon receipt and brought to the employer's attention immediately. If special-delivery or registered mail should come with the regular mail, you should process it without delay.

Routing Mail. What about the letter that should be seen by more than one executive or department? Your incoming mail may contain one or more of these letters that should be routed. Routing eliminates unnecessary handling and record keeping. It would not be advisable to send an order on account first to the sales department and then to the shipping department without the approval of the credit department. An order with a request for credit should be sent first to the credit department for approval before it is sent to the sales department.

Many businesses use a rubber stamp or routing slip with the names of all the departments or executives of the firm to whom the mail might be sent. The names are listed in the order in which the departments or individuals should receive the letter. Two examples are shown below.

REFERRED TO		ROUTE TO	
Credit Dept.	_____	Mr. Keller	_____
Sales Dept.	_____	Mr. Swenson	_____
Shipping Dept.	_____	Mr. Denton	_____
Accounting Dept.	_____	Mr. Wiley	_____
Purchasing Dept.	_____	Mr. Peterson	_____
Initial and refer to next department listed.		Please check and send to next person listed.	

Your employer will usually give his immediate attention to routed letters so that they can be sent to the other listed departments or executives without delay. You may have to remind him about any that he is holding.

Special Memorandums. As you read certain letters, you will note promises of materials under separate cover. To be sure that you receive them, it will often be desirable for you to keep a record of mail expected under a separate cover. Check at least twice a week to see what items have not been received so that you can follow up on delayed mail. This mail will also have to be referred to the department or the person to whom the original letter was referred if it was routed. One type of record for separate-cover mail is illustrated below.

DATE OF ENTRY	ARTICLE	FROM WHOM	DATE SENT	DEPARTMENT	INDIVIDUAL	DATE RECEIVED
3-12	Catalog	A. H. Martin & Co	3-11	Purchasing		3-14
3-14	Book	I. Stevens	3-12	Advertising		3-18
3-18	Tickets	G. H. Simms	3-15		P. L. Martin	3-21
3-20	Folders	Kimball Bros.	3-18	Filing		3-23
3-22	Catalog	Bryce & Maye	3-20	Purchasing		

Register of expected mail

The register shows that the first four items have been received and the last item has not yet arrived.

You may find it necessary to keep a record of the receipt of mail that is insured, special delivery, or registered. Use a form similar to the one illustrated below.

RECEIVED		FROM WHOM		FOR	KIND OF MAIL RECEIVED
DATE	TIME	NAME	ADDRESS	DEPARTMENT OR INDIVIDUAL	
10-1	8:15 a m	R J Walker	New York City	Accounting	Registered
10-1	9:20 a m	Mrs V Jones	Denver, Colo	O Miller	Insured
10-2	2:15 p m	Art Shop, Inc	Chicago, Ill	Sales	Special-Delivery

Register of insured, special-delivery, and registered mail

Study Questions

1. Why should every office worker know efficient methods of handling incoming mail?

2. When opening letters by a machine, how does the operator of the machine avoid cutting the contents of the envelopes?

3. Some concerns require that each letter and its enclosures be inspected as soon as they are removed from the envelope. For what specific things should you look?

4. A letter is received and the enclosure is missing. What should you do about it?

5. Under what circumstances is it desirable for an envelope to be attached to its contents by the one who opens the mail?

6. Why are letters dated and timed upon their receipt?

7. When should a letter be routed?

8. A letter is received in which reference is made to a package coming under separate cover. How can you remind yourself to look for the package in future deliveries?

What Do You Think?

1. Under what circumstances is incoming mail likely to be opened by hand? by machine?

2. In a certain office, rush mail is not being attended to promptly. What would you do to insure prompt attention?

3. In a certain business, there were a number of difficulties in the handling of the incoming mail. When you studied the situation, you found that these difficulties were:

   a. The mail was opened by hand by the receptionist who also handled the switchboard. When the mail was too heavy for her to take care of by herself, she was helped by any of the stenographers in the office who happened not to be busy. As a result, when any letters or enclosures were lost or when other errors were made, it was difficult, if not impossible, to fix the responsibility.

b. Enclosures that were referred to in letters frequently were not with the letters that were distributed to the various executives. The executives were, therefore, uncertain whether the enclosures had not been received or whether they had been received and separated from the letters.

c. Often a letter was not answered until some time after having been written, but the executives did not know whether the delay was in their own offices or whether the letter had not been delivered to the recipient promptly.

d. Before an order was filled, it was handled by the credit department, the sales department, and the order department. In some instances it went first to one department and in other instances first to another department, according to where the mail clerk was going first.

Describe methods by which these difficulties might be eliminated.

Your Personal Qualities

Miss Helen Young, chief clerk in the office of the comptroller, opens and reads the comptroller's mail when his secretary is on vacation, and then places it on his desk for reply. After opening and reading a letter from the President of the Company questioning some of the comptroller's financial policies, she notices that the envelope had been clearly marked "Confidential."

Question: How would you meet this situation if you were Miss Young?

How's Your English?

After reading about the use of quotation marks in Appendix B, insert quotation marks and other punctuation in the appropriate places in the following:

1. The mail clerk said I am going to deliver all the mail so promptly that there will be no room for complaint

2. The executive said as I have said before the mail must be handled efficiently

3. Did you see the film It Must Be Somewhere when it was shown last year

4. Her Four OClocks were famous

5. We went to see Ben Hur at the Apollo Theater

Office Work

Collect five to ten sales letters, preferably with enclosures and envelopes. Magazine and other sales letters frequently received at home would be good to use. Follow the suggested system of opening them, dating them, and making sure enclosures will not become lost. Be prepared to demonstrate in class how such mail should be handled.

Office Work Assignments

24: Mail Expected Under Separate Cover

It is necessary for you to make a record of the mail expected under separate cover. You will prepare a record similar to that shown in the illustration on page 152.

April 1–A letter from James R. Franklin refers to a package of folders that he shipped under separate cover on March 31 to our research department.

April 1–In a letter of March 30, Oscar J. Trumble stated that he was returning by parcel post a package of our merchandise. When the package is received, it is to be referred to our shipping department.

April 2–In a letter dated March 28 addressed to our company, the Acme Furniture Company said that it was sending the company one of its latest catalogs. The letter was referred to our purchasing department.

April 3–In a letter dated March 29, Mr. Harlan F. Brooks stated that he had sent under separate cover a booklet on salesmanship to Mr. Edward F. Tuttle.

April 3–In his letter of March 31, Mr. Arthur F. James said that he had mailed a pamphlet to Mr. Ernest N. George.

April 3–Folders are received from James R. Franklin.

April 3–In a letter of March 31, Mr. Ralph A. Brackett said that he was returning a chair to the service department.

April 4–Received shipment of merchandise from Oscar J. Trumble.

April 4–A letter from the branch office in St. Louis, Missouri, states that on April 2 they mailed a book. This book is to be referred to Mr. O. Harding.

April 4–In a letter addressed to our duplicating department, the J. F. Whitman Company said it was sending 30 reams of S-20, white, 8½″ x 11″ mimeograph paper. The shipment was sent April 2.

April 4–Received a booklet on salesmanship from Mr. Harlan F. Brooks.

25: Insured, Special-Delivery, and Registered Mail

The following insured, special-delivery, and registered mail has been received. Make a record similar to the illustration on page 153.

April 1–At 8:30 a.m. a registered letter was received from Mr. William G. Parsons, Norfolk, Virginia. It was referred to the accounting department.

April 1–At 10:15 a.m. a special-delivery letter was received from Mrs. Vilma C. Keene, Savannah, Georgia, for the sales department.

April 1–At 1:15 p.m. a special-delivery letter was received from Mrs. Carl Wilson, Chicago, Illinois. It was referred to the purchasing department.

April 2–At 11:15 a.m. a registered letter was received from Mr. Roland L. Baker, Kansas City, Missouri, for Dr. Ray Folsom.

April 2–At 2:15 p.m. an insured package was received from Mr. Franklin G. Davis, Knoxville, Tennessee, for the maintenance department.

April 3–At 8:05 a.m. a certified letter was received from Mr. Herman X. Graham, Chicago. It was referred to the credit department.

April 3–At 10:30 a.m. a special-delivery letter was received from Mr. Everett N. Spencer, Cleveland, for the accounting department.

April 3–At 2:30 p.m. a registered letter was received from the Miller Company, Phoenix, Arizona, for the sales department.

UNIT 6 | Mail and Telegrams

PART 2:

Outgoing Mail

Your employer has signed the letters, and other materials are also ready for mailing. Perhaps he has asked you to find out when the contract you are sending out can be expected to arrive at its destination. Should you send the mail first, second, third, or fourth class? Perhaps a certain letter should be sent airmail? Is it necessary to register a particular letter? What other service does the post office offer to enable you to get mail delivered rapidly, and how much does it cost? Where will you find the answers to these questions?

A complete listing of the postal services with detailed regulations and procedures covering these services is given in the Postal Manual of the United States Post Office Department. The postal services and rates are changed from time to time; therefore, it is essential that you have an up-to-date copy of the Postal Manual in your office. It may be purchased for a nominal fee from the Superintendent of Documents, Government Printing Office, Washington, D.C. 20402.

You should be able to select the proper mailing service for all the different types of outgoing mail. For instance, a letter may be sent by special delivery to insure prompt delivery, by airmail if it is to go a great distance, or by registered mail if it contains valuable papers. Newspapers and magazines are usually sent as second-class mail, circulars as third-class mail, and packages as fourth-class mail. A fee for special delivery or for special handling may be added to the fourth-class mail rate to insure the prompt delivery or the expeditious handling of parcel post packages. For a small fee, a return receipt, which is proof that an item has been received, may be requested.

Handling Outgoing Mail The system of handling outgoing mail, like the system of handling incoming mail, depends upon the size and the type of business in which you are employed. In a small office, the secretary, who may be the sole office worker, probably is responsible for all details connected with outgoing mail. In a large office, the mail is periodically collected in each department throughout the day by a messenger or a mail clerk and taken to the mailing department, where it is sealed, metered, and then stacked near the postage meter. The postage meter is a machine that automatically prints the amount of postage, the postmark, and the date of mailing.

Precautions Before Releasing Outgoing Mail. Before releasing your outgoing mail to the mailing department, check to be sure that:

1) The address on the envelope agrees with the inside address.
2) Any enclosures noted at the bottom of the letter are actually enclosed in the envelope.
3) Special notations such as "Registered," "Special Delivery," "Airmail," and "Personal" have been properly noted on the envelope in capital letters. Special envelopes are sometimes used for airmail. Rubber stamps or special stickers are also used in some offices to bring these notations to the attention of all concerned.
4) Foreign mail has been properly indicated on the envelope in the corner below the stamps.
5) "Personal" and "Confidential" letters have been sealed.
6) Carbon copies for others have been prepared for mailing.
7) Reference numbers, order numbers, or special key or department numbers referred to in previous correspondence are correct.
8) Any stamps that have to be enclosed have been placed in a wax-paper container.
9) Labels have been typed for packages to be sent separately.

Folding and Inserting Letters. Folding a business letter properly is not a difficult process, but care should be taken that the creases are straight and that they are made without detracting from the neatness of the letter. Paper 8½″ by 11″ to be inserted in an ordinary envelope (6½″ by 3⅝″) is folded and inserted as follows:

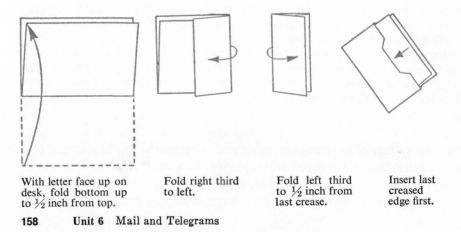

| With letter face up on desk, fold bottom up to ½ inch from top. | Fold right third to left. | Fold left third to ½ inch from last crease. | Insert last creased edge first. |

Only two folds are necessary if the letter is to be placed in a large envelope (9½″ by 4⅛″):

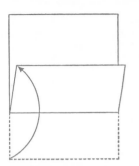
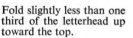
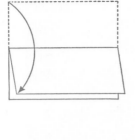
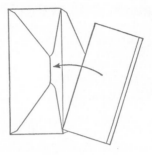

| Fold slightly less than one third of the letterhead up toward the top. | Fold down the top of the letterhead to within ½ inch of the bottom fold. | Insert the letter into the envelope with the last crease toward the bottom of the envelope. |

A letter should be inserted into an envelope in such a way that it will be in a normal reading position when it is removed from the envelope and unfolded. The enclosures that accompany the letter should be folded with the letter or inserted into the fold so that they will be pulled out of the envelope at the same time the letter is removed.

For a large-size window envelope, 8½″ by 11″ letter sheets are folded as shown below:

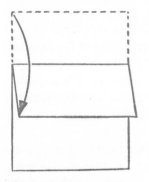
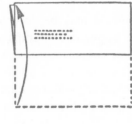
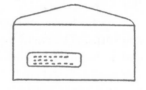

| With the sheet face down, top toward you, fold the upper third down. | Fold the lower third up so the address is showing. | Insert the sheet into the envelope with the last crease at the bottom. |

Small-size window envelopes are also available; they are used primarily for bills or statements that are designed to fit with only a single, horizontal fold.

Sealing Envelopes. If you should have to seal a large number of envelopes without the use of a sealing machine, spread about ten envelopes

A mail room

This scene is typical of a large mail room, showing the many kinds of equipment necessary to process the daily incoming and outgoing mail.

Pitney-Bowes, Inc.

on a table, address down, flap open, one on top of the other with the gummed edges showing, and with the top envelope nearest you. Brush over the gummed edges with a moist sponge or a moistener to soften the glue so that the flaps can be closed quickly and sealed. When sealing, start with the top envelope, the one nearest you, and work down to the first one placed on the table.

Stamps. You may also affix postage stamps rapidly by arranging six to eight envelopes on top of each other, showing just the upper right part of each one. Moisten the strip of stamps with a damp sponge and affix one after the other. You can save time and increase your efficiency this way.

Ordinary postage stamps may be purchased in sheet, booklet, or coil form. The small bound booklets of stamps are preferred for personal and home use; business firms find it more convenient to work with the 100-stamp sheets or the coiled stamps. Coiled stamps are often used in business because they can be quickly affixed to envelopes and because they are less likely to be lost or mutilated than are individual stamps.

Precanceled Stamps and Envelopes. In his advertising campaign, your employer may wish to use precanceled stamped envelopes. He must, in this case, obtain a permit from the post office to use them. They can be used on second-, third-, and fourth-class mail only at the post office where they were purchased. They cannot be used for first-class mail. Their use reduces the time and cost of mail handling. Precanceled mail, sorted and tied in packages by the mailer, requires less processing time in the post office and is therefore dispatched more quickly.

Stamped Envelopes and Cards. Another means of saving your time is through the use of stamped envelopes of different denominations, which

Postage meter mailing machine

his is a hand-operated machine. Automatic achines are available which, in addition to amping and postmarking, seal the letters, count em, and record the postage. They also may be dividualized for a business firm as shown in the lustration above.

Pitney-Bowes, Inc.

may be purchased in various sizes, singly or in quantity lots. The return request and address will be imprinted on them by the post office for a nominal fee if the envelopes are purchased in quantity lots.

First-class postal cards may be purchased in single or double form; the double form is used when a reply is requested on the attached card. Airmail postal cards are also available, but only in the single form.

If you are left with unserviceable and spoiled stamped envelopes and cards (if uncanceled), you may exchange them for stamps, stamped envelopes, or postal cards. You may also obtain an exchange on stamps if you happen to buy the wrong denomination.

Metered Mail. The most efficient device you can use to affix postage to any class of mail is the postage meter machine. This machine prints the postmark and the proper amount of postage on each piece of mail. The imprint of a fully automatic metering machine may also carry a slogan or a line or two of advertising, such as IT'S SMART TO BE THRIFTY, next to the postmark. Metered mail is neither canceled nor postmarked at the post office; therefore, it is processed and dispatched more quickly than mail that must be fully handled at the post office.

The meter of the postage machine is set at the post office for the amount paid at the time. The meter registers the amount of postage used on each piece of mail, the amount of postage remaining in the meter, and the number of pieces that have passed through the machine. The meter locks when the amount paid for has been used; it is then necessary to take it to the post office again to pay for more postage. Additional postage should be bought before the meter locks. You will find the postage meter very easy to operate, and it will save you a great deal of time.

Classes of Domestic Mail. Day after day, you can expedite your employer's business by using the right class of mail — the right service at the right time. You will be expected to become thoroughly familiar with the different categories of domestic mail widely used by business firms. After you understand what type of mail is included in each, you will be able to select more intelligently the services best suited for the transmittal of all kinds of outgoing mail. The seven categories listed below will be discussed separately in this unit:

1) First-class mail
2) Second-class mail
3) Third-class mail
4) Fourth-class mail or parcel post
5) Special postal rates
6) Airmail
7) Mixed classes of mail

First-Class Mail. One young lady sent her friend a present in a sealed package that weighed a pound. Much to her surprise the postal clerk applied considerable postage. Since the package was sealed, first-class rates were charged.

In another instance, an office worker mailed a package containing a typed manuscript without claiming the educational materials rate and was charged first-class rates.

Let's look at the kinds of mail that must be sent at first-class rates.

1) Letters: handwritten, typewritten, photocopies, or carbon copies
2) Matter partly in written form, such as bills, checks, punched cards, and filled-in forms
3) Other matter in written form, such as typewritten reports and documents
4) All matter sealed against inspection
5) Postal cards (government cards with stamps imprinted on them) and postcards (private mailing cards on which stamps must be affixed), either single or double
6) Business reply cards and envelopes

The rates for business reply cards and business reply envelopes are slightly higher than the rates for ordinary cards and letters. Before distributing reply cards and envelopes, the company must first obtain a permit from the post office where the cards or envelopes will be returned.

Second-Class Mail. In today's news-conscious world, many newspapers and periodicals are sent through the mails at a lower rate than parcel post or third class. They are mailed at the second-class rates. The basic rate applies to each two ounces or fraction of an ounce. Publishers and news agencies are granted second-class rates, which are lower than third-class rates, if they file the proper forms, pay the required fees, and comply with the regulations. The mail must carry notice of second-class entry.

Third-Class Mail. What is third-class mail? Every day you receive in your own home many circulars and advertisements that have been sent through the mails at third-class rates. This class is used for matter that cannot be classified as first- or second-class mail and that weighs less than 16 ounces. The same matter in parcels of 16 ounces and over is considered fourth-class mail.

The following matter may be sent by third-class mail service:

1) Circulars and other printed matter

2) Books and catalogs having 24 pages or more

3) Hotel keys and identification devices mailed unenclosed

To send third-class mail (not bulk), you merely affix the proper postage and drop it in the mailbox. Bulk mail must be taken to the post office.

Fourth-Class Mail. Fourth-class mail is known by most of us as *parcel post.* This class is used for sending merchandise, books, printed matter, and all other mailable matter not in the first, second, or third class that weighs 16 ounces or over. Parcel post rates are determined according to (1) the weight of the parcel, and (2) the distance the parcel is being transported, or the zone of delivery. Every local post office charts the country into eight zones. The present zones by mileage are:

ZONE	DISTANCE
Local	Local Limits
1 and 2	Up to 150 miles
3	150 to 300 miles
4	300 to 600 miles
5	600 to 1,000 miles
6	1,000 to 1,400 miles
7	1,400 to 1,800 miles
8	— Over 1,800 miles

There are limitations on the weight and the size of parcel post packages. You should procure these limitations from a current edition of the *Postal Manual.*

Special Postal Rates. Certain kinds of packaged mail are given special, low rates. For instance, packages containing books may be mailed at the *Educational Materials Rate.* The rate is the same for all zones. In order to obtain this rate, one must mark the package EDUCATIONAL MATERIALS. Consult the *Postal Manual* for other special rates.

Airmail. Did you know that California, Canada, Mexico, Hawaii, and Alaska are only one working day apart if you use airmail? Airmail is carried by air and the fastest connecting ground carriers. It is given the quickest handling in dispatch and delivery, but it is not given special delivery unless a special-delivery fee is paid. A standard rate per ounce applies to all airmail letters and packages not exceeding eight ounces in weight. A lower rate is charged for air postal cards and postcards. Packages sent by air that weigh over eight ounces are considered air parcel post; the rates for such parcels vary according to the weight and the zone of delivery.

You should know when the mail truck leaves the post office in your vicinity for the airport. Knowing the schedule will enable you to get letters out in time to take advantage of fast delivery.

Mixed Classes of Mail. Sometimes you may find it expedient to send two pieces of mail of different classes together as a single mailing to be sure that they will both arrive at the same time. A first-class letter may be attached to a larger envelope or parcel of mail, or it may be enclosed in the larger envelope or parcel. When a first-class letter is *attached*, the correct postage is affixed to each part separately. When a first-class letter is *enclosed*, the postage is computed on each parcel separately but is affixed together on the outside of the package. The words "First-Class Mail Enclosed" must be written, typed, or stamped below the postage and above the address.

Foreign Mail. There was a time when few companies sent letters out of the continental United States, but many firms today have worldwide contacts. Therefore, you will find the *Postal Manual* a necessary reference book for complete information on mail to foreign countries.

If you are employed by a firm engaged in international trade, it will be to your advantage to become familiar with the regulations covering foreign mail to the countries in which your firm has business.

The first-class rate for letters to Canada and Mexico is the same as the United States domestic rate; to all other countries, the rate is higher, the weight limited.

The airmail rate to Canada and Mexico is also the same as the United States domestic rate. Airmail rates to all countries can be obtained from the local post office or in an up-to-date copy of the *Postal Manual* or the *Directory of International Mail.* Also, excerpts of these larger volumes are usually available at your local post office.

Special Postal Services. In addition to transmitting the mail, the post office provides many special services for you. The major services listed below will be discussed separately in this unit.

1) Special Handling
2) Special Delivery
3) Registered Mail
4) Insured Mail
5) Certified Mail
6) C.O.D. Service
7) Tracing Mail

Special Handling. Only parcel-post packages may be sent with *special handling* service. On payment of a fee in addition to the regular postage, a parcel-post package labeled SPECIAL HANDLING will be accorded the same prompt delivery service given to first-class mail. The fee varies, depending on the weight.

Special Delivery. All classes of mail may be sent *special delivery*. Special-delivery mail is handled at the destination post office with the same promptness given to first-class mail, and, in addition, it is given immediate delivery (within prescribed hours and distances) from the post office to the addressee. The fees vary according to the weight of the letter or package. Thus, by affixing additional postage after you have stamped your envelope and marked it SPECIAL DELIVERY, the letter you put in the mail will be delivered by special messenger after it gets to the post office nearest the address on the letter.

Registered Mail. There will be times when you will send something very valuable and important through the mail. A contract, a diamond ring, a notarized application that must be delivered by a certain date, an application for a patent or copyright are some of the kinds of communications that should be sent by *registered mail*. This mail may be registered for insurance up to $10,000 if no other insurance is carried. If other insurance is carried, postal insurance liability is limited to a maximum of $1,000. Whenever postal insurance and other insurance both apply to the first $1,000 of value or any part thereof, postal liability is assumed on a co-insurance basis and prorated in accordance with a formula prepared by the Post Office Department and presented in the *Postal Manual*.

Parcel-post packages, however, may be registered only if first-class postage rates are paid. In case of loss, rifling, or damage, the Post Office Department will indemnify the sender for the full value of the mail up to $1,000 or for the registered value, whichever is smaller.

You are always given a receipt showing that the post office has accepted the registered mail for transmittal and delivery. For an additional fee, you may obtain a *return receipt* as evidence of the delivery of the registered mail.

Insured Mail. What about provision for insuring third-class and fourth-class mail, and airmail containing third-class or fourth-class matter? You may obtain insurance on these classes of mail up to $200. If a package is lost or damaged, the post office reimburses you for the value of the merchandise or the amount for which it was insured, whichever is smaller. A receipt is given for insured mail also.

Certified Mail. Airmail and first-class mail may be certified. How will this help you? You may wish to have a means of tracing a letter that the addressee complains he did not receive. For example, a check you mailed to a client in California is not received. If this mail was certified, the post office can quickly trace it. For a fee, the post office provides a numbered receipt which gives you the means of checking on the delivery of the letter. Certified mail is not insured.

C.O.D. Service. Merchandise may be sent to a purchaser C.O.D., that is, *collect on delivery*, if the shipment is based on an order by the buyer or on an agreement between sender and addressee. The seller may obtain C.O.D. service by paying a fee in addition to the regular postage. The maximum amount collectible on one package is $200. The total fee varies with the amount to be collected, the weight of the package, and the distance to the purchaser's post office address. Detailed information on mailing C.O.D. parcels is found in the *Postal Manual*.

Tracing Mail. If mail has not been delivered within a reasonable time, you may make a written request to your post office to have it traced. Although the post office will cooperate in every possible way, it is very difficult to trace unregistered, uninsured, or uncertified mail. Consequently, important or valuable mail should be registered, certified, or insured.

Other Services Connected with Outgoing Mail. There are other services available to business offices in connection with advertising campaigns, sales promotion, and information.

Mailing Lists. A mailing list is an extensive list of the names and addresses of customers or prospective customers of a firm. A firm may use a number of mailing lists: one made up of regular customers; another of prospective customers, compiled by the advertising and sales staff; and perhaps a third one of prospects for a particular product or service. Mailing lists may also be purchased: a manufacturer of office furniture may buy a mailing list of office managers; an air-conditioning dealer, a list of home-owners; and an investment house, a list of professional people. Special mailing lists of all kinds are available.

Mailing Lists on File Cards. The names and addresses of a master mailing list are frequently kept on 5″ by 3″ cards that may be filed in alphabetic order. These cards may be grouped under various classifications, such as doctors, druggists, jewelers, and stationers. The different groupings may be indicated by colored tabs, or the cards for each group may be filed in separate drawers or compartments in the card file.

The cards may also be filed by subject — the subject that the prospective customer has been interested in or may be interested in later.

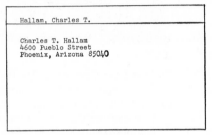

File cards in address style and index style for a mailing list

Up-to-Date Mailing Lists. Unless mailing lists are kept up to date, they soon lose much of their effectiveness. The names on all mailing lists are constantly changing as newcomers move into the sales area and others move out. Additions, deletions, and corrections of names and addresses should be made whenever the information is received. You learn of many of the necessary changes in addresses when mail is returned.

A notice of a change of address may be obtained from the post office by having a brief statement printed on the envelope or on the wrapper used to send third- and fourth-class mail. The postmaster then mails back a card giving the correspondent's new address. There is a small charge for this service.

Chain Feeding of Envelopes for a Mailing List. The names and addresses on a mailing list are usually typed on the envelopes if the list is used infrequently. A chain-feeding method of inserting and addressing the envelopes will save a great deal of time in typing from the list. The four steps in the widely used front-feed method follow:

1) Stack the envelopes *face down*, with the flaps toward you, at the side of the typewriter.
2) Address the first envelope; then roll it back (toward you) until a half inch shows above the alignment scale.

The front-feed method
of chain feeding of
envelopes

IBM Corporation

3) Insert the next envelope from the front, placing it between the first envelope and the cylinder.
4) Turn the cylinder back to remove the first envelope and to position the second one. Continue the "chain" by feeding all envelopes from the front of the cylinder.
5) The envelopes will stack themselves in order at the back of the cylinder. Remove them after about every sixth envelope is typed.

Addressing Machines and Addressing Services. You may use an addressing service or, if your office has it, an addressing machine in addressing a large number of envelopes. Because mailing lists are used over and over again, the names and addresses are often stenciled or embossed so that the envelopes can be automatically addressed on an addressing machine. Two styles of machines are widely used: the Addressograph, which prints from a metal plate; and the Elliott, which prints from a stencil plate.

(1) The Addressograph. The Addressograph is often used for the addressing of envelopes and cards for permanent mailing lists. It may also be used to print the inside addresses on letters or to print names, addresses, numbers, and other identifying information on bank statements, monthly bills, timecards, paychecks, dividend checks, and other business forms.

The metal plates used in the Addressograph are prepared on a lettering machine called the Graphotype, which embosses the name, address, date, number, or other required information on a small metal plate. The plates can be coded so that an automatic selecting device can be used as the letters are addressed. Classification tabs can be attached to the address plates of a particular list, and the automatic selector will then select and print only these plates without changing the order of any of the others.

An addressing machine

Addressograph-Multigraph Corporation

(2) *Elliott Addressing Machine.* The stencil address plates used in the Elliott addressing machine can be prepared on a typewriter. When a small attachment is used, the small stencil plates are typed in much the same manner as ordinary stencils. The stencil addressing equipment is not often used to print inside addresses on letters or other material that should give the appearance of being completely typed. The plates are, however, often used for mailing lists with frequently changing addresses.

Although the Post Office Department has not heretofore advised the use of abbreviations in the envelope address, because of the addition of the ZIP code (consisting of five digits), it has now published an approved list of two-letter state abbreviations which may be used on envelope addresses. These are mainly for the benefit of bulk mail users and those using addressing equipment, but anybody may use them. The new abbreviations, however, must be used *along with* the ZIP code; otherwise the mail is subject to return. A list of these abbreviations is given in Appendix D.

Study Questions

1. What information is found in the *Postal Manual?*

2. What items should be checked before the outgoing mail is released?

3. How can a large number of envelopes be sealed rapidly without the use of a sealing machine?

4. What disposition is made of

government-stamped envelopes that have been spoiled?

5. What is a postage meter machine?

6. When is payment made for postage used in a postage meter machine?

7. What kinds of mail must be sent at first-class rates?

8. What are the special characteristics of second-class matter?

9. What would be sent in third-class mail?

10. Parcel post is another name for what class of mail? In what ways does it differ from other classes of mail?

11. How are rates set for parcel post matter?

12. The special-handling service applies to what class of mail?

13. What is registered mail?

14. What is the difference between insured mail and registered mail?

15. What determines the fee for C.O.D. parcels?

16. What is the purpose of a mailing list?

17. How is a mailing list kept up to date?

18. How may one obtain from the post office an official notice of the change of address of a correspondent?

19. What laborsaving devices are used to simplify and accelerate the work relating to mailing lists?

20. What is the major difference between the Addressograph and the Elliott addressing machine?

What Do You Think?

1. In a business office in which you are working (a) several letters are returned for insufficient postage, and (b) several are returned because of incorrect addresses. What would you suggest to correct such occurrences?

2. Suppose that the firm for which you work is considering using a postage meter machine instead of ordinary postage stamps for its outgoing letters. What are the advantages that might come from the use of such a machine? The disadvantages?

3. Why does the government divide mail into a number of classes with different rates?

4. For what reasons should you make a special effort to keep a mailing list up to date, and how can it be done?

Your Personal Qualities

Just before closing time, Mr. Arnold prepares a request for important information to one of the branch managers and asks Miss Reynolds to send it by airmail. In the rush to get it out before 5 o'clock, she momentarily forgets that the letter is to be sent by airmail. The letter is metered and goes out at the regular rate.

Three days later Mr. Arnold wonders aloud why he has not received a reply from the branch manager, who is usually very prompt in supplying requested information.

Question: Should Miss Reynolds explain that the letter was accidentally mailed at the first-class rate and that the branch manager probably had not yet had time to reply, or should she offer no explanation and hope for the best?

How's Your English?

In Appendix B, read about spacing after punctuation marks, and type the following, properly punctuated and spaced:

1. The letter telling the manager that the price per pound was two dollars and ten cents 2.10 was delivered at 10 a.m. He replied by telegraph asking

Is this your best price

2. The report indicated that the total sales for the day was 2476892 shares and that the industrial average was down four point ninety seven 497 for the day. The customer asked dont you think that the market should go up tomorrow

Office Work

1. Using an 8½″ by 11″ sheet of paper and an ordinary envelope, fold the sheet and insert it into the envelope.

2. Using three sheets of 8½″ by 11″ paper and a large envelope, fold the three sheets together and insert them into the envelope.

3. Using an 8½″ by 11″ sheet of paper and a large window envelope (or an ordinary large envelope if you do not have a window envelope), fold the sheet and insert it into the envelope.

4. Address envelopes of either 3⅝″ by 6½″ or 4⅛″ by 9½″ for the following names and addresses. If envelopes are not available, type the addresses on slips of paper of approximately one of these sizes. You may assume that these names and addresses were taken from the classified telephone directory of New York.

Acme File Company, 30 Warren Street, 10007

Airport Duplicating Service, 510 East End Avenue, 10028

American Stationery Company, 59 East 44 Street, 10017

Apollo Supply Company, 139 Varick Street, 10013

Buckeye Printing Company, 30 West 59 Street, 10019

Chase Office Supply Company, 10 West 35 Street, 10001

City Systems, 59 Ann Street, 10038

Columbia Stationers, 199 East 14 Street, 10003

Cosmopolitan Supply Company, 410 West 24 Street, 10011

Dale Ribbons, 92 Park Avenue, 10016

Diamond Equipment Company, 210 East 27 Street, 10016

Duplicating Service, Inc., 10 Park Row, 10038

Embassy Manufacturing Company, 400 West 50 Street, 10019

Empire Filing Equipment, 192 Seventh Avenue, 10011

Equity Equipment, 310 West 46 Street, 10036

Globe Service Corporation, 10 East 39 Street, 10016

General Equipment Company, 92 Fourth Avenue, 10003

Guide Systems, Inc., 179 West 37 Street, 10018

Howard Stationery Company, 92 John Street, 10038

Hygrade Desk Company, 129 Fifth Avenue, 10003

5. On September 8, the Johnson Candy Company mailed the following items to out-of-town addresses. Find the total cost of postage.

18 letters, each weighing 1 ounce

2 letters, each weighing 1⅛ ounces

5 letters, each weighing 2 ounces

3 letters, each weighing 1½ ounces, special delivery

6 letters, each weighing 2½ ounces, special delivery

7 letters, each weighing 2¼ ounces, airmail

2 letters, each weighing 1 ounce, airmail, special delivery

1 package, first class, weighing 1 pound, special delivery

1 parcel-post package, weighing 4 pounds, addressed to a city in the third zone

4 parcel-post packages, each weighing 2½ pounds, mailed to the fourth zone

1 parcel-post package, weighing 4½ pounds, to be sent to the thrid zone, marked "Special Handling"

Use current postal rates, which may be secured from the local post office or from the current issue of the *Postal Manual*.

6. Type or write the addresses in the following list on file cards or on slips of paper about 5″ by 3″. Arrange the names and addresses in address style. After the cards have been completed, place them in alphabetic order.

a. Auto Radiator Works, 1120 Grand Street, Crawford, New Jersey 07016

b. Mason Coal Company, 1735 West Third Street, Pittsburgh, Pennsylvania 15238

c. Mundy Service Stations, 10 Thomas Avenue, Houston, Texas 77009

d. Albany Metal Company, 1002 Broad Street, Albany, New York 12202

e. Grande Vista Subdivision, 106 Main Avenue, Omaha, Nebraska 68106

f. Daniels Air Conditioning Service, 210–212 Harlinway, Cincinnati, Ohio 45204

g. Browne Accessories, Inc., 1096 Second Street, Chattanooga, Tennessee 37403

h. Loring Jewelry Store, 504 Plum Drive, Monroe, Louisiana 71201

i. Ellerson Department Store, 1501 Superior Road, Portland, Oregon 97203

j. Kynnard Art Gallery, Parkway and Oak, Salt Lake City, Utah 84103

k. Browning Advertising Agency, 1016 Gwynne Drive, Kansas City, Missouri 64107

l. Albans Nut Products, Albans Building, Atlanta, Georgia 30302

m. Danish Pastry Shop, 14 East Elm Avenue, Augusta, Maine 04301

n. Kyne Hardware Equipment, Carew Tower, Chicago, Illinois 60608

o. Masonic Auditorium, Fountain Square, Dover, Delaware 19901

p. Brown Publishing Company, 336–338 Race Street, Duluth, Minnesota 55803

Office Work Assignments

26: Order Letter

Mr. Randolph, general manager of Randolph Office Equipment and Supply Company, has instructed you to order the latest edition of the *Postal Manual*. Inasmuch as you do not have an order form for this purpose, write a letter. If necessary, check with the library or the post office to determine the amount of the remittance that should accompany the order.

Remember that in this office all letters are written in modified block form (no paragraph indentions) with mixed punctuation.

UNIT 6 | Mail and Telegrams

PART 3:

Telegraph Service

When you want to send the most rapid written communication, send a telegram. It can be transmitted from coast to coast and delivered in a few minutes. You can be sure, too, of getting attention, for a telegram carries with it a note of urgency and importance.

More than 500,000 telegraph messages and money orders are sent over Western Union wires every business day. They are sent to all of the states on the continent including Alaska, and to Canada and Mexico. Most of the messages relate to business transactions: buying and selling merchandise, dealing in securities, making reservations, or sending money.

A telegram will cost your employer approximately 20 percent less than the minimum charge for a person-to-person telephone call to the same locality. A telegram can be sent a distance of 1,500 miles and delivered at once, while the average business letter would spend at least one full day en route, even if it were sent by airmail.

After you are employed in an office, you will be expected to know when to send a telegram and which type of service to use. You will also be expected to know how to compose telegrams and how to get your messages to the telegraph office.

Selecting the Service. The telegraph company provides three different types of message service. Messages are transmitted and delivered according to the type of service used. Some are transmitted and delivered immediately; others are transmitted during the night and delivered during the following morning. The three types of service are:

1) The full-rate telegram
2) The day letter
3) The night letter

Full-Rate Telegram. When there is great urgency about the message, when speed in having the message received is important, you will send the full-rate telegram. A full-rate telegram, usually referred to simply as a telegram, is the fastest type of telegraph service. The message is transmitted immediately at any time during the day or night, and, if it is received during business hours, it is telephoned or delivered to the addressee at once. If it is received after business hours, it is relayed to the addressee as soon as possible. A full-rate telegram takes precedence over all other types of telegraph service. Although it is the most expensive type of service, it is used most frequently by businessmen because of the speed of transmission and delivery. The basic charge is made for a message of 15 words or less; a small additional charge is made for each additional word in the message.

Day Letter. If the message to be sent is a long one (over fifty words) and should be delivered today, but not necessarily within the hour, the service you should choose is the day letter. A day letter (DL) may be sent at any time of the day or night. This type of service is used for longer messages which can be deferred in handling and still serve their purpose. Ordinarily a day letter is delivered the same day that it is sent. The basic charge is made for a message of 50 words or less, with an additional charge for each additional group of five words.

Night Letter. When your employer wishes to send a long message at closing time, you may send it as a night letter. The night letter (NL), as the name implies, is a telegraphic message that is transmitted during the night. It will be accepted by the telegraph office at any time up to two o'clock in the morning for delivery the next morning. It is the slowest and the least expensive type of service. It is used primarily for deferred messages of considerable length. The basic rate is for 50 words or less, with an additional charge for each additional group of five words.

Preparing a Telegram. You must prepare a telegram carefully if it is to be delivered without delay and clearly understood by the recipient. The following suggestions should be followed in preparing a telegram:

1) *Use Western Union telegraph blanks.* You can obtain pads of telegraph blanks free of charge from any telegraph office.
2) *Indicate the type of service desired.* Under the heading "Domestic Service" at the upper left of the blank, type an "X" in the appropriate service box; otherwise the message will go full-rate.
3) *Type at least three copies of the telegram.* Ordinarily the original goes to the telegraph company; the second copy, to the correspondence file; the third, to the addressee as confirmation.
4) *Type the message with capital and lower-case letters.* The message should be double spaced but it need not be typed in all capitals. Do not divide words.

WESTERN UNION
TELEGRAM

1206 (4-55)

W. P. MARSHALL, PRESIDENT

Class of service

Paid or Collect

NO. WDS.-CL. OF SVC.	PD. OR COLL.	CASH NO.	CHARGE TO THE ACCOUNT OF	TIME FILED
Pd				10:20 a.m.

Time

Send the following message, subject to the terms on back hereof, which are hereby agreed to

Boston, Massachusetts, October 9, 19--

Date

Point of origin

Name, Address, and Telephone Number of Addressee

Mr. Bruce J. Harrison
B. J. Harrison and Company
244 State Street
Cincinnati, Ohio 45202
Telephone: 621-4400

Have no record of the order referred to in your telegram.

Please send a duplicate.

There will be no increase in price before the beginning of

the next quarter. No important change is expected then.

Body of Telegram

Gordon A. Eaton
The Boston Machine Company
2205 Barter Street
Boston, Massachusetts 02116
Telephone: 781-1620

Name, Address, and Telephone Number of Sender

Telegram

5) *Indicate whether the message is sent paid, collect, or charge.* If it is to be charged, indicate the account below the heading "Charge to the Account of."

6) *Type the date, time, and point of origin.*

7) *Type the full name of the addressee.* Always type the full name of the person to whom you send a telegram.

8) *Type the complete address and telephone number.* Whenever possible, give the office number. Spell out such words as "North" and "South." Do not use suffixes with street numbers (34 not 34th Street).

9) *Write the message clearly and include punctuation.* The use of punctuation marks makes the message clearer. There is no extra charge for them.

10) *Include your address and telephone number.* After the signature type the sender's telephone number, name, and address. This is important if hotel or travel reservations are requested.

Counting the Chargeable Words. Since the cost of a telegram is based upon a minimum number of words in the message plus an additional charge for extra words, it is important that you know how to count the chargeable words. The following summarizes the rules for counting words:

1) One address and one signature are free.

2) The following punctuation marks are transmitted as written but not counted or charged for:

. (period or decimal point)   ( ) (parentheses)
, (comma)   ? (question mark)
: (colon)   " " (quotation marks)
; (semicolon)   ' (apostrophe)
- (hyphen or dash)

3) Figures are counted as one word for every five characters. When used with figures the decimal point, the comma, and the dash are considered as punctuation marks and not counted.

34,785 (five figures with comma as punctuation).....1 word
378,534 (six figures with comma as punctuation)......2 words
4.333 (four figures with decimal point as punctuation) 1 word
10—160 (five figures with dash as punctuation).......1 word

4) The following special characters can be transmitted and charged for at the rate of one word for each five characters:

$, &, # (for number or pounds), " (for inches or seconds), ' (for feet or minutes), / (for the fraction mark)

The percent sign is transmitted as o/o and counts as three characters.

83.33% (four figures and % — decimal point as punctuation)...............................2 words
$44.50   (four figures and $ — decimal point as punctuation)...............................1 word
$450.25   (five figures and $ — decimal point as punctuation)...............................2 words
#4,960   (# and four figures — comma as punctuation) 1 word

5) The special characters ¢ (for cents), @ (for at), and ° (for degree) cannot be transmitted. They are written out and sent as words.

6) Dictionary words from the English, German, French, Italian, Dutch, Portuguese, Spanish, and Latin languages are counted as one word each, regardless of length. Nondictionary words and words from all other languages are counted as one word for every five characters.

7) Geographic names are counted according to the number of individual words contained in them even when they are written without spaces.

ST. LOUIS.......................................2 words
ST.LOUIS..2 words
NEW YORK CITY..............................3 words
NORTH DAKOTA.............................2 words
FARGO, N. D..................................3 words

8) Abbreviations of single words are counted as full words.

9) Common abbreviations are counted as one word for every five characters. Spaces between the abbreviations increase the word count. Periods are considered punctuation and are not counted.

NYC..1 word
N. Y. C..3 words
F.O.B...1 word
F. O. B..3 words
a.m...1 word

10) Initials in names are counted as separate words. A surname prefix, such as "Du" in DuBois, does not count as a separate word if it is not followed by a space. Initials, when separated by spaces, are counted as separate words, but when written together are counted at the rate of one word for each five letters.

```
JOHN F. KELLER...............................3 words
JAMES O'DONNELL.............................2 words
CARL VAN TIL.................................3 words
RALPH DUMONT...............................2 words
J. J. WILLIAMS...............................3 words
W.A.R. DAVIS................................2 words
```

Filing a Telegram. How can you file a telegraphic message? When it is filed, a message is turned over to Western Union for transmission and delivery. A message can be filed in any one of eight different ways:

1) *Over the Counter.* A prepared message can be taken to a Western Union office or a message can be written at the counter.

2) *Over the Telephone.* A telegram can be filed over the telephone. When a message is telephoned to a Western Union office, care must be taken to be sure that names and unusual words are transmitted accurately. Such words should be spelled out to the operator to avoid confusion.

3) *Call Boxes and Messenger Service.* Call boxes are kept in many offices where telegrams are sent frequently. They are wired to the nearest telegraph office. When a message is ready for filing, the key of the call box is turned. The telegraph office receives the signal and sends a messenger to pick up the telegram.

4) *Tie Line Service.* Tie lines are used when the volume of telegraph business justifies the installation. A tie line is a system of direct wires between the office of the patron and the office of the telegraph company provided by the telegraph company.

5) *Facsimile Service.* A handwritten or typewritten message can be transmitted from a business office on a *Desk-Fax,* a small, desk-sized facsimile sending and receiving machine. The message is

Desk-Fax

Western Union Telegraph Company

placed on the cylinder of the machine and the outgoing button is pressed. An electronic eye then scans the message and flashes an exact copy of it to a similar machine at the nearest high-speed telegraph center, which in turn flashes it to its destination. The Desk-Fax also receives telegrams by the same process with equal speed and simplicity.

A telegram may also be sent by dropping it into a panel of a *Telefax*, another facsimile machine which scans and transmits exact copies of messages electronically.

Intrafax, the newest facsimile service, is leased by Western Union to customers for fast, efficient communication within an organization.

6) *Teleprinter Service.* A telegraphic message can be sent on a specially installed printing telegraph machine with a teletype-writer-like keyboard called a *teleprinter*. As the message is typed in the patron's office on the teleprinter, it is recorded instantaneously on a tape or message form in the telegraph office. The message is transferred immediately to a trunk circuit and transmitted to its destination.

7) *Telex.* The dial-a-wire service, called Telex, permits users to dial other subscribers instantly, regardless of distance. This two-way, customer-to-customer teleprinter service links major cities in the United States, and also serves many countries in other parts of the world.

Tel(t)ex combines Telex with other Western Union services in cases where the ultimate receiver is not hooked into the direct dialing system.

8) *Private Wire Systems.* Many telegraph users, with a large volume of communications, require private telegraph systems of their own. Such private networks are engineered, installed, and maintained by Western Union on a lease basis. A system may extend hundreds, or even thousands, of miles and interconnect a company's offices and plants in a few, or as many as 100, cities.

One of the new and growing developments in the business world is automation (See Unit 5) — the use of machines to speed the processing of vast amounts of paper work. Since it is necessary to gather sales, payroll, inventory, shipping, and other data from distant cities and branch offices for processing at a central point, and do it quickly, many business firms use a private wire system for this purpose. Western Union has engineered private wire systems, called data communication, that, in addition to handling business messages, will also transmit data, either in punched card or tape form, ready for instant processing at destination by business machines and computers.

Special Telegram Services.

Repeat Back. At the time the message is filed with the telegraph company, you may decide that the message is important enough to warrant special attention. For example, the message may contain figures, names to be published, or dates. For an additional charge, a message may be repeated back from its destination to the sending office to be checked for possible errors. If errors are discovered, the corrected message is then sent at no additional charge. *Repeat Back* must be typed at the top of the telegraph blank if this additional service is desired.

Report Delivery. Occasionally written evidence of the time of delivery and the address of the person or firm to whom the telegram was delivered is considered necessary. To secure this additional information, you must pay the cost of a return telegram and type *Report Delivery* or *Report Delivery Address* at the top of the telegraph blank. These words of instruction are counted and charged for.

Cash, Charge, and Collect Service. Telegraph service may be paid for in any one of four ways:
1) With cash at the time the message is sent. Cash may be required of an infrequent telegraph user.
2) Through business charge accounts. Charge accounts are carried by the telegraph company, particularly for large firms that send many telegrams every business day. These accounts are carried on a monthly basis.
3) Through telephone subscribers' accounts. An individual may send a telegram from a telephone or from a Western Union office and have it charged to his telephone bill.
4) By the person receiving the message. A message may be sent "collect." This means that the receiver of the telegram pays for it upon delivery. To send a telegram collect, type the word *Collect* beneath the heading PD. or COLL. at the top of the blank.

Telegraph Money Orders. One of the quickest and safest ways for you to send money is to send it by telegraph money order. The amount to be transmitted is turned over to the telegraph office together with the name and address of the recipient and any accompanying message. There is a charge for sending the money order and a slight additional charge for any accompanying message. You will be given a receipt for the amount of money dispatched.

The recipient's telegraph office notifies him when the money order arrives; however, he must furnish evidence of his identity before the money is given to him.

Delivery of Telegrams. A telegraphic message may be delivered in any one of four ways:
1) *By messenger.* The message may be delivered in a sealed envelope by a Western Union messenger.
2) *By telephone.* The telephone is often used instead of the messenger for speed and convenience, especially when the addressee

```
                                                           72 (Rev. 8-56)
YOU CAN SEND          WESTERN UNION              THE FASTEST
A MESSAGE                                        AND SAFEST
WITH YOUR             TELEGRAPHIC                WAY TO SEND
MONEY                                            OR RECEIVE
Only                 MONEY ORDER                 MONEY
A FEW CENTS
MORE               W. P. MARSHALL, PRESIDENT
```

Send the following Money Order subject to conditions below and on back hereof, which are hereby agreed to:

ACCTG. INFM.	CHECK	OFFICE	DATE AND FILING TIME		
		Louisville, Ky.	May 12, 19--		

DO NOT WRITE ABOVE THIS LINE

PAY AMOUNT: One Hundred Sixty-Three - - - - DOLLARS AND 75 CENTS

TO: Peter J. Hancock

ADDRESS: 1422 Taylor Avenue   Tampa, Florida 33615

SENDER'S NAME: Arthur M. Pennington

DELIVER THE FOLLOWING MESSAGE WITH THE MONEY:

Balance will follow May 19. Regular commission deducted.

Unless signed below the Telegraph Company is directed to pay this money order at my risk to such person as its paying agent believes to be the above named payee, personal identification being waived. Foreign money orders excepted.

Arthur M. Pennington

Louisville, Kentucky.   621-3456

Information for test question:

Telegraph money order

is located at a distance from the telegraph office. The Western Union operator will mail a copy of a telephoned message to the addressee upon request.

3) *By teleprinter*. This machine, described under "Filing a Telegram" on page 178, automatically receives and prints messages.

4) *By facsimile*. Facsimile copies of messages are received by Desk-Fax and Telefax users.

If the telegraph company fails to deliver a message or makes an error in the transmission of the message, it is liable for damages. The limits of liability are stated on the back of each telegraph blank.

Differences in Time Zones. A subsidiary in Seattle wishes to contact your office. It is 5 p.m. in Seattle. It is a long message which will be reported at a branch meeting on the following afternoon. It was wisely sent by night letter. You will receive it when you arrive at work the next day. If a telegram is to be sent any great distance east or west, the sender should be aware of the time difference between the sending office and the receiving office to decide upon the correct service. A main office located on the East Coast is opened and closed three hours earlier than a branch office in San Francisco; a telegram sent anytime after 2 p.m. from a branch office on the West Coast would not arrive in a Boston main office until after closing hours. The message could be sent more economically as a night letter for delivery the following morning. As an office worker dealing with telegraphic communications, you will be expected to know the different time zones and the comparative time in each of them.

International Telegraph Service. To reach your employer quickly when he is in London, you *cable* him full rate. Cable and radio service are used to transmit overseas telegraph messages. Both of these services are offered by domestic telegraph offices. The messages are written on telegraph blanks and differ only in the way they are transmitted, either as cablegrams or radiograms.

Three types of international telegraphic communication services are available to business firms: *Full-Rate* (FR) messages, *Letter Telegrams* (LT), and *Ship Radiograms*.

Full-Rate Messages. A full-rate message is the fastest type of overseas service. It takes precedence over all other types of messages and is

```
┌─────────────────────────────────────────────────────────────────────────┐
│ ┌─DOMESTIC SERVICE─┐        WESTERN UNION      ┌INTERNATIONAL SERVICE┐     │
│ Check the class of service desired;                     Check the class of service desired; │
│ otherwise this message will be $ S      TELEGRAM        otherwise the message will be       │
│ sent as a fast telegram   1206 (4-55)                   sent at the full rate              │
│ TELEGRAM         S     W. P. MARSHALL, PRESIDENT  FULL RATE          X                     │
│ DAY LETTER       E                              LETTER TELEGRAM                            │
│ NIGHT LETTER                                    SHORE-SHIP                                 │
│ ┌NO. WDS.-CL. OF SVC.│PD. OR COLL.│CASH NO.│  CHARGE TO THE ACCOUNT OF │   TIME FILED ┐    │
│ │                    │            │        │        LAECO             │  3:15 p.m.   │    │
│ Send the following message, subject to the terms on back hereof, which are hereby agreed to │
│                                                                                           │
│                           Seattle, Washington, April 28, 19--                             │
│                                                                                           │
│      John C. Langley                                                                       │
│      Hotel Pierre                                                                          │
│      Paris, France                                                                         │
│                                                                                           │
│          Contact Doumier to expedite delivery contract.  Imperative                       │
│      get goods before May 10.                                                             │
│                                                                                           │
│                           LAECO                                                           │
│                                                                                           │
└─────────────────────────────────────────────────────────────────────────┘
```

A cable

transmitted and delivered as quickly as possible. It may be written in any language that can be expressed in letters of ordinary type, or it can be written in code or in cipher. A minimum charge is made for a message of five words or less.

Letter Telegrams. A letter telegram is transmitted during the night and delivered at its destination the following morning. The message must be written in plain language but code words may be used for the address and signature. A minimum charge is made for a message of 22 words or less. The rate is one half of the full rate.

Ship Radiograms. Plain language or code may be used in sending radiograms to and from ships at sea. A minimum charge is made for a message of five words or less. Only full-rate messages may be transmitted.

Counting the Chargeable Words in an Overseas Message. Cablegrams and radiograms are much more expensive than domestic telegrams. Not only are the rates higher, but many more words are counted and charged for. To avoid incurring unnecessary expense for your employer when you compose overseas messages, you should become familiar with the following regulations:

1) *Address and signature.* Each word in the address (except the country of destination and routing indicator) and signature are counted and charged for.
2) *Dictionary words.* Each plain language dictionary word is counted at the rate of 15 letters per word.
3) *Code words.* Each nondictionary or code word is counted at the rate of five letters per word. Code words are permitted only in full-rate cablegrams.
4) *Cipher.* Groups of figures, letters, signs, or a mixture thereof are counted at the rate of five characters per word.
5) *Punctuation marks.* The following punctuation marks when used in their normal sense in the text of a message are each counted as one word and are transmitted only at your specific request:

   , (comma)   " " (quotation marks)
   . (period)   ( ) (parentheses)
   : (colon)   ? (question mark)
   — (dash)   ' (apostrophe)
   - (hyphen)   / (fraction mark)

6) *Symbols.* The following special characters or symbols should be spelled out in the text of an international message because they cannot be transmitted: ¢, $, @, &, #, £.

Code Messages. You may send cablegrams, radiograms, and telegrams in "plain" or "code" language. Code is used primarily in overseas messages. A code message is simply a group of words or letters that stand for certain thoughts, expressions, or phrases. Long messages may be abbreviated to a few words by using code, thereby reducing the cost of the message. A code is unfamiliar to most people, and it tends to give the message a confidential nature that is sometimes necessary.

Code messages are of two types: (1) those that are made up of code words — that is, of dictionary words with special meanings other than their usual meanings; and (2) those that are written in cipher, that is, in groups of figures or letters that are not dictionary words.

Leaflets of code words may be obtained from Western Union and from code book publishers. In the leaflets the code words are arranged in alphabetic order so that you can use the leaflet as you would a dictionary.

It is impossible, of course, to provide for every contingency in a condensed code. Plain language, therefore, is permissible in a coded message and may be mixed with the code words when the code does not express the thought completely.

The following message is written in cipher code. It is written and counted as six words in a cablegram.

OBVEG MAHUP MEHJU ODIBY ODFUF MIPTI

OBVEG	Leaving for
MAHUP	London
MEHJU	Wednesday
ODIBY	Will not have sufficient money
ODFUF	Please cable at once
MIPTI	$500

The cipher code has two advantages: it uses fewer letters — the longest word containing but five — and it is easily adapted to the particular needs of any business.

Cable Code Addresses. Because each word in the address is counted in a cablegram, a business firm engaged in international trade, or any other firm with extensive overseas communications, registers and uses a single code word as the firm's cable address. The cable address of the South-Western Publishing Company of Cincinnati, Ohio, for example, is "SOWEPCO." There is a small annual charge for registering the cable address with the telegraph company.

Differences in Time. Time differences will determine, in part, the service you choose. If you work in an office with extensive overseas communication, be sure you have at hand a chart of time differences around the world.

Study Questions

1. What are three types of telegraph service?

2. Give the essential features of each class of service and the relative cost of each.

3. What suggestions should be followed in preparing a telegram?

4. What punctuation marks are sent without charge?

5. How are common abbreviations and figures counted in telegrams?

6. What are the eight ways in which telegrams may be filed?

7. What is meant by a repeat-back message? Is there a charge for such service?

8. In what four ways may telegraph service be paid for?

9. How is money sent by telegraph?

10. How may telegrams be delivered?

11. In what way is a knowledge of time zones important when sending telegrams?

12. Name and describe the various international telegraph services.

13. What is a code message?

14. What are the advantages of a code message?

15. What are the advantages of the cipher code system?

16. What are cable code addresses?

What Do You Think?

1. At 4:30 p.m. an employee in Philadelphia, Pennsylvania, is instructed to send a 17-word telegraphic message to a customer in Denver, Colorado. It is important that the message be delivered as quickly as possible. Which type of service should be used?

2. At 3:00 p.m. an employee in Portland, Oregon, is instructed to send a 30-word telegraphic message to the home office in Boston, Massachusetts. The office in Boston closes at 5:00 p.m. The message should be delivered as quickly as possible. Which type of service should be used?

3. At 10:00 a.m. an employee in San Antonio, Texas, is instructed to send a 115-word telegraphic message to a firm in Seattle, Washington. Although the message should be delivered rather quickly, a delay of a few hours is not important. Which type of service should be used?

4. At 4:30 p.m. an employee in Baltimore, Maryland, is instructed to send a 40-word message to a firm in Cheyenne, Wyoming. The message should be delivered the same day, although a delay of a few hours is not important. Which type of service should be used?

5. At 3:30 p.m. an employee in New Orleans, Louisiana, is instructed to send a 20-word message to a firm in St. Paul, Minnesota. It is important that the message be delivered as quickly as possible. Which type of service should be used?

6. At 3:30 p.m. an employee in San Francisco, California, is instructed to send a 15-word message to a firm in Chicago, Illinois, whose office closes at 5:00 p.m. The message should be delivered as quickly as possible. Which type of service should be used?

7. How many telegram words are in each of the following combinations?

a. $1,925.50

b. $50.00

c. New Jersey

d. C. A. Van Dyke

e. C.O.D.

f. f.o.b.

8. Under what conditions do you think a telegraph money order would most likely be used by an office?

9. Why is the responsibility of the telegraph company increased when a message is sent at the repeat-back rate?

10. The executive for whom you work wants to send a message to a business associate who has left for London by ship. What communication service should be used?

Your Personal Qualities

Mr. Edward Collins telephones his New York office from a hotel in Chicago at noon. The call is collect because his wallet with currency, travelers' checks, and credit cards has been either mislaid or stolen. In any event, he needs $200, and he needs it immediately. The employee who took the call promises to send the money immediately, but later realizes that in the excitement Mr. Collins failed to indicate how the money should be sent.

The money was sent in the form of a cashier's check in a special-delivery airmail letter.

Question: 1. What method of sending the money could have been used?

2. If you were handling the situation, what would you have done?

How's Your English?

Read about paragraphing in Appendix B, and then type a letter addressed to a local law office presenting the advantages and disadvantages of communicating by telegram as opposed to regular mail. The letter should be based on the material presented in this unit. Be sure to use paragraphing to the best advantage.

Office Work

In each of the following problems, compose the message and select the type of message to be sent.

1. At 10:00 a.m. on October 15, 19--, your employer, Thomas A. Evans, office manager of the Davis Advertising Agency, San Francisco, California, asked you to send a telegraphic message to the Grand Hotel, St. Louis, Missouri, reserving an $11.50 single room for the night of October 17, 19--. He will arrive in St. Louis about 8:00 p.m. on the 17th. Ask the hotel to wire confirmation collect immediately. The message is to be sent prepaid and charged to the company. It must be delivered as quickly as possible.

2. Write a telegraphic message to be sent by the Superior Paint Company, Cleveland, Ohio, to the Ingram Paint Store, 1152 Main Street, Newburgh, New York, at 9:15 a.m. on March 5, 19--. The message is to be sent prepaid and charged to the Superior Paint Company. It is important that this message be delivered in time to get a reply the same day, but a delay of an hour or two is not important. The Ingram Paint Store ordered 1,500 pounds of white lead to be shipped immediately, but they did not state the size of the containers. The lead can be supplied in units of 5- to 100-pound kegs. The price of kegs of less than a hundred pounds is 2 percent more than the 100-pound price.

3. At 4:30 p.m. on December 10, 19--, you are asked to send a telegraphic message for H. R. Harris, president of the Harris Construction Company, El Paso, Texas, to the Warner Manufacturing Company, Pittsburgh, Pennsylvania, whose office closes at 5:00 p.m. Ask them to cancel order #8675 of December 9. Tell them that a letter will follow the telegram.

4. On February 4, 19--, your employer, Mr. E. O. Colby, asked you to prepare a telegraph money order form for $100 to be sent to the firm's sales representative, Mr. S. D. Browning, at the White Beach Hotel, Atlantic City, New Jersey. You are to include a message informing Mr. Browning that a special sales meeting has been scheduled for February 15 at the Statler Hotel in Boston.

 Office Work Assignments

27: Typing Telegrams

If blanks are available, type the messages composed in the exercises under Office Work above, or type each message on a plain sheet of paper that would be satisfactory to submit to the telegraph office. Make a carbon copy of each message.

UNIT 7 | The Telephone

PART 1:

You on the Telephone

Can you imagine the office of today without a telephone? "Impossible!" is your quick response. The telephone is used in conversations to check information, to ask questions, to give explanations, to make contracts, to buy, to sell, to cancel orders. Because it is a most convenient means of communication, the telephone plays a part in the completion of every kind of business transaction.

As an office worker you will be called upon to make and answer all types of telephone calls. The effectiveness of each of your calls will, to a large extent, depend upon how well your callers understand you. Therefore, it is essential that you know the proper techniques for using the telephone in every business situation.

Telephone Personality. Your telephone personality will require very thoughtful consideration because you cannot be seen; you cannot rely upon your careful grooming and your attractive appearance to create a favorable impression. Nor can your smile, your friendly gesture, or your warm handclasp — all parts of your individual personality — be reflected in a telephone conversation. You must rely entirely upon your voice, your speech, your vocabulary, and your manner to create the desired impression. You should think of every telephone call as an opportunity to build goodwill for your firm. You can acquire a good telephone personality if you are consistently courteous, sincere, understanding, and helpful.

Courtesy and Sincerity. Courtesy is just as important in a telephone call as it is in a face-to-face conversation. The spirit of courtesy is best shown by the use of words, expression, and a manner which are natural and sincere. Trite words and phrases become boring to the listener and are definitely not necessary. Slang expressions should be avoided because they sound unbusinesslike. Your telephone conversation should

187

always conform to the generally accepted requirements of good business etiquette.

To reflect courtesy and sincerity, an incoming call should be acknowledged in the proper frame of mind. A call should not be considered as an interruption of work but rather as a part of it — and an important part. You have often heard of the "voice with a smile." Notice the difference in your voice if you smile while talking.

Telephone Speech. A voice can convey a spirit of interest, alertness, and helpfulness over the telephone or it can reflect an attitude of indifference, impatience, or inattention. It is so often true that "it is not what is said, but the way it is said" that really counts in a telephone conversation.

Telephone companies offer the following suggestions for improving your telephone habits:

1) *Speak distinctly.* Distinct speech is essential, since the listener can neither read your lips nor see your expression.

2) *Be heard clearly.* A normal conversational tone of voice — neither too loud nor too soft — carries best over the telephone.

3) *Talk at an appropriate pace.* A moderate rate of speech is more easily understood, but the pace should be related to the ideas you are expressing. You should give some information more deliberately, such as: technical information, lists, information the listener is writing down, numbers, names, and foreign or unusual words and expressions.

4) *Choose the right word.* Your ideas should be expressed simply with descriptive words where they are appropriate. Technical, cumbersome, and unnecessarily lengthy words may confuse the other person and may require an explanation or may even cause a misunderstanding.

5) *Use a low-pitched voice.* A low-pitched voice carries better over the telephone and is kinder to your listener's ears. A high-pitched voice tends to become shrill and irritating.

6) *Use emphasis with words.* The stress or emphasis placed on words, or groups of words, may change the meaning of what you are saying. A thoughtful use of emphasis will also help to give flexibility to your voice.

7) *Use voice inflection.* The rise and fall of your voice not only helps your thoughts but also adds personality to your voice. A monotonous voice may sound disinterested because it is flat and lacks spirit.

INCOMING CALLS

Answer Promptly. You should answer all incoming calls promptly and pleasantly. No one likes to wait; furthermore, you have no way of knowing who is calling — it may be a very important call. In fact, no matter who is calling, if he thought enough of your business to make a call,

Use of the telephone

When you use the telephone, your voice and manner should be pleasant, courteous, and sincere so that the calling party will receive a favorable impression of the firm you represent.

American Telephone & Telegraph Co.

you must give it prompt attention. It is best for all concerned if the telephone is answered at the end of the first ring.

As you reach for the receiver, reach for your pad of telephone message forms. You should be ready to take the message immediately. *Hold the mouthpiece about an inch from your lips* and speak directly into the telephone in a normal conversational tone of voice.

Identify Yourself. A telephone conversation cannot really begin until the caller knows that he has reached the right number. You should always identify yourself and your firm, office, or department immediately. Never answer by saying "Hello" or "Yes?" — these greetings add nothing to the identification.

If you answer an outside line, give your firm's name, followed by your name, as "Northern Construction Company, Miss Roberts." If your company has a switchboard, your operator has already identified the company; and you may answer your employer's telephone by saying, "Mr. Keller's office, Miss Roberts." When answering an office extension in a department, identify the department and give your name, as: "Personnel Department, Miss Roberts."

Screening Calls. One of your most important duties as an office worker may be to screen your employer's incoming telephone calls when he is away from his office, has someone with him, or is talking on another line. Explain why your employer cannot talk; and if possible, suggest an alternative, such as:

> Mr. White, Mr. Keller is attending a committee meeting. Is there anything I can do to help you?
>
> Mr. White, Mr. Keller is holding a conference. Would you care to talk to his assistant, Mr. Goetz?

Giving Information. You must exercise a great deal of discretion and tact to avoid giving out explicit information when your employer is not available for telephone calls. For instance, a reply such as, "Mr. Keller left for Minneapolis this morning," may be just enough information to let a competitor know that Mr. Keller is interested enough in a pending construction contract to make a personal trip to the construction site. Unless you are absolutely sure that your employer would want them to have the information, do not give out specific details over the telephone to outside callers.

Say:	*Rather Than:*
He is out of the city. May I ask him to call you when he returns on Monday?	He was called to New York to help close the Jones contract.
He is not at his desk. May I take a message?	He is discussing the pending merger with the comptroller.
He won't be in again until tomorrow morning. May I ask him to call you then?	He is at the Bonnie Brook Country Club.

Getting Information. Some telephone callers do not care to give their names; others prefer not to say why they are calling. As an office worker you will frequently have to find out *who* is calling and, if the name does not help you, *why* he is calling. Try to get the information as tactfully as possible by using an appropriate response, such as:

> Mr. Keller has a visitor at the moment. If you'll give me your name and telephone number, I'll ask him to call you just as soon as he is free.
>
> Mr. Keller is not at his desk just now. May I give him a message for you?
>
> Mr. Keller is talking on another line. May I help you?

If you must ask a direct question to get the information, state it as a request, rather than a demand, as: "May I tell Mr. Keller who is calling?"

Taking Messages Accurately. A pad of forms for recording the details of incoming telephone calls should always be kept on your desk next to the telephone to take messages when your employer is out. When your employer returns he can use the messages to return the calls, a practice which promotes better customer relations. It is imperative, therefore, that you record all of the details of every message accurately.

The message, written legibly, should include:

1) The exact time of the call and the date.

2) The name of the caller and his company (verify the spelling of any unusual name).

3) The telephone number, the caller's extension, and area code, if it's a long-distance call (verify the number).

4) The details of the message.

5) The initials of the person who wrote the message.

A.T.&T. CO.	MEMO OF CALL	GS-185 (6-60)

To M*r* *Keller*

M*r* *Robertson*

311 555-2368 —
AREA CODE   TEL. NO.   EXT.

☑ Telephoned   ☑ Will call you later
☐ Please call   ☐ Called to see you
☐ In response to your call   ☐ Wishes to see you

Message *acceptance of preliminary contract*

Rec'd by: *___* Date: *3/9* Time: *1:10*

Transfer Calls Carefully. You should transfer incoming calls only when it is necessary. Tell the caller why the transfer is necessary, and be sure that the call is being transferred to the proper person or department. Calls are usually transferred when the caller has reached a telephone by mistake, when he wishes to speak to someone else, or when his request can be more appropriately handled by someone else. In these instances you may say to the caller:

I am sorry, you have reached the wrong extension. What extension were you calling? . . . . . . I can transfer your call. Just a minute, please.

I shall be glad to transfer you to Mr. Williams. His extension is 2368. Just a minute, please.

Mr. Young has all the information on that matter. May I transfer your call to him?

To transfer a call you should depress and release the plunger of the telephone *slowly*. If you are using a *Call Director*, move the hanger *slowly*. This action flashes a signal light on the switchboard which will attract the operator's attention. After the operator acknowledges your signal, you might say: "Please transfer this call to Mr. Williams," or "Please place this incoming call on Extension 2368."

If you are disconnected during a call made *to* you, hang up, but try to keep your line free to receive the call back. If you placed the call, signal the operator and ask her to reestablish the connection; or if you dialed the call, dial it again. If you dialed a long-distance call, dial "0" for Operator and explain that you were disconnected.

Telephones for "Hands-Free" Talking. You need not pick up the receiver at all when you use the *Speakerphone*. When a call comes in, you press a button and talk as you would to a visitor in your office. The caller's voice comes from a small rectangular loudspeaker on your desk. He can hear you even if you are several feet from the set.

To make a call, press the button, dial the number, and converse. Both hands will be free to make notes or to consult records. When you want privacy with the Speakerphone, you can lift the receiver and use the telephone in the usual way.

Automatic Answering Sets. A telephone answering and recording set will automatically answer the telephone and record a message when no one is in the office. Here is how it works. Before the executive leaves the office for the day, he dictates a message to the set, for instance:

> This is John Keller speaking. You are listening to a recording of my voice. If it is urgent, you may reach me at 555-2368. When you hear the tone, you can record a message for me if you would like to do so. Thank you.

Upon returning to the office, the employer or one of his assistants can play back the messages left by the callers.

Recording Telephone Conversations. There will be times when your employer will want a written report of the conversation he is having. With the approval of the other party, he will ask you to take notes during the conversation or to record it on a tape recording machine. A typewritten copy of the recorded conversation may, of course, be sent to the person to whom your employer is speaking.

When You Hear a "Beep" Tone. A short "beep" tone heard on your telephone line about every 15 seconds means that the person with whom you are talking is recording your conversation. This signal is provided by the telephone company for your protection. *Use of a recorder without recorder-connector equipment containing a tone-warning device is contrary to the company's tariffs and not permitted.* If you do not want a record made of what you are saying, ask the person with whom you are

The Speakerphone

This "hands-free" telephone is equipped with an amplifier, permitting group conversations. It is useful for conference calls. It can also be used in a normal manner when privacy is desired.

American Telephone & Telegraph Co.

talking to disconnect the recording machine. When he disconnects, the signal is no longer heard.

OUTGOING CALLS

Making Telephone Calls. More and more executives are saving telephone time by answering and placing their own telephone calls. However, you may be expected to make telephone calls and to place calls for your employer. In order to make calls courteously and efficiently, you should have a fairly clear idea of the purpose of each call before you make it. You may find it advisable to make a list of the points you wish to cover before making an important call. Be sure that your employer is free to talk before you place a call for him, for when you say: "This is Mr. Keller's office. Mr. Keller would like to speak to Mr. Jones," you may be speaking to Mr. Jones.

Using Telephone Directories Correctly. Before making calls, you should know how to get information from the telephone directories quickly and how to operate the telephone properly. Three different telephone directories may be consulted to make outgoing calls: the alphabetical directory, the Yellow Pages, and your own personal directory of frequently called persons and firms. Most telephone directories have two general sections: the alphabetical section (white pages) and the Yellow Pages.

The Alphabetical Directory. The names of subscribers are listed alphabetically in this directory. Individual names and firm names are easily located, unless the spelling of a name is unusual, and then it is cross-referenced as:

```
Gray      — See also Grey
Hoffman — See also Hoffmann, Hofmann
Rees      — See also Reis, Reiss, Riess
```

Business and professional people frequently list their residence numbers directly below their business listings as:

```
Banks Jacob groc 4740 ReistwRd...................   555-3469
       Res 3516 VaAv................................   555-4092
```

It is often necessary to call various government agencies to secure information, obtain forms, licenses, and to get answers to various questions which are constantly arising about government regulations. Government agencies are listed under three categories:

Federal agencies under "United
States Government" as..............U.S. Government
                                    Agriculture Dept of —
                                    Labor Dept of

State agencies under state
governments as...................North Dakota State of —
                                    Employment Service
                                    Highway Dept

County and municipal agencies under
local governments as...............Minneapolis City of —
                                    Education Board of
                                    Fire Dept
                                    Police Dept

The first few pages of the alphabetical directory contain useful information including instructions for making emergency calls, local and long-distance calls, service calls (repair, assistance, etc.), and special calls (overseas, conference, collect, etc.). In addition, area codes for the United States and Canada, sample rates, and telephone company business office addresses and telephone numbers are listed.

The Yellow Pages. The Yellow Pages are used when you wish to find out quickly where you may obtain a particular product or service. The names, addresses, and telephone numbers of business subscribers are listed alphabetically under the appropriate product or service. Many business organizations use advertising space and artwork to tell their customers about the organization's operations, including brands carried, hours, and services. Nationally advertised or trademarked products may be listed with the names, addresses, and telephone numbers of most of the local dealers arranged alphabetically under a word or trademark design.

For instance, your employer may ask you to reorder master sets and copy paper for the Ditto spirit duplicator. Under the heading *Duplicating Machines and Supplies,* the familiar Ditto trademark, a ditto mark within a circle, is displayed. Many of the local dealers are listed below "WHERE TO BUY THEM."

At another time your employer may ask you to call a certified public accountant named Smith who has an office on North Fifth Street. Since there are so many Smiths listed in the alphabetical section, it will be much easier to refer to the heading in the Yellow Pages *Accountants — Certified Public* to find a Mr. Smith with an office on North Fifth Street:

Smith R R 209 N 5............................. 555-2626

Personal Telephone Directory. An up-to-date list of frequently called local and out-of-town telephone numbers will save you and your employer a great deal of telephoning time. Booklets to be used as personal telephone directories can be obtained from most of the telephone companies. For the small firm or office, an "automatic finder" can be used. By manipulating the indicator to the correct letter of the alphabet, you can reach the desired page immediately. A large personal listing can be kept more conveniently on cards in a revolving visible file on your desk. Telephone numbers can be obtained from Information service, but a more efficient way to get a particular number is through the use of an up-to-date personal directory. If it is necessary to use Information service to get a certain number, record it in the personal directory for future use.

To reach an out-of-town Information operator, dial the proper area code, then 555-1212. The number 555-1212 is the nationwide Information number. For numbers in your own area, call Information by dialing the number listed in the front of the telephone directory.

Be sure you have the correct number before making a call. If you are not sure of the number, refer to a telephone directory to avoid possible delay and embarrassment.

Numbers in Telephone Calls. If numbers must be given to the operator, the telephone company recommends careful enunciation. The following pronunciation of numbers may prevent misunderstandings:

Number	Pronunciation	Formation of Sound
0	OH	Long O
1	W u N	Strong W and N
2	T o o	Strong T and long oo
3	Th R-ee	Strong R and long ee
4	fo-eR	Long o and strong R
5	fi-iV	First i long, the second short, and a strong V
6	SiKS	Strong S and KS
7	SeV-eN	Strong S and V and a "rounded" N
8	aTe	Long a and strong T
9	Ni-eN	First N strong, long i and mild emphasis on the eN

How to Dial. Dialing instructions must be followed carefully to prevent mistakes:

1) *Listen for the dial tone.* Lift the receiver and listen for the *dial tone* — a steady humming sound which indicates that the equipment is ready for a call.
2) *Dial carefully.* Dial the numbers (or two letters and numbers) in the order in which they appear in the telephone directory.
   To dial 555-1357 you would:
   a. Place the forefinger firmly in the dial opening for the number "5."
   b. Turn the dial around in a clockwise direction until the finger strikes the finger stop.
   c. Remove the finger and let the dial return to its normal position *without forcing or retarding* its movement.
   d. Dial the following numerals in the same manner.
3) *If a mistake is made while dialing* or if your finger slips from the dial before it reaches the finger stop, hang up the receiver for a few seconds, then start to dial your call again.

In dialing, be careful to distinguish between the letter "O" and the numeral "0." The same is true of the letter "I" and the numeral "1." Mistaking one for the other will result in a wrong number. The transposing of numbers also causes errors in dialing: dialing 8864 as 8846 or 1191 as 1911.

Touch-Tone Telephones. Touch-Tone telephones have push buttons instead of the rotary dials. Listen for the dial tone, then push the numbered buttons to correspond with the telephone number. As each button is pushed you will hear a tone.

Touch-Tone dialing systems are being installed in all major cities and will be available to both residence and business users on an optional basis within the next few years. The major advantage to this system is increased speed in placing calls.

Button Telephones. Button telephones have almost completely replaced the two or three separate telephones formerly found on the busy executive's desk. They may have anywhere from one to six buttons along the base of the instrument, but the six-button variety is most commonly used. The buttons on a six-button set, with access to three central office lines, would be arranged and labeled in this order:

The *hold* button is the button on the left side of the key set. When it is depressed, you will be able to hold a call while you make or answer another call. The first caller is then *unable to overhear your second conversation.* The hold button does not remain depressed but returns to normal when you release it. However, if you do not use it before pressing another button, the call will be cut off.

Six-button telephone set

With this telephone it is possible to handle more than one call on an extension.

American Telephone & Telegraph Co.

Button #1	Button #2	Button #3	Button #4	Button #5	Button #6
Hold	2368	2369	2370	5621	Int.

The *pickup* buttons, buttons #2, #3, #4, and #5 above, are used to make and receive outside calls. A line will be connected with the central telephone office when you depress the corresponding pickup push button.

The *intercom* button, button #6, is depressed to permit you to speak to other persons, such as a secretary or a supervisor, within your own firm.

Operating a Button Telephone. A number of calls can be handled on a push-button telephone at the same time. The steps in the receiving and handling of two incoming calls follow:

1) Depress the *pickup* button connected with the ringing line before lifting the receiver. (Pickup buttons usually light up when in use.)
2) If a call comes in while you are talking on another line, excuse yourself, depress the *hold* button, then depress the *pickup* button connected with the ringing line and answer it.
3) If it is necessary to announce the second call to another person on the intercommunicating line, you would:
   a. Depress the *hold* button (you are now holding two calls).
   b. Depress the *intercom* button.
   c. Dial the intercom code for the person.
   d. When he answers announce the call and tell him on which line it is being held.
   e. Return to the call only long enough to be assured that it has been picked up properly.
4) Return to the first call by depressing the button for that line.

Shown above is the standard arrangement of push buttons. "Tailor-made" arrangements, designed to meet the special needs of a particular office, may be encountered on the job. For instance, a *signal* button, frequently a buzzer, may be used to signal a secretary.

American Telephone & Telegraph Co.

Call Director

Not usually considered a switchboard, the Call Director does not require a full-time attendant.

Call Director telephones can handle up to 29 lines and come in 12-, 18-, 24-, and 30-button consoles. As in the six-button telephone, there are lighted keys for hold, intercom, and signaling. The placement of the lines on the console varies with the particular office needs and requirements.

The Call Director is not usually considered a switchboard, for it does not require the services of a full-time operator. The individual employees receive and make their own calls, and the attendant handles only incoming calls of a general nature and transfer calls to other lines. She may make outgoing calls for employees who do not have their own lines. She also may take calls for an employee during his absence if so directed.

Automatic Dialing Telephones. There are several automatic dialing telephones commonly used in business offices. The *Card Dialer* uses small plastic cards for numbers you expect to call frequently. These should be coded and placed in the storage area in the unit. To place a call, you insert the proper card in the dial slot, lift the receiver, and, on hearing the dial tone, press the start bar.

The *Rapidial* repertory dialer, a separate unit associated with the telephone, stores names and numbers on magnetic tape. To record a

Card Dialer

An example of the automatic dialing telephones.

American Telephone & Telegraph Co.

number, turn the selector knob to a blank space on the tape, open the window over the tape and write in the name. Then dial the number for recording. To make a call, turn the selector knob to the desired name, lift the telephone receiver, and, on hearing the dial tone, press the automatic dialing bar. The Rapidial stores up to 290 names.

The *Magicall* automatic memory dialer is equipped to remember 400 telephone numbers but is also available to handle up to 1,000 numbers. The Magicall dialer handles intercom office calls, local outside calls, and long-distance calls. Its operation is similar to the Rapidial described above.

Terminating Calls. Try to leave a favorable impression by ending each telephone conversation in a friendly, unhurried manner. It is very bad manners to end a call by hanging up brusquely. As the caller closes the conversation, thank him for his call before you say "Good-bye" with an appropriate remark such as:

"Thank you very much for calling, Mr. Ames."

"Thank you for your message. I'll ask Mr. Keller to telephone you as soon as he returns."

"Thank you for the information. I'll be happy to pass it along to Mr. Keller."

Be sure to say "Good-bye." After the caller has hung up, replace the receiver *gently*.

Personal Telephone Calls. The policy of using a business telephone for personal calls varies in different offices. Some firms permit a limited number of personal calls; others permit none at all. However, all firms oppose the excessive use of a business telephone for personal calls. In the interest of efficiency and harmony, you should limit your personal calls. Callers who wish to discuss personal matters with you during business hours should be politely discouraged. Personal calls should be made only when they are necessary.

Cost for Local Calls. There are many ways of charging telephone calls. In most communities you receive unlimited service within the area. In more and more communities, extended area service provides for a flat rate for all calls within a wider area. In a few large cities the rate is based on message units (based on time and distance). The base rate provides for a specified number of units with a charge for additional units. The introductory page of the telephone directory in these cities shows how many units a call will consume to a particular region for the time-based period.

LONG-DISTANCE TELEPHONE CALLS

Charges are made for all out-of-town telephone calls or calls made beyond the local service area. The amount of the charge depends upon the distance, the type of call, the time of the day or night that the call is made, and the length of the conversation. The two most generally used types of out-of-town calls are the *station-to-station* and the *person-to-person* calls. You will be expected to know when it would be advisable to make each type of call and the relative costs of the calls.

Station-to-Station Calls. A station-to-station call is made to a given telephone number. The charge begins when the called number answers. Make this type of call if you are willing to talk to anyone who may answer the telephone or if you are fairly certain that the desired person is within reach of his telephone.

Person-to-Person Calls. When you want to speak to a specific person in a large company, place a person-to-person call. A person-to-person call is directed to a specific person, room number, extension number, or department at the called telephone number. A charge does not begin until the person or extension telephone called is reached. Make this type of call if you want to talk to a specific person and you are not sure he is within reach of his telephone. This may be much less expensive if the person is frequently not at his desk or if you have to go from the main switchboard operator to the secretary's desk, then to another office. In the station-to-station call you will be charged the moment the called firm's switchboard operator answers. If a person-to-person call is not completed, place the call later.

Relative Costs. The cost of a station-to-station call is about 30 percent less than the cost of a person-to-person call because a call can be made to a particular number in considerably less time than a call to a particular person. The rates for both types of calls are based on an initial charge for three minutes.

A table of the rates to the larger cities in the United States and Canada is given in the front of most telephone directories. The larger directories also list the charges to the major overseas countries.

Rates. Lower rates are in effect between 5 p.m. and 7 a.m. on weekdays and all day Saturday and Sunday for both station-to-station and person-to-person interstate calls. For these rates to apply, the time must be after 5 p.m. in the locality where the call is placed.

An evening rate applies to station-to-station calls made between 5 p.m. and 7 a.m. Monday through Friday; the night rate applies for calls made between 7 p.m. and 7 a.m. on weekdays and all day Saturday and Sunday. A late night direct distance dialing rate is available between midnight and 7 a.m. every day.

For person-to-person calls, the day rates apply from 7 a.m. until 5 p.m. Monday through Friday. Night rates are in effect between 5 p.m. and 7 a.m. Monday through Friday and all day Saturday and Sunday.

Time Factor. It is important that you be aware of the time differences across the country. The United States is divided into four standard time zones: Eastern, Central, Mountain, and Pacific. Each zone is one hour earlier than the zone immediately to the east of it. When it is 3 p.m. Eastern Standard Time, it is 2 p.m. in the Central zone, 1 p.m. in the Mountain zone, and noon in the Pacific zone. Because of time differences, you must remember not to call Los Angeles from New York before 12 noon because it is only 9 a.m. in California, or New York from California after 2 p.m. because it is then after 5 p.m. in New York and the office you want is likely to be closed. A map showing the four time zones, as well as the area codes for the United States, is shown on page 202.

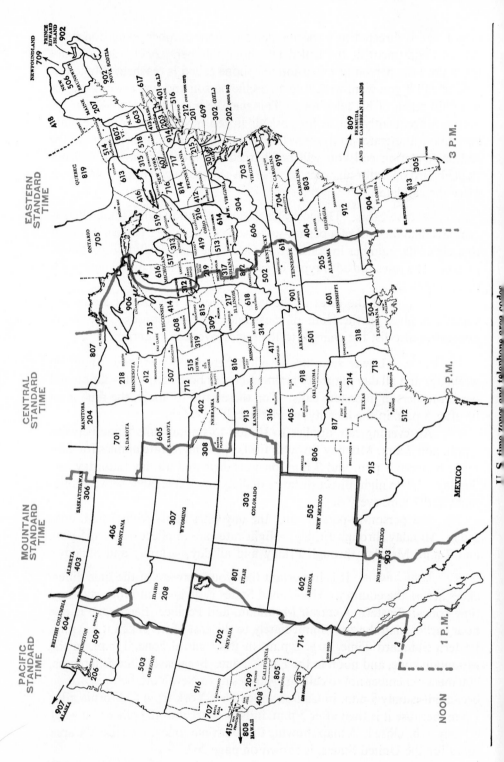

U.S. time zones and telephone area codes

Direct Distance Dialing. DDD makes it possible to dial most station-to-station long-distance calls. In many areas of the nation, it is necessary to dial a "prefix" code to get access to long-distance lines. The front pages of the telephone directory tell you how to place a long-distance call, and give the prefix code if one is required.

The first three digits of a long-distance number represent the area code for the geographical area; the following seven digits represent a specific telephone within that area. Area codes are required when calling from one area to another. They are seldom used when calling a telephone within the same area; however, the prefix code may then be required.

In more and more cities, it is also possible to dial person-to-person calls. Dial the "0" for "Operator" and then dial the number. When the operator identifies herself, give her the name of the person you are calling. When that person answers, the operator notes the start of the call. This is required for billing purposes.

If you cannot dial the person-to-person call directly, you dial the long-distance operator who will say: "Operator." Place the call in this order: city, state, area code, telephone number, and the name of the person wanted. For example, say: "I'm calling Oakland, Pennsylvania, area code 311, 555-8912, Mr. James Gordon, please."

To permit the most rapid handling of a long-distance call, do not give the number from which you are calling unless the operator asks for it.

Remain at the telephone until your call is completed or until you receive a report from the operator. If your call cannot be completed at the time it is placed, ask the operator to keep trying and remain near the telephone to be ready to talk when the number does answer or to give the operator any further details. Postpone the call if you cannot stay within reach of the telephone.

Special Long-Distance Calls. Special long-distance services include collect calls, conference calls, and overseas telephone service. Before placing these calls, check the front pages of the telephone directory for instructions to reach special operators. Usually you dial a code such as "0" for Operator.

Collect Calls. If you want the charges reversed — if you want the station or the person you are calling to pay the charges — notify the operator when you place the call. This gives the called station or person an opportunity to accept or refuse the call before the connection is made. The charges may be reversed on both station-to-station and person-to-person calls with no extra cost.

Conference Calls. A conference call is placed when an executive wishes to talk to several persons at different locations at the same time.

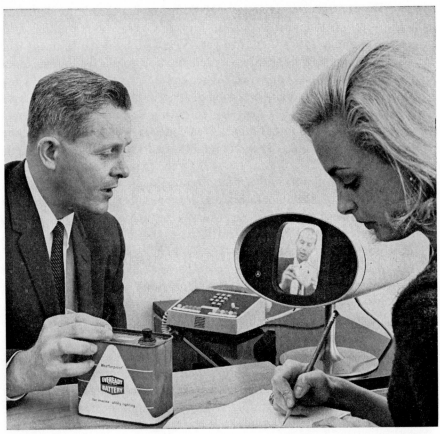

American Telephone & Telegraph Co.

The Picturephone set

This service is no longer experimental and may be brought into wider use in the business office in the near future.

As many as ten locations can be connected for a conference call. To arrange such a call you would give the operator the names, telephone numbers, and locations of the persons to be connected for the call. Be certain to give the specific time that the call is to be put through. Then, be certain that *your* executive is ready to receive this call!

Overseas Telephone Service. Overseas calling is increasing at an amazing rate — and the calls are as clear as local ones. You may obtain information on telephone calls to overseas points from the long-distance operator. A typical weekday rate for a three-minute person-to-person call from the central part of the United States to Argentina, Australia, Denmark, or Great Britain is $12; a typical station-to-station call to Puerto Rico is $6.50, and to Hawaii, $7.50.

When you wish to place an overseas call, dial the long-distance operator and ask for the overseas operator.

An appointment should be made for certain countries, and particularly for calls on holidays. It is also important to consider time zones. A call from Chicago at 9 a.m. Monday (Central Daylight Time) would be 2 p.m. Monday in London; 11 p.m. Monday in Tokyo; midnight Monday in Sydney, Australia; and 3 a.m. Monday in Pago Pago, American Samoa.

Picturephone Calls. The *Picturephone* service has a Touch-Tone telephone with buttons to make calls and to control the video screen. When you use the new service, you can control whether you want to be seen, whether you want to see yourself or the person you are calling, or whether you want a darkened screen.

Study Questions

1. On what does "telephone personality" rely?

2. Give several suggestions for improving telephone speech habits.

3. How should you identify yourself when answering a business call?

4. What information should be recorded when taking a telephone message?

5. How can calls be transferred?

6. Describe three functions of an automatic answering set.

7. Under what circumstances might you use the alphabetic telephone directory?

8. When would you be more likely to use the Yellow Pages?

9. What would you put in a personal telephone directory?

10. Describe the method of dialing a call.

11. What is the best way of terminating telephone calls?

12. What is the quickest and cheapest type of long-distance telephone call?

13. Under what set of circumstances would you recommend the placing of a person-to-person call?

14. What is a conference call?

15. What information should you furnish when a long-distance call is made?

16. What is Direct Distance Dialing and how is it used?

What Do You Think?

1. Your employer asks you to get a certain customer on the telephone. Should you connect your employer when you receive an answer at the switchboard of the other company, or should you wait until the particular person called answers?

2. Your employer is very busy and wants to be interrupted with as few telephone calls as possible. How would you know which calls to answer yourself and which calls to refer to your employer?

3. An office worker sometimes places calls for her employer. A number of these calls go to the same firms. How should the office worker be prepared so that these calls can be made quickly?

4. The assistant to the office manager of a business buys almost all of the miscellaneous office supplies. Some of the calls coming to the office are therefore for the office manager and some for the assistant. What should the assistant say when answering the telephone?

5. Charles Allen, a traveling salesman, makes the long-distance calls described in the following paragraphs. What type of service should he ask for in each case?

    a. Mr. Allen wishes to telephone to his home as cheaply as possible.

    b. A customer asks for information about a special contract. It is necessary for Mr. Allen to talk personally with the general manager to get this information.

    c. Mr. Allen receives an order from a customer who asks that the order be telephoned to the company at once.

    d. Mr. Allen calls the office to get prices on a new item.

6. The number of overseas telephone calls from the United States increased from 11,750 calls in 1927 to more than 8,000,000 in 1965. Discuss the reasons for this tremendous increase.

7. Discuss the probable business uses of Picturephone service.

8. Discuss the advantages of a "Touch-Tone" telephone over the traditional rotary-dial telephone.

Your Personal Qualities

Mr. Baldwin has left instructions with the receptionist, Alice Kirby, "that he is not to be interrupted with visitors or telephone calls." He is checking the departmental budget for the coming year and must have it ready for the comptroller Monday morning. If anyone calls, the receptionist is to say that Mr. Baldwin is not in.

Mr. Downs of the purchasing division calls to ask about a conference table which Mr. Baldwin ordered for his office. On the requisition, Mr. Baldwin failed to indicate the color he wanted. Miss Kirby answers the telephone and tells Mr. Downs that Mr. Baldwin is not in. She assures him that Mr. Baldwin will return the call just as soon as he returns, whereupon Mr. Baldwin picks up his telephone and tells Mr. Downs that he wants the table finished in desert sage.

Question: Miss Kirby feels quite embarrassed about what has happened. She feels there are three courses of action she can take:

    1. Tell Mr. Baldwin that he had given specific instructions that he was not in and that he embarrassed her.

    2. Call Mr. Downs and tell him that she was merely following Mr. Baldwin's orders when she told him Mr. Baldwin was not in.

    3. Do nothing and try to forget what happened.

What should she do?

How's Your English?

Read Appendix C and correct any inaccuracies in the following sentences:

1. He worked in the guideance department of the school.

2. The mimograph salesman said, do you get good mileage on your car.

3. In your judgement is any one make of machine any better than the others.

4. I knew he was lying when he siad, How lonly he was.

5. She was dying her dress.

Office Work

1. Using your telephone book, look up and list the telephone numbers for:

   a. All emergency calls (Fire, Police, Ambulance, Doctor, etc.)

   b. Telephone service calls (business office, telephone repairs, communications consultant, etc.)

   c. Calls to get time and weather (if available)

   d. The public library

   e. The public high school

   f. One of the larger business firms

   g. One of the banks

   h. The area codes for New York, Chicago, Los Angeles, and Philadelphia

2. This question requires the use of the Yellow Pages:

   a. If you were asked to get an attorney on the telephone, would you look in the Yellow Pages under the heading *Attorneys* or *Lawyers*?

   b. If you were asked to get a minister on the telephone, would you look under the heading *Ministers* or *Clergymen*?

   c. If you were asked to get an interior decorator on the telephone, would you look under the heading *Decorators* or *Interior Decorators*?

   d. If you were asked to get a dealer of metal window screens on the telephone, would you look under the heading *Screens* or *Window Screens*?

Office Work Assignments

28: Reporting Telephone Calls

The following telephone calls were received on March 5, 19--, while the persons called were out of the office. Prepare a report of each call on a form similar to the one shown in the illustration on page 191.

1. William C. Adams of Chicago called Alfred Rogers at 10:30 in regard to an order. Mr. Adams' telephone number is 312 555-3456. He will call again at 2:00.

2. Mrs. James Arthur called Mr. Arthur (her husband) at 12:30.

3. Mr. James Linden of Philadelphia called William Spencer at 11:45. He said that he had received order No. 10256 but had not received order No. 10245, which had been placed a week before the other order. His telephone number is 215 555-8230.

4. Earl Kramer called Alfred Rogers at 4:15. He will meet Mr. Rogers at 5:30 at the club.

Select a member of the Clerical Practice class to work with you in acting out this typical office telephone conversation. One of the parties should be prepared to make the call and the other prepared to answer it. If the Yellow Pages in your telephone directory do not list office machine service, use the following information:

Adding and Calculating Machines &
    Supplies
    Monroe — Sales, Service,
        and Rental......... 687-1456

As other members of your class make and place the service call, evaluate each call under the following general headings: the Placing and Beginning of the Call, the Development of the Call and the Giving of Information, the Closing of the Call, and the Voice Personalities of the Callers.

All of the information needed for a telephone call should be obtained before the call is placed if the message is to be transmitted properly.

1. Assume that you are a clerk in the billing department of a department store. The adding machine you have been using has broken down, and you are asked to call a service man. You will need to know the make, model, and serial number of the machine before placing the call. Use the Yellow Pages to find the name and telephone number of the manufacturer under the heading *Adding & Calculating Machines*.

2. Assume that you are taking service calls for the Standard Adding and Calculating Machine Company. When the call comes in from the billing clerk, verify the information about the machine, the address of the department store, and the room number and floor of the billing department. Tell the billing clerk approximately when the service man will call.

3. If evaluation forms are available, use them to make comments on the making and answering of the service calls. The comments are to be listed under four main headings: Beginning of the Call, Development of the Call, Closing of the Call, and Voice Personality.

UNIT 7 | The Telephone

PART 2:

Switchboard Operations

If you work for an average-size or a large business firm, in all probability there will be a private branch exchange (PBX) or telephone switchboard system in your office. Telephone companies lease PBX systems to business firms. The type of system installed in each office is determined by the communication services required by the particular business. Consequently, a PBX system may vary in capacity from 20 station lines to over a thousand.

A PBX system has three main functions:

1) *To receive incoming calls.* Any central office line can be connected with any extension line in the office.
2) *To place outgoing calls.* Any extension line can be connected with any central office line.
3) *To make interoffice calls.* Any extension line can be connected with any other extension line within the office (even in different buildings) without going through the central telephone office.

There are many different types of PBX systems. However, the basic types are: (1) cord switchboards and Centrex systems for larger businesses, (2) push-button dial switchboards for medium-size businesses, and (3) Dial Pak service and cordless, touch-key switchboards for small businesses.

Cord Switchboards. Cord switchboards are still used when there are many central office (outside) lines and hundreds of extension lines, although they are being replaced, where possible, with more modern timesaving equipment. An interoffice (inside) call is made by dialing the extension number. An outside call is placed by dialing a code number (usually number 9) for connection with an outside line. When the dial tone changes, you then dial the number as usual. Many incoming calls

The switchboard

The operator is answering an incoming call on the cord switchboard.

American Telephone & Telegraph Co.

are received and connected to the called extensions by the switchboard attendant.

Centrex. In all federal government agencies and in many other firms each extension is also a telephone number which you can dial directly without the assistance of a switchboard operator. This timesaving direct inward dialing and direct outward dialing service applies to both local and long-distance calls. One of its major advantages is that it saves time.

Button Dial Switchboards. The push-button dial switchboard is housed in a compact console that takes up about as much room on the attendant's desk as a typewriter. It provides for as many as 60 extension telephones and ten central office lines.

Some of the features of the push-button dial switchboard are the "automatic disconnect" on all calls, the "camp-on" for intracompany calls, and the "direct station selector" for incoming calls. As soon as you hang up your receiver, your telephone is automatically disconnected and your extension is immediately available for another call. If someone from within the company calls when your line is busy, he may "camp-on" your line, not overhearing your call, and then be connected automatically when your telephone is free. Incoming calls are completed almost instantly.

Dial Pak Service. A new type of communication service, called *20-40 Dial Pak*, has been especially designed for the approximately 30,000 American business firms which have from 20 to 40 telephones. The basic unit serves up to 20 telephones and may be expanded to 40 lines. The attendant, at a compact *Call Director*, is no longer tied to a full-time manual switchboard. Calls to key employees come directly to their own telephones which are also used for outgoing calls. The attendant answers only the general incoming calls and places calls for office employees who do not have outside lines on their telephones. She is left with time to type information on business forms, to sort and file business correspondence, and to do other clerical work. Dial Pak service sometimes eliminates the need for a switchboard attendant altogether by the placement of two or three Call Directors on the desks of various employees.

Another feature of the 20-40 Dial Pak is that as many as 12 people within the office can be connected for a conference-type call.

The PBX Attendant. The switchboard attendant is the "voice" receptionist of all incoming calls, and an efficient and resourceful "girl Friday" for the entire office staff. Her personality is a vital part of the character of the firm because she is in constant communication with callers and her fellow employees. Her day-to-day spirit of helpfulness can contribute much to the morale of the staff and the success of the business.

The attendant should acknowledge calls promptly and courteously. If she cannot complete calls at once, she might handle them in this fashion:

An incompleted call:

ATTENDANT: Northern Construction Company, good morning.
CALLER: Mr. Keller, please.
ATTENDANT: Mr. Keller's line is busy. Would you care to wait?
                   or May I take a message?
CALLER: I'll wait, thank you.
ATTENDANT: (about 15 seconds later) Mr. Keller's line is still busy.
CALLER: I'll wait.
ATTENDANT: (about 20 seconds later) Mr. Keller's line is still busy. May I have him call you?
CALLER: Yes. Would you ask him to call H. B. Nelson, extension 3243 at the First National Bank, 555-4700.

Desk top switchboard

This cordless board is capable of handling 10 trunks and 60 telephones.

American Telephone & Telegraph Co.

ATTENDANT: That's Mr. H. B. Nelson (N as in Nellie), extension 3243 at 555-4700. Thank you, Mr. Nelson.

A delayed call:

ATTENDANT: Northern Construction Company, good morning.
CALLER: The purchasing agent, please.
ATTENDANT: Mr. Miller's extension is busy. Will you wait?
CALLER: Yes.
ATTENDANT: (about 15 seconds later) His extension is still busy.
CALLER: I'll wait.
ATTENDANT: (later) You may have Mr. Miller's extension now. Thank you for waiting.

In smaller offices employees are often asked to fill in at the switchboard during the noon hour or at other times during the business day. If you are asked to operate the switchboard, it would be well for you to obtain switchboard training from the telephone company. A staff of instructors is employed by them to give individual instruction to office workers on the type of switchboards installed in their respective offices. The request for training is made by the employing firm.

Auxiliary PBX Services. Auxiliary switchboard services, when business conditions require them, add a great deal to an organization's communcation system. Six of the major auxiliary services are:

1) Conference Calls — Manually Arranged
   The attendant can arrange a conference call over your regular telephone with up to four office people and one outside person.
2) Conference Calls — Dial Arranged
   An internal conference with up to 10 people in your firm can be held on regular telephones when this service is available.
3) Telephone Dictation
   Your regular telephone can be used to dictate to a recording machine at a central point when you have this service. You can use one-digit dialing controls to START, STOP, CORRECT, and PLAYBACK your dictation.
4) Code Call Signaling
   With this auxiliary PBX service, your regular telephone can be used to dial a code signal and to locate employees away from their telephones.
5) Loudspeaker Paging Service
   This service connects the switchboard with your loudspeaker paging equipment.
6) After-Hours Service — Dial
   This after-hours service affords complete telephone coverage from a button-type telephone during those hours when the

switchboard is unattended. All incoming calls are answered by a regular after-hours employee, and all office employees working after hours have the assurance that calls will reach them quickly over their regular telephones.

Study Questions

1. What do the initials PBX mean?

2. What are the three main functions of PBX service?

3. Dial Pak service is designed for firms with approximately how many telephones?

4. What is the advantage of the "camp-on" feature of the push-button dial switchboard?

5. What is the main advantage of Centrex service?

6. How would you characterize the PBX attendant?

7. How should the switchboard attendant handle a call that cannot be completed immediately?

8. Under what circumstances can your telephone be used for recording dictation?

What Do You Think?

1. What are the advantages of having had telephone switchboard training when applying for a beginning office position?

2. Why are courtesy and alertness so important in switchboard operation?

Your Personal Qualities

Claire Rogers and Ann Brown fill in as relief switchboard operators during the noon hour. Claire handles a delayed call in this fashion:
"Mr. Smith's extension is busy."
After about 15 seconds she says, "Still busy."
When the extension is free she says, "I'll ring him now."

Ann handles a similar call in this fashion:

"Mr. Clark's extension is busy. Will you wait, please?"
After about 15 seconds she says, "Mr. Clark is still busy."
When the extension is free she says, "You may have Mr. Clark's extension now. Thank you for waiting."

Question: Which of the two approaches to the handling of a delayed call is more likely to make a favorable impression on the caller? Why?

How's Your English?

After reading Appendix C on spelling and word choice, correct the spelling of the following words:

gastly

offence
pleges
vacume
volentary

Office Work

1. Use the telephone directory to type an alphabetical list of the names, addresses, and telephone numbers of ten business firms in your area that might employ you after you graduate.

2. Visit your local telephone office. Become thoroughly acquainted with the latest dial services, including the switchboard systems. Prepare and submit a typewritten report on your visit.

3. When you make regular business telephone calls, note how the switchboard attendants handle your calls. Do they answer promptly? Do they identify their firms clearly? Do they handle your calls courteously?

Prepare typewritten comments on your observations.

4. Certain words and phrases of ancient vintage still used in telephone conversations bear little relation to the telephone of today. The following list of trite and poor expressions are too frequently heard in telephone conversations. Submit a rephrased courteous statement for each of them in typewritten form.

a. Please put Mr. Davis on the phone.

b. He's tied up now, can I have him call you back?

c. He's engaged at the moment, hold the line.

d. OK, I'll have him call you back.

e. Who do you want to talk to?

f. What do you want to talk to him about?

g. I'll put Mr. White on the wire.

h. I'll have to hang up now.

i. Hello, Mr. Ames, National Slippers.

j. Put the receiver on the hook.*

*There is no hook anymore — it's a cradle.

UNIT 7 | The Telephone

PART 3:

Intercom Systems

"Get Joe on that immediately," your employer may say. This does not mean later this afternoon but within the half hour. "Ship this order for delivery tomorrow," means the shipping department must get the order within the next ten minutes.

Interoffice communication systems are installed in business offices for voice transmission, for the transfer of business papers, and for the sending and receiving of written messages. The loudspeaker systems are used to make announcements, issue orders, make requests, receive replies, and to carry on other routine business conversations. Their use greatly reduces the number of interoffice telephone calls, leaving both the switchboard and the extension telephones more accessible for incoming and outgoing calls. Pneumatic tubes and other carrier systems are used to transfer business papers, documents, checks, and cash from one department to another. These conveyor systems do away with a great deal of the slower personal messenger service. Special interoffice writing machines send and receive typewritten and handwritten messages. They may be sent from office to office within an organization and to branch offices in other parts of the country. Automatic devices print tape as orders and bills are typed. The tapes are transmitted to other sections of the country within minutes.

Business Interphone. A recent addition to the field of intercommunications is the Business Interphone developed by the Bell System. Built into the existing telephone, its most advantageous feature is "hands-free" answering and talking, which frees you to take notes, refer to records, and move around while you listen and talk. Stations may be reached by merely dialing one or two digits or pushing a button. Privacy is possible by picking up the receiver.

Some additional features of the Business Interphone are the conference feature, which enables you to confer with as many as five others; direct station selection, which lets you call an intercom station by pushing

The Executone

An Executone system is an independent channel of communication used only for inside calls. It usually consists of a compact desk-top unit for initiating two-way conversations with up to 40 connected staff stations. Calls are announced by a soft chime, and may be answered from anywhere in the room.

Executone Systems

a button; the "Add-On" feature, which connects an intercom station to an outside call; and visual and audible signals which announce incoming calls, tell you when a line is available, and indicate when the line is busy.

Voice Transmission. The Dictograph is one of many non-telephone interoffice communicating devices used for two-way voice transmission. An executive can press a button on the Dictograph to speak to an employee in another unit, or, if he chooses, he can speak to the employees at all units at the same time. Your employer may prefer to use the Dictograph on his desk in his private office to speak to the receptionist in the outer office. He may also find it a more convenient means of direct oral communication with such frequently called locations as the stock room and the shipping room. A separate handset or watchcase earpiece, much like a telephone receiver, can be used instead of the loudspeaker system for private interoffice conversations.

Among the other available intercommunicating devices are the Executone, the Operadio, the Amplicall, the Teletalk, and the Bel-fone.

Teletypewriters. Imagine! You can walk into the TWX (teletypewriter exchange) room in New York City, ask the operator to send a message to your plant in Detroit, and wait while they type an answer.

A teletypewriter operates on the same principle as a telephone except that the typewritten, rather than the spoken, word is transmitted. Messages typed on the standard typewriter keyboard of a teletypewriter

The teletypewriter

A fast, efficient way to communicate in written form, the TWX dial service gives your business versatile and reliable written communications on a message rate basis. Messages may be transmitted at 100 WPM.

American Telephone & Telegraph Co.

can be transmitted and reproduced as they are typed. A message may be reproduced on a single machine or on a whole network of machines, depending upon the central-office connection. Teletypewriters are frequently used for interoffice communication when speed is an important factor and when a written record of the message is preferred.

There are two types of teletypewriter service — teletypewriter exchange service and teletypewriter private-line service. Teletypewriter exchange service (TWX) operates through a central telephone office. Each subscriber has a teletypewriter number and is furnished with a directory of all teletypewriter subscribers in the United States. The rates for teletypewriter messages are considerably lower than the rates for comparable station-to-station long-distance telephone calls.

Before sending a message, the teletypewriter attendant signals the central office and types the exchange and the number she wishes to reach. After the connection has been made and the called unit is ready to receive, the attendant types her message.

Teletypewriter private-line service (TWPL) or leased-wire service messages do not go through a central telephone office. The machines are connected by direct wires. They are used extensively for interoffice communication by firms with a number of branch offices and plants throughout the country.

Both types of service can be used to produce punched paper tape which can be used for filing and/or for sending over high-speed transmission equipment.

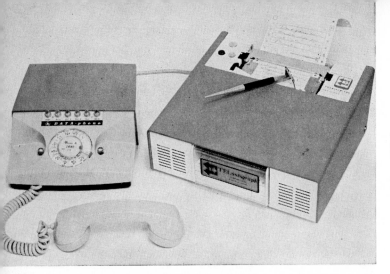

The TELautograph and the DATA-phone

The message is reproduced instantly on the receiving unit.

TELautograph Corporation

DATA-phone Service. DATA-phone service provides the means of transmitting information between business machines over regular telephone lines. This information may be in the form of punched cards, punched paper tape, magnetic tape, or facsimile (drawings, charts, photographs, and handwriting). DATA-phone service is not limited to the transmission of business information. Office workers in medical centers and hospitals use the service to transmit electrocardiograms of the heart and electroencephalograms of the brain.

DATA-phone sets are capable of transmitting at speeds ranging from 100 to 2,700 words per minute. The charge for the service is the same as it would be for a regular long-distance call.

The TELautograph. This intercommunicating device will electrically transmit and receive handwritten messages. A message is written with a metal stylus on a metal plate. As it is written, the message is reproduced instantly by the pen of the receiving unit on a roll of paper.

The TELautograph is usually used for high-speed written communication over short distances: between the warehouse and the main office, between floors in a hotel, and between a paying teller in a bank and an account clerk on a floor above.

Mobile Telephone Service. Radio telephones are frequently installed in automobiles and trucks so that calls may be made directly to and from the vehicle. If you are working for a trucking concern, you will use them continually. Business and residence calls can be made to and from a mobile telephone. City officials, doctors, lawyers, and businessmen who have need of quick communications frequently have mobile service. Mobile telephones are widely used for intercommunication between the vehicles of a single organization and the main office of the organization. Emergency vehicles — fire apparatus, police cars, and ambulances — are usually equipped with privately owned radio telephones. Fleets of taxicabs are frequently equipped with radio telephones to facilitate dispatching.

Television. Closed-circuit television is being used as an intercommunication device by large business organizations. Executives at widespread branches may now hold conferences at which they can see each other as well as talk to each other. In order to help set up such a conference and to arrange agenda and materials with the office workers in other branches before the conference, you, too, may need to use the TV circuit. It is also used in banks and department stores where constant observation is desired. Some railroad lines are now using closed-circuit television to visually assign seats, chairs, rooms, or other space as he reservations are made.

Study Questions

1. What are the principal reasons for installing interoffice communicating systems in business offices?

2. In what instances would you use interoffice voice transmission devices instead of telephones?

3. What is a Dictograph and how does it differ from a Dictaphone?

4. What is a teletypewriter? From a business viewpoint, what advantage does it have over a telephone?

5. What types of messages are transmitted on TELautograph?

6. Who are the most frequent users of mobile telephone service?

7. What are three forms of business information that may be transmitted by DATA-phones?

8. What are some features of the Business Interphone?

What Do You Think?

1. Discuss the reasons for making punched paper tapes of teletypewriter messages.

2. Discuss the business use of closed-circuit television.

Your Personal Qualities

Miss Loretta Jones, the receptionist in the president's office, was asked to find Mr. Albert Williams and request that he see the president as soon as possible about a problem that had come up. Miss Jones called him on the "intercom" system and said: "Mr. Williams — Report to the president at once!"

Question: Is that the way Miss Jones should have conveyed the message? What would be your suggestion for improving the method of her request to Mr. Williams?

How's Your English?

After reading Appendix C, add a suffix to the following words:

hope   tie

shoe   add
sale   drug
love   plan
pale   army

Office Work

1. Visit a newspaper office in your community to study the operation of the teletypewriter and the inter-office communication systems used by the newspaper. Try to decide why each system was installed and how each of them expedites the publication of the paper. Submit a typewritten report of your visit, and be prepared to talk about your visit in the clerical practice class.

2. Prepare an office telephone directory for John Carl Warner and Associates, a firm of architects and planning consultants, from the following list of officers and associates. Arrange the names of the 25 officials in alphabetical order before typing them with their respective titles and Centrex telephone numbers. Type the last name of each official first — in solid capitals.

Name	Title	Centrex Telephone Number
John Carl Warner	President	566-0101
Carl T. Warner	Executive Vice President	566-0102
Martin C. Hunter	Vice President	566-0103
Leonard T. Hart	Vice President	566-0104
James J. Carroll	Secretary	566-0105
Arthur D. Brown, Jr.	Treasurer	566-0106
Donald R. Stewart	Project Manager	566-0110
Joseph C. Margolo	Systems Manager	566-0109
Emery Hirschman	Personnel Director	566-0107
Eugene C. Davis	Construction Supervisor	566-0108
Jean Wiley	Interior Designer	566-0111
Wallace D. Russell	Comptroller	566-0115
Walter E. Nelson	Office Manager	566-0113
Arthur A. Schiller	Construction Supervisor	566-0112
Josef Ausubel	Chief Draftsman	566-0114
David C. Palmer	Project Manager	566-0120
Walter J. Roberts, Jr.	Transportation Engineer	566-0117
Thomas M. White	Public Relations Director	566-0121
Wayburn Evans	Chief of Shop Drawings	566-0118
Lisa T. Guthrie	Landscape Designer	566-0116
Thomas F. O'Brien	Construction Supervisor	566-0119
Ralph T. Spencer	Project Manager	566-0122
Lawrence A. Adams	Construction Supervisor	566-0124
Joseph A. McMurray	Estimator	566-0123
William C. Peterson	Construction Supervisor	566-0125

UNIT 8 | The Receptionist

PART 1:

Meeting People

Although all people have many character-istics in common, a receptionist in her associations with people learns clearly how different each person is from every other person. The reception-ist finds that there are quiet people and noisy ones, shy ones and aggressive ones, uncertain ones and certain ones who approach her desk for informa-tion, advice, entrance to an executive's office, or for a number of other purposes. They must be received by the receptionist with the graciousness that will put each of them at ease and will allow the receptionist to act responsibly in her position.

Receiving Callers. The receptionist possesses, so it seems, a sixth sense, for she must be immediately aware that someone has come to her desk. She must greet the caller promptly, courteously, and if possible, by name. A typical conversation between a receptionist and a caller might be this one:

THE RECEPTIONIST: Good morning, Mr. Norman. How are you today?

THE CALLER: Fine, thank you, Miss Jones, and how are you? I was in the building for a conference and thought I'd stop to see Mr. Nelson for a few minutes about the contract we talked about on the telephone yesterday. Is he free?

THE RECEPTIONIST: Mr. Nelson is talking with a client on a long-distance call, but I'm sure that he will be happy to talk with you as soon as he is fin-ished. Would you care to hang up your coat and hat?

THE CALLER: Thank you, but I'll leave them right here since this will be a very brief conference.

THE RECEPTIONIST: Please have a seat and I'll let Mr. Nelson know you are here as soon as he is free.

Receiving a caller

The receptionist should greet a caller courteously and promptly. She should be interested, alert, and sympathetic.

If the receptionist is on the telephone or busy at the time a caller arrives, she should welcome him briefly and indicate that she will be with him as soon as she has finished with the task that has her attention at the moment.

Be Interested. Every caller deserves the interest and attention of the receptionist. While the caller may be asking for information that the receptionist has provided over and over again to many previous callers, the receptionist must never convey a feeling of annoyance or boredom. Each caller should receive a courteous and complete answer every time the request is made. A possible conversation concerning a much-repeated request is:

> CALLER: Is your company still hiring workers for the new plant on the west side of town?
>
> RECEPTIONIST: Yes, I believe we still need additional personnel. Are you interested in a position with our company at its new plant?

CALLER:	Yes, I am and I would like to fill out an application blank and talk with someone here who can tell me about the opportunities in your new plant. Is there somebody I can talk to?
RECEPTIONIST:	Yes, our employment office is on the third floor. The interviewing hours are from 10 to 12 and 1:30 to 3:30 daily. I would suggest that you go to that office now if you have time.
CALLER:	How long would it take?
RECEPTIONIST:	I am not absolutely sure. However, as soon as you arrive, the receptionist in the employment office will give you an application form which you can fill out, and she will schedule you for an interview immediately. You should be able to see an interviewer within a half hour after you have completed your application form.
CALLER:	Thank you very much. I'll go right up to the employment office.

Be Businesslike in Your Work. A receptionist who obviously appears to be at work creates a favorable impression on the caller who is approaching her desk. A receptionist who seems to be doing nothing, or reading a novel, or eating, drinking, or smoking will hardly convey to the caller that here is an organization of people with definite tasks that must be performed.

While a receptionist should be at work, she does interrupt what she is doing as soon as the caller reaches her desk and gives to him her full attention. The receptionist has the ability to shift her attention so completely that, for the time she is conversing with the caller, he has no feeling that her mind is on the task she interrupted.

Classifications of Callers. Several types of callers will come to the typical business organization in the course of a week. There will be customers, prospective customers, salesmen, creditors, applicants for positions, friends and members of the employer's family, and friends and members of the families of other office employees. Sometimes there will be those with projects and proposals of some general community interest. There will be callers from other offices within the organization and from other branches of the company.

The receptionist must learn the manner in which each type of caller is to be received. You must interpret the wishes of your company with intelligence and flexibility. Most general rules for handling callers must be applied with full awareness that exceptions will need to be made from time to time. To turn away a caller with whom an executive has wanted to talk for several days can create an unfortunate situation.

Customers and prospective customers are usually welcome at any hour. In some offices salesmen are admitted only at specified times so that the executives in charge of purchasing can plan the use of their time to their best advantage. Many firms have definite rules to guide the receptionist in keeping out certain types of callers; for example, many companies do not allow direct solicitation for funds on the premises.

The receptionist will also know the manner in which applicants are to be received. In large organizations they are immediately referred to the personnel department; in smaller offices they may be asked to fill out application blanks.

Members of the executives' families and their friends are usually welcome at any time. If executives are busy when they call, they may be asked to wait. As a rule, personal callers are infrequent in a busy office. In fact, in many companies personal callers and personal telephone calls are not looked upon with favor. Personal emergencies, of course, are graciously handled by the receptionist and other personnel.

Fellow executives and their associates are generally welcome at any time in most offices. Whether or not an executive will see an employee on his staff depends upon the working relationships that have been established in the office. In some instances, the executive maintains a so-called open-door policy, which allows freedom to his staff to come to him as long as he is not otherwise busy. In other instances, an executive expects the receptionist to determine the nature of an employee's request and at that point to decide if it is of a nature to require an appointment with the executive.

Registering Callers. In some companies a record is maintained of all callers. Usually the record will include the caller's name, his business affiliation, the location of his business, the purpose of his call, and the name or title of the executive upon whom he is calling.

REGISTER OF CALLERS____ Monday - May 16, 19--

TIME	NAME AND AFFILIATON	PERSON ASKED FOR	PERSON SEEN	PURPOSE OF CALL
9:30	H. Arnold - Grove Lighting Fixt. Co.	B. D.	✓	Salesman
10:30	L. Crowe - Standard Plumbing	R. J.	✓	"
11:45	C. Apple - Contr. on Merrill Bldg. for lunch appt.	B. D.	✓	Discuss Progress
1:40	L. Rehula - Flexwood Consultant	B. D.	R. J.	Hammer Job
3:50	Messenger from Flexwood	—	✓	Brought Samples

Register of callers

The receptionist can easily approach the caller and request such information if the caller does not provide a business card with the needed information.

Many offices keep a card-file record of the names and other pertinent information about their callers. Often the business card of the caller is stapled to the card and any additional information is recorded below the business card or on the back of the file card. Sometimes there are listed such things as the dates on which calls have been made and any comments that the executive may add that will help the receptionist in dealing with the caller in the future.

This card file of callers should be reviewed from time to time by the receptionist so that the cards of those who no longer call may be discarded.

Scheduling Appointments. In some offices, executives will see no one from outside the organization without an appointment. In other offices, executives will see people only if it is convenient; and in still other places, executives reserve a part of each day for appointments.

Some executives like to make their own appointments, which means that a receptionist must check each request with the executive before she can schedule the desired appointment. In many more instances, however, the receptionist is given the responsibility of making appointments for those callers who have legitimate reasons to see the executive.

The receptionist must be very careful to check her employer's time schedule to avoid conflicting and overlapping appointments.

Making Appointments. The receptionist will receive requests for appointments in a variety of ways. There will be callers who request appointments; there will be telephone calls from prospective callers; and there will be letters requesting appointments. All such requests deserve immediate attention.

If the appointment is requested by a caller, the receptionist should record on a small card the date and hour of the appointment so that the caller will have a record of the pending appointment. When the appointment is requested by telephone, the receptionist should be sure to state very clearly the details of the appointment. Also, when an appointment is requested by letter, the return letter should be complete concerning the details of the appointment.

Recording Appointments. The receptionist must be sure to get the name, address, telephone number, and business affiliation of the person requesting the appointment. Also, there must be recorded the date and the exact time of the appointment; the name of the executive with whom the appointment is made, in case there is more than one executive for whom appointments are made; and the amount of time to be set aside for it.

The details of appointments may be recorded on an ordinary desk calendar if the number of appointments for each day is limited; or they may be recorded on ruled appointment schedule forms if the number of daily appointments is great, or if you are required to schedule appointments for a number of people. The appointment record should also include the executives' appointments away from their offices. Some executives will expect the receptionist to keep appointments of a personal nature on the appointment calendar, such as a luncheon with friends or a shopping date with their wives.

Often the executives will maintain calendars. In such instances, it is important that the receptionist check the executives' calendars frequently to be sure that there are no conflicts. All appointments which the executives make on their own should be recorded on the receptionist's calendar so that she has a complete listing of all appointments. The receptionist will also keep the executives' calendars up to date with appointments she has made. Sometimes the executives' secretaries will perform this task.

The receptionist will prepare for the executives, or for their secretaries, copies of their record of appointments for the day and place them on the appropriate desks. Forthcoming appointments that might require some preliminary planning on the part of the executives might also be noted.

Cancellation of Appointments. From time to time, an executive will find it necessary to cancel an appointment. He may have to leave town earlier than anticipated or not return until a date later than scheduled. As soon as the receptionist knows that an appointment must be canceled, she should talk with the person with whom the appointment is scheduled so that the inconvenience that might be caused by the cancellation can be held to a minimum. If possible, the receptionist should be able to suggest some alternate times for the appointment that must be canceled if the need for the appointment still exists.

Once in a while an appointment will not be canceled until very near the hour of the appointment, which means that the caller will arrive for his appointment only to learn that it must be canceled. It is in such circumstances that the receptionist must be very tactful and very considerate toward the caller.

Conserving Office Time. As a receptionist, you can be of great assistance by referring certain callers to departments or individuals in the firm who can provide information just as well as, or better than, the executive for whom the caller asks. In a number of cases you will be able to supply the information. A conversation that will save the caller's and the executive's time follows:

CALLER: Good morning. I'm George Williams of the Globe Paper Company. I'd like to talk to Mr. Keller about our new mimeograph bond paper. It will greatly improve the appearance of your mimeographing.

Calendar pad appointment record

APPOINTMENTS
WEDNESDAY, MAY 18, 19 —

Time	Engagements	Memorandums
9:00	Mr. Wilson	
		Call C. D. Moore re contract
9:30		
10:00	Mr. L. F. Dawson	
		Call Mr. Calhoun re
10:30		United Fund Drive
	Conference on	
11:00	Personnel Policies	
11:30	Dr. Campbell	
12:00		
12:30	Lunch — D D L — Wilson	Work on Adv. Club talk

Appointment schedule

RECEPTIONIST: All of our office supplies and stationery are ordered by the purchasing department. You should see Mr. Daniels in the purchasing department.

CALLER: But I understand that Mr. Keller has to OK all larger orders.

RECEPTIONIST: I doubt if he would be consulted about an order for duplicating paper. The order would have to come from the purchasing department.

CALLER: Who did you say does the ordering of stationery?

RECEPTIONIST: Mr. Daniels in the purchasing department. His office is on the first floor, Room 100.

CALLER: Thank you. I'll try to see him right away.

Great care must be exercised in referring callers to other offices. Many visitors will insist upon seeing the person in charge of an operation even if the matter could be handled more efficiently by a subordinate. Most callers, however, will appreciate your timesaving suggestions when they learn that their problems can be handled to their satisfaction by another member of the organization.

Refusing Requests for Interviews. When you find it necessary to refuse a caller's request for an interview, you should do so as tactfully as possible. The typical business caller will accept a logical reason for denying the interview, such as: "Mr. Keller is out of town this week," or "Mr. Keller has a full calendar of appointments today," or "Mr. Keller has nothing to do with our advertising program."

There is no magic formula that you can follow in all cases, other than to use good judgment and tact, and to make your refusal sound very impersonal. If the caller is insistent, you can suggest that he leave a note to be given to the executive or that he write a letter requesting an appointment and giving the purpose of his visit. Occasionally a caller will not accept any excuse and you will have to tell him that the executive does not wish to see him.

The Difficult Caller. Occasionally you will encounter a caller who has called to register a personal complaint. The complaint may be real or imaginary, justified or unjustified, depending upon the caller. It is usually against a person within the organization or concerns an error that has been made; rarely is it against a policy of the organization. As a rule, the difficult caller does not have an appointment but insists upon speaking to the president of the firm or some other top executive immediately. He is invariably out of sorts, infuriated, and may even be rude. In a situation like this, it is important that you overlook the caller's apparent rudeness and that you remain calm and courteous. Try to avoid an argument with a caller in this frame of mind. Get him to explain all the details of his complaint and listen sympathetically without committing yourself or your firm.

After you are thoroughly familiar with all the details, you must then decide if the complaint warrants the personal attention of the executive. If you decide against a personal interview, assure the caller that the complaint will be called to the executive's personal attention immediately. The caller may then be willing to submit a written statement if you provide the stationery, or he may be willing to talk to a junior executive of the firm. Above all, do not let the caller leave with the impression that his complaint is without merit or that it will not be given full attention. Many times the receptionist's deft handling of a difficult situation has resulted in keeping a customer for her firm.

Another difficult caller is the nuisance caller, the peddler of knick-knacks, or the solicitor for a very dubious organization, who will use every artful approach to get beyond the reception desk. As a receptionist, you should hesitate before admitting an individual who refuses to give his name or who refuses to state the purpose of his visit. In such cases it is often prudent to consult your employer and to allow him to make the decision.

The Caller Who Must Wait. If it is necessary for the caller to wait before being admitted to the appropriate office, you should try to make the delay as pleasant as possible. The reception room should be well lighted and well ventilated; it should be attractively decorated and well supplied with current reading material. Some firms display their house organs, stockholders' reports, and other business publications in their reception rooms; others display models of the products they manufacture or sell.

When the executive is ready to see the caller, you should tell him and direct him to the executive's office. If a caller is making his first visit to your company, you should escort him to the executive's office and make the necessary introduction in a friendly, informal manner, such as:

> Mr. Keller, may I present Miss Steele? *or*
> Mr. Keller, may I introduce Miss Steele from Standard Systems?
>
> Mr. Keller, this is Mr. Nelson from Standard Products, *or*
> Mr. Keller, this is Mr. Nelson, sales manager for Standard Products.

Interrupting and Terminating Conferences. You should avoid interruptions unless they are absolutely necessary. You may, on the other hand, find executives who wish to have their conferences interrupted for routine business affairs. If an executive follows this practice, he should make his policy known to you at the outset. When interruptions are necessary, they should be made quietly and with as little distraction as possible. You may have to call an executive to take a very important or a very urgent telephone call during an interview. You may also interrupt by quietly bringing in a message written on a small slip of paper, placing it on the executive's desk, and leaving without comment.

Some executives will ask you to help them close interviews with callers who have overstayed their allotted time. As you usher a caller into your employer's office for a short conference at 10:45, you might say: "Mr. Keller, you asked me to remind you of your meeting with the chairman of the board at eleven o'clock." This comment should serve as a tactful reminder to the caller that he should not stay more than fifteen minutes. In some cases the executive may use a buzzer signal, or some other intercommunicating device, to secure your assistance in terminating an interview. After you have heard the buzzer signal, you might enter the office and say: "Mr. Keller, I am sorry, but I must remind you that you are supposed to attend a meeting in the president's conference room in just a few minutes."

No matter how or when the appointment ends, you should be as gracious and sincere when you bid the visitor good-bye as you were when you said hello.

Emergencies. The receptionist should maintain in a very convenient place the telephone numbers of the firm's doctor, a nearby hospital, the nearest police station, the fire department, the firm's maintenance department, and all other sources of immediate help in case of an emergency. In the face of an emergency, the receptionist must maintain a calmness and composure that will enable her to handle the situation wisely.

Reception Desk Coverage. A reception desk should never be left unattended. If you are serving at that desk, you should not leave without asking someone to take your place while you are away. It is important that you conduct yourself in a businesslike manner at the reception desk. Personal telephone calls should be avoided, and long personal chats with fellow employees who happen to go by are never appropriate. The tasks of the receptionist are important, and only through conscientious awareness of their importance can the receptionist do her job in a completely satisfactory manner.

Study Questions

1. What should the receptionist do when a caller approaches her desk?

2. Is it important for the receptionist to be interested in the caller's reason for calling? Explain.

3. "Oh, when I have nothing to do I read a novel or a fashion magazine at the desk." What is your reaction to a receptionist who makes this remark?

4. What types of callers may the receptionist be expected to handle in the course of her work?

5. For what purpose would a receptionist register callers?

6. What kind of information is generally recorded if a register of callers is maintained?

7. Describe briefly the type of information that would be maintained in a card-file record of callers.

8. In what ways may appointments be made?

9. What information does the receptionist need for each person requesting an appointment?

10. What kind of record does the receptionist make of each appointment which she makes?

11. How does the receptionist know of the appointments made by an executive?

12. What may be the receptionist's responsibilities concerning the reception desk?

13. How should the receptionist handle the person who is refused an appointment?

14. Describe how the receptionist might interrupt an executive when he is in the middle of an appointment.

15. What sources of assistance should the receptionist know in order to handle emergencies?

What Do You Think?

1. One of the executives for whom you work calls you into his office to tell you that he must leave town at noon instead of at 6 p.m. as originally scheduled. You note that he has three appointments for the afternoon. What would you do about these appointments?

2. An out-of-town caller comes to see an executive without an appointment. The executive has set aside certain morning hours to receive callers. It is now afternoon. The caller says that he is leaving town that night. What would you do?

3. Two callers appear for 3 p.m. appointments. One is listed on your calendar; the other is not. The one that is not listed was apparently made by the executive when he met the caller at a downtown restaurant earlier in the week. What will you do about this matter?

4. One of the executives has a crowded appointment schedule for the afternoon. Shortly before 2:30 a caller appears who says he must see this executive for a few minutes immediately. At the time there is someone in the office with the executive and a person waiting to see him at 2:30. What would you do?

5. A caller asks to see an executive. However, he refuses to give you his name or indicate the purpose of his visit. What would you do?

Your Personal Qualities

Miss Jane Layman was asked to relieve the receptionist while she went on an errand for one of the executives. While the receptionist was away, a caller appeared who wanted to see Mr. Smith, one of the company executives. The caller did not have an appointment, but since Mr. Smith was in his office alone, Jane told the caller to walk into Mr. Smith's office and pointed out to him which office was Mr. Smith's. After fifteen minutes, the caller leaves and shortly thereafter Mr. Smith comes out of his office and angrily states: "Why did you let that man in my office? Didn't you know that I don't see callers during the morning hours? I reserve the morning hours for desk work."

Questions: 1. What was wrong in the way Jane handled the caller?

2. In what way could Jane have avoided the annoyance caused Mr. Smith?

How's Your English?

After reviewing the rules on the use of the period, comma, semicolon, question mark, exclamation point, apostrophe, and colon in Appendix B, place the proper punctuation marks in the following recorded conversation:

RECEPTIONIST: Good morning Mr Booth May I help you

VISITOR: Yes Miss Heller I would like to see Mr Atwood Its an emergency

RECEPTIONIST: Im sorry Mr Booth Mr Atwood is not in yet

VISITOR: Not in yet When do you expect him I must see him and no one else

RECEPTIONIST: He telephoned to say that he would make a call on his way in He should get here by 1015

VISITOR: 1015 Thats almost an hour from now I'll make another call and be back not later than 1030 Tell him its vital that I see him

RECEPTIONIST: I shall make an appointment for you for 1030 Mr Atwood has a meeting scheduled for 1100 will that give you time enough

VISITOR: Yes if I can see him promptly at 1030

Office Work

The Modernaire Cosmetics Company has executive offices in New York City. Mr. Carl Able is vice-president in charge of promotional activities. The following situations take place during the course of one morning:

1. Mrs. Suzy Walls, a fashion editor for a popular magazine, arrives at 9:20 for an appointment scheduled for 9:30.

2. A caller with a suitcase comes in at 10 and requests an appointment with Mr. Able. He tells the receptionist that he has a very interesting display that can be adapted to the products that are sold by this company and he is sure that Mr. Able will want to use the display for the exhibition.

3. A young lady comes in and tells the receptionist that she is interested in working in the company. Her major in college was art, and she believes she would enjoy working in a department that is in charge of promotion. The young lady does not know that there is a central employment office for the company.

4. Mrs. Able, the wife of the vice-president, comes in at 11:50. Her husband is to have lunch with her at 12:00. Someone is in Mr. Able's office when she arrives.

Consider what the receptionist and the caller might say in each of these situations. Be prepared to act as either the receptionist or the caller before your class. Also, be prepared to evaluate the manner in which your classmates handle each of the situations that you observe.

Office Work Assignments

30: Recording Appointments

The receptionist makes the following appointments for one of her employers, Mr. Burns, for Thursday, November 15. The date preceding each item is the date on which each appointment for November 15 is recorded:

November 1 — A 9:30 appointment is scheduled for Mr. T. F. Ford, who wrote requesting a morning appointment on the 15th.

November 6 — Mr. Sherwood, a close business associate of Mr. Burns, calls to see if Mr. Burns can meet him for lunch at the Essex Club on the 15th at 12. You check with Mr. Burns; his answer is "Yes."

November 8 — Mr. Wells of the sales department calls to schedule a meeting for four company officials and himself in Mr. Burns' office at 11 on the morning of the 15th. This will last a half hour.

November 9 — Mr. Burns asks you to call Mr. T. Myers of a local advertising agency to see if Mr. Myers can come to the office at 2 on the 15th. Mr. Myers is free to come.

November 12 — Mr. Burns asks you to make appointments with two of his staff for Thursday. He would like to see Mr. Cansler at 3:15 and Mr. Derwood at 3:30.

November 14 — Mr. T. F. Jackson calls from another town to see if he can talk with Mr. Burns for a few minutes early the next morning. You schedule an appointment for 9.

November 14 — Mr. Ford's secretary calls to cancel the appointment at 9:30 tomorrow, inasmuch as Mr. Ford will be unable to arrive in town as early as scheduled. He would like a late afternoon appointment. An appointment is scheduled for 4 p.m.

November 14 — Mr. B. H. Mellon calls to see if he can have an appointment tomorrow morning with Mr. Burns. A 30-minute meeting is scheduled for 9:30.

November 14 — Mr. Burns asks you to check on a possible appointment at 10 the next day with Miss Jennie Gales of personnel. She is free to come.

November 14 — Mr. Jack Colman of the advertising department calls to see if he can talk with Mr. Burns the next day. An appointment is scheduled for 3 p.m.

Record Mr. Burns' appointments for November 15, in the order in which they were made, on a form similar to that illustrated on page 227. Then type a copy of these appointments for Mr. Burns on a form similar to that illustrated on page 227.

UNIT 8 | The Receptionist

PART 2:

Business Speech

       The receptionist represents her company and its executives each time she meets and talks with someone. The impressions that many visitors to a company have are formed through associations with the people in that company. The receptionist must always be mindful of her manner and her approach to people. While the large company may have women who serve full time as receptionists, few office workers can do their work without meeting callers and company associates who deal with their employers.

    The Personality of the Receptionist. When an office worker turns to greet a caller, it is the sum total of her personality and appearance that confronts the visitor. Her poise, her self-confidence, her gestures, her voice, her hairstyle, her dress, and her words are all ingredients of the impression that develops. The competent receptionist is a poised, self-confident young woman who moves graciously as she turns to greet the caller. She is a young woman who dresses attractively, yet quietly. Her voice is well modulated, her words are appropriate and soft-spoken.

    As a receptionist, you will have the opportunity to deal with many different people. You must have a deep liking and respect for others in order to convey a sincere interest in those with whom you must associate as receptionist.

    Your Appearance. You have already spent some time in discussing the types of clothing that are suited for the business office. You are also acquainted with the need to "know yourself" — to know the types of clothing that are best for your figure and your personality. You will want to wear clothes that enhance your self-confidence and that are comfortable, yet attractive.

    The well-groomed look is one that can be acquired by every young lady who takes time to keep her hair clean and becomingly styled, her

The receptionist

The receptionist assumes the role of office hostess.

clothes impeccably clean and pressed, her face and hands well scrubbed. Her shoes and stockings, too, should be clean and in good condition.

The first impression is largely related to the way you look. Be sure your appearance is in harmony with your personality and conveys to the visitor the kind of person you are.

Manners. The accepted way of behaving in a variety of situations is what we mean by "manners." As a child you were taught the manners for talking to those older than you, the manners that were expected in a shop, at an afternoon tea, at a meeting. So, too, in the business office there is a code of etiquette that the receptionist knows well and uses naturally and with graciousness.

The receptionist knows how to greet people, how to introduce an executive to a visitor who is a stranger, and how to create an atmosphere of friendliness and helpfulness.

A receptionist knows that she must temporarily shift from the work she is doing to give full attention to the person who has come to her desk. To appear annoyed at the visitor because she feels she has been interrupted is not appropriate behavior. The receptionist should remain calm and be attentive to the visitor, for she knows that dealing with people effectively is one of the most important tasks which she performs.

Business Speech. One's speech habits are a very important factor in the person's total personality. When you have seen an impersonator of some famous person, have you noted that quite frequently it is the voice and gestures related to speaking that the impersonator has assumed that convey the famous person's identity to the audience? Your speech habits reflect you. You want to be sure, then, that they serve you in the most favorable fashion. You may have acquired speech habits that are bothersome to others. Therefore, you will want to spend some time in understanding how you speak.

Proper pronunciation, good enunciation, careful choice of words all contribute to effectiveness in business speech. The receptionist who wants to be fully qualified for her position will strive to improve her speech habits.

Expressing Ideas. Have you heard the comment, "I know what I want to say, but I don't know how to say it"? Now, the person who makes such a comment is really saying that up to this point he doesn't know *what he wants to say.* Much mental activity precedes the spoken words that convey an idea. The person who is an effective speaker is one who thinks well, who is able to outline mentally what he hopes to express. If ideas are worth presenting, they deserve your careful and thorough attention preliminary to being shared with others.

In the business office it is extremely important that what is said is clearly understood. Misunderstandings can cause conflict between people and may be disastrous for the business enterprise. As an office worker you will want what you say to mean what you intend it to mean. Much time is lost by the person who makes a comment which is followed by another person's comment and then must be followed by the first person saying, "Oh, you didn't understand what *I meant.* . . ." If the first person had carefully expressed his idea, this dialogue would not have been necessary.

Ideas must be presented clearly so that (1) the speaker conveys what is on his mind; (2) the person listening understands what the speaker is saying; and (3) the two persons talking can make progress in their conversation.

Voice. A pleasing voice is a valuable asset in the business office. Do you not like to listen to a person whose voice is of fine quality? A harsh, monotonous voice is not so pleasant to hear as one that is mellow and flexible. The quality of the voice is determined by the manner in which the speaker uses his speech mechanism. The effective speaker is one who had learned to control his breathing so that the strength of his voice varies with the thoughts he wishes to convey. Such a speaker has a relaxed throat and neck and he makes full use of the jaws, lips, and tongue.

The voice automatically will register emotions, so it is important for you to mean what you say. For example, to say, "I am very sorry that Mr. Jones is not in," but have no *feeling* of "being sorry" will not have the meaning intended, for your voice will convey a counteremotion to the listener.

You have heard others say, "She has a wonderful telephone voice." Such a comment usually refers to the quality of the speaker's voice. You will want to cultivate good control of your speaking so that your voice will be well modulated and interesting for those who will listen to you.

Pronunciation. As a receptionist, you will want to use the pronunciation of words most readily understood and accepted in the office in which you are employed. It is sometimes difficult to find an acceptable standard of pronunciation inasmuch as standards differ from place to place. What is an acceptable pronunciation in Boston may not be acceptable in Atlanta. Speech authorities say that a person should attempt to follow the usage of the educated people of the community. Of course, if you should be working in a community that is in a different part of the country from the one in which you grew up, you will find that people are very tolerant of the differences they will find in your pronunciation. In fact, to attempt immediately to imitate the speech of a new area is to make your speech sound affected. Affectation in speech means that you are attempting to speak in a manner that is unfamiliar to you under normal conditions. A young lady from Atlanta who is working in Boston, let us say, will not be able to assume the pronunciation of the new city without sounding affected. Most people find such assumed speech patterns unattractive.

You will want to be careful to avoid pronunciation errors that are caused by careless speech habits. Some errors that are made frequently include:

	FAULTY	CORRECT
Dropping the sound of "g" in words ending in "ing"	— "workin"	for "working"
	"goin"	for "going"
	"typin"	for "typing"
Dropping the sound of "r" in words ending in "r"	— "fatha"	for "father"
	"numba"	for "number"
Adding the sound of "r" when it is not called for	— "idear"	for "idea"
	"Cubar"	for "Cuba"
Using the wrong vowel sound	— "fur"	for "for"
	"git"	for "get"
	"Toosday"	for "Tuesday"
Substituting one syllable for another	— "chimley"	for "chimney"
	"punkin"	for "pumpkin"
	"libery"	for "library"

As you know, the dictionary will aid you when you are uncertain of the pronunciation of a word. Consult it when you are unfamiliar with the correct pronunciation of a word you wish to use in your business speech.

Enunciation. The precision with which you pronounce each word is what is meant by "enunciation." The office worker must strive to develop precision in pronunciation because it is very important that she be understood. Two of the most common errors in enunciation are running words together and the failure to sound all the syllables of a word. "*Didya*" for "*did you*," "*gimme*" for "*give me*," "*whatchagonna*" for "*what are you going*," "*uster*" for "*used to*," "*lemme*" for "*let me*" are examples.

There are many words in the English language that are very similar to at least one other word. It is important, therefore, that such words be enunciated well if the listener is to grasp the word intended. Words of this nature include the following:

ascend-assent	immigration-emigration
cease-seize	irrelevant-irreverent
council-counsel	picture-pitcher
descend-descent	sense-since
eminent-imminent	statue-stature-statute
incidents-incidence	while-wild-wile
attack-attach	worth-work-word

Diction. The use, choice, and arrangement of words is known as *diction.* Good diction is an asset to any worker in the modern business office. If you are to speak properly, you must choose words that are recognized as correct by authorities in the American language. You must choose words that will be acceptable to the people you address and will lead to a favorable response.

Colloquial Words and Expressions. As you know, the spoken language of a society is constantly changing, and there will always be at a given time certain words and expressions that are considered satisfactory for informal communication but are not appropriate for more formal situations, such as communication in the business office. Often these colloquial words and expressions lend ease and naturalness to what is said; however, they must be used with care. Seldom are they as appropriate as the more fully accepted words that convey the same meaning. Some examples are:

PREFERRED USAGE

around for about	I will leave the office *about* five o'clock.
contact for get in touch with or call or talk with	I will *call* Mr. Jones when I arrive in Chicago tomorrow.

| posted for informed | Please be sure to keep Mr. Pearson *informed* of your progress. |
| wait on for wait for | Will you be able to *wait for* Mr. Ray tonight? |

Slang. Although colloquialisms are sometimes acceptable, slang cannot be condoned in the business office. Slang is made up of widely used current terms which have a forced meaning such as "to get with it" meaning "to cooperate" or "dig this" meaning "understand this." Words or expressions of this type are used in direct defiance of good language usage.

The wide usage of certain slang words and phrases as "on the ball" or "to miss the boat" have caused them to lose some of the undesirable quality that they had in the past; however, their usage in the business office should be very limited. A vocabulary made up of *"swell," "lousy," "guy," "pencil pusher,"* and other slang reflects a very weak English background.

Mannerisms. Most people use more than their vocal mechanisms when they utter words to convey thoughts. They use eyes, facial expressions, gestures with the hands and arms, and their whole body at times to assist them in expressing their thoughts. The proper use of the supporting movements can enhance a person's ability to communicate. At the same time, improper use can be highly distracting. There are many unattractive mannerisms that one should avoid. Excessive use of the hands, unnatural use of the eyes, distorted facial expressions can detract from a conversation. The office worker wants to be sure that she has no mannerisms that are unpleasant to her associates or anyone else with whom she deals.

Speech Courtesy. In the process of communicating with others in the business office, the receptionist must give attention to the need to be courteous. Courtesy requires that she be a good listener. To "do all the talking" is seldom, if ever, the appropriate thing to do. Furthermore, interrupting a person while he is still talking is considered highly discourteous. For example, when the receptionist steps into an executive's office to give him verbally some information he has requested for a conference that is under way, the receptionist should wait quietly at the door until there is an appropriate pause in the conversation.

Also, courtesy requires that the receptionist give attention to the person she is addressing or to the one who is talking to her. To talk with one person while you are looking at another person or some part of the room is inexcusable behavior. Effective public speakers are said to be those who can establish "eye-contact" with their audiences. Then the listeners feel the speaker is talking to them personally. So it is in a two-way conversation. To talk directly to the person by looking at the person is to convey to the listener that you are talking to him.

Effectiveness in oral communication, which is the heart of your task as a receptionist, can improve if you give attention to what you say and how you say it.

Study Questions

1. Why should the clerical practice student study the tasks a receptionist performs?

2. What personal qualities of a receptionist will a visitor most likely notice initially?

3. What constitutes good grooming for a receptionist?

4. Why should the receptionist use good manners "naturally"?

5. Give some examples of rules of manners that the receptionist must know thoroughly.

6. Why is it necessary to express an idea clearly?

7. Why should the office worker avoid affectation in her speech?

8. Cite examples of pronunciation errors that can occur when an office worker is careless about her speech.

9. Illustrate each of the two types of errors in enunciation which are discussed in this Part.

10. Why must a receptionist give attention to diction when speaking with callers?

11. What advice would you give an office worker who asked you if it is proper to use colloquial words and expressions?

12. Why should slang be avoided in an office?

13. Cite some mannerisms that can be annoying to listeners.

14. In what way can a receptionist convey the fact that she is a good listener?

15. Why is speech courtesy of importance to the receptionist as well as all other office workers?

What Do You Think?

1. You see the following classified advertisement in the "Help Wanted" section of your newspaper: "Needed: Receptionist for large manufacturing company. Must know how to type-write."

What personal qualities do you think an interviewer for the company will want to evaluate when he interviews candidates for the position?

2. In what ways would you think the personality of a receptionist might differ from that of a bookkeeping machine operator?

Your Personal Qualities

Betty Sands is the receptionist at the Smith Iron Works Company. As the receptionist, Betty overhears much of the business affairs of her company. One day a junior executive, Mr. Tanner, asks Betty:

"Someone was in my office this morning and he told me that the company is moving out of this town. I had never heard this before. Is this rumor true, Betty?"

"Mr. Tanner," said Betty, "I have no information for *you* on this matter. I would suggest that you forget about the matter. Why do you listen to such rumors?"

Mr. Tanner became very angry, hurried out of the office, and on his way out said, "Well, I have other sources for finding out what I want to know."

Questions: 1. Did Betty handle the situation in the most effective way?

2. Did Mr. Tanner behave appropriately?

3. What should Betty do next?

How's Your English?

Read the information on the use of the semicolon in Appendix B. Read each of the following sentences, indicating whether or not the semicolon has been used correctly:

1. Good grooming is important for the receptionist; therefore, it deserves careful attention.

2. You will want a hairstyle that is becoming for you; and it need not be the high-fashion style at the moment.

3. A competent receptionist uses good diction; the wise use, selection, and arrangement of words.

4. Dropping the "g" on words ending in "ing" reflects a careless speech pattern; therefore this practice should be avoided.

5. The receptionist must possess certain personal qualities, for example, flawless manners, pleasant voice; and correct speech habits.

Office Work

1. Make a list of words and expressions that you have heard that illustrate the slurring or improper sounding of syllables. What suggestions would you make to help your fellow students eliminate these habits?

2. Make a list of colloquial words and expressions that you and your classmates use that you feel would not be appropriate in a business office. Opposite each word indicate what you would say if you were talking to an office associate.

3. Make a list of slang words and expressions that you hear daily. Opposite each word or expression write its equivalent.

4. Listen to the voice quality of others. Identify a voice that you feel is pleasant and that you enjoy hearing. Describe in as much detail as possible what makes the voice pleasing to you.

Office Work Assignments

31: Effective Business Speech

Each member of the class is to prepare a two-minute speech on one of the following topics or on a topic chosen by you and approved by the instructor:

The Personality of a Good Receptionist

Why Good Diction Is Important to the Receptionist

Why a Business Office Needs a Competent Receptionist

A Receptionist I Know

In preparing your speech, plan to use the following checklist as a reminder of some of the characteristics of effective speech. You will use this checklist in rating other students who present their speeches to the class.

Expression of Ideas

Did the speaker —

1. have a clear idea of his topic?
2. make clear what his main points were?
3. express his ideas with precision?
4. develop each idea adequately to communicate what was intended?

Voice

Did the speaker —

5. talk at a pace that was appropriate?
6. talk with proper emphasis and variation in expression?
7. talk with adequate force so that everyone could hear easily?

Pronunciation

Did the speaker —

8. pronounce all words correctly? (List words mispronounced.)

Enunciation

Did the speaker —

9. use proper enunciation? (List all words and expressions that were poorly enunciated.)

Diction

Did the speaker —

10. express his thoughts with the most appropriate words and phrases? (List words and expressions that you feel were not good choices.)

Colloquial Words and Expressions

Did the speaker —

11. avoid colloquial words and expressions? (What colloquial words or expressions were used that you feel were not appropriate?)

Slang

Did the speaker —

12. avoid slang words and expressions? (List slang words and expressions that were undesirable.)

Mannerisms

Did the speaker —

13. use gestures and facial expressions that contributed to the effectiveness of expression?

14. avoid mannerisms that were distracting and unbecoming? (List mannerisms which you felt detracted from the effectiveness of expression.)

UNIT 9 | Business Filing and Records Control

PART 1:

Records Management

Every day millions of documents are created in offices throughout the United States. Each year business and government organizations spend billions of dollars recording and retaining information.

Because of the growth and complexity of business, the need for information is receiving considerable attention in today's business office.

Records management is concerned with developing and controlling effective information systems. Since information is created and disseminated in so many different ways, a records management program will play an important role in the "business intelligence" of the organization for which you work.

Specifically, records management is concerned with these six broad areas:

1) *Records Retention and Disposition:* Determining what records should be retained, where and for how long; determining when and how obsolete records should be destroyed; establishing and maintaining record centers.

2) *Files Management:* Developing effective information (or file) systems; determining the specific type of equipment and supplies needed for each system; controlling and improving the system.

3) *Information Retrieval:* Developing effective and rapid methods of retrieving information, either manually or mechanically, photographically or automatically.

4) *Records Protection:* Determining the vital records of an organization and developing a program for protecting these records. (Vital records are those needed to continue operating after a disaster.)

245

The file clerk

Beginning office workers can expect to have a part in files management. An office worker's responsibility in helping administer that phase of an information system is important.

5) *Correspondence Management:* Determining and developing the most effective way of communicating by letter.

6) *Forms and Report Control:* Determining the need for specific information; developing the proper method of obtaining and disseminating needed information.

The Need for Records. Any records which you file presumably are essential for the continued and successful operation of your firm. These records are the "memory" of the organization. In today's business office, vital decisions are based upon available, up-to-date information. The risks are too great for the executive's decisions to be based upon guesses, hunches, or hearsay. A businessman cannot hope to remain in a competitive field without a comprehensive information system.

As a beginning office worker, you will be particularly concerned with one important segment of records management: *files management.* The files are an important link in the information system of every office. The importance of a well-planned and well-administered filing system cannot be overemphasized. The files are more than paper, guides, folders, and equipment — they are *information systems.* Your responsibility in administering a system is an important one.

The Files. "Where is it? I know I put it away carefully so that I could find it quickly — but where?" These are thoughts that race through the mind of the file clerk who searches nervously for the contract, the report, or the letter for which the employer is impatiently waiting. If only it had been filed correctly! Don't let this happen to you!

What is *filing*? It is a system of arranging and storing business papers, cards, forms, catalogs, and other items in a neat, orderly, and efficient manner so that they may be located readily when they are wanted.

Filing is one of the most important — yet one of the most neglected — of all the duties performed by office workers. Errors in filing may appear to be humorous in cartoons, but they are expensive and exasperating in a business situation. Your employer doesn't expect to have to wait for filed copies of his correspondence and other business papers. In order to find material efficiently, you must follow standard rules and procedures of filing. You cannot make numerous exceptions to the rules and then rely entirely upon your memory to locate every business paper.

Not only must you know the rules of filing and apply them, but you must also keep your files up to date by devoting some part of every day to filing. Otherwise, you may have to search through the files and then the unfiled material on your desk when you receive a request for filed material.

Systems of Filing. Making it possible to locate information quickly is an important objective of filing. Filing systems are usually developed around the way records are used or requested. Since a great many business records refer to the name of a person or company, these names often determine the type of system that will be used. This system of filing is known as an *alphabetic name file* and is widely used. When you look up a telephone number in the directory, you are using this basic system.

Another filing system found in a business office is an *alphabetic subject file*. A sales office might have such a file in which some of the subjects might be: "Applications for Sales Positions," "Sales Quotas," "Agenda for Sales Meetings," and so on. The classified section of the telephone directory — the Yellow Pages — is an example of alphabetic subject filing. Most offices maintain both an alphabetic name file and an alphabetic subject file.

In order to locate the names of customers and prospects by the part of the country in which they are located, many offices maintain a *geographic file*. A geographic file might be devised around the names of certain states and then further subdivided by cities, towns, or sales territories. Sales offices and publishers often use geographic systems.

Since many documents are identified by number rather than name, *numeric files* are frequently used in business offices. Large insurance companies, for example, file insurance policies by policy number. In addition to the main numeric file, an alphabetic name file of all policyholders (listing their policy numbers) is also maintained.

One more basic filing system is the *chronological file*, a file maintained by dates. A publisher might maintain a chronological file to show the expiration dates of magazine subscriptions. Such a file would enable the publisher to send out letters to subscribers urging renewal before the expiration date of their subscriptions.

The Care of Records. For business purposes, records are classified in four categories: vital, important, useful, and nonessential. All records considered essential for the re-creation of an organization (such as those which may be used as a basis for loans or those needed to prove loss after any type of disaster) are classified as *vital records*. Over 40 percent of the business firms that lose their vital records find it impossible to continue operating. These records may be protected in fireproof safes or vaults, by microfilming, or by duplicating and storing copies in another location or vital records center.

Now let us consider the next two classifications: important and useful. *Important records* are those which could be replaced — but at considerable expense. These records should also receive a degree of protection. *Useful records* are those which can be replaced — but at some inconvenience. They should be retained in ordinary steel filing equipment.

Finally, you will be concerned with nonessential records. Nonessential records are those which soon outlive their usefulness — perhaps they should not have been filed in the first place. They should be destroyed to save valuable floor and file space as well as to reduce the hazard of fire. Records management experts have estimated that at least 40 percent of all material in office files is nonessential and may be safely destroyed.

Files Used by the Office Worker. You may be expected to decide what material should be filed and where. A great deal of the material that reaches your employer's desk (advertisements, announcements, etc.) need not be filed at all. Briefing sessions with your employer will help you determine the retention value of many of these records. Many companies are now adopting record retention schedules, which will simplify your problem. In addition to the regular office files, you may also be asked to maintain a separate file of your employer's personal correspondence as well as keep the records of his civic or professional work.

To help your employer's day run smoothly, you will use a *chronological file*. These files are kept for appointments, conferences, and other important business engagements. A desk calendar is one form of chronological file. More elaborate chronological files of pending or follow-up work may be maintained in a *tickler file*, a file arranged in a calendar

Peerless Steel Equipment Company

Vertical files

sequence. Since it is impossible to remember all the things that must be acted upon on a certain day, such a file must be developed and continually "watched" so that appropriate and prompt action may be taken.

Central Files. Many firms maintain a central file of all materials of interest to related departments or to the entire organization. It is also possible that a department within an organization may centralize its files.

Since the files operators in a central file are well trained and supervised, better and faster record service is possible. A central file also eliminates the retention of duplicate material and makes possible more efficient use of floor space and filing equipment. The central file should always serve as an active information file — not a place for filing inactive records. You should know what materials are sent to the central files and how to use the central files for maximum effectiveness.

Vertical Files. Vertical file cabinets are commonly made in five heights: two-drawer, three-drawer, four-drawer, five-drawer, and six-drawer. The two-drawer cabinet is often placed beside a desk and is used for filing very active records. Three-drawer cabinets are frequently used as counters, as well as filing cabinets, and are often called counter-height cabinets. Although the five-drawer cabinet is growing in popularity, the four-drawer height is still the most commonly used cabinet. The five-drawer cabinet can hold 20 percent more records in the same amount of floor space occupied by a four-drawer file. The six-drawer file is also receiving acceptance in the office, although both the fifth and sixth drawers are out of the reach of office workers and ladders are required in filing and retrieving records from them.

Since a great variety of file equipment, in size, quality, and effectiveness, is available, careful attention must be given when selecting the

Open-shelf file

proper equipment to be used for the particular filing system maintained by your organization.

Shelf Files. Because of the increasing number of records that must be maintained in expensive office space, many organizations are installing shelf files. In shelf filing, papers are held in folders placed on shelves in a vertical position. The folders resemble those used in drawer file cabinets except the tabs on the folders and guides are on the side (instead of the top). Some shelf files are built with open shelves; others are equipped with sliding doors to protect the records. Some can be equipped with sliding shelves which serve as a work area. Units that are seven or eight shelves high conserve the maximum amount of floor space while retaining adequate reference accessibility.

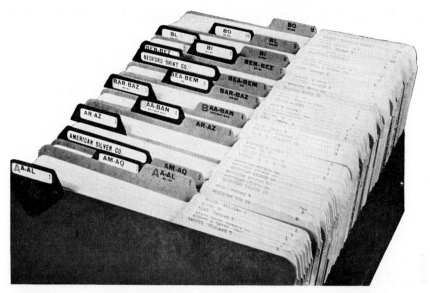

Shaw-Walker Company

Alphabetic index for a correspondence file

While considerable floor space can be saved by using shelf files, many authorities believe that individual records cannot be filed or retrieved as quickly as in vertical files, particularly when sliding doors are used. They feel shelf filing is most effective for the retention of semiactive or inactive records.

Alphabetic Correspondence Filing. As an office worker, you will be most concerned with an alphabetic name or subject file (often combined in one system). Let's take a look inside a file drawer.

Each drawer in a vertical correspondence file contains two different kinds of filing supplies: guides and folders. The *guides* in an alphabetic correspondence file divide the drawer into alphabetic sections and serve as signposts for quick reference. They also provide support for the folders, adding body to the files.

File folders hold the papers in a vertical position in the file drawer. They are made of heavy sheets of paper and serve as a container to keep papers together.

Guides. Guides are heavy cardboard, pressboard, or bristol-board sheets the same size as the folders. Extending over the top of each guide is a tab upon which is marked or printed a notation or title called a caption. The caption indicates the alphabetic range of the material filed in folders behind the guide. This tab may be an extension of the guide itself, or it may be an attached metal or plastic tab. Sets of guides may be purchased with printed letters or combinations of letters and numbers that may be used with any standard filing system. Other guide tabs are blank, and the specific captions are made in the user's office.

Guides may be obtained with a rod projection that extends below the body of the guide. The projection contains a metal eyelet through which a file drawer rod may be run, thus holding the guides in place and preventing the folders from slipping down in the drawer.

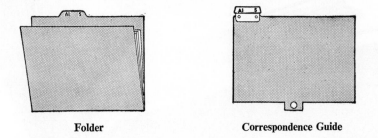

Folder   Correspondence Guide

For rapid retrieval, no more than ten folders should be filed behind any one guide. The number of guides needed, however, will depend on the activity of the file and the amount of material in each folder. Anywhere from 15 to 25 guides per file drawer will facilitate finding and filing in most filing systems.

Kinds of Guides. Guides are classified as primary and auxiliary (or secondary). The *primary guides* indicate the major divisions — alphabetic, numeric, subject, geographic, or chronological — into which the filing system is divided. *Auxiliary guides* are subdivisions of the primary guide and are used to highlight certain types of information, for example, to indicate the placement of special folders (such as those for "Applications" or "Branch Offices"). They are also used to indicate a section of the file in which many folders with the same first indexing unit are placed. For example, if a file contains many individual folders for the name "Brown," an auxiliary guide with the caption "Brown" might be placed in the file drawer to facilitate retrieval.

Folders. A folder is made of a sheet of heavy paper (manila, kraft, pressboard, or red rope stock) that has been folded once so that the back is about one-half inch higher than the front. Folders are larger than the papers they contain so as to protect them. Two standard folder sizes are "letter size" for papers that are 8 1/2″ x 11″ and "legal cap" for papers that are 8 1/2″ x 13″.

Folders are cut across the top in two ways: so that the back is straight (straight-cut), or so that the back has a tab that projects above the top of the folder. Such tabs bear captions that identify the contents of each folder. Tabs vary in width and position. The tabs of a set of folders that are "one-half cut" are half the width of the folder, and have only two positions. "One-third cut" folders have three positions, each tab occupying a third of the width of the folder. Another standard tabbing is "one-fifth cut" which, as you can guess, has five positions. There are also folders with "two-fifths cut," with the tabs in the third and fourth, or fourth and fifth, positions. Some folders have plastic tabs, usually third or fifth cut, into which a typed identification is inserted. Other folders "hang" from a metal frame placed inside the file drawer.

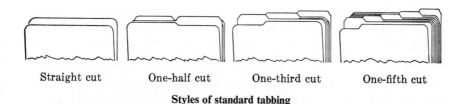

Straight cut   One-half cut   One-third cut   One-fifth cut

Styles of standard tabbing

Miscellaneous Folders. A miscellaneous folder is maintained for every alphabetic primary guide. When there are fewer than six documents to, from, or about the same person or firm, these documents are placed in a folder bearing the identical caption of the primary guide it serves. They are called miscellaneous folders because they contain documents of more than one person or firm.

Individual Folders. When six documents to, from, or about one person or subject have accumulated in the miscellaneous folder, an individual folder for this material is prepared. The caption on the tab of an individual folder identifies the correspondent. Obviously, materials will be retrieved faster if filed in an individual folder instead of a miscellaneous folder.

Special Folders. When an organization files a large amount of material that relates to one subject (such as applications for employment or correspondence with a branch office), all this related material is placed in a special folder. The caption identifies the subject or the name describing the material. A special folder might be prepared to file all identical surnames, thus removing them from the miscellaneous folder. For example, all the "Smiths" might be removed from the miscellaneous folder and placed in a special folder, thus allowing faster retrieval.

Positions of Folders. Since the tabs of the folders occupy only part of the top of the folders, they may appear in several positions. In any filing system, the tabs in each position should be uniform in width; that is, all the tabs at first position are the same width, all the tabs in the next position are the same width, and so on.

A specific position should be designated for each type of folder. Folders with tabs in the second position of a one-fifth cut may be used for miscellaneous folders; folders with tabs in third position may be used for special folders; and folders in the last position may be used for individual folders. Naturally, the selection of the cut and position will depend on the type of system devised for each office.

Capacity of Folders. Folders should never become overcrowded. They should contain no more than one inch of filing material. Most file folders have *score lines* at the bottom that are used to expand the capacity of each folder. When the folder begins to fill up, the first score is creased; as more paper accumulates, the remaining scores are creased. If the scores are creased too soon, the documents will curl in the folder. On the other hand, the folder will bulge if the score is not creased when necessary. If it is necessary to have a large number of papers accumulate in one folder, expansion folders should be used.

When the capacity of a folder is finally reached, the material should be subdivided into two or more folders. These subdivisions can be made chronologically (Jones Company — *Jan–Mar*, *Apr–June*, etc.) or by subject (Jones Company — *Orders*, Jones Company — *Receipts*). The subdivision information should appear on the folder tab to identify properly the contents. Merely putting "Folder No. 1" or "Folder No. 2" on the tab doesn't tell you what is in the folder. The miscellaneous folders should always be examined so that individual and special folders can be prepared, thus logically expanding the filing system.

Folder Labels. The captions on folder labels may be printed or typewritten; the latter is preferable as they can be typed as needed. Although either gummed or adhesive (pressure-sensitive) folder labels can be used, adhesive labels are preferred. Adhesive labels are easily placed on the tab and stand up better through continued use. If gummed labels are used, a blotter should be used when folding the labels over the tab; otherwise, the typing may be smeared or air bubbles may remain under the label.

Consistency in typing captions on the labels is important. The captions should always be typed in exact indexing order (Brown, John A. *not* John A. Brown). Punctuation other than a hyphen or dash is usually omitted. In order to insure uniformity in the files, you should type the first letter in the caption at the same point on each label, usually two spaces from the left edge. Type the name on the label so that after the labels have been attached to the folders, the names will appear at the top edge of each tab. For ease in reading, upper- and lower-case letters should be used. In a subject file, however, the caption of the main subject is sometimes typed all in upper case for emphasis, and the subdivisions, in upper and lower case.

The label must be kept in good condition and be replaced when torn or difficult to read. Hard-to-read or torn labels will slow retrieval.

Positions of Guides and Folders. Like the tabs of folders, the tabs of guides also vary in position across the file drawer. Therefore, certain positions should be reserved for each type of guide. If guide positions are assigned in relation to the position of the folders, order is brought into the filing system. An example of this is an alphabetic system in which four filing positions are used:

1) First position: Reserved for the primary guides indicating the major divisions of the system.

2) Second position: Reserved for miscellaneous folders. Miscellaneous folders carry the same caption as the primary guides and are placed at the end of each category, *immediately preceding the next primary guide.*

3) Third position: Reserved for individual (or special) folders filed directly behind the primary guides.

4) Fourth position: Reserved for out-guides or substitution cards, indicating the material has been borrowed.

Again, these positions will vary from system to system. Every office must consider what is best for its own particular filing situation.

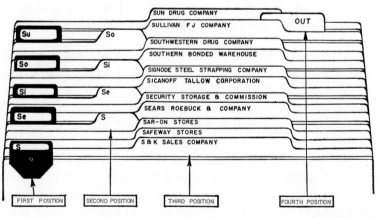

Lever Brothers Company

Drawer Labels. Drawer labels are used to identify the contents of each file drawer. For speedy retrieval, the labels must be specific, easily read, and current. The following information should appear on the label, which is inserted in a frame on the front of the file drawer:

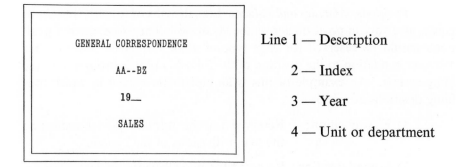

GENERAL CORRESPONDENCE   Line 1 — Description

AA--BZ   2 — Index

19__   3 — Year

SALES   4 — Unit or department

The labels should be covered with acetate windows to keep them neat and clean. When the contents of a cabinet are changed in any way, the drawer label must be corrected immediately.

Filing Accessories. In addition to filing cabinets, guides, and folders, a complete filing system should include other items which contribute to the efficiency of the system: a table or desk to be used by persons arranging material for the files; file boxes or baskets into which material is placed; a sorter or distributor for arranging papers in order prior to filing; a stool to sit on when working at the lower file drawers or shelves.

A file shelf is also a valuable accessory. It is a small "table-at-the-file drawer" that may be hooked onto the filing cabinet. Since both hands are needed to insert or remove papers from the folders, it is important to have a file shelf on which to place the materials with which you are working.

Alphabetic Card Files. In many instances, you will need an alphabetic vertical card file. A card file is probably the easiest system to organize and use. You will use this type of file when it is desirable to keep an alphabetic record of separate items of information that can be conveniently listed on cards. It is essential as a cross-reference to a numeric or subject filing system.

Although the file cards in alphabetic card files vary in size, they are usually 5" x 3" cards with one horizontal rule across the top and one vertical rule at the right side. The item of information that determines its order in the files (such as the name of a person or of an organization or subject) is written above the horizontal rule. If a number has been assigned to that

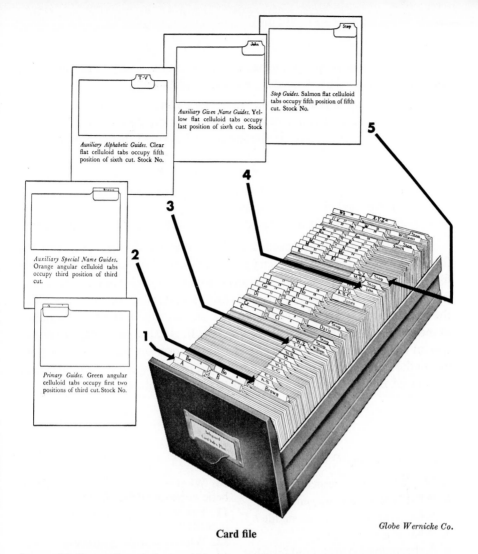

Auxiliary Alphabetic Guides. Clear flat celluloid tabs occupy fifth position of sixth cut. Stock No.

Auxiliary Given Name Guides. Yellow flat celluloid tabs occupy last position of sixth cut. Stock

Stop Guides. Salmon flat celluloid tabs occupy fifth position of fifth cut. Stock No.

Auxiliary Special Name Guides. Orange angular celluloid tabs occupy third position of third cut.

Primary Guides. Green angular celluloid tabs occupy first two positions of third cut. Stock No.

Card file

Globe Wernicke Co.

item of information, it is typed in the upper right corner. The illustration below shows a file card for the American Rug Cleaning Company, to which number 163 has been assigned.

| American Rug Cleaning Company | 163 |

465 Gilbert Avenue
Salem, Massachusetts 01970

File card

Card guides with metal tabs

For ease in retrieving needed information, every card should be uniformly typed. This procedure should be followed:

1) Type the name in exact indexing order.
2) If the card is not ruled, begin typing on the third line from the top of the card. If the index card is ruled, begin typing above the printed line.
3) Indent two spaces from the left edge of the card and set margin.
4) Use upper- and lower-case letters. They are easier to read.
5) Abbreviations may be used since space is limited.
6) Be consistent in style, spacing, capitalization, and punctuation.

Just as guides are needed to divide the file drawer and keep the folders in order, it is also necessary to divide the cards in an alphabetic card file into convenient alphabetic sections with a set of *card guides*. These card guides indicate on projecting tabs the various alphabetic sections into which the file drawer is divided. The notations on the tabs of the guides consist in most cases of letters, such as *A*, *Ad*, *Ae*, *Al*, *All*, but they may consist of special names as you will notice in the illustration on page 257. They indicate the alphabetic range of the cards filed in each section. The file cards are placed in alphabetic order behind the appropriate guides.

Study Questions

1. Why are records needed?
2. What is records management?
3. What is an alphabetic name file?
4. What is a numeric file?
5. A chronological file is used for what types of documents?
6. How should records be cared for?
7. What kinds of files does the office worker in a small office use?
8. What should you know about the central files?
9. Describe a vertical file.

10. What are the basic tools of alphabetic correspondence filing?
11. For what purpose are guides used in a file?
12. What are primary guides?
13. What are miscellaneous, individual, and special folders?
14. Of what value are the various positions of folder and guide tabs?
15. How should folder and drawer labels be prepared?
16. When would you keep an alphabetic card file?

What Do You Think?

1. What are the relative merits of the various sizes of vertical filing cabinets?
2. What kinds of materials should be filed in the executive's office? What should be sent to the central files, and what should be discarded?

Your Personal Qualities

Miss Lois Fowler is employed in the central files division of the Adams Electric Company. When Bill Stone, one of the young men in the accounting department, phones for information about invoices and other records, he always identifies himself as J. B. Adams, who is president of the company. Lois has become fully aware of the fact that he is joking and invariably gives him a flippant answer.

One day Lois received a telephone call from a man who identified himself as J. B. Adams. Assuming the caller to be the humorist in the accounting department, Lois gave him a flippant answer. Her caller proved to be the astonished president of the company!

Lois recovered from the shock and supplied Mr. Adams with the information he desired. Later, she began to worry about what had happened and about her general conduct in telephone conversations, particularly when dealing with the young man in the accounting department.

Questions: 1. Should Lois call the president and try to explain her behavior, or should she try to forget the incident and hope that the president will forget it, too?

2. What recommendations would you make concerning Lois' behavior?

How's Your English?

After reading about spelling rules in Appendix C, inspect the following words and indicate which are spelled incorrectly.

wilfull	shyness	enrollment	payible
		drugist	hopefull
		carrage	attorneys
		armys	occurred

Office Work

1. Contact five office workers, asking each the following questions:

  a. What kinds of files do you have in your office?

  b. Who does the major portion of the filing in your company?

  c. Do you consider the files and filing important and valuable to your firm? Why?

2. With one or more of your classmates visit a local office and study the filing system or systems in use. Prepare a written report, but be ready to make an oral report to the class if the teacher requests you to do so.

UNIT 9 | Business Filing and Records Control

PART 2:

Alphabetic Filing Rules

Every information system makes use of filing rules — whether the system is based on manual, mechanical, or automatic retrieval methods.

As you already know, information is costly to create and maintain. Therefore, if the system you are in charge of is to be worth this high operating cost, information must be available immediately when it is needed. This means the information must have been arranged (or "filed") in some exact and predetermined order.

Filing Rules. There are two basic methods of filing: *alphabetic* and *numeric*. Because of special office needs (usually the complexity of material or the high volume of information retained), many information systems have been developed by combining these two methods. In certain cases, you will need on-the-job training in order to work with these combined systems. But since every organization, regardless of its size or the number of its records, uses an alphabetic file, it is important that you learn the following alphabetic filing rules.

By adhering strictly to one set of filing rules and recognizing the importance of all phases of records management, you will soon become known as an "information conscious" person. And you will play a vital role in the successful operation of your office.

Indexing. The first step in filing procedure is indexing. When you arrange names for filing purposes, you are indexing. The following are rules for alphabetic indexing:

1. Names of Individuals

When you consider the name *Walter B. Anderson*, each word and each initial or abbreviation is a separate indexing unit. Thus you have

```
┌─────────────────────────────────┬────────┐
│ Anderson, Walter B.             │   72   │
│                                 │        │
├─────────────────────────────────┤        │
│                                 │        │
│ Mr. Walter B. Anderson          │        │
│ 575 Crane Road                  │        │
│ Middletown, N. Y. 10940         │        │
│                                 │        │
└─────────────────────────────────┴────────┘
```

three indexing units. The units of an individual's name are considered in this order: (a) surname, or last name; (b) first name, initial, or abbreviation; (c) middle name, initial, or abbreviation. Therefore *Anderson* is the first indexing unit, *Walter* is the second, and *B.* is the third. (In the examples, the names are in alphabetic order.)

Index Order of Units

Names	Unit 1	Unit 2	Unit 3
Walter B. Anderson	Anderson	Walter	B.
Henry David Brown	Brown	Henry	David
Edw. J. Cox	Cox	Edward	J.
J. B. Davis	Davis	J.	B.

2. Surnames

When the surnames of individuals are different, the alphabetic order is determined by the surnames alone. In the following lists, the italicized letter in each surname determines the alphabetic order of that name in relationship to the preceding name. Note that when one surname is the same as the first part of a longer surname, the shorter name precedes the longer. This is often called the "nothing before something" rule of filing order.

Names	Names
H*a*ll	Johns
H*i*ll	Johns*t*on
H*u*ll	Johnston*e*

3. Compound Surnames

A compound surname (Fuller-Smith, for example) is indexed as two separate units. The hyphen is disregarded. In a surname such as *St. Claire*, "St." is considered to be the first unit (in spelled-out form), and "Claire" the second unit.

Index Order of Units

Names	Unit 1	Unit 2	Unit 3
Michael F. Ross-Harris	Ross-	Harris	Michael
Robert J. Ross	Ross	Robert	J.
Allen Ross-Sanders	Ross-	Sanders	Allen
George J. Rosse	Rosse	George	J.
Alice Roswell-Kent	Roswell-	Kent	Alice
Edwin St. Claire	Saint	Claire	Edwin
Gerald St. John	Saint	John	Gerald

4. Surnames Containing Prefixes

A surname containing a prefix is considered as one indexing unit. The common prefixes include *D', Da, De, Del, Della, Des, Di, Du, Fitz, La, Le, Les, Mac, Mc, O', Van, Vanden, Van der, Von,* and *Von der.* Spacing between the prefix and the rest of the surname, or capitalization of the prefix is of no significance.

Names	Index Order of Units		
	Unit 1	Unit 2	Unit 3
Ralph J. D'Andre	D'Andre	Ralph	J.
Elizabeth Mary da Vinci	da Vinci	Elizabeth	Mary
Mario L. Del Favero	Del Favero	Mario	L.
Anthony F. Della Robia	Della Robia	Anthony	F.
Charles La Croix	La Croix	Charles	
Martin J. MacDonald	MacDonald	Martin	J.
Malcolm Paul McDonald	McDonald	Malcolm	Paul
Mary M. O'Shea	O'Shea	Mary	M.
Henry T. Van Allan	Van Allan	Henry	T.
Ruth Van der Water	Van der Water	Ruth	
John E. von Stein	von Stein	John	E.

5. Given Names

When the surnames are alike, you then consider the first names of individuals in determining alphabetic order. When the surnames and the first names are alike, the middle names determine alphabetic order.

Names	Index Order of Units		
	Unit 1	Unit 2	Unit 3
William A. Smith	Smith	William	A.
Zelda Smith	Smith	Zelda	
Walter Clark Thompson	Thompson	Walter	Clark
Walter Crane Thompson	Thompson	Walter	Crane

6. Unusual Names

When it is difficult to decide which part of an individual name (usually a foreign name) is the surname, the last part of the name as written should be considered the surname. This type of name is often cross-referenced as explained on page 273.

Names	Index Order of Units		
	Unit 1	Unit 2	Unit 3
Farah Farit Abdullah	Abdullah	Farah	Farit
Thomas George	George	Thomas	
Sharda Ptai	Ptai	Sharda	
Pan Chin Shih	Shih	Pan	Chin

7. Initials and Abbreviated First or Middle Names

A first or middle initial is considered an indexing unit and precedes all names that begin with the same letter. An abbreviated first or middle name is usually treated as if it were spelled in full if the full name is known. (Originally a nickname — *Bob* for *Robert*, *Larry* for *Lawrence*, etc. — was always indexed as if written in full. Recently, however, many names formerly considered nicknames have become given names. Unless the first name is known to be a nickname — *Tom* for *Thomas* — it should be indexed as written.)

		Index Order of Units	
Names	Unit 1	Unit 2	Unit 3
R. Robert Brogran	Brogran	R.	Robert
Robt. R. Brogran	Brogran	Robert	R.
Robert Richard Brogran	Brogran	Robert	Richard
Sam F. Brogran	Brogran	Sam	F.
Sam'l George Brogran	Brogran	Samuel	George

8. Titles

   (a) A personal or professional title or degree is usually disregarded in filing but is enclosed in parentheses at the end of the name.
   (b) When a religious or foreign title is followed by a given name only, it is indexed as written.

		Index Order of Units	
Names	Unit 1	Unit 2	Unit 3
(a) Dr. Alfred Brown	Brown	Alfred (Dr.)	
Arthur E. Brown, M.D.	Brown	Arthur	E. (M.D.)
Raymond C. Ellis, Ph.D.	Ellis	Raymond	C. (Ph.D.)
Mr. Edward Frantz	Frantz	Edward (Mr.)	
Francis Fuller, Esq.	Fuller	Francis (Esq.)	
Mme. Jeannine Patou	Patou	Jeannine (Mme.)	
Mayor John J. Ryan	Ryan	John	J. (Mayor)
Lieut. Earl T. Smith	Smith	Earl	T. (Lieut.)
Sen. Ralph Wilson	Wilson	Ralph (Senator)	
(b) Brother Andrew	Brother	Andrew	
Father Pierre	Father	Pierre	
Lady Anabel	Lady	Anabel	
Princess Margaret	Princess	Margaret	
Sister Mary Martha	Sister	Mary	Martha

9. Seniority Titles in Identical Names

A term designating seniority, such as "Junior" or "Senior," or "II (Second)" or "III (Third)," is not considered an indexing unit. The term is merely used as an "identifying element" (a secondary means of determining alphabetic sequence).

Names	Unit 1	Unit 2	Identifying Element
John Young	Young	John	
John Young, IV	Young	John	(Fourth)
John Young, Jr.	Young	John	(Junior)
John Young, Sr.	Young	John	(Senior)
John Young, III	Young	John	(Third)

10. Identical Personal Names

When identical names are encountered in filing, the sequence is determined by the parts of the address as follows:

(a) Town or City Name
(b) State Name
(c) Street Name
(d) House Number (numeric order)

Names	Identifying Elements			
John Smith 145 Beech St. Kingston, Ill. 60145	Kingston	Illinois		
John Smith 204 Pearl St. Kingston, N.Y. 10124	Kingston	New York	Pearl	
John Smith 177 State St. Kingston, N.Y. 10124	Kingston	New York	State	177
John Smith 350 State St. Kingston, N.Y. 10124	Kingston	New York	State	350

11. Names of Married Women

If it is known, the legal name of a married woman (her first name, her maiden surname, and her husband's surname; or her first and middle names, with her husband's surname) should be used rather than her husband's name. The title "Mrs." is placed in parentheses after the name *but is disregarded in filing*. Her husband's name is given in parentheses below her legal name.

Names	Index Order of Units		
	Unit 1	Unit 2	Unit 3
Mrs. Thomas (Mary Parker) Smith	Smith (Mrs. Thomas Smith)	Mary	Parker (Mrs.)
Mrs. Theodore Smith	Smith	Theodore (Mrs.)	
Mrs. Frank (Evelyn Marie) Zeller	Zeller (Mrs. Frank Zeller)	Evelyn	Marie (Mrs.)

12. Business or Firm Names

The following rules determine the indexing of a business or firm name:

(a) As a general rule, the units in a firm name are indexed in the order in which they are written. The word "and" is not considered an indexing unit.

(b) When a firm name includes the *full name of an individual*, the name is transposed and indexed as are individual names.

(c) Occasionally, a business name contains the name of an individual (for example, Arthur Murray or Fanny Farmer) who is so well known that confusion would result by transposing the name. In such cases, the name is indexed as it is popularly known; cross-referencing should be used.

(d) The name of a hotel or motel is usually indexed in the order in which it is written. However, if the word "Hotel" or "Motel" appears first, it is transposed to allow the most clearly identifying word to become the first indexing unit (for example, Hotel McKitrick is indexed as McKitrick Hotel). This rule applies to all the services or departments located in the hotel which use the hotel name.

	Index Order of Units			
Names	**Unit 1**	**Unit 2**	**Unit 3**	**Unit 4**
Ames Art Shop	Ames	Art	Shop	
Hotel Ames	Ames	Hotel		
Brown and Son Realty Co.	Brown (and)	Son	Realty	Company
Campbell Dress Shop, Inc.	Campbell	Dress	Shop	Incorporated
Citizens National Bank	Citizens	National	Bank	
John Hancock Mutual Life Insurance Co.	John	Hancock	Mutual	Life
John H. Kramer Shoe Repair Shop	Kramer	John	H.	Shoe
Michigan Savings and Loan Co.	Michigan	Savings (and)	Loan	Company
Modern Tile Store	Modern	Tile	Store	
Montgomery Ward and Company	Montgomery Ward (and)		Company	
Motel Morris Gift Shoppe	Morris	Motel	Gift	Shoppe
L. Morrison Moss Supply Co.	Moss	L.	Morrison	Supply

13. Alphabetic Order of Business or Firm Names

The first units of firm names determine the alphabetic order when those units are different. The second units determine alphabetic order when the first units are alike. The third units determine alphabetic order when the first and second units are alike. The first unit that is different in the names determines alphabetic order.

	Index Order of Units		
Names	**Unit 1**	**Unit 2**	**Unit 3**
Gunn Printing Company	Gunn	Printing	Company
Gunnell Radio Shop	Gunnell	Radio	Shop
Hess Beauty Shoppe	Hess	Beauty	Shoppe
Mary Hess Beauty Salon	Hess	Mary	Beauty
Hess Specialty Shop	Hess	Specialty	Shop
Irwin Shoe Distributors	Irwin	Shoe	Distributors
Irwin Shoe Mart	Irwin	Shoe	Mart

14. Articles, Prepositions, and Conjunctions

   (a) The articles (a, an, the); prepositions (of, on, for, by, etc.); and conjunctions (and, &, or) are *not* considered as indexing units and should be enclosed in parentheses.

   (b) However, when a preposition is the first word in a business name (as in *At Home Bakery* or *In Town Motel*), the preposition is treated as the first indexing unit.

	Index Order of Units			
Names	**Unit 1**	**Unit 2**	**Unit 3**	**Unit 4**
L. S. Andrews & Co.	Andrews	L.	S. (and)	Company
A Bit of Scotland	Bit (of)	Scotland (A)		
By the Sea Inn	By (the)	Sea	Inn	
First National Bank of Cincinnati	First	National	Bank (of)	Cincinnati
The House of Design	House (of)	Design (The)		
In Between Book Store	In	Between	Book	Store
Walker the Magician	Walker (the)	Magician		

15. Abbreviations

   An abbreviation in a firm name is indexed as if it were spelled in full. Single-letter abbreviations are also indexed as though spelled in full. If the meaning of the abbreviation is not *definitely* known, however, the name should be indexed as it is written.

	Index Order of Units			
Names	**Unit 1**	**Unit 2**	**Unit 3**	**Unit 4**
Amer. Paper Co.	American	Paper	Company	
Ft. Lee Stores Inc.	Fort	Lee	Stores	Incorporated
New York Central R.R.	New	York	Central	Railroad
St. Vincent's Hosp.	Saint	Vincent's	Hospital	
U.S. Rubber Co.	United	States	Rubber	Company
Y.W.C.A.	Young	Women's	Christian	Association

16. Single Letters

Firm names made up of single letters which are not abbreviations are filed before words beginning with the same letter. Each letter is considered as a separate filing unit. The spacing between the single letters is of no significance.

Names	Unit 1	Unit 2	Unit 3	Unit 4
			Index Order of Units	
A & A Auto Parts	A (&)	A	Auto	Parts
ABC Printers	A	B	C	Printers
A C Cleaners	A	C	Cleaners	
A–Z Dry Cleaners	A (–)	Z	Dry	Cleaners
Acme Rug Co.	Acme	Rug	Company	
WRCA	W	R	C	A
X Y Z Packers	X	Y	Z	Packers

17. Hyphened and Compound Names and Words

(a) Hyphened firm names are indexed as if they were separate words; therefore, they are separate indexing units (as Allis-Chalmers, for example).

(b) Each part of a hyphened "coined" word (such as The Do-It-Ur-Self Shop) is considered to be a separate indexing unit.

(c) A single word written with a hyphen (a word containing a prefix, such as ante-, anti-, bi-, co-, de-, dis-, inter-, mid-, non-, pan-, per-, pre-, re-, trans-, tri-, un-) is filed as one indexing unit.

Names	Unit 1	Unit 2	Unit 3	Unit 4
			Index Order of Units	
(a)				
Pitney-Bowes Mailing Co.	Pitney-	Bowes	Mailing	Company
The Shaw-Walker Company	Shaw-	Walker	Company (The)	
Stokens-Van Buren, Inc.	Stokens-	Van Buren	Incorporated	
(b)				
Bar-B-Q Drive-Inn	Bar-	B-	Q	Drive-
C-Thru Window Company	C-	Thru	Window	Company
Econ-O-Me Cleaners	Econ-	O-	Me	Cleaners
(c)				
Inter-State Truckers Assoc.	Inter-State	Truckers	Association	
Mid-City Garage	Mid-City	Garage		
Pre-Cast Industries	Pre-Cast	Industries		

18. One Versus Two Units — Words Considered As One

If separate words in a firm name are frequently considered or written as one word, these words as a group should be treated as one indexing unit. The use of a hyphen or the spacing is of no indexing significance. This rule eliminates separating similar names in the files. Examples of such words include: *airport, carload, crossroads, downtown, eastside, goodwill, halfway, mainland, railroad, seaboard*; and points of the compass words such as *northeast, northwest, southeast,* and *southeastern.*

Index Order of Units

Names	Unit 1	Unit 2
Good Will Agency	Goodwill	Agency
The Half-Way Restaurant	Halfway	Restaurant (The)
North Eastern Haulers	Northeastern	Haulers
Trans Caribbean Airlines	TransCaribbean	Airlines

19. Titles in Business Names

(a) A title *in a business name* is treated as a separate unit and is indexed in the order in which it is written.

(b) The titles "Mr." or "Mrs." are indexed as written *rather than* spelled in full.

Index Order of Units

Names	Unit 1	Unit 2	Unit 3
Dr. Allen's Health Club	Doctor	Allen's	Health
Madame Cecile's Hats	Madame	Cecile's	Hats
Mr. Tod's Barber Shop	Mr.	Tod's	Barber
Sir Reginald's Men's Wear	Sir	Reginald's	Men's

20. Compound Geographic Names

Compound geographic names containing two English words (such as New York) are treated as two separate indexing units; but compound names written as one word (such as Lakewood) are considered to be one indexing unit.

Index Order of Units

Names	Unit 1	Unit 2	Unit 3
Ft. Wayne Drug Co.	Fort	Wayne	Drug
New Jersey Res't. Assoc.	New	Jersey	Restaurant
Newport Travel Bureau	Newport	Travel	Bureau
St. Louis Air Port Store	Saint	Louis	Airport

21. Foreign Names

(a) Each separately written word in a compound foreign name is considered to be a separate indexing unit. The words "San" and "Santa" mean Saint and are, therefore, indexed separately.

(b) A foreign prefix is combined with the word that follows it and indexed as one filing unit (as explained in rule 4).

(c) Obscure foreign names are processed as written.

Index Order of Units				
Names	**Unit 1**	**Unit 2**	**Unit 3**	**Unit 4**
(a)				
Mesa Verde Dist.	Mesa	Verde	Distributors	
Puerto Rico Imports	Puerto	Rico	Imports	
San Diego Meat Market	San	Diego	Meat	Market
Terre Haute Fence Service	Terre	Haute	Fence	Service
(b)				
Du Bois Stationery Shop	Du Bois	Stationery	Shop	
LaBelle Cleaner's	LaBelle	Cleaner's		
Las Vegas Equipment, Inc.	Las Vegas	Equipment	Incorporated	
Los Angeles Letter Shop	Los Angeles	Letter	Shop	
(c)				
Ambulancias Hispano Mexicana	Ambulancias	Hispano	Mexicana	
Iino Kauin Kaisha Imports	Iino	Kauin	Kaisha	Imports
Mohamed Esber, Cia	Mohamed	Esber	Cia	
N. V. Ned. Wolspinnerij	N.	V.	Ned.	Wolspinnerij

22. Numbers

A number in a business name is considered as though it were written in full and is treated as one indexing unit (regardless of the length or number of digits). Four-digit numbers are written out in hundreds; five digit numbers are written out in thousands, etc.

Index Order of Units		
Names	**Unit 1**	**Unit 2**	**Unit 3**
A-1 Register Service	A-	One	Register
40 Winks Motel	Forty	Winks	Motel
44th St. Garage	Forty-fourth	Street	Garage
40,050 Investment Assoc.	Forty thousand fifty	Investment	Association
400 Park Avenue Club	Four Hundred	Park	Avenue
4th Avenue Shopping Center	Fourth	Avenue	Shopping

23. Possessives

The "apostrophe s" ('s), the singular possessive, is disregarded in filing. An "s apostrophe" (s'), the plural possessive, is considered as part of the word. Very simply, consider all letters to be in the indexing unit up to the apostrophe; drop those after it.

Index Order of Units		
Names	**Unit 1**	**Unit 2**	**Unit 3**
Boy's Life Magazine	Boy's	Life	Magazine
Boys' Baseball Outfitters	Boys'	Baseball	Outfitters
Brook's Garage	Brook's	Garage	
Brooks' Bros. Clothing	Brooks'	Brothers	Clothing
Paul's Barber Shop	Paul's	Barber	Shop
Pauls' Automatic Washers	Pauls'	Automatic	Washers

24. Identical Business Names

    (a) Identical names of two or more businesses are arranged in alphabetical order according to names of the cities. Names of states are disregarded unless names of towns are same.

    (b) If several branches of one business are located in the same city, names are arranged alphabetically or numerically by streets. If more than one branch is located on the same street in the same city, they are arranged according to the numeric order of building numbers. Names of buildings are not considered unless street names are not given.

Names	Index Order of Units			
	Unit 1	Unit 2	Unit 3	Identifying Elements
(a) Office Supplies Company Akron, Ohio	Office	Supplies	Company	Akron
Office Supplies Company Canton, Ohio	Office	Supplies	Company	Canton
Office Supplies Company Lansing, Michigan	Office	Supplies	Company	Lansing
(b) National Food Market 225 Main Street Columbus, Ohio	National	Food	Market	Main
National Food Market 187 Prospect Street Columbus, Ohio	National	Food	Market	Prospect
National Food Market United Building 341 Stone Drive Columbus, Ohio	National	Food	Market	Stone 341
National Food Market 722 Stone Drive Columbus, Ohio	National	Food	Market	Stone 722
National Food Market Young Building Columbus, Ohio	National	Food	Market	Young

25. Federal Government Offices

    The names of all federal government agencies and offices are indexed under United States Government. They are indexed as follows:

(a) United States Government

(b) Name of the department

(c) Name of the bureau

(d) Name of the division or subdivision

(e) Location of the office

(f) Title of official, if given

```
United States Government
────────────────────────
Treasury (Department of)
Internal Revenue Service
Indianapolis
District Director

District Director
Internal Revenue Service
Indianapolis, Indiana 46204
```

Examples	Index Order
The Postmaster Buffalo, New York	United States Government Post Office (Department) Buffalo Postmaster
Division of Employment Statistics Bureau of Labor Statistics U.S. Department of Labor Cleveland, Ohio	United States Government Labor (Department of) Labor Statistics (Bureau of) Employment Statistics (Division of) Cleveland
District Director Agricultural Research Service Federal Building Tallahassee, Florida	United States Government Agriculture (Department of) Agricultural Research Service Tallahassee District Director

(Note: Rule 25 also applies to foreign government names.)

26. Other Political Subdivisions

The names of other political subdivisions — state, county, city, or town governments — are indexed (a) according to the geographic name of the subdivision as: New Jersey, State (of), Westchester, County (of), or Philadelphia, City (of); (b) according to the name of the department, board, or office; (c) the location of the office; and (d) the title of the official, if it is given.

	Index Order of Units			
Names	Unit 1	Unit 2	Unit 3	Unit 4
Local Police Department Alliance, Ohio	Alliance	City (of)	Police (Dept.)	
Clinton Cty. Park Commission Dubuque, Iowa	Clinton	County (of)	Park	Commission
Municipal Public Works Div. Lancaster, Pa.	Lancaster	City (of)	Public	Works
State Health Department Columbus, Ohio	Ohio	State (of)	Health (Dept.)	

27. Churches, Synagogues, and Other Organizations

(a) The name of a church or synagogue is indexed in the order in which it is written unless some other word in the name more clearly identifies the organization.

	Index Order of Units		
Names	Unit 1	Unit 2	Unit 3
The Chapel at Brown & Vine	Chapel (at)	Brown (and)	Vine (The)
First Baptist Church	Baptist	Church	First
Congregation of Moses	Congregation (of)	Moses	
Trinity Lutheran Church	Lutheran	Church	Trinity
St. Paul's Church	Saint	Paul's	Church

(b) The name of a club or any other organization is indexed according to the most clearly identifying unit in its name.

	Index Order of Units		
Names	Unit 1	Unit 2	Unit 3
Local 200, Retail Store Employees Union	Retail	Store	Employees
Fraternal Order of Eagles	Eagles	Fraternal	Order (of)
Rotary Club	Rotary	Club	
Loyal Order of Moose	Moose	Loyal	Order (of)

28. Schools

(a) The names of elementary and secondary schools are indexed first according to the name of the city in which the schools are located, and then by the most distinctive word in the name.

	Index Order of Units			
Names	Unit 1	Unit 2	Unit 3	Unit 4
Indian Prairie School Kalamazoo, Michigan	Kalamazoo	Indian	Prairie	School
Oakwood Elementary School Kalamazoo, Michigan	Kalamazoo	Oakwood	Elementary	School
Oakwood Junior High Kalamazoo, Michigan	Kalamazoo	Oakwood	Junior	High
Pershing School Portage, Michigan	Portage	Pershing	School	

(b) The names of colleges or universities are indexed according to the most clearly identifying word in the name.

	Index Order of Units		
Names	Unit 1	Unit 2	Unit 3
Indiana Business School	Indiana	Business	School
Iowa State University	Iowa	State	University
University of Iowa	Iowa	University (of)	
Northwestern University	Northwestern	University	

29. Newspapers and Periodicals

(a) The name of a newspaper is indexed in the order in which it is written unless the city of publication does not appear in its name. In that case, the name of the city is inserted before the name of the newspaper.

	Index Order of Units			
Names	Unit 1	Unit 2	Unit 3	Unit 4
Wall Street Journal New York, New York	New	York	Wall	Street
The Canton Herald	Canton	Herald (The)		
The Journal Gazette Ft. Wayne, Indiana	Fort	Wayne	Journal	Gazette (The)

(b) The name of a periodical is indexed in the order in which the name is written. A cross-reference may be made listing the publisher, as described below.

	Index Order of Units		
Names	Unit 1	Unit 2	Unit 3
Administrative Management	Administrative	Management	
Harvard Business Review	Harvard	Business	Review
The Office	Office (The)		

30. Subjects

Certain related materials are indexed according to the subjects to which they pertain rather than according to the name of the correspondents. The reason for this special treatment is that the subjects are more important than the names of the correspondents and are therefore the basis on which materials are called for. Applications for employment are examples of this type of indexing. The applications are of major importance; the names of the applicants are of secondary importance.

	Index Order of Units			
Names	Unit 1	Unit 2	Unit 3	Unit 4
C. J. Browning (Advertiser)	Advertisers:	Browning	C.	J.
R. M. Smith (Advertiser)	Advertisers:	Smith	R.	M.
H. L. Kramer (Application)	Applications:	Kramer	H.	L.
Jack Myer (Application)	Applications:	Myer	Jack	
J. Frank Smith (Application)	Applications:	Smith	J.	Frank

Cross-Referencing. What will you do when a letter or other material to be filed could be asked for by more than one name? Examples are firm names that consist of two or more surnames, the names of married women, and the names of magazines. You may look for the name according to an indexing order that is not shown on the piece of correspondence or on the file card. For example, you may remember only the name *Goodman* in the firm name *Bergdorf-Goodman*; you may not remember a married woman's legal name — you may remember only that her husband's name is *Thomas Devine*; or you may remember the name of a magazine, *Life*, but not the name of the publisher, *Time, Inc.*

If a copy-making machine is available, it is more efficient to prepare a facsimile copy of the document, thereby saving time when the document is requested from the files.

Although cross-referencing is important for rapid information retrieval, care should be exercised in deciding what records need to be cross-referenced. Too much cross-referencing is both time- and space-consuming. Too little will cause needless and costly delays in obtaining important information.

CROSS-REFERENCE SHEET

Name or Subject ___Whitmore, Earl R.___
Kansas City, Missouri   64151

Date of Item ___June 14, 196-___

Regarding ___Request for further information as
basis for quotation on printing a
booklet___

SEE

Name or Subject ___Carter, William, Company___
615 Lakeland Drive
Kansas City, Missouri   64151

WILLIAM CARTER COMPANY
815 LAKELAND DRIVE · KANSAS CITY, MISSOURI 64151 · TReed 1-1120

June 14, 196-

JUN 15   2 12 PM 196-

Allis-Rowen Products, Inc.
9621 East Tracy Street
Los Angeles, California 90028

Attention Mr. B. P. Warren

Gentlemen:

Thank you for your letter of June 12 in which you inquired about the possibility of our printing for you a small booklet giving a short description of your company and an illustrated description of the products which you manufacture.

Before we are able to quote prices on a publication of this kind, we need the following information:

1. An estimate of the length of the booklet

2. The approximate number and dimensions of illustrations

3. The size of the page desired

4. The kind and quality of paper and cover stock

We shall be glad to give you an exact quotation on cost of the booklet as soon as we receive this information.

At the present time we are in a position to give you prompt as well as efficient service. We can assure you of an attractive book with suitable type, clear illustrations, and strong binding.

Sincerely yours

Earl R. Whitmore

Earl R. Whitmore

eob

Coded letter

The line drawn under the name William Carter in the letterhead above indicates the name under which the letter should be filed. The line drawn under the signature *Earl R. Whitmore*, which is extended into the margin and marked with an "x," indicates that the letter may be called for by Whitmore's name rather than by the name of the company. Consequently the cross-reference sheet above was prepared and should be filed under the name *Earl R. Whitmore*.

Cross-reference sheet

Cross-Reference for a Company Known By More Than One Name.
If the name of a certain company is *Rogers-Turner Food Mart*, the original document should be indexed as it is written. You should, however, make a cross-reference card or sheet for the second surname in the title. Thus, if you remember only the second surname, *Turner*, you will find on the cross-reference for *Turner* "See Rogers-Turner Food Mart."

Cross-Reference for the Name of a Married Woman. You will file the original document for a married woman under her legal name; that is, her given first name, maiden surname, and her husband's surname. Her husband's given name might be cross-referenced in order to speed information retrieval. If the legal name of a married woman is Mrs. Dorothy Lee Hall, this name should be indexed on the original document; and a cross-reference card or sheet based on her husband's name should be prepared.

```
Hall, Dorothy Lee (Mrs.)
_____

Mrs. Raymond C. Hall
1230 Fifth Street
Marion, Iowa 52302
```

```
Hall, Raymond C. (Mrs.)
_____

See Hall, Dorothy Lee (Mrs.)
```

Study Questions

1. How many indexing units are there in the name *Gerald V. Wilcox*?

2. What is meant by the "nothing before something" rule?

3. Is *Van Der Veer* considered one filing unit or two?

4. What happens when surnames are alike?

5. Under what circumstances is a name indexed as it is written?

6. How is an abbreviated first name like *Wm.* treated?

7. What is done about the *Dr.* in *Dr. James B. Moulton*?

8. Are religious and foreign titles treated in a special way?

9. Which is the correct order: Jr., Sr., III, IV; or Fourth, Junior, Senior, Third?

10. Is the city or state considered first when filing identical names?

11. What is the legal name of a married woman?

12. In what order are the units of a business name considered for filing purposes?

13. What is done with units of an individual name that are included in a firm name?

14. How are the words *and, of,* and *for* treated in indexing?

15. In a firm name what distinction is made between two words combined with a hyphen and a single word containing a hyphen?

16. What are the rules for geographic names?

17. Give examples of subject titles that would be used in preference to the names of the persons or businesses that are concerned.

18. What is a cross-reference card?

19. Give two examples of types of names that are frequently cross-referenced.

20. What is the advantage of using facsimile cross-reference copies?

What Do You Think?

1. What confusion might be caused if surnames containing a prefix were not considered as one unit?

2. Why are foreign names frequently indexed as they are written?

3. Why is each word in a geographic name usually treated as a separate indexing unit?

4. For what purposes other than filing may the office clerk make use of the rules for alphabetic indexing?

5. Why should caution be exercised in cross-referencing?

Your Personal Qualities

Miss Bertha Lewis has been with the firm since it was started over thirty years ago. She originated the filing system for the firm and is now supervisor of the central files.

She has her own ideas about filing rules; for instance, the customers' names beginning with *Mac* and *Mc* are placed ahead of all the other names in the "M" section of the alphabetic files. This is but one of the variations in alphabetic filing at the Lily Soap Company.

New employees are confused because the system varies so much from the rules they have been taught. They waste considerable time and energy filing and finding correspondence and business forms. Miss Lewis is not willing to accept any suggestions for change, claiming that the system has been operating successfully for over thirty years. The turnover of employees and the requests for transfers from the central filing department are very high.

Questions: 1. If you were to be employed as a file clerk at the Lily Soap Company, how would you reconcile differences between company practice and what you learned about filing in school?

2. How would you plan to get along with Miss Lewis?

How's Your English?

After reading in Appendix C about homonyms, give a homonym for each of the words listed below:

allowed	herd	
bare	capitol	
two	meddle	
there	through	
brake	course	

Office Work

1. In each of the following names of individuals select the *first* indexing unit:
- **a.** R. Harold Dana
- **b.** Hubert Smith-Johnson, Jr.
- **c.** Lois J. McDowell
- **d.** Veronica Blake
- **e.** Father Francis
- **f.** Chairman Frank Simpson
- **g.** Mrs. John Hanson
- **h.** President Walter C. Schott
- **i.** T. J. Fairleigh
  News Commentator
- **j.** Attorney Edward K. Wilcox

2. In each of the following business names select the *second* indexing unit:
- **a.** The Holden Paper Company
- **b.** Woodward & Lothrop
  Department Store
- **c.** A to Z Cleaning Service
- **d.** Pre-eminent Products, Inc.
- **e.** North West Wholesale Furriers
- **f.** Tommy Tucker's Toys
- **g.** Johnson-Hardin Produce
  Company
- **h.** San Bruno Public Warehouse
- **i.** A-1 Window Washers
- **j.** St. Louis Pharmaceuticals, Inc.

3. In each of the following names select the *first* indexing unit:
- **a.** Provident Bank & Trust
  Company of Cleveland
- **b.** Michigan State University
- **c.** National Association of
  Life Underwriters
- **d.** Exchange Club
- **e.** St. Gertrude's Church
- **f.** University of Cincinnati
- **g.** Disabled American Veterans
- **h.** Camden Savings and Loan
- **i.** Yale Alumni Association
- **j.** Miss Wallis' Preparatory
  School for Girls

4. Is the order of the names in each of the following pairs correct?
- **a.** H. M. Jones
  Henry M. Jonas
- **b.** Carl O'Bannon
  J. B. Obannon
- **c.** Mrs. Rena Lawson Carter
  Harold Lawson-Carter
- **d.** Professor Walter Hampton
  Walter Charles Hampton
- **e.** George Carpenter, II
  George Carpenter, III
- **f.** Sister Julia
  Julia Sisson
- **g.** Ernest V. Mellon, Sr.
  Ernest V. Mellon, Jr.
- **h.** Dr. Frank Tarkington
  Frank D. Tarkington
- **i.** Francine the Florist
  Francis J. Flanagan
- **j.** Charlie's Place
  Charlie Porter, Plumbing

5. Indicate the order in which the parts of the following titles are considered in indexing:
- **a.** Board of Education
  Hamilton County, Oregon
- **b.** Pennsylvania State
  Department of Highways
- **c.** Central Trust Company of
  Delaware
- **d.** Department of Public Welfare
  City of Minneapolis, Minnesota
- **e.** Phillips & Woods (Real Estate)
- **f.** Division of Unemployment
  Compensation
  Ohio State Employment Service
- **g.** Oakwood First National Bank
- **h.** M. Meredith Weatherby
  (Application for Employment)
- **i.** The Gerald Gerrard Gun Shop
- **j.** The War College
  U.S. Department of Defense

6. Arrange the following names in correct alphabetic order in each group:

Group 1
- **a.** H. Duncan McCampbell
- **b.** Mack Campbell
- **c.** The Campbell Soup Company
- **d.** J. C. MacCampbell

Group 2
- **a.** Martin and Ulberg
- **b.** Martin C. Ulberg
- **c.** Martin-Ulberg, Inc.
- **d.** K. Martin Ulberg, M.D.

Group 3
a. Rosewood Delicatessen
b. Olde Rosewood Tea Shoppe
c. Rose Wood (Mrs.)
d. Roselawn Public Library

Group 4
a. Five Corners Car Wash
b. Five-Corners Creamery
c. Five O'Clock Shop
d. 15th Avenue Apartments

Group 5
a. Williams Ave. Brake Service
b. William's Coiffures
c. Williams' Sons (Brokers)
d. Williamson Heater Company

Group 6
a. La Maisonette
b. Lamson & Towers Advertising
c. Lamps & Lighting, Inc.
d. Laap Brothers Furniture

Group 7
a. 2 in 1 Cleaning Service
b. 22d Street Theater
c. Twenty-One (Restaurant)
d. Twosome Dance Club

Group 8
a. Mrs. J. C. (Barbara) Sands
b. Santa Barbara Police Dept.
c. St. Barnaby's Episcopal Church
d. Barbara St. John

Group 9
a. Boy Scouts of America
b. Boy's Scouting Club
c. Boy and Bike Shop
d. Boys' and Dads' Day Committee

Group 10
a. J. & L. Fruit Market
b. Jones & Laughlin Steel
c. J. L. Jones, Jr.
d. J. L. Jones, Sr.

Group 11
a. Southern Railway
b. South Boston Beanery
c. South Western Printing Company
d. Rachael W. Souther

Group 12
a. Black's
b. Blacks'
c. Blacks' Super Market
d. S. Black & Son

Group 13
a. K-P Kitchenware
b. Kennedy-Porter Fencing
c. Arthur P. Kennedy
d. P. Kennedy Arthur

Group 14
a. St. Joseph's Orphanage
b. St. Joseph (Missouri) Railroad Depot
c. San Jose Growers' Assn.
d. Sanjor Coffee House

 Office Work Assignments

32: Alphabetic Indexing No. 1

In completing the exercises in this unit on filing, you will need one hundred 5″ x 3″ file cards, or plain paper cut to about that size.

a. Type each of the following names in index form at the top of a card. Type the number of each name in the upper right corner of the card. (These numbers will aid in checking the answers.) Type the name and address below the indexed name. (See illustration on page 261.)

b. After the names, numbers, and addresses have been typed, arrange the cards alphabetically.

c. Save these cards for use in assignments following Parts 3 and 6.

1. Janitrol Heating Service, 6602 N. Clark St., Chicago, Illinois

2. Kitty's Korner Kitchen, Cooper Bldg., Marietta, Ohio

3. Mlle. Jeanette Cecil Sagan, 3 Rue de la Pais, Paris, France

4. Janitor Supplies & Equipment Co., 9 W. Seventh St., Akron, Ohio

5. Robert P. Van der Meer, 2231 Watervliet St., Detroit, Michigan

6. Jerome Labelson, Apt. 3B, 60 Sutton Place, South, New York, New York

7. Williams & Williams, Tax Consultants, Suite 12, Statler Hotel Bldg., Cleveland, Ohio

8. Jasper J. Seaman, Chalfonte Hall, Campus Station, Durham, North Carolina

9. Meyer Lufkin & Son, Commercial Bldg., Sixth & Walnut, Omaha, Nebraska

10. Meyer, E. Jones, & Millikin Co., 210 N. State St., Albany, New York

11. Youman & Garties Mfg. Company, 316 Spring St., N.W., Atlanta, Georgia

12. The World-Telegram News, Dallas, Texas

13. Raymond J. Vandermeer, 3920 Alamo Drive, Houston, Texas

14. Mid Way Service Station, Junction State Routes 7 & 9, Owensburg, Idaho

15. Ringling Bros.-Barnum & Bailey Circus, Winter Headquarters, Sarasota, Florida

16. Greendale Zion Reform Temple, Cor. Reading & Vine Sts., Greendale, Pennsylvania

17. William's U-Fix-It Shop, 4920 Carthage Rd., Richmond, Virginia

18. Seamen's Rest, 60 Front St., New Orleans, Louisiana

19. Wati Rajhma, Room 2100, United Nations Secretariat, New York, New York

20. Oberhelman Bros. Flooring, Inc., 420 Vine St., Seattle, Washington

21. P. M. Diners' Clubhouse, 22 Regent St., Louisville, Kentucky

22. Society for the Sightless, 1404 K St., N.W., Washington, D.C.

23. J. & K. Seaman Hauling Line, 160 N. First St., Ottumwa, Iowa

24. 91st Street Mission, 13 - 91 St., San Francisco, California

25. La Belle Dresses, 18 Circle Drive, Roselawn, Connecticut

26. Rosenswig's Dept. Store, 6920 Appletree Rd., Wilmington, Delaware

27. R. & L. Benjamin & Company, 14 West Decatur St., Ft. Smith, Arkansas

28. Mayor Michael O'Berne, City Hall, Baltimore, Maryland

29. Midway Seafood House, 3109 Collins Ave., Miami Beach, Florida

30. Boy's Hobby Shop, 1010 Pacific Blvd., Portland, Oregon

31. Automatic Food Dispenser Co., 112 High St., Colorado Springs, Colorado

32. Automatic Food Dispenser Co., 19 & Ewald Sts., Camden, New Jersey

33. Automatic Food Dispenser Co., Camden, Ohio

34. Boys' Hobby Haven, 730 Pine St., St. Joseph, Missouri

35. Lufkin Central Savings Society, 9 S. Main St., Lufkin, Texas

36. Rosen's Fresh Fruit Market, 1403 La Cienega St., Los Angeles, California

37. Kitty-Kat Products, Ashtabula, Tennessee

38. Long Island Railroad, 69–75 Rockefeller Plaza, New York, New York

39. Adolph G. Meier Lumber Co., First St. at B. & O. R.R., Columbus, Ohio

40. Dr. John W. Barnhart, 22 Medical Arts Bldg., Oak Park, Illinois

41. John Barnhart, 635 Capitol Ave., Springfield, Illinois

42. Drury Hill Farms, Inc., Box 10, Route 4, Drury, Pennsylvania

43. Carthage Mills, Inc., Spring Valley, Georgia

44. Police Department, Drury, Pennsylvania

45. P. M. Dinersman Company, 1614 Meridian St., Indianapolis, Indiana

46. Branford & Branford Co., Aurora Mississippi

47. Branford, Branford and Branford, Attorneys, Union Life Bldg., St. Louis, Missouri

48. Olde Seaport Inn, Front and Plum Sts., Alexandria, Virginia

49. John L. Barnhart, Sr., 2226 Washington Avenue, Fargo, North Dakota

50. Ninety and Ninth Apartments, 90 St. at Ninth Ave., New York, New York

UNIT 9 | Business Filing and Records Control

PART 3:

Filing Procedures

Effective filing procedures begin long before any material is actually placed in the files. Efficient filing procedures will save time as well as conserve your energy for other office duties. But even more important, well-developed filing practices insure the prompt retrieval of needed records.

The following steps will help in the successful administration of your filing system:

Collecting Papers for the File. The first step in preparing papers for the files is developing a well-planned collection routine. In a small office, records to be filed are placed in "file trays" on the various desks. Several times during the day these documents should be removed and prepared for filing. Occasionally, it may be necessary to go through your employer's desk (with his permission, of course) and uncover documents that should be filed. In larger offices, a messenger collects the papers at regular intervals and delivers them to the central filing department.

When records are not needed for immediate use, they should be filed. A definite collection routine will remove records from desk tops and place them in the files where they are protected and controlled.

Inspection. The next step in the filing process is inspecting each document that is sent to the files. During the inspection step, you look for a *release mark*, which is your authority to file each document. This mark indicates that action has been taken on the document and it is released for filing. The release mark is usually indicated by the initials of the person who has used the document. These initials are placed in the upper left corner of the document.

Since it is assumed that carbon copies are ready to file, they do not bear release marks. Many firms prepare carbon copies on paper with the words "file copy" printed in large outline letters across the face of the sheet. Some firms use a "piggy-back" method. This means that the back of the original document is used for the carbon sheet; thus, the inquiry is on one side of the document and the response on the other — saving filing space.

In addition to checking for the release mark, one should examine documents for completeness. All documents that are clipped together are examined and stapled (if they belong together) in the upper left corner. The reply is stapled on top of the incoming letter. Paper clips, rubber bands, or straight pins are never placed in the file drawer. Torn documents should be mended at this time.

Indexing. Although every step in the filing process is important, the *indexing* (or reading) step is particularly significant. Indexing is the mental process that determines how a document is to be filed. An incorrect decision at this time may mean a lost document. At the very least, it means lost time in locating the record. Several names or subjects may appear in each record. It is necessary, therefore, to scan or read each record carefully to determine the *key name* or title that best identifies the document.

The way records are requested usually determines the way they should be indexed. An incoming letter could be filed under the name appearing on the letterhead, the name of the person signing the letter, the name of a person or business mentioned in the body of the letter, or the subject of the letter. For example, a letter announcing a new fire-resistant filing cabinet would probably be filed under the heading "Office Equipment" in a folder labeled "Filing Cabinets" rather than under the name of the distributor appearing on the letterhead.

Copies of outgoing letters could be filed under the name of the addressee, the name of a person or business mentioned in the letter, or the subject of the letter. If a letter is of a personal nature, it is filed under the name of the person to or by whom it is written, even though the letter may have been written on company letterhead.

If there is any doubt about how a document should be indexed, the person who has released the record for filing should be consulted.

Coding. After the exact indexing order has been chosen, the document is marked or coded. A document may be coded in several different ways. The indexing units may be numbered:

<pre>
        1   2   3   4
      Acme / Dry / Cleaning / Corporation

        2   3   1
      R. / Robert / Wagner
</pre>

or the units may be underlined:

Acme Dry Cleaning Corporation

R. Robert Wagner

If the name or subject does not appear in the letter, it must be written in, preferably in the upper right portion of the paper. All coding is done with a colored pencil. Coding facilitates filing the record each time it is removed from the file.

Cross-Referencing. Although selecting the indexing caption is relatively simple in most cases, there are always some records that might be requested in different ways. For example, a company might receive a letter from a good customer recommending an applicant for a position. Obviously this letter of recommendation should be filed with other records referring to the applicant and would be filed in the applicant's folder in the "Applications" section. It may be well, however, to keep a record of the letter in the customer's folder. The name of the applicant, therefore, is underlined on the letter as the primary indexing unit. An "X" is then written in the margin to indicate that the document should be cross-referenced. A cross-reference sheet (usually of some distinctive color) is prepared with the name and address of the customer, the date of the letter, a brief description of the letter, and where the letter is filed. This cross-reference sheet is then placed in the customer's folder as a record of the letter.

If the name to be cross-referenced does not appear in a letter, or if the letter is to be cross-referenced by a subject not clearly indicated in the letter, you should write the name in the margin.

Rather than prepare regular cross-reference sheets, many companies prefer using a photocopy of the original document. This speeds retrieval since a complete copy of the record is available at either file point.

Many "hard to index" documents should be cross-referenced. Too much cross-referencing, however, requires considerable time and considerable file drawer space; too little cross-referencing may delay retrieval.

If a permanent cross-reference is desired, a cross-reference guide is prepared. This is a manila card the same size as a file folder, with a tab in the same position as those used for individual folders. A situation requiring a permanent cross-reference guide might be as follows: The name of a company you do considerable business with is changed. Another folder is prepared for the new name and all the material placed in this folder. The old folder is now replaced with a cross-reference guide with the necessary retrieval information on its tab:

Adams and Smith Manufacturing Co.

See Adams and Son Manufacturing Co.

Correspondence sorter

Yawman & Erbe

If a special form is not available, the front flap of an individual folder may be cut off at the score line and the back portion of the folder used as a cross-reference guide. The cross-reference guide remains in the file as long as the name or subject is still active.

Sorting. After the records have been coded and the necessary cross-reference sheets prepared, the material is ready to be sorted. *Sorting* is the process of arranging the records in indexing order before placing them in the folders.

Sorting serves two important purposes. First, it saves actual filing time. Since the records are in exact indexing order, you are able to move systematically from drawer to drawer; thus, time and energy are conserved. Second, if documents are requested before filed, they can be found quickly.

If the volume of filing is high, special sorting trays or compartments should be used. Sorting trays are equipped with alphabetic, numeric, or geographic guides, depending upon the classification system being used. When one sorts materials alphabetically, for example, records beginning with the letter "A" are placed behind an *A* guide; those beginning with "B," behind a *B* guide, and so on through the alphabet. After the materials have been rough sorted, they are removed from the sorting tray and placed in exact alphabetic order (fine sorting). If the volume of material is low, this same general procedure may be followed on your desk top.

Papers should be filed daily. If this is not possible because of an unusual office situation, records should be fine sorted several times a day.

Placing Records in the File. After the records have been fine sorted, they are taken either as a unit or in alphabetic sections to the files and placed in the folders. A systematic routine should always be followed:

1) Locate the proper file drawer by examining drawer labels.
2) Scan the primary guides in the drawer to locate the major alphabetic section desired.
3) Check to see if an individual or special folder has been prepared for this material. If so, file the record there.
4) If no individual or special folder is available for this particular record, file the document in the miscellaneous folder for the section.

Arrangement of Materials in Folders. Records should always be placed in folders with the front of the record facing the front of the folder and the top of the record at the left side. Uniformity is essential for prompt retrieval.

In "individual" folders, records are arranged according to date, with the *most recent* record in front. In "miscellaneous" folders, documents are arranged alphabetically by name; if two or more records are for the same individual or company, they are arranged according to date, with the most recent record first. In a "special" folder, the records are arranged alphabetically by name and then by date in each group of names.

Twenty Filing Hints. Here are twenty filing "hints" that should be incorporated into your daily filing procedures. They have been recommended by experienced file clerks.

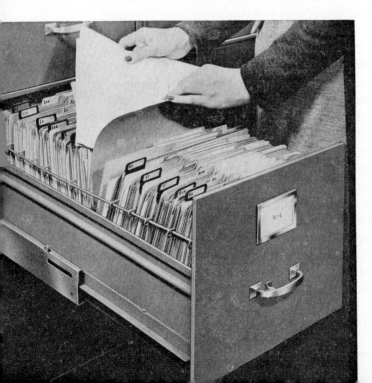

Filing correspondence

The file clerk raises the folder from the file drawer as she places the correspondence, with the top edge at the left, in the front of the folder.

Remington Rand

1) Be a good housekeeper. Well-organized, carefully administered files encourage accurate filing and rapid retrieval. What is more, you will enjoy filing!

2) Don't foolishly economize on file supplies. Good-quality supplies hold up through continued hard use; poor-quality supplies soon wear out and hinder the efficiency of the system. Pick the right supplies for the right records with a particular system in mind.

3) Before refiling any folder that has been removed from the files, quickly examine its contents. You may find a lost document by performing this simple procedure. Always "jog" the contents of a folder before returning it to the file.

4) Set aside a definite time each day for filing. Remember: records belong in the file — not in or on desks.

5) Constantly analyze your filing system and recommend ways in which it can be improved. Your employer will appreciate any suggestion for an improved information system. Seek the advice of your office supplies dealer. Constantly review the various business publications. They'll keep you informed on the latest products and new developments in the field of records management.

6) Let color help. Use different color labels for different file years or periods. A well-planned color scheme will aid in prompt filing and retrieving.

7) Keep your system simple. If others must use your files, be certain they understand how the system works, but insist that you do all the filing and refiling. Provide a handy place for them to place the materials they have removed from the files. They will be glad to cooperate — and it will guarantee file accuracy.

8) File the most active records in the most accessible parts of the file cabinets. Active records belong in the top drawers, less active documents in bottom drawers. This saves both time and energy.

9) Use your filing cabinets only for filing, not for storing office supplies and other items. File only vital records in the special fire-resistant equipment that has been purchased for their protection.

10) Don't allow folders to bulge. Bulging folders encourage filing errors. When necessary, divide individual folders into monthly folders. Expand your system by preparing special and individual folders whenever possible.

11) Separate records that must be maintained in the files for long periods of time from those of temporary value. It's easier to purge the files.

12) If small or substandard documents are placed in file folders, glue them to standard-size paper. They'll be easier to find.

13) If a particular document was difficult to retrieve, cross-reference (or reclassify) it when it's finally found. It will save time when it is requested again.

14) Protect the tabs on guides and folders. Always lift a folder or guide by the side — never by the tab. Replace folder labels immediately when they become difficult to read.

15) Don't fill a file drawer to capacity. Leave at least six inches of working space in each file drawer. It speeds up your work and prevents papers from being torn.

16) For safety's sake, close a file drawer immediately after using it; and open only one drawer at a time.

17) Use the proper filing tools. A rubber finger helps separate documents; a file shelf makes you more efficient at the file; a file stool conserves your energy (yes, you can file sitting down).

18) Mend all torn documents before placing them in a file folder.

19) Follow a regular program of removing inactive records from the active files (more about this in Part 4).

20) Be certain to follow, without variation, the office procedures that have been established to protect vital records.

Study Questions

1. How are letters and other papers gathered together for filing and by whom?

2. Do carbon copies of outgoing letters need to bear release marks?

3. Is *indexing* something that is written?

4. What are the various captions under which incoming letters could be filed?

5. Under what captions may copies of outgoing letters be filed?

6. Under what caption is a personal letter filed?

7. What is coding and how is it done?

8. What is cross-referencing?

9. What is used to establish a permanent cross-reference?

10. Why are materials sorted before they are filed?

11. What is a sorting tray?

12. How are letters arranged in "individual" folders? in "miscellaneous" folders? in "special" folders?

13. What are the twenty filing hints that are recommended by experienced file clerks?

What Do You Think?

1. Why are indexing and coding so important in filing?

2. It is said that cross-referencing can be overdone. Under what circumstances might this be true?

3. Why is the most recent letter placed in front in an "individual" folder?

Your Personal Qualities

In the office of the Walters Shoe Company, Mr. J. B. Wilkins has received a letter asking for an answer to an earlier letter written by the National Leather Company. The unanswered letter was found in the "special" folder of the National Leather Company. The letter bears the initials JBW as a release-for-filing mark, but Mr. Wilkins says he does not remember initialing the letter. The initials were actually placed there by mistake by a clerk in Mr. Wilkins' office.

Question: What should be done in this case?

How's Your English?

After reading rule 10 on spelling in Appendix C, fill in the correct letters in the following words:

w—ght   pr—st   n—ghbor

fr—ght   rec—ved   —ther
bel—f   s—ze   counterf—t
interv—w   v—l   rec—pt
conc—t   c—ling   for—gn

Office Work

1. The following letters pertaining to the application of John A. Dillon are filed in the "Applications" folder of the firm where you work. Indicate the order, from front to back, in which the letters should be placed in this folder.

a. Henry & Currier Company's March 8 letter of recommendation

b. John A. Dillon's March 12 letter stating that he will call on March 15

c. Your firm's March 3 letter to Mr. Dillon asking him to come in for an interview

d. John A. Dillon's March 18 letter accepting the position

e. Your firm's March 5 letter to the Henry & Currier Company asking for information about Mr. John A. Dillon

f. Your firm's March 11 letter to Mr. Dillon asking him to come in for a second interview

g. Your firm's March 17 letter offering Mr. Dillon a position in the cost accounting department

h. John A. Dillon's March 1 letter of application

i. Your firm's March 9 letter to Henry & Currier Company thanking them for their cooperation

2. The following letters are filed in the Harvey O. Jackson individual folder. Indicate the order, from front to back, in which the letters should be placed in this folder.

a. Harvey O. Jackson's order of April 1

b. Your firm's letter of April 8 enclosing the April 6 invoice

c. Harvey O. Jackson's letter of April 30 enclosing a check

d. A cross-reference sheet dated April 10

e. Your firm's letter of May 3 acknowledging the check of April 30

f. Your firm's invoice of April 6 for the April 1 order

3. The following letters are filed in the "To-Tw" miscellaneous folder. Indicate the order, from front to back, in which the letters should be placed in this folder.

   a. Your firm's letter of September 30 to Arthur Towne, Jr.

b. The receipted invoice sent to you on September 21 by Albert Town

c. Towne and Lovitt's order of September 2

d. Your firm's letter of September 28 to Richard G. Twitchell

e. Your firm's invoice of September 6 covering the September 2 order from Towne and Lovitt

f. An advertising circular and letter dated September 14 sent to your employer by H. J. Tweed

Office Work Assignments

33: Alphabetic Indexing No. 2

a. Type the following 25 names in index form on 25 more of your file cards. Type the number in the upper right-hand corner and the name and address below the indexed name as you did in Part 2.

b. Integrate these 25 cards in proper filing order with the 50 cards prepared in Part 2.

c. Save the cards for the assignment following Part 6.

51. X-Cel Paints & Varnishes, 532 Mill St., Pittsburgh, Pennsylvania

52. Theodore C. Haller, 59 E. Tenth St., Charleston, West Virginia

53. Henry R. Elston, II, 660 N. Michigan Ave., Chicago, Illinois

54. XYZ Electrical Repair Service, Second and Main Sts., Lexington, Kentucky

55. Countess Flora's Dance Academy, Chase Hotel, St. Louis, Missouri

56. Mrs. K. D. Ingles (Hazel Parks), 40 Sheridan Dr., Providence, Rhode Island

57. Quick Brothers Florists, 6720 Turkey Run Rd., Nashville, Tennessee

58. Charles T. Hallam, 4600 Pueblo St., Phoenix, Arizona

59. Hall-Kramer Printing Co., Inc., 7700 S. Wells St., Chicago, Illinois

60. R. Nelson Forrester, 377 Desert Drive, Reno, Nevada

61. Robert N. Forrest, 781 University Ave., Minneapolis, Minnesota

62. Sister Julietta, Sacred Heart Academy, Racine, Wisconsin

63. William A. Graves, 239 N. Vineyard Drive, Kenosha, Wisconsin

64. Mrs. Arthur P. Matthews (Helen), 5229 Crest Drive, Cleveland, Ohio

65. Town & Country Furniture Co., Town & Country Shop-In, Centerville, Indiana

66. U.S. Electrotype Corp., 2101 — 19 St., Long Island City, New York

67. Prince George Hotel, St. Thomas, Virgin Islands

68. Les Trois Chats Inn, 48 Henri St., Quebec, Province of Quebec, Canada

69. 29 Palms Motel, U.S. 60 at First St., Twenty-Nine Palms, California

70. Vera Cruz Yacht Club, 29 Oceanside Drive, Vera Cruz, California

71. Mt. Morris Book Store, Sixth & Pike St., Mt. Morris, Illinois

72. State Auditor, Columbus, Ohio

73. Hire-the-Handicapped Committee, 30 LeVeque Tower, Denver, Colorado

74. Hamilton County S. P. C. A., Colerain & Blue Rock Sts., Cincinnati, Ohio

75. Port-au-Prince Imports, Inc., 21 Main St., Gulfport, Mississippi

UNIT 9 | Business Filing and Records Control

PART 4:

Charge, Follow-Up, Transfer, Storage, and Microfilming

Records are retained because they contain needed information; filing systems are developed in order to retrieve this information promptly and efficiently. Yet, if records are continually removed from the files without "charging" them to the borrower, the system will soon become ineffective. It will certainly not be worth the considerable amount of time, effort, and money that has gone into its development.

Since the people who borrow records from the files are busy, they may neglect to return these documents to the files. Although every worker should feel responsible for maintaining an effective office information system, it is your responsibility to protect the records placed under your control. Therefore, some type of charge-out and follow-up system must be developed to insure the return of borrowed documents to the files.

Charging. Requests for material from the files may be made in person, over the phone, or through interoffice mail. Regardless of the method that is used, a form should be prepared that fully identifies the records removed from the files. This form (usually 5″ x 3″ or 5″ x 4″) is known as a *requisition card* and has spaces for a full description of the material borrowed, the name and department of the borrower, the date the material was removed from the file, and the date it is to be returned.

Charge Forms. In addition to the requisition card, four other forms are commonly used when material is withdrawn from the files. They are out guides, out folders, carrier folders, and substitution cards.

Out Guides. An out guide is a pressboard guide with the word "OUT" printed on its tab. It is placed in the files when an entire folder is borrowed. There are two forms of out guides. One type is ruled on both sides and the charge information written directly on the guide. When the

289

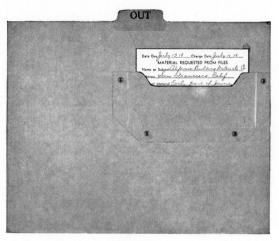

Out guide

folder is returned, the out guide is removed and the charge information crossed out. The guide is then ready for further use.

The other form of out guide has a pocket into which a requisition card is placed. This form is preferred since it is faster to use and the charge information is usually more legible. The requisition cards may later be used to analyze the activity of the files (a tabulation of the cards will determine how often the files are used and which records are most active).

Out Folders. Some firms prefer using out folders when an entire folder is requested from the files. If additional material reaches the files before the regular folder is returned, it is temporarily filed in the out folder. This material is then filed in the regular folder when it is returned. The out folder is also available in the two formats described earlier.

Carrier Folder. A carrier folder is useful in reminding the borrower to return records to the files. It is of some distinctive color with the words "RETURN TO FILES" printed on it. The requested material is removed from the regular folder and sent to the borrower in a carrier folder. An out card or guide is placed in the regular folder containing the charge information. The regular folder remains in the file to hold any material placed in the file before the carrier folder is returned. A carrier folder saves the regular folder from the wear and tear it would receive when removed from the files.

Substitution Cards. A substitution card is a tabbed card, usually salmon-colored, that is placed in a folder when single documents are borrowed. The word "OUT" is printed on the tab. The charge information

OUT

SUBSTITUTION CARD   FILE AT EXTREME RIGHT OF FOLDER

Name or Subject   Tickler date

Gibson Hotel, Los Angeles   *Oct. 20*

Re: Date of letter

                                             Sometime
Quotation on room prices   *in August*

Taken by   Date taken

D. M. Cannon   *Oct. 18*

Signed *J. R.*   Dept. *Advertising*

REQUISITION OR TICKLER

Remington Rand

Substitution card

may be recorded on the card itself or a requisition form inserted into a pocket on the subsitution card.

Facsimile Copies. To avoid removing important documents from the files, many firms prepare facsimile copies of a requested record. When this method is used, the document is removed from the files and copied on a copying machine. The original document is then refiled and the photocopy sent to the borrower with instructions to destroy it after use. This method is generally used when single documents are requested rather than an entire folder.

Length of Charge Time. Borrowed materials are usually used by the borrower upon receipt and should be returned to the files immediately. The longer records are away from the files, the more difficult it is to get them back; furthermore, they are likely to be lost or discarded. Most firms charge out records for only one week (with weekly extensions, if found necessary). It is best to have short charge periods and prompt follow-up of materials not returned to the files.

Follow-Up Methods. How will you remember to give attention to the many matters that require future attention? Since you cannot rely on

Remington Rand

Card tickler file and card

your memory, you will find it necessary to devise a system that will call your attention to these matters at the exact date when action must be taken. A file that is designed for this purpose is called a *follow-up file* and is arranged in chronological order. Three common follow-up files include the card tickler file, the dated follow-up folder file, and signal folders.

Card Tickler Files. A card tickler file consists of a set of twelve monthly primary guides and thirty-one daily secondary guides. Important matters to be followed up are recorded on cards and placed behind the appropriate month and day guides in the file. A card tickler file may be used to follow up records that have been borrowed from the files or to follow up other matters that require attention.

Dated Follow-Up Folders. This file resembles the card tickler file except that a folder is available for each day of the month. Items that require follow-up are placed in the correct day folder and the folder is placed behind the appropriate monthly guide. For example, a folder may contain a facsimile copy of a purchase order or an extra carbon of an invoice that should be checked on a specific future date. On that particular date you will see if the goods have been received or other matters referring to the purchase order or invoice in question have been taken care of, or if further follow-up action is necessary. By using facsimiles and extra carbons for follow-up, the original documents can be filed in their proper place and the official folder is always complete.

Signal Folders for Follow-Up. Some types of material, such as contracts, franchises, and sales reports, are on perpetual follow-up at irregular periods and the entire folder is always wanted. A special type of folder may be used for this purpose. This is a folder with a straight-edge back printed from left to right with numbers 1 to 31, corresponding to the days of the month. The follow-up date that applies to the folder is checked in pencil or a movable color signal is placed over the date. The folder would be filed by name. When the follow-up date is reached, the folder is pulled out and turned over to the person who takes action on the matter.

Transferring Records. Office files should contain only those records that are needed to operate efficiently. If inactive or obsolete records are never removed from the files, needed information becomes more and more difficult to retain and retrieve. Every organization should adopt a plan of removing inactive documents from the active files and *transferring* these records to a *records center.*

Removing inactive records from the office files serves three important purposes: (1) active records can be filed and retrieved quickly; (2) expensive office space and file equipment is kept to a minimum; (3) costs are reduced since transferred records are housed in inexpensive file equipment, usually cardboard transfer cases.

It is important to remember that not every document received should be filed; not every document retained in the active file should be transferred.

Transferring File Folders. Records that must be retained for long periods of time should be segregated from those of temporary value when placing records into transfer cases. Miscellaneous, special, and individual folders are usually transferred from the active to the inactive files. File guides, however, are not transferred. These guides are too expensive and more detailed than necessary for inactive records. Each transferred folder should be stamped "Transfer File" to prevent it from being returned to the active files should it be requested from the records center. Many firms use different colored folder labels to identify different file periods.

Transfer Methods. There are two methods of transferring material to inactive files: *perpetual* and *periodic.*

The Perpetual Method. The perpetual method is a method of continually removing inactive material from the active files. It can be used only when work is completed in easily defined units, such as the legal cases handled by lawyers or the building projects of contractors. When a case is closed or completed, the folder is transferred to a records center.

Periodic Methods. The transfer of inactive matter to record centers at stated intervals is known as periodic transfer. Three different methods may be used: the *one-period plan*, the *two-period* or *duplicate equipment plan*, and the *maximum-minimum plan*.

1) One-Period Plan. When this plan is used, *all* material is removed from the active files on a certain date (usually once or twice a year) and placed in the records center. New folders are prepared and a new active file is started. The major objection to this method of transfer is that many active documents are suddenly removed from the files and frequent trips to the inactive files are necessary.

2) Two-Period Plan. Under the two-period plan, duplicate files are maintained in the office, one active and one semiactive. These records are usually maintained in the same or adjacent filing cabinets. Quite often the upper drawers of the filing cabinets are used for filing active records and the lower drawers reserved for semiactive records. At the end of each file period (six months or a year), the semiactive files are transferred to the records center and the material in the active files, in turn, transferred to the semiactive section. The advantage of this plan is that both active and semiactive records are readily available in the office. This method is successfully used in many offices, both large and small.

3) Maximum-Minimum Plan. When this plan is used, only the inactive material is transferred at regular intervals.

The following example illustrates how the plan works. In a particular office, records are transferred each year on June 30. All records dated during the current calendar year remain in the active files, while all records dated during the preceding year are transferred. This means that records are kept in the active files for at least six months (January 1 to June 30 of the current year, when transfer is made) but not more than eighteen months (January 1 of the preceding year to June 30 of the transfer year). In other words, every record that is transferred is at least six months old and may vary in age at the time of transfer from six to eighteen months. It is from these minimum and maximum periods of time that the method receives its name.

The Records Center. A records center is an important part of any transfer program. This center houses documents no longer needed for daily reference. Records may be retained at the center indefinitely or for a temporary period only. Inactive records are inexpensively maintained in the center since all the floor space can be utilized (floor to ceiling filing) and inexpensive equipment can be used to house the records.

Documents maintained in the center must be accurately indexed and controlled so that they are available when requested. Without adequate indexing, protection, and control of these inactive records, all the time and effort spent in the transfer program would be wasted.

The Retention of Records. Every organization is faced with the problem of how long to retain their records. Because of the growing volume of paper work, many firms are establishing *record retention schedules.* This schedule identifies the retention value of every record created or received by an organization and determines what records must be retained and for how long. Useless records occupy expensive floor space and costly equipment; they hinder the rapid retrieval of needed information.

While certain documents must be retained permanently, most of the records created and received in the average business organization have a limited period of usefulness. The National Records Management Council estimates that 95 percent of all corporate paper work over a year old is rarely, if ever, referred to again. Most record authorities estimate that 40 percent of all stored records can be legally destroyed.

Even though every organization must develop its own retention schedule, factors that may affect the retention value of business records include: (1) legal requirements (federal, state, and local); (2) office use (those records needed to operate on a daily basis); (3) historical documents; (4) vital records.

A retention schedule can be adopted only after a thorough study of the record requirements of a particular organization. Legal counsel should always be sought. Once a schedule is adopted, it must be continually revised to meet changing conditions and needs.

Protecting Vital Records. Vital records are documents a company must have in order to resume operations after a fire or some other disaster. Usually they are related to the legal and financial matters of a corporation or company and include information regarding customers, employees, stockholders, and other equally important matters. These records are sometimes kept in fire-resistant filing equipment or in special vaults. Some companies make duplicate copies of these essential records and have copies stored at a location other than the principal office of the company. These duplicate copies are sometimes facsimile reproductions of the documents, but they are frequently reproduced on microfilm or on magnetic tape. A few commercially operated record centers have been established in the country, sometimes located in caves or old mines. In offices where vital records are worked on and kept, the employees should file records promptly after use and be certain that all such records are off the desks and are deposited in the fire-resistant filing equipment before they leave for the night.

Microfilming. Because of increasing information requirements, many organizations are using microfilm as a solution to certain of their information problems. Microfilm is a method of copying records in miniature. Since microfilm cannot be viewed by the naked eye, the microimages are magnified by a reader or reader-printer.

Microfilm was originally used as a method of saving space or protecting vital records. Today, however, it is widely used as a method of processing, distributing, and retrieving information. Schools, banks, department stores, libraries, government offices, and research centers are among the many active users of microfilm.

A few examples of the information capabilities of microfilm are as follows:

Duplication and Copying. With the development and refinement of the reader-printer, *hard copies* of microimages are quickly obtained by pressing a button. The term "hard copy" applies to copy that can be read without the use of a magnifying device. Duplication by microfilm also eliminates time-consuming manual transcribing and also provides error-free copies.

Retrieval. The retrieval of microimages is no longer a slow and tiresome job. Motorized and electronic equipment capable of retrieving microimages at very high speeds and producing hard copies almost instantaneously is available. The Social Security Administration, for

Microfilming checks in a bank

Recordak Corporation

example, maintains microfilm records of over 130 million people — and can obtain a hard copy of any record in 90 seconds.

Communications. Many organizations (particularly builders and engineers) transmit information exclusively by microfilm. A large number of engineering drawings, for example, can be mailed in an ordinary envelope when reduced to microfilm.

Publishing. Microfilm makes possible the preservation and distribution of rare books, reference materials, newspapers, and periodicals to schools and libraries all over the world.

Microfilm Formats. Once documents have been photographed by a microfilm camera and the film processed and inspected, the microimages are ready to be used. In its original state, microfilm is in 100- or 200-foot lengths of film. Other formats include: film magazines, microfilm tape, chips, micro-opaque cards, acetate jackets, microfilm sheets, and aperture cards. The roll, acetate jacket, and aperture card are commonly used in many business offices.

Roll. About 3,000 letter-size documents or 30,000 check-size documents can be photographed on a 100-foot roll of microfilm. Roll film is the most economical format, provided no additions or corrections must be made to the roll. Fast and accurate reference to the records will depend on how well the film is indexed. Motorized viewing machines allow rapid retrieval of records stored on rolls.

Jackets. Jackets are transparent acetate envelopes with narrow chambers that hold strips of microfilm. Since the standard microfilm jacket is 4″ x 6″ (the same size as a standard file card), the jacket and a card file may be combined as an integrated information system. The images can be read and hard copies produced without removing them from the jacket. Obsolete images are easily removed and new images inserted in the jacket. Jackets are frequently used in hospitals and in large personnel departments.

Aperture Cards. The aperture card is a file or standard tabulating card with a die-cut hole in which a microimage (or frame) is mounted. If the images are mounted in tabulating cards, indexing information may be punched on the cards and the cards arranged and retrieved mechanically by using a sorter.

The aperture card is used in many microfilm retrieval systems and has found popular use in engineering offices. For example, the U.S. Army Rocket Guided Missile Agency "files" over 100,000 engineering drawings on aperture cards in only four square feet of floor space.

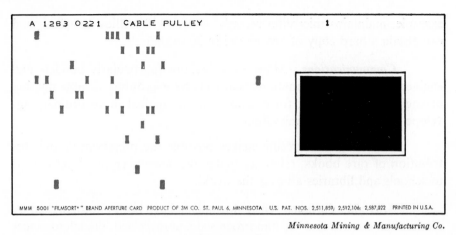

MMM 5001 "FILMSORT*" BRAND APERTURE CARD   PRODUCT OF 3M CO.   ST. PAUL 6, MINNESOTA   U.S. PAT. NOS. 2,511,859; 2,512,106; 2,587,022   PRINTED IN U.S.A.

Minnesota Mining & Manufacturing Co.

Aperture card

What to Microfilm? All documents should not be microfilmed. Although documents reduced to microfilm occupy about two percent of the space required by regular records, microfilm should not be used only as a method of saving space, except in unusual situations. Inactive records should be transferred to low-cost record centers after realistic retention periods have been adopted. The expense of microfilm cannot be justified if infrequent use is made of too many office records. In most cases, records must be retained for fifteen years or more before it is economical to microfilm only to save space. Newly created vital records, however, may be microfilmed immediately in order to protect vital information.

Information Retrieval Systems. Eastman Kodak, IBM, and Magnavox are among several organizations that are developing automatic information retrieval systems combining microfilm with electronic data processing equipment. For the most part, these systems have been designed for governmental and military operations. These micromemory systems, however, are commercially available and some of them will eventually be installed in business offices.

In general, these systems provide for the filming of many related documents along with indexing information on a "chip" of film. In a less advanced system, these images would be placed on one or more aperture cards with the indexing information keypunched on the cards. In a micromemory system, the indexing information might be produced on perforated tape and then fed through a machine that electronically converts the information into a dot-code pattern on the chip that contains the greatly miniaturized records. In one system, a chip of film smaller than a postage stamp contains twelve letter-size documents as well as the indexing code. These systems provide for almost unlimited cross-indexing and high-speed retrieval and print-out capabilities. One firm, for example, is developing a micromemory system that will be able to retrieve any one of 99 million documents in about five seconds.

Study Questions

1. Why should all materials taken from files be "charged" to the person taking them?

2. What is a requisition card?

3. What are the two types of out guides? Which is better?

4. What is the difference between an out guide and a substitution card?

5. How is the out folder used?

6. Describe a card tickler file and tell of its use.

7. What are signal folders? How are they used?

8. What are the commonly used plans for transferring old papers from active files? Describe each.

9. Why are business papers micro-filmed?

10. For what purpose is a microfilm reader used?

What Do You Think?

1. The filing department of a certain business is so small that no one person is responsible for the keeping of a record of materials borrowed. Each person who needs correspondence from the files removes it from the folders, signs his name in a record book kept for this purpose, and takes the correspondence with him. Can you recommend any improvement in this system?

2. In what way does transferring filed materials at regular intervals tend to cut down the cost of labor? How does it often save rent? How does it save in the cost of filing equipment?

3. How long should a business keep general correspondence? interdepartmental correspondence?

Your Personal Qualities

Your company has a rule that all materials requisitioned from the files must be returned within 48 hours. One of the company executives has a habit of holding folders for a week or more, frequently creating problems in the filing room.

Question: What action might the chief file clerk take to try to improve this situation?

How's Your English?

After reading Appendix C on spelling and word choice, correct the spelling of the following words:

acceptible

affidavid
colateral
complience
customery

Office Work

1. The filing department of the A to Z Novelty Supply Company transfers its correspondence once a year, on December 31, according to the two-period plan. If a letter is dated August 2, of last year, on what date is it removed to the semiactive files? to the transfer files?

2. The filing department of the General Products Corp. transfers its correspondence twice a year, on June 30 and December 31, according to the two-period method. If a letter is dated October 14 of last year, on what date is it transferred to the semiactive files? to the transfer files?

3. Visit a local office and learn what procedures are used in transfer and storage. Write your report, but be ready to make an oral report to the class if your teacher asks you to do so.

UNIT 9 | Business Filing and Records Control

PART 5:

Numeric, Subject, and Geographic Filing

Records must be filed in the manner by which they will be requested in order to justify keeping them at all. When you follow your executive's direction to send copies of a particular report to all the salesmen in each territory, you will make use of a geographic file. In another instance, you may determine which checks are outstanding, according to a numeric file. Instead of remembering the name of the man who wrote your employer about wage-incentive plans, you may look for the letter under the subject "Wage-Incentive Plans." So you see that, although most material is filed alphabetically because it will be asked for by a company or individual name, other materials are identified and requested by number, by subject, or by geographic location.

The distribution of the copies of a sales order is another example of filing records in the manner in which they are most useful or will be requested. Orders are usually written on multipart forms with a preprinted number in the upper right portion of the form. A typical distribution of a seven-part form would be:

Copy 1 — Acknowledgment — sent to the customer.

2 — Manufacturing or production department — as an "order to manufacture" or to withdraw the item or items from stock. This copy is filed in consecutive numeric order and related correspondence on production schedules, back orders, shipping dates, and complaints is attached.

3 — Accounting department — as a record of "accounts receivable." This copy is filed alphabetically by customer's name.

4 — Sales department — as a record of business from a customer. This copy is usually filed alphabetically, and related intraoffice correspondence or letters to and from the customer are attached. Frequently, when products are manufactured specifically for a customer, each order will be filed in an individual folder which will be identified by order number as well as by name.

5 — Sales department — as a statistical record for products sold and /or sales in a territory. This copy may be filed by product number, product name (by subject), or by territory (geographically), then by product number or name within the territory.

6 — Purchasing department — as a requisition to buy needed materials. This copy is usually filed numerically.

7 — Shipping department — as a packing slip for enclosure with merchandise. Before shipment, these copies are filed alphabetically by name of customer.

NUMERIC FILING

With the widespread use of data processing systems for repetitive and statistical operations in many organizations, numbers have become prevalent as identifiers of records in today's businesses. In general, only large systems would probably use numeric filing unless the number already is part of the document. Records that are frequently identified by number and filed in a numeric sequence include such things as stock and /or inventory items and stock records, requisitions, purchase orders, sales orders, vouchers, contracts, projects, jobs, cases, licenses, customers' charge accounts, and credit-card accounts. Many large government agencies such as the Social Security Administration, the Veterans Administration, and state motor vehicle bureaus file their records in numerical order.

Since it would be impossible to remember the file number of every account, claim, or business paper, an alphabetic index (either cards or one copy of a multiple-part form) of the numerically filed material is maintained by name or by subject as a cross-reference. Numeric filing systems are indirect in finding and filing because in most instances reference must be made to the alphabetic card index before a document is found or coded.

Organization of a Numeric File. A numeric file usually consists of three parts:

1) The file itself, in which the documents are filed by an assigned number and in which both guides and folders bear numeric captions.

2) A supplementary index card control file in which names or subject titles are arranged alphabetically.

3) An accession book in which a consecutive record of assigned numbers is kept. The company, name, or subject, and in the case of orders, the customer's order number, also may be listed next to the number.

Numeric Arrangements. There are several arrangements of numbers that may be used in numeric filing. The numbers may be in consecutive order; or certain portions of a long number may be used as the first indexing unit; or the numbers may be assigned to maintain both an alphabetic and numeric sequence; or the number may be combined with letters of the alphabet. Expansion is almost unlimited in numeric filing, and each arrangement has specific applications for which it is most suitable.

Consecutive Number Filing. In this arrangement, documents are filed in strict numeric sequence. The next available number from the accession book is assigned to the project, job, order, or document as the papers are initially received. The number is written in the upper right portion of the paper and the alphabetic card typed as a cross-reference to the assigned number. The papers are filed in numerical sequence in folders, and the cards are filed alphabetically in the index. Subsequent papers for the same matter are checked against the card index and coded with the previously assigned number.

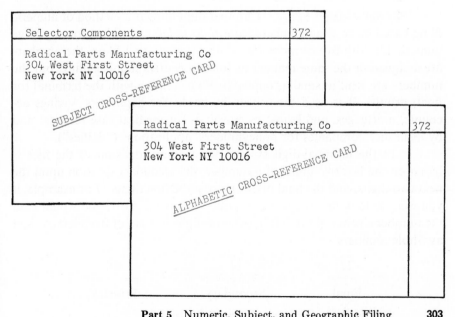

Project and Job Files. Consecutive numeric filing is used for these two types of records primarily because there are related drawings, blueprints, and artwork connected with the correspondence. Such material is controlled more readily through a numbering system. Almost always it is necessary to subdivide the correspondence by subject. Drawings will have subsidiary numbers for parts of the project or job, and dates for revisions of drawings become an important identifying factor. Numbers are obtained from the accession book. The alphabetical card index is an essential key for locating material by name or subject.

Legal Files. In legal firms, a number (for example, 607) is assigned to a client and as additional matters are handled for the same client, they are given a subsidiary number (607-1) to separate the new matter. An alphabetic cross-reference card is made for each client as well as for each subsidiary matter. Individual folders are prepared for each and are filed numerically: 607, 607-1, 607-2, and so on.

Numeric Correspondence Files. Because it is a slow and indirect method, ordinary correspondence today is seldom filed numerically. The need to keep papers confidential is the primary reason for using this system. Numbers are assigned in consecutive order from the accession book, and individual folders are made for each correspondent. All papers for this correspondent are placed in this folder, with the most recent material in the front. An alphabetic index card is made. Both the accession book and the card index are not accessible to unauthorized personnel.

Terminal-Digit Filing. Terminal-digit filing is a method of numeric filing based on reading numbers from *right to left*. It is ideal for any large numeric file with five or more digits. In terminal-digit filing, the numbers are assigned in the same manner as for consecutive number filing, but the numbers are read in small groups (00–99) beginning with the terminal (or final) group. It is used extensively by banks for depositors' savings accounts, mortgages, and loans; by hospitals for medical case records; and by insurance companies for policyholders' applications ("dailies").

In the terminal-digit system, the primary division of the files is based on the last two digits of a number, the secondary division upon the next two digits, and the final division upon the first digits. For example, if you were to look up life insurance policy number 225101, you would read the numbers from right to left in pairs of digits instead of from left to right as whole numbers.

22	51	01
Final	Secondary	Primary

You would first locate the drawer containing those materials or records whose numbers end with 01. Then you would search down the guides in that drawer for the number 51. Lastly, you would file or find the material in proper order behind the number 22. Numbers of fewer than six digits are brought up to that figure by adding zeros to the left of the number.

When even larger numbers are common, they may be broken down for filing in groups of three digits, 000 to 999.

Since it is basically a method of interfiling, the terminal-digit filing system assures an even distribution of material in all parts of the file, thereby avoiding congestion. Workloads are distributed more evenly among operating personnel. Drawer contents do not have to be shifted constantly to fill in numeric gaps when "closed" files are transferred to storage areas. It is easier to remember two- or three-digit numbers accurately. Sorting and handling of records is faster and more efficient. The following chart compares consecutive-numeric, and terminal-digit filing arrangements and illustrates how congestion will occur with consecutive numbers.

Consecutive Numeric →

00	01	02	03	04	05	06	07	08	09
10	11	12	13	14	15	16	17	18	19
20	21	22	23	24	25	26	27	28	29
30	31	32	33	34	35	36	37	38	39
40	41	42	43	44	45	46	47	48	49
50	51	52	53	54	55	56	57	58	59
60	61	62	63	64	65	66	67	68	69
70	71	72	73	74	75	76	77	78	79
80	81	82	83	84	85	86	87	88	89
90	91	92	93	94	95	96	97	98	99

Terminal Digit →

The Office — February 1955

Time savings of 25 to 50 percent have been realized by some companies in changing from consecutive-number to terminal-digit filing. Printed forms, such as insurance applications, frequently are printed with spaces or dashes between the digit groups to further facilitate filing:

22 51 01   or   22-51-01

Middle-Digit Filing.   One modification of terminal-digit filing is middle-digit filing. In this system, the middle (secondary) series of digits is considered first, then the final series, and lastly (if necessary) the primary series. The number 225101, would be filed in this order:

22	51	01
Final	Primary	Secondary

If a company prefers to assign numbers in blocks rather than singly, it is possible in middle-digit filing to have the entire block filed in one place. For example, a sales organization may assign orders with the middle digits of 40 to the Western territory, 60 to the Midwestern, 80 to the Southern, and 00 to the Eastern (main office).

Middle-digit filing has the same advantages and uses as terminal-digit filing, plus other benefits when applied to electronic accounting.

Comparison of Consecutive, Terminal-Digit, and Middle-Digit Sequences

This table compares the sequence of seven numbers filed in consecutive, terminal-digit, and middle-digit files. The same numbers are used in the three columns.

Back	Consecutive-Number Filing	Terminal-Digit Filing	Middle-Digit Filing	Back
↑	74 27 18	12 34 56	53 96 24	↑
	53 96 24	34 37 49	53 95 27	
	53 95 27	34 34 49	34 37 49	
	46 29 18	53 95 27	12 34 56	
	34 37 49	53 96 24	34 34 49	
	34 34 49	46 29 18	46 29 18	
Front	12 34 56	74 27 18	74 27 18	Front
		Sequence Folder Drawer	Sequence Drawer Folder	

Alpha-Numeric Filing. Banks now identify the checking accounts of their depositors by numbers. In some banks, an individual account number is assigned to each depositor according to an *alpha-numeric plan*. This is a method of assigning numbers to accounts in such a way that even with additions and deletions, the accounts filed in numeric sequence will also be in alphabetic sequence. Originally, the accounts are arranged in exact alphabetic sequence and assigned account numbers with uniform gaps between numbers to allow for additional accounts. This number (MICR) is printed with a special magnetic ink on a set of blank checks before the checks are given to the depositor. After a check has been drawn, cashed, and returned to the bank, a machine automatically "reads" the MICR number and charges the account of the depositor. The canceled checks are filed daily, in front of checksize guides which usually contain the signature card of the depositor, and are accumulated until the time of the month when the statement and canceled checks for the period are returned to the depositor.

Other Alpha-Numeric Systems. There are other applications and many possible variations of alpha-numeric filing systems. Two such variations are the Soundex system and the Triple Check Automatic system, both of which are manufactured by Remington Office Systems, a division of Sperry Rand Corporation.

The Soundex system is designed to bring all names that sound the same but are spelled differently (such as Patin, Paton, Patten, and Patton) into one section of a file by assigning alpha-numeric codes to the names on the basis of pronunciation rather than spelling.

The Triple Check Automatic System is based upon a system of alpha-numeric codes assigned to correspondence according to a chart for coding primary indexing units and a chart for coding secondary indexing units. Filing of papers is done on the basis of the codes assigned rather than on the basis of the alphabetic units themselves. Color is also used to aid in the filing and finding of folders.

Both Soundex and Triple Check Automatic are highly specialized systems and are typically used in large filing departments with special problems that these systems are designed to solve. Before a files operator is assigned to the operation of such a system, in-service training should be given. For that reason these systems are not covered in detail in this book.

Guides and Folders Used in Numeric Filing. The type and quantity of supplies used in numeric filing will depend on the arrangement that is used. Single numbered sheets can be filed 50 or 100 to a folder, with the tabs numbered in skips of 50 or 100. Sheets with two or three papers attached can be filed ten numbers to a folder, with the tabs numbered in skips of 10. Individual folders can be made for each number, with the number on the tab, or the number and name typed on a label affixed to the tab. Folder tabs can be straight cut, one-half cut (even numbers can be placed on the left tab, odd numbers on the right tab, to further facilitate filing operations), or one-fifth cut in all five positions (00, 05, 10, 15, etc., are always on the tab in the first position, another aid in speed). Guides are normally inserted for every ten folders. Colored acetate windows in the guides for 00, 25, 50, and 75 in a terminal-digit system, or for every 100 in a consecutive-numeric system, will highlight areas and speed finding.

SUBJECT FILING

Every organization has materials which are of prime significance because of their content rather than by whom or to whom they are written, and for these materials a *subject filing system* would be necessary. These letters relate to the administration, management, and operational functions of the business and are the basis for company policies and procedures. Other areas in which subject filing is important are in the research and development, product or manufacturing, sales and engineering departments, where technical data and information are constantly being used. Today's "knowledge explosion" is being stressed, and rapid information retrieval is a necessity.

In almost every filing system you will find that some materials are called for by subject rather than by name, so there are usually a few folders in every system that are labeled according to the subject matter of their contents. A folder labeled "Applications" with the subheading "Salesmen" is an example. The names of all the sales applicants are not easily remembered; therefore the names are of minor importance in filing, and the letters should be placed in a special subject folder labeled "Applications — Salesmen." As long as there are only a few subject-matter folders, they are filed in a regular alphabetic or numeric system along with the other folders.

If subject matter becomes the predominating element in most of the correspondence, the filing system, or a part of it, should be arranged in terms of subjects rather than names. Separate subject files are commonly used in departmental and branch offices for materials that pertain to those departments or branches as separate units of the business rather than to the business as a whole. If the whole filing system is arranged on a subject-matter basis, great care must be taken to outline divisions and subdivisions of subjects so that letters may be readily filed and found.

Arrangement of a Subject File. An alphabetic arrangement of subjects permits direct reference to the filed material. The two methods of arranging subject matter alphabetically are: (1) a straight *dictionary arrangement* of subjects without relation to each other, and (2) *group method*, an alphabetic arrangement of main subjects, with the subdivisions of each subject also arranged alphabetically. For example, if the files of a firm were arranged according to the group method, one of the main subjects could be "SAFETY," and the subheadings under the main heading "SAFETY" would be "Accident Prevention," "Emergency Procedures," "Fire Prevention," "Fire Protection," "Plant Protection," and "Standards." Subdivisions under "Plant Protection" could be "Clearances," "Guards," "Passes," "Regulations," and "Visitors."

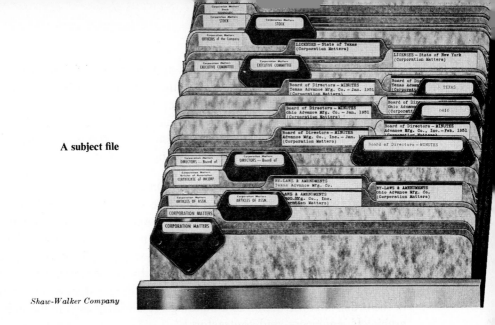

A subject file

Shaw-Walker Company

The terms must be clear and concise, adequately descriptive, and designed to meet the needs of the business. The system must be designed around the *functions* of the business, but the use of department or division names as main subjects will not necessarily be properly descriptive or eliminate overlapping. Another hazard is that frequent departmental name changes would necessitate changing the file terminology and contents. The use of simple terms (not so broad as to become "catch-alls") and an uncomplicated system as a whole will provide a most useful working "tool" for the executives in a company in bringing together all papers on a related subject.

The following list shows some typical subject filing captions:

Advertising	Equipment	Payroll
Applications	Executive Matters	Periodicals
Appropriations		Personnel
Associations	Finance	Price Lists
Audit Reports		Public Relations
	Government	Publications
Balance Sheets		Real Estate
Bulletins	Instructions	Reports
By-Laws	Insurance	Research
Catalogs	Legal Matters	Safety
Charts		Sales Reports
Clippings	Magazines	Speaking Invitations
Conferences	Maps	Speeches
Contracts	Methods	Statistical Data
Conventions	Minutes	Surveys
Credits and Collections	Mortgages	
		Taxes — Federal
		Taxes — Municipal
Directors' Meetings	Operating Policies	Taxes — State

The selection of main subjects and their subdivisions is not easy. Printed subject headings, or a subject filing system used by a similar type of business, can serve as a guide for selection of topics, but they rarely can be used without many adaptations and changes. The operation of a subject filing system requires thoughtful consideration on the part of the indexer in the correct designation of the right filing place for each paper.

Numeric Subject Filing Systems. Once the basic subject terms have been established, it may be found that the main subjects and their subdivisions would be better arranged by the *sequence of operations* than in alphabetic order. In this case, consecutive numbers, an Alpha-Numeric, Duplex-Numeric, or decimal classification system, could be applied to the subjects. The standard filing system issued by the American Institute of Architects is an example of a Duplex-Numeric filing system that is arranged in the order of construction of a building. It is widely used in the offices of architects, engineers, and contractors.

Guides and Folders in a Subject File. In a subject file, you will make use of several different types of guides and folders. The main subject titles are used as captions for primary guides. These serve the same purpose as primary guides in an alphabetic file. Auxiliary guides are used for the subordinate titles that are related to the main subjects on the primary guides behind which they are placed.

There is a miscellaneous folder for each main subject in which all papers relative to that topic are filed. Individual folders are made for subdivisions of the main subject when sufficient papers (usually 6 or 7) accumulate for the subtopic. The subdivisions may be made by subject (*Accident Prevention* under "Safety"), by name (*Administrative Management Society* under "Associations"), and /or by date periods (semiannually, quarterly, monthly) as, "Production — Heat Treatment — Reports — *Jan–June 19--*."

When individual folders are used in a subject file, they are placed behind the primary or auxiliary guides that classify the subject matter of the correspondence in those folders. In this way correspondence is doubly identified: by subject, as shown by the guide captions, and by the titles shown on the folder captions. Main subject and all subdivisions must be shown on each folder tab.

Cross-Reference to a Subject File. An alphabetic cross-reference is essential in a subject file for maintaining consistency in assigning subjects. Cross-referencing may be done by using a 5″ x 3″ card index, which is very flexible as additions can be readily made, or by a listing, which is known as a *relative index*.

```
RELATIVE INDEX

        SUBJECT                              FILE UNDER

                              A

Ability Tests                     EMP  - Testing
                                         General Ability

Absence Records                   PR   - Attendance & Absence Records

Absenteeism                       PR   - Attendance & Absence Records

Accident Insurance Plan           EB   - Accident Insurance Plan

Accident Prevention               S&S  - Accident Prevention

Accident Reports                  MS   - Medical Records
                                         Reports - Accident

Accidents                         S&S  - Accidents

Accounting Department             A/F  - Accounting Department

ACCOUNTING & FINANCE              A/F  - ACCOUNTING & FINANCE

Achievement Tests                 EMP  - Testing
                                         Achievement

Activities & Welfare - Employee   EA   - EMPLOYEE ACTIVITIES & WELFARE

Adding Machines & Calculators     ADM  - Equipment & Supplies
                                         Machines
```

Some companies will distribute copies of the main subjects of the filing system (and possibly a definition of each) to each department for their use in dictating letters or when requesting materials from the files.

The card index and relative index are cross-references of a "permanent" nature and do not replace the cross-reference *sheets* which are made on a *single letter*.

Subject Filing Procedure. The person handling the records for a subject file should follow this procedure:

Inspection. Each letter should be checked to see that it has been released for filing.

Coding. The letter must be read carefully to determine under which subject it should be filed. Thorough familiarity with the outline of subjects and their subdivisions is essential. When the subject of a letter has been determined, the caption is written on the letter in the upper right corner or it is underlined if it appears in the letter.

Note that in the sample section of the relative index above, symbols (EMP for "Employment," PR for "Personnel Records," EB for "Employee Benefits") are used as abbreviations of the main subject.

Cross-References. If more than one subject is involved in a letter — a very frequent occurrence — an extra carbon, a facsimile copy of the letter, or a cross-reference sheet should be prepared. If a new product is being discussed, for example, a 5″ x 3″ index card should also be prepared for inclusion in the alphabetic card index.

Follow-ups. Material that needs to be referred to the writer of the letter at a future date should be recorded, using the type of follow-up system that has been adopted for use in the office.

Sorting. Material is sorted first according to the main subjects and second by the main subdivisions.

Placing Material in Folders. Material that is placed in an individual subdivision folder is filed with the latest date in front. If there is no sub-division folder, the material is filed in the miscellaneous folder for the main subject in alphabetic order according to subdivisions or in date order, latest date to front.

Charge Out. When letters are borrowed from the files, use the same procedures of making a record that you would for an alphabetic file. The subject or subdivision is used as the description, instead of the name, on the out guide, out folder, or substitution card which replaces the folder or letter in the file.

The following considerations are extremely important in setting up and operating a subject filing system:

1) The list of subjects must be carefully and intelligently prepared. It should be based upon the material in the files; therefore, it can be prepared only by an office employee who is thoroughly familiar with the files and company operations.
2) Only a trained employee can classify material on a subject basis accurately; therefore, the cost of coding is relatively high.
3) There must be extensive cross-referencing because a number of subjects are sometimes covered in a single letter.

GEOGRAPHIC FILING

If you are using a geographic filing system, geographic location is the prime indexing factor. In the United States, for instance, materials would be arranged alphabetically first by states, then by cities or towns within the states, and finally alphabetically by the names of the corre-spondents in the cities or towns. A geographic file may also be based upon territories of salesmen, upon cities in a single state, or upon districts or streets for local correspondence.

Typical users of geographic filing systems are publishing houses, mail-order houses, radio and television advertisers, real estate firms, and organizations dealing with a large number of small businesses scattered over a wide area. The personnel in many of these small businesses change frequently; therefore, the name of the individual owner or manager is often less important than the location of the business.

Geographic filing is an indirect method for locating folders for individual correspondents. It is slower to operate as papers must be sorted as many as three times, depending on the geographic arrangement that is selected.

Arrangement of a Geographic File. The primary guides in a geographic filing system bear the names of the largest geographic divisions. The specific arrangement will depend on the referral needs of the company and the volume of records. For example, a geographic filing system based on states would have each guide tab printed with the name of a state, and all correspondence with people in that state would be filed behind that guide. These state guides are usually arranged alphabetically; thus, Alabama is first, followed by Alaska and the other states in alphabetic order. They could also be arranged by a division of the country into areas, such as "West Coast"; and behind these guides the secondary guides or folders for the states of Washington, Oregon, and California would be filed.

The secondary guides bear the names of the geographic subdivisions. For example, behind each primary state guide there are secondary guides with captions that provide for the alphabetic arrangement of cities and towns within that state, and interspersed among these are other secondary guides with city names as captions for cities with a sufficient amount of correspondence to warrant this division.

A geographic file may include several different kinds of folders, such as individual folders, city folders, and alphabetic folders. Individual folders in a geographic file are used in the same manner as they are in an alphabetic file. They differ, however, in their captions, because in a geographic file, the caption on an individual folder includes the name of the city and state, as well as the name of the correspondent. The geographic identification should appear on the top line; the correspondent, on the second. This arrangement of the captions facilitates the correct placement of the folders behind the appropriate state and city guides.

Geographic file

Shaw-Walker Company

If there is no individual folder for a correspondent, his communication is filed in a city folder. If there is not enough correspondence to warrant the use of a separate city folder, the communication is placed in a miscellaneous state folder at the back of the appropriate state section of the file.

For larger cities, several city folders are sometimes necessary. These are assigned alphabetic captions and placed behind an auxiliary city guide. For example, five Chicago folders might be used, the first for those Chicago correspondents whose names fall into the alphabetic range of A–C; the second, D–H; the third, I–M; the fourth, N–R; and the fifth, S–Z.

Procedure. The filing procedure for a geographic file is similar to that for alphabetic filing, except that the state and city are of primary importance in coding and filing. In coding, it is desirable to mark on each letter the city and state as well as the name of the correspondent. The location may be circled and the name of the correspondent underlined.

As in alphabetic filing, there are times when cross-references must be prepared on a letter. The geographic location, the correspondent's name, and other information about the letter are written in the proper spaces on the form. Facsimile copies of incoming letters and extra carbon copies of outgoing letters are also appropriately used as cross-references.

Cross-reference sheet for a geographic file

The letter for which this cross-reference sheet was prepared was filed according to the geographic location of the Fifth Avenue Clothing Mart. The cross-reference sheet should be filed according to the geographic location of the R. D. Gallagher Apparel Shop so that a person who examines the material in the folder for this shop will know that he can find related information under Fifth Avenue Clothing Mart.

CROSS REFERENCE SHEET

Name or Subject   Massachusetts, Boston 02151

        R. D. Gallagher Apparel Shop

        7348 Pine Road

Date   June 2, 19--

Regarding   Committee to study retail dealers'

        problems

                                SEE

Name or Subject   New York, New York 10006

        Fifth Avenue Clothing Mart

        1926 Fifth Avenue

Permanent *cross-reference guides* may be prepared when, for example, a correspondent has branches in several cities but all correspondence is handled with a main office. A different color label may be used for the cross-reference guides.

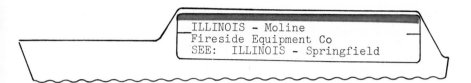

```
ILLINOIS - Moline
Fireside Equipment Co
SEE:   ILLINOIS - Springfield
```

When a correspondent has branches in several cities, the correspondence in one folder frequently pertains to problems and conditions in other branches. As a cross-reference, the tabs on each of the branch folders would refer to all the others, as:

```
ILLINOIS - Chicago
Ipswich Manufacturing Co
SEE:   COLO - Denver;  FLA - Tampa;
       MASS - Boston;  MO  - St Louis
```

Materials are sorted by geographic units, starting with the key unit for the first sorting and continuing until all the units involved in the filing system have been used. For example, the first sorting might be on the basis of states, the second sorting on the basis of cities or towns, and the final sorting on the basis of correspondents.

Letters are arranged in the folders as follows: (1) in an individual folder by date, (2) in a city folder by the names of the correspondents and then by date, (3) in an alphabetic state folder by the names of cities or towns and then by the names of correspondents according to date. In each case, of course, the most recent letter is placed in front.

Card Index. In geographic filing you must know the name of the city and state in which a person or business firm is located to find a letter referring to that correspondent. Because this information is not always known, it is advantageous to keep a card index with a geographic correspondence file. This is usually a 5″ x 3″ card file, which includes a card for each correspondent giving the name and address of the correspondent. The card index is arranged alphabetically according to the names of the correspondents.

Study Questions

1. What three parts are considered necessary in a numeric filing system? What is the purpose of each?

2. How is a number assigned to a correspondent in a numeric file?

3. How is a number assigned to a subject? Give an example.

4. What are some of the advantages and disadvantages of the numeric system?

5. When is a subject filing system used in preference to other methods?

6. What are the two methods of arranging subject captions alphabetically?

7. What is the major problem in a subject file?

8. How is a letter coded in a subject system?

9. Explain the procedure of cross-referencing in a subject file.

10. What are the advantages and disadvantages of subject filing?

11. What is the basis for geographic filing?

12. What kinds of guides and folders are used in this type of filing system?

13. When is a folder for a given city started? for an individual correspondent?

14. What is one method of indicating the essential words in geographic coding?

15. Under what name or names are cross-references prepared?

16. How are materials arranged in an individual folder? in a city folder? in an alphabetic state folder?

17. Why is it advantageous to have a card index for a geographic file?

What Do You Think?

1. What are the advantages of using numbers as well as subjects for guide and folder captions?

2. How should an office decide whether it ought to arrange its files by number, subject, or geographic location?

3. What is a practical situation where terminal-digit filing may promote office efficiency?

Your Personal Qualities

A file clerk filing under a subject system must read letters and papers carefully, as they may contain references to more than one subject. Miss Caryl Carson, with whom you work, fails to read the material to be filed, and, as a result, there is much misfiling and improper cross-referencing.

Whenever the chief file clerk corrects her, Caryl either cries or tells the chief clerk the system is "stupid" and does not make sense.

Question: How might you help Caryl to improve her work habits and to understand the importance of proper operation of the filing system?

How's Your English?

Review punctuation in Appendix B and punctuate the following:

1. Yes she said Ill take the folder with me

2. What are these Xs for

3. Carsons folder contains twenty 20 pieces of correspondence

4. Folders removed before 1145 am on Tuesday should be returned by 1145 am on Thursday

5. Out guides substitution cards and out folders these are the forms most commonly used

Office Work

Type the following twenty business firm names, addresses, and account numbers on 5″ x 3″ cards. File them three ways: (1) alphabetically, (2) geographically, and (3) numerically.

5001 Cobin & Sons, Washington, D.C.

5004 Connell Manufacturing Co., Seattle, Washington

5009 The Cole Manufacturing Co., San Francisco, California

5006 Crawford, Crawford, and Croll, Cincinnati, Ohio

5003 Cone, Lambert, and Ulysses, Chicago, Illinois

5002 Corn and Frederick, Dallas, Texas

5005 Max Collier & Sons, Tallahassee, Florida

5007 Conwit Tailors, Gainesville, Florida

5008 Cone, Arnold & Co., New York, New York

5010 Cobbs Corporation, Boston, Massachusetts

5019 Conklin Company, Erie, Pennsylvania

5015 Conner Corporation, Cleveland, Ohio

5016 The Samuel Collins Company, St. Louis, Missouri

5013 Colton Company, Boise, Idaho

5012 Conrad & Matthew, Reno, Nevada

5011 Coyne Corporation, Los Angeles, California

5014 Craig & Stanton Corporation, San Luis Obispo, California

5017 Cole & Monford Co., Nashville, Tennessee

5018 Conners Metal Manufacturing, Inc., Cicero, Illinois

5020 Conover & Sterling, Baton Rouge, Louisiana

UNIT 9 | Business Filing and Records Control

PART 6:

Special Files and Filing Systems

A number of special files involve the use of cards. Sometimes these cards stand on edge in vertical arrangement; sometimes they are placed in various kinds of files referred to as visible files; at other times they appear in specially constructed equipment known as wheel files. Still other types have cards arranged at random and located by the use of special rods. And still others involve the use of power-driven equipment usually referred to as elevator files.

Card Records. From small to large, practically all offices use some kind of card file. You may have located in your desk a small card file that includes the most frequently called telephone numbers. Doctors and dentists usually have card files relating to their patients; schoolteachers will usually have a card file covering the students in their classrooms; libraries, of course, have card files — quite often voluminous card files — referring to all the books in the library. Cards used in filing are usually 5″ x 3″, 6″ x 4″, or 8″ x 5″. Size selection usually depends upon the amount of information that appears to be needed on the card. By far the most popular size is 5″ x 3″. Card files are used in practically every business, including the shipping and receiving department, purchasing and inventory department, personnel, payroll, and stock departments.

Vertical Card Files. These are the types of files in which the card stands on edge, usually the longer edge. Thus, a 5″ x 3″ card rests on the 5-inch edge; the 6″ x 4″ card rests on the 6-inch edge; the 8″ x 5″ card rests on the 8-inch edge. There are, however, exceptions to this; some cards are kept the other way. The cards may be ruled or not ruled, depending upon whether or not they are likely to be typed or written on by hand. In a small card file, an ordinary 25-division set of guides is used. For more involved systems, 40-division, 60-division, or even a greater number of

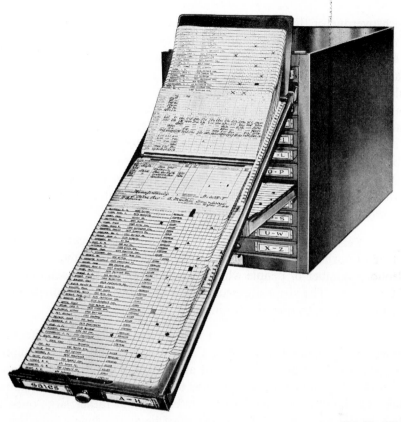

Visible record card cabinet

guides may be used. In some places, special primary and secondary guides are used; and color frequently plays an important part.

Visible Card File. These are files in which a portion of the card is visible at all times, that portion generally showing the name, department, or product to which the card record refers. These cards are generally placed in pockets on horizontal trays, or on vertical sheets, or in files that appear in book form. The total card becomes visible as the overlapping cards are raised to provide a view of the whole card.

Signals on Visible Records. In addition to cards that are specially printed for use with visible files, small metal or plastic signals are available. These may be placed in various positions on the cards to indicate something regarding the record. For example, if a visible file is used for collection records, the signal may indicate that the account is in good standing, or that it is overdue. Some signals may be used to indicate that it is very much overdue or that the firm with the account is no longer to be given any credit because of poor standing. These signals are sometimes placed in special positions on the card and frequently are in different colors. For example, blue may indicate a good credit standing; yellow may suggest mildly overdue; orange may mean very much overdue; and red may tell you no further credit is to be extended. Some visible card systems are placed in looseleaf binders and are overlapping. These are frequently used in connection with bookkeeping records, especially where machine posting is being used. The cards are usually kept in a wide, tublike type of equipment with the edge of each card showing and overlapping the next card to the right. The machine operator can lift a card out, make an entry on it, and return it to its place without difficulty.

Reference Visible Systems. These files usually carry only a strip instead of a whole card, the strip containing perhaps a name, address, and telephone number of people who are called with some reasonable degree of frequency. The strips are usually referred to as visible panels and are generally limited to one or two lines.

Wheel Files. These are cards to be used where ready reference is needed to a large number of cards. Cards used with this type of equipment are punched or cut at the bottom or at the side, depending upon the style of wheel. They can be readily attached to or detached from the equipment. There are small ones used for desk reference and rather large ones used when a large amount of information must be at someone's fingertips.

Random Filing. In this kind of system, the cards not only have typed or printed information on them, but also are equipped with strips of metal teeth which are attached to the bottom edge of the card. These teeth are cut in relation to magnetic rods that run under the cards. These files are operated by a keyboard, and the depression of certain keys causes one or more cards to be pushed up, thus locating them and making them available to the person trying to find a particular card. The system has the advantage of allowing one card to be identified under one of several possible captions.

Elevator Files. This type of file is power driven and is in a sense a glorified card file with trays arranged on shelves which may be brought to the level of the operator by the use of an elevator or power-driven system. The shelves in this kind of a file operate on the same principle as a ferris wheel at an amusement park. The shelves may be wide enough to take four, five, or more trays of 5″ x 3″ cards; and any single machine may include a large number of shelves. The operator pushes a button to move any particular shelf into position in front of his work station. At that point, he may work directly on some cards, or he may remove a complete tray of cards and turn them over to someone else to work on.

Commercial Alphabetic Files. If a filing system is to be effective, considerable planning must be spent in its development. Effective systems are not haphazardly devised; unfortunately, the solution to a records problem is not always a simple one. The development of an effective filing system must be based on planning, analysis, and experience.

Here are some factors that should be considered when developing a filing system:

1) *The record requirements of the office for which the system is being devised.* What kinds of records are retained? How are these records created or received? What is the total volume of records retained each week, month, or year? What about future expansion of the system?

2) *Using the system.* How are the records requested and used? How active are the records? How long must the records be retained?

3) *Storing the records.* What type of classification system should be used? Will a centralized or decentralized file plan be most effective? Where will the inactive records be stored?

4) *Equipment and supplies.* What specific types of equipment and supplies — out of the vast array available — would be most appropriate for this system and this office?

Since every office has different records requirements, a system devised for one office is not always suitable for another. Remember: you are retaining important information that must be quickly retrieved — you are not merely storing pieces of paper.

Every filing system should be as simple as possible to use. In addition, the system should be efficient and reliable in providing needed information as well as economical to operate and maintain.

When an office decides to install a new filing system or revise an old one, two methods may be considered. A qualified person in the office may analyze the particular information requirements and develop an "office-made" system, or a system may be purchased from a file equipment and supplies manufacturer. These "commercial" systems have been developed and tested by filing experts.

Since the office in which you are employed may be using a commercial system, you should be familiar with its operation. In general, you will find that a commercial filing system is characterized by one or more of the following features:

1) Captions of guides and folders that include numeric symbols as well as alphabetic notations. The numeric symbols reduce the time that is required to locate the proper guides and folders in the file drawers.

2) Special positions for guides and folders. Many systems arrange guides and folders so that the captions read from left to right; that is, primary guide captions at the left and individual folder captions at the right. Some systems use only one position for primary guides; others stagger these guides in two or three positions.

3) The use of color schemes to facilitate the location of guides and folders. Different colors on guide and folder tabs serve as signals for the location of different sections in the file drawer.

The trade names of some of the commercially manufactured filing systems include Direct-Name, Bee Line, Ideal Index, NUAL Alphabetic, Safeguard, Tailor-Made, Tel-I-Vision, Triple Check, Super-Ideal, and Variadex.

Four of the more widely used systems — the Variadex, Super-Ideal, Safeguard, and Direct-Name — are described briefly below.

Variadex. Color is used on the guides and folders in this Remington Rand system to help you file and find material faster and more accurately. The color of the guide or folder is determined by the *second* letter in each name. Five colors are used to set off the five divisions of the alphabet: A through D are orange; E through H are yellow; I through N are green; O, P, and Q are blue; R through Z are violet. The letters and related colors of the tabs and folders are shown in the following table of surnames. Note that the color is determined by the second letter in each surname and not the first letter.

THE OPERATION OF THE VARIADEX COLOR PRINCIPLE

When the second letter in the surname is:	A B C D	E F G H	I J K L M N	O P Q	R S T U V W X Y Z
The color on the guide and folders is:	ORANGE	YELLOW	GREEN	BLUE	VIOLET
	Adams	Benson	Anderson	Appleby	Atkins
	Bates	Henderson	Bingham	Coyle	Brown
	Garrison	Kellogg	Higgins	Hoover	Gross
	Harris	Peterson	King	Johnson	Hubbell
	Karpen	Sherman	Pitman	Kohler	Kresge
	Waterman	Wendel			

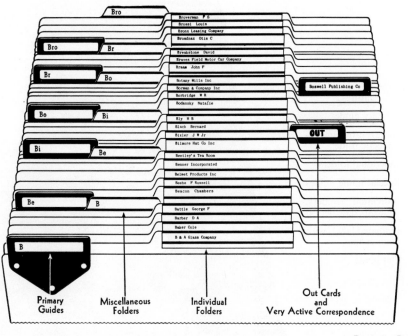

| | | | | Bro | | | | |

Broverman F S
Brossi Louis
Bronx Leasing Company
Broadnax Otis C
Breakstone David
Braves Field Motor Car Company
Brass John F
Botany Mills Inc
Borman & Company Inc
Borbridge W R
Bodansky Natalie
Bly H B
Black Bernard
Bixler J W Jr
Bilmore Hat Co Inc
Bentley's Tea Room
Benner Incorporated
Belnet Products Inc
Beebe F Russell
Beacon Chambers
Battle George F
Barber D A
Baker Cole
B & A Glass Company

Boswell Publishing Co

OUT

Primary Guides · Miscellaneous Folders · Individual Folders · Out Cards and Very Active Correspondence

Remington Rand

Variadex

In this system, first position is reserved for primary guides; second position is used for miscellaneous folders; third position is used for individual folders with double tabs; and fourth position is used for special and OUT guides.

Super-Ideal. The Super-Ideal index is one of the more widely used Shaw-Walker vertical filing systems. Since it was found that 51 percent of all names came under the letters *B, C, H, M, S* and *W*, in the Super-Ideal index half of the alphabetic guides represent these six letters. Thus, in a 25-guide A to Z Super-Ideal filing system there would be guides as follows:

First Letter of Name	Percent of Total Volume	Number of Guides	Guide Captions		
B	9.4	2	BA–BL	BO–BY	
C	6.6	2	CA–CL	CO–CY	
H	8.0	2	HA–HE	HI–HY	
M	8.9	2	MA–MC	ME–MY	
S	11.2	3	SA–SE	SH–SM	SN–SY
W	6.8	2	WA–WH	WI–WY	

The other 12 guides would cover all the other letters in the alphabet.

Primary guides are staggered in first and second positions. Miscellaneous folders are in first position. Individual folders occupy third and

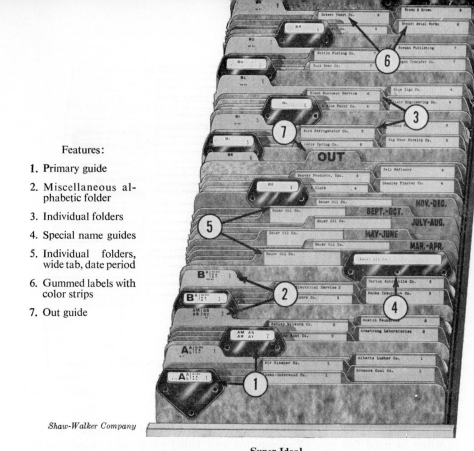

Features:

1. Primary guide

2. Miscellaneous alphabetic folder

3. Individual folders

4. Special name guides

5. Individual folders, wide tab, date period

6. Gummed labels with color strips

7. Out guide

Shaw-Walker Company

Super-Ideal

fourth positions. Special guides are in fourth position, and the folders behind them can be in second, third, or fourth positions.

Safeguard. Another adaptation of alphabetic filing is the Safeguard plan manufactured by The Globe Wernicke Company. This system offers a well-planned color scheme for guide and folder tabs as well as a scientific arrangement of guides and folders throughout the file drawer.

Primary guides (green) and miscellaneous folders (red) are staggered in the first three positions. Fourth position is used for special name or title guides, date section guides, and alphabetic auxiliary guides; all are blocked out in different colors. Individual folders with double tabs appear in last position and are grouped into color blocks as an aid to filing and finding.

Direct-Name. Lastly we shall consider the Direct-Name system manufactured by Yawman and Erbe. In this system, numbered folders in first and last position are filed behind numbered alphabetic guides in second and third position. The tabs of guides with odd numbers are in second position, and those with even numbers are in third position. There

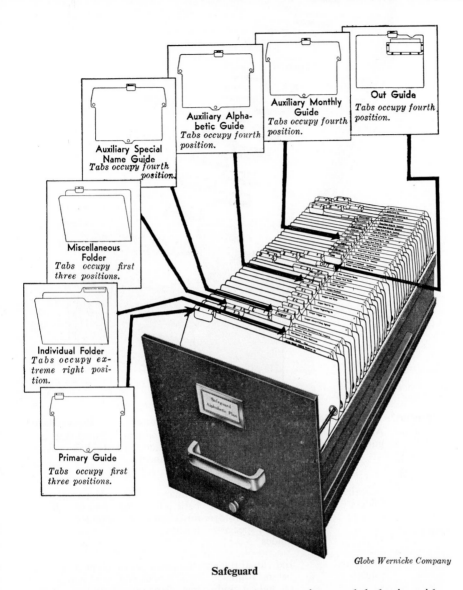

Auxiliary Special Name Guide
Tabs occupy fourth position.

Auxiliary Alphabetic Guide
Tabs occupy fourth position.

Auxiliary Monthly Guide
Tabs occupy fourth position.

Out Guide
Tabs occupy fourth position.

Miscellaneous Folder
Tabs occupy first three positions.

Individual Folder
Tabs occupy extreme right position.

Primary Guide
Tabs occupy first three positions.

Globe Wernicke Company

Safeguard

are five components in this alphabetic system: primary alphabetic guides, special guides, miscellaneous and individual folders, and period folders. Period folders are individual folders with extended tabs used to divide voluminous filing material for one correspondent by time period. The tabs on these folders show not only the names of the correspondents but the time periods in proper chronological order.

Summary of Filing Positions. Let's look inside the file drawers of these four commercial systems. We shall see the following arrangement of guides and folders from left to right in the drawers:

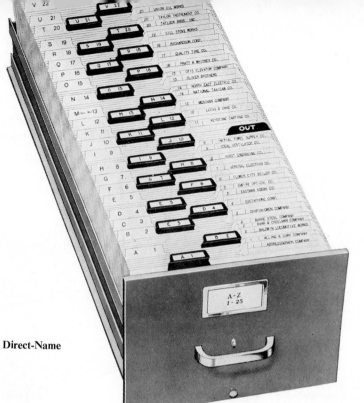

Direct-Name

Yawman and Erbe

Position*	Variadex	Super-Ideal	Safeguard	Direct-Name
1	Alphabetic guides	Primary alphabetic guides; miscellaneous folders	Primary alphabetic guides and miscellaneous folders	Miscellaneous folders
2	Miscellaneous folders	Primary alphabetic guides and individual folders behind special guides	Primary alphabetic guides and miscellaneous folders	Alphabetic and special guides
3	Individual folders	Individual folders behind primary, secondary, and special guides; out guides	Primary alphabetic guides and miscellaneous folders	Alphabetic and special guides
4	OUT guides: special guides	Individual folders behind primary and secondary guides; special guides and folders	Special, date, and auxiliary alphabetic guides; OUT guides	Individual folders
5				Individual folders

*Position does not refer to the tab cuts but to the order in which the tabs appear from left to right in the file drawer.

Study Questions

1. What are three of the characteristic features of commercial alphabetic filing systems?

2. In what way is color used in the Variadex index?

3. What is the principle behind the use of guides in the Super-Ideal index?

4. What kinds of guides and folders are used in Safeguard Alphabetic Filing?

5. For what are the four folder cuts in the Direct-Name filing system used?

What Do You Think?

1. Of the following types of guide captions, which do you think contribute most to accurate and rapid alphabetic filing: (a) letters only, (b) letters and numbers, (c) letters and colors, (d) letters, numbers, and colors?

2. Which do you think is the better plan — to have primary guide tabs limited to one position or to have them staggered in two or three positions?

Your Personal Qualities

Miss Danker and Miss Olsen were working together on the files when Miss Danker caught her sleeve in a file drawer that was closed by Miss Olsen. The girls had words during which Miss Danker accused Miss Olsen of being careless. Miss Olsen suggested that Miss Danker should not come to the office in fancy dresses, the sleeves of which can be so easily caught in a file drawer.

Questions: 1. How should the situation have been handled by these two girls?

2. What is appropriate dress for the office?

How's Your English?

Read about emphasis and listing of itemized data in Appendix B. Make a typewritten copy of the section on Variadex in this part, indicating emphasis and rearranging the tabulated material in an attractive fashion.

Office Work

Visit a local office to observe the filing system in use. Write a report on the major features of the system. Be sure to include in your report a statement by the person in charge of the filing operation as to why the particular system was adopted. On the basis of your observation, what features were particularly impressive? Were there any apparent violations of basic principles of filing?

Office Work Assignments

34: Alphabetic Indexing No. 3

This assignment is similar to the one at the end of Part 3. Prepare your last 25 index cards from the names below, and integrate them with the 75 cards you now have from the assignments following Part 2 and Part 3.

76. Henry R. Elston, IV, 2728 Germantown Rd., Germantown, Pennsylvania

77. Chamber of Commerce, 12th & Olive Sts., Joliet, Illinois

78. Chief Engineer, Safety Division, Arkansas State Highway Dept., Ft. Smith, Arkansas

79. Horace Mann Junior High School, 2500 Euclid Ave., Erie, Pennsylvania

80. St. Mark's Episcopal Church, Oakwood, Missouri

81. University of New Mexico, Albuquerque, New Mexico

82. Wm. A. Graves, 1620 N. Vernon Place, Winnetka, Illinois

83. Second National Bank, Eighth & Race Sts., Spokane, Washington

84. Ye Olde Garden Gate Antiques, 49 W. Elm St., Independence, Kansas

85. Security Savings Society, 74 Ohio Ave., Watertown, New York

86. Vera's Beauty Salon, 29 W. Adams St., Bennington, Vermont

87. Jack the Tailor, 536 S. 29 St., Oklahoma City, Oklahoma

88. Downtown Merchants Assn., 1200 Transportation Bldg., Wheeling, West Virginia

89. Lady Constance Cosmetics, 128 W. 63 St., New York, New York

90. Citizens Bank & Trust Co., Manchester, New Hampshire

91. Hartford Water Department, Hartford, Connecticut

92. U.S. Marshal, Justice Dept., Federal Bldg., Boise, Idaho

93. Arnold A. Townley-Jones, 5021 Eastman Blvd., Chicago, Illinois

94. Chief Inspector, Food & Drug Administration, Health & Welfare Dept., Post Office Bldg., Butte, Montana

95. United Fine Arts Fund, Terminal Bldg., Dallas, Texas

96. Baldwin-Wallace College, Berea, Ohio

97. Harold McArthur & Sons, 4587 Roland Ave., Glendale, California

98. MacArthur Sportswear, 688 Jefferson St., Kalamazoo, Michigan

99. Bernice L. McAdoo, 3 Alpine Terrace, Trenton, New Jersey

100. Perkins-Reynolds Insurance Agency, 200 Nicollet Ave., Minneapolis, Minnesota

UNIT 10 | Copying and Duplicating

PART 1:

Copying Processes

Office copying machines may be defined as equipment which copies material exactly and directly without requiring the relatively time-consuming preparation of intermediate material such as a master or a stencil. Duplicates of letters, forms, drawings, and designs can be made in less than a minute. They are acceptable as evidence in courts of law and by government agencies because they are exact photographic reproductions of the original documents.

Ordinarily, copying machines are used for making from one to ten copies. They are intended for short runs since, *per copy*, they are slower to process and are more expensive than copies produced on longer-run duplicators, such as stencil or fluid.

Copying machines are used in small offices as well as large offices to save time and money in making brief replies to business letters. An executive may answer a letter by writing his reply on the face of the letter itself instead of having a return letter typed. A copy is then made on a copying machine to go into the company files; the original is mailed back to the sender. This procedure is efficient because: (1) it saves the executive's time (he does not need to compose a complete reply letter); (2) it saves the typist's time (she does not need to type and proofread a reply letter); (3) it saves office file space (the reply is included on the original incoming letter, so only one sheet of paper is involved).

The five copying processes you are most likely to encounter include diazo, infrared, diffusion-transfer, dye-transfer, and electrostatic-transfer.

Diazo. The basic characteristics of the diazo process are described in the following paragraphs:

329

Minnesota Mining & Mfg. Co.

A copying machine

Exposure. In addition to the diazo process machine, a *translucent original* and a sheet of copy paper especially treated on one side with azo-dye are necessary. The copy paper, sensitized side up, is placed directly beneath the translucent original, image side up. Both are exposed to an ultra-violet light source. Light passes through the *nonimage areas* of the original to the sensitized side of the copy sheet, leaving those areas de-activated; that is, nothing will reproduce in those areas. Since the image areas on the original prevent light from passing to the copy sheet, those areas remain "activated" so that they will develop.

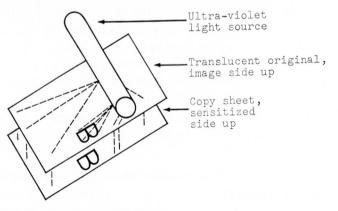

Ultra-violet
light source

Translucent original,
image side up

Copy sheet,
sensitized
side up

Development. After the image has been copied chemically on the copy sheet through the exposing process, the image must then be developed so that the image areas are visible.

Some diazo copying machines are designed so that development is the result of passing the exposed copy sheet through ammonia vapors. Since copies emerging from the machine are dry, this process is sometimes called "dry diazo." The Ozalid Division of General Aniline and Film Corporation produces popular dry diazo process machines.

In the "moist diazo" process, the exposed copy sheet is developed by being squeezed between two rollers moistened with developer. The "Copyflex" model, manufactured by the Charles Bruning Company, Incorporated, is a popular moist diazo process machine.

In either dry or moist processes, only two sheets are involved: the translucent original and the specially treated copy sheet on which the print is made.

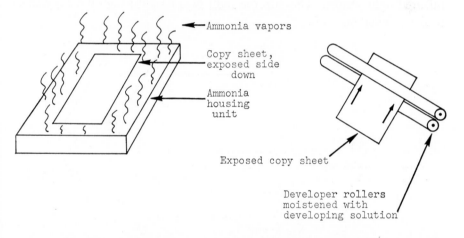

Special azo-dyed copy sheets are available to reproduce colored image areas on either the dry or moist diazo process. Colors are chosen by means of appropriate selection of copy paper. Prints are possible on a wide variety of materials: standard weights, translucent paper, foil, or even cloth. Equipment ranges in size from desk-top models to units which produce prints up to 54 inches wide.

The main advantages of this process are its speed and its relatively inexpensive cost per copy. A copy can be produced less expensively by this process than by any of the other copying processes. Manufacturers claim that a diazo process print can be made in 15 to 30 seconds at approximately one cent per copy.

The diazo processes have some disadvantages, however. Opaque one-sided originals or any two-sided original cannot be reproduced because light must pass through the original material. The image areas to be re-produced, however, must be opaque. Black ink images on the original produce best. Blue and purple inks usually are not so opaque, and reproduction of these images is not as satisfactory. For best results, the developing unit of the moist diazo machine must be cleaned completely every day.

Infrared. In this process a heat-sensitive sheet of copy paper and the original to be reproduced are necessary. "Thermofax" models, manufactured by Minnesota Mining and Manufacturing Company, are widely used infrared-process machines.

Either the copy sheet or the original to be copied must be translucent. If an opaque one- or two-sided original is used, the copy sheet must be translucent. The method of exposure would be the following: The translucent copy, heat sensitive coating up, is placed on top of the original image to be copied face up. In the machine, both sheets are exposed to an infrared light source. The infrared light rays pass through the copy sheet to the original beneath.

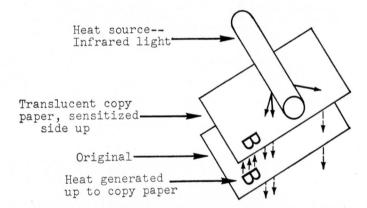

Heat source-- Infrared light

Translucent copy paper, sensitized side up

Original

Heat generated up to copy paper

Have you noticed that when you wear dark clothing in the sunlight on a hot summer day you are warmer than when wearing light-colored clothing? This is true because the dark clothing absorbs the sun's rays and generates heat to the body.

The infrared process, sometimes called the heat process, works on this same principle. Dark substances, such as black office ink or carbon deposits, absorb more light than light-colored substances. Where the infrared light strikes the dark image areas on the original, it is absorbed, and through absorption generates heat up to the copy paper above. Thus, the portions of the copy paper directly above the image areas turn dark on the copy sheet. The image to be copied, therefore, is "burned" onto the copy sheet above.

If an opaque copy is desired, a *translucent original* is necessary. Materials would be arranged as follows: The translucent original, image side up, would be placed on top of the opaque copy sheet, heat-sensitive side up. In the machine, both sheets are exposed to an infrared light source. The infrared light rays are absorbed in the image areas on the original and generate heat to the sensitized copy paper immediately below. Therefore, the image to be copied is burned onto the copy paper *beneath*.

This process is the fastest of the copying processes: an 8½" x 11" sheet can be reproduced in approximately five seconds. This speed is possible because it is a single-step process, contrasting to the two-step procedure — exposing and developing — involved in many of the other copying processes.

By varying the arrangement of materials as they are fitted into the machine, either one- or two-sided opaque originals, or translucent originals

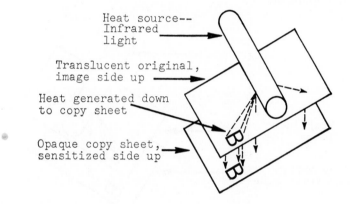

Heat source--
Infrared
light

Translucent original,
image side up

Heat generated down
to copy sheet

Opaque copy sheet,
sensitized side up

may be copied. The only requirement is that either the copy sheet or the original to be copied must be translucent.

Because chemical solutions are unnecessary, the infrared machine requires no special care. These machines are capable of preparing fluid masters and offset masters with no special equipment.

This process does have one limitation, however. The image to be reproduced must be capable of generating sufficient heat to "burn" an image onto the copy paper. Carbon-based or metal-based deposits are necessary in the image to be reproduced. Most ordinary pencil marks, black ink marks, and standard typing and printing can be copied easily. Certain inks — particularly blue inks — may not reproduce at all.

Diffusion-Transfer. Some diffusion-transfer machines produce a positive copy from the original in one step. Other machines produce, first, a negative from the original; and, from the negative, a positive copy is made in a two-step process.

One-Step Procedure. The one-step procedure is sometimes called the "direct" or "autopositive" method.

Exposure. A translucent original and a special light-sensitive copy sheet are required. The translucent original is placed, image side up, on top of the sensitized side of the copy sheet. Both are exposed to a light source. Light passes through the nonimage areas of the original to the copy sheet. Where light strikes, the copy sheet is deactivated in those areas; that is, those areas will not reproduce when developed. Light is stopped from passing to the copy sheet when it strikes the opaque image areas on the original; those areas remain activated. Thus, after exposure, on the copy sheet only the areas corresponding to the image areas on the original remain for development.

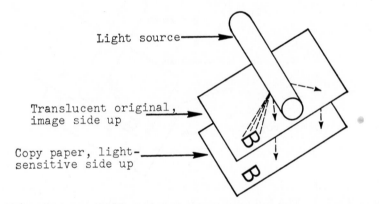

Light source

Translucent original, image side up

Copy paper, light-sensitive side up

Development. The exposed copy sheet is passed through a special developing solution and then through two rollers which squeeze out the excess developing solution.

Two-Step Procedure. This is sometimes referred to as the "face-to-face-reflex," or "transfer," diffusion-transfer method.

Exposure. The two-step procedure requires the following materials: a translucent or an opaque one- or two-sided original, a translucent light-sensitive negative sheet, and a specially-sensitized positive copy sheet. The negative sheet, sometimes called a "matrix," is placed, light-sensitive side down, on the image side of the original. Both are exposed to a light source. Light passes through the translucent negative sheet to the original beneath. The image areas on the original absorb the light rays as they strike. The nonimage areas of the original, however, *reflect* the light back up to the light-sensitive negative, causing such a reaction in the chemical coating of the paper that it turns dark when developed. The image area, when the negative is developed, remains white.

Development. When the exposed negative sheet is immersed into developing solution, a reverse-reading white image on a dark background results. The negative is then placed face to face with the photographically-sensitized side of the positive copy sheet; both are then passed through the

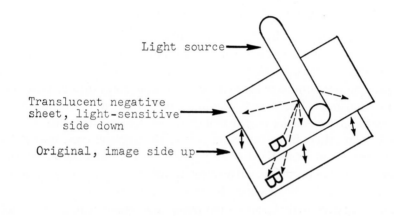

developing solution. The developing solution is squeezed out as the two sheets, face to face, are pressed together between two rollers. When the negative and positive sheets are separated, a positive (black right-reading image on a white background) copy of the original has been reproduced.

The main advantage of the diffusion-transfer copying process is its high quality of reproduction on any color of paper. It is also fairly speedy to process; most manufacturers claim that a single copy can be produced within 30 seconds. Equipment is available which will produce copies up to 20 inches wide. Common trade names include Apēco, manufactured by American Photocopy Equipment Company; Copease, by Copease Corporation; and Photocopier, by A. B. Dick Company.

On two-step machines, any type of original can be used: translucent, or opaque one- or two-sided. On one-step machines, however, only translucent originals will reproduce.

Expense, per copy, on diffusion-transfer machines ranges from four to nine cents. On two-step machines, the expense per copy is higher since to produce a single copy of an original, both a negative sheet and a positive sheet are necessary. A standard-size 8½″ x 11″ set of one positive and one negative copy can be purchased for a little less than ten cents. On one-step machines, a single copy is less expensive since only one sensitized sheet — the positive copy sheet — is necessary.

Dye-Transfer. The basic characteristics of the dye-transfer process are described in the following paragraphs:

Exposure. An original and a special translucent light-sensitive negative sheet (matrix) are necessary to process dye-transfer copies. A photographically-sensitized positive sheet is not necessary; any nonsensitized sheet of copy paper may be used. The same face-to-face reflex method of exposure as is used on two-step diffusion-transfer machines is utilized in the dye-transfer process. (See page 335 for illustration.)

Development. The exposed negative sheet is immersed in an activator solution where it remains for approximately 20 seconds. During this time the image areas, as well as the nonimage areas, turn dark; but the substance on the nonimage areas hardens so that that portion of the sheet will not transfer. The reverse-reading image areas develop into a soft, transferable dye. As the negative sheet is withdrawn from the activator solution, two rollers force the image side of the negative copy into contact with a sheet of nonsensitized copy paper. This contact permits a small portion of the dye on the negative sheet to transfer to the copy sheet, thus producing a copy of the original. By repeating the developing process with the same negative matrix, up to ten acceptable copies can be produced. Copies become lighter, however, with each successive reactivation and transference.

Advantages of the dye-transfer copying process are similar to the advantages of the two-step diffusion-transfer process since they are so similar. Any type of original may be used — either translucent, or opaque one- or two-sided. Reproduction is of high quality. Unlike the diffusion-transfer method, however, any type of copy paper can be used.

If only one copy is processed from the exposed negative, the cost per copy is comparable to that of the diffusion-transfer two-step method — a little less than ten cents. If more than one copy is made from the matrix, however, cost per copy is reduced.

Because of the 20-second activation time allowed for the matrix to develop, the total processing time for this method is a little longer than for the diffusion-transfer method. Manufacturers claim that the first copy can be processed in approximately 50 seconds (as compared with 15 to 30 seconds for the diffusion-transfer), but that up to five extra copies can be reproduced in one minute.

Dye-transfer machines are capable of producing paper offset masters for offset duplicators. The most widely publicized trade name among dye-transfer machines is Verifax, manufactured by Eastman Kodak Company.

Electrostatic-Transfer. This process of office copying is based on the fact that unlike electrical charges attract, whereas like charges repel. A common term for this process is "xerography," a name similar to "Xerox," a trade name for electrostatic-transfer machines manufactured by Haloid Xerox, Incorporated.

A copy is produced as a result of five basic steps:

1) A selenium-coated plate is given a positive electrical charge by passing it under a series of special wires designed for this purpose.

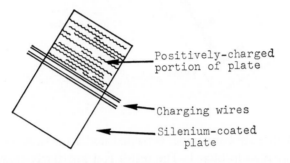

Positively-charged portion of plate

Charging wires

Silenium-coated plate

2) The image areas from the original are then projected on the positively-charged plate through a camera lens. Where light rays strike the plate — the nonimage areas on the original — the positive electrical charge is canceled. Light, however, is stopped in the image areas; therefore, the positive electrical charges remain on the plate in those areas. At this point, there remains on the plate only an invisible positively-charged reverse-reading image, representing the image areas of the original.

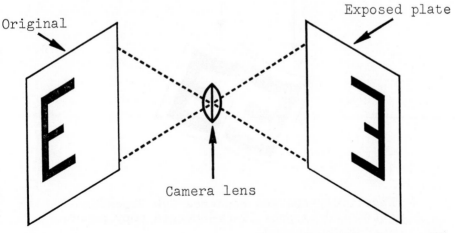

Original

Exposed plate

Camera lens

3) The plate is then placed in contact with negatively-charged powdered ink. Since unlike electrical charges attract, the negatively-charged ink powder particles adhere to the positively-charged image on the plate, making the reverse-reading image on the plate visible. Thus, at this point in the process, a *visible negatively-charged reverse-reading image* remains on the plate.

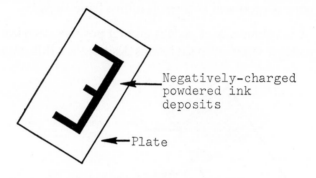

Negatively-charged powdered ink deposits

Plate

4) A sheet of copy paper is passed under the same positive charging wires described in Step 1. The result is a positively-charged sheet of copy paper. The plate containing the negatively-charged image is placed face to face with the positively-charged copy sheet. The negatively-charged powdered ink deposits on the plate are attracted to, and thus transferred to, the positively-charged copy sheet, resulting in a right-reading image on the copy paper.

Copy
sheet   Plate

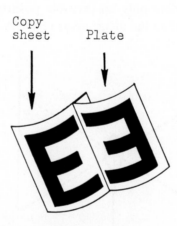

Negatively-charged powdered ink deposits
attracted by positively-charged copy paper

5) The plate is then wiped clean and laid aside for reuse. The copy sheet, on which the image from the original is now printed, is then exposed to heat for a few seconds. The heat fuses the ink deposits forming the image areas, resulting in a permanent image on the copy paper.

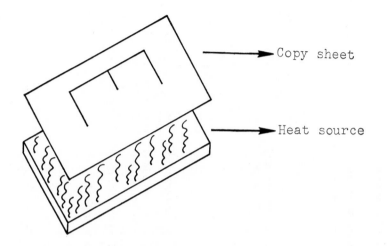

Copy sheet

Heat source

The advantages of this copying process are many, whereas the disadvantages are few. For that reason it is becoming more and more common in modern business offices.

Since it is a dry process, the operator is not concerned with changing developing solutions. The image to be copied may be typing, handwriting, printing, drawings, or even photographs. The original image may be on any type, weight, or color of material. The original image may be on translucent or opaque material, one or two sided. Enough powdered ink is deposited on the plate so that up to eight copies can be produced from a processed plate. Reproduction is of the highest quality. Electrostatic-transfer machines can be used to produce single copies on plain paper, fluid-process masters, offset paper or metal masters. With the use of a camera, copy can be enlarged or reduced. Cost per copy has been estimated at five cents on standard office bond paper.

Until the manufacture of continuous-flow type electrostatic process machines, a semiskilled operator was required. A single copy took approximately three minutes to complete. However, in the continuous-flow type of machine, the process proceeds automatically once the material has been fed into the machine, thus making higher speeds and less skilled operators possible.

SUMMARY OF COPYING PROCESSES

Process	Approximate Cost Per Copy	Necessary Materials	Features of the Process
1. Diazo (Ozalid — dry) (Copyflex — moist)	1 cent	(1) Translucent original and (2) Specially sensitized positive copy sheet	Ultra-violet light source. Positive is made from a positive; no intermediate agent. Sensitive to most colors — less so to blues and purples. Least expensive of the copying processes. "Dry" diazo machines develop with the use of ammonia vapors. "Moist" diazo machines develop by passing exposed copy sheet between two rollers moistened with developing solution. Will produce colored images. Original must be translucent.
2. Infrared (Thermofax)	5 cents	(1) Translucent heat-sensitive copy sheet and (2) Opaque one- or two-sided original, or translucent original; or (1) Opaque heat-sensitive copy sheet and (2) Translucent original	Infrared light source. Image is "burned" onto copy paper by heat generated from the absorption of the image areas on the original. Dry process. Fastest of the copying processes — five seconds. Capable of producing, with no extra equipment, fluid masters and offset masters. Image areas on the original must be carbon- or metal-based. Most blue office inks will not reproduce.
3a. Diffusion-Transfer One-Step Procedure	4-9 cents	(1) Translucent original and (2) Light-sensitive copy sheet	Sensitive to wide range of colors. Copies on white or colored coated paper. High-quality reproduction. Positive is made from a positive; no intermediate agent. Some machines, with special units, capable of making paper offset masters.

Process	Approximate Cost Per Copy	Necessary Materials	Features of the Process
3b. Diffusion-Transfer Two-Step Procedure (Apēco, Copease, Photocopier)	8–10 cents for single copy, less if more than one positive is produced from negative	(1) Translucent negative copy sheet and (2) Photographically-sensitized positive sheet and (3) Translucent original or opaque one- or two-sided original	Sensitive to wide range of colors. Copies on white or colored coated paper. High-quality reproduction. A two-step process: A negative is made from the original; then the positive is made from the negative. Multicopy negative copy paper available which will produce up to five positive copies from one exposed negative. With special units, some machines capable of making offset masters.
4. Dye-Transfer (Verifax)	9–10 cents (1 cent for each extra copy)	(1) Translucent negative sheet and (2) Translucent original or opaque one- or two-sided original	Copies are positives on nonsensitized paper, white or colored. Sensitive to wide range of color. High-quality reproduction. Up to ten copies can be made from one exposed negative sheet. Machines with special adapters capable of producing superior-quality offset masters.
5. Electrostatic-Transfer (Xerox)	5 cents for single copies made on average office bond paper	(1) Selenium-coated plate and (2) Translucent original, or opaque one- or two-sided original	Copies made on nonsensitized paper, one or both sides, any color. Will copy typing, handwriting, printing, line drawings, lettering, rubber stamp, crayon, and/or photographs involving different tones. Sensitive to any color. Very high-quality reproduction. Commonly used for making paper or metal offset masters, and fluid masters. Principle of operation: unlike electrical charges attract; like electrical charges repel.

Study Questions

1. What kind of paper must the original be for the diazo process? Why?

2. Explain the difference in "moist diazo" and "dry diazo" development.

3. Which of the copying processes is the fastest? Why?

4. Describe the one-step method of exposure in the diffusion-transfer copying process.

5. Describe the two-step method of exposure in the diffusion-transfer copying process.

6. What is the main advantage of the diffusion-transfer copying process?

7. What is an advantage of the dye-transfer process over the diffusion-transfer process?

8. The electrostatic-transfer copying process is based on what principle?

9. Which copying processes are commonly used to produce offset masters? fluid masters?

What Do You Think?

1. What are several office situations in which a copying machine might be used?

2. How would you help your employer decide which type of copying machine or duplicator should be purchased for your office?

Your Personal Qualities

A new copying machine has been installed in the personnel department to reduce copying expense. The Director of Personnel has decided that it would be more efficient to have just one person in the department operate the machine and control the supplies, and he has asked Miss Sherwood, a new employee, to assume this responsibility.

Immediately after the machine was installed, Mr. Yates, a chief clerk in the payroll department, asked Miss Sherwood to make a copy of a newspaper clipping covering an account of a naval battle of World War II. Mr. Yates is interested in naval history and considers himself an authority in this field. Miss Sherwood graciously made the copy of the clipping for Mr. Yates. Since that time he has brought in an ever-increasing number of clippings, photographs, and diagrams of naval battles to be reproduced on the copying machine.

The photocopying paper costs more than five cents a sheet. If Miss Sherwood continues to do all of Mr. Yates's work, she will use up her copy paper stock in half the expected time. Sensing that a difficult or embarrassing time lies ahead, Miss Sherwood wonders what she should do.

Questions: 1. What courses of action could Miss Sherwood take?

2. Which course of action would you take?

How's Your English?

Refer in Appendix C to the paragraph on words that should not be pronounced alike but often are, then fill in the correct word in each of the following statements:

1. The man was_____at dodging.
2. I'll_____remember.
3. The change will not_____me.
4. He did not get a good grade on the_____.
5. The police were called to_____ the crowd.

Office Work

The following material is to be reproduced on an office copier. Type a copy that can be transferred to a master by a photocopying machine. Set it up in a more attractive style.

PROGRAM FOR THE SEVENTH ANNUAL BUSINESS EDUCATION CONFERENCE

WEDNESDAY, July 6, 19--. 12:00 Noon — Registration, Conference Lounge, Student Union Building, East Wing. 2:00 p.m. — First Session, Baldwin Auditorium: Speaker, Dr. Robert G. Ball, Central Teachers College, Pittsburgh, Pennsylvania, "A Changing, Progressing Business Education." 2:45 p.m. — Intermission. 3:00 p.m. — Speaker, Mr. Henry Reynolds, Philadelphia Public Schools, Philadelphia, Pennsylvania, "Curricular Problems in Business Education — As Viewed by a Supervisor of Business Education"; Speaker, Miss Marilyn Donnell, Illinois Junior College, Chicago, Illinois, "Answering the Needs of Today's Business World." 4:15 p.m. — Forum: Moderator, Dr. T. J. Collins, Department of Business Education, Eastern Academy, Newark, New Jersey; Discussants, Dr. Robert G. Ball, Mr. Henry Reynolds, Miss Marilyn Donnell. 6:45 p.m. — Dinner, State Room, Student Union Building, East Wing: Presiding, Mrs. Edith R. Jones, Department of Business Education, Southern University, Atlanta, Georgia; Speaker, Dr. K. T. Lerner, Director of Business Education, Ohio Western College, Toledo, Ohio.

UNIT 10 | Copying and Duplicating

PART 2:

Stencil Duplicating

One of your duties may be to prepare or "cut" stencils and to run the stencil machine. The care with which you prepare the stencil is a most important factor in determining the quality of reproduction on the finished copies. A stencil duplicator is also known as a "mimeograph" duplicator.

THE STENCIL ASSEMBLY

The stencil assembly is composed of three parts, and sometimes a fourth part: the stencil sheet, the cushion sheet, the backing sheet, and sometimes a cellophane film.

The stencil sheet is made of fibrous tissue coated on both sides with a waxlike substance. This nonabsorbent waxlike coating makes the entire surface ink-repellent until some of the surface is pushed aside by a sharp instrument.

Probably you will use a standard stencil more than any other type. By looking at the illustration on the opposite page, you can see that stencils are designed to aid you in placing properly the material to be duplicated. Strict observance of the guide lines and numerals shown will insure attractively positioned copies.

Specially designed stencil sheets with appropriate guide markings can be purchased for duplicating special jobs such as address labels, newspapers, and four-page folders.

Affixed to the top and behind the stencil sheet is the backing sheet. This heavily oiled, smooth paper provides a firm backing for the stencil sheet and helps to equalize the irregularities of a typewriter platen.

The cushion sheet is placed between the backing sheet and the stencil sheet to absorb the force of the cutting instrument. The contrast in color between the stencil sheet and backing sheet makes proofreading easier.

344

STENCIL SHEET MARKINGS

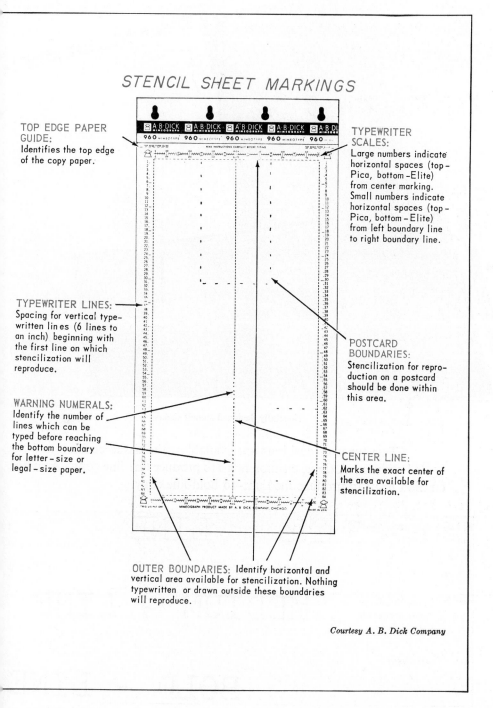

TOP EDGE PAPER GUIDE: Identifies the top edge of the copy paper.

TYPEWRITER SCALES: Large numbers indicate horizontal spaces (top – Pica, bottom – Elite) from center marking. Small numbers indicate horizontal spaces (top – Pica, bottom – Elite) from left boundary line to right boundary line.

TYPEWRITER LINES: Spacing for vertical type-written lines (6 lines to an inch) beginning with the first line on which stencilization will reproduce.

POSTCARD BOUNDARIES: Stencilization for reproduction on a postcard should be done within this area.

WARNING NUMERALS: Identify the number of lines which can be typed before reaching the bottom boundary for letter – size or legal – size paper.

CENTER LINE: Marks the exact center of the area available for stencilization.

OUTER BOUNDARIES: Identify horizontal and vertical area available for stencilization. Nothing typewritten or drawn outside these boundaries will reproduce.

Courtesy A. B. Dick Company

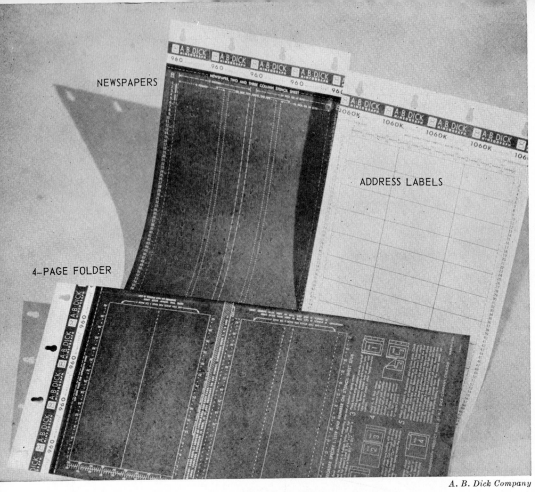

NEWSPAPERS

ADDRESS LABELS

4—PAGE FOLDER

Specially designed stencil sheets

Two types of cushions are available: the tissue cushion and the coated cushion. A tissue cushion helps to produce fine-line copy. A coated cushion helps to produce medium- to bold-line copy.

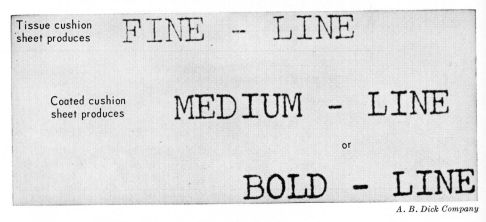

Tissue cushion sheet produces FINE - LINE

Coated cushion sheet produces MEDIUM - LINE

or

BOLD - LINE

A cellophane film may be placed on top of the stencil sheet to assist the sharp type face in pushing aside more of the stencil coating. Since broader stencil openings result, darker, bolder copies may be produced. This film also protects the stencil sheet from letter cutout when the platen is too hard or the type face is excessively sharp.

Stencil assemblies are available in various sizes, qualities, and designs. Some are capable of producing more copies than others; some are better suited for artwork than others. The most widely used sizes are the standard letter size, 8 1/2" x 11", and the standard legal size, 8 1/2" x 14".

Before purchasing stencils, read the advertising literature available from manufacturers to see which type best fits your particular purposes.

Although stencil assemblies can be purchased one at a time, they are most commonly purchased in quantities of 24, called "quires."

STENCILIZATION

The process of exposing the porous surface of the stencil sheet is called "stencilization." Another term is "cutting a stencil." Stencilization is possible through use of a typewriter or sharp instruments called "styli."

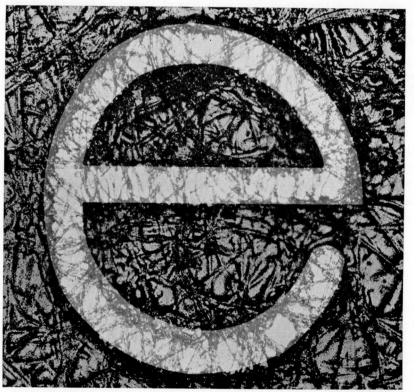

A. B. Dick Company

Typing a Stencil. The following steps are involved in typing a stencil:

1) *PREPARE THE GUIDE COPY.* To assure proper positioning on the stencil sheet, the material to be stencilized should be typed on ordinary typing paper first. (Be sure to use the same size paper that will be used to run off the duplicated copies.) Remember that you must plan to stay within the boundary lines on the stencil sheet.

2) *PREPARE THE TYPEWRITER.* Shift the ribbon control to "stencil" position. This disengages the ribbon and allows the type face to strike the stencil sheet directly.

Clean the type. Type face covered with ink deposits from the ribbon can interfere with the "cutting" process.

Move the paper bail rollers so that they are just outside the boundary markings on the stencil sheet.

3) *PREPARE THE STENCIL ASSEMBLY.* Place the guide copy directly beneath the stencil sheet, making sure that the top edge of the guide copy is aligned with the top edge paper guide marking on the stencil sheet. Since the stencil sheet is translucent, it is easy to see the guide copy beneath. Mark the stencil sheet with dots of correction fluid to aid you in positioning the material when the stencil sheet is inserted into the typewriter. Remove the guide copy and lay it aside.

Insert the cushion sheet between the stencil sheet and the backing sheet. Remember that a coated cushion helps to produce medium- to bold-line copies. The tissue cushion helps to produce fine-line copies.

4) *INSERT THE STENCIL ASSEMBLY INTO THE TYPEWRITER.* With the backing sheet next to the platen, carefully roll the stencil assembly into the typewriter, taking care to avoid wrinkling the stencil sheet. Straighten the stencil assembly in the same manner that you would an ordinary sheet of typing paper. (Disengage the paper release, match top and bottom right corners, top and bottom left corners. Engage the paper release.)

5) *TYPE THE STENCIL.* Stroking on an electric typewriter is no problem since the force with which the type face strikes the stencil sheet is controlled electrically. If a manual typewriter is used, however, you will probably obtain better results if you type a little slower than your usual rate. Use a uniformly firm, but not heavy, staccato touch. Strike with greater force those letters and special characters that have a large printing surface, such as M, W, E, A, $, #, %, and @, so that the entire type-face area will cut through the stencil. Strike with less force letters and punctuation marks having small sharp printing surfaces such as c and o, the comma, and the period.

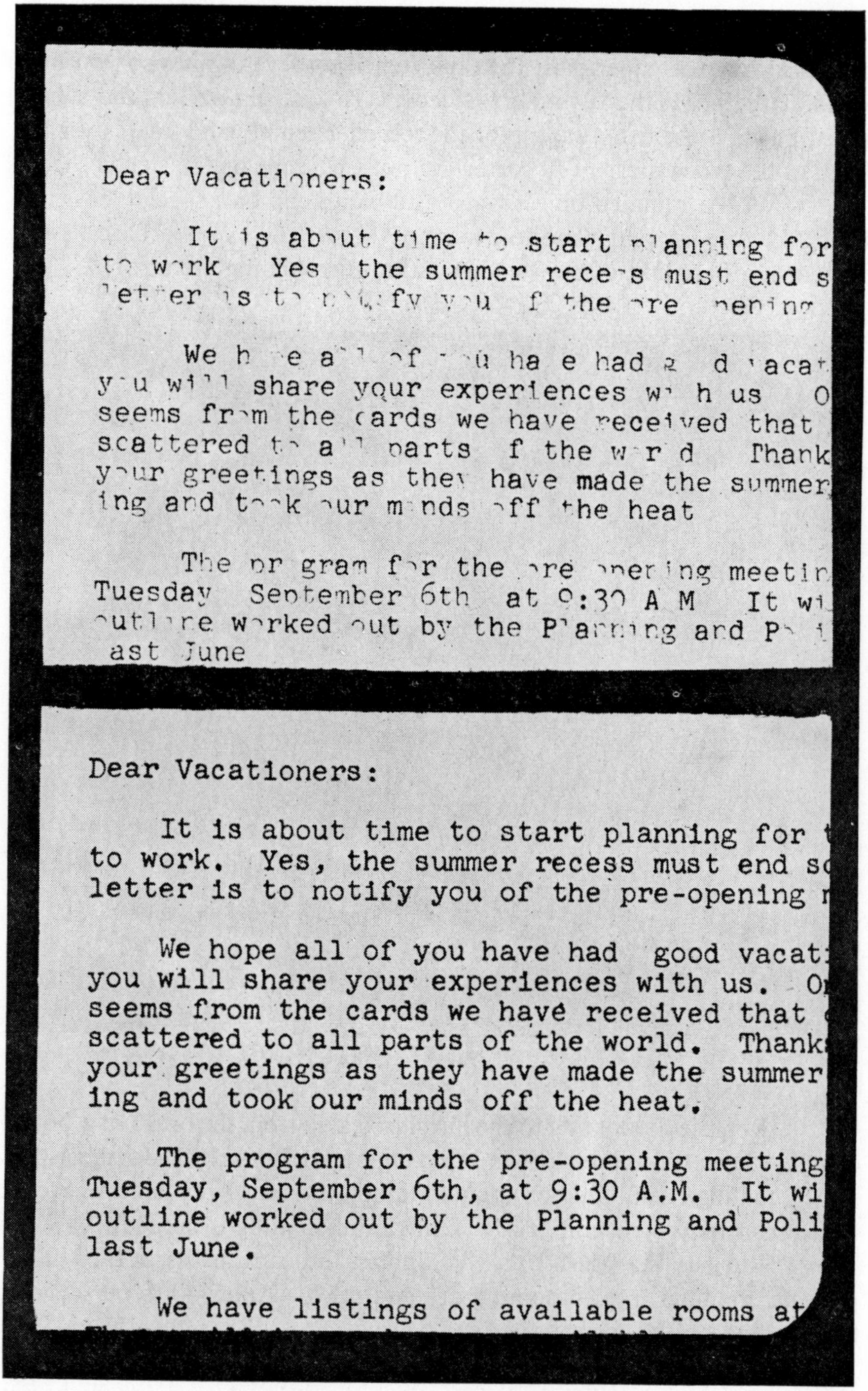

Dear Vacationers:

It is about time to start planning for
to work Yes the summer recess must end s
letter is to notify you f the pre opening

We hope all of you have had a good vacat
you will share your experiences with us   O
seems from the cards we have received that
scattered to all parts f the world Thank
your greetings as they have made the summer
ing and took our minds off the heat

The program for the pre opening meetin
Tuesday September 6th at 9:30 A M   It wi
outline worked out by the Planning and P i
ast June

Dear Vacationers:

It is about time to start planning for t
to work. Yes, the summer recess must end so
letter is to notify you of the pre-opening r

We hope all of you have had good vacat
you will share your experiences with us. Or
seems from the cards we have received that
scattered to all parts of the world. Thank
your greetings as they have made the summer
ing and took our minds off the heat.

The program for the pre-opening meeting
Tuesday, September 6th, at 9:30 A.M. It wi
outline worked out by the Planning and Poli
last June.

We have listings of available rooms at

A. B. Dick Company

Top illustration shows poor stencilization.
Bottom illustration shows correct stencilization.

6) *CORRECT ERRORS IMMEDIATELY AFTER THEY ARE MADE.* Lift the paper bail; turn the stencil up several lines so you may work at the point the typing error occurred. If a film covers the stencil sheet, pull it loose from the top of the stencil assembly and lay it over the front of the typewriter. (The correcting must be done on the stencil sheet.)

With a rounded object, such as a paper clip or a special glass rod burnisher, use a circular motion to smooth over the exposed base tissues with a small amount of the stencil coating surrounding the error.

Replace the coating to the burnished area from the brush of a bottle of stencil correction fluid, a chemical compound essentially the same as the stencil coating itself. Before applying fluid, be sure to remove the excess liquid from the correction brush. Only a thin coating is needed.

Replace the brush quickly; tighten the cap on the bottle. This prevents the fluid from becoming dry and thick. Allow 30 to 60 seconds for the fluid on the correction area to dry.

Roll the stencil back to typing position and then type the correction, using a stroke slightly lighter than normal. An extremely heavy stroke may cut too deeply into the weakened stencil fiber.

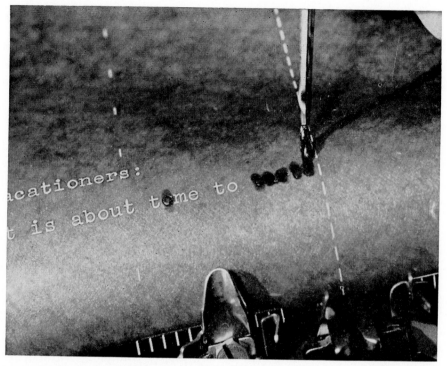

7) *PROOFREAD.* It is always wise to proofread carefully and make corrections before removing the stencil assembly from the typewriter. If an error is discovered after the stencil assembly has been removed, it is necessary to realign the stencil in the typewriter so that it is in the same position as when the copy was first typed.

8) *REMOVE THE STENCIL ASSEMBLY FROM THE TYPE-WRITER.* To avoid wrinkling the stencil sheet, be sure to disengage the paper release before attempting to remove the stencil.

Preparing a Stencil Involving Artwork and/or Lettering. Follow these detailed steps in preparing artwork and/or lettering:

1) *PREPARE A GUIDE COPY.* As is true for typewritten stencils, the use of a guide copy assures proper positioning. Since art stencilization can be fairly time-consuming, it is especially important that a guide copy always be made. A paste-up guide copy, however, will serve the purpose satisfactorily and is relatively fast to prepare. Paste or tape the design to be reproduced on the sheet of guide paper. Remember to plan to stencilize only within the area inside the boundary lines.

2) *ASSEMBLE ACCESSORY EQUIPMENT AND SUPPLIES.*

a) *Illuminated drawing board*—a boxlike frame housing a sheet of translucent glass over a light source serves as a working surface for stencilization. The light beneath illuminates the stencil sheet so that the design on the guide copy, positioned securely on top of the translucent glass, is clearly visible.

b) *Flexible writing sheet*—a flexible, translucent sheet of grained cellulose which serves as a cushion to the pressure exerted manually by the artist on the stencil sheet. This sheet prevents the fibrous base of the stencil sheet from being torn as the sharp instrument pushes the coating aside. It is placed directly beneath the stencil sheet and on top of the guide copy.

c) *Styli*—special pencil-like sharp instruments with which stencilization is accomplished. Many types and designs are available; the stylus chosen will depend on the work to be accomplished. The five most frequently used styli are: (1) wire-loop — for ruling or drawing, (2) ball-point — for fine detail work, (3) roll-point — for handwritten work, (4) curved-point — for use with lettering guides, and (5) burnisher — for shading.

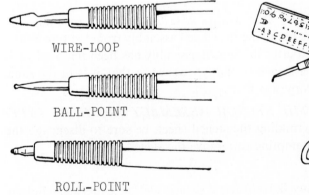

WIRE-LOOP

BALL-POINT

ROLL-POINT

CURVED-POINT

BURNISHER

Courtesy A. B. Dick Company

d) *Shading screen plates*—metal or plastic sheets with embossed surfaces which make possible attractive shading. To produce a shaded effect, the raised surface of the plate is held firmly beneath the area to be shaded. The stencil sheet is placed on top of the embossed surface and, using a burnishing stylus, the artist rubs back and forth briskly over the area.

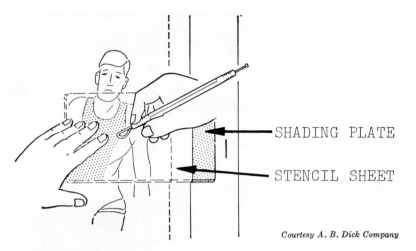

SHADING PLATE

STENCIL SHEET

Courtesy A. B. Dick Company

e) *Lettering guides*—plastic or paper strips with cutout areas in alphabetic designs which aid in reproducing professional-looking lettering. A variety of styles and sizes may be purchased. The lettering guide is placed carefully on top of the stencil sheet. A curved-point stylus is used to stencilize the cutout areas of the guide.

f) *T-square*—a metal, plastic, or wooden t-shaped frame which serves as a base on which the lettering guide rests. It is also useful in stencilizing straight vertical and/or horizontal lines.

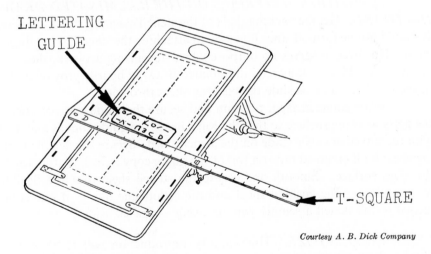

LETTERING GUIDE

T-SQUARE

Courtesy A. B. Dick Company

g) *Commercially-stencilized insets* — small, precut illustrations which may be used to add a professional touch to an especially important stencil involving artwork. Instead of tracing or drawing a design manually with styli onto a stencil sheet, you may cut a window opening and affix, with cement, the small prestenciled design.

A. B. Dick Company

3) *POSITION MATERIALS ON THE ILLUMINATED DRAW-ING BOARD.* Get the backing sheet of the stencil assembly out of the way. It should not be torn off since it is used in attaching the stencil to the duplicator. However, it serves no purpose when stencilizing artwork, shading, or lettering. Most commercial illuminated drawing boards provide a slot in the boxlike frame to slide the backing sheet through.

With gummed tape, position and secure the guide copy on top of the glass working surface so that the top edge of the guide copy is matched with the top edge paper guide on the stencil sheet. Secure the flexible writing sheet with gummed tape on top of the guide copy, which is attached to the glass surface. Smooth and secure the stencil sheet over the flexible writing plate. The cushion sheet and the cellophane film — if one is attached to the stencil assembly you are using — are set aside.

4) *STENCILIZE.* High-quality reproduction will result if you observe the following points:

Apply hard, even pressure to the stylus. Inadequate application of pressure results in having insufficient coating pushed aside on the stencil.

When shading, *outline* the area to be shaded; then place the shading plate, embossed side up, directly beneath the stencil sheet. Hold the shading plate secure while the area is burnished. Movement of the shading plate during the shading process may result in an unattractive shading pattern.

Approach a corner (or junction of two lines) from opposite directions. This should be remembered especially when using lettering guides.

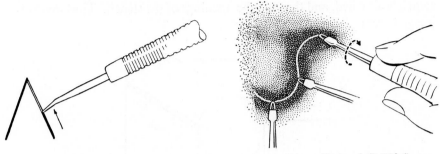

Courtesy A. B. Dick Company

Never pull a wire loop stylus broadside. To avoid tearing the stencil, always hold the stylus in such a manner that the thinnest part of the loop is parallel to the line being drawn. Curved lines present a problem because the stylus must be rolled between the thumb and index finger so that the thinnest part of the loop is kept on the line.

5) *RUN THE COPIES.*

a) *Ink-pad machine — one cylinder.* This duplicator has a single perforated cylinder, around which is placed a flannel absorbent cloth called an ink pad. Ink is placed within the cylinder and, through the openings, the pad becomes absorbed with ink. The "cut" stencil adheres to the inked pad. Each time the cylinder rotates, a sheet of clean copy paper is fed into the machine and pressed, by means of the impression roller, against the stencil. Ink is squeezed through the "cut" portions of the stencil, resulting in an image on the copy paper. The completed copies are ejected into a receiving tray which stacks the paper.

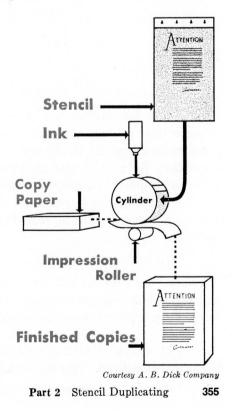

Courtesy A. B. Dick Company

b) *Silk-screen machine — two cylinders.* This machine is a two-cylinder duplicator, around which a sheet of screen made of silk is attached. Two small oscillating ink rollers distribute ink from a tube to the surface of the two cylinders. As the cylinders rotate and paper is fed into the machine, ink is pressed through the tiny pores in the screen around which the stencil is attached, and through the openings of the stencil. Thus the desired image is reproduced.

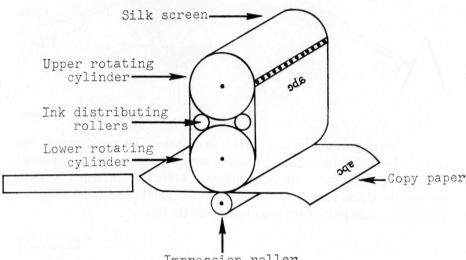

DUPLICATING

Detailed instructions of operation may be obtained from the manufacturer of your machine. Some machines have step-by-step directions mounted on the duplicator. Since these instructions are designed specifically for a particular machine, it is wise to study these carefully before attempting to duplicate copies.

The following is an outline of the general steps involved in duplicating on a stencil machine, regardless of the brand of machine that may be used:

1) *PREPARE THE STENCIL AND THE DUPLICATOR.* After the stencil has been cut and proofread, remove the cushion sheet and the cellophane film — if one was used. Detach the protective cover (a piece of nonabsorbent paper) from the machine and lay it aside for reuse.

2) *ATTACH THE STENCIL.* With the backing sheet up, attach the stencil face down. Tear the backing sheet from the stencil sheet along

the perforation. Shifting both hands to the end of the stencil, stretch the stencil sheet carefully around the cylinder(s). Push with your finger tips toward the outside edges of the stencil to remove any wrinkles which may occur; avoid touching any of the stencilized areas.

A. B. Dick Company

If a letter-size stencil is being attached, place toward the bottom end of the ink pad a part of the protective cover, or a piece of the cellophane film from the stencil sheet. The entire inking area must be completely covered when the machine is in operation.

3) *LOAD THE FEED TABLE.* Place a supply of copy paper — the number of sheets depending on the amount suggested by the machine's manufacturer — on the feed table. Adjust the left and right paper guides so that the paper fits snugly into the area appropriate to the size paper you are using.

4) *PREPARE THE RECEIVING TRAY.* It is desirable that the completed copies, as they are ejected from the machine, be stacked neatly

in the receiving tray. This is particularly important when duplication is necessary on both sides of the paper. As is true of the feed table, the receiving tray can be adjusted to accommodate various lengths and widths of paper. Specific directions for these adjustments may be found in the instruction booklet which accompanies your machine.

5) *REVIEW AND FOLLOW CAREFULLY THE INSTRUCTIONS GIVEN FOR INKING AND OPERATING THE MACHINE.* Duplicate a trial copy; inspect it to see if marginal adjustments are necessary. Copy may be raised or lowered and, on some machines, even leveled by adjusting simple controls on the machine. Side margins can easily be adjusted by moving the left and right paper guides on the feed tray.

If copies are too light, the pad, or silk screen, may be receiving an inadequate supply of ink. Check the source of ink supply. If necessary, add ink according to instructions for the machine. Run off a few more copies. If copies are dark enough and evenly inked, run off the desired number.

All machines have some mechanism by which copies may be automatically counted as they are run through the machine. Some machines register one on the counting device each time a sheet of paper is fed through. When the machine begins to produce the quality desired, the operator sets the counter register at zero and operates the machine until the counter shows that the desired number has been reproduced.

On other models, it is possible to preset the counting device to the number of copies desired. When that number has been fed through the machine, a bell will sound and the feeding mechanism will automatically stop the flow of paper into the machine.

6) *MAINTAIN A CONSTANT CHECK ON THE QUALITY OF THE COPIES.* Occasionally, while the cylinder is still rotating, stop the flow of paper being fed into the machine and inspect, front and back, a copy from the receiving tray. If you discover any unwanted ink deposits, or if you notice inconsistent reproduction, cut off the motor and remedy the trouble.

7) *REMOVE THE STENCIL.* If the stencil is not to be reused, discard it by placing it inside an old newspaper and depositing it in the wastebasket.

If the stencil should be saved for possible reuse, an absorbent stencil file folder is needed. So that the stencil may be readily identifiable from the outside, an impression of the image reproduced by the stencil contained inside may be placed on the front of the folder. This may be accomplished in one of three ways: (a) attach to the front of the folder with gummed tape one of the copies produced; (b) before removing the stencil from the machine, place one of the absorbent folders face down over the stencil and rub lightly over the folder's entire surface (this produces an image on the folder); (c) hand feed the absorbent folder through the machine so that a copy is made on the front of the folder in the same manner in which regular copies are reproduced.

Place the detached stencil, ink side up, on one side of the folder. Close the folder and rub your hand lightly over the entire surface of the folder front so the stencil adheres to the folder and the ink on the surface is absorbed. The folder containing the stencil is now ready for filing.

8) *PREPARE THE MACHINE FOR DISUSE.* Do not leave the ink pad, or silk screen, exposed after you have removed the stencil. Particles of dust and dirt may adhere to it and hinder the ink flow, or the ink may drop down from the lower edges onto the impression roller. Attach the protective cover in the same manner as a stencil. Feed a few sheets of copy paper through to be sure that the cover has adhered completely to the pad or screen beneath. Position the revolving mechanism at the position suggested by the manufacturer. Clean the ink accumulations from the machine with a soft cloth dampened with a cleaning fluid. Wipe off any lint or dust deposits. Clean up the surrounding work area.

COLOR REPRODUCTION

Ink-Pad Machine. Copy can be reproduced in several colors at one time on all ink-pad stencil duplicators. The colored inks are not put inside the cylinder; they are applied directly to the outside of a clean cloth pad attached to the cylinder. Thus, more than one color can be applied in one run as long as the colors do not overlap.

For color work on the ink-pad duplicator:

1) Prepare a guide copy, designating the different color areas. Allow a space of at least *one inch* between the color areas.

2) Prepare the cylinder for color work by removing the protective cover; removing the black ink pad; wiping the edges only of the cylinder with a clean cloth to remove the black ink; placing a protective cover over the cylinder and smoothing it down, being sure that all the cylinder holes are completely covered to keep the black ink inside the cylinder from coming out; attaching the clean cloth ink pad over the protective cover.

3) On the front side of the stencil sheet before it is attached to the cylinder, paint an ink boundary in the color desired for each area.

4) Attach the stencil. Lay the backing sheet over the stencil sheet and rub gently. This identifies the various colored areas in the appropriate color of ink on the ink pad. Remove the stencil sheet temporarily.

5) Paint the pad with the colored inks within the boundary of each colored area.

6) Attach the stencil.

7) Duplicate one or two copies and check them for inking and positioning. If more ink is required, lift the stencil and brush more ink into the pad where ink is needed. Complete the run.

8) When the color runs are finished, remove the colored ink pad; remove the protective cover used to block out the black ink from within the machine; attach either a clean pad or the one that was originally removed from the machine. Clean and cover the machine as described on page 359. Colored ink pads may be stored for reuse in stencil file folders in the same manner as stencils are stored.

You may want to duplicate many copies of a color not contained in the cylinder. In this case, the entire cylinder on the machine may be lifted out and replaced with another cylinder containing ink of a different color.

Silk-Screen Machine. Only one color at a time can be reproduced on the silk-screen machine. It is a relatively rapid and simple process to remove and replace the silk screen and the oscillating ink rollers, clean the two cylinders, and attach a tube of colored ink.

Another method satisfactory for producing short runs is to turn off the automatic inking system and apply the colored ink manually to the upper cylinder. The rotation of the cylinders distributes the ink to the other cylinder.

Study Questions

1. What are the three primary parts of a stencil assembly? What is a fourth optional part of a stencil assembly?

2. What is the purpose of each of the four parts?

3. Describe the guide markings on a standard stencil sheet.

4. Name three special-purpose stencils.

5. What is a "quire" of stencils?

6. Define "stencilization."

7. With what common instruments is stencilization accomplished?

8. Why is it advisable to prepare a guide copy?

9. How is the typewriter prepared for typing a stencil?

10. When typing on a manual typewriter, what kind of typewriter keys should be struck with heavier force than normal? lighter force?

11. Describe how to make a correction on a stencil.

12. What are the five most frequently used styli? For what type of work is each best suited?

13. Explain how to stencilize shaded areas.

14. Describe how to position materials on the illuminated drawing board.

15. What point must be remembered when designing a guide copy for reproduction involving more than one color at a time on the ink-pad machine?

What Do You Think?

1. Which is more valuable to you as a prospective office employee: experience in preparing stencils that are mostly straight typing or experience in preparing those that include drawing, lettering, shading, and insets?

2. To what extent is creative or artistic ability needed to prepare good work on an illuminated drawing board?

Your Personal Qualities

The stencils typed by Mary Brady, an employee in the publicity department, failed to produce the sharp, clear, and clean copies so essential for publicity purposes. At first she attributed the difficulty to the fact that the rubber surface on the typewriter cylinder was slightly pitted, so she had the cylinder replaced. Later she increased the pressure on the type bars, but both changes, though they brought about improvements, failed to produce the desired quality.

Finally she noticed that duplicated copy bearing the initials of the director's secretary was invariably sharp and clean. She asked the secretary for suggestions for improving her copy and received two:

a. Always clean the type before typing a stencil.

b. Brush the keys occasionally as you type the stencil to prevent paper lint from collecting on the type faces.

Mary had never cleaned the type before or during the typing of a stencil, so she frankly told the director's secretary that her suggestions were worthless.

Questions: 1. If you were Mary, how would you handle the suggestions that were made?

2. What is your evaluation of the manner in which Mary dealt with the director's secretary?

How's Your English?

After reading the rules on spelling in Appendix C, indicate which of the following are the correct spellings:

1. secede   seceed   sesede

2. exceed   excede   exsede

3. procede   proceed   prosede

4. intersede   interceed   intercede

5. preceed   precede   presede

Office Work

1. Type as guide copy for stencil duplication the following material arranged in tabular form. Rule the form.

Comparison of Estimated and Actual Expenses.

Last year:

Sales Salaries: Estimated, $7,000.00; Actual, $7,118.00

Office Salaries: Estimated, $7,500.00; Actual, $7,556.00

Delivery Expense: Estimated, $1,600.00; Actual, $1,591.05

Advertising: Estimated, $300.00; Actual, $312.95

Rent: Estimated, $1,500.00; Actual, $1,500.00

Supplies: Estimated, $300.00; Actual, $287.60

Insurance: Estimated, $2,100.00; Actual, $2,100.00

Depreciation: Estimated, $500.00; Actual, $521.16

Miscellaneous: Estimated, $350.00; Actual, $357.35

This year:

Sales Salaries: Estimated, $7,500.00; Actual, $7,439.00

Office Salaries: Estimated, $7,800.00; Actual, $7,780.00

Delivery Expense: Estimated, $1,650.00; Actual, $1,612.45

Advertising: Estimated, $350.00; Actual, $365.75

Rent: Estimated, $1,500.00; Actual, $1,500.00

Supplies: Estimated, $350.00; Actual, $342.75

Insurance: Estimated, $2,250.00; Actual, $2,250.00

Depreciation: Estimated, $550.00; Actual, $565.32

Miscellaneous: Estimated, $400.00; Actual, $392.40

2. Be prepared to demonstrate before the class any one of the steps involved in stencil duplicating.

3. Secure from your instructor an assignment for work to be done on a stencil. Prepare enough copies for your instructor and all members of your class.

UNIT 10 | Copying and Duplicating

PART 3:

Fluid Duplicating

Copies of the minutes of the weekly meeting must be sent to all who attended, or an interoffice memorandum must be sent to all department heads concerning safety rules. What duplicating process would best be used? Fluid duplicators are used successfully for duplicating copies which must be produced in quantities sufficient to make the use of carbon copies impractical, and the appearance of which is not so important as the cost and speed of reproduction. Up to 300 copies can be produced from a single fluid-process master, but generally the required number of copies from a single master copy ranges from 15 to 50. Fluid duplicating is utilized extensively by relatively large business firms in the distribution of interoffice communications: reports, memos, bulletins, etc.

PRINCIPLE OF OPERATION

There are five basic elements in the fluid duplicating process: the glossy master sheet, special carbon paper, the fluid duplicator, the moistening fluid, and the copy paper.

The master is attached, carbon side up, to a revolving drum. As clean copy paper is fed into the machine, it is moistened with an alcohol-like fluid by means of a dampened roller and a felt wick which distributes the fluid evenly onto each sheet. As the drum revolves, an impression roller presses the moist blank paper against the carbon side of the master, causing a minute portion of the carbon to be transferred to the copy paper. The impression roller then ejects the duplicated copy into the receiving tray of the machine.

Because the image produced is made directly from the carbon image on the master sheet, this process is sometimes called the "direct" process. Because of the watery nature of the moistening fluid or liquid, the terms "fluid" and/or "liquid" process may be used. Because the moistening fluid is of chemical composition, it is referred to as the "chemical" or "spirit" process. All these names refer to the process being discussed.

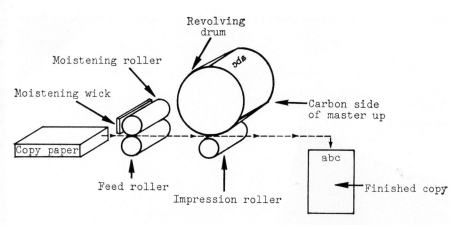

Copies of documents involving handwriting and/or artwork may be produced simply and speedily by this method, even though typewritten material is more common in business offices.

PREPARING THE MASTER COPY

Typing a Master Copy. For best results when preparing a typewritten master, be guided by the instructions that follow:

1) *PREPARE A GUIDE COPY TO ASSURE PROPER HORIZONTAL AND VERTICAL POSITIONING.* Leave at least one-half inch blank at the top or at the bottom so that the master copy may be clamped onto the drum of the duplicating machine. (The master copy may be attached to the revolving drum at either end.)

2) *PREPARE THE PACK.* The "pack" refers to the sheet of master paper and the sheet of carbon.

Many typists use combined assemblies called "Mastersets." A Masterset consists of one sheet of glazed, hard-surfaced white master paper attached to a sheet of special carbon-coated paper, with a loose protective tissue sheet interleaved between the two. The main advantage of the Masterset is that the operator can avoid handling the glossy side of the carbon sheet and can, therefore, keep his hands relatively free of carbon smudges.

If a preassembled Masterset is not available, it is simple to assemble a master sheet, a carbon sheet, and a sheet of heavy paper or resilient plastic to serve as a backing sheet. The carbon paper is placed between the master sheet and the backing sheet with the glossy (active) side of the carbon toward you. When you type, the carbon will be deposited on the back of the sheet on which you type, thus making a reverse-reading copy.

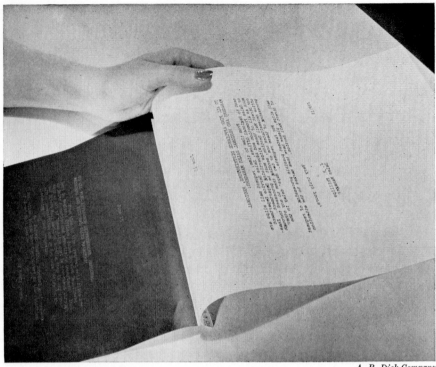

A. B. Dick Company

3) *PREPARE THE TYPEWRITER.* Clean the type well, giving extra attention to type faces where ink is likely to accumulate, such as *e, a, W, g.*

4) *INSERT THE PACK INTO THE TYPEWRITER.* As you see it in your typewriter, the white master sheet is nearest you; the carbon is next, carbon side toward you. The backing sheet is last against the platen. If a Masterset is used, be sure to remove the tissue interleaved between the master sheet and the carbon sheet before inserting it into the typewriter.

5) *TYPE WITH FIRM, RHYTHMIC STROKES.* Type capital letters a little sharper than normal; punctuation marks, a little more lightly than normal. Notice that by nature of the positioning of the materials into the typewriter, typing results in a positive ribbon image on the front of the master sheet — which facilitates proofreading — and a reverse-reading carbon image on the back.

6) *PROOFREAD.* If corrections are necessary, make them according to the information which follows:

When you type a master copy, your typing simply puts carbon deposits on the back of the master sheet. When you make an error, you have carbon where you do not want it. Be sure that you do the correcting on the carbon-deposit side of the master sheet.

If you do not need to type over the mistake, you can follow one of three procedures:

a) Cut it out of the master with a razor blade or knife. This procedure would be appropriate for eliminating relatively large areas; for example, an entire paragraph.

b) Cover the error with cellophane tape or gummed label. This procedure would be appropriate for eliminating relatively small areas; for example, an unwanted word at the end of a line or the last sentence of a paragraph.

c) Lightly scrape off the unwanted carbon deposit with a razor blade or knife. This procedure would be especially appropriate for eliminating an unwanted character (letter or punctuation mark) between words.

If you must type a correction at the point of the error (as in a misspelled word), you must first eliminate the error. The most satisfactory procedure for this type of correction is to scrape off lightly the unwanted carbon deposit with a razor blade or knife. After the error has been disposed of, you are ready to type the correction.

However, remember that *fluid carbon paper can be used only once,* and that you have used up the carbon at that point where you typed the error and must provide some new carbon there. So, insert a slip of fresh carbon (cut from the bottom of the carbon sheet or from another carbon sheet) under the master at the point where you must type the correction; then remove the extra carbon slip before going on.

7) *DISENGAGE THE PAPER RELEASE AND REMOVE THE PACK FROM THE TYPEWRITER.* Carefully separate the master copy from the carbon sheet, and discard the carbon sheet. Cover the carbon side of the master copy with paper (the tissue sheet if a Masterset was used) to protect it until it is attached to the machine for duplicating.

Preparing a Master Involving Artwork, Lettering, Shading, and/or Handwriting. For best results when preparing a master involving other than typewriting, follow these general instructions:

1) *PREPARE A GUIDE COPY.* This step may not be necessary if only handwriting is involved. If artwork and/or lettering are included in your design, for best positioning results, a guide copy should be prepared.

2) *PREPARE THE MASTER COPY.* The *fastest* way to prepare the master copy is the following:

a) If a Masterset is used, remove the tissue sheet.

b) Secure the pack with gummed tape to a *resilient,* smooth working surface. If a wooden working surface is utilized, a plastic backing sheet beneath the pack will provide the resiliency needed.

c) Cover the master sheet with the guide copy; secure it with gummed tape to the working surface.

d) Outline the image area, applying hard, even pressure with a sharp-pointed instrument (hard-lead pencil, ball-point pen, or stylus). Enough pressure must be exerted to result in a carbon image on the back side of the master sheet. Remember that the pressure must pass through two thicknesses: the guide copy and the master sheet.

A more satisfactory method, in terms of *quality of reproduction,* however, may be the following:

a) Separate the carbon from the master sheet.

b) Trace lightly, with the use of an illuminated drawing board and a pencil or pen, the image area onto the front of the master sheet.

c) Remove the guide copy from the working surface.

d) Position the carbon sheet, glossy side up, under the master sheet.

e) Outline the image area.

Since the pressure from the writing instrument must pass through only one thickness — that of the master sheet — a more uniform carbon deposit is usually possible.

Lettering guides and t-squares can be used in the same manner as they are in preparing a stencil.

To secure shaded effects, the embossed surface of the shading plate is placed beneath the carbon sheet. Rubbing lightly on the front of the master sheet with a blunt instrument, such as a burnishing stylus, will result in carbon deposited in a patterned shaded area on the carbon-deposit side of the master sheet.

RUNNING THE FLUID DUPLICATOR

In a large office with a separate duplicating department, you would be expected to run off copies only in an emergency. In a small office, however, preparing masters and turning out copies on a fluid duplicator may be one of your regular duties. As you would expect, the specific instructions for producing copies on the various makes of fluid duplicators vary slightly. Nevertheless, the following general instructions apply to all makes.

1) *ATTACH THE MASTER.* Clamp the master copy to the cylinder, carbon side up. To avoid wrinkling the master copy, take care to insert the master copy across the width of the drum into the slot *evenly*; then hold lightly to the unattached end while you turn the drum one complete revolution.

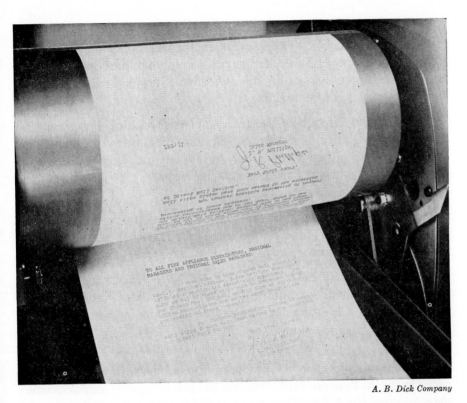

2) *ADJUST THE FLUID CONTROL.* This mechanism determines how much the paper being fed into the machine is moistened. The wetter the paper when it comes in contact with the master copy, the more carbon deposit transferred from the master copy to the paper. Therefore, when this mechanism is set on "high," each individual copy produced will have relatively dark color strength. However, fewer copies can be produced from the master copy.

3) *POSITION THE CLEAN COPY PAPER IN THE FEED TRAY.* Copy paper should be relatively slick-surfaced and nonabsorbent. Align the side of the clean copy paper on the feed tray with the sides of the master copy on the drum. This permits the duplicated copies to have the same margins as the master copy.

4) *SET THE PRESSURE CONTROL.* This mechanism controls the force with which the impression roller presses the moistened clean paper against the carbon side of the master copy. When the mechanism is adjusted to a "low" setting, each moistened sheet will be pressed only *slightly* against the master, resulting in relatively light copies. More copies, even though light in color of duplication, can be produced in this manner.

5) *RUN THE COPIES.* Both electrically-operated and manual machines are available. The speed of manual machines may be varied. The greater the speed, the weaker the color strength of the copies produced and the greater the number of copies possible. Slower speeds give shorter runs with greater color strength.

Caution: Be sure to effect a complete revolution once you start the rotation of the drum. Hesitation will cause the copy to be darker at the point of hesitation than at any other, since the pause allows more carbon to be deposited onto the copy paper at that point.

6) *RELEASE THE MASTER.* Remove the master from the machine. If it is desirable to save the master for possible reuse, attach the protective tissue sheet to the carbon side of the master sheet and file it. If the tissue has been thrown away, any sheet of paper will serve satisfactorily.

7) *PREPARE THE MACHINE FOR DISUSE.* After the copies have been duplicated, discontinue the flow of fluid and adjust the pressure control to zero. Clean the machine and the surrounding work area.

COLOR DUPLICATION

Several colors may be produced at one time with no adjustments necessary to the fluid duplicator because *the color of carbon used determines the color reproduced.* Therefore, one part of a master copy may be prepared using a purple carbon sheet; another part, a green carbon sheet; another part, a red carbon sheet, and so on.

The most common fluid carbon color is purple; but red, blue, green, and black carbon sheets may be used. Even though you may use different colors close together, you should not let the colors cross or touch.

THE AZOGRAPH PROCESS

The Azograph process, which works essentially the same as other fluid duplicating processes, is designed to eliminate the problem of keeping hands and clothing free from carbon smudges when preparing the master copy. This is possible because no printing dye is formed on the master copy until the copies are in the process of being run on the duplicator. A chemical agent included in the moistening fluid reacts on the master copy to form the blue printing dye.

Azograph duplicators are versatile because they can be used to produce copies from regular fluid-process masters as well as special Azograph masters. Regular fluid duplicators, however, unless equipped with the special Azograph moistening fluid, will not produce copies from Azograph masters.

Study Questions

1. For what kind of work is the fluid duplicator widely used?

2. Explain the principle of operation for the fluid process.

3. What other names are common for the fluid process?

4. Elaborate on the statement: "One-half inch should be left blank on the master copy at the top or at the bottom."

5. What is the primary advantage of the Masterset?

6. Describe the sequence of the pack as it is positioned in the typewriter.

7. What are three satisfactory procedures used to correct an error if you do not need to type over the error?

8. Explain how to correct an error if you must type a correction at the point of the error.

9. What two machine controls can be adjusted to determine color strength of copies and length of run? Explain.

10. What is the relationship of the speed of operation to color strength and length of run?

11. What is the special feature of the Azograph process?

What Do You Think?

1. In your office considerable time is spent in preparing carbon copies of certain reports for as many as twenty people. What better method could be used for making this number of copies plus additional copies for incidental use and for the files?

2. What factors would help you decide whether your employer should order a regular fluid duplicator or an Azograph?

3. Which typewriter do you think prepares better masters or stencils — one with pica type or one with elite type? If you think that there is a difference, how do you account for it?

Your Personal Qualities

You work in the office of an insurance company that has a fluid duplicator used by nine of the employees. It seems that the machine is frequently out of order when you want to use it. On several occasions you notice that the pressure has been left on and the fluid has not been turned off when you want to use the machine. Also, there always seems to be a great deal of waste copy paper around the machine because users are not getting good copy all of the time. This seems to be a case of "everyone's responsibility is no one's responsibility." What should you do?

How's Your English?

Read about compound words in Appendix C, and then write the following words correctly, inserting hyphens where they are required:

fifty /seven	by /line
one /half	hand /made
can /not	by /laws

trade /in /value	take /off
ex /president	bond /holder
head /line	lay /man
parcel /post	passer /by
half /dollar	self /help
per /cent	north /east
trade /union	trade /name

Office Work

1. The following announcement is to be reproduced on a fluid duplicator and sent to all salesmen in the field. Type it up in good form preparatory to making a master.

To all company salesmen:

Because of rising costs it will be necessary to raise prices in our line of canned fruits. The new prices indicated below will go into effect on the first day of next month.

Stock Numbers	Name	Old Price Per Case	New Price Per Case
CF 27	Sliced Apples	6.18	6.48
CF 28	Applesauce	5.10	5.45
CF 31	Fruit Cocktail	8.04	8.55
CF 36	Peaches (Halves)	6.22	6.53
CF 38	Peaches (Sliced)	6.15	6.45
CF 41	Pears (Halves)	8.15	8.60
CF 45	Pineapple (Sliced)	7.56	8.04
CF 50	Pineapple (Crushed)	6.14	6.45

UNIT 10 | Copying and Duplicating

PART 4:

Offset and Other

Reproduction Processes

When contacting customers or clients with duplicated material, you may want not only large quantities but also superior quality. To get copies that are often as attractive as professional print-shop work, offset duplicators are used. Letterheads, envelopes, and business forms of all kinds are printed on offset machines. They are also used to produce illustrated sales letters, folders, and bulletins.

Until recently only large, expensive, complex offset duplicators were available. Today, however, smaller, less expensive models of offset duplicators are becoming very popular. These machines have many automatic features which make operation of the machine fairly simple. As a result, more and more office workers are required to know about the offset process.

OFFSET PROCESS

Principle of Operation. The offset process is based on the principle that oil (or grease) and water will not readily mix — in this instance, an oil-based printing ink and a water-based repellent.

Copies are produced from a paper or metal master (sometimes referred to as a "plate"). A grease-receptive direct-reading image — in the form of handwriting, typewriting, artwork, and/or lettering — is deposited on the master. The master is attached, image side up, around a rotating cylinder, called the "master" cylinder. As the master cylinder revolves, the master is brought into contact with a small roller moistened with a water-based repellent (water roller). The repellent solution adheres to nonimage areas on the master, but is repelled by greasy image areas.

As the master cylinder continues to rotate, another small roller (ink roller) moistened with oil-based ink contacts the master. The ink from the ink roller adheres to the greasy image areas, but is repelled by the non-image areas, which have been moistened with the water-based repellent. (Grease adheres to grease, but is repelled by water.) The image now appears in the form of ink on a wet background.

As the master cylinder rotates still farther, the master contacts another large cylinder, which is approximately the same size as that around which the master is placed. Wrapped around this cylinder is a large sheet of thick rubber called a "blanket." Thus, this cylinder is often called the "blanket" cylinder. As both cylinders rotate, the greasy right-reading image areas are transferred from the master cylinder to the blanket cylinder in the form of a reverse-reading image.

This three-step cycle — moistening the master with water, moistening the master with ink, and transferring the grease image to the blanket — occurs with each rotation of the master cylinder.

Through means of an impression roller, the clean copy paper is pressed against the imaged blanket cylinder, and the ink deposits on the blanket are transferred to the copy paper as it is ejected from the machine.

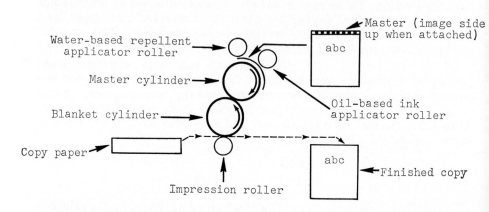

Preparing Offset Masters. Preparing a paper master with the use of a typewriter or special writing tools is a relatively simple process. A few precautions, however, are necessary if best results are to be obtained.

Typing a Master

1) *PREPARE THE TYPEWRITER.* As is true with typing any master copy — whether stencil, fluid, or offset — care should be taken to see that the typewriter is prepared appropriately. Type faces should be clean; feed rolls and platen should be free of ink smudges and deposits.

A special ribbon — one capable of leaving greasy ink deposits — is necessary when preparing typewritten offset masters. Carbon ribbons produce best results. Carbon *plastic* ribbons produce sharper print than carbon *paper* ribbons. If your typewriter is not equipped for use with a carbon ribbon, then a special fabric "grease" ribbon may be used. Remember, only grease-receptive images will reproduce.

Move the paper bail rollers to the extreme right and left edges of the master. This prevents the rollers from smearing the greasy deposits down the page.

2) *INSERT THE MASTER.* The side on which nonreproducible guide markings are printed is the side on which typing should be done. Therefore, after insertion into the typewriter, these markings should be visible to the typist. Common guide markings on paper masters include center markings for both 8-inch and 8 1/2-inch wide paper, warning numerals for use when typing near the bottom of 11-inch and 14-inch long paper, and top-edge paper guide. (Note that the markings are similar to those on stencil sheets.)

3) *TYPE THE MASTER.* Use a uniform touch in typing, sufficient to deposit an even, uniformly dark image.

Too heavy a touch results in embossing on the opposite side of the master. Embossment is undesirable since the embossed letters may be pressed beyond the reach of the ink roller, resulting in hollow-looking reproduction. On an electric typewriter, the pressure control should be set to the lowest position where all characters will print.

4) *CORRECT ERRORS.* A very soft, nongreasy eraser should be used. Special offset erasers produce best results.

Erase the image very lightly. It is necessary only to remove the greasy deposit. It is not necessary to remove the stain or ghost image left by the dye from the imaging medium, as this stain will not reproduce. It is necessary, however, that the slick surface of the area being erased is left unharmed. Be sure to keep the eraser clean by frequently rubbing it on a piece of clean paper.

Preparing a Paper Master Involving Artwork, Lettering, and/or Signatures. A special offset reproducing pencil, ball-point reproducing pen, offset drawing crayon, or offset drawing fluid may be selected as the imaging medium. For signatures, even a rubber stamp wet with ink from an offset ink pad may be used. Use these instruments as you would use them on a plain sheet of paper. Most paper masters are translucent enough so that, when used in conjunction with an illuminated drawing board, the image may be traced onto the master. Again, only medium pressure is required; take care not to emboss the master. Lettering guides are used in much the same manner as they are when preparing a fluid master. Special nonreproducing pencils which will not cut into the special coating on the master are available for writing in notations which should not be reproduced on the final copies.

Photo-Offset Masters. There are two basic types of offset duplicating masters: paper masters and metal masters (sometimes referred to as aluminum plates). Short-run, medium-run, and long-run paper masters may be purchased. Up to 10,000 copies can be obtained from a single long-run paper master, but 25,000 or more copies can be run from an aluminum plate. The short-run paper masters are the least expensive — less than ten cents; the aluminum plates are most expensive — approximately fifty cents.

One of the most satisfactory, but most expensive, ways of "imaging" offset masters is the photo-negative method. A photo negative is prepared, and from it the image is transferred to the "positive" — the master. Even though this method is most commonly used to image metal masters for long runs, it may be used to image special long-run plastic-coated paper masters.

Any corrections must be made on the original copy *before* it is photographed, that is, before the negative is made. An incorrect word, for example "lokos," may be cut out of the original. The correct word, "looks," which has been typed on another sheet or in the top, bottom, right, or left margins of the original sheet, is cut out and substituted in the cutout area on the original. Mending tape is applied to the *back* of the original to hold the substitution in place.

Another way you can make a correction is to rub over the error with white chalk until it is completely covered. Then type the correction over the covered area.

One of the main advantages of the photo-negative method of preparing masters is that the image from the original can be enlarged or reduced as the photo negative is made from the original.

Some of the copying processes described in Part 1 have recently become very popular in the preparation of masters for offset machines. This is true because, generally, preparing offset masters through the use of copying machines is speedier, less expensive, and simpler to accomplish than preparation by the photo-negative method. The four copying processes most widely used for this purpose are dye-transfer and infrared, which image paper masters; diffusion-transfer, which images paper or metal masters depending on the brand of machine used; and electrostatic-transfer, which images either paper or metal masters. The image can be enlarged or reduced on some electrostatic-transfer copying machines, but not on the other copying processes mentioned here.

A. B. Dick Company

Advantages and Disadvantages of the Offset Process. One of the major advantages of the offset process is its ability to produce copies of superior quality. Printing can be done in a variety of colors; simply use the color of ink desired for the image area. Registration is exact enough so that multicolor jobs can be run, although a separate master and a separate run are required for each color. The offset process is considered to be a high-speed duplication process (from 4,500 to 8,000 copies an hour is common), although the machine model and the weight of copy paper used determine exactly how many copies may be produced in an hour. Offset machines will reproduce on a variety of paper weights, sizes, colors, and qualities of paper.

More skill is required in the operation of an offset machine than in some of the other duplicating processes, such as fluid or stencil. Designs of office models now on the market have made operation much less complex than on larger commercial models.

Expense per copy depends on the quality of materials used — paper or metal masters, size, weight, quality of copy paper — as well as on the length of run. On long runs, the expense per copy should be small; in most cases, only a small fraction of a cent.

RELIEF PROCESS

The relief process works on the same principle as reproduction on a regular typewriter or a rubber hand stamp; all make copies through the use of embossed, or raised, letters and /or designs.

The embossed master is prepared in one of two ways. Metal embossed strips may be typed on a machine similar to a typewriter. As the individual key is struck, the embossed typeface strikes the metal strip with such force that the design of the character is punched into the metal strip. These metal strips are fitted on raised buttons appropriately projected from the "blanket," which is curved to fit the rotating cylinder on the relief machine.

Another way of preparing the embossed master involves setting type by hand with the use of individual rubber or metal typeface (similar to that on a typewriter) and an instrument called a "composing fork." The typesetter picks up the appropriate typefaces with the composing fork and slips them into grooves on the cylinder. Thus, the completed cylinder is a series of embossed individual typefaces assembled in grooves, which correspond to typewritten lines.

Just as there are two methods for preparing the embossed master from which copies are made, there are two possible methods of inking for relief process duplicators. One uses a large inked ribbon which is pressed by means of an impression roller between the embossed image areas and the copy paper. This method of inking works on the same principle as an ordinary typewriter. On a typewriter, as each key is struck, the embossed surface of the typeface is pressed through an ink ribbon to the copy paper, where an ink image of the embossed area is deposited.

On the relief process machines, however, an entire page of material is printed with each revolution of the drum. It is obvious, then, that material duplicated with this particular method of inking can hardly be differentiated from material which was actually typed on an ordinary typewriter. For this reason, this process is used extensively for correspondence which may be "personalized" by later filling in, on a typewriter, the name and address of the individual recipient.

The second method of inking involves ink applied to the embossed surface of the cylinder by means of an *inked roller* before contact with the copy paper. The rubber hand stamp works on this principle. The embossed surface of the hand stamp picks up ink when pressed against an ink pad. The ink is then transferred from the embossed areas to the copy paper when pressure is applied.

Color of reproduction can be controlled easily and simply in either method of inking. Printing colors are limited only by availability of colored ribbons or colored inks.

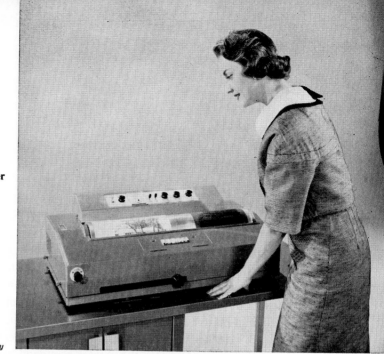

An electronic facsimile copier

A. B. Dick Company

In the relief process, reproduction on one or both sides of the copy paper is possible on a variety of weights, grades, colors, and sizes of copy paper.

Very long runs are not only possible, but advisable, for the relief process, since preparation of the embossed master is a relatively time-consuming task. Because of the durability of the metal typefaces described in the composing-fork method of typesetting, runs of several hundred thousand are fairly common.

Excluding the expense of preparation of the embossed master, duplicating cost per copy is low. Expense varies with the quality of the copy paper used as well as length of run. Less than $.002 per copy is common.

Relief machines, due to the initial expense of equipment, the complexity of the process, and the expensive preparation of relief masters, are not common office duplicators.

SPECIAL AUXILIARY MACHINES

Electronic Facsimile Copiers. This process is becoming more and more popular in preparing, electronically, master copies for some of the other duplicating processes: offset paper masters, fluid masters, and even stencils for long-run stencil duplicating.

Two cylinders, turning at the same speed, are used in the facsimile process. The original copy is wrapped around the left cylinder; and an

The Vari-Typer

Vari-Typer Corporation

offset paper master, fluid master sheet, or vinyl-plastic stencil is wrapped around the right cylinder. When the "start" button is pressed, the original copy is scanned photoelectrically as the synchronized cylinders rotate; and an exact facsimile image is recorded on the offset master, fluid master, or stencil in a matter of minutes. The process is much faster than the manual typing of paper masters or stencils. Furthermore, it completely eliminates the need for proofreading the master or stencil because an exact facsimile is produced, whether it be an engineer's drawing, a complicated tabulation, a detailed business form, or an office communication.

The original copy for facsimile duplicating is limited to sheets up to 8 1/2" x 14 1/2". The sheets must be of a stock which can be wrapped around a cylinder with a diameter of six inches. Copies cannot be made from a book or a magazine without removing the pages. Up to 5,000 copies can be run off from a facsimile-produced offset paper master; over 5,000, from a single vinyl-plastic stencil; and up to 300, from a fluid master.

The Vari-Typer. The Vari-Typer is a semiautomatic composing machine with a wide variety of typefaces. It is used primarily in the initial stages of the duplicating process to prepare master copy. The typing pressure is uniform and can be set for any one of seven degrees of strength to make the proper impression on the master sheet. Fluid masters, offset paper masters, and stencils can be typed on this machine. It is also used to type copy which is to be pasted up in a layout and photographed in the photo-negative copying process.

Copy composed and typed on the Vari-Typer has a professional, printed appearance because the letters of the alphabet are automatically spaced according to their individual widths. Thus, the wider letters like *M* and *W* are set in wider spaces than the narrower letters of the alphabet like *i* and *l*.

By typing the copy twice, you can justify (make even) the right margin to give it an added resemblance to typeset copy. As the rough draft is typed, it is converted into a justified line. A tabular key sets into motion a mechanism which automatically computes the space differential in a line of copy needed to bring it out to an even right margin.

The copy can be typed in many different typefaces, set in type *fonts* or bands. The different typefaces vary in size from tiny 6-point type to large 16-point type; more than 300 styles are available, some for foreign languages. Two fonts can be fitted into the operating anvil of the machine at one time. They can be changed quickly from one to the other, thereby permitting the use, for instance, of italics and bold-faced type matching the main type style used in the copy.

The wide selection of styles and sizes of typefaces makes the machine ideal for the composition and typing of masters for printed materials. It is used extensively in business offices to prepare bulletins, booklets, brochures, house organs, reports, business forms, etc.

The Automatic Typewriter. The automatic typewriter is used for form letters to obtain more favorable consideration from the recipient than those reproduced by ordinary methods. The automatic typewriter produces original typewritten letters in large quantities for selected mailing lists. The automatically typed letters are *individually* typed letters, and so they do not look like form letters. This, of course, is the most expensive type of quantity reproduction.

The automatic typewriter operates on the principle of the player piano. A perforated roll or paper tape of the copy to be written automatically must first be typed on the "perforator." Provision can be made to stop the roll or tape at specific points in the letter to allow the operator to type in manually variable information. The manually typed information usually includes the date, the inside address, the salutation, and inserts, such as a specific amount of money, a date, or some other item that changes from letter to letter.

After a master copy has been typed for each machine, one typist can look after as many as four or five machines at one time. Some automatics have an attachment for embossing the signature on each letter.

Collators. A duplicated job of two or more pages must be collated — the pages gathered together in proper order and fastened into separate sets — before it is delivered. The simplest method of collating is stacking the copies of each page in individual stacks on a table, then lifting the top page from each stack until the last page in the set is removed. This method, however, is both tiring and time-consuming. You can increase your collating speed by picking up pages with both hands at the same time. In collating a four-page set, for example, you would start by picking up

American Automatic Typewriter Company

The Auto-Typist

page one with your right hand; then as you pick up page two with your right hand, simultaneously pick up page one with your left, and so forth. As you are turning down the completed right-hand set, you are picking up page four of the left-hand set. The last step is to crisscross the left-hand pack on top of the right-hand set as you put it down. If a gathering rack is available, you can arrange a number of duplicated stacks in it and place it immediately in front of you on a table.

Sometimes a rotating circular table is used. With this device, individual stacks of papers are placed in proper sequence along the edge of the table. As the table rotates, you simply take the top sheet from each stack as it passes your fixed position.

SUMMARY OF DUPLICATING PROCESSES

Process	Length of Run For Which Best Suited	Characteristics
Fluid	10–300	Prints on glossy-finished paper of any color. Various colored images can be duplicated in one run. Purple reproduces best. Masters can be saved for reuse. Used commonly in reproducing typewritten interoffice communications.
Azograph	10–100	Variation of the fluid process. Masters cleaner to handle since printing dye is not formed until master is moistened during the process of duplication. Reproduction is gray-blue in color.
Stencil	10–5,000	Most commonly printed on absorbent, rough-finished paper of any color; although when used with special quick-drying inks, bond paper may be used. Colored images possible through use of colored ink. On ink-pad stencil machines, it is possible to print more than one color at a time for short runs. Silk-screen machines print only one color at a time.
Offset	100–many thousands	High-quality reproduction. Uses paper or aluminum masters, oil-based ink, and water-based repellent solution. Prints on various sizes, weights, grades of paper. Colored images possible — one color at a time — through control of color of ink.
Relief	300–100,000	Embossed master required. Copies resemble typing or printing. Colored images controlled by color of ribbon used or color of ink used. Any color copy paper may be used. Very high quality of reproduction.

Electric collating machines are often used in duplicating departments of offices where there is a great deal of duplicating and collating. The pages of a duplicated job are stacked in separate compartments of the collator. A rubber-tipped metal rod rests on each stack and pushes a page out of each compartment as the foot control is depressed. The pages are gathered in sets and crisscrossed for stapling or binding after each depression of the foot control. Available also are automatic collators that mechanically gather the pages together and bind them into sets.

Study Questions

1. On what principle is offset duplication based?

2. Identify the following offset machine parts and tell the purpose of each:

a. water roller   **d.** blanket cylinder
b. ink roller   **e.** impression roller
c. master cylinder

3. Describe the typewriter ribbon(s) which may be used to produce offset masters.

4. What causes embossment on typewritten offset masters? How does an embossed character reproduce?

5. Describe the type of eraser which should be used on offset masters.

6. Besides the typewriter, what other writing instruments may be used to image offset masters?

7. What is the main advantage of the photo-negative method of preparing offset masters?

8. How can a color image be reproduced on the offset machine?

9. What distinguishes a relief-process master from masters used for other processes of duplication?

10. Describe the two methods of inking which may be used in duplicating on relief-process machines.

11. Electronic facsimile copying may be used to prepare master copies for what duplicating processes?

12. Describe the Vari-Typer and tell how it differs from an ordinary typewriter.

13. Explain the use of the automatic typewriter.

What Do You Think?

1. Most operators of the special types of duplicating and copying machines learn the method of operation on the job. What then are the advantages, if any, of becoming familiar with these machines while in school?

2. Under what circumstances would you use each of the following methods of preparing several copies of material in preference to the other methods?

a. Typewriter   **c.** Fluid duplicator
b. Stencil   **d.** Offset duplicator
 duplicator   **e.** Copier

Your Personal Qualities

Howard Lansing, the assistant office manager, is also secretary of a local service organization. Almost every week he brings in a job to be done on one of the duplicating machines. With equal frequency he also brings in several papers to be reproduced on one or more of the copying devices. He never offers to pay for any of this service, not even for any of the supplies.

Some companies permit this practice as a goodwill gesture to the local service clubs when one of their own men is an officer. Others charge for the service and supplies at cost. Still others have a rigid rule against such practices.

Question: Assume that you are in charge of the duplicating service for the firm. If you were asked to do this work, what steps would you take?

How's Your English?

Review Appendix B on punctuation and correct the following:

1. Are you going home soon

2. Will you telephone to Mr. H C Hotton

3. Tell him to send our order C O D

4. The voice with a smile wins customer confidence

5. Please call at 2:45 p m

Office Work

1. Visit one of the local offices or an office in a nearby city and make a study of their business paper reproduction methods. Before you go, prepare a checklist or questionnaire based on this unit. Write a report and be prepared to make an oral presentation to the class.

Office Work Assignments

35: Copy for an Offset Master

Type a guide copy for a master for the following report to stockholders of the Wakefield Gypsum Company. Use your best judgment in planning the layout of the guide copy. Correct all errors and make the layout as attractive as possible.

To the stockholders—
Profits for the first nine months and the third quarter of this year, compared with corresponding periods of last year, were as follows —

	this year		*last year*	
	Amount	Per share	Amount	Per share (1)
9 months				
Consolidated Companies;				
Profit before income taxes...	$13,894,71	$4.86	$12,474,298	$4.36
Less United States and Foreign Taxes on Income...	7,030,558	2.46	6,405,100	2.24
Profit after income taxes	6,863,813 (2)	$2.40	6,069,198	$ 2.12
Dividends from *Subsidiaries* NOT CONSOLIDATED......	$84,725 (3)	.03	188,140	.07
3rd Quarter				
Consolidated Companies;				
Profit before Income Taxes....	4,808,157	$1.68	$4,407,167	$1.54
Less United states and foreign Taxes on Income.........	2,469,15	.86	2,253,296	.79
PROFIT AFTER INCOME TAXES...................	$2,338,982	$.82	$2,153,871	$.75
Dividends from SUBSIDIARIES NOT CONSOLIDATED.....	22,887,00	.01	71,199.00	.03
NET Income...............	$2,361,869	$.83	$2,225,070	.78

1. Based on 2860005 Shares now outstanding

2. Includes profit on sales of Canadian factory property, $183,118.00 or $.06 per share NET AFTER TAXES.

3. Operating profits of unconsolidated subsidiaries (before exchange devaluation of approximately $84,000.00) exceeded dividends received by $64,418 or $.02 per share in the first nine months of this year, after deducting estimated u.s. taxes applicable.

THE FIGURES ARE SUBJECT TO AUDIT AT THE END OF THE YEAR

UNIT 11 | The Mailable Letter

PART 1:

Placement

Letters are costly to produce. To justify the costs, a company wishes its letters to be attractive and impressive, for they provide an important medium of communication. Everyone in the company who in some way aids in the preparation of letters — from the dictator to the typist — must be fully appreciative of the value of doing each part of the task in a businesslike manner and using standards that result in quality work.

The First Impression. The recipient of a letter sees the total letter on the sheet of letterhead and forms an impression before he begins to read the message. A well-placed letter with clean, even typescript will make a very favorable first impression. Such a letter will encourage the recipient to read the letter with the care and attention that your employer would like his letter to receive. A poorly typewritten, carelessly placed letter may fail to get the consideration it deserves. It is your responsibility to assess each letter you typewrite in a critical fashion and with the question in mind: "How will this letter look to the recipient?"

The factors of a letter which provide a good first impression are as follows:

1) Margins, indentions, and spacing that are artistically pleasing
2) Parts of the letter that are correctly placed according to the style selected
3) Copy on which there are no obvious erasures and no strikeovers
4) A letter that is clean — has no smudges or fingermarks
5) Typescript that is even and clear

Margins and Spacing. Placement of a letter on a sheet of letterhead paper is a skill that is developed with experience. You will be able with practice to place attractively each letter you typewrite and not need to retype letters because the placement is off balance.

Ordinarily, the width of a letter should be no less than four inches nor more than six inches. The side margins should also have a desirable relation to the bottom margin and the space between the letterhead and the body of the letter. Usually the most appealing arrangement is when the side margins are even and the bottom margin is slightly wider than the side margins. In some business offices, however, a standard line length is used for all business letters, and the spacing between the date line and the inside address is varied according to the length of the letter.

A letter-placement table like the one below will guide you as you develop experience in estimating the proper spacing for a particular letter. This placement table is for letters typed on 8 1/2-inch by 11-inch paper and is simple to follow. It assumes that the date line is placed about fourteen spaces from the top of the page or approximately two spaces below the printed heading. The number of spaces between the date line and the address varies from three to nine, depending upon the length of the letter. Note that there are different specifications for elite and pica types. If your typewriter has pica type, you have ten horizontal spaces per inch; if elite type, twelve horizontal spaces per inch.

LETTER-PLACEMENT TABLE

Letter Length	Actual Words in Body of Letter*	Length of Line** Pica Spaces	Elite Spaces	Blank Lines Between Date Line and Address
Short	Under 100	50	50	7, 8, or 9
Medium	101–200	60	60	5, 6, or 7
Long	201–300	60	70	3, 4, or 5
Two-page	Over 300	60	70	At least 3

*ACTUAL WORDS IN BODY OF LETTER represents the complete words — not the average 5-stroke words used to measure typing speed.

**Some business offices use standard margins (a set line length) for all business letters. This may necessitate greater variations in the space left between date and address.

Assume that you have a letter of approximately 130 words. Now the table indicates that a 60-space line should be used. Seven spaces should be allowed between the date and the address because the number of words, 130, is not quite one third of the distance between 101 and 200 words (the range of the medium-length letter).

Letter Styles. The office worker knows which letter styles are used for correspondence in the company where she is employed. Often there is a correspondence manual that gives the instructions for typewriting the various types of letters that are used in the company.

There are a number of letter styles and many variations of the basic styles. The ones most commonly used in the business office today are (1) the modified block, (2) the block, and (3) the simplified. These are discussed in the following paragraphs along with (4) the official style.

TRUXELL UNLOADING SERVICE

ESTABLISHED 1938 · FAST FREIGHT SERVICE TO MANY POINTS · 410 MAIN STREET

BUTLER, PENNSYLVANIA 16001

April 14, 19 — —

Ferguson & Walters
634 Main Street
Harrisburg, Pennsylvania 17101

Attention Mr. James C. Ferguson

Gentlemen:

It required six months for us to gather and to
condense into a 28-page booklet all the information the shipper needs for the selection, packing, sealing, and shipping of corrugated fiber
shipping boxes.

This booklet shows how to select the proper
style of box construction, how to pack various
commodities to conform to transportation regulations, how to seal every sort of corrugated box,
and how to specify just what you require when
you are ordering boxes or packing supplies.

We shall be glad to mail you a copy of this useful little booklet with our compliments and to
supply, without cost or obligation, any further
information that you may wish to have. Just
check and mail the enclosed card at once, while
you have it in hand.

Yours very truly,

William A. Johnson

William A. Johnson
Sales Manager

ve

Enclosure

Business letter

This letter is typed in modified block form with mixed punctuation. It is the form most widely
used in business offices.

(1) Modified Block Style. This commonly used style is attractive and relatively easy to set up. While there are a number of variations, in all instances the address is blocked at the left margin. The complimentary close and signature lines are usually blocked beginning slightly to the left of the center of the page. The date may be typed at the same position as the closing lines or at some point in harmony with the heading. In some instances the paragraphs are blocked; in others the first line of each paragraph is indented. On page 391 you will see an example of the modified block style with paragraph indentions and with the date line typed in harmony with the heading.

(2) Block Style. In this style all lines of the letter begin at the left margin. Because the letter can be typed without using tabular stops, it is easy to type. It is considered a modern style and is used in many offices. You have an illustration of this letter style on page 391.

(3) Simplified Style. The simplified style as you will note in the illustration on page 391 eliminates the salutation and the complimentary close. All lines begin at the left-hand margin. This style was introduced and promoted by the Administrative Management Society.

(4) Official Letter Style. The official style is considered a formal, somewhat dignified style. It differs from other business letter styles only in the position of the address. The address is placed at the end of the letter, after the signature, and is typed flush with the left margin, two to five line spaces below the signature, depending upon the length of the letter. The reference initials are placed two spaces below the final line of the address.

The official letter style, shown on page 391, is similar to the modified block style except for the placement of the address. When you use this style, you may indent paragraphs or begin each paragraph flush with the left margin.

Letter Punctuation. There are several possible patterns of punctuation for the special lines of a letter. Special lines include the date, the lines of the address, the salutation, the complimentary close, and the typed name of the company and dictator. The three styles of punctuation for these special parts of a letter are known as open, close, and mixed. The most commonly used styles are open and mixed.

The open style leaves out punctuation marks at the ends of the special lines — the date, each line of the address, and the complimentary close. In the mixed style of punctuation, a colon is typed after the salutation and a comma after the complimentary close. In the close style, there is a period after the date, commas at the end of each line of the address except the last line which ends with a period, a colon after the salutation,

PITTSBURGH, PENNSYLVANIA 15218

CONSOLIDATED STEEL COMPANY

September 29, 19—

Mr. David W. Griffin, Manager
Admiral Steel Products Company
179 Moore Street
Brooklyn, New York 11206

Dear Mr. Griffin:

Thank you for your order for 12 steel racks
of commercial heavy weight, size 12" x 36" x 75".
We are pleased to have this order from you.

A large shipment of these racks is on its way
from our factory. It should reach us within a few
days. We are, therefore, holding your order until
our shipment arrives. Unless we hear from you to
the contrary, we shall assume that this action is
satisfactory. We shall ship the racks as soon as
they arrive.

The enclosed booklet on steel shelving may be
of interest to you. Let us know if we can serve
you further.

Sincerely yours,

James C. Davis
James C. Davis, Manager
Order Department

EE

Enclosure

Modified block style, mixed punctuation, indented paragraphs

STANDARD METALS PRODUCTS, INC.

2901 Brunswick Place • Trenton, New Jersey 08608 • 609-911-4800

September 5, 19—

Stanley Powers Company
8311 Whitehall Avenue
St. Louis, Missouri 63144

Gentlemen

This letter will confirm our telephone conversation
of yesterday afternoon. We shall appreciate your
sending us information on surplus raw materials for
electronics that you have available for sale.

We are particularly interested right now in cold
rolled steel and pretinned nickel silver. We are
interested, also, in coils of extra-tough hard
copper.

Keep us in mind when additional lots of materials
for electronics become available. We are suppliers
for South American outlets and are in constant need
of all types of electronic materials.

Yours very truly

Foster Palmer
Foster Palmer, Manager
Purchasing Department

Jm

Block style, open punctuation

PEMBERTON PRODUCTS, INC.

371 Ashdale Avenue   Minneapolis, Minnesota 55426

May 17, 19—

Mr. William S. Scott, Manager
Four Seasons Cruises, Incorporated
178 Fifth Avenue
New York, New York 10010

AMS SIMPLIFIED LETTER

This letter is written in the style recommended by
the Administrative Management Society. The formal
salutation and complimentary close are omitted.
These are not the only changes that have been made,
however. Other improvements are given below:

1. The extreme left block format is used.

2. A subject heading is used and should be typed
   in capitals a triple space below the address.

3. Paragraphs are blocked (no indentions).

4. The writer's name and title are typed in capitals at the left margin at least three blank
   lines below the body of the letter.

5. The initials of the typist are typed at the
   left a double space below the writer's name.

Please show this letter to the correspondents in
your company. You will find that its use reduces
your letter-writing costs.

William C. Kane
WILLIAM C. KANE - PRESIDENT

MRC

Simplified style

Office of William R. Biel ATTORNEY AT LAW

601 TIMES BUILDING • BALTIMORE, MARYLAND 21202

WOodward 7-9178

October 23, 19—

Dear Mary Jane:

I am glad to accept your invitation to meet with
the Thomas Jefferson High School Business Club.
Thank you very much for giving me a choice of
three dates. I would prefer to be with you on
March 20 at 2:30 p.m.

I understand from what you told me over the telephone that you would like me to speak on office
procedures and practices. I shall be very happy
to do so. Within the next week or ten days I shall
send you the exact title of my remarks so that you
will be able to include that item of information in
your program.

May I suggest that I talk for approximately twenty
minutes so that about half of the time will be available for the question and answer period that you
would like to have.

It will be good to return to the school where I
received my own training. I am looking forward
with pleasure to your meeting of March 20.

Very truly yours,

William R. Biel
William R. Biel

Miss Mary Jane Harris
Secretary, Business Club
Thomas Jefferson High School
Baltimore, Maryland 21212

WRB/ec

Official style

Four business letter forms

and a comma after the complimentary close. On page 391, you will see examples of open and mixed styles of punctuation for letters.

Simplifying the Typewriting of Letters. In recent years many office managers have attempted to reduce the costs of letters. Among the time-saving procedures that have been developed, you will find the following in use in many offices:

1) The typewriting of letters in block, modified block, or simplified style. Block-style and simplified style letters can be typed faster than all other letters because every line is started at the left margin and the tabular mechanism is not used. The modified block letter takes slightly more time, but some employers prefer this style.

2) The use of open or mixed punctuation. Eliminating the need to type marks of punctuation is clearly a timesaving feature of open punctuation and, to a lesser degree, of mixed punctuation.

3) The use of a standard line length for all letters. When the length of letters varies considerably, a great deal of time can be saved by establishing a standard line length and varying the distance between the date and the address and between the complimentary close and the reference initials. Many offices use a six-inch line for all letters, and the skillful office worker can make each letter attractive with this standardization.

4) The omission of names that appear in the letterhead. For example, there is no need to typewrite the name of the company below the complimentary close if it appears at the top of the letterhead. Also, the typewritten name and title of the dictator need not appear if they are in the letterhead.

 Study Questions

1. If you were to determine the costs of letters in a particular office, what factors must you include?

2. What will the recipient of a letter note initially as a basis for forming an impression?

3. What is the most appealing arrangement for side and bottom margins?

4. What is the difference between pica and elite type?

5. How would you determine the placement of a letter of approximately 190 words?

6. How does the modified block style differ from the block style?

7. What are the special features of the simplified style of letter?

8. Where is the inside address typed in the official style of letter?

9. How does mixed punctuation differ from open punctuation?

10. Why is the use of a standard line length considered a timesaving technique?

What Do You Think?

1. In what ways can an efficient office worker assist in keeping the costs of letters at a minimum?

2. Why do you think the office worker should strive to have each letter correctly placed the first time it is typed?

3. Why do you think close punctuation is less popular for business letters than mixed punctuation?

4. Why would the block style be considered a modern style?

5. Which style is considered more formal — the official letter style or the modified block style?

Your Personal Qualities

Sally Quinn is a typist in a clerical pool. She spends most of the day typewriting letters. Although there is a supervisor in the pool, there is very little supervision of the workers. Sally finds that she must retype practically every letter because, when she finishes one, she finds that it is not placed properly on the page. She knows that she should not have to do this, and she feels very uncomfortable about her job competency. She realizes that she could do twice as much as she presently does. However, no one else seems to be paying any attention to her, and she has not been reprimanded for her low production.

Question: If you were Sally, what would you do at this point?

How's Your English?

Refer to Appendix D on abbreviations, and select the correct words in the following sentences:

1. As a general rule, the names of states and territories (should — should not) be abbreviated.

2. The approved abbreviation for Pennsylvania is (Pa. — Pn.).

3. South Carolina should be abbreviated as (S.C. — So. Car.).

4. The accepted abbreviation for New Mexico is (N.Mx. — N. Mex.).

5. (V.I. — V. Is.) is the approved abbreviation for the Virgin Islands.

Office Work

1. Assume that you are a typist who has been given a number of handwritten letters to typewrite. The letters were all written by the same executive who has a rather large writing style. You check the number of words he has written to a line in four or five lines, taken at random, and find that there are approximately 6 words to each line. The lengths of the letters are indicated below. You are using a typewriter with elite type. For each letter, determine the line length you would use and the number of spaces you would allow between the date and the address.

a. Letter No. 1 is a full page, or 30 lines in length.

b. Letter No. 2 is approximately a page and a half, or 45 lines in length.

c. Letter No. 3 is approximately a half page, or 15 lines in length.

2. Make a collection of five to ten business letters. For each letter, describe briefly what might have been done to make the letter more attractive.

3. For the letters collected in 2 above, make a record of the style of letter and the style of punctuation used in each. Tally the number of letters in your collection for each of the forms and punctuation styles. Be prepared to report these figures during a class meeting. The totals for the entire class will give you an idea of what modern business letters look like.

 Office Work Assignments

36: Letter in Modified Block Form

Compose a brief letter in which you describe the modified block form. Type the letter, addressing it to your teacher, in modified block form. Use open punctuation.

37: Letter in Block Form

Compose a brief letter in which you describe the block form. Type the letter, addressing it to your teacher, in block form. Use the mixed style of punctuation.

38: Letter in Simplified Form

Compose a brief letter in which you describe the simplified form. Type the letter, addressing it to your teacher, in simplified form. Use the open style of punctuation.

UNIT 11 | The Mailable Letter

PART 2:

Styling

Proper styling of each letter you typewrite requires careful attention to many details. How well you take care of these details will determine the kind of impression your letters will make when they are read by the recipients. In this part, there will be described the more commonly accepted forms for the details of a business letter. You must remember that in every instance there may be some exceptions which you may find used in a particular business office.

Date Line. The date of a piece of correspondence is very important; therefore, you must date every letter you typewrite. The date line contains the name of the month written in full, the day, and the year. This line is usually typed in relation to the heading on the letterhead. It may be typed so that the end of the line is either flush with the heading or centered in relation to the heading. Sometimes the date line is typed flush with the right margin of the letter. In block form, of course, the date line is typed flush with the left margin. A comma is placed after the day. A period is used after the year only when the close style of punctuation is being used.

The most common business practice is to use figures for the day and the year, although you may find some exception to this, especially in more formal letters. Abbreviated forms of the date, such as "11/13/6-" or "11-13-6-," should be avoided in letters.

Address. It has long been the custom to type the address of the recipient immediately above the salutation. The address provides a complete reference for filing the carbon copy at the home company; and it also gives complete information to the recipient, for frequently the envelope is discarded when the letter is opened. If there were no address, a salutation such as "Dear Sir" would not be any clue to a company as to whom the letter should be directed, for example.

The address is typed flush with the left margin and from three to nine spaces below the date line. As you learned in the previous part, the variability between the date line and the address allows the typist to arrange the letter attractively on the page. In official, personal, and formal government correspondence, the address is usually placed below the dictator's signature, flush with the left margin.

The address in the letter should correspond exactly with the address that will be typed on the envelope. No abbreviations should be used, except in those cases where an abbreviation will make a more balanced line. The address should contain the name, title (when appropriate), and the complete address of the person or the organization to whom the letter is to be sent.

Satisfactory forms for the address are:

```
Mr. William F. Wells, Vice President
The American Copying Company
3546 Broad Street, N. W.
Philadelphia, Pennsylvania  19140

Mr. James A. Satterfield
President, Consultants Limited
465 Avenue of the Americas
New York, New York  10011
```

You will note that in the first illustration the title is placed after the person's name and is separated from the name by a comma, while in the second instance the title is typed on the second line, followed by a comma and the name of the organization. Both forms are correct; the one the typist selects is determined on the basis of which would be more attractive for the length of words involved.

Attention Line. There are times when a letter is addressed to a company, but one person in the company should see the letter. In such an instance, an attention line is typed a double space below the address. The salutation in those cases where there is an attention line agrees with the name in the address.

Preferred placements of the attention line in relation to the other parts of the letter are illustrated below:

```
Almond Construction Company
321 Forbes Boulevard
Pittsburgh, Pennsylvania  15222

Attention Mr. Whitney T. Drews

Gentlemen:
```

Attention Line Blocked at the Left Margin

This arrangement may be used with any letter form.

Almond Construction Company
321 Forbes Boulevard
Pittsburgh, Pennsylvania   15222
                    Attention Mr. Whitney T. Drews
Gentlemen:

Attention Line Centered on the Page

This arrangement may be used with the modified block form.

Salutation. The salutation is a greeting to the recipient. It is typed a double space below the address if there is no attention line. The body of the letter begins a double space below the salutation. A salutation may be as informal as *Dear Joe* or as formal as *Sir.*

The salutations given below are arranged from the least formal to the most formal. Please note the capitalization used in each.

For Men	*For Women*
Dear John:	Dear Jane:
My dear John:	My dear Jane:
Dear Mr. Simon:	Dear Mrs. (Miss) Whitman:
My dear Mr. Simon:	My dear Mrs. (Miss) Whitman:
Dear Sir:	Dear Madam:
My dear Sir:	My dear Madam:
Sir:	Madam:

For a Corporation	*For a Firm of Women*
Gentlemen:	Ladies:
	Mesdames:

For a Firm of Men	*For a Firm of Men and Women*
Gentlemen:	Gentlemen:
	Ladies and Gentlemen:
	My dear Mrs. Smith and Mr. Jones:

Subject Line. In some instances, the writer of a letter will want to use a subject line as a way of headlining the key concern of the letter. When a subject line is used, it will be typed a double space below the salutation, and a double space will follow it. The phrase is usually preceded by the word *Subject.* Sometimes, *Re* or *In re* will precede the phrase. It may be typed flush with the left margin or centered on the page.

Illustrations of subject lines are:

Gentlemen:

    Subject: Insurance Requirements for Small Companies

    There are many considerations that must be care-
fully understood by a company . . . .

Centered Subject Line

```
Gentlemen:

Re: Insurance Requirements for Small Companies

There are many considerations that must be carefully
understood by a company . . . .
```
Subject Line Typed Flush with Left Margin

Body of the Letter. A double space follows the salutation (or the subject line if there is one) before the typist begins the body of the letter. You want to be sure to paragraph the body of the letter so that it will be easier to read. Use double spacing between paragraphs to give the letter a more attractive appearance.

You will want to keep the right margin relatively even and approximately as wide as the left margin. You can do this by setting the right margin stop from five to eight spaces beyond the point where you want the line to end so that the bell will ring close to the space where the line should end. Yet, you will have space to complete a short word or add a hyphen for a word that must be hyphenated before the carriage stops moving.

Second Page. On letters of more than one page, one of the following forms may be used at the top of the second and succeeding pages for identification purposes:

```
Mr. Arthur C. Reilly        2            June 16, 19—
Mr. Arthur C. Reilly
Page 2
June 16, 19—
```

The space between the top of the second sheet and the first line of the identification should be about an inch (6 line spaces). Three line spaces should be left between the second-page heading and the body of the letter. Carry over at least two lines of a paragraph to the second page, and type at least two lines on the first page.

Usually the stationery you will use for the second page will be plain bond paper of the same quality as the letterhead.

Complimentary Close. The complimentary close, which is written on the second line below the body of the letter, is the "good-bye" of the letter. In the block style, it begins at the left margin. In the modified block style, it begins slightly to the left of the center. It should be started far enough to the left so that the longest of the closing lines of the letter will not extend noticeably beyond the right margin. Only the first word of the complimentary close is capitalized.

Acceptable Complimentary Closings

Regular Business Letters —

Yours truly,
Yours very truly,
Very truly yours,

Yours sincerely,
Sincerely yours,
Very sincerely yours,
Yours very sincerely,

Formal Letters —

Respectfully yours,
Very respectfully yours,

Yours respectfully,

Friendly Letters —

Cordially yours,
Yours cordially,
Sincerely yours,

Yours sincerely,
Faithfully yours,

Signature. Your employer signs his name between the complimentary close and his typed signature. The typed signature eliminates the difficulties created by a poorly written signature. The firm name is not typed as part of the signature except in formal documents, and the official position of the dictator need not be typed as part of the signature if it is printed on the letterhead.

If the company name is used, it is typed in capital letters on the second line below the complimentary close. The name of the dictator is typed four spaces below the company name. If the company name is not used, the dictator's name is typed four spaces below the complimentary close. When both the name of the dictator and his title are used, they are typed on the same line, or the title is typed on the line below the typed name.

The following illustrations show different types of complimentary closings and typewritten signature styles:

Yours truly,

*Signature with
the Dictator's
Name and Title,
Modified Block
Style*

Frederick W. Pendleton
Purchasing Agent

Very truly yours,

*Signature with
Company Name and
Dictator's Name and
Title, Modified
Block Style*

UNION TRUCKING AND STORAGE CO.

M. O. Thomas, Vice President

When you type your employer's signature, you should not use his title before the name, such as *Dr.* or *Mr.* An unmarried woman, however, should sign her full name and may place *Miss* in parentheses before it. The practice of omitting *Miss* seems to be growing. A married woman should sign her full name and should place either her married name below in parentheses or *Mrs.* in parentheses before her signature. It is equally correct to type *Miss* or *Mrs.* in the signature line without the parentheses.

The following illustrations indicate the accepted forms for signatures of women:

Yours sincerely,

(Miss) Eva M. Kelly

Signature of an Unmarried Woman

Very truly yours,   Very truly yours,

Elaine E. Brooks
(Mrs. W. R. Brooks) *(Mrs.) Alice Canter*

Signature of a Married Woman   **Signature of a Married Woman or Widow**

If you are requested to sign your employer's name to a letter, be sure to initial the signature as you see below:

Very truly yours,   Sincerely yours,

Robert E. Maxwell   *Robert E. Maxwell*
M.H.

Robert E. Maxwell

by M.H.

You must be sure that each letter is signed before you fold it and insert it into an envelope for mailing.

Reference Line. In order to indicate who dictated a letter and who typed it, the dictator's initials and the typist's initials are usually typed two single spaces below the last line of the signature and flush with the left margin. If the employer's name is not included in the typed signature, it is sometimes given in full in place of his initials. On the other hand, when the employer's name is typed as part of the signature, his initials are sometimes omitted from the reference line. In some instances, the typist of the letter may be indicated by a number rather than by initials.

If the letter does not carry an official title or the typewritten name of the employer, the reference initials are typed on the fourth line below the company signature. If the letter does not have a company signature, the typed name of the employer, or an official title, six to eight spaces are left between the complimentary close and the reference initials. Typical reference initials are:

```
HIL:RT       HIL/RT       MD:12       TEBlack--GHM       ghm
```

Enclosure Notations. Any enclosures you send with a letter should be indicated at the end of the letter. This is an efficient procedure to insure including the enclosures and a service to the addressee who can quickly check to see if material is included in the envelope. The enclosure notation should be typed at the left margin two spaces below the reference initials. One enclosure is indicated by the word *Enclosure*. More than one enclosure is indicated by the correct figure typed after the word *Enclosures*. If it is desired, more than one enclosure may also be indicated by the word *Enclosures* typed on one line, followed by a list of the enclosures, each enclosure being listed on a separate line and indented five spaces from the left margin. Typical enclosure notations are:

```
Enclosure          Enclosures 2          Enclosures
                                            Price List
                                            Circular
                                            Sample X-14
```

Separate-Cover Notations. When the letter refers to items sent under separate cover — that is, in an envelope or package that is not included with the letter — you should type the proper notation at the left margin two lines below the last enclosure line, or two lines below the reference line if there are no enclosures. One item sent under separate cover is indicated by the words *Separate Cover*. Two or more separate-cover items are usually indicated by the correct figure typed after the words *Separate Cover*. In some offices the means of transportation used for sending the separate-cover material is indicated. If it is desired, the nature of the item or items may be indicated in the same manner as enclosure items. The following are typical separate-cover notations:

```
          Separate Cover--Express

          Separate Cover 2

          Separate Cover--Mail
              Price List C12
```

UNIVERSITY OF CALIFORNIA, LOS ANGELES

BERKELEY · DAVIS · IRVINE · LOS ANGELES · RIVERSIDE · SAN DIEGO · SAN FRANCISCO   SANTA BARBARA · SANTA CRUZ

DEPARTMENT OF EDUCATION
LOS ANGELES, CALIFORNIA 90024

1 October 17, 19--

2 Central High School Commercial Club
Central High School
Denver, Colorado 80215

3 Attention Mr. Richard Graham, Secretary

4 Gentlemen

5 Subject: The Business Letter

I am glad to discuss the questions that you raised
in your letter of October 13 about the placement
of certain parts of the business letter.

6 The attention line is usually written two spaces
below the inside address and two spaces above the
salutation. It may begin at the paragraph point,
be centered on the page, or be blocked at the left
margin. The attention line may, however, be written on the same line with the salutation and is
then centered on the page.

The salutation is typed flush with the left margin,
two spaces below the inside address. If the attention line is used, the salutation is typed two
spaces below the attention line.

The subject line may be blocked at the left margin,
begun at the paragraph point, or centered. It is
typed on the second line below the salutation. The
phrase may be preceded by the word "Subject."

7 Very truly yours

8 *[signature]*

9 S. J. Wanous
Professor of Education

10 ad

11 A postscript is typed on the second line below the
additional data. It may be preceded by the abbreviation "P.S.," or it may be written in the same
form as any paragraph in the letter.

Business letter

(1) Date; (2) Address; (3) Attention line; (4) Salutation; (5) Subject line; (6) Body; (7) Complimentary close; (8) Pen-written signature; (9) Typed signature and title; (10) Reference initials; (11) Postscript.

Mailing Notations. When a special postal service such as special delivery or registered mail is to be used, a mailing notation to that effect is typed even with the left margin (a) two lines below the last line of typing or (b) between the date line and the first line of the address. The notations are usually typed in all capitals. Some firms type mailing notations only on carbon copies. Some firms make no notation at all.

Carbon Copy Notations. When you prepare a carbon copy for the information of a person other than the addressee of the letter, the notation *cc*, followed by the name of that person, may be typed at the left margin two spaces below the last line of typing. If it is not desirable for the addressee to know that a carbon copy has been sent to someone else, the carbon copy notation may be placed on the copy only, preferably at the top.

Postscript. Once in a while a postscript is added to a letter. A postscript is a short message that is typed on the second line below all other notations. It may be preceded by the abbreviation *P.S.*, but the modern trend is to write it in the same form as any paragraph in the letter.

The postscript is sometimes used to take care of some detail inadvertently omitted from the letter. It is frequently used, however, to emphasize a particular point by setting it apart from the rest of the letter.

Addressing the Envelope. If the letter is to be handled efficiently by the postal clerks, it is very important that the address on the envelope be accurate and easily read. Writing all parts of the address without abbreviations will make for ease in reading.

When the name of the street is a number from one to ten, inclusive, the street name is spelled out; figures are used for street names that are numbers above ten. When a street name is written in figures, the house number is separated from the street number by a hyphen with a space on either side. If, however, the street number is preceded by *East*, *West*, *North*, or *South*, the hyphen is not necessary. For example:

```
367 Second Avenue      589 South 117 Street
157 - 179 Street       381 Tenth Street
36 East 42 Street
```

The name of the city is separated from the name of the state by a comma. The ZIP Code number should be typed on the same line with the city and state and at least two spaces after the state with no mark of punctuation between the state and ZIP Code number. The ZIP Code numbers for cities and towns in the United States are listed in the *Directory of Post Offices*, P.O.D. Publication No. 26, available from the Superintendent of Documents, Government Printing Office, Washington, D.C. 20402.

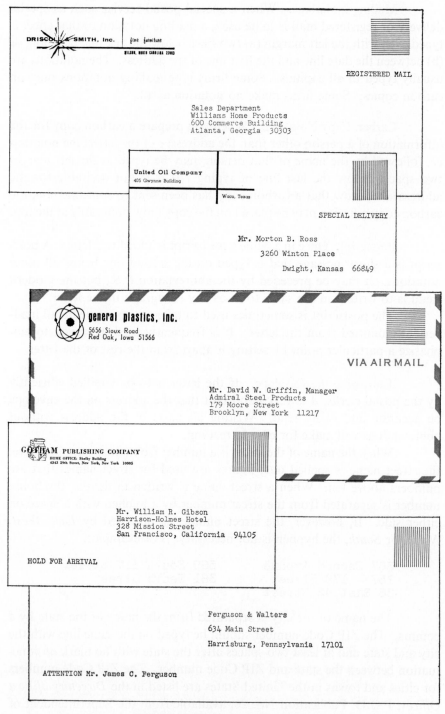

DRISCOLL & SMITH, Inc. | fine furniture
WILSON, NORTH CAROLINA 27803

REGISTERED MAIL

Sales Department
Williams Home Products
600 Commerce Building
Atlanta, Georgia 30303

United Oil Company
405 Gwynne Building

Waco, Texas

SPECIAL DELIVERY

Mr. Morton B. Ross

3260 Winton Place

Dwight, Kansas 66849

general plastics, inc.
5656 Sioux Road
Red Oak, Iowa 51566

VIA AIR MAIL

Mr. David W. Griffin, Manager
Admiral Steel Products
179 Moore Street
Brooklyn, New York 11217

GOTHAM PUBLISHING COMPANY
HOME OFFICE: Shelby Building
4343 29th Street, New York, New York 10005

Mr. William R. Gibson
Harrison-Holmes Hotel
328 Mission Street
San Francisco, California 94105

HOLD FOR ARRIVAL

Ferguson & Walters

634 Main Street

Harrisburg, Pennsylvania 17101

ATTENTION Mr. James C. Ferguson

Addressed envelopes for business letters

The address is typed with the same style of punctuation as that used in the letter. Three-line addresses may be double spaced, while addresses of more than three lines are generally single spaced. An attention line should be typed in the lower left corner or immediately below the name of the company in the address itself. Special notations such as *Hold for Arrival* and *Please Forward* are typed in the lower left corner of the envelope. Mailing notations such as *Special Delivery* and *Registered Mail* are typed in capital letters below the stamp. *Airmail* envelopes should be used for airmail letters, or if they are not available, the word *Airmail* is typed in capital letters below the stamp. Note illustrations of typed envelopes on page 404.

Study Questions

1. What are some of the details of a business letter that require special attention on the part of the typist?

2. Where are the possible places for typewriting the date line?

3. Why is the address of the recipient typed in a letter?

4. Where may the title of the recipient be typed in the address?

5. What are some examples of informal salutations? formal salutations?

6. What salutation is generally used for a corporation?

7. What is the purpose of a subject line?

8. Where does the subject line appear in a letter?

9. Where does the attention line appear in a letter?

10. Where does the body of a letter begin?

11. Where is the complimentary close typed?

12. What are reference initials? Where are they typed?

13. Why should there be a notation for enclosures?

14. When is double spacing used on an envelope?

15. How does a typist indicate that a letter is to be held for arrival of recipient?

What Do You Think?

1. Why are abbreviations avoided in letters and on envelopes?

2. Why should a woman use *Miss* or *Mrs.* in her signature, yet a man never precedes his signature with *Mr.*?

Your Personal Qualities

Irene has just been hired as a typist for a new company. On her first day she is asked to do some filing of correspondence in order to become acquainted with the style of letters she will be asked to type. She notices that there are many differences between the styles of these letters and what she was taught in school. For example, she notes abbreviations in the date line and in the address, the date line typed flush with the left margin, and the closing lines centered.

Questions: 1. What standard of letter styling should Irene follow?

2. How and when should Irene make suggestions for improvements in letter styling?

How's Your English?

After studying the list of abbreviations presented in Appendix D, indicate the terms for which the following abbreviations stand:

c/o	cf.
COD	No.
et seq.	hp.
WB	mfg.
treas.	reg.

Office Work

The following exercises may be completed on one sheet of paper in the following manner: top half of front page, Exercise 1; bottom half of front page, Exercise 2; top half of back page, Exercise 3; bottom of back page, Exercise 4.

1. Your employer has written in longhand to the McConnell Engineering Company, 296 Walnut Street, Denver, Colorado 80204. The letter is to be delivered to Mr. Thomas Hamilton of that firm. Write the date, address, attention line, and salutation. Block the attention line.

2. Write the appropriate salutation for a business letter to each of the following people:

a. Mr. J. Sommers

b. Miss Nancy Hall

c. Patricia Trent and Jane Taylor

d. John Myers and Mary Standley

3. Write an appropriate heading for the second page of a letter written to Mr. F. M. Randall on May 16, 19—.

4. C. W. Graham, president of the Graham Advertising Agency, has written in longhand a letter to be sent to an old client. Write an appropriate complimentary close, typewritten company name, dictator's name and official title, and reference initials. There will be two enclosures.

Office Work Assignments

NOTE: In all the following problems that require the typing of business letters, type the specified number of carbon copies; and type the address on an envelope of appropriate size if the necessary supplies are available.

39: Letter in Modified Block Form

Type the letter in the illustration on page 402 in modified block form with no paragraph indentions. Use the mixed style of punctuation.

40: Letter in Block Form

Type the letter in the illustration on page 402 in block form with open punctuation. Prepare one carbon copy.

41: Letter in Modified Block Form

Type the following letter in modified block form with mixed punctuation. Make one carbon copy. The sign ¶ means *paragraph*.

Hawley, Hayes & Miller 496 Dana Avenue Englewood, New Jersey 07631 October 10, 19-- Dr. Cyril J. Small 410 Grant Street White Plains, New York 10604
Dear Dr. Small Subject: Location for Dental Office Thank you for your inquiry about a possible location for a dental office in Englewood, New Jersey. We are glad to be able to tell you that we are soon going to start the construction of eight apartment houses that will provide for 124 families. These apartments will be located on Chestnut Street, just outside the main business district. Any one of the first-floor apartments in these buildings would be admirably suited for a dentist's or a physician's office. The rents are reasonable, and we feel the layouts are unusually well designed. (¶) We have already rented some of the apartments and expect that by the time construction is completed, practically all apartments will be rented. As many of these families will move to Englewood from other communities, they will doubtless want to make connections with a dentist. (¶) We are enclosing a floor plan of one of the apartments that we feel could be particularly well adapted to your purposes. We should be glad to discuss it with you whenever it is convenient. Will you come to our office and talk this matter over, or may we ask our Mr. Williams, who is in charge of renting this property, to call on you sometime soon? Very truly yours HAWLEY, HAYES & MILLER Norman C. Hayes, President

42: Two-Page Letter

Type the following letter in modified block form with open punctuation. Make one carbon copy.
Los Angeles and Suburban Bell Telephone Company 690–694 Broadway Los Angeles, California 90014 June 29, 19-- Mr. Earl F. Sawyer, Manager, Harold Dean Mfg. Company, 928 Harrison Building, 1258 Columbus Drive, Los Angeles, California 90012 Dear Mr. Sawyer Irritated customers . . . lost orders . . . tied-up lines . . . delays and misunderstandings . . . garbled messages . . . excessive phone bills . . . wasted sales effort. These are some of the costly results of the bad telephone practices so common today in business. (¶) But they don't have to be common in *your* business. You can make sure *all* your calls — incoming and outgoing — are handled courteously, efficiently, and economically by using our unique training program, BETTER BUSINESS BY TELEPHONE. (¶) And right now, as a new subscriber, you will get a free BONUS PORTFOLIO of past issues which cover both the right and the wrong way to handle many common telephone situations, for example —
— The 15 rules of telephone courtesy that *everyone* should follow.
— Why no office worker should *ever* use the blunt phrase "Who's calling?"

— How to build sales and goodwill when taking telephone orders.

— What to say — and what *not* to say — in handling complaint calls.

— Why so many executives now make and take their own 'phone calls.

— The six ways to save time — and money — on all telephone calls.

— Why *new employees* need telephone training — and how to give it.

— How to handle the caller who doesn't want to give his name.

— *Why* and *how* to use the telephone to collect past-due accounts.

— How to turn more of your telephone *inquiries* into actual *sales.*

(¶) BETTER BUSINESS BY TELEPHONE has already helped more than 16,000 companies, of every size and type, make more effective use of their telephones. Included are one-man-and-a-girl offices — and such companies as Du Pont, American Airlines, Ford, Sears Roebuck, General Electric, Arthur Murray Studios, Wall Street Journal, etc., etc. (¶) BETTER BUSINESS BY TELEPHONE will help you with every phase of your telephone operation, from handling routine calls to planning a complete telephone sales campaign. (¶) Regular twice-monthly bulletins bring you the latest in tested telephone techniques . . . case histories showing how other progressive companies are solving telephone problems and making the most of telephone opportunities . . . hints on time- and money-saving procedures . . . ideas that spark your own thinking on how you can make your company's telephone contacts a sales and public relations *asset* rather than a liability. (¶) Along with the bulletins for management, you get regular twice-monthly *Fone-Talks* for employees . . . all *Special Reports* and *Supplements* as issued . . . easy access to all past issues that may help you . . . and unlimited use of our *free mail consultation service* on your individual telephone problems. And your subscription starts with a "Telephone Improvement Kit" which shows you exactly how to make the best possible use of our material. (¶) As a BETTER BUSINESS BY TELEPHONE subscriber, you'll have everything you need to make your company's handling of the telephone as good as that of any company in the country . . . and to *keep* it that way. And you'll quickly see why we receive such comments as this from Harvard C. Wood, President, H. C. Wood, Inc., Lansdowne, Pennsylvania: (¶) "I have a warm feeling toward your organization because I feel you are rendering a splendid service to those businessmen who want to use the telephone effectively and efficiently." (¶) You'll find full information on rates on the enclosed order form. Just tell us how many copies of each bulletin you will need to cover your department heads and key employees. We'll do the rest. Sincerely yours, Arthur Downing, Manager, Customer Service.

UNIT 11 | The Mailable Letter

PART 3:

Composing Business Letters

Letter writing is a very important activity in every business office. Some of the letters that are sent are routine letters and may be taken care of by an office worker who is fully acquainted with the matter involved in the correspondence. There are also occasions when an executive may give the basic facts needed in a letter to an office worker and ask her to write the letter.

An office worker will not be asked to compose letters until the employer is confident that the responsibility can be handled with considerable ease and accuracy. Although the letters to be written may appear to be of a routine nature, it is important to remember that such letters may include details that are critical to the completion of a transaction. The office worker wants to be sure that the letters written reflect the best usage in modern letter writing and that they represent the company in a favorable fashion.

Preparing to Write a Letter. A business letter is frequently ineffective because the writer is not fully acquainted with all the necessary details. These should all be known before the letter is started. If the essential facts pertaining to the subject are not known to you, investigate. Have the essential facts written down, perhaps in the margin of the letter to be answered. Do not depend upon your memory — especially if the facts pertain to such matters as amounts, dates, names of persons, or other specific data. When the information has been gathered, consider the plan and content of the letter before writing.

If you have had little or no experience in writing business letters, you may find it wise to make a brief outline. As you become more experienced, you should not need a written outline, but you should always make mental notes of the steps you are to follow.

Basic Business Letters. As a clerical office worker, you may be asked to compose and type the following routine business letters:

Composing at the typewriter

Office workers frequently compose letters, announcements, and reports. Sometimes the employer supplies the basic facts needed to write the letter; at other times the letter is written without instructions.

(1) Letter of Acknowledgment. A letter of acknowledgment is written as a matter of courtesy when your employer is out of the office for an extended period. The acknowledgment of a letter should say that the letter has been received and that it will be called to your employer's attention when he returns.

(2) Letter Concerning Appointments. The appointment letters you compose should give the purpose, as well as the time, date, and place of the appointment.

(3) Letter Making Reservations. A request for reservations should include the name and business affiliation of the person for whom the reservation is being made, the accommodations desired, the time and place of arrival and departure, and the destination.

(4) Letter Regarding Meetings. When acknowledging a notice of a meeting, you should restate the time, place, and date of the meeting.

If your employer is unable to attend the meeting, you should give the reason.

(5) Letter of Transmittal. A brief letter of transmittal should always accompany a valuable enclosure such as a contract, deed, mortgage, or stock certificate.

(6) Follow-Up Letter. You should send a follow-up letter when an assignment is not completed within a reasonable time. The date of the first letter is given and its contents restated, or a copy of the original letter is enclosed.

(7) Thank-You Letter. Letters of thanks for help, gifts, compliments, or congratulations received are always appreciated. These letters should express sincere appreciation in simple English completely without affectation.

(8) Miscellaneous Routine Letters. Letters in this category deal with a variety of matters such as requests for references and letters offering congratulations.

Standard Business Letters. In addition to the routine letters you may be expected to write for your employer, it may be necessary for you to write letters of a more important nature. You will, therefore, want to become acquainted with the essential features and outstanding characteristics of these more important standard types of business letters.

Letter of Inquiry. A letter of inquiry seeks information. Since specific information is desired, the letter must be worded clearly. Questions must be asked in such a way that their meaning cannot be misunderstood. If it is necessary to get data on a comprehensive subject or problem, a series of numbered questions should be asked. Follow this plan when you are composing a detailed letter of inquiry:

1) Give the subject of your inquiry at the outset.

2) Give the reason for your inquiry and explain why the letter was addressed to the reader.

3) Add explanatory material that may be of help to the reader, such as specific details, definitions, dates, and the description of an item.

4) End the letter courteously. Avoid stock phrases, such as *Thanking you in advance* . . . or *Awaiting your reply, we remain* . . . Instead, use *Any assistance you may give us will be greatly appreciated*, or *We shall appreciate any assistance you give us.*

When the answer to a letter of inquiry will be a favor to you, enclose a stamped, self-addressed envelope of convenient size.

A routine letter of inquiry is easy to write. A brief paragraph on one's business letterhead and the signature may fill all the requisities of a good routine letter of inquiry. To illustrate:

Gentlemen:

I believe some time ago you published a booklet, <u>An Office Manager's Guide for the Selection of New Office Equipment</u>. This booklet should be helpful in selecting equipment for our new branch office in Fargo. If it is still available, will you please send me a copy.

Sincerely yours,

The answer to a letter of inquiry should be brief, adequate in covering all the questions asked, and courteous. An illustration follows:

Dear Mr. Williams:

The booklet you requested, <u>An Office Manager's Guide for the Selection of New Office Equipment</u>, has just been reprinted. A copy is being mailed to you with our compliments.

Your interest in this booklet is appreciated. We hope it will prove helpful to you in selecting office equipment for your new branch office in Fargo.

Yours very truly,

You should answer a letter of inquiry promptly. Promptness is a matter of courtesy and affords a real opportunity to build goodwill. A reply that leaves the business office the day the inquiry is received is certain to gain respect and has a better chance of satisfying the inquirer.

Letters Ordering Goods or Services. A letter written to purchase goods or services is an order letter. The order should be clear, specific, and complete. Misinterpretation means delay and inconvenience to both firms.

Unless there is some previous arrangement, every order for goods should show the following essential facts: quantity, price, catalog number (if there is one), destination of shipment, method of shipment, desired date of delivery (this determines the method of shipment, to some degree), and the method of payment.

Order blanks are often distributed to regular customers by the seller. It is common practice, however, for business firms to print their own order forms. The use of these forms reduces the chances of making mistakes or omitting required information in ordering goods and does away with the need for writing order letters.

Hillman-Robbins

DUnkirk 3-1475 • 400 PARK PLAZA • DALLAS, TEXAS 75204

September 16, 19--

Gates, Daley & Walker
124 Federal Street
Boston, Massachusetts 02110

Gentlemen:

Please ship the following items to our branch office
at 15 North Pearl Street, Albany, New York. You gave
us quotations on these items on September 10.

   3 four-drawer letter-size files, stock
     number V1070, Silvertone finish, list
     price $99.50 ea.

   2 secretarial desks, stock number 6045 PRH,
     typewriter platform at the right, 60" x 32"
     top, Silvertone finish, list price $210.50
     ea.

   2 secretarial chairs, stock number 8315-61,
     Silvertone grospoint frieze covering, list
     price $71.25 ea.

   1 work table, stock number 2020T, 70" x 36"
     top, Silvertone finish, list price $94.50

We need this office furniture immediately, and we
would appreciate your making shipment during the
week of September 21. Payment will be made within
ten days after the furniture is received at the
Albany branch office.

                    Yours very truly,

                    Thomas J. Clark

                    Thomas J. Clark
                    Purchasing Agent

emk

Letter placing an order

Part 3 Composing Business Letters   413

Remittance Letters. Many remittances, especially checks (frequently voucher checks), are self-explanatory and require no letter of remittance. This is especially true when the remittance is in payment of a regular invoice or usual monthly bills. When a remittance is for an exceptional or unusual payment, a remittance letter should be sent. The letter should indicate the purpose of the remittance, the amount, and the form in which it is sent: check, draft, or money order. It should also include any necessary explanation. A remittance letter should include an enclosure notation. The notation is typed two spaces below the reference initials.

An illustration of a remittance letter follows:

```
Gentlemen:

    A check for $255.93, in payment of Invoice
No. 3960, is enclosed.  You will note we have
deducted $43.38 from the original amount of
the invoice to cover the cost of goods we re-
turned to you.

                        Yours very truly,

                        S. E. Walker, Treasurer
ve
Enclosure
    Check for $255.93
```

All remittances, except checks, should be acknowledged. Canceled checks become their own receipts.

Order Acknowledgment Letters. An acknowledgment of an order, in general, expresses the thanks of the firm for an order, restates the order briefly, and tells the customer how and when the goods will be shipped. A letter of acknowledgment of an order for goods or services should be written and mailed on the day the order is received. Such a procedure shows the company's appreciation for the confidence the customer has in the business. Orders lacking complete information and orders that the company itself cannot fill or on which there may be a delay must, of course, be handled differently.

If an order is received with incomplete information, a letter of inquiry must be sent to ascertain the exact order. The inquiry must be tactfully worded so that the customer will give the needed additional information without feeling too much at fault. An assurance that more information will prevent delay and insure greater accuracy in filling the order will make the customer feel that the firm is exceedingly careful. At the same time, the customer will not consider himself at fault.

If the delivery of the order is to be delayed, the letter of acknowledgment must minimize the inconvenience and delay without specifically calling it a disappointment. The customer must be made to feel that the delay will be offset by the quality of the goods he will receive in a comparatively short time. He must also be made to feel that not only his order but also his willingness to cooperate in giving the firm an opportunity to overcome an unforeseen difficulty are appreciated. An expression of a desire to give him the best and promptest service possible makes the customer feel that the firm has a genuine interest in him.

Adjustment Letter. Because it is human to make a mistake now and then, it is necessary to adjust errors occasionally. Such adjustments are neither pleasant nor easy to handle. In all the difficulties that arise because of someone's blunder, however, little should be said about who is at fault. Most of the emphasis should be given to the handling of the problem with the least amount of annoyance to those affected. Unless a conciliatory spirit prevails, goodwill is bound to be lost.

There is a possibility that the firm, its customer, or perhaps a third agency (the transportation company) is at fault; or it may be that the firm and its customer are both at fault. When you are asked to write an adjustment letter, you should know what to do in each case. You should know, first of all, how far you are permitted to go in making the adjustment. The firm should be willing to shoulder its share of any loss and to see that the transportation company assumes its fair share.

You can best settle a complaint through a personal interview; but because of the time, distance, and expense, it will often be necessary for you to write an adjustment letter. The letter usually contains the following elements:

1) A cordial acknowledgment of the letter with a reference to the complaint
2) An explanation and an expression of regret
3) A suggestion for the adjustment of the complaint

You should present the facts in a forthright way, without anger and with no charge of incompetence or blame. Suggest the adjustment in a tone and manner that will reassure your customer. A grudging, negative tone will achieve far less than a positive, cheerful, and sincere tone expressed in a persuasive and tactful manner. *Your unsupported claim, Your unjustified complaint, You neglected to, We are at a loss as to what to do,* and *It never happened before* are tactless expressions that will soon lose a customer, whereas a tactful adjustment of the matter, in all probability, will recoup any loss of sales. Agreement with a customer does not necessarily mean that you are granting his every wish. Expressions of concern such as *Our desire to give you satisfactory service* and *Let us see if we cannot work this out* give a pleasing tone to an unpleasant subject and are usually conciliatory in their effects.

Davis Equipment Company

485 HALLECK STREET ■ MILWAUKEE, WISCONSIN 53207

September 10, 19--

Mr. Harry T. Williams
1201 Washington Boulevard
Janesville, Wisconsin 53545

Dear Mr. Williams:

Thank you for your letter of September 7, 196-, and for returning the Model 20J-NP desk set.

We are sending you a new desk set with our compliments. We hope that you enjoy using it in your new office.

To be sure that this does not happen again, we are checking with our dealer in Janesville to see that all defective sets are returned to us.

We regret any inconvenience that you may have been caused. Please let us know how you like the new set.

Cordially yours,

Lawrence A. Lewis

Lawrence A. Lewis

LAL:emk

Mention the customer's share of the burden tactfully and as impersonally as possible. Your explanations must be adequate so that the customer will know that you are being fair. Close the adjustment letter with a word to the effect that an incident of this type seldom occurs and that you hope all future transactions will be completely satisfactory. If it is your company's fault, you may close with: *We hope you will give us the opportunity to serve you more satisfactorily in the future.*

Credit Letters. Modern business is built upon the foundation of credit. The success of credit transactions depends upon *character, capital,* and *capacity* of the customer. These three — the customer's character (desire for honest dealing), his capital (net worth), and his capacity (ability to pay) — are the real determining factors in the customer's ability to obtain credit. Every business should check these factors before extending credit to a customer.

In answer to an application for credit, credit application forms are sometimes used. These forms are usually questionnaires, formal and appropriate for the type of information desired. A form is sent to the customer with a courteous letter asking for a prompt return of the form filled in with the desired information.

After the credit application form is returned by the customer, letters are sent to the references that he gives. The letters may be written to chambers of commerce, banks, credit rating houses, and other concerns that have had dealings with the customer. Worded in a direct, impersonal style, the letters are designed to obtain definite answers to questions bearing upon the customer's character, type of business, capital, ability to pay, and promptness in paying.

Fortunately, a letter refusing credit is not often written. It is hard to write to a prospective customer and tell him, in effect, that he cannot be trusted. The statement is not made in these words, of course. The customer is thanked for his order and told frankly why the business cannot extend credit to him. A possible solution (such as cash dealings) is offered, and the letter is ended with an expressed wish that credit can be extended later. The letter should leave as favorable an impression as is possible under the circumstances.

Collection Letters. The purpose of a collection letter is to collect an outstanding account by encouraging or urging the customer to pay the money owed by him for services or goods already delivered. Customers fail to pay their obligations on time for various reasons:

1) They disregard the due date of small amounts.
2) They overlook debts because of their poor system of keeping records.

3) They are habitually slow.
4) They are temporarily short of funds.
5) They are verging on insolvency or are actually insolvent.
6) They are deliberately fraudulent.

The type of collection letter you should write depends to a large extent upon the customer's reputation, his ability to pay, and his desire to pay. A collection letter is not unlike other letters, but it carries a serious message. The customer must be made to feel that it is to his advantage to pay.

Usually a statement, a formal notice, a series of form letters, and finally, a series of emphatic personal letters make up the collection sequence. The tone of each communication gradually grows more demanding until the account is settled. A collection letter should strive to obtain the payment but also to retain the customer's goodwill. You should always maintain a courteous tone. And your letter will be successful to the extent that you are able to judge the reaction of the reader. All of your letters in the collection series should avoid the appearance of being curt, for curtness suggests the tone of dunning.

The first letter in a collection series is usually a statement of the time the account has been overdue and the number of notices that have been sent. It is merely a letter of notification. A second letter should ask why no response has been made to the previous letter. The third and fourth letters are a trifle more persistent and should appeal to the debtor's pride and sense of fair play. A reasoning tone should be maintained throughout the series of letters. Inducements for payment — such as an offer permitting a partial payment or installment payments on the debt — may be offered. These inducements, however, should not offer favors that will tempt the debtor to delay further in the hope of gaining additional favors. The series may be as long as needed. The last letter of the series is usually a formal notification that the account will be placed in the hands of a lawyer. Sometimes, at this point, a firm may send a telegram asking for some evidence of good faith in preference to taking court action.

Sales Letters. The sales letter is an attempt to sell services, goods, or ideas. The amount of business attracted by sales letters is so important that some firms employ specialists to write them. Regardless of the volume of business attracted, it is important that sales letters be well written, for every sales letter affects goodwill.

Before beginning to write a sales letter, you must know certain facts: what there is to sell, who will be interested, and how to develop interest. The question most difficult to answer is how to develop interest.

The structure and the purpose of a sales letter are much the same as that of any other business letter. The message must attract favorable

Safety Equipment Company

October 23, 19--

Williams & Smith, Inc.
1508 Walnut Street
Philadelphia, Pennsylvania 19102

Gentlemen:

We are sorry that we have not heard from you regarding our July 3 invoice, amounting to $926. Since you have not answered our previous communications, we feel that it is only fair to you that we make our position clear.

In many cases we have been willing to grant extensions of time to customers who have been prevented by circumstances beyond their control from making payments on due dates. We feel, though, that we are justified in expecting you to tell us your reasons for defaulting and to give us concrete evidence of your desire to make full payment, before we can grant any further extension on your account.

We cannot believe that you are attempting to evade your obligation. The length of time your account has run, with no word from you, however, requires that we ask that you either offer us some explanation or mail us a check without delay.

You still have time to preserve the good credit rating that you had when the account was opened. Why not settle in full now, for your own benefit as well as ours?

Sincerely yours,

Vincent J. Collins
Vincent J. Collins
Credit Manager

cf

Collection letter

attention, arouse interest, create desire, convince the reader, and, finally, stimulate the reader to act immediately.

There are many successful ways of attracting the reader's attention in a sales letter. Aurner and Burtness suggest that one of the following be used:

"1) Flash a 'Short-Short' Story
2) Paint an Action Picture
3) Offer a Miniature Testimonial
4) Ask a Question
5) Flash a Piece of News
6) Strike a Parallel
7) Supply a Startling Fact
8) Use an 'If' Opening
9) Make a Pleasant and Agreeable Assertion
10) Use a Quotation
11) Refer to Current Events
12) Use a 'Power'-Phrase That Compresses the Point"[1]

There are other effective ways of getting the reader to follow through the letter. The use of color may help to strengthen the initial impression — color in the stationery, color in the letterhead, color in the type, or color in the illustrations printed on the stationery.

The description following the initial sentence or paragraph should be vital. In the sale of goods this description may vividly portray physical appearance, that is, the size, shape, color, texture, or taste of the object offered for sale. In this connection it is often desirable to arouse an emotional feeling in the reader. Whenever possible, both the pleasure, or satisfaction, and the practicability of the object should be stressed. There is nothing so effective in breaking down sales resistance as an emotional appeal. It creates a desire and justifies the cost of goods as no other method of appeal does. Such an emotional appeal convinces the prospective purchaser and causes him to buy things for which he felt no immediate need before he read the letter.

The descriptions in a sales letter should also be dynamic. For instance, a vivid phrase concerning a piece of cloth, a sample of which may be found with the letter, carries a great deal of weight. This vividness turned into facts, figures, and scientific description greatly emphasizes the merits of the product.

Action must be approached gradually; but once the crucial point is reached, the message must move rapidly to immediate action. The good sales-letter writer offers the reader inducements for action; he makes it easy for the prospective customer to act. "No money needed," "article

[1] Robert R. Aurner and Paul S. Burtness, *Effective English for Business* (5th ed.; Cincinnati: South-Western Publishing Company, 1962), pp. 552–553.

will be sent on approval," "unqualified guarantee," "to be paid in install-ments," "offer good until——," and "a special discount for immediate purchase" are only a few of the inducements that may be offered to a pro-spect to effect immediate action.

An order blank to be filled out with check marks or a self-addressed and stamped envelope may win a prospect. A suggestion to "fill out and mail TODAY" or "mail the enclosed card now" induces many prospective customers to act so that they will not "miss this splendid opportunity."

Follow-Up Sales Letters. If a number of sales letters are written to the same prospective customer in a systematic campaign, those that follow the initial letter are known as follow-up letters. They follow up inquiries, stimulate action, introduce improvements, sell direct, keep the customer's goodwill, and acquaint him with the firm and its products for future sales possibilities.

There are several types of follow-up campaigns: the campaign series, the wear-out series, and the continuous series. The *campaign series* consists of a complete set of letters prepared in advance in a predetermined style to be sent to the customer in a fixed order, one after the other, until the series has been exhausted. In the *wear-out series*, sales letters continue until the customer is "sold." The *continuous series* is likely to be composed of the type of letter sent to people who are already customers. The series acts primarily to introduce improvements and to keep the customers' goodwill.

There are many variable factors in a follow-up series, such as the length of the letter, the length of the series, the intervals between mailings, the nature of the article, the size of the mailing list, and the selling points. All of these variables must be considered in the organization of any follow-up system.

Form Letters. Many letters are classified as *form letters*. A form sales letter is written so that it can appropriately be sent to many prospects. It should possess a certain appeal; however, the appeal is often limited to specific customers. For instance, form letters written to sell transistor radios or portable television sets can be mailed to almost anyone, but a form letter written to sell aluminum storm windows should be sent only to homeowners.

Duplicated form letters create almost as favorable an impression as separately dictated letters if the letterheads and envelopes are of good quality, if the typing of addresses and other fill-ins matches the typing in the bodies of the letters, and if the letters are individually signed. Many companies that send out form letters to prospective customers make no attempt at individualizing them by inserting the name and address of the prospect but depend upon the style and content of the letter itself to sell the product.

There are form letters and form paragraphs for many other purposes: for collection letters, for letters of inquiry or answers to inquiries, for acknowledgment letters, and for credit letters. For instance, a typist may use the same opening paragraph in acknowledging all the letters received during an employer's absence or the same form letter to acknowledge the receipt of all unsolicited applications for employment. Form letters save a considerable amount of time; consequently, they have their place in the efficient operation of a business office.

You may someday be in a position to design your own file of form letters and of opening and closing paragraphs; it will then be easier for you to process many of the business letters you will be asked to write.

 Study Questions

1. When composing letters, what should the office worker do before typewriting?

2. What types of letters are called routine business letters? What is the purpose of each type?

3. What plan should you follow in composing a detailed letter of inquiry?

4. What should an answer to a letter of inquiry be like?

5. What information should be included in a letter ordering goods?

6. How should an order acknowledgment letter be written when delivery of the order is to be delayed?

7. When an order is received with incomplete information, what should be done?

8. Name the elements that should be included in an adjustment letter.

9. What is the purpose of credit letters?

10. Suggest a series of actions that may make up a collection series.

11. What are some of the important purposes of sales letters?

12. Give twelve ways in which a sales letter may attract the reader's attention.

13. What are follow-up letters?

14. What is a *wear-out series* in a follow-up campaign?

15. What are some of the instances in which form letters and form paragraphs may be used?

 What Do You Think?

1. A clerical office worker is writing a letter in which she must include the date that Mr. T. F. Smith will be in Chicago. She is not sure when he will arrive for the convention that he will be attending. What should she do?

2. A clerical office worker dated a letter three days earlier than the date on which she typed the letter. What do you think of this procedure?

3. Why is an adjustment letter sometimes difficult to write?

4. "Every letter is a sales letter." In what respects is this statement true?

5. When might you be asked to compose letters as a clerical office worker?

Your Personal Qualities

W. F. Block Company received a letter from Mrs. Theodore Lewis in which she said that two cups in her order of six cups and saucers were broken when she received the package about four weeks earlier. The adjustment department wrote her the following letter:

Dear Mrs. Lewis

We are surprised to hear at this late date that you received two broken cups. Apparently you did not report the breakage to the post office as you should have done immediately upon opening the package.

You should have taken care of the breakage as soon as you noted it. We do not take care of such an adjustment unless it is brought to our attention within a week of delivery of the package. We hope you will keep this policy in mind in the future.

Very truly yours

W. F. Block and Company

R. C. Van Wright
Adjustments

Questions: 1. What personal qualities are reflected in this letter?

2. What personal qualities should an adjustment letter reflect?

3. How would you suggest that this letter be written?

How's Your English?

After reading the text material in Appendix D, indicate any improper usage in the following sentences:

1. I shall leave in the a.m.

2. He expects to arrive at 5.30 pm.

3. The YMCA is a boys' organization.

4. The carpet was 12 ft long and 9 feet wide.

5. A woman asked for one pound of butter 2 lbs of sugar and 5 # of flour.

Office Work

1. You have been asked to write letters to the three airlines that serve your city requesting copies of their new schedules. Compose the letter that you would send to each of the three airlines.

2. Your office has received an order for a file cabinet of four drawers. This cabinet is available in three colors, grey, tan, or black. The customer has not indicated the color desired. Write a letter to the customer, Quick-Service Printers, 3547 Monroe Avenue, Chicago, Illinois 60603, requesting a color choice.

3. You are a clerk-typist in the order department of a large retail mail-order company. You have been asked to write a form letter that will be sent to all customers when the merchandise they have ordered is out of stock. Compose a letter that will help the company maintain the goodwill of the customers.

 Office Work Assignments

43: Letter of Inquiry

Assume for this letter that you have the responsibility of securing the prices for carpeting that might be used in the exhibit area of your company during the forthcoming conventions. You need the prices for wool pile broadloom and wool random sheared broadloom for an area that is 6 by 9 feet in size. The color needed is royal blue. Write a letter to T. F. Simon, Fifth Avenue at 38 Street, New York, New York 10036, seeking prices for the carpeting desired.

44: Order Letter

Write a letter to Harper and Brothers, 45 Fifth Avenue, New York, New York 10010, ordering the following books:

    3 copies of IMPROVING OFFICE EFFICIENCY by T. C. Felman at $4.95 per copy

    1 copy of RECORDS MANAGEMENT FOR THE MODERN OFFICE by George B. Blaney at $5.50 per copy

45: Adjustment Letter

Write a letter to Mr. T. F. Kerr, 468 Stony Road, Clarksburg, West Virginia 26301. He wrote that the two-drawer file cabinet that he ordered had come without the drawer handles. In your letter express regret that the handles were missing and tell Mr. Kerr that they have been sent to him by special handling.

46: Collection Letter

Rewrite the following letter with a more courteous tone:

Howard's Stationery Store
75 Market Street
Newark, New Jersey 07102

Gentlemen

Under the date of November 11, we very nicely requested that you send us your check, immediately, in the amount of $62.55 to cover our invoice of August 11; but up to the present date we have not heard a word from you. Our terms are 30 days, but this item is more than two months overdue. We ask you to send us a check by return mail.

Yours truly

UNIT 11 | The Mailable Letter

PART 4:

Typewriting from Voice Recording and Transcribing Machines

Voice recording and companion transcribing machines are used in many offices to facilitate the tasks of the executives in recording the messages they wish to prepare. This equipment makes it possible for the executive to prepare reports while he is away from his office. The belts or discs can be mailed back to the company and copies prepared for his signature. In many companies there are centralized transcribing pools where many persons work as transcription operators. These operators are invaluable workers, for they are proficient in typewriting mailable transcripts quickly and accurately.

Types of Equipment. There are at the present time over 100 different models of dictating and transcribing machines manufactured by 17 companies. Several media are used for the recording function: there are plastic and magnetic belts, plastic discs, magnetic sheets, and magnetic tape media.

Plastic and Magnetic Belt Recorders. Several manufacturers of dictating and transcribing equipment use the belt as the recording medium. One type of belt is made of plastic and the dictator's voice is engraved into the surface of the belt, as is done with recordings on phonograph records; another type is coated with a magnetically sensitive covering which captures the dictator's voice.

The Dictaphone Corporation is the only company that provides a plastic belt, which is a one-time recording medium. The visible tone grooves allow the dictator to find his place quickly. The machine is equipped with an indication slip that guides the transcriber to corrections and to the end of each letter.

Machines manufactured by Victor, Comptometer, International Business Machines, and Stenocord use magnetic belts that record from 12 to 14 minutes of dictation. These belts are reusable, allowing the dictator

425

to change a portion of his material by merely redictating over the portion
he wishes to change. Many users consider this "ability to erase" what has
been said in error an important advantage of the magnetic type of recording device. However, there is always the possibility that material may
accidentally be "erased."

Disc Recorders. A small disc, of the general nature of a phonograph record, is the recording medium for a number of dictating units
now available. All the manufacturers, except one, use a plastic type disc
which is used only once. Some manufacturers do provide a resurfacing
service that makes discs reusable for a number of times. There is one
manufacturer, Telefunken, which makes a machine that uses a magnetic
disc of 10-minute duration. Such a magnetic disc has all the features of the
magnetic belt described in the preceding section. The companies who
manufacture machines that require plastic discs are: McGraw-Edison,
Gray Manufacturing, and SoundScriber. Discs come in varying sizes
capable of recording dictation for periods of approximately ten minutes
to an hour.

Magnetic Paper Recorder. The Cole Steel Company manufactures
a machine called Vanguard V-3. This machine records on a magnetic sheet

which can hold as much as 45 minutes of dictation and can be folded and mailed as simply as a letter. It is also possible to make, from the original copy, a second copy which can be kept in the originating office in those instances where the dictation is not transcribed. The sheets of paper can be reused indefinitely, as the surface is comparable to that of the magnetic belt or magnetic disc.

Magnetic Tape Recorders. A number of companies manufacture tape recording machines that are equipped with transcription facilities so that they can be used in the business office. Cole Steel Company, DeJur-Amsco Corporation, Dictaphone, and McGraw-Edison, as well as a number of other manufacturers, provide machines that use magnetic tape as the recording medium. Tapes that will hold as much as two hours of dictation are available. Tape recording machines are especially useful in conferences and in other instances where there is a considerable period of recording.

Types of Units Available. As stated above, there is a considerable range of types of equipment available in the dictating-transcribing field. In addition, there are small, transistorized, portable units that weigh under five pounds, and there are also large network dictation systems. The more typical units that are available include:

1) *Dictation Unit* which is designed for the dictator's office and is for dictating purposes only.

2) *Transcription Unit* which is designed for the transcriber who will make typewritten copies of the dictation.

3) *Combination Unit* which can be used for both dictating and transcribing. This unit is practical in those instances where limited use is made of the equipment.

4) *Network Dictation System* where the dictation is transmitted over a telephone-like mechanism to a central place where the transcription is handled.

5) *Portable Dictation Unit* which allows for dictation out of the office. Some units can be operated by battery or through the battery of an automobile.

Dictating Skill Needed. While you may not be called upon to dictate often, you will want to know good techniques of machine dictation.

A hand microphone is used to record dictation on a machine in the office, or an instrument resembling a telephone is used to record dictation in a central transcription room. The operation of the hand microphone varies slightly with the different makes of dictating machines. They all

SoundScriber Corporation

Machine dictation

An employer can help you transcribe more efficiently and more accurately if he uses proper dictation techniques.

follow a basic pattern of providing a bar for starting and stopping the dictation and labeled keys or buttons for repeating a few words of the dictation and for indicating corrections and the length of each letter.

When you begin dictating, set the record in motion by a slight pressure on the starter device on the side or front of the mouthpiece, which is really a small microphone. Keep the microphone close to your lips. The record stops revolving when the pressure on the microphone is released. This mechanism enables you to stop the record while thinking and to keep the record in motion only when actually dictating.

Some manufacturers furnish desk microphones which may be used in place of the manual electronic mouthpiece. The use of the hand mouthpiece is advisable when the machine is to be used in open offices or in places that are somewhat noisy or not too private. The desk microphone is used in private or relatively quiet offices. Desk microphones are available with either hand or foot controls for starting or stopping the machine.

The foot control on the desk microphone frees both hands for telephoning or making notes.

The dictating unit will not only record but will also play back the dictation that has been completed. Thus you may have the machine repeat your dictation for you at any point.

Special instructions to the transcriber may be dictated on the belt, disc, tape, or sheet along with the regular dictation. Greater efficiency can be developed, however, by standardizing a system of marks covering some of the routine instructions, including stating the number of carbon copies desired or indicating a "rush" letter. These marks may be made on a strip of scaled paper called an *indication slip*, which on most models is placed in a special holder attached to the dictating unit. The marks referring to a particular letter are written on or cut into the part of the indication slip that is directly in front of the dictating machine. The beginning and the ending of a letter are also marked on this indication slip in order to give the transcriber the opportunity to judge the length of the letter and to plan its placement on the letterhead. When either the dictation is finished or the record is filled, the belt, disc, tape, or sheet and its accompanying indication slip are removed from the machine. The record and the indication slip are then delivered or sent to the person who is to transcribe the dictation.

Dictating Instructions. Efficient machine transcription depends to a large extent upon the quality of the dictation. The following five hints for improving machine dictation were prepared by the Gray Manufacturing Company:

1) Relax — be natural — you're talking to another person.
2) Hold the microphone within 2–3 inches of your lips and speak across its face.
3) Until it is a habit, be careful in the use of the start-stop control so you don't lose the first or last part of your dictation.
4) Have a mental outline of what you want to say and say it clearly in a conversational tone at normal speed.
5) To help your secretary, tell her the number of copies before you dictate a letter, indicate paragraphs, and pronounce unusual names with special care or spell them out.

Transcribing. If you are assigned the work of transcribing dictated material from a machine, you have many of the same problems that are encountered by the stenographer who transcribes from shorthand notes. The chief difference is that as a machine operator, you must depend upon your hearing. You have the advantage of being able to check the accuracy of your typing and the arrangement of your letters as you transcribe, while the stenographer must devote much of her attention to the reading of her shorthand notes as she transcribes.

Transcribing Machines. Most of the transcribing machines are equipped with single earpieces or headsets that either fit into the ears or rest gently against the ears. The operator places the dictated record on the transcribing machine, then places the indication slip on the special tray provided for it, and proceeds to transcribe.

For ease in the operation of the transcribing machine, adjust the controls to suit your particular needs: the speed control, until the voice is clear (neither too fast nor too slow); the volume control, to suit your own hearing; and the tone control, for pleasant listening.

The indication slip which accompanies each recording should serve as a guide for efficient transcription. You should listen to the corrections and special instructions before beginning to type from the recording. Then note the length of each letter as it is marked on the slip and set the margin stops and the vertical spacing on the typewriter for the correct placement of the letter on the letterhead.

At first, transcription is usually performed by starting the machine, listening for a few words, a phrase, or a sentence, stopping the machine, typewriting the words, starting the machine again, listening for a few more words, and so on until each letter (or other material dictated) has been transcribed.

As proficiency is increased, you should be able to type more or less continuously. It is then usually unnecessary to stop and start the transcribing machine to pick up lost words or phrases. If dictation is not too rapid, it may be possible to type along with the voice. It is most important, however, that you learn to stop and start the machine without pausing in typing.

Suggestions for Improving Machine Transcription. The rate of machine transcription can be increased and the number of time-consuming errors can be reduced if the following suggestions of experienced transcribers are adopted:

1) Listen to the corrections and special instructions *before* transcribing any of the letters, memorandums, or other matter.
2) Use the indication slip as a guide for the proper placement of material.
3) Be sure that you understand the meaning of the dictation before typing so that you will avoid:
   a. errors in grammar
   b. errors in punctuation
   c. errors in spelling
   d. confusion of homonyms, such as *bare* for *bear*
4) Develop the power to carry dictation in your mind in order to avoid the overuse of the repeat key.
5) Develop the pattern of the expert machine transcriber — keep the typewriter moving, but stop the dictator. Listen to one phrase ahead of your typewriting.

6) Use the parts of the typewriter to advantage, especially the tabular key and the variable line spacer.

7) Avoid errors in syllabication:
    a. dividing the last word in a paragraph
    b. dividing after re-, de-, etc.
    c. carrying over two letters: ly, ed, ty, etc.

8) Proofread. Read as you type a letter; reread after finishing a letter.

Study Questions

1. What are the advantages of machine transcription over shorthand transcription?

2. How does business use voice recording machines today?

3. Name four media that are used for the recording function in dictating and transcribing machines.

4. How much dictation can be recorded on a recording disc?

5. What is the maximum amount of dictation that a tape will hold?

6. For what purposes is the tape recorder especially useful?

7. What is the prime advantage of a foot control over a hand control on a desk microphone?

8. How may the dictator give special instructions to the transcriber?

9. Give four hints for improving machine dictation.

10. How may the transcriber judge the length of a letter dictated on a dictating machine?

11. List five suggestions which will make the use of machine transcription more efficient.

12. How should the transcriber use the indication slip?

What Do You Think?

1. In what way does the use of dictating and transcribing machines effect a saving for an employer?

2. Can you think of any disadvantage of having only the combination unit dictating-transcribing machine?

3. Give some circumstances under which a portable dictation unit would be advantageous.

4. What are the advantages of a network dictation system?

5. Need a transcribing-machine operator be less qualified than the secretary who transcribes her letters from shorthand notes?

6. Whenever Mr. Adams dictates, he fails to prepare an indication slip. How would you ask him to remember to prepare one for you?

7. What skills and abilities should an office worker possess in order to become an efficient transcribing-machine operator?

Your Personal Qualities

Miss Virginia Hall has been assigned to transcribe the dictation of James Murray, the purchasing agent, referred to as "Mumbling Jim." He dictates slowly, in a very low voice, but he mumbles and swallows his words. It takes Miss Hall many hours to transcribe the recorded dictation because she has difficulty understanding Mr. Murray's words. Even then she is not always sure that she has transcribed correctly.

Miss Hall receives a pamphlet called "Ten Commandments for Dictators" from a dictating machine company and she places it on Mr. Murray's desk. He cannot understand why it was left on his desk; he considers himself to be an excellent dictator.

Questions: 1. What do you think of Miss Hall's action?

2. Should Miss Hall tell Mr. Murray that his dictation could be improved?

How's Your English?

After reading Appendixes D and E, indicate which of the following is correct:

1. I expect to arrive at 12:45 (pm — p.m.)

2. You should have received your order on (May 12 — May 12th.)

3. In order to reach the station you should (first — 1st) walk three blocks south, (second — 2nd) walk one block west, and (third — 3rd) use the entrance on the northeast corner of Seventh Avenue and (14 St. — 14th St.)

4. Bill of Lading is abbreviated by using (B/L — B.Lad.)

5. What are the plurals of the following abbreviations?

    a. ct.   **d.** deg.

    b. lb.   **e.** chg.

    c. ft.

Office Work

1. Prepare a brief report of no more than 100 words in which you discuss the topic "How a Busy Office Can Save Time by Using Dictating and Transcribing Equipment."

2. If dictating and transcribing equipment is available, plan a demonstration on such equipment, highlighting the manner in which the machine is to be used effectively.

3. If dictating and transcribing equipment is available, dictate a letter in which you discuss the efficient use of the dictating unit; then transcribe your letter. After you have done this assignment, write a brief report indicating the ways in which you could improve your use of the equipment.

4. Transcribe letters from a record selected by your instructor if machines for transcription are available.

UNIT 12 | Typing Tasks

PART 1:

Business Reports and Manuscripts

Most business executives devote almost half of their business day and extra time at home each evening to reading the business reports, correspondence, and other business publications mailed or routed to their offices. They are also expected to prepare a number of the reports required by management to supply information that may be incorporated into other reports, such as the annual report to the stockholders. These reports have increased in importance and in volume as business operations have become more diversified and more widely removed from the home office. Furthermore, an ever-increasing number of reports of all kinds are now required by municipal, state, and federal government agencies.

As a competent office worker, you may be expected to work with your employer in compiling, drafting, and editing the factual information contained in his business reports. You will also be responsible for their final typing, collating, and distribution. When you have learned how and where to obtain the related information required for each report and how to present it most effectively, you will become of invaluable assistance to your employer in his efforts to produce reports of a superior quality.

Kinds of Business Reports. Business reports vary in their purpose, in their length, and in the extent of their distribution. A one-page interoffice memorandum is a business report of a confidential nature to be circulated only within the confines of an office. The typical business report is designed for wider distribution; consequently, it is either typed together with several carbon copies or is duplicated. It varies in its length and in its form. It may contain only a few pages or more than fifty.

A manuscript is a typewritten copy of a document to be sent to the printer for publication. If this document is properly printed, it is likely to receive ready and favorable acceptance from the reader.

The Form of Business Reports. The form of a business report is usually determined by its purpose, its reader or readers, and its length. A short report may consist of only a title page and the text; a long, comprehensive report may consist of many parts. In either event, you will be responsible for the final preparation of your employer's reports. If the contents are to receive favorable consideration from the reader, the report must be attractively presented, neatly and accurately typed, and easy to read.

Steps in Report Writing. There is no "one" set way to write a report; there are many ways. However, in drafting and revising a business report until it finally meets with his approval, an executive usually takes these eight steps:

1) He develops a broad concept of the scope of the problem to be covered in the report.
2) He prepares either a sketchy or a detailed outline of the contents.
3) He composes a preliminary draft. He may write the entire draft in longhand; he may record it on a dictating machine; or he may dictate it directly to a member of his staff.
4) He has the preliminary draft typed in rough-draft form.
5) He reorganizes and edits the preliminary draft for content, wording, and sentence structure.
6) He has a second draft typed.
7) He edits the second draft to insure the most effective presentation of the contents.
8) He has the report typed in final form.

The Outline. After the scope of the problem to be covered in a business report has been determined, the author prepares an outline. Outlining the report forces the writer to think through the entire problem and to organize his thoughts in logical sequence — a sequence that can be readily followed by the reader. It is also a framework for the initial draft.

An outline may be written in topical form — preferably with nouns — or in complete sentence form. Parallel construction should be maintained; if one part of the outline is in sentence form, the next part should be a sentence, too. Words, phrases, and sentences should not be mixed throughout the outline. No main heading or subheading should be left to stand alone. For every Roman numeral "I," there should be a Roman numeral "II"; for every letter "A," a letter "B"; for every Arabic "1," an Arabic "2."

In the outline on the opposite page, each identifying number or letter is followed by a period and two spaces and begins just below the first word of the preceding line.

An Outline of a Report on

PUNCHED-CARD DATA PROCESSING OPERATIONS

I. Introduction

    A. Purpose
        1. To review present operations
        2. To develop an improved system
    B. Approach
        1. To make detailed studies of present equipment
        2. To prepare flow charts of present operations
            a. Accounting department
            b. Payroll department
            c. Purchasing department

II. Proposed system

    A. Staff requirements
        1. To retrain present personnel
        2. To employ systems manager
    B. Equipment requirements
        1. To study rental costs of additional machines
        2. To study other costs
            a. Auxiliary equipment
            b. Additional cards and tapes
        3. To study additional wiring costs

An outline of a report

The Rough Draft. A rough draft is the writer's first attempt to get his thoughts down on paper where they can be edited and improved. Before it is finally accepted, the draft may be revised and retyped many times; therefore, you will find the following ten suggestions helpful:

1) Use typing paper strong enough to withstand erasing easily. Do not use expensive letterhead paper nor fragile onionskin paper.
2) Type double or triple space so that the changes can be clearly marked and easily seen and followed.
3) Allow ample margins (1 1/2 to 2 inches) at the top, bottom, and on both sides of each page to provide enough room for corrections and insertions.
4) "X" out typing errors and deletions in the preliminary draft instead of taking the time to erase them.
5) Make only the number of copies that you are asked to make.
6) Number each page in the draft in its proper sequence. Also assign a number to each successive revision of a draft and type the date on it.
7) Type a long insertion on a separate sheet of paper and give it a corresponding page number and letter. For example, the first insertion to be included on page 8 should be numbered "8A" and clearly marked "Insert 8A" at the point where it is to be inserted.

(Nov.) 3, 19— (SP)

Cap Mr. John C. Clark, Office manager
Electronic Data Processing Corporation
521 Fifth Avenue
New York, New York 10036

Dear Mr. Clark

tr We understand that you have just been appointed office   #
manager of the Electronic Data Processing Corporation.
tr We congratulate you on your well-deserved promotions.   §

[*Cap* [The Equity Insurance company has just put out a   #
special term insurance policy for office employees.
This policy will give you full protection when you need
it most--and at the very lowest rates. We enclosed   §
a circular explaining in detail the complete coverage.

We are in a position to *give* offer you a $10,000 term policy *stet*
for 20 years, with the option of renewing for another
10 years, at an annual premium of $150. If you are
interested, we ~~would~~ appreciate your signing and returning the enclosed card.

shall.   Cordially yours

                         Robert Graham, Manager
                         Group Insurance Division

ve

Enclosure

Rough draft of a business letter

8) Type quoted matter of four lines or more single space and indent
it in the same form as it will appear in the final draft.

9) Type footnotes single space at the bottom of the page, on a
separate sheet, or, preferably, insert them in this manner immediately after the reference but separated from the text by solid lines:

---

[1]Peter L. Agnew, James R. Meehan, and
William R. Pasewark, Clerical Office Prac-
tice (4th ed.; Cincinnati: South-Western
Publishing Company, 1967), p. 152.

---

10) Keep all rough drafts in a file folder until the final draft has been
approved. Your employer may decide to include words, phrases,
sentences, and other materials deleted from previous drafts in the
final draft of his report.

Proofreaders' Marks. Proofreaders' marks are used primarily to indicate corrections on typeset printer's proof for the printer of a document. However, they are used more and more by executives to indicate corrections and revisions in typed rough drafts of business reports because they are clearly understood and easily followed. Their use greatly reduces the chance of error in the retyping of a draft. Standard proofreaders' marks, as they are indicated in a rough draft and corrected in the text, are shown on the next page. You will need to know their meanings to type rough drafts of business documents efficiently.

Typing the Report. The final draft of a business report should be typed on white bond paper (8 1/2 x 11 inches in size) of good quality, preferably of 20-pound substance. The body of the report, except for footnotes and extensive quotations, should be double spaced. The typing line should be 6 to 6 1/2 inches long: 60–65 pica spaces or 72–78 elite type spaces.

The vertical and side margins for typed reports are determined by the binding. If the following table of margins for unbound, side-bound, and top-bound reports is carefully followed, the format or general appearance of the report will be greatly enhanced.

MARGINS FOR TYPING BUSINESS REPORTS

Margins	Unbound	Side Bound	Top Bound
Top margin			
First page	2 inches	2 inches	2½ inches
All other pages	1 inch	1 inch	1½ inches
Side margins			
Left	1 inch	1½ inches	1 inch
Right	1 inch	1 inch	1 inch
Bottom margin	1 inch	1 inch	1 inch

A black carbon ribbon or a fresh silk or nylon typewriter ribbon should be used to give a clear, sharp, black impression. The type should be cleaned frequently to maintain a consistently clear impression throughout the entire report. A good quality of carbon paper should be used, and it should be replaced often enough to insure clean and distinct copies and to avoid creasing and treeing.

Erasures should be made so carefully and so well that they cannot be detected in the typed report. An erasing shield and a clean abrasive eraser should be used to make corrections on the hard-finish bond paper; a softer eraser, to make corrections on carbon copies.

Mark in Margin	Meaning of Mark	Correction or Change Marked in Text	Corrected or Changed Copy
∧	caret; indicates insertion is to be made	If you are interested∧we	If you are interested, we
⊙	period	Send the copy to the printer⊙Do not fasten	Send the copy to the printer. Do not fasten
(sp)	spell out	(Prof.) Hill	Professor Hill
◯	write it out	① Park Avenue	One Park Avenue
SS	single space	You will produce \n SS\n more attractive \n material in	You will produce \n more attractive \n material in
⌒	close up	on the pay⌒roll	on the payroll
lc	lower case	Building And Loan Co.	Building and Loan Co.
≡ or caps	capitalize	Mutual life of New York	Mutual Life of New York
no ¶	no paragraph	continued on the next \n page. \n no ¶ If a short letter	continued on the next \n page. If a short letter
¶	new paragraph	two or more lines.¶One \n caution	two or more lines. \n One caution
]	move to right	centered over the \n]columns and then typed	centered over the \n columns and then typed
[	move to left	cc: Joseph H. Morrow \n [Gerald A. Porter \n Allen A. Smith	cc: Joseph H. Morrow \n Gerald A. Porter \n Allen A. Smith
#	more space	has a press#release ready	has a press release ready
tr	transpose	monthly beenfits	monthly benefits
͜	take out; delete	We wished you	We wish you
stet	leave it as it was originally	commencing \n starting next month	starting next month
ds	double space	When you are busy at a \n typewriter performing \n clerical duties	When you are busy at a \n typewriter performing \n clerical duties
>	leave a line space	Change Spacing \n >This line should be \n another line below \n the heading.	Change Spacing \n \n This line should be \n another line below \n the heading.

Proofreaders' marks

Parts of a Report. A comprehensive business report or a manuscript may contain a dozen, more or less, specific parts which are classified under three main headings: the introductory parts, the body of the report, and the supplementary parts. In the final assembly before binding, they are arranged in this order:

A. Introductory Parts
 1. Cover
 2. Title page
 3. Preface or letter of transmittal, including acknowledgments
 4. Table of contents
 5. List of tables
 6. List of illustrations

B. Body of the Report
 1. Summary or synopsis
 2. Introduction
 3. Main body or text
 4. Conclusions and recommendations

C. Supplementary Parts
 1. Appendix
 2. Bibliography
 3. Index

The body of the report must be developed first; consequently, it is usually typed first, followed by the supplementary parts. Finally the introductory parts of the report are typed.

The Cover. The cover of the report should be of a bright color so that it can be easily identified. The label on the cover should contain this information: the title of the report, the name of the person submitting it, and the date it was submitted.

The Title Page. The items of information that usually appear on the title page are the title of the report, the name of the author, the date, and the place of preparation. Sometimes reports include the name of the person (with his title) for whom the report was prepared. The items of information may be typed in traditional or nontraditional form. If traditional form is used, all the items are centered horizontally, starting with the title which is placed at least two inches from the top of the page, or three if the report is bound at the top. For effective display, the other items are separated by at least four line spaces. A nontraditional title page affords you an opportunity to use artistic typing effectively. All the items of information may be typed at the left in block form. The title may be typed at the left with the author's name at the right, or other variations in placement

A REPORT ON DATA PROCESSING OPERATIONS
AT PALMER PRODUCTS INCORPORATED

For
William Lawrence Henderson
Executive Vice President

By
Michaels, Singer, and Smith
Management Consultants
San Francisco

November 14, 19--

REPORT ON DATA PROCESSING OPERATIONS

PALMER PRODUCTS INCORPORATED

For
William Lawrence Henderson
Executive Vice President

By
Michaels, Singer, and Smith
Management Consultants
San Francisco, California

November 14, 19--

REPORT ON DATA PROCESSING OPERATIONS

At . . .
          .
          .
          Palmer Products Incorporated

For. . .
          .
          .
          William Lawrence Henderson
          Executive Vice President

By . . .
          .
          .
          Michaels, Singer, and Smith
          Management Consultants
          San Francisco, California

On . . .
          .
          .
          November 14, 19--

Three sample title pages for reports

440   **Unit 12   Typing Tasks**

may be used. Special characters such as the asterisk and the hyphen are often used for artistic display work in a nontraditional title page.

Numbering Pages. Small Roman numerals (ii, iii, iv, etc.) are used to number the pages of the introductory parts of the report. The title page is considered as page "i" but no number is typed on it. The numbers are centered and typed one-half inch from the bottom of the page and they are not followed by periods or any other punctuation.

Arabic numerals, without punctuation, are used to number the pages in the rest of the report. They begin with "1" and run consecutively throughout the report. The number on the first page of each section is centered and typed one-half inch from the bottom of the page. Remaining page numbers are one-half inch from the top and even with the right margin.

Types of Headings. You will choose from several types of headings to set off the appearance of typed matter and to indicate the relationship of its parts. If the material is well organized, the headings and subheadings will serve as a basic outline for the article.

Main Headings and Subheadings. Main headings are usually centered when the material is of considerable length and requires the use of side subheadings as well. When the material is short and does not include subheadings, the main headings may be typed at the left side of the page.

A subheading is usually typed on the left side of the page and consists of a complete sentence or of key words at the beginning of a paragraph. In either case some device, such as underlining, must be used to give proper emphasis to the subheadings by setting them apart from the rest of the copy. If the material is typed in block style, the subheadings should be written flush with the left margin. If the indented paragraph style is used, the subheadings should also be indented.

Another arrangement for subheadings is that of placing them on separate lines set apart from the preceding and following paragraphs by double or triple spacing. This type of heading is usually placed flush with the left margin even though the indented style of paragraph is used.

Emphasis in Headings. Titles, main headings, and subheadings may be given different degrees of emphasis by using spaced-out capital letters, by underlining, by typing letters twice to get a bold-faced effect, and by combinations of these devices. On the next page you will find a number of possible arrangements. It is not likely that all of these would be used in a single paper or report. After a particular method of emphasis has been selected for a heading or subheading, care must be exercised so that all headings of the same rank are typed in the same way. When spaced-out letters are used, three spaces must be left between words.

RETENTION PLAN FOR CENTRAL FILES OF ACME CORPORATION

The following report has been prepared by Frank Henry (in charge of Records Management Department) after consultation with the heads of all major departments, Helen Jones of the central filing unit, Mary Shay of Shaw-Walker Company, and Edward J. Leahy, whose work in the field of records management is most significant.

Need for Developing a Plan

Background of the Problem. The Acme Corporation has been in operation fifteen years. It has grown in size from a one-story plant in a suburban area to a large central factory with five subsidiaries in rural centers and a central office operation in Chicago in a high-rent district. The volume of paper work has increased greatly, and the expense of storage space has grown with transfer of administration to a metropolitan location. On a national average it costs more than $1\frac{1}{2}$ cents a year to keep a paper in the files. An analysis of expenses shows that it costs $2\frac{1}{2}$ cents in the Acme Corporation.

Method of Making the Analysis. The manager of each major department in the Chicago office (see attached chart

Page of manuscript illustrating the use of headings

H E A D I N G S	Caps spaced and underscored
W I T H L E S S	Caps spaced
AND LESS EMPHASIS	Caps underscored
FROM THE	Caps
M a i n H e a d i n g s	Spaced and underscored small letters
T o t h e M i n o r	Spaced small letters
Subheadings	Underscored small letters

Preface or Letter of Transmittal. The preface or letter of transmittal is written in a less formal and more personal style than the body of the report. Nevertheless, it must be carefully planned and well written if it is to accomplish its major objectives — to interest the reader and to put him in a proper frame of mind to read the entire report.

In its simplest form, the letter of transmittal indicates who authorized the preparation of the report and transmits it to the reader. If a separate summary is not included in the report, it is usually included in the letter. The length and content of the letter of transmittal depend upon the length of the report and the number of subdivisions contained in it. It may include these five items of information about the report, not necessarily in this order:

1) Authorization of its preparation
2) Prime purpose of the report
3) Scope of the report
4) Time given to its preparation
5) Acknowledgments of assistance in its preparation

Table of Contents. The table of contents precedes the report and gives an overview of the material covered in it by listing the main topics or chapter titles with their page numbers. The heading, *Table of Contents*, should be centered two inches from the top of the page and typed entirely in capital letters. Double spacing is used before the titles of chapters or main topics, and single spacing in all other instances. All important words in the chapter or main topic title should be capitalized. Each chapter should be preceded by its number, which is typed in Roman numerals and followed by a period and two spaces. The Roman numerals should be in vertical alignment with the periods directly beneath each other. Leaders (periods and spaces alternated) should extend across the page from each title to guide the reader in finding the page number at the right.

The periods in the leaders should be in vertical alignment also. This can be done easily by typing all periods at even numbers on the typewriter line scale. Before it is finally typed, the table of contents should be checked for correctness of titles and accuracy of page numbers.

List of Tables. The heading *List of Tables*, like all other headings, is centered two inches from the top of the page and typed entirely in capital letters. The table numbers are typed in Arabic numerals followed by a period and two spaces. The first letter of every important word in the title of a table is typed with a capital letter. Leaders extend from the title to the Arabic page numbers at the right. Lists of charts and other illustrations are typed in the same form as the list of tables.

TABLE OF CONTENTS

MICHAELS, SINGER, and SMITH

Management Consultants

San Francisco

November 14, 19--

Mr. William Lawrence Henderson
Executive Vice President
Palmer Products Incorporated
555 Madison Avenue
New York, New York 10022

Dear Mr. Henderson

Accompanying this letter is the report covering our study of data processing operations at Palmer Products Incorporated. The report proposes a new data processing system for your firm, first in principle and then in detail, and suggests a plan of action.

The system proposed would eliminate the need for a punched-card installation in any of your branch offices and would provide you with weekly reports of the expenditures and remaining funds in all of your branches.

We estimate that annual savings of $26,000 would result from installing the new system. An initial outlay, however, of about $6,500 would be required for the new equipment which we are recommending.

We were materially assisted in our study by the cooperation of your staff and the others we interviewed. We would be pleased to discuss the contents of this report with you after you have had an opportunity to review it.

Very truly yours

MICHAELS, SINGER, and SMITH

David R. Singer
David R. Singer

rkm

Summary, Recommendations, or Conclusions. Although the summary, recommendations, or conclusions of a report are prepared after the main section has been written, they usually follow the table of contents because they are intended to give the reader a quick overview of the complete report. They are prepared to save the reader's time and to make it easier for him to understand the detailed statements contained in the body of the report. In general, the summary contains four major statements:

1) The nature of the problem covered in the report
2) The principal findings or results of the report
3) The major conclusions of the report
4) The major recommendations for future action

The Body of the Report. The main divisions of the body of a report are called chapters, sections, topics, or parts. The division headings in the body of the report should correspond to the titles as they appear in the table of contents. Each division should begin on a new page with the word *Chapter* or *Section* centered two inches from the top of the page. It should be typed entirely in capital letters and followed by a chapter or section number typed in large Roman numerals. The title of the chapter or section is centered two line spaces below and also typed in capital letters. A very long title should be broken into two or more lines and divided with the thought if that is possible. With a long title the inverted pyramid type may be used — the top line longer than the second, and the second line longer than the third. Three line spaces should be left between the title and the first paragraph of the report.

Quoted Material. Material from other sources is frequently quoted in a business report to increase the effectiveness of the writer's point of view. All direct quotations should be typed exactly as they are written in the quoted source: in wording, spelling, punctuation, and paragraphing.

1) A brief quotation of fewer than four lines is typed in the text and enclosed with quotation marks.
2) A quotation of four lines or more is started on a new line and typed on shorter, single-spaced lines — indented from both the left and right margins. No quotation marks are used.
3) A quotation of several paragraphs need not be indented, but a quotation mark should precede each paragraph and should follow the final word of the last quoted paragraph.
4) A quotation within a quotation (an inside quotation) is enclosed with single quotation marks. The apostrophe is usually used to indicate a single quotation in typed material.
5) Omissions in a quotation are shown by typing an ellipsis — three spaced periods for an omission within a sentence or between sentences, four periods for an omission at the end of a sentence.

CHAPTER III

PROPOSED SYSTEM IN PRINCIPLE

The system outlined below would eliminate the need for all
punched-card installations in any of the branch offices. This
would virtually eliminate the need for overtime during the peak
season. It would also provide weekly reports of the expenses
and remaining balances in all branches. An improved method for
planning and controlling the work is outlined to enable the
Computer Center to handle this system.

Savings under the proposed system are estimated at about
$26,000 annually. The system anticipates continued growth in
the size of Palmer Products and contemplates that, in the future,
other processing functions will be added to those now processed
by the Computer Center.

The following procedures are recommended for developing
branch office budgets, for ordering all goods and services, for
processing payments, and for preparing budgetary reports. The
Budget Office would consolidate all funds for each branch office,
regardless of the source, into single-line amounts for each of the
various items in order to facilitate control over expenditures.
The line items would differ among branches, depending on what the
largest expense items were. Many branches, however, would require
the following line items: personal services, supplies, office

A typed page of a report

Permission should be obtained to quote copyrighted material if it
is to be widely distributed in duplicated reports or printed manuscripts.
Material may be quoted from government publications without permission.

Footnotes. Footnotes refer the reader to information outside the text of a report. They are inserted to acknowledge and identify the source of the quoted information, to "prove the point" made by the writer or to support his arguments, to provide additional material for the reader, or to elaborate on the meaning within the text. The Arabic number of a footnote is typed in the text just after the statement to be documented but slightly above the line of writing. The footnote itself, if it is the first reference to a particular work, should identify the author and the title of the work referred to, give facts about the publication of the work and the copyright date, and cite a specific page reference.

Later references to the same source need not repeat all these details; only *ibid.* and the page number are used when references to the same work follow each other. The author's name, *op. cit.*, and the page number are used when a previous reference has been made to the same source but other references intervene. The author's name and *loc. cit.* are used to refer to the same passage in a reference previously cited.

The following footnotes illustrate the use of *ibid., op. cit.*, and *loc. cit.*:

---

[1] H. Webster Johnson, How to Use the Business Library (3d ed.; Cincinnati: South-Western Publishing Company, 1964), p. 148.

[2] Robert R. Aurner and Paul S. Burtness, Effective English for Business (5th ed.; Cincinnati: South-Western Publishing Company, 1962), pp. 537-592.

[3] Ibid., p. 646.

[4] Johnson, op. cit., pp. 142-146.

[5] Aurner and Burtness, loc. cit.

Footnotes should be typed according to the following practices:

1) They are separated from the text by a short, solid, horizontal line of 15 pica or 18 elite spaces typed with the underscore key a line below the last line of the text.
2) The first line of the first footnote is typed two lines below the short horizontal line. It is indented the same number of spaces as the paragraphs in the report. The succeeding lines of the footnote begin at the left margin.
3) The reference number, which corresponds with the footnote number in the text, is also typed slightly above the line of writing. It is typed without punctuation or a space between it and the first word of the footnote.
4) All footnotes are typed single space. A double space is used to separate them.
5) Footnotes are usually numbered consecutively throughout a report or manuscript.

An Appendix. The text of a comprehensive report or a manuscript may be followed by an appendix; it is omitted in a short report. It usually contains supplementary reference material not easily included in the text. The appendix may also contain general reference tables, tables containing complete original data, and other materials which will help to interpret and to add interest in the report.

The Bibliography. All documentary sources referred to in a business report or a manuscript — books, articles, periodicals, and primary source materials — should be included in the bibliography. It should also include all the references consulted which yield worthwhile material related to the report. The items listed in the bibliography should be arranged in alphabetical order by authors, by editors, or by titles if the authors' names are not available. Examples of references to books, magazine articles, and primary source materials in a bibliography follow:

BIBLIOGRAPHY

Yearbook — Business Education for the Automated Office, The Eastern Business Teachers Association Yearbook, 1964. The Eastern Business Teachers Association, 1964.

Unpublished Material — Erickson, L. W. Selected Business Education Practices in the California Senior High Schools. Ed.D. dissertation, University of California, Los Angeles, 1955. 461 numbered leaves.

Newspaper Article — New York Herald Tribune. October 21, 1964.

One-Author Book — Lamb, Marion M. Word Studies, 5th ed. Cincinnati: South-Western Publishing Company, 1963.

Two-Author Book — Niswonger, C. Rollin, and Philip E. Fess. Accounting Principles, 9th ed. Cincinnati: South-Western Publishing Company, 1965.

Three-Author Book — Lessenberry, D. D., T. James Crawford, and Lawrence W. Erickson. 20th Century Typewriting, 9th ed. Cincinnati: South-Western Publishing Company, 1967.

Magazine Article — Prentis, Henning W. Jr. "Managing by Principle," Office Executive. XXXIII (July, 1958), 9-11.

Government Document — U.S. Congress, Senate, Committee on the Judiciary. The Many Crises of the Soviet Economy. 88th Congress, 2d. session. Washington: U.S. Government Printing Office, 1964.

Examples of bibliographical form

Your Responsibilities. You are probably thinking that an employer may not know all the information that is needed to complete either the footnotes or the bibliography. He may have only scant information to give you such as, "I think the title of the book is *Business Organization and Management* and the author is Tyler, but I'm not sure." Of course, he may not remember the author's first name or even how to spell his name. As for the newspaper article he referred to, all he may remember is that it was in the *Times* last week. The rest is up to you.

There is even more to it than that. Very often in quoting material, the executive may not remember each and every word; he may not have the statistics exact, or the dates exact. This, too, is your responsibility. Checking the original sources, you make the changes that are necessary without annoying your executive with such details.

You will, therefore, need to check reference books like the *Reader's Guide to Periodical Literature, The New York Times Index, The World Almanac.* You may also have to call the public library for help. Thus, you will find that, in connection with manuscript writing, you will need to know where to look, what to look for, and how to get the information rapidly and correctly. Appendix G will help you.

An Index. An index is necessary only in a comprehensive report or manuscript for which a table of contents would not be an adequate key to the entire document.

Proofreading. All typewritten reports and manuscripts should be proofread before they are duplicated or printed. The text can be checked most effectively, particularly if it contains statistics, by having one of your co-workers read the original copy aloud to you while you check the reading against the final copy.

The first printer's proof of a manuscript is called galley proof — long sheets of printed material to permit corrections before it is made up into the final printed pages. Every error or change in the galley proof should be indicated by a proofreaders' mark (illustrated on page 438). If you catch and correct even one error in the galley proof, the manuscript is thus made more nearly perfect. You should, therefore, proofread and correct the contents of all reports and manuscripts with extreme care. Pride in workmanship is evident in manuscript work.

You must also be absolutely sure that all figures in the proof are accurate. An incorrect letter in a word is considered undesirable, but seldom does this type of error cause the reader to misunderstand the entire document. An incorrect figure, on the other hand, may mean the difference between a profit and a loss on a business transaction. You will find the following suggestions for reading and checking figures helpful:

1) Read *2948* as *two nine four eight*.
2) Read *0* (zero) as *oh*.
3) Read a decimal point as *point*.
4) Read *.00032* as *point 0 0 0 three two*.
5) Read down columns, not up or across.
6) Verify totals by addition. This is a double check on the original and on the copy.

The names of persons, places, and other proper nouns should be spelled by the reader, at least the first time that they appear in the copy, in order to avoid errors.

Interoffice Memorandums. In the office in which you will be employed, you may type many short business reports on forms called interoffice memorandums. These memorandums remain within the organization itself. They are brief and to the point because their only purpose is to communicate with other members of the organization quickly and clearly. The chief advantage of these forms is that they can be typed quickly. Titles (*Mr.*, *Mrs.*, *Dr.*, *etc.*), the salutation, the complimentary close, and the formal signature are usually omitted.

The forms, with the heading *Interoffice Memorandum*, are usually printed on half sheets of paper. The printed words *To*, *Date*, *File*, and *Subject*, with enough writing space after each of them, may be included in the heading of the form. The word *From* is included in the heading if a signature line is not printed at the bottom of the form.

You should leave a triple space between the last line of the heading and the first line of the message. Short messages of not more than five lines may be typed double space; longer messages should be typed single space. Reference initials should be typed at the left margin two spaces below the last line of the message. When enclosures are sent with a memorandum, the enclosure notation should be typed a double space below the reference initials.

An interoffice memorandum is often sent to a number of people within the organization. In such cases carbon copies may be used. The names of all who are to receive copies, however, should be listed on the original and on all carbon copies. Another practice is to type two copies: one original with the names of the recipients and one file copy. The original, with any special enclosures, is sent to the first person on the list. When he is finished with it, he draws a line through his name and sends the memorandum along to the next person on the list. This is repeated until all the interested persons have seen it. This practice is most satisfactory when there is an enclosure or an attachment with the interoffice memorandum that is either too long or too difficult to reproduce.

Study Questions

1. What are an office worker's responsibilities in the preparation of business reports and manuscripts?

2. What are the three factors that determine the form of a business report?

3. Why should an outline be prepared before a report is written?

4. What are the advantages of using proofreaders' marks to indicate corrections in reports and manuscripts?

5. What determines the side and vertical margins of typed reports?

6. What is the length of a typewritten line in the average business report?

7. What kind of typewriter ribbon should be used to give a clear, sharp impression in a typewritten report?

8. Why are the recommendations and summary of a report placed after the table of contents and before the body of the report?

9. What are the three main parts of a business report?

10. Give the two kinds of numerals used to number the pages of a report or a manuscript, and indicate where each kind is used.

11. List the items of information usually given on the title page of a report.

12. What is the purpose of a letter of transmittal?

13. Why are materials from other sources quoted in business reports and manuscripts?

14. What specific information is contained in a footnote?

15. When is the word *From* included in the heading of an interoffice memorandum?

16. What is the major advantage of writing a short business report in the form of an interoffice memorandum?

What Do You Think?

1. Discuss the reference books and handbooks that you might use to aid you in editing a preliminary draft for content, wording, and sentence structure.

2. To what extent is an office worker responsible for the designing of the form and style of a business report?

3. Why is a typist permitted to "X" out errors and deletions in a preliminary draft of a report?

4. Why are footnotes sometimes used by a writer to prove his point?

5. What advantage does a written report have over direct oral communication?

Your Personal Qualities

Mildred Alexander read proof hurriedly and failed to check some computations in it. She told the executive for whom she worked, however, that it had been carefully checked and rechecked. On the basis of her statement, he approved the proof and returned it to the printer. After the material was in print and distributed, a very serious error was discovered that caused some loss and considerable embarrassment to the company.

Questions: **1.** What explanation should Miss Alexander make?

2. What action should the executive take?

How's Your English?

After reading Appendix E, indicate which of the following is correct:

1. For a more vivid description, refer to chapter XII, page 463 (Chapter XII, page 463).

2. His talk entitled "Making Progress In The World" ("Making Progress in the World") was well received.

3. The Ohio River (Ohio river) is considered by many to be the dividing line between the north and the south (the North and the South).

4. Mr. John B. Reynolds is Executive Secretary (executive secretary) of the local chapter of the club.

Office Work

1. Type the following five items of information in the form of a title page for a report:

a. Title: RESEARCH REPORT ON NEW PRODUCTS

b. For: Thomas B. Carleton, President of the Smith Paper Company

c. By: Walter A. Starr, Director of Research and Development

d. At: Chester, Pennsylvania

e. On: November 30, 19--

2. Type the following TABLE OF CONTENTS with appropriate margins on a single page:

	Page
Letter of Transmittal	ii
Table of Contents	iii
List of Tables	iv
List of Charts	v

Chapter	
I. Introduction	1
Prices	2
Outlook	3
Earnings and Dividends	4
Employment	5
II. Directors and Officers	6
III. Statement of Earnings	7
IV. Balance Sheet	8
V. Comparative Balance Sheets	9
VI. Accountants' Certificate	10
VII. Property, Plant, and Equipment	11
VIII. Inventories and Investments	13
IX. Disposition of Income	15
X. Research and Development	16

3. Type the following paragraphs with indented paragraph headings (see illustration on page 442):

Incorporating an Established Business. Owners of sole proprietorships or persons doing business as a partnership may wish to incorporate the business and continue its operations as a corporation. In such a case, the same type of information is provided in the application for a charter as that provided when a corporation is formed to promote a new business. Each subscriber to the capital stock of the corporation indicates on the subscription list the number of shares of stock subscribed and the method of paying the subscription when the charter has been granted. The owner or owners of the established business usually take stock in payment for their interest in the business.

Goodwill. Frequently the incorporators of a corporation being formed to continue the operations of an established business will agree to pay the owner of the established business more than the value of his proprietary interest in the assets of the business as shown by the balance sheet. This excess value is known as goodwill. The incorporators agree to pay more for the assets of the business than the owner's proprietary interest because the owner has an established trade, and the customers he has served will continue as customers of the corporation.

4. Type the following letter of transmittal in block form with open punctuation (current date):

Mr. Thomas B. Carleton President Smith Paper Company Chester, Pennsylvania 12055 Dear Mr. Carleton (¶) The report which accompanies this letter covers the research on new products and the development of new markets for the Smith Paper Company. (¶) Our employees made dramatic progress last year in developing new products and new markets which will contribute importantly to the Company's future growth. Some of the new products are shown elsewhere in this report; still others — not yet ready for the market — are in various stages of development. Our research and development expenses for last year were almost 25% greater than the previous year. After very careful study of the long-range opportunities open to us through research in the physical sciences and in marketing — as well as gains to be made in mechanical development — we think it is safe to say that our total budgets for these important activities will probably be increased by as much as 50% over the next three years. (¶) Smith employees at all levels are committed to a policy of improving the quality of our products and continuing the war against waste and inefficiency in every form. The credit for what we consider to be a truly remarkable achievement in research and development by the Smith Paper Company belongs not only to the Research Division but to all the men and women employed by the Company. Sincerely yours Walter A. Starr Director of Research

5. Type the following page from an annual report to the stockholders. The page is to be typed double space with margins set for binding at the side. The subheading is *Research and Development.*

The Corporation's long-standing emphasis on research and development continues to be directed to new products, to improved products, and to more economical processes and equipment. These activities, located at Yorktown Heights, New York, are conducted to assure the future success of the Corporation. The organization is composed of separate groups with personnel well trained in scientific fields related to the Corporation's business, that is, in chemistry, in physics, in engineering, and in textile technology. Each group has adequate up-to-date facilities and equipment to do modern research in fields of expanding technology. (¶) The combination of the various technical talents at one location enables groups to conduct coordinated research on new fibers and packaging firms — and basic or exploratory research directed toward the discovery of new products. In fiber research during the past year, the competitive position of rayon tire yarn has been improved by developing stronger yarns and better bond for rayon cord and rubber. This latter development has been particularly important for two-ply rayon cord pas-senger car tires, as it has made them even more durable under difficult road conditions.

Office Work Assignments

47: Proofreading

Set up a finished copy of the rough draft given below. Make three carbon copies if you have the materials. Arrange the copy to fit an interoffice memorandum form 8 1/2" x 5 1/2".

Put on interoffice memorandum form

Memorandum about [Meeting of Committee on Retirement Party]
└ use as subject

TO: Mary Miller, ~~Doctor~~ *Harold* Fielding, and ~~Mr.~~ *Leo* Spaulding

FROM: John Fleming   *Single Space*

    organization
The/meeting of the Committee, which was set up by Mr. Combs, will *body*

be held on Friday, September ~~31~~ *30*, in the Executive Dining Room at

12:30. Please have in mind when you come ~~y~~ : (1) ~~a proposed~~ *when the*
party should be held
~~date for the party~~; (2) ~~the kind of party you prefer~~ whether you

prefer a dinner or a late afternoon reception, (3) whether we

should present retirement gifts, and, if so, what kind, ~~and~~ (4)

who should be invi*t*ed*, and* *(5)* ~~whether~~ *we*

Mr. Combs checked and discovered that there are four people re-

tiring.

Should ~~we~~ have an outside speaker?.

Maybe you should ~~examine~~ discuss the matter with some of your

colleagues before the meeting so that we can give Mr. Combs a

sampling of the thinking of the entire group.

tabo
ite
to b
disc

UNIT 12 | Typing Tasks

PART 2:

Financial Reports and Statements

Most business firms issue financial reports to their owners and to prospective investors. The first of these reports is a prospectus, a business report designed to present a new enterprise in a most favorable manner. The financial structure, estimated earnings, and probable future growth of the proposed business venture are included in the prospectus. It should contain all the information that would be required by any prudent individual or organization before investing money in the business. If the securities of a proposed enterprise are to be offered in interstate commerce and registered with the Securities and Exchange Commission, a complete prospectus is required by law.

After a business firm has been established, the board of directors periodically supplies business information to the firm's investors. The larger corporations furnish brief financial reports to their shareholders at quarterly intervals during the year and well-illustrated complete annual reports at the end of the fiscal year. An annual report usually contains a letter to the shareholders from the president of the corporation accompanied by a statistical report of the highlights of the year, an account of newly developed products and recently acquired markets, and a number of financial statements with supporting schedules. Ordinarily, the financial statements include a statement of income, a statement of retained earnings, and a balance sheet. Some of the supporting statistical information, such as a report of the volume of sales in the different territories, may be presented in columnar form in carefully structured tables. Other statistical information, such as the distribution of the sales dollar or the fluctuation in annual sales, is often presented more vividly in graphic form.

Highlights of the Year. In each annual report, the statistical highlights of the year usually precede the president's letter to the shareholders

455

of the corporation. The highlights offer, in tabular form, a comparison of significant figures for the year with those of the preceding year. These comparative figures are usually headed by Net Sales, Net Earnings or Net Income, Net Earnings per Share, Dividends Paid, and Dividends Paid per Share. Other significant figures compared are: Provisions for Depreciation, Expenditures for Plant and Equipment, Investments, and Capital Invested in the Business. The yearly comparisons of the number of shares of stock outstanding, the number of shareholders, and the number of people employed by the corporation are usually listed as the final significant figures in the highlights. A typical tabular report of the highlights of a corporation for the present and the preceding year follows:

HIGHLIGHTS OF THE YEAR

	This Year	Last Year
Net Sales.	$239,000,000	$219,000,000
Net Earnings	14,000,000	9,800,000
Net Earnings per Share	$2.95	$2.06
Dividends Paid	9,500,000	9,400,000
Dividends per Share.	$2.00	$2.00
Provision for Depreciation . . .	14,300,000	14,700,000
Expenditures for Plant and Equipment	4,300,000	5,300,000
Investment and Advances to Avis Corporation during the year.	3,100,000	3,800,000
Capital Invested in Business at the end of the year. . . .	293,700,000	288,800,000
Book Value per Share	$61.81	$60.93
Number of Shares Outstanding . .	4,751,995	4,738,805
Number of Shareholders	25,600	27,000
Number of Employees.	12,800	13,400

Portion of a tabular report

Financial Statements. , Most financial reports contain three financial statements: a balance sheet, an income statement, and a statement of retained earnings.

A *balance sheet* is a summary of the condition of a business on a specific date. It contains three kinds of information: (1) the assets (what the business owns); (2) the liabilities (what the business owes); and (3) the proprietorship (the owners' equity or net worth). On every balance sheet the total assets always equal the total liabilities plus the proprietorship. By the same token, we can also say that assets minus liabilities equal proprietorship.

An *income statement* shows the progress of the business for the fiscal period stated in the heading; for example, "For the Year Ended December 31, 1967." Below the heading, the income statement shows in convenient form the income of the business, the cost of merchandise sold, the expenses, and the net income that resulted from the operation of the business during the fiscal period. An income statement may be quickly analyzed by relating the Net Sales to each of the other items on the statement. This is accomplished by adding a column to the income statement to show the percent that each item is of Net Sales. For example, notice in the income statement on page 459 that Merchandise Inventory, January 1, is 10 percent of sales; that Gross Profit is 13.9 percent; and that Net Income After Deducting Federal Income Taxes is 1.4 percent.

A *statement of retained earnings* shows the amount of retained earnings remaining in the business at the *end* of the fiscal period. This amount is obtained by adding the amount of retained earnings at the *beginning* of the fiscal period and the amount of Net Income After Federal Income Taxes. From this total the amount of Dividends Paid to Stockholders is subtracted, leaving as a remainder the amount of the Retained Earnings. A statement of retained earnings is shown below. Samples of a balance sheet and an income statement appear on pages 458 and 459.

THE PALMER CORPORATION
Statement of Retained Earnings
December 31, 1967

Retained Earnings, January 1, 1967. . . . . $38,306
Plus: Net Income After Federal Income Taxes.   28,594
                                                          $66,900
Less: Dividends Paid to Stockholders   17,500
Retained Earnings, December 31, 1967. . . . . $49,400

A statement of retained earnings

THE PALMER CORPORATION
Balance Sheet
December 31, 1967

Assets

Current Assets:

Cash			$ 31,534
Notes Receivable			26,120
Accounts Receivable.	$96,500		
Less Allowance for Bad Debts. . . .	1,900		94,600
Merchandise Inventory.			232,600
Store Supplies			4,817
Office Supplies.			154
Prepaid Insurance.			209
Total Current Assets			$390,034

Fixed Assets:

Store Equipment.	27,000		
Less Allow. for Depr. of Store Eqp.	8,860	18,140	
Delivery Equipment	20,000		
Less Allow. for Depr. of Del. Equip	5,940	14,060	
Office Equipment	8,000		
Less Allow. for Depr. of Off. Equip	4,200	3,800	
Buildings.	75,000		
Less Allow. for Depr. of Buildings.	21,600	53,400	
Land		20,000	
Total Fixed Assets			109,400

Total Assets. $499,434

Liabilities

Current Liabilities

Notes Payable.	$ 40,900	
Accounts Payable	71,614	
Employees' Income Taxes Payable	1,490	
FICA Taxes Payable	435	
State Unemployment Taxes Payable . . .	147	
Federal Unemployment Taxes Payable . .	930	
Federal Income Taxes Payable	19,518	
Total Current Liabilities.		$135,034

Long-Term Liabilities:

Mortgage Payable (20-year, 5%)		65,000

Total Liabilities $200,034

Proprietorship

Capital Stock	250,000	
Retained Earnings	49,400	
Total Proprietorship.		299,400

Total Liabilities and Proprietorship. . . $499,434

A balance sheet

THE PALMER CORPORATION
Income Statement
For Year Ended December 31, 1967

			% of Net Sales
Income from Sales:			
Sales.		$2,111,755	100.6
Less: Sales Returns and Allowances. . $ 5,642			
Discount on Sales 6,113		11,755	.6
Net Sales.		$2,100,000	100.0
Cost of Merchandise Sold:			
Merchandise Inventory, January 1, 1967	$ 209,800		10.0
Purchases. $2,288,650			
Less: Pur. Returns and Allow .$152,900			
Discount on Purchases. . 304,850 457,750			
Net Purchases.	1,830,900		87.2
Cost of Merchandise Available for Sale	$2,040,700		97.2
Less Merchandise Inventory, Dec.31,1967	232,600		11.1
Cost of Merchandise Sold		1,808,100	86.1
Gross Profit on Sales.		$ 291,900	13.9
Operating Expenses:			
Selling Expenses:			
Delivery Expense . . . . $ 20,573			1.0
Depreciation of Delivery Equipment . 4,813			.2
Depreciation of Store Equipment. . . 2,420			.1
Miscellaneous Selling Expense. . . . 6,294			.3
Sales Salary Expense 112,894			5.4
Store Supplies Expense 15,117			.7
Total Selling Expenses	$ 162,111		7.7
Administrative Expenses:			
Bad Debts Expense. . . . . $ 1,100			.1
Depreciation of Buildings. 3,000			.1
Depreciation of Office Equipment . . 932			*
FICA Taxes 5,800			.3
Federal Unemployment Taxes 930			*
Insurance Expense. 2,037			.1
Miscellaneous Administrative Expense 3,195			.2
Office Salary Expense. 58,403			2.8
Office Supplies Expense. 1,951			.1
State Unemployment Taxes 3,139			.1
Total Administrative Expenses. . .	80,487		3.8
Total Operating Expenses		242,598	11.6
Net Income from Operations		$ 49,302	2.3
Other Income:			
Interest Income. . . . . $ 940			*
Other Expense:			
Interest Expense	2,130		.1
Net Subtraction.		1,190	.1
Net Income Before Deducting Federal Income Taxes		$ 48,112	2.3
Less Federal Income Taxes.		19,518	.9
Net Income After Deducting Federal Income Taxes		$ 28,594	1.4

*Percent is less than .1

An income statement

Tables. Tables are used in reports to present clear and concise comparisons of figures. The structure of a well-balanced table must be carefully planned before it can be typed. Your best method of planning a table is to make a penciled rough draft of it first. If you are using the backspacing centering method of tabulating, you should follow these steps in preparing a table:

1) *Machine Adjustments.*
   a. Set the paper guide so that the paper is centered when it is inserted into the machine.
   b. Clear the tab stops.

2) *Planning the Setup of the Problem.*
   a. Note the number of columns to be used and the length of the longest item in each column. An even number of spaces is usually left between columns (4, 6, 8, 10, or more, depending upon the number of columns to be used).
   b. For simple tables containing a few narrow columns, you may base your decision regarding the number of spaces between columns solely on judgment. As a rule, leave not less than 2 nor more than 12 spaces between columns.

3) *Planning the Vertical Placement.*
   a. Count the lines required to type the problem; include the main heading, the columnar headings when used, and the blank lines as well as the lines in the table itself. Allow one blank line (a double space) between the main heading and the secondary heading and after columnar headings. Allow two blank lines (a triple space) between the main heading and the columnar headings when no subheading is used. If a subheading is used, two blank lines should separate it from the columnar headings. Be sure to count the blank lines.
   b. Subtract the number of lines to be used from the total lines on the page — 66 on a standard page 11 inches long.
   c. Divide by two. The result is the number of lines to be left at the top of the paper before typing the main heading.
   d. A newer practice in centering material vertically on a full page is to center it according to *reading position*, three spaces above the actual center. To center vertically according to the reading position, determine the top margin (Steps 3a through 3c) and start three vertical spaces higher on the page.

4) *Determine the Horizontal Placement of the Columns.*
   a. *Left Margin Stop.* From the center of the page, backspace once for each two spaces in the longest line in each column. Decide upon the number of spaces to be left between columns, and backspace once for each two spaces between the columns. Set the *left margin stop* at this point. The first column will begin at this point.

b. *Tab Stops.* From the left margin, use the space bar to space forward one space for each space in the longest line in the first column and one space for each space to be left between the first and second columns. *Set the first tab stop at this point.* It is the point at which the second column will start. Continue in this manner until the tab stops for all columns have been set.

5) *Type the Columnar Headings.* The columnar headings (if used) are usually centered over the columns. One way to do this is to space forward, from the point where the column is to begin, one space for each two spaces in the longest line in the column. This will bring the machine to the center of the column; from that point backspace once for each two spaces in the columnar heading. Type the columnar heading. It will be exactly centered over the column. Another way is to add the figures from the alignment scale for the first and last strokes in the column. Dividing this sum by two will result in the center point of the column.

Reading
Position
Vertical
Spacing

TABLE 1

EARNINGS ON COMMON SHARES

Year	INCOME BEFORE TAXES		NET INCOME		Per Common Share
	Amount	% of Net Sales	Amount	% of Net Sales	
	(000)		(000)		
1966	$44,409	15.6	$22,214	7.8	$2.75
1965	42,560	15.5	21,560	7.8	2.68
1964	42,956	15.9	22,356	8.3	2.78
1963	41,866	17.0	21,336	8.6	2.65
1962	37,740	16.5	18,820	8.2	2.33
1961	26,755	16.2	11,695	7.1	1.80
1960	25,782	17.6	10,707	7.3	1.72
1959	27,622	18.5	10,886	7.3	1.75
1958	14,645	15.1	7,195	7.4	1.95
1957	9,527	11.4	5,627	6.7	1.52
1956	6,314	8.6	3,839	5.2	1.04
1955	4,714	8.2	2,857	5.0	.76
1954	3,347	7.2	2,020	4.4	.52
1953	3,154	8.4	1,756	4.7	.50
1952	2,972	9.4	1,620	5.1	.51
1951	2,705	8.8	1,271	4.2	.38
1950	3,824	12.0	1,811	5.7	.58
1949	3,416	12.6	2,014	7.4	.66
1948	2,718	13.3	1,901	9.3	.62
1947	2,522	11.1	1,833	8.8	.60

Pica   Spaces

Horizontal and vertical tabulation on a full sheet of paper

Graphs. Statistical data in business and financial reports are frequently presented by means of pictorial devices known as *graphs*, in which horizontal and vertical bars of varying lengths, solid and broken lines, sections of a circle, or symbols in a pictograph are used to represent figures or the relationships among figures.

Quantities presented in graphic form are often more easily understood and remembered than they would be if they were presented in tabular form. Sometimes the same figures in a report are presented through the use of both tables and graphs so that the reader can refer to actual amounts in the table if he wishes to, and can visualize the significance of the figures by referring to the graph.

There are many different kinds of graphs used for many different types of business data, and some of them can be prepared effectively only by using graph paper and special drawing instruments. Some graphs can be prepared in typewritten form, however, and you should know how to prepare them for typewritten reports.

Line Graph. The most widely used type of graph is the *line graph*. It is a most effective means of showing changes over a period of time, such as fluctuations in sales, costs, income, or net profits over a period of days, weeks, months, or years. An illustration of a line graph prepared on the typewriter for the following data appears on page 463.

AVERAGE DAILY SALES	1965	1966
Monday.	$5,129	$5,610
Tuesday.	4,912	5,240
Wednesday	5,307	5,433
Thursday.	4,848	4,951
Friday	5,087	5,125
Saturday.	5,410	5,577

Bar Graph. The bar graph presents quantities by means of horizontally or vertically extended bars. It is most effective in showing comparisons of a limited number of factors, generally not more than four or five.

Follow these suggestions for preparing bar graphs:

1) All the bars should be the same width. They should differ only in their length.
2) The space between bars should be at least one half the width of the bars.
3) When possible, arrange the bars in the order of their length either in ascending or descending order.
4) If the bars are arranged according to a period of time, chart the earliest period first.

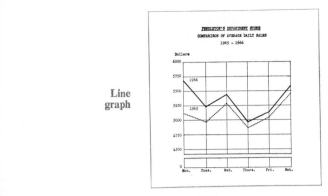

Line graph

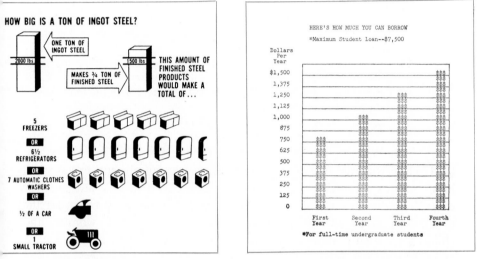

Pictograph

Bar graph

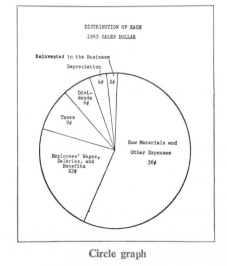

Circle graph

Part 2   Financial Reports and Statements   463

Circle Graph. The circle graph or pie chart is used to show graphically how a given quantity, represented by an entire circle or pie, is divided into parts or pieces. The size of each part shows how it compares to every other part. This type of graph is often used to show how the tax dollar is spent by the local, state, or federal government; it is also used by business firms to show how the sales dollar is spent.

You will need a compass and a protractor to construct a circle graph, and you should keep these points in mind while you construct it:

1) The parts should be shown on a percentage basis; therefore, the 360° shown as the circumference of a circle on the protractor is equivalent to 100 percent.
2) Multiply the percent for each part by 3.6. For example, 15 percent would be 54 degrees on the protractor scale. (15 × 3.6 = 54.0)
3) Arrange the parts in the order of their size, and show them in clockwise order, beginning with the largest at twelve o'clock.
4) Keep the graph simple. If you have the space, type the name of each part inside the section.
5) Type the names of the parts horizontally.

The Pictograph. Small sketches of the actual items in a report are used in a pictograph, one of the most effective ways of presenting statistical information graphically. Each drawing represents a specific amount; for example, each drawing of a dial telephone in a series may represent the installation of 100,000 telephones. Small figures of men, women, and children are used to denote population trends; passenger cars, coal cars, and oil drums are used to show the production of automobiles, coal, and petroleum.

 **Study Questions**

1. What is the purpose of a prospectus?

2. What three kinds of information are contained in a balance sheet?

3. What is the purpose of an income statement?

4. What is the first step in the planning of a typewritten table?

5. What is the minimum and what is the maximum number of spaces to be left between columns in a tabulated table?

6. How is the vertical placement of a tabulated table determined?

7. Explain what is meant by the *reading position* in vertical placement.

8. What is the most widely used type of graph?

9. What is the minimum amount of space to be left between bars in a bar graph?

10. How are the parts in a circle graph arranged?

11. At what point is the largest part of a circle graph begun?

12. How would you equate parts expressed on a percentage basis with the 360° in the circumference of a circle?

13. How is statistical information presented in a pictograph?

What Do You Think?

1. A certain business report contained a title page, letter of transmittal, table of contents, statement of conclusions and recommendations, statement of findings, and appendix. What criticism might be made of the order of presentation of the report?

2. It is frequently said that a picture is worth a thousand words. In what way would this apply to some business reports, although the reports do not have photographic reproductions?

3. To what extent should an office employee take it upon herself to redesign the form and style of business reports?

Your Personal Qualities

After she graduated from high school, Miss Roberta Butler was employed by an export-import firm as a statistical typist. She was responsible for typing all the financial statements and reports. When she was interviewed for the position, she was specifically told that her immediate superior would be Miss Hayes, the transcription supervisor.

Miss Butler became quite disturbed when Miss Davis, the typist at the next desk, gave her instructions about the typing of the financial statements because Miss Davis' instructions conflicted with those given by Miss Hayes.

Every afternoon Miss Davis gave Miss Butler some of her own work. Miss Davis said that she had too much work, but she made a practice of taking a lunch hour that frequently extended to two hours.

Questions: 1. Should Miss Butler tell Miss Hayes that Miss Davis gave her conflicting instructions?

2. Suppose Miss Butler does not tell Miss Hayes. How might she handle the situation by herself?

How's Your English?

Read the section on numbers in Appendix E and then indicate which is the correct way of writing the numbers in the following:

1. Eleven (or 11) men worked on the installation.

2. Enclosed is our check for two dollars (or $2).

3. He paid seventy-five cents (or 75 cents) for the call.

4. A monthly salary of $250.00 (or $250) was paid for the job.

5. There are 20 (or twenty) girls in the office.

6. As many as ten (or 10) of our two-hundred ninety (or 290) employees are over 65 (or sixty-five).

7. Eighteen hundred (or one thousand eight hundred)

8. In your letter of May 20 (or 20th) (or twentieth)

9. The stores on Fifth (or 5th) Avenue have beautiful window displays.

10. Twenty-seven (or 27 —) 78 Street

11. Ninety-two (or 92) 4 (or Fourth) Avenue

12. 8:00 p.m. (or eight p.m.)

Office Work

1. Type the following information in the form of a title page. Use a border design.
The Financial Condition of the Powers Development Company, Tuscaloosa, Alabama, prepared by Darwin K. Marshall, Certified Public Accountant, June 30, 19--.

2. Type the following information in the form of a full-page table of contents:

Section I.   Introduction, page 1
Section II.   Balance Sheet, page 2
               Schedule 1 — Notes Receivable, page 4
               Schedule 2 — Accounts Receivable, page 5
               Schedule 3 — Notes Payable, page 7
               Schedule 4 — Accounts Payable, page 8
Section III.   Income Statement, page 10
Section IV.   Conclusions, page 12

3. Prepare a vertical bar graph similar to the one on page 463 to show a comparison of the figures given below. Use the typewriter in preparing the graph.
Title: HERE'S HOW MUCH YOU CAN BORROW
Subtitle: **Maximum Student Loan — $7,500
First Year $375; Second Year $500;
Third Year $625; Fourth Year $750.
**For part-time undergraduate students.

4. Prepare a circle graph similar to the one on page 463 to show the DISTRIBUTION OF INCOME FOR 1965. The percentages are: Manufacturing Cost, 52%; Selling Expense, 22%; Administrative Expense, 16%; Net Profit, 10%.

5. Select an appropriate heading for the following article; set it up and type it on a half sheet of paper:
    Hundreds of new companies come into existence each year — and go out of existence in a short time, too. What makes businessmen fail? Here are the seven major reasons.

1. They don't sell enough to get over the initial hump.

2. They lack experience.

3. They are poor administrators — keep skimpy records, let operating costs get out of hand, overcommit themselves on fixed assets.

4. They start with too little capital.

5. They choose poor locations.

6. They give credit too loosely.

7. They just don't tend to business enough.

Source: *Changing Times*

UNIT 12 | Typing Tasks

PART 3:

Legal Papers, Minutes, and Resolutions

"Please type the architect's contract so that Mr. Brown can take it with him on the eleven o'clock flight," may be your employer's request. Or he may say, "Please fill out the lease so that we can mail it out this afternoon." So, you, a typist for a manufacturing, industrial, or service firm, may find yourself busily engaged in typing legal forms. The amount of legal work you will perform will vary in different offices. If you are employed by an attorney or in the legal department of a large firm, you may devote most of your time to the drafting, typing, and proofreading of legal papers. If you are employed by a real estate firm, an insurance company, or a bank, you may spend almost half of your time preparing legal documents. In other types of offices, however, the legal work that you will be asked to do may be limited to the occasional typing of a legal form. In any event, as a prospective office employee you should be familiar with the preparation and purpose of each of the more widely used legal papers.

LEGAL PAPERS

Typewritten Legal Papers. Some legal documents are completely prepared on the typewriter; others are finished by typing specific information on printed legal forms. The typed documents may be written on ordinary paper of the standard 8 1/2″ by 11″ size. Many legal documents, however, are typed on legal-size paper which is 8 1/2 inches wide and may vary from 13 to 15 inches in length. This paper may have printed left and right margin lines. The left margin rule is usually a double line; the right margin, a single line. In typing material on legal paper with printed margin rules, you should set the margin stops on your typewriter so that the margins of the typewritten material will be at least two spaces within the printed margin lines. If paper without printed margin rules is used for typing a legal paper, you should allow a 1 1/2-inch left margin and a 1/2-inch right margin. Minimum margins of 2 inches at the top and 1 inch at the bottom are usually allowed. You should prepare two or more carbon copies of all legal papers so that each person affected by the paper will have a copy, including at least one copy for the lawyer and one for the court record.

Spacing. Typewritten legal documents are usually double spaced, but you may type some of them, including wills and affidavits, single spaced. A type of legal paper may be purchased with consecutive numbers printed down the page at the left of the printed left margin line. The number "1" is approximately two inches from the top edge and indicates the position of the typewritten title. The other numbers indicate the positions of the typewritten lines of material and make possible easy reference to any particular part of the legal paper when its contents are under discussion. If the legal paper used does not contain these printed numbers, and if your employer wants to have them on the completed document, it will be a simple matter for you to type them as you type the document.

Erasures. Because a legal paper states the rights or privileges and duties or obligations of the parties who sign it, and later may be submitted in a court of law as evidence, you should prepare each paper accurately and proofread it carefully. You may erase and correct some errors in typing legal papers; others may not be corrected. If the error and erasure affect only one or two letters in a relatively unimportant word, you may erase and make the correction. If, on the other hand, the error you make involves a word which might have a bearing upon the meaning of that part of the contract, substituting the word *may* for *must*, for example, or if an error involves an amount of money, the erasure should not be made, but the complete paper should be retyped. In some cases, however, such corrections may be made if the corrected paper is initialed by all parties. If you are in doubt, you should ask your employer if it is necessary to retype the legal paper or if it is permissible to erase and correct the error.

Numbers, Dates, and Titles. Quantities in legal documents are usually written in both words and figures, as:

A scholarship of one thousand dollars ($1,000)
Under the terms of the will he will receive five thousand (5,000) dollars
A twenty- (20) year mortgage
Fifty (50) shares of Woolworth common stock
Five (5) percent interest

Dates are written in several forms. No one form, however, is more legal than another; therefore, there is no reason why you should not type a date in a legal form as you would type it in a letter. Variations are:

Two-inch top
margin for
all pages

Testator's
name in all
capital
letters

Double
spacing

Copy typed
within
marginal
rules

Introductory
words in a
paragraph
usually typed
in all capi-
tal letters

LAST WILL AND TESTAMENT OF WILLIAM H. STEWART

I, WILLIAM H. STEWART, a resident of the City of Trenton, State of New Jersey, declare this to be my Last Will and Testament, and revoke all former Wills and Codicils.

FIRST: I declare that I am married, and my wife's name is MARJORIE DAVIS STEWART; I have two children now living, DAVID H. STEWART and STEPHEN C. STEWART.

SECOND: I direct that my just debts and funeral expenses be paid.

THIRD: I give, devise, and bequeath to my wife, MARJORIE DAVIS STEWART, all the rest of my estate both real and personal and wheresoever situated, which I may own or have the right to dispose of at the time of my decease.

FOURTH: I appoint as Executrix of my Will my wife, MARJORIE DAVIS STEWART, to serve without bond. In the event she is unable or unwilling to serve, or to complete such service as Executrix, then it is my wish that DR. HOWARD PATTON, a long-time friend of mine, shall be appointed as Executor.

This Will and Testament is subscribed by me on the eighth day of December, 19--, at Trenton, New Jersey.

William H. Stewart

The foregoing instrument, consisting of one page, was subscribed on the date which it bears, by the testator, WILLIAM H. STEWART, and at the time of subscribing was declared by him to be his Last Will and Testament; and we, at the testator's request and in his presence and in the presence of each other, have signed such instrument as witnesses.

Jane Nicholson residing at 703 Bunker Hill Avenue
Trenton, New Jersey

Ida May Turner residing at 513 New York Avenue
Elizabeth, New Jersey

On this, the third day of November, 19—
This 16th day of June in the year 19—
This sixteenth day of June, in the year of our Lord, one thousand
nine hundred and ——————

Personal titles — Mr., Mrs., Miss — are not used with names in legal documents. Professional titles are not ordinarily used either.

Printed Legal Forms. As an office worker you may prepare a legal document by typing pertinent information on a printed legal form. Standard forms for bills of sale, deeds, leases, mortgages, and wills may be purchased in stationery stores. It should be noted, however, that important legal documents should be checked by a competent lawyer before they are executed. This is particularly true of deeds and wills. A *deed* is a formal written instrument by which title to real property is conveyed from one person to another. All the details of the transaction should be approved by a lawyer before the deed is registered with the proper government agency.

A *will* is a legal document in which a person provides for the distribution of his property after his death. The person who makes the will is the *testator* (man) or *testatrix* (woman). He may designate an *executor* (man) or *executrix* (woman) to *probate* his will — prove its validity to the court for the purpose of carrying out its provisions. The drawing of a will is a technical matter and should be entrusted only to a qualified attorney.

When material is to be typed on a line that also includes some printed matter, you should use the variable line spacer on the typewriter to be certain that the filled-in matter has the same base line as the printed matter. If the space allowed is greater than that needed, the necessary words should be centered in the space. If the item of information that is filled in is important, such as a sum of money, the space that remains on either side of the item after it is typed should be filled in with hyphens. This device eliminates the possibility of figures, letters, or words being added later to change the meaning of the typewritten insertion.

The same margins that are set for the printed matter should be kept for the typewritten matter. When one or more carbon copies are prepared, the position of the printed matter on the separate copies must be checked carefully so that the typewritten additions will appear in the proper places on all copies. Unless this check is made, it may happen that the typewritten matter on a carbon copy will be written over some of the printed matter, and the copy will be illegible. If a number of copies are to be made, it is recommended that an envelope opened at the flap be placed over the top of the assembled copies before they are inserted into the typewriter and that a paper clip be fastened on them after they have been inserted in the machine and the envelope has been removed to assure constant correct alignment of the carbon copies.

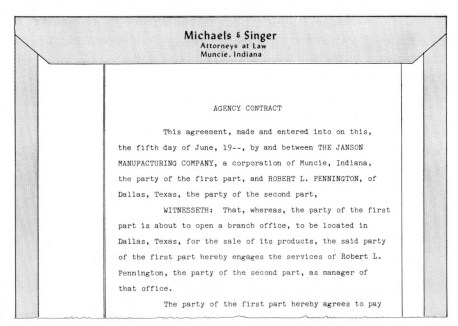

Michaels & Singer
Attorneys at Law
Muncie, Indiana

AGENCY CONTRACT

This agreement, made and entered into on this,
the fifth day of June, 19--, by and between THE JANSON
MANUFACTURING COMPANY, a corporation of Muncie, Indiana,
the party of the first part, and ROBERT L. PENNINGTON, of
Dallas, Texas, the party of the second part,

WITNESSETH: That, whereas, the party of the first
part is about to open a branch office, to be located in
Dallas, Texas, for the sale of its products, the said party
of the first part hereby engages the services of Robert L.
Pennington, the party of the second part, as manager of
that office.

The party of the first part hereby agrees to pay

Portion of a legal document with a backing sheet

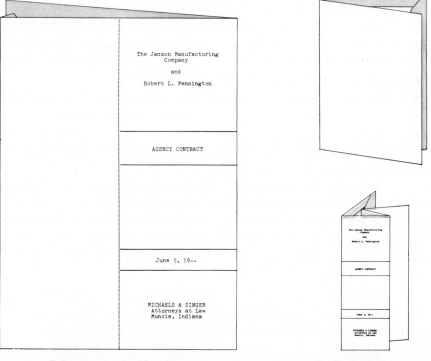

The Janson Manufacturing
Company

and

Robert L. Pennington

AGENCY CONTRACT

June 5, 19--

MICHAELS & SINGER
Attorneys at Law
Muncie, Indiana

Indorsement on backing sheet

Folding a legal document

Typical Legal Documents. An examination of a simple contract, a lease, an affidavit, and a power of attorney, four of the legal papers that are frequently prepared in a business office, will show you the typing problems connected with the preparation of legal papers.

Simple Contract. A *contract* is an agreement that can be enforced at law. It creates legal rights and responsibilities. It may be either oral or written; however, some contracts, such as those for the purchase of real estate, must be in writing. Before you type a contract, you should check to see that it includes the following essential information:

1) The date and the place of the agreement
2) The names of the parties entering into the agreement
3) The purpose of the contract
4) The duties of each party
5) The money, services, or goods given in consideration of the contract
6) The signatures of all the parties

The illustration on page 471 shows parts of a simple contract prepared on legal paper with printed margin lines. Note particularly the space between the printed margin lines and the left and right margins of the typewritten material, the spacing (triple spacing between the title and the first line, double spacing thereafter), the use of all capitals for certain words in the contract, and the punctuation. Many special types of contracts are typewritten in this form. Be sure to type enough copies of each contract so that each party will have one for his files.

Lease. A contract that establishes the relation of landlord and tenant is a *lease*. This relationship exists when one person, the tenant or *lessee*, under an express or implied agreement, is given possession and control of the real property of another, the landlord or *lessor*. The consideration given by the tenant is *rent*.

The lease shown on page 473 illustrates the typing problems involved in completing a printed form for a legal document. Observe the even base lines where typewritten material has been inserted, the method of indicating the amount in words and figures, and the completion of certain words by adding letters that keep the sentences containing those words consistently in plural form.

Affidavit. An affidavit is a written declaration made under oath that the facts set forth are sworn to be true and correct. It must be sworn to before a proper official, such as a judge, justice of the peace, or a notary.

Power of Attorney. An executive may give an experienced employee his *power of attorney* — the power to act for him. It may authorize the

This Lease Witnesseth:

THAT John E. Hansen and Evelyn M. Hansen, husband and wife,

HEREBY LEASE TO Charles L. Burroughs

the premises situate in the City of Miami in the County of

Dade and State of Florida described as follows:

Building to be used as a restaurant located at 232 Collins Avenue, Miami, Florida,

with the appurtenances thereto, for the term of ten (10) years commencing

June 1, 19 --, at a rental of Two hundred fifty (250)

dollars per month , payable monthly

SAID LESSEE AGREE S to pay said rent, unless said premises shall be destroyed or rendered untenantable by fire or other unavoidable accident; to not commit or suffer waste; to not use said premises for any unlawful purpose; to not assign this lease, or underlet said premises, or any part thereof, or permit the sale of his interest herein by legal process, without the written consent of said lessor ; to not use said premises or any part thereof in violation of any law relating to intoxicating liquors; and at the expiration of this lease, to surrender said premises in as good condition as they now are, or may be put by said lessor , reasonable wear and unavoidable casualties, condemnation or appropriation excepted. Upon nonpayment of any of said rent for thirty days, after it shall become due, and without demand made therefor; or if said lessee or any assignee of this lease shall make an assignment for the benefit of his creditors; or if proceedings in bankruptcy shall be instituted by or against lessee or any assignee; or if a receiver or trustee be appointed for the property of the lessee or any assignee; or if this lease by operation of law pass to any person or persons; or if said lessee or any assignee shall fail to keep any of the other covenants of this lease, it shall be lawful for said lessor s their heirs or assigns, into said premises to re-enter, and the same to have again, re-possess and enjoy, as in their first and former estate; and thereupon this lease and everything herein contained on the said lessor S ' behalf to be done and performed, shall cease, determine, and be utterly void

SAID LESSORS AGREE (said lessee having performed his obligations under this lease) that said lessee shall quietly hold and occupy said premises during said term without any hindrance or molestation by said lessors, their heir or any person lawfully claiming under them.

Signed this first day of May A. D. 19 --

IN THE PRESENCE OF:

Louis K. Whitfield   John E Hansen
Robert R. Crowell   Evelyn M. Hansen
                        Charles L. Burroughs

Statement of a notary public

employee to sign checks and other legal documents for him. The power of attorney specifies the acts which the agent is authorized to perform for the principal. It may be granted for an indefinite period, for a specific period, or for a specific purpose only. It must be signed by the principal and should be notarized.

Notarizing Legal Papers. Many legal documents are notarized. This means a signed statement is added by a notary public (a public official authorized by the state) to show that the paper has been signed in the notary's presence and that the signers have sworn that they are the same persons referred to in the document.

Do not be surprised if your employer wishes you to become a notary public. In larger offices one of the employees usually acts in this capacity. In an office building containing a number of small offices, an office worker employed in one of them may act as a notary public for all offices in the building.

The laws governing the procedure for becoming a notary public differ in the various states, but the procedure is not complicated and is usually handled by the businessman or executive who is interested in having an employee act in this capacity. In many states an application accompanied by statements that show that the applicant is a citizen and a resident of the state, of the required age, and of good character is submitted to the governor's office. If the application is granted, the notary public secures a notary's seal, which is a metal, hand-operated instrument that embosses on a legal paper the design of a seal containing the name of the notary. A notary's commission is for a limited period of time, usually for two years, but it may be renewed.

MINUTES

In our busy business world, with an executive's responsibility covering a wide range of activities, with the need for interchange of ideas, for mutual understandings, for decision making based not on one man's point of view but on many, meetings are frequent and necessary. What you do in planning and in taking minutes can improve the effectiveness of a meeting. If you are called upon to take and type minutes regularly, a knowledge of parliamentary procedure will be most helpful. This can be acquired by reading either Robert's *Rules of Order*, the standard guide for presiding officers and parliamentarians, or Sturgis' *Standard Code for Parliamentary Procedure*.

Minutes are the official records of meetings and the action taken in them. Minutes should be characterized by a clear, concise presentation of factual information, properly arranged. Since minutes are frequently used for reference, every detail included in them should be complete and accurate.

The planning for a committee meeting, conference, or official meeting is usually done by an employee in the chairman's office. If you are asked to plan for a meeting, you will be expected to reserve the meeting room and to notify the members well in advance of the meeting. A reasonable time before the meeting each member should receive an agenda, which is a schedule of business to be covered at the meeting. After the meeting, as a general rule, the minutes are edited for omissions and corrections by the chairman or the recording secretary before they are duplicated and distributed to the members.

Securing Information for Minutes. If you are asked to take the minutes of a meeting, you should have the following information before the meeting starts: the name of the organization, the place, the date, the time of the meeting, and the agenda. You should know, or obtain, the names of those who should attend the meeting. With such a list you can quickly check attendance and thereby know the names of those present and absent.

You should have available at the meeting the minutes of the previous meetings, particularly those of the last meeting, and any figures, letters, bulletins, reports, and legal papers that might be referred to in the course of the meeting. This foresight on your part will help to keep the meeting running smoothly. The presiding officer or committee chairman may suggest to you the data that should be available at the meeting. Under no circumstances should you leave the meeting to obtain information unless the chairman asks you to do so.

As the meeting progresses, you should take notes on the points that you think are of importance and interest, and, insofar as possible, you should couple the discussion and the resolutions with the names of those who participate. The names of those who make and second each motion should be recorded. Motions and resolutions, whether passed or not, should be recorded word for word because future proceedings are often governed by the interpretation placed on the wording.

Arranging the Minutes. Minutes are usually arranged in accordance with the customary steps in parliamentary procedure:

1) Calling the meeting to order — duty of the presiding officer
2) Checking of attendance — duty of the secretary, either orally or by observation
3) Reading and approval of the minutes of the previous meeting (If they have been distributed in advance of the meeting, they are usually approved without being read.)
4) Treasurer's report — copy given to secretary
5) Reports of standing committees — copies given to secretary
6) Reports of special committees — copies given to secretary
7) Unfinished business
8) New business
9) Date of next meeting
10) Time of adjournment

Typing of Minutes. The completeness of the typed minutes depends upon the formality of the meeting. The minutes of an informal meeting are brief and cover only the essential points; the minutes of a formal meeting are typed in detail according to a routine pattern. In most sets of minutes, the following points are covered:

1) The name of the group, committee, organization, or business; the time, date, and place of the meeting, and whether it is a regular meeting or a special meeting.
2) The names of the presiding officer, secretary, and those present (also those absent if that can be determined). In the case of a meeting of a large organization, only the number of members present need be recorded to indicate that there was a quorum (the minimum number of members necessary for conducting the business of the group).
3) The reading of the minutes of the previous meeting, and the approval, amendment, or correction of those minutes.
4) The reports of the committees or persons who previously were assigned special duties.
5) The unfinished business and the action taken on it.
6) The new business, the discussion, and the action taken.
7) The time, date, and place of the next meeting.
8) The time of adjournment.
9) The signature of the secretary or one responsible for the minutes.

MINUTES OF THE MEETING

of the

E X E C U T I V E   B O A R D

Administrative Management Society

e and
ce of
ting

The regular monthly meeting of the Executive Board was held on Friday, October 31, 19--, in the conference room of the Palmer Mailing Company. The meeting was called to order at 5:30 p.m. by the President, Robert C. Ellis.

endance

Present: Virginia E. Allen, Robert C. Ellis, Henry A. Foster, Eleanor J. Gage, Helen E. Henderson, Martha M. Lester, James P. Sullivan, and Henry J. Townsend.

oval of
ites

The minutes of the September meeting, which had been mailed to all of the members of the Board, were approved.

asurer's
ort

The Treasurer, Henry A. Foster, presented his report showing a balance of $1,536.75 on October 24. He was authorized to pay a bill for $168.75 from the Standard Printing Company.

rt of
iding
ittee

Miss Allen reported for the Publicity Committee. She said that the release on the Salary Report had been prepared and would be given to the press on November 15.

rt of
ial
ittee

The Special Committee on Corollary Information reported that the average workweek had been reduced from 40 hours to 37½ hours and that two firms had a basic workweek of less than 35 hours. Only one firm reported a workweek of over 40 hours.

nished
ness

The Secretary submitted two additional estimates for the cost of tabulating the Salary Report. After extended discussion, the members of the Board voted unanimously to accept the bid of $125 submitted by the Reynolds Company.

ness

Mr. Foster moved that the cost of the Salary Report for nonmembers be increased to $5. The motion was carried.

of
Meeting

The next meeting of the Board will be held on Friday, November 28, in Parlor A of the Statler Hotel.

The meeting was adjourned at 6:45 p.m.

Respectfully submitted,

Helen E. Henderson

Helen E. Henderson
Secretary

Correction of Minutes. When minutes are being typed, they should be corrected, even rewritten if necessary, to be certain that they are as nearly perfect as possible when they are read at the next meeting. At the meeting it is sometimes necessary to make corrections in the minutes. If only a few words are affected, lines may be drawn through the incorrect words and the proper insertions made above them. If more than a few words are affected, lines may be drawn through the sentences or paragraphs to be corrected and the corrections written on a new page. The page number of the corrections should be indicated on the original minutes. The minutes should not, however, be rewritten after they have been read and approved at the meeting.

RESOLUTIONS

During the course of a meeting, you may be given the responsibility of typing a resolution. Resolutions are framed to express appreciation, to do honor, to indicate action, to express regret, to offer congratulations, to commemorate, or to present a program of action.

"WHEREAS" and "RESOLVED," which are characteristic introductory terms in formal resolutions, are typed in capital letters. The first word after "WHEREAS" is not capitalized unless it is a proper name. No comma follows "WHEREAS" unless one is necessary to make the sentence clear. "RESOLVED" or "RESOLVED further" is usually followed by a comma and the first word after it is capitalized.

Some resolutions are less formal. In an informal resolution the terms "WHEREAS," "RESOLVED," and "Therefore be it" are eliminated, and the facts or events leading up to the resolution are stated simply and directly. For example, "The following resolution was unanimously adopted:

> The Trustees of Martin College accept with thanks the sum of $25,000 representing a gift from the friends and colleagues of the late Harriet Simons for the establishment of the *Harriet Simons Scholarship Fund.* The income from the invested principal is to be used to assist able and needy high school graduates who have selected Martin College for their undergraduate studies. The Fund is to be administered by the Dean of Students."

Study Questions

1. In what ways does legal paper differ from ordinary paper?

2. What are the minimum margins usually allowed on legal papers?

3. What is the advantage of using legal paper on which the lines are numbered?

4. What type of error may be erased and corrected in a legal paper?

5. How are quantities usually written in legal papers?

6. How should words be filled in on a printed legal form?

7. What is meant by the term *notarized*?

8. What are minutes?

9. Why must every detail in the minutes be accurate and complete?

10. In what divisions are minutes usually arranged and what specific points are covered?

11. What is an agenda?

12. If you were asked to take the minutes of a meeting, what information should you have before the meeting?

13. What should you bring to the meeting if you are asked to take the minutes?

14. How may the minutes be corrected?

15. What is the purpose of a resolution?

What Do You Think?

1. Is a typing error in a legal paper more serious than a similar error in an important business letter?

2. In your opinion, is it an advantage or a disadvantage for an office worker to be a notary public?

3. Why do you believe the person taking minutes should not leave a meeting, even during the discussion, unless instructed to do so?

4. What should you do if a resolution or a motion is presented in such a way that you are not able to take it down verbatim? What procedure might be used to avoid this difficulty?

5. What should you do if you are taking the minutes and do not know the name of the person making or seconding a motion and you have been instructed to keep a record of the names of such persons?

6. If a motion is not seconded or if it is not approved, why should the text of the motion be included in the minutes?

7. To what extent should the office employee assigned to take minutes of a meeting be familiar with the rules of parliamentary procedure for conducting meetings?

Your Personal Qualities

Just before lunch Miss Irene Harper completed the typing of a legal form for a lease covering the rental of floor space in a building owned by her employer. You and Irene are joined at lunch by Marion Baler, an office worker from another firm. Marion leads the conversation around to the lease and asks Miss Harper pointed questions about the annual rent and about other items covered by the lease.

Miss Baler and Miss Harper have been friends for several years. Miss Harper tells Miss Baler about many of the terms and conditions of the lease.

Question: Had you been in Miss Harper's place, how would you have handled the situation?

How's Your English?

After reading about titles in Appendix E, write the following names with the correct title for each:

Stanley F. Ingalls
Elsie C. Field (unmarried woman)
Adele G. Findley (wife of Morton D. Findley)
Frances W. Folsom (widow of Joseph W. Folsom)
Keller and Arnold (law partners)
Alice and Margaret Linton (sisters — both unmarried)

Josephine C. Meredith (wife of Dr. Samuel G. Meredith)
Cecil J. Overbrook (minister) and wife
Arthur F. Ralston and Jordan L. Meader (two ministers to whom a letter is being addressed jointly)
Lawrence J. Ronson, Junior
Albert Lee Pennbrook the Third
Frederick W. Rogers (M.D. and secretary of the local medical association)

Office Work

1. From the following brief notes, write the minutes for a meeting of the Holten High School Business Club:

Regular meeting — Business Club— Room 26 — 3:15 p.m — November 17, 19--.

James Ingram, pres., in charge. All members present. Minutes read — approved.

Inez Carson, treas. — cash balance, $42.75.

Mildred Pearce, chairman of membership com. — Sam Nugent and David Engle applied for membership — eligible — pd. dues.

Sally Seymour, ch. of special events com., considering project for raising money — annual school carnival. Recommended exhibit of old and modern office equipment — tickets 25 cents. Discussion — feeling exhibit would not produce enough revenue. Motion by Donna Thomas — club sponsor booth at carnival — ice cream and candy. Motion seconded — Lawrence Steele — vote 26 to 14.

Charles Becker, ch. of program com. — introduced Miss Phyllis Chapman, former student and grad. of dept. — talked on "How My Secretarial Training in School Helped Me in My First Job."

Date of next meeting — Dec. 15 at 3:15 p.m. — Room 26.

Motion made and seconded — meeting adjourned at 4:30 p.m.

2. Type the following power of attorney on legal paper, making one carbon copy. Use the current date. If ruled legal paper is not available, rule in ink the necessary vertical lines on regular 8 1/2" x 11" paper.

NOTE: *A power of attorney is a formal written document used for the appointment of an agent.*

Know All Men by These Presents, That I, Ernest W. Dunn, of the City of Beverly, County of Essex, State of Massachusetts, have made, constituted, and appointed, and by these presents do make, constitute, and appoint, Merrill J. Martin, of the City of Salem, County of Essex, State of Massachusetts, my true and lawful attorney, for me and in my name, place, and stead, to sign my name to any and all checks drawn on the First National Bank against my deposits in the same, for the purchase of the property situated at the corner of State Avenue and Congress Street, known as the Randolph property; and I hereby ratify and confirm all that my said agent or attorney will lawfully do, or cause to be done, in connection with this purchase. (¶) IN WITNESS WHEREOF, I have hereunto set my hand and seal this_____day of____ ————————in the year of our Lord one thousand nine hundred and————.

_____

Witnesses:

_____

_____

State of Massachusetts⎫ ss.
County of Essex ⎭

The above-signed authority, Ernest W. Dunn, personally appeared before me on the_____day of _____in the year of our Lord one thousand nine hundred and _____, and in due form achnowledged the attached instrument to be his act and deed and declared that it may be recorded as such.

(SEAL)   _____
            Notary Public

3. Type the following partnership agreement on legal paper, making two carbon copies. Use the current date. If ruled legal paper is not available, rule in ink the necessary vertical lines on regular 8 1/2″ x 11″ paper.

NOTE: *The written contract of partners in a business is known as the partnership agreement.*

PARTNERSHIP AGREEMENT

This contract, made and entered into on this_____day of_____ _____, 19____, by and between LYLE J. POOR, of San Francisco, California, FRED W. EATON, of Sacramento, California, and LAWRENCE A. GEDNEY, of Fresno, California, (¶) WITNESSETH: That the said parties have on this day formed a partnership for the purpose of engaging in and conducting a wholesale hardware business under the following stipulations, which are made a part of this agreement: (¶) FIRST: The said partnership is to continue for a term of ten (10) years from the date hereof. (¶) SECOND: The business is to be conducted under the firm name of Northern California Wholesale Hardware Company, at Tenth and Mission Streets, San Francisco, California. (¶) THIRD: Each partner to this agreement shall, at the signing of these presents, pay into the partnership the sum of One Hundred Thousand (100,000) Dollars in cash. (¶) FOURTH: Each partner is to devote his entire time and attention to the business and is to engage in no other business enterprise without the written consent of the other partners. (¶) FIFTH: Lyle J. Poor will have general supervision of the business; Fred W. Eaton will have charge of the sales, credits, and collections; and Lawrence A. Gedney will have supervision of the buying and of the accounting records. In addition, each partner is to attend to such other duties as shall be deemed necessary for the successful operation of the business. (¶) SIXTH: Each partner is to receive a salary of Nine Thousand Six Hundred (9,600) Dollars a year, payable in installments of Eight Hundred (800) Dollars in cash on the last business day of each month. At the end of the annual fiscal period, the net profit or the net loss after salaries have been allowed is to be shared equally. (¶) SEVENTH: No partner is to withdraw assets in excess of his share of the profits without the written consent of the other partners. (¶) EIGHTH: During the operation of this partnership, no partner is to become surety or bondsman for anyone without the written consent of the other partners. (¶) NINTH: The investment and all transactions completed in the operation of the business are to be recorded in books of account in accordance with standard accounting procedure. These books of account are to be open for the inspection of each partner at all times. (¶) TENTH: At the conclusion of this contract, unless it is mutually agreed to continue to operate the business under a new contract, the assets of the partnership, after the liabilities are paid, are to be divided in proportion to the net credit to each partner's capital account on that date. (¶) IN WITNESS WHERE-OF, the parties aforesaid have hereunto set their hands and affixed their seals on the day and in the year first above written.

Lyle J. Poor

Fred W. Eaton

Lawrence A. Gedney

Witnesses:

Office Work Assignments

48: Power of Attorney

If printed forms for a power of attorney are available, complete the original copy and one carbon copy of that form by adding those parts of the following information that are printed in boldface type. Use the current date.

If printed forms are not available, type an original copy and one carbon copy of the following power of attorney:

KNOW ALL MEN BY THESE PRESENTS:

That **I, David O. Westley, of the City of Phoenix, County of Maricopa, State of Arizona,** have made, constituted, and appointed, and by these presents do make, constitute, and appoint **Michael D. Morris, of the City of Phoenix, County of Maricopa, State of Arizona,** my true and lawful attorney, for **me** and in **my** name, place, and stead, **to act for me in connection with my business of wholesale groceries at Phoenix: 1. To draw checks against my account in the Peoples Trust and Savings Bank; 2. To indorse notes, checks, drafts, or bills of exchange that may require my indorsement for deposit as cash or for collection in said bank; 3. To accept all drafts or bills of exchange that may be drawn upon me;** giving and granting unto **my** said attorney full power and authority to do and perform all and every act and thing whatsoever requisite and necessary to be done in and about the premises, as fully to all intents and purposes as **I** might or could do, if personally present, with full power of substitution and revocation; hereby ratifying and confirming all that **my** said attorney or his substitute shall lawfully do, or cause to be done, by virtue hereof. (¶) IN WITNESS WHEREOF, **I** have hereunto set **my** hand, this_____day of_____ in the year one thousand nine hundred and_____.

Signed and acknowledged in the presence of us:

49: Lease

If printed forms for a lease are available, complete an original copy and one carbon copy of that form by adding those parts of the following information that are printed in boldface type. Use the current date.

If printed forms are not available, type an original copy and one carbon copy of all parts of the following lease:

THIS LEASE WITNESSETH:

That **M. L. Rolfe and A. N. Franklin, partners,** Hereby Lease To **James Wright** the premises situated in the City of **Seattle** in the County of **King** and State of **Washington,** described as follows: **Building to be used as a garage located at 345 West Center Street, Seattle, Washington,** with the appurtenances thereto, for the term of **five (5) years** commencing **July 1, 19--,** at a rental of **One Hundred Fifty (150)** Dollars per **month** payable **monthly.**

Said Lessee Agrees to pay said rent, unless said premises shall be destroyed or rendered untenantable by fire or other unavoidable accident; to not commit or suffer waste; to not use said premises for any unlawful purpose; to not assign this lease, or underlet said premises, or any part thereof, or permit the sale of **his** interest herein by legal process, without the written consent of said lessors; to not use said premises or any part thereof in violation of any law relating to intoxicating liquors; and at the expiration of this lease, to surrender said premises in as good condition as they now are, or may be put by said lessors, reasonable wear and unavoidable casualties, condemnation or appropriation excepted. Upon nonpayment of any of said rent for **ten (10)** days after it shall become due, and without demand made thereof; or if said lessee or any assignee of this lease shall make an assignment for the benefit of **his** creditors; or if proceedings in bankruptcy shall be instituted by or against lessee or any assignee; or if a receiver or trustee be appointed for the property of the lessee or any assignee; or if this lease by operation of law pass to any person or persons; or if said lessee or any assignee shall

fail to keep any of the other covenants of this lease, it shall be lawful for said lessors, **their** heirs or assigns, into said premises to re-enter, and the same to have again, repossess and enjoy, as in **their** first and former estate; and thereupon this lease and everything herein contained on the said lessors' behalf to be done and performed shall cease, determine, and be utterly void.

Said Lessors Agree (said lessee having performed **his** obligations under this lease) that said lessee shall quietly hold and occupy said premises during said term without any hindrance or molestation by said lessors, **their** heirs or any persons lawfully claiming under **them.**

Signed this_____day of _____, A. D. 19____.

_____

_____

_____

STATE OF **WASHINGTON**
KING COUNTY. ss.

This day, before me, a **notary public** in and for said county, personally came **M. L. Rolfe and A. N. Franklin, partners, and James Wright,** the parties to the foregoing Lease, and acknowledged the signing thereof to be their voluntary act.

Witness my hand and official seal this_____day of_____, A. D. 19__.

(SEAL)   _____

50: Warranty Deed

If printed forms for a warranty deed are available, complete an original copy and one carbon copy of that form by adding those parts of the following information that are printed in boldface type. Use the current date.

If printed forms are not available, type an original copy and one carbon copy of all parts of the following warranty deed:

KNOW ALL MEN BY THESE
PRESENTS:

That **I, William W. Fredericks, of Rochester, in the County of Strafford and State of New Hampshire** for and in consideration of the sum of **One Dollar and other valuable consideration** to **me** in hand before the delivery hereof, well and truly paid by **James McGuire, of said Rochester,** the receipt whereof **I** do hereby acknowledge, have granted, bargained and sold, and by these presents do give, grant, sell, alien, enfeoff, convey and confirm unto the said **James McGuire, his** heirs and assigns, forever, **a certain tract of land situated in Wakefield, in the County of Carroll and State of New Hampshire, on the easterly side of Route 16, so-called, the same being the highway from Wakefield to North Wakefield, bounded as follows:**

Beginning on the easterly sideline of said highway at a stone wall at land formerly of B. Hull, **thence by said wall easterly and thence northerly by wall and by stakes and stones and by trees marked "line" to land formerly of M. C. Denicore at Blake field, so-called; thence easterly by said field to land formerly of John C. Peak and the Peter Carroll lot, so-called, formerly owned by John W. Matthews; thence southerly by said Carroll lot to the Peter Carroll place, as it was once called; thence westerly by said Carroll lot and George L. Williams lot, as it was once called, to the aforesaid highway; thence northerly by said highway to the bounds begun at, the same containing forty (40) acres, more or less.**

For title reference see deed of Edward Daniels to Albert Swain dated July 30, 1914, recorded Carroll County Records, Book 160, Page 306, the grantor hereof having obtained his title by devise under the will of the late Albert Swain, see Carroll County Probate Records.

To have and to hold the said premises, with all the privileges and appurtenances to the same belonging, to **him** the said **James McGuire** and **his** heirs and assigns, to **their** and **their** only proper use and benefit forever, and **I** the said **William W. Fredericks** and **my** heirs, executors and administrators do hereby covenant, grant and agree, to and with the said **James McGuire** and **his** heirs and assigns, that until the delivery hereof **I am** the lawful owner of the said premises, and **am** seized and possessed thereof in **my** own right in fee simple; and have full power and lawful authority to grant

and convey the same in manner aforesaid; that the premises are free and clear from all and every incumbrance whatsoever, except _____ and that **I** and **my** heirs, executors and administrators, shall and will WARRANT and DEFEND the same to the said **James McGuire** and **his** heirs and assigns, against the lawful claims and demands of any person or persons whomsoever.

And I, **Josephine Fredericks,** wife of the said **William W. Fredericks,** in consideration aforesaid, do hereby relinquish my right of dower in the before-mentioned premises.

And we, and each of us, do hereby release, discharge, and waive all such rights of exemption from attachment and levy or sale on execution, and such other rights whatsoever in said premises, and in each and every part thereof, as our Family Homestead, as are reserved, or secured to us, or either of us, by Chapter 260, Revised Laws of the State of New Hampshire, or by any other statute or statutes of said State.

IN WITNESS WHEREOF, **we** have hereunto set **our** hands and seals this **23rd** day of **January** A. D. 19--.

———————————————

———————————————

STATE OF NEW HAMPSHIRE
County of **Strafford**

On this **23rd** day of **January** 19--, before me, the undersigned officer, personally appeared **William W. Fredericks and Josephine Fredericks** known to me (or satisfactorily proven) to be the persons whose names **are** subscribed to the within instrument and acknowledged that they executed the same for the purposes therein contained.

IN WITNESS WHEREOF, I hereunto set my hand and official seal.

(SEAL)

———————————————

———————————————
Title of Officer

UNIT 13 | Financial Duties

PART 1:

The Checkbook and the Bank

Have you thought that you might be handling bank accounts of hundreds, thousands, or hundreds of thousands of dollars? As with most of your other duties, the size and type of firm for which you work will determine the extent of your contact with banks. For example, if you are employed by a large firm with a separate accounting department, your dealings with banks may be limited to handling the personal financial affairs of your immediate employer. On the other hand, if you are employed by a firm engaged primarily in financial transactions, whether it is a large brokerage house or a small collection agency, dealing with banks may be one of your most important daily tasks.

When you deal with a bank or handle money in any other capacity for your firm, you must take care that all transactions are completed accurately and promptly and that all information about them is kept strictly confidential.

Bank Accounts. You know that business firms prefer to use the services of commercial banks rather than endure the risks that are always present when large sums of money are kept on the premises. Funds are deposited in commercial accounts, regular checking accounts, and special checking accounts, and checks are drawn against these accounts to make payments. Generally, cash is used to pay only minor business expenses.

Payment by check is usually preferred because the canceled check is ultimately returned to the one who wrote it and serves as a receipt for payment. Furthermore, a person receiving a check can easily transfer it to someone else or deposit it in his own bank account. When a check is deposited in an account, the bank in which it is deposited will collect the amount from the bank on which the check was drawn.

If you are handling bank accounts, it will be your responsibility to make deposits, draw checks, keep the checkbook stubs up to date, indorse checks, and reconcile bank statements. You may even have to take

485

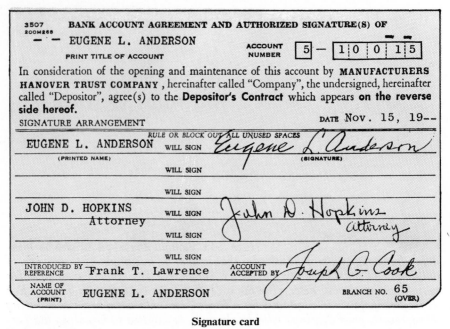

Signature card

the initial step of opening the bank account. Let's look at these various duties to see how you can handle them.

Opening a Bank Account. When you open a personal bank account, the bank may want to have you identified and introduced by one of its depositors. Ordinarily, however, the bank will ask for one or more references — preferably a reference from another bank where you may have had an account, or a reference from your present employer. This request is made so that the bank may check the references to be reasonably sure that it is dealing with a responsible person who will use the account properly.

Before your account is opened you will be asked to fill out a *signature card*, which will be kept on file at the bank. The signature which you use to sign your checks should consistently agree with your signature on the card. If you have used a first name and a middle name on the signature card, *Mary Alice Downs*, for example, you should not use initials, as *M. A. Downs*, when you sign your checks.

When more than one person is to sign checks for a firm — the president, vice-president, and the treasurer, for example — all must fill out signature cards. When you are asked to handle an active account for a businessman, a letter must be presented to the bank authorizing your signature, and you will have to fill out a signature card before you will be permitted to sign checks. Frequently, the letter must be accompanied by a power of attorney giving you authority to act for the businessman; and,

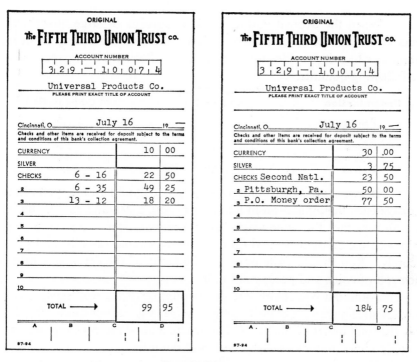

ORIGINAL		
The FIFTH THIRD UNION TRUST co.		
ACCOUNT NUMBER		
3 2 9 — 1 0 0 7 4		
Universal Products Co.		
PLEASE PRINT EXACT TITLE OF ACCOUNT		
Cincinnati, O. July 16 19—		
Checks and other items are received for deposit subject to the terms and conditions of this bank's collection agreement.		
CURRENCY	10	00
SILVER		
CHECKS 6 – 16	22	50
2 6 – 35	49	25
3 13 – 12	18	20
4		
5		
6		
7		
8		
9		
10		
TOTAL ⟶	99	95

ORIGINAL		
The FIFTH THIRD UNION TRUST co.		
ACCOUNT NUMBER		
3 2 9 — 1 0 0 7 4		
Universal Products Co.		
PLEASE PRINT EXACT TITLE OF ACCOUNT		
Cincinnati, O. July 16 19—		
Checks and other items are received for deposit subject to the terms and conditions of this bank's collection agreement.		
CURRENCY	30	.00
SILVER	3	75
CHECKS Second Natl.	23	50
2 Pittsburgh, Pa.	50	00
3 P.O. Money order	77	50
4		
5		
6		
7		
8		
9		
10		
TOTAL ⟶	184	75

Deposit tickets

when you sign checks for him, you sign your name and add "Attorney" or "Attorney in Fact" after your name. Most banks will print up checks with one of the above titles printed on them.

Making Deposits. Before making a bank deposit for your firm, you must list all of the amounts in detail on a deposit slip. This form is supplied at the bank's writing counters, and you should have a supply of them on hand so that you may complete and double-check all entries before you go to the bank with your deposits. A deposit slip is usually prepared in duplicate or triplicate form. Some banks, however, use a four-part slip. Typical deposit slips are illustrated on this page. This is the information you must fill in: the name of the depositor, the date, and the items to be deposited. The deposit may consist of currency (paper money), silver (coins), indorsed checks, and/or money orders. There is a place on the deposit slip for showing the amounts of each by category. In listing checks, you may identify them in one of three ways:

1) By transit number which appears in fraction form in the upper righthand corner of the check and is assigned to each bank by The American Bankers Association — see check on page 489.
2) By name, if the bank is a local one.
3) By the city and state of out-of-town banks.

When the deposit you are making consists of large quantities of coins and bills, the bank prefers to have you put the money in money wrappers which it provides for its depositors. Pack coins in paper rolls in the following quantities:

Denomination	Number of Coins to a Roll	Total Value of Coins in Roll
Pennies	50	$ .50
Nickels	40	2.00
Dimes	50	5.00
Quarters	40	10.00
Halves	20	10.00

If you have many bills of different denominations, you should package each denomination in amounts of $50, $100, and so on. Be sure that all bills face the same way. Wrap a bill wrapper — a narrow paper strip with the amount printed on it — tightly around the bills and glue it securely. You should write or stamp the name of the depositing firm on each roll of coins and package of bills.

Although you should list the amount of each check separately on the deposit slip with the transit number, some large corporations may show only the total under "Checks" and attach an adding machine tape showing the individual amount of each check and the total.

Now you are ready to make your trip to the bank. When you present the deposit slip together with the cash and the checks to the bank teller, he will check the items against the deposit slip. In some banks the teller then places the deposit slip in a machine which stamps the name of the bank and the date on it. One of the copies of the deposit slip is then returned to you as your deposit receipt. In other banks a receipt of deposit is recorded on the teller's machine as the amount of the deposit is registered, and this receipt is given to you instead of a copy of the deposit slip.

Writing Checks. As you know, a check is a written order directing a bank to pay out the money of a depositor; therefore, it should be written with extreme care. You should always type checks or write them in ink — never in pencil. The following suggestions will be helpful:

1) *Number* each check, if numbers are not printed on them, and be sure that the number of the check corresponds with that of the check stub.

2) The *date* of the check must be the exact date that it is being written. Do not postdate a check; that is, date it ahead with the hope that there will be sufficient funds in the account by that time to cover the check.

3) Write the *name of the payee*, the person who is to receive the money, in full. If you are not sure of the correct spelling, try to verify it in the telephone directory or from previous correspondence. Omit titles such as Mr., Mrs., Miss, Dr., or Prof.

4) Write the *amount* of the check in large, bold figures next to the printed dollar sign and sufficiently close together to prevent the insertion of other figures. In spelling out the amount, start at the extreme left, capitalize the first letter only, and express cents as fractions of one hundred:

> Three hundred thirty-four no/100- - - - - - - - - - - -*Dollars*
> One thousand five hundred fifty 75/100- - - - - - -*Dollars*

If you should write a check for less than a dollar, precede the spelled-out amount with the word "Only," and cross out the printed word "Dollars" as:

> Only eighty-nine cents- - - - - - - - - - - - - - - - - - - -*Dollars*

5) Fill in all *blank spaces* before and after the name of the payee and after the written amount with hyphens, periods, or a line.

6) You may wish to write the *purpose* of the check, such as "In Payment of Invoice #3960," in the lower left corner of the check.

7) *Do not erase* on a check. If you should make an error in writing a check, write the word "Void" across the face of both the check and the check stub. Save the voided check and file it in numerical order with the canceled checks when they are returned by the bank.

8) *Do not sign blank checks.* Anyone can fill them out and cash them.

9) *Do not make a check payable to "Cash"* unless you plan to cash it at once.

10) *Write legibly.* An illegible signature creates difficulties at the bank and is no protection against forgery.

A firm issuing a large number of checks usually will print the amount on each check with a checkwriter, a machine that perforates and inks the amount into the check paper to prevent any alteration.

The Check Stub. Don't run the risk of overdrawing an account! Fill out the check stub *before* you write a check. Otherwise, you may forget to fill it out and to deduct the amount from the account balance. You will then have no record of the check except a blank stub until the bank returns your canceled checks or notifies you that your account has been overdrawn.

Check with stub

The check stub is bound into the checkbook to the left of the blank checks. It provides space for recording the original balance, new balances, deposits, and information about each check you write. This information includes the check number, the date, the name of the payee, the amount, and the purpose. The amount should be deducted from the previously recorded account balance and the new balance entered on the stub.

Duplicate Checks. Your firm may prefer to prepare checks in duplicate with a ball-point pen, a typewriter, or some other writing machine instead of taking the time to fill out regular check stubs. The original copy of each check is sent out, but the duplicate copy is retained for reference purposes and to serve as a basis for entering the transaction in the company records.

Indorsing Checks. When your firm gives a check to a person for his services, he cannot cash, deposit, or transfer his rights in that check until he indorses it. The checks your firm receives must also be indorsed. The indorsement is made by signing the check across the back at the top of the left end. There are different types of indorsements which you will see and use. The most common types of business indorsements are restrictive, full or special, and blank indorsements. A knowledge of indorsements will help you safeguard checks.

A *restrictive indorsement* allows you to send an indorsed check safely through the mail. It transfers the ownership for a specific, stated purpose. For example, the following words may be written above the signature of the indorser: "Pay to the order of the Guilford National Bank for deposit." If you indorse a check in this way, it can only be deposited in your account. Since the check cannot be cashed by anyone else, there is little danger if the check is misplaced, lost, or stolen.

Indorsements are ordinarily written in ink, but restrictive indorsements made with rubber stamps are frequently used for depositing checks. This type of indorsement is satisfactory because it makes the checks payable only to the account of the depositor and would not benefit anyone who might obtain a rubber stamp and attempt to use it improperly.

> Pay to the order of
> Guilford National Bank
> for deposit
> to the account of
> The Apex Corporation

> Pay to Guilford National Bank
> for collection.
>
> THE APEX CORPORATION

Restrictive indorsements

Indorsement in full	Blank indorsement

An *indorsement in full*, or a special indorsement as it is sometimes called, shows the name of the person to whose order the check is being transferred. For example, the words: "Pay to the order of Lawrence Trent," may be written before the indorser's signature. A check indorsed in this way cannot be cashed by anyone without Lawrence Trent's signature. Therefore, you may send a check indorsed in this manner through the mail without danger in case of loss.

A *blank indorsement* consists only of a signature across the back of the check. It makes the check payable to anyone who may possess it. You should use this type of indorsement only when you plan to cash or deposit a check immediately. It is not a satisfactory indorsement for a check that is being sent through the mail or for a check that could be lost or misplaced because the check can be cashed by anyone who holds it — even if he has no right to it.

Stopping Payment on Checks. One of the firm's employees calls to say that he has lost his paycheck. You must call the bank immediately to tell them to stop payment on the check. If the check has not already cleared, the bank will refuse payment when it is presented. Payment can be stopped if a check is lost or stolen, if it has been made out incorrectly, if it represents payment for goods or services which have been canceled, or for any of a number of other reasons.

You must give the following information to stop payment on a check: the name of the drawer (the one who signed the check), the date of the check, the amount of the check, and the name of the payee. You should also send a confirming letter to the bank immediately or fill out a stop-payment form supplied by the bank. This form gives the bank written instructions not to cash the check described.

Overdrafts. An overdraft occurs when a depositor draws a check on an account in which he does not have sufficient funds to cover the full payment. This frequently happens when checks that have not been entered and deducted on the check stubs are cashed or when an error is made in computing or recording the checkbook balance on the stubs. An occasional overdraft is embarrassing but excusable; but if you should consistently overdraw your employer's account, you will jeopardize his credit standing with the bank.

With personal checking accounts, an overdraft may very well result in a check's being returned marked "Insufficient Funds," and a charge made by the bank for handling the overdraft. Thus, overdrafts are expensive as well as embarrassing.

Reconciliation of the Bank Statement. Now you are ready to learn about the last duty in connection with your banking transactions. Sometime during each month you will receive a bank statement and the canceled checks that the bank paid out of your firm's account during the previous month. Some banks send such a statement early in the month to all of their customers. Other banks use a system whereby customers' statements are sent out at different times of the month; that is, statements might be mailed on the tenth of each month to customers whose surnames begin with the letters A–H, on the twentieth, I–Q, and so forth. The account balance at the beginning of the period is listed at the top of the statement, followed by the date and the amount of each deposit and withdrawal, and the service charge deducted by the bank for handling the account. The account balance at the end of the period is shown on the statement. This banking service permits you to check the accuracy of your checkbook with the bank records and to file the canceled checks as proof of the firm's payments.

After you have received the canceled checks and the bank statement, you should compare the final balance on the bank statement with the checkbook balance and account for the difference. This process of accounting for the difference is called *reconciling the bank statement*. For the convenience of their depositors, many banks print a reconciliation form on the back of the monthly statement. The following steps should be taken systematically to reconcile an account:

1) Compare the amount of each canceled check with the amount listed on the bank statement. This step will disclose any error made by the bank or the depositor in recording a check. Place a check mark beside each verified amount.
2) Arrange the canceled checks in numerical order.
3) Compare the returned checks with the stubs in the checkbook. Place a check mark on the stub of each check returned.
4) Make a list of the outstanding checks — those that have not been paid and returned. Include on the list the number of each outstanding check and the amount.
5) Add the amounts of outstanding checks and deduct the total from the balance shown on the bank statement.
6) Subtract the amount of the service charges listed on the bank statement from the checkbook balance.
7) After the service charge has been deducted from the checkbook balance, the remaining amount should agree with the balance shown on the bank statement after the total of the outstanding checks has been deducted.

Here is an example of a reconciliation:

RECONCILIATION OF BANK ACCOUNT

June 30, 19—

Balance as shown on bank statement..	$530.00		Balance as shown by checkbook.......	$375.50
Less checks outstanding:			Less June service charge.........	1.50
No. 143. $50.00				
No. 144. 16.00				
No. 147. 90.00	156.00			
Adjusted bank balance........	$374.00		Adjusted Checkbook balance....	$374.00

Now, you have seen the duties you will be expected to perform in reference to either your employer's or your firm's banking transactions. They are not difficult, but they demand accuracy, neatness, dependability, and efficiency on your part.

Study Questions

1. As an office worker why should you understand banking procedures?
2. Why is actual cash seldom used in business transactions?
3. Enumerate the duties of an office worker who handles a bank account.
4. How is a bank account opened?
5. What is the purpose of a signature card?
6. A deposit slip contains what information?
7. Present ten suggestions that will enable you to write checks correctly.
8. What is a checkwriter?
9. When should the check stub be filled in, and what information should be on it?
10. For what purposes are duplicate checks used?
11. Name the various types of indorsements and explain the use of each.
12. Under what conditions should payment be stopped on a check, and what procedure should be followed?
13. What causes overdrafts and why should they be avoided?
14. What information is included on a bank statement?
15. How is a reconciliation of the bank statement made?

What Do You Think?

1. Under what circumstances would you recommend that indorsement in full be used?

2. If you were going into a bank to cash a check, which form of indorsement would you use?

3. If you were indorsing a check to be sent through the mail, what form of indorsement would you use?

4. If you were unable to go to your bank and were planning to send checks through the mail for deposit, which form of indorsement would you use?

5. Who, if anyone, loses when payment on a check is stopped?

6. Need the records that are kept by a clerk be as accurate as those kept by a bookkeeper who devotes his full time to that type of work?

7. What measures may be taken to make it less likely that a check could be altered?

8. Some persons believe that making a bank reconciliation is too much trouble. What is your reaction to this attitude?

Your Personal Qualities

By a carefully designed system of manipulation, Mr. Howard A. Tuttle is defrauding the firm for which he works of considerable sums.

Miss Dever, who has been working for Mr. Tuttle for several months, discovers the situation and realizes that she has unwittingly been a party to the fraudulent practice.

Question: What should she do?

How's Your English?

Read Appendix E on titles, capitalization, and numbers. Indicate any improper usage and suggest corrections in the following:

1. Mr. John Henry Wilbur, Esq.

2. Enclosed is a check for twenty seven dollars.

3. The Sixth Corps will parade on Tuesday.

4. The County of Essex in the state of Massachusetts

5. The spanish speaking countries of the western hemisphere

6. Dr. James G. Mullin, Ph.D.

7. He is secretary of the chamber of commerce.

8. 92 w. 57 st.

9. We employ 692 people, fifty of whom work in the office.

10. He used 175 — 5 cent stamps.

Office Work

1. The checking account balance of the Art Craft Company on the first of March was $932.15. During the month it deposited $2,530.15 and issued checks totaling $2,777.81. Checks amounting to $298.60 have not been cashed. What is the checkbook balance at the end of the month? What is the bank balance?

2. With a committee of fellow students, visit a local bank, interview one or more of the bank officers, and procure copies of the more commonly used forms provided for use of customers of the bank. Prepare a written report on bank services to business firms. Be prepared to present the report orally to the class. Also make a bulletin board display of the forms you collected and be prepared to explain the use of each form.

Office Work Assignments

51: Checks, Deposit Slips, and Check Stubs

You are employed by Johnson & Sears and have been authorized to write and sign the checks and keep the checkbook during the absence of the employee who ordinarily does it. During this period, the following checks were written and deposits made. Write the checks, prepare the deposit slips, and complete the check stubs.

Nov. 10. Balance according to last check stub, $1,073.51.

11. Check No. 532, Washington Square Service Company, $169.25, for invoice of November 2.

12. Check No. 533, Howard A. Johnson, $50, for personal use.

13. Deposit: currency, $14; silver, $2.25; checks — First National Bank, $59.70; Syracuse, New York, $212.75; Cincinnati, Ohio, $193.80.

15. Check No. 534, J. W. Combs Co., $549.62, for invoice of November 5.

15. Check No. 535, City Electric Co., $13.95, for electric bill.

16. Check No. 536, Franklin Paper Co., $42.50, for wrapping paper and cartons.

18. Deposit: currency, $15; checks—Central Trust Company, $221.40; First National Bank, $129.62; Rochester, New York, $279.33.

52: Reconciliation of a Bank Statement

During the month of June the following checks were issued by the Fuel Oil Products Company:

No. 146	$ 16.10	No. 162	$ 46.81
No. 147	4.31	No. 163	5.00
No. 148	4.24	No. 164	8.50
No. 149	10.23	No. 165	105.25
No. 150	166.81	No. 166	65.00
No. 151	204.68	No. 167	191.84
No. 152	15.31	No. 168	84.56
No. 153	4.06	No. 169	2.04
No. 154	.52	No. 170	254.68
No. 155	18.93	No. 171	27.13
No. 156	16.77	No. 172	19.00
No. 157	22.54	No. 173	118.34
No. 158	18.30	No. 174	125.00
No. 159	281.69	No. 175	50.00
No. 160	346.06	No. 176	6.60
No. 161	2.85	No. 177	8.14

No. 178	$ 14.67	No. 182	$219.00
No. 179	178.34	No. 183	1.92
No. 180	101.47	No. 184	10.13
No. 181	11.12		

The check-stub balance on June 1 was $932.15. The deposits for the month were as follows: $401.68; $664.00; $593.45; $432.18; $187.67; $251.17.

The bank statement for the month of June showed a balance of $981.59. A service charge of $1.50 had been deducted. All of the checks written were returned with the bank statement except checks No. 173, 179, 183, and 184.

Prepare the reconciliation of the bank statement.

UNIT 13 | Financial Duties

PART 2:

Making Cash Payments

"*Here is a C.O.D., Miss Ryan,*" *the deliveryman says. Miss Ryan must pay cash to get the package. So, as one of her regular office duties, she makes a cash payment for her firm. One office worker may be responsible for making cash payments from the petty cash fund for such small items as postage due, collect telegrams, and messenger fees. Another may also make out and mail checks to pay the monthly bills and statements received for telephone and other services. And still another girl, if she is employed in a small office, may be expected to handle the petty cash fund, pay the monthly bills, and verify and pay the invoices received from other firms.*

As a prospective office worker, you should be thoroughly familiar with the correct procedure to be followed in making all types of cash payments.

The Petty Cash Fund. The petty cash fund is for incidental expenses and is ordinarily handled by one person, usually the receptionist or some other office worker. In case you are asked to handle the fund, you should understand how it is established, how payments are made from it, and how the fund is replenished. In the average office, about $25 is set aside for the petty cash fund; however, the amount may range from $10 to $100, depending upon the demands normally made upon the fund. The money in the fund is usually kept locked in a metal cashbox in the desk of the person handling it, and is placed in the office safe at night.

Establishing the Fund. To establish a petty cash fund:

1) Write a check payable to "Petty Cash" for the amount to be maintained in the fund, $25 for example.
2) Have the check signed by an authorized person and cashed at the firm's bank.
3) Place the money in the petty cash box.

CARSON & WHITE

PETTY CASH RECEIPT

No. _3 11_   Date _November 10_ 19 _—_

Received of Carson & White $ _2 75_

Two 75/100 _____ Dollars

For _Miscellaneous store supplies_

Account Charged: _Store supplies_ Signed _J. D. Dean_

Petty cash receipt

Making Payments from the Fund. When that C.O.D. package comes, you should immediately make out a receipt which the parcel deliveryman signs when you pay him. Each time that you make a payment from the petty cash fund, you should make out a receipt for the amount and have it signed by the person receiving the money. The receipts should be numbered consecutively. Each should show the date, to whom the payment is to be made, and the purpose of the payment. The signed receipts should be kept in the petty cash box. At all times the cash on hand plus the total amount of the receipts should equal the original amount set aside to maintain the fund. You should get a book of receipts which can be filled out quickly and easily as part of your usual procedure. Be sure to get a receipt each time you make a payment because *you* are accountable for the money, and receipts are proof of your proper use of the fund.

Replenishing the Fund. The petty cash fund should be replenished whenever the amount of cash gets low. To replenish the fund, follow these steps:

1) Add all receipts and count the cash in the petty cash box.
2) "Prove" the petty cash fund by adding the amount of cash on hand to the total of all petty cash receipts. The sum should equal the amount originally set aside for the fund. An illustration of a proof follows:

Total of petty cash receipts.....................	$22.04
Petty cash on hand.............................	2.96
Total..	$25.00

3) Prepare a summary report of petty cash expenditures (illustrated above) and attach the receipts for them.
4) Write a check payable to "Petty Cash" for the total amount of the receipts shown in the summary report ($22.04 in the illustration on page 499).

DATE		EXPLANATION	RECEIVED		PAID	
19 Nov.	1	Balance	25	—		
	3	Telegram				75
	30	Postage stamps			3	—
	30	Totals	25	—	23	65
	30	Balance			1	35
			25	—	25	—
	30	Balance	1	35		
	30	Check No. 315	23	65		

Simple petty cash book

DATE		EXPLANATION	RECEIPTS		PAYMENTS		DISTRIBUTION OF PAYMENTS				
							OFFICE SUPPLIES	STORE SUPPLIES	ADVERTISING	MESSENGER	MISCEL- LANEOUS
19 July	1	Balance	25	—							
	2	Ad on program			1	75			1 75		
	3	Ink			1	50	1 50				
	6	Immediate delivery of a sale				35				35	
	8	Cleaning office			2	50					2 50
	10	Miscellaneous supplies			1	25		1 25			
	12	Telegram				55					55
	13	Postage stamps			2	—	2 —				
	15	Immediate delivery of a sale				50				50	
	16	Ad in school program			3	—			3 —		
	17	Miscellaneous supplies				75		75			
	19	Twine for store			1	35		1 35			
	21	Registered letter				35					35
	23	Cleaning office			2	50					2 50
	26	Delivery of contract				50				50	
	27	Entertaining a customer			2	50					2 50
	29	Miscellaneous supplies				69	69				
	31	Totals	25	—	22	04	4 19	3 35	4 75	1 35	8 40
	31	Balance			2	96					
			25	—	25	—					
	31	Balance	2	96							
	31	Check No. 475	22	04							

Columnar petty cash book

SUMMARY REPORT OF PETTY CASH

July 1 to 31, 19--

Balance on hand, July 1		$25.00
Expenditures:		
Office Supplies	$4.19	
Store Supplies	3.35	
Advertising	4.75	
Messenger	1.35	
Miscellaneous	8.40	
Total expenditures		22.04
Balance on hand, July 31		$ 2.96

Report of petty cash

5) Submit the summary report and the attached receipts to your employer with the check payable to the petty cash fund.
6) After your employer has signed the check, cash it and place the money in the petty cash box, thus replenishing the fund.

Paying Monthly Bills. To pay the monthly bills for such services as light, rent, and telephone, you will draw ordinary checks upon a commercial account. Before writing the checks, you should verify the brought-forward balances of all bills to be sure that you are not being charged for service for which you have already paid. Your last check might have been received after the bill had been prepared, so the payment was not deducted from the new bill. Your records will tell you what has been paid and when.

Voucher Checks. Look at the illustration of the voucher check below to see what is different about it. Your company may adopt the

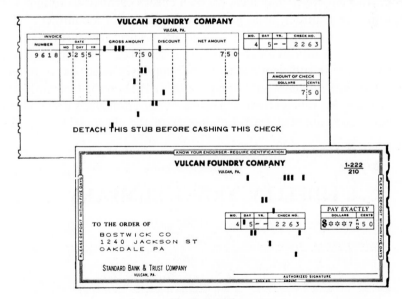

Voucher check

use of voucher checks instead of regular checks because by using this type of check it can indicate on the face of the check, or on a detachable stub, the specific invoice, bill, or service for which payment is made. When the invoices are being paid, the invoice number, the amount of the invoice, the amount of the discount, and the net amount of the check are recorded in a special block at the left end of the voucher check or on the stub.

You should check the accuracy of all computations on an invoice — the extensions, additional charges, discounts, and the net amount — before preparing a check in payment. When you receive a voucher check with a detachable stub, the stub should be detached and filed before the check is deposited.

Other Forms for Cash Payments. There are other forms you can use to make cash payments. In addition to ordinary checks and voucher checks, the various forms that are used in making cash payments include:

1) Certified check
2) Bank draft
3) Cashier's check
4) Postal and express money orders

Certified Check. Sometimes a check must be *certified* before it will be accepted by a firm. If your employer does not know the credit standing of a new customer, he may ask that a certified check accompany the order. Since a stop-payment order cannot be issued against a certified check, your employer may have his own checks certified to submit with a bid, to bind a contract, or to guarantee fulfillment of a contract.

If your employer asked you to get a check certified, you would take it to a bank official and ask to have it certified. After investigating to see that there are sufficient funds in your employer's account to cover the check, the bank official would stamp CERTIFIED on the face of the check and then add his official bank signature. Your employer's account would be immediately charged with the amount of the check. This amount is

No. 2311	DES MOINES, IOWA	May 21, 19--

FIDELITY TRUST COMPANY 34-13/764

Pay to the order of Edward J. Templeton---------------------------------$7000.00

Seven thousand no/100--DOLLARS

CERTIFIED
FIDELITY TRUST COMPANY
Cashier
J. L. Harvey
Jay Robbins

Certified check

Bank draft

transferred by the bank to a special account to be used in paying the check when it is returned. The bank, and not the drawer of the check (in this instance, your employer), becomes responsible for the payment of the certified check. Because the bank guarantees payment of a certified check, any payee will gladly accept it. Like an ordinary check, however, it should be cashed or deposited promptly.

Bank Draft. Another type of cash payment is the bank draft. If you are ordering paper from Nome, Alaska, you may send a bank draft to bind the contract. A bank draft is an order drawn by one bank on its deposit in another bank, to pay a third party. Since this type of draft, like a certified check, has the bank's assurance of payment, it is accepted more freely than an ordinary check. In the illustration, The Omaha National Bank is the drawer; the Guaranty Trust Company of New York, the drawee, is the bank that must pay the draft; and the payee is C. A. Lester. The cashier of The Omaha National Bank, W. B. Pullen, merely signs for the drawer.

You may purchase a bank draft by presenting cash or your employer's check to a bank. The cashier will make out the draft, which is merely a bank's check drawn on its deposits in another bank. Ordinarily, banks make a small charge for bank drafts.

A bank draft is usually used to remit to an individual or firm in a distant city who might not care to accept an ordinary check from a person or firm unknown to them. Although bank drafts and certified checks should be passed with equal confidence, business firms prefer bank drafts.

Cashier's Check. Another type of cash payment you or your employer might use is the cashier's check. A cashier's check is written by a bank on its own funds. It serves somewhat the same purpose as a bank draft. It differs in that it is drawn by the cashier on funds in his own bank, whereas a bank draft is drawn upon deposits in another bank.

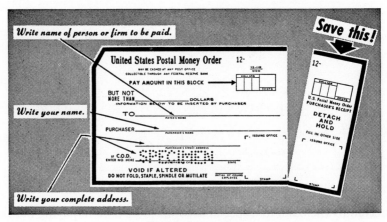

Postal money order

When you wish to pay a person who is unaware of your credit standing or to cash a check in a distant city where you are not known and your personal check might be questioned, you could use a cashier's check.

You need not be a depositor in a bank to purchase a cashier's check. You may give the cashier your employer's check or cash to cover the amount of the cashier's check. He will then write a check for the specific amount, payable to the payee whom you designate. A small charge is usually made by the bank for issuing a cashier's check.

Postal and Express Money Orders. Finally, you may make remittance by sending domestic and international postal money orders or express money orders. You may send a money order to your salesman in Seattle or Honolulu. Domestic postal money orders may be purchased at all post offices, branches, and stations in the United States and its possessions; international postal money orders, at many of them. Express money orders may be purchased at any American Express or any REA Express office.

If you are sending an international money order, you must fill out a printed application form. None is required for a domestic money order or an express money order. When you purchase a domestic money order, you are required to enter on the appropriate lines the name of the payee, your own name, and your address. The fees for domestic postal money orders and American Express money orders are the same; the fees for international money orders are double the domestic fees. Postal money orders are limited to $100, but two or more may be purchased to make up any desired amount. For example, to send $450, four for $100 and one for $50 are required; to send $500.06, six money orders are necessary. If equally convenient, it normally would be better to send one cashier's check or American Express Money Order for the full amount.

To cash a postal money order, take it to any money order office within thirty days after issue; after that time, the orders will be paid only at the office designated on the order.

You may cash express money orders either at express offices or at banks.

Study Questions

1. What is a petty cash fund?
2. How is a petty cash fund established?
3. Why should a receipt for each payment from the petty cash fund be kept?
4. What steps are necessary to have the petty cash fund replenished?
5. Describe a voucher check.
6. How and why would your employer have a check certified?

7. Name the three parties to a bank draft.

8. What is a cashier's check and under what circumstances might you use one?

9. Where and in what amounts may postal money orders be procured?

10. Where may express money orders be purchased?

What Do You Think?

1. Why should you exercise care in maintaining a petty cash fund?
2. Describe circumstances in which a businessman might use:

    a. a bank draft
    b. a cashier's check
    c. a postal money order
    d. an express money order

Your Personal Qualities

Rosanne Morrow, a clerk in the office of Mr. Stanley Walker, president of the National Jewelers' Association, was asked to serve at the registration desk at the Association's convention. It was her duty to collect the registration fees.

At the end of the day, she had taken in $1,395 in cash, and checks amount-ing to $415. She was most anxious to send the fees to the national treasurer in Cleveland. The checks presented no problem as she could send them by mail, but the large amount of cash presented a real problem. She considered the possibilities of sending the money itself through the mail and of sending the amount by postal money order or cashier's check. She finally decided to send the money by cashier's check. Her employer told her that she had made the right decision.

Question: 1. What problems would be created by sending the money through the mail? by sending the money by postal money order?

2. Why do you think that Mr. Walker approved of sending the money by cashier's check?

 How's Your English?

After reading about capitalization in Appendix E, indicate the words in the following sentences that should be capitalized:

on wednesday i met with a committee that was planning a picnic. it will be held on july fourth at the glenwood city park located on the banks of the ohio river. mr. james j kay will act as chairman of the committee. he is vice-president of the peoples savings bank of watertown. he is a westerner by birth but has made his home in the state of kentucky for many years. mr. kay has invited charles de forest, of brookfield township, to take charge of the sporting event of the day. de forest is a vice-president of the howard hardware company and is treasurer-elect of the watertown rotary club. a group of policemen from division g will control traffic at the picnic grounds, and a reporter from the watertown herald will be on hand to give the affair good news coverage.

 Office Work

Which of the following types of remittances would you send under each of the following conditions? Give the reason for your choice in each case.

  Postal money order
  Check
  Bank draft
  Express money order
  Certified check

1. We desire to pay in full an account with a firm in Denver with whom we have done business for seven years. The amount is $156.86.

2. It is necessary to send a salesman his salary while he is on the road.

3. We order a few items from The Chicago Implement Company. They desire payment with the order, for we have never done business with them before.

4. We have made a bid on a construction job in our city and have been asked to accompany the bid with a $100 check to show our good faith and to bind the bid.

Office Work Assignments

53: Petty Cash Summary and Receipts

The following transactions pertain to the petty cash fund kept by the Jones Drug Company during the months of September and October:

Sept. 1 Check No. 175 for $25 was cashed to establish a petty cash fund.

3 Paid Bill Smith $6 for cleaning the store and office.

8 Paid Mr. Jones $6 for entertaining a customer.

13 Paid the Lake Supply Company 95 cents for miscellaneous supplies.

17 Paid Johnny Stone 75 cents for delivering merchandise.

24 Paid the Royal Repair Company $8 for repairs to a typewriter.

29 Paid the Stevens Hardware Company 50 cents for a duplicate key for the office.

30 Check No. 221 for $22.20 was cashed to replenish the petty cash fund.

Oct. 4 Paid the Peters Stationery Company $1.15 for miscellaneous office supplies.

10 Paid Bill Smith $6 for cleaning the store and office.

17 Paid Central High School $5 for advertisement in school paper.

22 Paid the Jackson Paper Company 85 cents for miscellaneous store supplies.

29 Paid the REA Express $6.75 for collect charges on merchandise purchased.

31 Check No. 256 for $19.75 was cashed to replenish the petty cash fund.

Fill out a page from a simple petty cash book similar to the one at the top of page 498. If receipt forms are available, write a receipt for each of the payments made during the month of September.

UNIT 13 | Financial Duties

PART 3:

Payroll Work

The procedure followed in the handling of the payroll in any business depends upon the size of the organization and whether or not the employees are paid by the hour, week, month, or on a piece-rate scale. As a general rule, the executives and the office and administrative groups of a business are paid their salaries on a weekly, biweekly, or a monthly basis. Most of the other employees are paid by the hour. Some employees are paid by the piece; that is, they are paid so much per unit or job completed. For example, a man who puts heels on shoes in a shoe factory is known as a "heeler," and he is paid a certain amount for every pair of heels that he applies.

Time Reports. The time an employee works during a given day must in some way be recorded. Some organizations use a time clock, which will be described later, while others use a less formal system of keeping records of days and hours which a person has worked or has not been at work.

On page 507 is shown a copy of a time report used in an office where the secretarial and clerical staff are paid on a weekly basis. You will note that the form provides double blocks for each day — the upper block for regular or lost time and the lower block for overtime. This form for any one week is generally started just before the beginning of the week by having someone in the office who is responsible for payroll records type on the form the names of employees, their number, and their basic salary. In many large organizations this general information is printed on forms from addressing machine plates.

In offices, the basic salary is usually listed as a weekly salary. This form is maintained from day to day by having someone in the office write appropriate information beside the name using the guide that is printed at the bottom of the form. At the end of the week whoever is responsible for completing the payroll record will compute the earnings on the basis of the day-to-day records. If a person has worked full time, he gets his regular

PAYROLL DEPT.
BY 10 A.M. OF → June , 19--

PAY PERIOD ENDING June 19, 19--

EMPLOYEE NUMBER	NAME	TIME REG OR LOST	MON.	TUE.	WED.	THU.	FRI.	SAT.	SUN.	WEEKLY SALARY	TOTAL HOURS REGULAR	TOTAL HOURS OVERTIME	RATE PER HOUR REGULAR	RATE PER HOUR OVERTIME	AMOUNT EARNED REGULAR	AMOUNT EARNED OVERTIME	GROSS EARNINGS
11	BUTLER, JOSEPH A.	REG/O.T.	X	X	X	X	X	---	---	60 00	40.0	—	1 50	2 25	60 00	—	60 00
32	CAVALLO, ROSE M.	REG/O.T.	7 / S	X	X	X	X	---	---	125 00	39.0	—	3 125	4 69	121 88	—	121 88
13	DYER, LENA B.	REG/O.T.	S	X	X	X	X	---	---	60 00	40.0	—	1 50	2 25	60 00	—	60 00
24	FAIRBANKS, JOHN	REG/O.T.	X	2	X	X	X	5	---	80 00	40.0	7.0	2 00	3 00	80 00	21 00	101 00
35	GROSSMAN, ISIDORE	REG/O.T.	X	X	X	X	X	3.5	---	140 00	40.0	3.5	3 50	5 25	140 00	18 38	158 38
26	JUNG, FOO Y.	REG/O.T.	X	O	X	X	X	---	---	100 00	32.0	—	2 50	3 75	80 00	—	80 00
9	KIRKLAND, MURRAY	REG/O.T.	X	X	X	T	---	---	---	60 00	32.0	—	1 50	2 25	48 00	—	48 00

2. REGULAR TIME – For each day worked insert "X" in upper box opposite employee's name.

3. For reporting other than regularly scheduled workday, insert actual hours of:

*NOTE. Circle this entry if it is not to be processed as gross change, i.e. Compensatory O.T. earned or used, excused lateness, etc.

4. REPORT FRACTIONAL HOURS IN DECIMALS AS FOLLOWS:

MINUTES → DECIMALS
15 → .3
30 → .5
45 → .8
60 → 1.0

4. NEW EMPLOYEE – Mark "N.E." in upper box for first day worked. Insert new employee's name if not on Time Report Form.

5. TERMINATION – Mark "T." in upper box for last day worked.

** NOTE – Process P/A forms as soon as possible for:
New Employees
Termination
Leave of Absence

6. FOR DAYS NOT WORKED INSERT APPROPRIATE SYMBOL IN UPPER BOX:
H - HOLIDAY OR STAFF DAY
V - VACATION
S - SICKNESS
W - INJURY ON JOB (WORKMEN'S COMP.)
J - JURY DUTY
D - DEATH IN FAMILY
M - MILITARY DUTY
E - EXCUSED ABSENCE - PAY
L - LEAVE OF ABSENCE
O - ABSENCE - DO NOT PAY

** N.E.
** T.

X LOST TIME →
--- OVERTIME →

PREPARED BY

APPROVED BY

Time report

pay. If he has been absent part of the day or one or more days, his pay is reduced by the proper amount using an hourly rate that is equivalent to 1/40 of his weekly salary. If he has worked overtime, he is paid extra on the basis of 1 1/2 hours for every overtime hour worked.

A number of items are mentioned at the lower part of this form that perhaps require explanation:

1) *Report Fractional Hours in Decimals as Follows:* The decimal system in reporting hours is increasingly common because of the ease with which decimals can be computed when using pencil and paper arithmetic, some kind of an adding or calculating machine, or in having the payroll put through one of the many currently available data processing systems.

2) *Regular Time:* You will notice that the person keeping this form is asked to put an "X" in the upper box opposite the employee's name. This, of course, is meant to be used when the employee has begun to work at the usual time in the morning, has taken the proper lunch period, and has left at the usual closing time at night.

3) *Less than scheduled workday:* If the person has worked less than a full day because (a) he has arrived late, (b) taken too long a period for lunch, or (c) left early, the number of hours and fractions thereof he has worked should be recorded in the upper block rather than an "X" being reported there.

4) *New Employee:* Frequently people are assigned at an office as new employees before the time report has been completed in some other office. Consequently, their names may not appear when the time report is issued to the office in question. Therefore, if a new employee is in the office and his name does not appear in the time report, the name should be added and "N.E." lettered in the upper box.

5) *Termination:* For many reasons people leave office employ-ment, i.e., because the family is moving to another town, because they are returning to school full time, because they are accepting a position with another organization, because they are getting married, or perhaps because their work has been unsatisfactory and they have been asked to leave. As suggested, the letter "T" is inserted in the upper block for the last day a person is employed.

6) *Days Not Worked:* A number of symbols are used to indicate days not worked, i.e., "H" for holiday, "V" for vacation, "S" for sickness, "W" when the person is injured on the job and therefore should collect under Workmen's Compensation, "D" for death in the family, "J" for jury duty, "M" for military duty, "E" for excused absence with pay, "L" for leave of absence, and "O" for absence for which payment is not to be made.

Timecards. Even though some organizations use an informal system for recording hours and days worked, a great many companies do use a time clock. Time clocks are usually located at the door where the employees enter. In an "out" rack on one side of the clock is a timecard for each employee. When an employee arrives at work, he takes his card from the "out" rack, puts it in the clock, depresses a key or lever to record the time of his arrival, removes the card from the clock, and places it in an "in" rack on the other side of the clock. The more up-to-date time clocks are automatic so that all the employee need do is insert the card to have it stamped. Some companies require punching in and out at lunchtime.

Timecards usually cover one week. In addition to a complete record of the times at which the employee arrives or departs, the card indicates the days for which the card is to be used, the name of the employee, and his card number.

Sometime during the day, or at the end of a week, the cards are removed from the clock racks and arranged in numerical order. If an employee is paid by the hour, the time for the preceding day is calculated and entered on the card. From these cards the time is usually transferred to a payroll record.

Payroll Register. This is a form illustrated on page 510, on which you will list the names of the employees, the number of exemptions, and gross earnings. This information is carried over from the time report. After these items have been listed on the payroll register, the various types of deductions should be entered and the form completed by doing the horizontal and vertical adding and subtracting that is necessary.

Piecework Slips. A piecework slip indicates the number of pieces completed by an employee. The slip is usually signed by the employee and his foreman and turned in at the end of each workday. It is the policy of some companies to pack goods into jobs or lots that have numbers. In such a case, the piecework employee is asked to indicate the number of the lot or the job upon which he worked. This is done to be certain that only one worker gets paid for doing a given job.

Hourly and Piecework Reports. If you were keeping payroll records for hourly workers or piecework employees, you would start them in advance of the pay period, which is usually a week. On time or piecework sheets you record the names of the employees, their numbers, and the rate of compensation per hour or per piece. In many large organizations, this general information is printed on forms from addressing machine plates.

After the record has been prepared, you enter on it the number of hours that those who work by the hour were employed each day. You get this information from the timecards. You then calculate this part of the

PAYROLL REGISTER

THE WAKEFIELD PUBLISHING COMPANY

DATE June 22, 19--

NUMBER	NAME	EXEMPTIONS	GROSS EARNINGS	DEDUCTIONS FEDERAL WITH. TAX	F.I.C.A.	GRP. INS.	HOSP.	BONDS	TOTAL DEDUCTIONS	NET EARNINGS
11	BUTLER, JOSEPH A.	4	60.00	0.30	2.64	0.60	0.75		4.29	55.71
32	CAVALLO, ROSE M.	2	121.88	13.80	5.36	0.85	1.00		21.01	100.87
13	DYER, LENA B.	1	60.00	6.70	2.64	0.60	0.75		10.69	49.31
24	FAIRBANKS, JOHN	2	101.00	10.60	4.44	0.60	0.75		16.39	84.61
35	GROSSMAN, ISIDORE	4	158.38	14.70	6.97	1.10	1.00	2.00	25.77	132.61
26	JUNG, FOO Y.	3	80.00	5.00	3.52	0.85	0.75	1.00	11.12	68.88
9	KIRKLAND, MURRAY	1	48.00	4.70	2.11	0.60	0.75		8.16	39.84
TOTAL			629.26	55.80	27.68	5.20	5.75	3.00	97.43	531.83

payroll by multiplying the hours by the rate per hour and by making the necessary adjustments for any overtime worked. Entries are also made for various payroll deductions.

To determine the wage of the piece-rate workers, enter on the payroll record the number of pieces or units completed and total them. You then multiply this total by the price per unit. A check with the time-card is sometimes made to see how much of the time spent in the factory was actually spent on work. After the pay of the pieceworker has been calculated, you subtract the deductions. Enter the remaining amount as the net amount to be paid. Separate payroll sheets are prepared for piece-workers and for hourly workers when conditions warrant.

Deductions. Quite a few deductions may be made from the payroll. These include federal, state, and/or city income taxes, social security (known as FICA after the Federal Insurance Contributions Act under which it is levied), and, in some states, unemployment insurance. Many firms deduct also for group life insurance, hospital insurance, mutual aid, government savings bonds, and pensions or annuities, union dues, community chest, uniforms, towels, and purchases of merchandise.

The rates of the deductions for income and social security taxes are established by the government and must be deducted under prescribed conditions. Deductions for unemployment insurance vary; they are determined according to the laws of the particular state in conjunction with federal law.

Group health and life insurance, including hospitalization and major medical insurance, are quite commonly found in large organizations, as are various annuity plans. In some organizations such insurance payment and annuity contributions are optional; in others, mandatory. Inasmuch as group plans are inexpensive, most employees subscribe even though they are not required to do so.

Mutual aid is a fund established by employees to help any of their number who need financial assistance. Usually contributions are voluntary, but frequently they are agreed upon at a meeting of the employees and are deducted accordingly from the employees' pay. Unions among the employees often have contracts that provide for payroll deduction of union dues. Community chest deductions are entirely voluntary. If employees wish to have money deducted for the fund, they authorize the deductions. Other voluntary deductions are handled in much the same way.

You may be employed by a company that permits you to buy company products on a payroll deduction plan. In such organizations you charge merchandise to a special account. The charges may be deducted at the end of the pay period, or you may be able to spread the deductions over a number of pay periods.

Employee's Earnings Record. An individual record is kept for each employee so that detailed information regarding all items affecting wage payments will be brought together in one place. This record is known as the *employee's earnings record.* The earnings records for all employees are usually kept in alphabetic order on cards in a file or on loose-leaf sheets in a binder. An employee's earnings record is illustrated on page 513.

The employee's earnings record is made with divisions providing information for thirteen weeks, a quarter of a year. The facts on each weekly payroll record for each employee are summarized on one line of that employee's earnings record each week. The form provides space for the totals for each quarter and for the year. These totals are needed for the quarterly and the annual reports that the employer is required to make to the government.

Paying Employees. After the payroll has been prepared, the next step is to pay each employee the amount due him. In many firms payment is by check; in other firms, in cash; in still others, certain ones are paid in cash and the rest are paid by check.

Paying by Check. Payroll checks are usually drawn on a special payroll bank account, the funds being transferred from a general checking account by a check or a voucher prepared by some person in authority.

Payroll checks, after being prepared by a clerk, must be signed by the person designated by the firm to do this. As a rule, however, if there are many checks, a check-signing machine is used. After being signed, the checks are verified and counted and the number verified by the register on the check-signing machine.

Deductions are frequently indicated on payroll checks in such a way that the employee will know the amount of each deduction. This information is sometimes imprinted on a special stub attached to the check that the employee removes before cashing the check.

Checks for office employees are frequently enclosed in envelopes for privacy and distributed in packets to department heads, who give them to the individuals in their departments. In some organizations checks are mailed to the employee's home or bank. Checks for salaried workers who are employed in the factory are sometimes enclosed in envelopes so that they will not become soiled from handling in the factory. They are distributed to the department heads or foremen, who pass them on to the employees. Checks for salaried store employees are generally given to department heads for distribution. While methods of payment vary with different businesses, the information provided on the check will always be the same information that is developed in the payroll register; therefore, the check should be prepared using the payroll register as a source of information. See payroll check and stub on page 514.

EMPLOYEE'S EARNINGS RECORD

LAST NAME: Reynolds FIRST: Raymond MIDDLE: D. SOC. SEC. NO.: 269-05-1568

| WEEK | PERIOD ENDING | EARNINGS | DEDUCTIONS | | | | | | NET PAY | |
			F.I.C.A.	FED. WITH. TAX	GRP. INS.	HOSP.	OTHER	TOTAL	AMOUNT	TAXABLE EARNINGS ACCUMULATED
TOTAL FIRST 3 QUARTERS		3537 60	155 65	99 20	24 00	10 00	35 00	323 85	3213 75	3537 60
1	10/8	65 00	2 86	1 95	0 50	0 75	3 00	9 06	55 94	3602 60
2	10/15	65 00	2 86	1 95	0 50	0 75		6 06	58 94	3667 60
3	10/22	73 50	3 23	2 10	0 50	0 75		6 58	66 92	3741 10
4	10/29	65 00	2 86	1 95	0 50	0 75		6 06	58 94	3806 10
5	11/5	81 00	3 56	3 20	0 50	0 75	3 00	11 01	69 99	3887 10
6										
7										
8										
9										
10										
11										
12										
13										
QUARTER TOTALS										
YEARLY TOTALS										

Employee's earnings record

YEAR TO DATE				GROSS		CURRENT PERIOD		
GROSS	FED. TAX	F.I.C.A.		BASE	FED. TAX	F.I.C.A.	GRP. INS.	HOSP.
893 60	88 20	39 32		158 38	14 70	6 97	1 10	1 00

	BONDS	OTHER DEDUCTIONS & ADJUSTMENTS			
	2 00				

EMPLOYEE NO.　　PERIOD ENDING

35　　June 19, 19--

S T A T E M E N T

NET PAY　　$　132 61

THE WAKEFIELD PUBLISHING COMPANY
STATEMENT OF EARNINGS AND DEDUCTIONS
KEEP THIS STUB FOR YOUR PERSONAL USE AND INFORMATION

CHECK NUMBER
1400

No. 1400　　**THE WAKEFIELD PUBLISHING COMPANY**　　1-30／210
181 W. 4th St., New York, N. Y. 10014

DATE

June 22, 19--

TO THE ORDER OF:

ISIDORE GROSSMAN

NOT VALID AFTER 60 DAYS
OFFICE PAYROLL ACCOUNT

PAY
EXACTLY →

DOLLARS	CENTS
132	61

MANUFACTURERS HANOVER
TRUST COMPANY
378 AVENUE OF THE AMERICAS, NEW YORK, N. Y.　　⑈0 2 10⑈0030⑈ 0065 5⑈ 2 24 16⑈ ⑈000 1 100000⑈

Payroll check and stub

Paying in Cash. As a general rule, employees need their money immediately on payday. Therefore some firms, as a service to their employees, make salary payments in cash rather than by check. This policy is also followed by companies in districts where there are no conveniently located banks.

When it is the policy to pay some or all of the employees in cash, a check is drawn for the net amount of the payroll, that is, the amount of the payroll less all deductions. The check is cashed, the money is placed in pay envelopes, and the envelopes are distributed. Before someone is sent to the bank for the payroll money, it is customary to prepare two forms — a payroll change sheet and a payroll cash slip.

Payroll Change Sheet. A *payroll change sheet* or *money tally* shows the name of each employee and the amount of money he has earned. In the columns to the right of each employee's name are indicated how many

PAYROLL CHANGE SHEET

DATE November 6, 19--

EMPLOYEE	AMOUNT PAID	$20	$10	$5	$1	50¢	25¢	10¢	5¢	1¢
Butler, Joseph A.	$ 55.71	2	1	1			2	2		1
Cavallo, Rose M.	100.87	3	3	2		1	1	1		2
Dyer, Lena B.	49.31	1	2	1	4		1		1	1
Fairbanks, John	84.61	3	2		4	1		1		1
Grossman, Isidore	132.61	4	3	4	2	1		1		1
Jung, Foo Y.	68.88	1	4	1	3	1	1	1		3
Kirkland, Murray	39.89		2	3	4	1	1	1		4
TOTAL	$531.88	14	17	12	17	5	6	7	1	13

Payroll change sheet

bills and coins of each denomination will be needed to pay the worker. For example, if James Harvey makes a net amount of $57.90, he would be given two $20 bills, one $10 bill, one $5 bill, and two $1 bills (or five $10 bills, one $5 bill, and two $1 bills), a half dollar, a quarter, a dime, and a nickel. After the salary amounts have been broken down into the various denominations and the various columns have been totaled, the totals are transferred to a payroll cash slip so that the bank will know how many of each of the various denominations are needed.

Payroll Cash Slip. Using the payroll change sheet as a source of information, the clerk prepares a *payroll cash slip* (see page 516). This form shows the amount of hundred-, fifty-, twenty-, ten-, five-, and one-dollar bills and the amount of silver dollars, half dollars, quarters, dimes, nickels, and pennies that are needed. Because the employee usually finds it difficult to change large bills, most firms use nothing larger than twenty-dollar bills.

Distribution of Payroll Money. After the money has been received from the bank, it is usually counted out in various denominations and

MANUFACTURERS HANOVER TRUST COMPANY

REQUISITION FOR PAYROLL

Wakefield Publishing Co.
NAME OF DEPOSITOR

DATE *November 6, 19--*

THIS COLUMN FOR USE BY BANK ONLY	DENOMINATIONS	DOLLAR AMOUNT ONLY	CENTS ONLY
	$100 BILLS		
	$ 50 "		
	$ 20 "	280	00
	$ 10 "	170	00
	$ 5 "	60	00
	$1 & $2 "	17	00
	HALVES	2	50
	QUARTERS	1	50
	DIMES		70
	NICKELS		05
	PENNIES		13
	TOTAL →	531	88

238
1250M 1-66

Payroll cash slip

inserted into pay envelopes which have been prepared in advance. In large organizations, these envelopes often are prepared with the names and numbers of the employees by an Addressograph machine, but in small organizations they are written by hand, as is the amount.

After the money has been inserted, the pay envelopes are ready for distribution. If there are only a few employees in an organization, the pay envelopes are usually distributed to them by an executive, the cashier, or the bookkeeper. In a large organization where it might be unsafe and inconvenient to carry all the pay envelopes of the employees around to them individually, the employees are asked to call at a certain place for them. The employees are often asked to sign a slip as a receipt when they receive their pay.

Payroll Accounting Machines. Many large offices use accounting machines in the preparation of their payroll records. The use of such machines saves time and helps to reduce errors. Time is saved because one payroll accounting machine can prepare several payroll records in one operation. Errors are reduced because there is no need to post from one record to another.

Earnings and deductions are usually computed by a payroll clerk and are recorded by hand on the timecards. From these timecards, the payroll accounting machine operator quickly and efficiently prepares the remaining payroll records. The machine imprints the information for each employee on the payroll register and on the employee's earnings record at the same time that it completes the payroll check and the employee's statement of earnings and deductions.

Electronically Computed Payrolls.

Increasingly you will find payrolls in the larger concerns being handled by electronic data processing equipment. Once the basic information regarding salary and hours or days worked is entered in the machine by an input clerk, the properly programmed machine will automatically complete all computations including deductions. As part of its operation, it will produce the paycheck and explanatory stub and all the supporting records. Some large firms now have their payrolls prepared at an off-the-premises data processing center. This type of service center is becoming increasingly popular and is used to supplement the company office.

Study Questions

1. What information is included in a time report and how is it indicated in the time report form that is illustrated?

2. What information does a timecard contain?

3. Why are piecework slips used?

4. What information, including deductions, will be found on a typical payroll register?

5. Which payroll deductions are mandatory?

6. What is the purpose of the employee's earnings record?

7. Explain the reason why some employees in business will be paid in cash while others will be paid by check.

8. What is the purpose of a payroll change sheet, and how does it help the payroll clerk to distribute the payroll?

9. Why is it necessary that a payroll cash slip be prepared by the payroll clerk?

10. In what ways may a cash payroll be made up and distributed to employees?

11. How does the use of payroll accounting machines save time and reduce errors?

12. How is electronic data processing equipment used in payroll work?

What Do You Think?

1. What are the advantages of the various types of wage returns for services rendered: weekly or monthly salary; piece-rate scale; hourly rate?

2. Do you consider it a sign of poor planning by certain employees when they prefer to be paid in cash because it would be inconvenient for them to wait until the following day to have a check cashed?

Your Personal Qualities

James Preston has just been hired as a payroll clerk. He finds that some of the procedures allow room for errors. After each pay period, several employees come into the office to complain of improper amounts in their paychecks. James feels that he could offer suggestions for improvement in procedures based on what he learned in school.

Questions: 1. How long should he wait before offering his suggestions?

2. How should he go about making suggestions for improvements?

How's Your English?

For each of the letters described below, indicate an appropriate salutation. You will find examples of salutations in Appendix F. Note especially the degree of formality in each instance.

1. A letter is to be written to John C. Doyle, President, Yosemite University.

2. A letter is to be written to the Vice President of the United States.

3. A letter is to be written to the U.S. Representative from your district.

4. A letter is to be written to the president of a large company. His name is Randolph Taylor Matthews.

Office Work

Visit the payroll department of one of the local business offices. Check the methods they use in computing payrolls. You should especially try to determine the way in which they compute withholding income tax for the federal government and also for the state, if such a tax is required. Also find out what the current rate of F.I.C.A. deduction is.

Office Work Assignments

54: Payroll Work

You are to prepare several of the payroll records of The Wakefield Publishing Company for the week of July 4–10 using the information given on page 519:

Employee			Working Time							Deductions			
Name	Exemp-tions	M	T	W	T	F	S	Weekly Salary	Fed. With. Tax	Grp. Ins.	Hosp.	Bonds
Butler, Joseph A.	4	H	8	8	8	8		60.00	0.30	0.60	0.75	
Cavallo, Rose M.	2	H	7	8	8	8		125.00	15.40	0.85	1.00	2.00
Dyer, Lena B.	1	H	8	8	8	8	3	60.00	8.00	0.60	0.75	
Fairbanks John	2	H	8	8	8	8		80.00	7.00	0.60	0.75	
Grossman, Isidore	4	H	8	8	9	8	2	140.00	14.70	1.10	1.00	2.00
Jung, Foo Y.	3	H	8	8	8	0		100.00	5.00	0.85	0.75	1.00
Kyoto Fusai	2	H	8	8	8	8		100.00	11.70	0.85	1.00	1.00
Maloney, Michael J.	1	H	V	V	V	V		75.00	9.30	0.60	0.75	
Nielsen, Ingar	1	H	8	E	E	8	5	75.00	11.70	0.60	0.75	
Presley, Thelma M.	2	H	2	5	8	8	3	75.00	5.00	0.60	0.75	
Reid, Ruth P.	2	H	7.3	8	8	8		90.00	8.50	0.85	0.75	
Sanchez, Julio P.	1	H	8	8	8	0		60.00	4.80	0.60	0.75	
Tenney, Mabel A.	3	H	8	8	8	9	2	100.00	10.00	0.85	1.00	1.00
Upton, Charlotte	1	H	10	8	8	8		75.00	10.30	0.60	0.75	
Walker, Arlene N.	2	H	8	8	8	5		70.00	5.30	0.60	0.75	

1. Prepare a weekly time report similar to that illustrated on page 507. List the names of the employees, the weekly salary, the total hours, regular and overtime, the rate per hour, regular and overtime. The regular rate is determined by dividing the weekly rate by 40. The overtime rate, which is 1 1/2 times the regular rate, should be used for all hours over 40 worked in any one week. Once you have determined the regular amount earned and the overtime amount earned, determine the gross earnings which is the total of the two preceding columns.

In entering the number of hours an employee has worked or not worked, you should use the symbols shown at the bottom of the time report form (see illustration on page 507). For example, you will notice that the Working Time area indicates that Monday, July 4, was a holiday for everyone. The letter "H" should be entered in the upper box of the time report, and in computing the number of hours worked during that week you should regard this as a full day's work. Mr. Maloney was on vacation for the rest of the week after the holiday, and several people worked fewer than eight hours, several more than eight hours, and some worked on Saturday. You will also note that Foo Y. Jung was absent on Friday — an absence that was not excused (indicated by a "0") and, therefore, he is not to be paid, while Ingar Nielsen was absent on Thursday but the absence was an excused absence indicated by the letter "E." An "X" is used to indicate that an employee has worked a full day. For reporting other than regularly scheduled workdays, the actual number of hours worked is inserted in the appropriate box.

2. When the time report is completed, you should then complete the payroll register on which you will list the names of the employees, the number of exemptions, and gross earnings. These items will be carried over from the time report. You should then fill in the various columns under the general heading of "Deductions." The federal tax to be withheld, the hospitalization, group insurance, and deductions for bonds are given above. You should compute the F.I.C.A. (Federal Insurance Contributions Act) tax at the rate of 4.4% of the total earnings of each employee.

After the various deductions have been filled in, add them across to get the total deductions. Deduct the total deductions from gross earnings in order to determine the net salary — the amount that should appear in the final column. Prove your work by adding all columns vertically. Add the totals of all deductions horizontally. This should equal the grand total of deductions, and this amount, subtracted from the total gross earnings, should equal the total net salaries.

3. Complete the payroll change sheet (see page 515).

4. Complete the payroll cash slip (see page 516).

55: Employee's Earnings Record

You are to complete the employee's earnings record of Thomas P. Randall, Social Security Number 123-26-7310, for the last quarter of the year.

1. Prepare an employee's earnings record (see page 513); enter the following information on it:

				Deductions			
Week	Period Ending	Earnings	F.I.C.A.*	Fed. With. Tax	Grp. Ins.	Hosp.	Other
Total Three	First Quarters	4,200.50	184.82	577.51	39.00	87.75	45.00
1	10/8	125.00	5.50	15.68	1.00	2.25	5.00
2	10/15	125.00	5.50	15.68	1.00	2.25	
3	10/22	142.85	6.28	22.10	1.00	2.25	
4	10/29	100.00	4.40	13.40	1.00	2.25	
5	11/5	135.71	5.97	21.10	1.00	2.25	5.00
6	11/12	75.00	3.30	9.30	1.00	2.25	
7	11/19	149.99	6.60	23.10	1.00	2.25	
8	11/26	125.00	5.50	15.68	1.00	2.25	
9	12/3	125.00	5.50	15.68	1.00	2.25	5.00
10	12/10	159.68	7.03	24.60	1.00	2.25	
11	12/17	130.00	5.72	19.10	1.00	2.25	
12	12/24	130.00	5.72	19.10	1.00	2.25	
13	12/31	152.26	6.70	24.60	1.00	2.25	

*F.I.C.A. Tax computed at 4.4%

2. Complete the employee's earnings record by (a) adding each line horizontally to find the total deductions; (b) subtracting the total deductions from the total earnings to find the net pay; (c) extending the total earnings for the first three quarters to the "Taxable Earnings Accumulated" column and adding the successive total earnings for each week to the accumulated total to find the taxable earnings accumulated; and (d) adding vertically all columns except the "Taxable Earnings Accumulated" column to find the totals for the quarter and for the year. After the totals have been recorded, check the accuracy of your work by subtracting the deductions total from the earnings total; the remainder should equal the total of the "Net Pay" column. The last entry in the "Taxable Earnings Accumulated" column should be equal to the earnings total. *NOTE:* The items in the "Other" column represent payments made by Mr. Randall for goods purchased from the company store.

UNIT 13 | Financial Duties

PART 4:

Income Tax Records

Many millions of people in the United States are required to file income tax returns each year. Your employer will be required to file a tax return, and, if you have a reasonable amount of income, you, too, will be required to file such return. In order that accurate returns can be filed, it is essential that careful records be kept of personal income and expenditures. In order that you may file your own return accurately and be helpful to your employer in case that help is requested, you should be well informed about federal income tax requirements.

Current Regulations. Income tax regulations change from time to time. Consequently, you need to study the most recent regulations. The pamphlet *How to Prepare Your Income Tax Return* is mailed to all taxpayers annually by the Internal Revenue Service. The booklet *Your Federal Income Tax* may be purchased for a nominal fee from your District Director of Internal Revenue or from the Superintendent of Documents, United States Government Printing Office, Washington, D.C. 20402. It presents in considerable detail the federal income tax laws as they relate to individual taxpayers. You will find it very helpful because it is written in nontechnical language and contains many examples to illustrate the application of the tax laws to practical situations.

Two additional Internal Revenue Service publications which may be of particular assistance to you and which may be obtained from your District Director of Internal Revenue are *Tax Guide for Small Business* and *Employer's Tax Guide, Circular E.* Other references that may prove helpful are the *Federal Tax Guide* published by the Commerce Clearing House and Prentice-Hall's *Federal Tax Guide.*

In some states, there is a state income tax. If you should be employed in one of these states, it would be well for you to familiarize yourself with the current state tax requirements so that you can keep the records which are necessary to prepare state income tax returns.

To prepare a satisfactory income tax return, it is essential that all information regarding income and all information regarding expenses be recorded in such a way that this information may be used in preparing the necessary forms.

Income. In order to complete an income tax report, it will be necessary to have a record of all income received from:

1) *Wages or salaries*, including the name and address of each employer and the totals. All withholding (W-2) forms should be attached.

2) *Bonuses, commissions, and special fees*, with the name and address of the company making payment and the dates of payment.

3) *Stock transactions.* List the number of shares of stocks and bonds in the taxpayer's possession, with the name, price, and date of purchase; the number of stocks and bonds sold, including the sale price. Buy-and-sell slips should be attached. All expenses connected with the buying and selling of stocks and bonds, such as broker's fees, should be itemized and statements attached.

4) *Interest.* Furnish the name and address of each bank in which the taxpayer has an account, and the amount of interest earned in each; number of bonds, the issuing company, the amount of interest.

5) *Other sources*, such as:

   Rents from properties, listed by the month, with expenses to maintain such properties, including services, repairs. Original cost, costs and dates of improvements should be listed to determine depreciation.

   Profits from sales or exchanges of real estate. Original buying price, costs and dates of improvements, and selling price should be listed, with bills, receipts, and bills of sale attached.

   Royalties from books, patents, copyrights, listed individually. All *expenses connected with inventing or the writing of books* should be listed, with bills attached, including secretarial service, editing, retyping; printing; home and/or office expenses that may be charged to the writing or inventing; the value of the home, the office, the furniture and equipment, so you can compute a proportionate amount as depreciation in connection with the inventing or writing; costs of copyrights and/or patents.

   Estates and Trusts. The taxable portion will be determined based upon information furnished by the officers of any trust and those responsible for administration of any estates from which income is derived.

Expenses. The following is a list of expenses that should be recorded for income tax purposes:

Business Expenses (not reimbursed by the company): Hotel bills, credit association statements, gasoline costs, tolls, transportation charges, baggage expenses, cost of transporting sample cases and display material, reasonable tips, convention expenses, entertainment. Rather rigid rules are currently in effect covering deductions for travel, entertainment, and gift expenses. These are set forth in detail in Publication No. 463, which can be obtained at any Internal Revenue Service office. Receipts and itemized accounts must be furnished.

Personal Expenses:

Contributions, listing the name and address of each organization, date, and amount of contribution. Receipts or canceled checks should be attached.

Interest paid on loans and mortgages.

Taxes: real estate, personal property, state income, state or local retail sales, and state gasoline tax.

Medical Expenses: List the names and addresses of doctors, hospitals, dentists, and the amounts paid to each. Eyeglasses, artificial teeth, medical or surgical appliances, X-ray examinations and treatments, premiums on hospital or medical insurance, and the cost of drugs should be listed. Receipts must be attached.

Other Expenses: Losses due to fire, theft, vandalism; expenses for professional books, subscriptions to professional magazines, and memberships in professional associations; bank vault charges; advisory service charges in connection with stock, bond, and real estate investments; legal fees in connection with the preparation of income tax returns, both federal and state.

Declaration of Estimated Tax. You should keep monthly records. This will make it easier to file a more accurate declaration of estimated tax. Although income from salaries is subject to withholding tax, other income is not. By filing this Declaration of Estimated Tax (Form 1040-ES) and making quarterly payments in advance, one is not burdened at the end of the year with a large payment at one time.

Setting Up the Income Tax Record. Income tax records are required by law, and they must be accurate. A simple form for keeping income tax records is illustrated on page 524. Notice that the columns at the left provide space for recording various types of income received; the columns at the right provide space for recording various types of expenses.

It will be wise to add each month the recorded amounts in the income tax record and transfer these totals to a separate page, so that the monthly totals may be studied and added together at the end of the year to get the yearly total. This will also enable you to examine subtotals every three months in order to assist you in revising the estimates of income if they are not accurate.

Income Tax Record

Salary	Dividends	Interest	Rents & Royalties	Misc.	Date	Explanation	Contributions	Interest	Taxes	Medical & Dental	Misc.
	35.00				19-- Jan 3	Acme Mfg. Co. — dividend					
			75.00		5	A. C. Langton — rent					
					8	Merchants Bank — interest on mortgage		52.50			
					10	Dr. Thomas Wales — dental work				36.00	
				600.00	11	Profit on sale of Rentest Corp stock					
					14	Salem County — real estate taxes			52.50		
300.00					15	Salary					
					16	Sam's Auto Repair — repair from accident					39.75
		10.00			18	F. M. West — interest on loan					
					22	Red Cross — donation	25.00				
					23	State income tax			115.00		
	11.25				24	George & Co. — dividend					
					25	Queen Optical Co. — eyeglasses				30.00	
					28	Southern Publishing Co. — professional books					7.50
300.00					31	Salary					
					31	Christ Church — donations for month	20.00				
600.00	46.25	10.00	75.00	600.00	31	Totals	45.00	52.50	167.50	66.00	47.25

Income tax record

Selecting Your Own Income Tax Form. What about your own tax return? In order to make your reporting as simple as possible, the Internal Revenue Service has developed two individual income tax forms: Form 1040 and Form 1040A.

Form 1040 is the standard form which can be used regardless of the source or amount of income. Filling in this form involves four steps: (1) claiming your exemptions, (2) reporting your income, (3) claiming your deductions, and (4) figuring your tax.

Form 1040A is the simplest tax return. It is a tabulating machine card. You may use this form if:

1) Your gross income was less than $10,000, AND
2) It consisted of wages reported on withholding statements (Forms W-2) and not more than $200 total of other wages, interest, and dividends, AND
3) You wish to take the standard deduction (about 10% of your income) instead of itemizing deductions.

If your gross income was less than $5,000 and you choose to use Form 1040A, you may elect to have the Internal Revenue Service figure your tax for you.

Personal Qualities. If you are to assist in the preparation of income tax reports, it is essential that you possess certain personal qualities. Probably the most important of these is that you should be thoroughly honest. There should not be the slightest question in your mind about whether any deduction should or should not be made. If there is a question, ask a tax expert. If it is legal to make the deduction, it should be made; if it is not legal, then the deduction should not be made. Under no circumstances should you assist in the preparation of income tax returns that are in any way fraudulent.

In addition to being scrupulously honest, you should have a "head for figures" and a recognition of the fact that it is essential that your figures be absolutely accurate. When working with income tax records or reports, you should be certain that they are rechecked to see that all computations are accurate.

A third quality that is necessary is neatness. Tax reports should be prepared neatly so they can be checked in detail without undue effort.

As mentioned previously in this text, you should always regard business information entrusted to you as confidential, not to be discussed with associates and friends. Needless to say, this is doubly important when the employer's personal affairs are concerned, including his income tax records.

Study Questions

1. Why do you need to be well informed about federal and state income taxes?

2. What publications are available that contain tax information?

3. Name some types of taxable income.

4. Name a number of expense items that are deductible.

5. What kinds of business expenses may be deducted on a federal income tax return?

6. What kinds of personal expenses are deductible?

7. Name some of the medical expenses that may be deducted.

8. Why is a Declaration of Estimated Tax made?

9. Under what circumstances is each of the federal income tax return forms used?

10. What personal qualities are essential to one who works on tax records and returns?

What Do You Think?

1. In what ways can you be most helpful in connection with the income tax returns of your employer?

2. What precautions should you take to keep your employer's income confidential?

3. Mr. William J. Destry has an adjusted gross income of $4,500, which includes dividend income of $300. His deductible nonbusiness expenses amount to $600. What tax return form should he use?

Your Personal Qualities

Mr. Howard Downing has taken the carefully prepared records pertaining to his income tax and altered them considerably in order to reduce his tax. He then asks you to type the tax forms using the altered information, much of which is clearly fictitious and fraudulent.

Question: What should you do?

How's Your English?

Examples of address forms and salutations in Appendix F indicate that some salutations are more formal than others. Choose the most appropriate salutations for the following letters:

1. Your employer received an invitation to attend the ceremony in which his son is to receive recognition in a special college award program. The letter came from Ezra P. Logan, president of the college. Your employer is writing a letter of acceptance.

2. Your employer has dictated a letter to Frank Farrell, U.S. Senator from his district, in which he invites the Senator to go on a Canadian fishing trip. Your employer and the Senator have known each other for a short time and do not call each other by their first names.

3. Your employer dictates a letter to the State Representative from the district in which your employer's business is located. The letter expresses your employer's attitude in regard to a proposed new tax.

4. Your employer is program chairman for a local men's group and wishes to invite the mayor of your city to speak at the next luncheon meeting. Your employer knows the mayor.

5. Your employer has been requested by Dr. Warren Wilson's wife to participate in a local charity event. He dictates the answering letter to you and tells you, "Send this to Dr. Wilson's wife. Her name is Helen."

 Office Work

Robert A. Kendrick, who is 39 years old and has a wife and two dependent children, received for the year 19-- a salary of $9,500, from which his employer withheld $1,262.90 for income tax. During the year Mr. Kendrick received $25.97 interest on a savings account and $30 interest on a state turnpike authority bond. He also received stock dividends as follows:

General Motors............	$ 20.00
Stors Radio and Television Corporation.............	8.80
Sterling Drug Company.....	112.50
	$141.30

His expenditures were as follows:

Interest on a mortgage paid to the local bank.........	$150.11
Real estate taxes on his home	420.46
State income taxes..........	341.75
State sales tax, gasoline tax, etc.....................	43.40
	$955.72

During the year Mr. Kendrick suffered no losses from fire, storm, other casualty, or theft. He did incur, not reimbursed by insurance, medical expenses as follows:

Hospital bills..............	$ 75.00
Physician's bills............	127.50
Dentist's bills..............	147.00
Eyeglasses.................	27.50
	$377.00

Mr. Kendrick spent $175.70 on professional books and dues in professional organizations and $137.90 in travel to a professional convention. He donated $75 to his church, $10 to the Red Cross, $15 to the university from which he graduated, and $25 to the local Community Chest.

Procure from the nearest federal tax collector's office the proper tax form and its instruction booklet and compute Mr. Kendrick's income tax for last year.

Office Work Assignments

56: Income Tax Record

You have been asked by Dr. Arthur J. Boles, a professor at Central State University, to keep for him a record of (1) all income other than salary that he receives during the year, and (2) all expenditures made by him that are deductible for income tax purposes.

On October 1, the balances brought forward in the various columns of the income tax record you are keeping are as follows:

Income

Dividends................	$ 265.20
Interest..................	36.00
Rents and Royalties......	3,415.75
Honoraria...............	450.00
Miscellaneous...........	115.00

Deductible Expenses

Contributions...........	$ 325.00
Interest..................	157.50
Taxes...................	431.66
Medical and Dental.......	285.00
Miscellaneous...........	108.80

Dr. Boles reports income and expenditures for October, November, and December as follows. Not all of the expenditures reported are deductible expenses for income tax purposes. Using the tax booklet you obtained for your exercises in this part, record in the income tax record all income that is taxable and all expenditures that are deductible.

Oct. 5. Paid $25.35 to Cooper Publishing Co. for professional books.

7. Received $90 royalties from Century Film Company.

11. Received an honorarium of $25 from the Rotary Club for making a speech.

15. Paid $238.06 to the state tax commissioner for state income tax.

19. Paid $137.50 to Southern Life Insurance Co. for a premium on a life insurance policy.

21. Received a stock dividend of $17 from Patterson Metals, Inc.

22. Paid $20 dues to the Association of University Professors.

23. Received $500 as the result of winning a contest.

25. Received $27.23 dividend on his veterans insurance.

26. Paid $15 interest on a note to the First National Bank.

28. Contributed $25 to the American Foundation for Scholarships.

30. Paid $21.50 to American Investment Service for a year's subscription to their service.

30. Gave $10 to Trinity Church.

Nov. 2. Received royalties of $1,063.40 from Sutton Publishing Co.

5. Paid $18 to Dr. Ernest Sewall for medical services.

6. Gave $5 to a needy family.

9. Paid $3 for a dog license.

10. Received an honorarium of $15 from the Women's City Club for making a speech.

13. Received a dividend of $75 from the Ford Motor Company.

15. Paid $157.50 to First National Bank for interest on mortgage.

19. Paid $35 to Thomas Opticians for eyeglasses.

23. Paid $24 to Photographers, Inc., for professional pictures.

25. Paid $178.67 for a professional trip to Chicago for which he was not reimbursed.

27. Paid $45 to Harry's Garage for repairs to his automobile caused by a collision with another automobile. This loss was not covered by insurance.

28. Gave $10 to Trinity Church.

Dec. 1. Received a dividend of $12.50 from Radio Corporation of America.

4. Paid $114.40 to the Town of Westport, Connecticut, for taxes on real estate.

7. Paid $4 to Dr. Leonard Smith for dental services.

10. Lost his billfold containing $35 in cash on the way to the University on December 3. The billfold has not been returned, and the loss is not covered by insurance.

15. Received an honorarium of $50 from the Printers' Guild for making a speech.

18. Received $300 from Jack Callan for three months' rent of the Westport property.

22. Paid $30 to the Hartford Insurance Co. for a premium on a hospitalization insurance policy.

23. Received $200 as a Christmas gift from his father and mother.

28. Gave $20 to Trinity Church.

31. Received notice from the First National Bank that interest amounting to $19.78 had been credited to his savings account.

UNIT 13 | Financial Duties

PART 5:

Credit and Collections

You probably know that practically every business extends credit to its customers. In other words, goods or services are sold to the customer with the expectation that payment will be made at some future time. Credit, however, cannot be given to everyone who requests it, for not everyone is dependable or honest enough to be trusted. Hence, some one person or department in an organization is charged with the responsibility of determining good credit risks. This person or department usually is also responsible for collecting from the customers who have been granted credit.

In a small organization, the head of a firm or one of his chief assistants is usually responsible for credits and collections. In a larger organization, a special department is organized for taking care of this function of the business.

Ordinarily, as a clerical office worker, you will not be asked to take the responsibility of granting credit. You will, however, handle and record the various forms that are used in connection with credit transactions, and frequently you will summarize and record reports that are used. Hence, you should be acquainted with the work of the credit department.

The average length of time that retailers, wholesalers, and manufacturers remain in business in the United States is only a few years. Most of the failures occur among small business organizations because of poor business methods and practices. Many of these unsuccessful firms start in business with insufficient capital, keep poor records, or fail to exercise good judgment in extending credit. Thus they develop a large number of bad debts that eventually cause bankruptcy.

TYPES OF CREDIT

Open Account Sales. Most goods are sold on what is known as an *open account;* that is, the goods are sold to the customer on credit, and he

530

is expected to pay within a certain specified time, generally thirty days. Often the customer is offered a cash discount for making payment promptly. For example, goods may be sold on the terms of 2/10, n/30. These terms mean (1) that a discount of 2 percent will be allowed if payment is made within ten days after the date of the invoice, (2) that the full amount must be paid if settlement is made after the discount period, and (3) payment is due no later than thirty days after the invoice date.

Credit Information. When one firm asks another for credit, it generally has to submit a statement of its financial condition and the names of individuals or firms with whom it has been doing business on a credit basis. The seller then writes to the firms whose names are listed to gather information about their credit experiences with the prospective customer. Many businesses use a special form, called a *request for credit information*, which asks a number of questions pertaining to the credit experiences. These questions cover such points as how long the firm has been a customer, how frequently the account has been used, what amounts of credit have been extended, how promptly the customer has paid his bills, what discounts he has taken, and other related information.

In addition to the information that has been gained from these sources, the credit department may seek information on the customer from a general credit-rating agency, such as Dun & Bradstreet, Inc., or from a local or national credit exchange bureau. Banks also furnish credit information on customers, and most credit departments mail forms to banks to get this information.

Credit-Rating Agencies. Dun & Bradstreet, Inc., is a large national, general credit-rating organization, located in New York, that undertakes to list every business organization in the country in a credit-rating book, indicating financial strength and credit standing by a system of letters and symbols. In addition to the book containing the ratings, this firm issues confidential, up-to-date reports on the credit standing of businesses upon request. Firms that do business on a credit basis frequently use Dun & Bradstreet as one check on the credit rating of firms requesting credit.

Local or national credit agencies are located in various parts of the country. In many instances, they are a means of exchanging credit information. They are spoken of as *interchange bureaus* because various firms that have had dealings with a customer pool their knowledge about that customer's credit so that each member may know all about the credit relationships that other members have had with that customer. These interchange bureaus are also used as checks on the credit standing of individuals; hence they are especially valuable for retail stores that extend credit to customers.

Credit Files. In most credit departments you will find one or more special files maintained to carry credit information about customers. Frequently the regular credit file is composed of steady customers, and another card file is maintained for prospective customers. On these cards the essential elements of credit information about the individual or firm are kept for quick reference. Keeping these card files up to date is one of the important activities in the credit office. After all the information about a customer is gathered, the details are placed on a card, and the correspondence related to it is placed in a folder.

On the basis of the information on file, you can determine whether or not credit should be granted to a customer. If it is not granted, a notation is placed on the card and in the folder. If it is granted, there is usually a limit to the amount of credit to be extended, and this is recorded on the card. As the customer is billed for goods, the account is checked by the credit department to see that the amount charged does not exceed the amount of credit allowed. The account is also checked to see that the customer pays his bills on time. Steps are taken by the credit department to collect payment when the account is in arrears.

Credit Instruments. Not all of the credit activities of a business pertain to open-account sales. Quite frequently, written promises to pay are involved. Such promises, known as *credit instruments*, include promissory notes, commercial drafts, and trade acceptances.

Promissory Note. Sometimes a customer may give the seller a promissory note for goods that have been purchased. This promissory note may be given at the time that the purchase is made or at some time when an extension of credit is desired. Such note is usually for sixty to ninety days. The maker may, after making proper arrangements with the bank, be permitted to renew the note for a similar period of time.

| $ 2,000.00 | | December 3, | 19 -- |
| SIXTY DAYS | | after date I promise to pay to | |

the order of MANUFACTURERS HANOVER TRUST COMPANY

TWO THOUSAND AND NO/100---DOLLARS

at MANUFACTURERS HANOVER TRUST COMPANY at its Banking House in the City of New York, N. Y.

Value Received

No. 353   Due February 1, 19--   *Richard Bailey*

1396A 2-65-R.S.D.

Promissory note

A promissory note is not a remittance; it is simply a written promise to pay a certain amount with or without interest at some definite time in the future.

A note, like a check, should be written carefully so that no essential information can be changed. A note should contain the place and the date the note is written, the length of time of the loan, the due date, the amount written in words and in figures, and the signature of the borrower. The words *for value received* are usually placed on the note although they are not necessary. Other information, such as the rate of interest that the maker of the note is to pay or where the note is payable, may be given on the note.

A promissory note has several advantages over an oral promise. First, there is less chance of misunderstanding. Second, in the event of a lawsuit, a written promise to pay is better evidence of a debt than an oral promise. Third, a note may be taken to a bank and sold at any time before it is due. When a note is sold to a bank, the bank will pay to the firm selling the note the face of the note less a nominal sum called *discount*. In this manner, a business may discount a promissory note and use the money long before the maturity date of the note.

Collateral Note. A special form of the promissory note is known as a *collateral note*. It is like any other promissory note except that the maker deposits with the payee valuable securities. These securities may be sold by the payee in case the collateral note is not paid when it is due.

Bank Loans. Many individual and business organizations borrow money from a bank to carry them over periods when they do not have cash enough on hand to pay their obligations and meet their payroll. In such cases the bank usually requires the businessman to file a financial statement prepared by a CPA (Certified Public Accountant). This statement is used by the bank to evaluate the risks involved in making the loan.

Purpose of the Loan. Certain types of loans come under regulations established by the Board of Governors of the Federal Reserve System. Consequently, when a bank makes a loan it is necessary for them to have the person applying for the loan make a statement with respect to the purpose of the loan. If the loan is for the purpose of purchasing securities, it may be subject to certain special regulations. On the other hand, if it is not for the purpose of purchasing securities, it may be permissible but the person applying for the loan is required to indicate the purpose for which he needs the money. Some of the more common purposes for making loans are: (a) purchase or carrying of unlisted stock, (b) purchase or carrying of inventory, (c) improvement or purchase of real estate, (d) payment of taxes, (e) securing additional working capital, or (f) making household improvements.

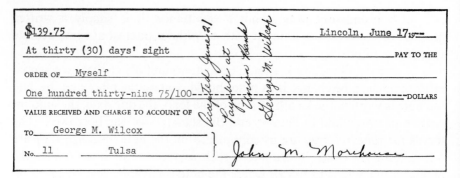

$139.75 _____ _____ Lincoln, June 17 19-- ____

At thirty (30) days' sight _____ PAY TO THE

ORDER OF___ Myself _____

One hundred thirty-nine 75/100---------------------------------DOLLARS

VALUE RECEIVED AND CHARGE TO ACCOUNT OF

TO___ George M. Wilcox _____

No.__11____ Tulsa _____ } John M. Morehouse

Accepted commercial draft

Type of Note. When money is borrowed from the bank, the bank may use the simple form of promissory note presented in the illustration on page 532. Under certain circumstances, the same bank, however, may prefer to use a form of note which includes all the information on a regular note and also includes various clauses that tend to make the note become due and payable immediately if certain conditions are present. For instance, it may become payable immediately if the business appears to be in danger of going bankrupt, if legal action is taken against the business for failure to pay taxes, or if various other conditions exist that might make it difficult or impossible for the maker to meet his obligation if he is allowed to wait to make payment when the note is due.

Commercial Draft. A commercial draft is an unconditional order written by one person directing another to pay on demand, or at a fixed or determinable future time, a certain sum of money to a designated person. This draft is largely a collection device.

Oftentimes when a debt is overdue, the creditor draws an order on the debtor requesting payment of the debt at once. This type of draft is called a *sight draft*, or *demand draft*, and the drawer frequently places it with his bank for collection. Sometimes a draft is drawn for a debt not yet due and states a specified time when payment is expected. If the drawee is willing to make payment, he writes his acceptance across the face of the instrument. When the draft is so accepted, it becomes in effect a note, since it is a written promise to pay.

Accepting a sight draft means paying it when it is presented for payment. Accepting a time draft means promising to pay it when it will become due at a fixed or determinable time after the date of the draft or of the acceptance.

Trade Acceptance. This negotiable instrument is defined as a bill of exchange or draft drawn by the seller on the purchaser of goods and accepted by such purchaser. In other words, a trade acceptance is signed by the purchaser at the time that the sale is completed. In the case of a promissory note, the written promise is usually made sometime after the transaction that created the debt.

Installment Sales. Installment sales are a special type of credit sale. Automobiles, refrigerators, vacuum cleaners, washing machines, television sets, and a host of other large items of consumer merchandise are frequently sold on the installment plan. In an installment sale, the customer is usually required to pay a certain amount of the total price, called a *down payment*, at the time the goods are purchased. The rest of the sale price is paid in equal installments spread over a number of months or years.

Until the final installment is paid, merchandise sold on the installment plan does not legally belong to the person who buys the commodity but to the firm financing the transaction. The goods are sold on a *conditional bill of sale*. The merchandise ordinarily is not delivered to the customer until a check on his credit standing has been made and the financing has been approved. Delivery is then made to him with the understanding that the goods will be returned to or repossessed by the firm selling the article or by the firm financing the transaction should he not be able to pay or maintain payments when they are due.

If the article is repossessed, usually nothing paid on account is returned to the customer. Because of this threatened loss, installment buyers usually make every effort to meet payments as they become due.

The credit information desired about a customer who is buying on the installment plan is essentially the same information that is required of a customer buying on open account. Although the procedure in installment sales is more complicated, that fact does not affect the work of the office clerk in many credit departments because the financing of such sales is usually turned over to a bank or to a company that specializes in such financing.

COLLECTION

No matter how carefully the credit department investigates the credit standing of prospective customers, it is inevitable that some approved customers will not meet their obligations. Because of this, it is imperative that every organization that sells on credit maintain a procedure for collecting from customers. Any irregularities in a customer's payment of an account are made a part of his credit record and may affect his over-all credit rating.

At the end of every month an open-account customer is sent a statement which has a twofold purpose: (1) to allow the customer to check his books with those of the company, and (2) to remind the customer of amounts still unpaid.

If the account remains unpaid until it is overdue, another statement is usually sent to the customer. This one is stamped with a simple reminder such as "Please remit," "Overdue account," "May we have your check?" or some such reminder. The statement of an overdue account may not be sent out until the account is more than a month overdue; on the other hand, many firms send it out in the middle of the month or within ten or fifteen days after the account is due. If the customer pays within a few days after the account has become due, nothing more is done. If the customer does not pay within a few days after payment is due, a series of collection letters is usually begun.

Collection Letters. As you learned in Part 3 of Unit 11, collection letters are usually form letters that are typed individually and addressed to the customer asking him to pay his bill. Most collection departments prepare a number of these letters, sometimes as many as seven or eight in a series. The first one is a very mild reminder. Each successive letter is more firm, and the last one usually contains a threat of legal action if the bill is not paid.

These letters are usually sent at fifteen-day intervals, although circumstances might sometimes call for shorter intervals between letters. For example, if a check on a customer who has always paid his obligations promptly shows that his finances are in a precarious condition, it may be advisable for the creditor to take special steps to collect the account as quickly as possible.

Installment-Sale Collections. Installment customers are treated somewhat differently because it is reasoned that if a customer defaults on an installment and does not pay within the next period, he will be even less likely to pay two installments by the time the next one comes due. Thus installment customers are usually sent a reminder within five days after the payment becomes due, and each successive notice is sent at ten-day intervals. This is done so that a customer will receive at least three reminders before the next payment is due. If a second installment payment is missed, even sterner reminders are sent. Frequently, after the second installment period passes without a payment, the necessary steps are taken to repossess the goods.

Most installment organizations do not allow the customer to be more than three payments in arrears, although sometimes there are extenuating circumstances that may alter conditions.

Study Questions

1. Why is credit checking considered important in the operation of a business?

2. What are the principal causes of business failures among small business organizations?

3. What is meant by a sale on an open account?

4. What is the procedure for establishing credit?

5. What service does Dun & Bradstreet, Inc., render?

6. What is a promissory note?

7. What information should a note contain?

8. What is some of the information that a note with special clauses might contain?

9. Give some of the purposes for which a bank might loan a businessman money.

10. What is a commercial draft?

11. What is a trade acceptance?

12. What is a conditional bill of sale?

13. What is the procedure that is followed to collect overdue open accounts?

14. What is the procedure to collect overdue installment accounts?

What Do You Think?

1. Why is a customer's bank able to supply credit information about him?

2. Is installment buying sound? Why?

Your Personal Qualities

Alfred Jameson is an employee in the credit department of a large firm. One of his duties is to determine which accounts are overdue and should receive reminders. There are more than twenty accounts with large balances to which additional charges are being made each month but on which no payments are being received. These accounts have been specially marked by Alfred's supervisor to indicate that they are *not* to receive overdue reminders. Alfred has asked his supervisor why this is so but he has not been given an answer.

Questions: 1. Why might the supervisor want no reminders to go to some charge customers?

2. If Alfred feels that the supervisor's actions are against company policy, what should he do about the situation?

How's Your English?

1. After referring to an appropriate reference book and Appendix F, type the address and a suitable salutation for:

  a. The president of your state university
  b. A professor at a college or university near your home
  c. The dean of a college in your state

2. In an appropriate reference book, look up the names and addresses of a local Protestant minister, a Catholic priest, and a Jewish rabbi. After referring to Appendix F, type the correct address and salutation for a letter to be addressed to each.

3. In an appropriate reference book, look up the names and Washington addresses of one of your senators and one of your representatives to Congress. After referring to Appendix F, type the correct address and salutation for a letter to be addressed to each.

Office Work

Visit a local credit office or financing organization and inquire about (a) the procedure followed in investigating the credit standing of a customer, and (b) the technique used in collecting from customers who are behind in their payments. If possible, procure forms used in these two activities. Prepare a written report of your visit and be prepared to report orally to the class if the teacher instructs you to do so.

Office Work Assignments

57: Note, Draft, and Trade Acceptance

Prepare in handwriting the following note, sight draft, and trade acceptance to be issued by Hanna & Hanna, Buffalo, New York, on June 15, 19--.

1. A note for $125 payable in 2 months with interest at 5 percent to Arthur L. Holmes, payable at the Syracuse Trust Company.

2. A 30-day sight draft for $110.50 drawn on George G. Grimm, Ithaca, New York, through the State Bank and Trust Company of Ithaca.

3. A 30-day trade acceptance for $258.64 to Harmeyer & Melvin, Albany, New York, for the merchandise sold today payable at the Albany State Bank. Make the trade acceptance payable to Hanna & Hanna.

UNIT 14 | You as an Office Worker

PART 1:

Occupational Information

What will you do when you are ready to hold an office position? Now is the time to give much thought and careful consideration to applying for the job for which you are best qualified. Specifically, you must be prepared to:

1) *Evaluate your qualifications and your special interests.*
2) *Obtain pertinent information about job opportunities in your employment area.*
3) *Write worthwhile letters of application.*
4) *Fill out application blanks intelligently.*
5) *Take one or more tests in production and speed typewriting, clerical aptitudes, English vocabulary, grammar, and spelling.*
6) *Discuss your qualifications and interests during an interview.*
7) *Take a physical examination or submit a statement as to your physical condition from your own physician.*
8) *Apply for a social security number at the nearest Social Security Administration office if you do not already have one.*
9) *Make a decision — accept the right position, and reject the other offers.*

THE JOB ITSELF

Classifications. What positions are open to you? It is reassuring to know that typewriting, one of your basic skills, is needed for over 50 percent of all office positions and that your other office skills will be most helpful in obtaining your first job. Of course, as a recent graduate with little or no actual office experience, you will have to start in a junior position. Positions such as audit clerk, tabular typist, accounting clerk, or senior general clerk which require tact, judgment, and on-the-job experience are seldom, if ever, held by a beginning office worker. You will probably start as a typist, clerk-typist, file clerk, junior general clerk, key-punch operator, mail clerk, or in any one of ten other junior office positions which may be open to inexperienced office employees. These beginning positions, however, offer you invaluable on-the-job experience.

539

Type of Firm. You may have decided, because of your special interests or because of the insight you may have gained from part-time office jobs, to apply for a position with a particular type of firm. If you have not made your decision, consider carefully whether or not you would like to work in the office of a:

1) Communications system: a television station; a newspaper, magazine, or book publisher
2) Financial institution: a bank, a brokerage office, or an insurance company
3) Federal or state agency: the Central Intelligence Agency (CIA), the State Department, the Federal Bureau of Investigation (FBI), the Internal Revenue Service, or one of many others
4) Industrial firm: a manufacturer, a processor, or a jobber
5) Municipal agency: a hospital, a school, a library, or a city department such as real estate, tax, or traffic
6) Professional man: a doctor, a lawyer, or an engineer
7) Retail firm: a department store, a chain store, or a specialty store
8) Transportation system: an airline, or a railroad

Size of Firm. You should consider not only the type of firm that would interest you but also the size of the firm. Would you prefer to work for a very small firm with fewer than 10 office employees, a small firm with from 10 to 50 employees, an average-size firm with from 50 to 100 employees, or a large firm with anywhere from 100 office employees to over 5,000? There are advantages and disadvantages to be considered when seeking employment in offices of all sizes.

In the smaller office you will have a wider range of duties coupled with greater opportunities to acquire diversified office experience. You may have to assume broad responsibilities for the handling of cash, communications, correspondence, and important business records. It must be admitted that there are fewer administrative posts in the smaller offices. Therefore, you may decide, after you have acquired sufficient experience, to move to a larger office to obtain advancement to a more challenging position at a higher salary.

While the opportunities for advancement within the firm are greater in the larger offices, the policies on job classification, starting salary, fringe benefits, and promotion are more rigid. Large firms tend to evaluate every office employee at least once every six months during his probationary period. Nevertheless, some employees feel that their service to the company is overlooked because of the size of the office staff.

Office Location. You may be interested in working in the downtown business district, in a suburban community, or in the office of a large industrial organization located in an outlying district. If you are employed in the business district, your starting salary will probably be slightly higher than it would be in other areas; but you will be expected to dress more attractively, and you may have to use some form of public transportation every day to get to and from your office. You will have many opportunities to meet and exchange ideas with countless other employees holding positions like yours in other downtown offices.

If you decide to work in a suburban community, you are more apt to find employment in a small office — a branch office, a district agency, a real estate agency, or the office of a professional man: a doctor, a dentist, or a lawyer. Starting salaries are slightly lower, but transportation expense may also be lower if you live in or near the suburb in which you work. Casual business dress, rather than the smart business dress required in the business district, is acceptable in outlying areas. Opportunities for changing to better jobs are limited.

If you should find employment with one of the large firms located in an outlying district, you may find that the company provides meals at cost for its employees in company-operated restaurants and coffee shops. This saving is often offset, however, by increased transportation expense. Attractive recreational facilities are often provided for the employees. Job opportunities are necessarily limited to the various departments of the firm by which you are employed.

LOCATING JOB OPENINGS

School Placement Bureaus. If your school has a placement bureau, you should register with it. Your school placement bureau will take a personal interest in you and try to place you in the position for which you are best qualified. The bureau will have your school record, including your extracurricular activities, and the recommendations of some of your teachers. It will, therefore, be in an excellent position to recommend you for suitable openings with its listed employers of office personnel. You should cooperate with the bureau by reporting back after every interview.

Employment Agencies. If your school does not have a placement bureau, you can obtain help from public and private employment agencies. The public agencies charge no fees for their placement service. You may, for example, register without charge with your state employment service. Registration includes a comprehensive interview and a test of your skills to determine the type of office work for which you are best suited.

Private employment agencies are in business for a profit and charge a placement fee based on a percentage of your first month's salary (at least equal to one week's salary). The fee is paid either by the employee or the employer, depending upon the arrangement, and may be paid in installments over a specified period of time. As a rule, private agencies screen applicants carefully before sending them to prospective employers. The screening consists of a series of tests and an interview in depth to determine the applicant's qualifications and placement possibilities. Private employment agencies of all types, for permanent and temporary positions, are listed in the Yellow Pages. They often list their available positions with starting salaries in the classified advertising sections of the newspapers.

Classified Advertisements. Employers constantly use the classified advertisement (Help Wanted) sections of newspapers to find suitable office help. They insert either signed or blind advertisements. A *signed* advertisement usually lists the firm's name, address, telephone number, and occasionally the interviewing hours.

A *blind* advertisement, on the other hand, lists only a box number. In answering, you need only to write to the given number at the newspaper office. To respond to the blind advertisement illustrated below, you would write to Box R3, World Journal Tribune Inc., New York, New York 10015, and use the salutation *Gentlemen*. A blind advertisement is used by an employer who wishes to interview only a selected number of applicants.

Help Wanted — Female

CLERK-TYPISTS
BEGINNERS CONSIDERED
GOOD SALARY
Liberal Benefits — 35 hours

Varied clerical duties in Sales Dept. medium-sized publishers.   Accurate typing required.   U. N. area

THE PSYCHOLOGICAL CORP
OR 9-7070   EXT 757

A signed advertisement for
clerk-typists

Help Wanted — Male

CLERKS
Trnee & Exp
TO $80

Large Midtown company in N.Y.C. has work range of positions for beginners or experienced clerks. Opportunities in data processing, sales administration and customer services. Excellent company paid benefits including tuition refund, profit-sharing and medical plan. State salary requirement and background in letter to R3 World Journal Tribune.
An equal opportunity employer M/F.

A blind advertisement for
trainees and experienced clerks

Recommendations of Office Employees. Surprising as it may seem, most office workers find their first jobs through the recommendations of their employed friends and relatives. An employee is usually aware of an opening in her department; and, if her own work is of a superior quality, she is often asked to recommend a qualified person to fill the vacancy. A recommendation of this type can be most helpful to you. The employee on the job can tell you when, where, and to whom you should apply. She can also give you a good idea of the nature of the job, the office hours, and the fringe benefits.

Civil Service Announcements. If you are interested in a position in a government office, you can secure information regarding the dates of civil service examinations from announcements that are posted in public buildings and usually reported in the daily newspapers. Announcements of city civil service examinations are usually posted in the city hall building; announcements of county and state examinations, in the county courthouse or principal county building; announcements of federal examinations, in first- and second-class post offices. Your name will be placed on a mailing list for notification of federal tests if you send such a request to the United States Civil Service Commission. This service is also rendered by many state and local civil service offices. Civil service is discussed in Part 4.

Study Questions

1. What are some of the steps you must be prepared to take when you apply for your first office position?
2. What are some positions open to beginning office workers?
3. What must you decide about the job itself?
4. What are some of the advantages and disadvantages of working for a large firm?
5. How may you learn of specific job opportunities?
6. Why should you register with your school placement bureau?
7. Why do private employment agencies charge a placement fee?
8. What is the difference between a *signed* and a *blind* classified ad?

What Do You Think?

1. How might you find out about various kinds of offices in order to make a decision on what kind would be right for you?
2. What are the advantages and dis- advantages of being recommended for a job by a friend or relative rather than procuring a position through an employment agency or a newspaper advertisement?

Your Personal Qualities

The graduating seniors in the business education department at Ballard High School made a survey of 32 office jobs. They found ten of them were open to students without previous business experience. The survey showed that the highest salaries are paid to accounting clerks (senior bookkeepers), tabulating machine operators, and executive secretaries, positions to which they hope to advance after gaining on-the-job experience and after additional study.

The students received an announcement that courses in accounting, data processing, and advanced secretarial studies are to be offered at a nearby community college during the next term.

Questions: 1. What are some of the office jobs that are open to students with no previous business experience?

2. What are some of the related courses that would be of help to prospective accountants? executive secretaries? data-processing supervisors?

3. Why do you think that the highest salaries are paid to accounting clerks, executive secretaries, and tabulating machine operators?

How's Your English?

After reading Appendix A on grammar, correct the errors in the following:
1. Mary and John said they did not like them people.
2. Every office worker should do their best.
3. If I were him I'd leave.
4. It is more better to work in a small office than in a large office.
5. If I was older I'd accept a job out of town.
6. Neither the public or private employment agencies had any jobs of that type listed.
7. She was very pleased to accept the job.
8. He said he did his work good.

Office Work

1. Make a list of the sources of placement information that are available to you in your locality.

2. From the newspapers usually read in your community, clip the advertisements for office positions that have appeared in the past week that you might be able to fill. Be ready to discuss these job opportunities in class, and tell why you think you could fill each position.

UNIT 14 | You as an Office Worker

PART 2:

The Personal Data Sheet and the Application

Once you have decided to apply for a specific office position, whether you have been recommended by the school placement bureau, by an employee of the firm, or whether you have read about the position in the Help Wanted columns of a newspaper, you will probably prepare a personal data sheet and write a letter of application. If you are sent for a job interview by an employment agency, usually the agency will make the appointment for you or know the interviewing hours; therefore, you will need a personal data sheet only.

The Personal Data Sheet. First, consider the purpose of your *personal data sheet*. It is designed to give the prospective employer a precise summary of your qualifications. It may be divided into five major sections as follows: personal information, education, extracurricular activities, experience, and references.

1) Personal information tells the interviewer who you are, where you live, how you can be reached (your telephone number, including the area code), your age in years, your height, your weight, your marital status, and your physical condition.

2) Your complete scholastic record should be listed under education. This includes: the name of the high school you attended with the date of your graduation, the curriculum you followed or the major courses you completed, office skills attained such as your typewriting speed, together with proficiency awards or certificates you may have earned. The office machines you have successfully operated in your clerical practice course, such as adding and listing machines, key-driven and rotary calculators, transcribing machines, and stencil, offset, and photocopy duplicators, would be of interest to a prospective employer and should be listed. Any post-high school work you may have taken at a business school,

545

2309 Vernon Avenue
Joliet, Illinois 60431
June 16, 19—

Mr. Frederick C. Moore
Personnel Director
Mutual Life Insurance Company
209 West Fourth Street
Joliet, Illinois 60432

Dear Mr. Moore

Miss Dorothy Fowler, one of your employees who attended Central High School with me, told me that there will be an opening in your machine transcription pool on July 1. I should like to apply for the position. As I have indicated on the enclosed personal data sheet, my qualifications meet the high standards of your company.

I graduated in the upper fourth of my high school class. During the fall term I plan to take courses in business and finance in the evening division of Joliet Community College. My application for admission has already been approved.

During the past two summers I have had experience as a clerk-typist with the Metropolitan Life Insurance Company, as listed on the data sheet. The office manager, Mr. Arthur T. Sweeney, has given me permission to list his name as one of my business references.

I enjoyed my work with the Metropolitan Life Insurance Company, and I should like to continue in the life insurance field. May I expect to be called for an interview? My telephone number is 555-2368.

Sincerely yours

Margaret Jean Collins

(Miss) Margaret Jean Collins

Enclosure

Application letter

P E R S O N A L   D A T A   S H E E T

NAME: Margaret Jean Collins   HEIGHT: 5'6"

ADDRESS: 2309 Vernon Avenue   WEIGHT: 116 pounds
Joliet, Illinois 60431

TELEPHONE: Area Code 815 555-2368   MARITAL STATUS: Single

AGE: 18 years   PHYSICAL CONDITION: Excellent

EDUCATION:

Graduated from Central High School, Joliet, Illinois, on June 13, 19—, after completing the Clerical Practice program. Admitted to the Evening Division of Joliet Community College for the fall semester of 19—.

Office Skills:
Typewriting rate—60 net words a minute
Machine transcription rate—35 words a minute
Awards and Certificates:
Central High School Student Service Award
Alphabetic Filing Certificate
Dictaphone Transcription Proficiency Certificate
Office Machines Operated:
Dictaphone, Mimeograph, Multigraph, Olivetti printing calculator, Call Director switchboard

EXTRACURRICULAR ACTIVITIES:

Treasurer of the Business Service Club
President of the Central High School Chapter of the Future Business Leaders of America
Reporter for Spot Light, school newspaper

EXPERIENCE:

Clerk-typist in the office of the Metropolitan Life Insurance Company in Joliet, Illinois, for the last two summers
Part-time clerk in the Placement Director's office during senior year at Central High School

REFERENCES:

Mr. Arthur T. Sweeney, Office Manager, Metropolitan Life Insurance Company, 236 Main Street, Joliet, Illinois 60634, Telephone 555-2200
Miss Helen C. Harris, Chairman, Commerce Department, Central High School, Joliet, Illinois 60433, Telephone 555-1715
Dr. August W. Brustat, Pastor, Trinity Church, 23 Crane Road, Joliet, Illinois 60432, Telephone 555-8230

Data sheet

technical school, evening school, or community college should also be listed, together with the courses you completed and any special office skills you may have acquired, such as the ability to operate a manual switchboard, a teletypewriter, a Comptometer, a printing calculator, or an alphabetic key-punch machine.

3) A detailed listing of your extracurricular activities is an indication of your special interests, your ability to work with others, and your qualities of leadership. You should list all your school clubs, the class or club offices you held, and any of your special activities, such as serving as a reporter for the school newspaper or as a cashier in the school cafeteria.

4) Beginning with the most recent, list all the jobs you have held. Give the job title first, then the name of the employing firm, and finally the approximate dates of your employment. If your experience is limited, list any voluntary work you may have done for a charitable or civic agency, or for a religious organization.

5) Employers are keenly interested in your references. They prefer different types of references; therefore, you should give at least one from each of the three following types, preferably in this order:

    a. Experience...the recommendations of present or former employers or supervisors, to indicate the quality of your work and your ability to get along on the job.

    b. Scholarship..the recommendations of some of your former teachers to give an indication of your scholastic accomplishments and your potential ability.

    c. Character....the recommendations of persons who have known you for a number of years (preferably clergymen, businessmen, and professional men but not relatives) to certify as to your integrity, loyalty, and reliability.

Your personal data sheet and its contents will make either a favorable or an unfavorable impression upon the interviewer long before he sees you. Therefore, you cannot be too careful. A careless erasure, a smudge, or an error in spelling would be unpardonable. Each personal data sheet that you send out should be a carefully typed original copy.

Letter of Application. Your letter of application accompanies the personal data sheet to the prospective employer and tells him that you wish to be considered an applicant for the position that is being offered.

First, don't fail to put your residence address at the top right above the date. Next, to whom will you address the letter of application? If you obtain the job lead from an advertisement in the classified section of a newspaper, you will address the firm or the box number at the newspaper office, depending upon whether you are answering a signed or blind advertisement.

If the job lead comes from the school placement bureau, an employed friend, or a teacher, you will know the name of the firm and perhaps the name of the person in charge of employment. Your letter then may be appropriately addressed:

The Stoddard Company, Inc.
115 Fourth Avenue
New York, New York 10003

Attention: Mr. James A. Young, Personnel Manager

The salutation, of course, would be *Gentlemen.* You may also write directly to the owner of the organization if he hires the employees:

Mr. Robert A. Smith, President
Case Construction Company
98 Broad Street
Newark, New Jersey 07104

Dear Mr. Smith:

The material to be included in the body of the application letter should be simple and to the point. Get right to the business at hand in the very first sentence by stating that you are applying for a specific position and by telling how you learned of the opening. For example, you might begin by saying, "I wish to apply for the office position which you advertised in the March 27 issue of the *Herald Tribune.*"

Your second paragraph can make reference to the personal data sheet which you will enclose. It should also highlight the main points that may be of interest to a prospective employer. You might say something like this:

"As I have indicated on the enclosed data sheet, I will be graduating from Hamilton High School in June with a business diploma. During my high school career I was awarded a proficiency certificate in Dictaphone transcription and a 60-word-per-minute award in typewriting. I have listed the many office machines which I learned to operate in the clerical office practice course.

"Although I have had no experience in office work, I have been active in assisting Miss Summers, the school's administrative assistant, by transcribing letters which she recorded on Dictaphone belts and typing reports, memorandums, and notices for her. Moreover, there have been opportunities for me to work in offices throughout the high school, filing, answering the telephone, and typing and duplicating material for the teachers. My résumé lists my other experience including retail selling in a department store and counseling in a summer day-camp."

Your last paragraph should request an interview and should give the time when you are free:

"I am looking forward to the opportunity of meeting you for a personal interview. Since classes end at two o'clock, I am free any afternoon after that time."

The closing will be a simple *Very truly yours,* with your name signed and typed below, with the *Enclosure* notation at the left indicating the enclosed data sheet.

You may want to include some reference to your desire to work in a specific type of firm or in a special department such as advertising or personnel. You may also want to mention your plans to continue your education in the evening division of a nearby college or business school by taking advanced courses in accounting, retailing, data processing, or some other field.

When you apply through an agency, you will usually go directly to the firm, so a letter won't be necessary; but be sure to take a copy of your personal data sheet with you.

The Application Blank. Unless the firm is very small, you will be expected to fill out an application blank, usually before leaving the office of the interviewer. Ordinarily, you will be asked to complete the blank in ink, and the legibility of your handwriting will be taken into consideration in evaluating your application. Nevertheless, you should use a typewriter if one is available. In either case, you must read the headings carefully, decide what information you will give and how you can fit it into the space provided. Often, the blank is not completed neatly because the applicant fails to check all the information to be included before he starts writing or typing in the spaces provided.

An application blank that is given to each prospective office employee of a large company is shown on pages 550 and 551. Notice the need for exact dates and addresses. You will have much of the information on your personal data sheet, so it is a good idea for you to have an extra copy of it with you.

In completing the application blank on pages 550 and 551, the applicant filled in *all* the blanks according to the directions. In those instances in which the applicant could not give an answer, she indicated by inserting dashes that she had not overlooked the question. When necessary, abbreviations can be used in firm names and addresses. Every item must be accurate; every date, correct. If you complete the blank on a typewriter, remember that your signature must be handwritten. Neatness and clarity are essential for the favorable consideration of your application.

Tests. Be prepared to take a test. Bring your pen, a pencil, a good typewriting eraser, and a small pocket dictionary. Brief discussions of the kinds of tests you may be expected to take follow.

Personnel Division

APPLICATION FOR POSITION

Date_June 22,_____19_--

I hereby apply for a position with the Acme Manufacturing Company and in connection therewith state the following:

1. Name____MILLER_____RUTH_____ESTHER_____
   (Print) Last Name   First Name   Middle Name

2. Address_3466 Poplar St., Spokane, Wash. 99203_3.Telephone_555-1046

4. Age	5. Date of Birth	6. Are you a citizen of the United States?_Yes____
	Month Day Year	"Yes" or "No"
21	May 12 1945	7. If not, have you taken out first papers?_____
		"Yes" or "No"

Sex

8. Male ☐ Female ☒ | 9. What is your Social Security No._368-05-6133___

10. Are you: Single__x_; Married____; Separated____; Widowed____; Divorced__

11. Full Name of Husband or Wife:_____

12. Family: Give the ages of your:

                How many dependents have you?_---

   Father living_Yes_ Brothers___25__ Relationship of dependents to you:
        "Yes" or "No" Sisters_____18__ _____

   Mother living_Yes_ Sons_____ _____
        "Yes" or "No" Daughters_____ _____

13. Do you live with your parents or other relatives, board, rent, or own your own home?__Live with parents

14. In case of emergency, notify:
    Mrs._John A._Miller,_3466_Poplar St.,_Spokane,_Wash._____
            Name   Address

15. Have you completed an application for employment in this Company previously? ___No_____When?__-_------If you were employed by this Company previously, in what capacity?_-_--

16. Are you related to anyone now in the employ of this Company?___No_ If so, give:
                                                   "Yes" or "No"
    Name__-_____Relationship_---____Division_---__

17. Education	NAME OF SCHOOL	ADDRESS OF SCHOOL	DATES OF ATTENDANCE		DID YOU GRADUATE?
			FROM	TO	
			Mo. YR.	Mo. YR.	
Last Grammar School Attended	Taylor School	Spokane	9-51	6-59	Yes
All High and Preparatory Schools Attended	South High School	Spokane	9-59	6-63	Yes
Business School	Norbert Business School	Spokane	Now attending		
					(Degree)
College or Univ.					

18. What course did you take in High School?_Business_in College?_____
    What were your major subjects?__English,_History,_Business_____
    _Principles, Economics, Accounting_____

19. What course if any are you now taking? *____Do you plan to study further?_Yes_
                                                           "Yes" or "No"
    What course or subjects? *Accounting_____Where?_Norbert_____

20. In what school activities such as athletic, dramatic, literary, honor societies, or school government did you participate?_____
    _High school:__Student Council, 3 years; Debating Club;____
    _____Dramatics Club; Honor Society._____
    _____

21. Are you a   What
    stenographer?_No_ speed?_---- Do you   Indicate _calculator___
                                   operate   the   Xerox_____
    Are you   What   any office type of Mimeograph____
    a typist?__Yes___ speed?_65__ machine_Yes_ machine bookkeeping____

(over)

An application blank — Page 1

Source of Applicant

Name

Div.

Sect.

Date of Appointment

Div.

Sect.

Pos.

Classification   Salary
                        $

Forms 4	Persl.	Section
Typed		
Checked		

EDUCATION COMPLETED
Years of High School
Years of College
Points Completed
Business School
Other
Clerical Aptitude Test
Typing Test
Steno Test

Inquiry	Chaser	Chaser	Checker

Disposition	Date	Initial

To Medical

MED. REPORT

| Case closed | | |

22. BUSINESS EXPERIENCE (LIST ALL EMPLOYERS)

	Inquiry	Chaser	Chaser	Checked

Present or last employer
Wm. Paulson & Associates
312 Myers St., Spokane, Wash.
Name and Address of Firm

EMPLOYED FROM MONTH YEAR: 7-63
TO MONTH YEAR: Present

WHY DID YOU LEAVE? ---

Jr. typist $75.00 wk.-Thomas Adams
Position Held   Salary   Dept.   Name of Dept. Head

Employer before above

Name and Address of Firm

EMPLOYED FROM MONTH YEAR:
TO MONTH YEAR:

WHY DID YOU LEAVE?

$
Position Held   Salary   Dept.   Name of Dept. Head

Employer before above

Name and Address of Firm

EMPLOYED FROM MONTH YEAR:
TO MONTH YEAR:

WHY DID YOU LEAVE?

$
Position Held   Salary   Dept.   Name of Dept. Head

Employer before above

Name and Address of Firm

EMPLOYED FROM MONTH YEAR:
TO MONTH YEAR:

WHY DID YOU LEAVE?

$
Position Held   Salary   Dept.   Name of Dept. Head

23. If you were unemployed at any time since leaving school, give the following information:

What were you doing during this time?

FROM MONTH YEAR | TO MONTH YEAR

24. Indicate the general nature of the duties in your former position or any special work you have done:
Clerical duties. Compute salesmen's expense accounts, compose routine letters, file, mimeograph weekly bulletin.

25. Were you ever discharged by any company? No If so, give: Name of Company
Reason for discharge

26. If you are now employed, why do you desire to make a change? There is little opportunity for advancement or promotion.

27. List any organizations of a civic, business, or professional nature, excluding organizations the name or character of which indicates the race, creed, color, or national origin of its membership, to which you belong:
National Honor Society; Spokane YWCA

28. Please use this space if you care to include any additional information:

Awarded the Dictaphone Transcription Proficiency Certificate for transcribing five full-page mailable letters in one hour.

29. Give the names of three persons who have known you six months or longer. Do not give relatives, former employers, or doctors.

NAME	ADDRESS	OCCUPATION
Mrs. C. C. Clark	3470 Poplar St., Spokane	Purchasing agent
Mr. John Calhoun	South High School, Spokane	Teacher, business subjects
Miss Mary Wagner	1312 Pearl St., Spokane	Owner of hardware store

Signature *Ruth Esther Miller*

An application blank — Page 2

Part 2   The Personal Data Sheet and the Application   551

Intelligence. One type of psychological test that is very frequently used in business offices is similar to the intelligence tests that are commonly used in schools. You have taken intelligence tests in school; therefore, you should have no difficulty in taking them in the employment office of a prospective employer.

Personality. Another type of psychological test that is given quite frequently in business offices is a personality inventory test. Several of these tests are available at the present time, and the business world has been making increasing use of them. Some of these tests are quite simple; others are quite complicated. The more complicated tests try to delve rather deeply into the psychological background of the applicant and should be interpreted only by professional psychologists. Some companies employ psychologists for this purpose.

Clerical Aptitude. Still another type of test that is quite commonly used for screening applicants is some form of clerical aptitude test. This test may have some of the characteristics of the regular psychological tests, but it will almost always include work with figures, work with the alphabet, and matching problems that reveal information about the applicant's clerical aptitude.

Job Competency. A job competency test is very commonly used to indicate the candidate's capacity to do the job for which he is applying. Of course, the most widely used of these tests is a simple typewriting test. Many firms also ask the candidate to take a test on vocabulary, spelling, punctuation, and English grammar. This kind of test is frequently given to applicants for all types of office positions.

Physical Examination. Some companies also require a physical examination. They may provide a form to be filled out after examination by the applicant's own physician, or the company doctor may give the examination.

 Study Questions

1. What information would you include in a personal data sheet?

2. What should be included in a letter of application?

3. When would you be required to fill in an application blank?

4. What are some of the tests you might be expected to take when making application for a position? What are some of their characteristics?

What Do You Think?

1. Why do you think business organizations ask so many questions on an application form?
2. What do companies expect to learn from the various tests that they may ask you to take when you apply for a position?
3. Why do a large number of firms require all applicants to take a physical examination?

Your Personal Qualities

When applying for a position in a local insurance company, Marilyn Conway was asked to take a series of tests. She took them, but throughout the test period she complained to the person who administered them. Marilyn complained that the vocabulary test was ridiculous — that it was too hard. She said that the typewriting test was impossible because the machine assigned to her did not work properly and that the third test was just like one she had taken at school, and her school record showed she had taken it. She voiced a number of other complaints.

Questions: 1. What is your evaluation of Marilyn's conduct during the series of tests?

2. What would you do if your typewriter failed to function properly during a test?

How's Your English?

Read Appendix B on punctuation; then punctuate the following paragraph:

Andrew B Hill Martha F Eaton and Elizabeth A Raymond all applied for a position at the office of the Jones Manufacturing Company Inc the interviewer Mr Howard Cannon talked to them as a group and then one by one he took each to a private office for a private chat the first to go in was Andrew who smiling pleasantly entered the office next Martha obviously nervous was asked to go in while Elizabeth calm as could be waited and was last Mr Cannon a pleasant little gray haired man was apparently well pleased with this group and overlooking the nervousness displayed by Martha said you have all done well we hope in a day or two to be able to tell you that we have a position for each of you.

Office Work

1. Type a letter of application in response to a local newspaper advertisement. Give only actual facts as related to your experience, education, and other qualifications. Include all of your qualifications in the body of the letter of application; that is, do not use a separate data sheet. Attach the advertisement to your letter. Submit your letter to your instructor for suggestions for improvement.

2. Using an assumed name of a business that has not advertised for help but which is the type of business in which you would like to secure office employment, type a letter of application with the details of your qualifications listed on an enclosed personal data sheet.

3. Collect three to five application forms from the business firms in your area. Compare them. Try to determine why each company asks for the information that it does.

Office Work Assignments

58: Application for Position

Assume that you have been asked to complete an application form for a position as a general clerk. If an application form is available, complete it carefully with pen and ink. If a form is not available, type a copy of the illustration on pages 550 and 551 and fill in the required information with pen and ink.

UNIT 14 | You as an Office Worker

PART 3:

The Interview

The day and hour are here. You are standing outside the personnel office of a large business firm. It is ten minutes before your scheduled interview, and you feel the nervous tension that usually accompanies a new experience. At this point, you take a deep breath, stand erect, and open the door to the waiting room of the personnel office. Since you are ten minutes early, you don't feel rushed; and as you walk up to the receptionist, you smile as you greet her: "Good morning, I have a ten o'clock appointment with Mr. Black. I'm Joan Roberts." (Was that you speaking in a well-modulated, softly pitched voice?) Just hearing yourself and seeing the smile on the receptionist's face as she tells you that she will inform Mr. Black you are here gives you confidence, and some of that nervous feeling begins to leave you.

At the suggestion of the receptionist to make yourself comfortable, you remove your coat and your gloves and sit down in one of the chairs. The glimpse you get of yourself in the mirror is even more reassuring — the suit and hat you have chosen are perfect for business, and you look down at your leather shoes and bag, and take a quick glance at your well-groomed nails. (Yes, you are pleased, and you should be. The time and thought that you gave to your appearance, to the way you walk, and to your posture are giving you today the poised appearance of an office worker.)

"Miss Roberts, Mr. Black will see you now," the receptionist is saying, and as you rise to go in, your coat, your gloves, and your purse are being held on your left arm and hand, leaving your right hand free just in case Mr. Black extends his hand for a friendly handshake. You no longer have to remember to stand erect — this has become a natural posture for you over the past months. You no longer have to remember your voice, for this, too, has improved naturally; as a result of long practice, it doesn't rise to high pitches, or rush along, or become too low to be heard. So, when you say, "Good morning, Mr. Black, I'm Joan Roberts," your poise is apparent.

There on his desk are your personal data sheet and your letter of application. There is no question that Mr. Black has read both with attention and has been impressed. (*How carefully you prepared that data sheet! And that letter of application. Was it three or four times that you rewrote it? How glad you are that you did! But you must not think of that now. Later, when you review this situation, you will evaluate it.*)

You now pay full attention to the interviewer. You no longer think of yourself, but only of the best way to answer his questions. Since you are no longer thinking of yourself, you are more at ease. Moreover, you hear Mr. Black say that he is pleased with the qualifications that you have indicated on the data sheet and that he has several positions open. You realize that his main interest is placing you in the department and position that will be best for you and the firm.

Knowing that you may have other job interviews scheduled and that you are also evaluating the firm he represents, Mr. Black outlines the various benefits (often called fringe benefits) you will obtain from this firm:

1) A two-week paid vacation each year
2) A 35-hour week, hours nine to five, one hour for lunch
3) Days off for all major holidays
4) A 15-minute coffee break in the morning and afternoon
5) Hospitalization program
6) A pension plan and an investment plan for company stock
7) Bonus at Christmas
8) Regular salary increases
9) Possibilities for advancement
10) Paid educational training

You have listened carefully, and Mr. Black has given you a brochure listing these benefits.

Now he asks you about your extracurricular activities. You are happy to tell him of your membership in the business club and your active participation in the committees that organized the field trips. Another activity which demanded a great deal of your time but gave you great satisfaction was your chairmanship of the student government's organization committee.

You are also ready for the next two questions which Mr. Black asks you. Why do you want to work for this firm? What salary do you want? You state quite honestly that you wish to work for a manufacturer of consumer products, that you also wish to work for a large firm, and that you hope to advance. As to salary, the ad you answered told what the starting salary would be for a general clerk in this firm, and you inform Mr. Black that this would be a satisfactory beginning for you.

(Your anticipation of these questions has enabled you to answer intelligently. You checked on the salary range in your area for a beginning general clerk. You discussed this firm with the placement officer of your school when you considered answering the advertisement. She told you that in a firm as large as this you would probably start as a trainee in the purchasing or sales division but that there would be opportunities for advancement later on.)

At this point, Mr. Black indicates that it is your turn to ask the questions if you have any. (Very often the interviewer will purposely omit pertinent information. Are you quick enough to ask about it? Think of a good way to ask one or two questions before the interview.) You hear yourself say, "I am interested in continuing my education in the evening, and I note from the brochure that your firm pays expenses. Does it pay for job-related courses only, or for general education courses, too?" You have another question tucked away in your memory, "May I ask if the Company has a lunchroom?" The answers to these questions are very important for you to evaluate this job opportunity with others that you may have. Mr. Black understands this.

Now Mr. Black makes you very happy by telling you that you will receive a letter this week offering you a position as a general clerk in the sales division. You had not expected him to tell you this, and, indeed, Mr. Black usually tells the applicant that he will let her know. He was so favorably impressed with you, however, that he informed you of his decision immediately. Of course, you thank him. You would like to make up your mind at this moment that this is the position you want; however, you have told the placement officer that you will go to another company tomorrow. You explain to Mr. Black that you have another interview tomorrow but that you will be glad to answer his letter immediately after tomorrow's interview. You are sure to thank him for the interview and for offering you this opportunity.

Before you leave, he asks you to complete the company's application blank. This is another of those little jobs for which you are prepared. In fact, you have with you a copy of your data sheet so that you will have exact dates, names, and addresses.

The Interviewer's Evaluation. You know that Mr. Black was making an evaluation of you and your qualifications, although he was not filling out any forms during the interview. After you have left his office, he will complete a rather long questionnaire which will be filed with your application.

Here are some of the personal qualities which he was considering as he spoke to you and discussed your qualifications. He may even have asked direct questions about some of them.

Appearance. Is the general impression of appearance favorable? How careful is the applicant of her person and her clothing? Is her clothing appropriate and attractive? Is her posture good? Does her facial expression indicate a favorable or an unfavorable physical, mental, and emotional condition? And what about her nerves? Is she relaxed or tense — as indicated by her facial expression and bodily movements? (A competent interviewer can rate an applicant on almost all these things before the applicant has walked the few steps from the office door to the interviewer's desk. All are vitally important in getting and holding a job.)

Auditory Impression. After the applicant has seated herself and started talking, the interviewer is alert for other qualities that the applicant should have. Is her voice good? Is it pleasing in sound, quality, and inflection? Is its volume normal? Are her spoken words fully and distinctly articulated? Does her speech conform to good grammatical usage? Is her pronunciation of words accurate, and does her use of words indicate both simplicity and maturity? Does she talk freely but not glibly?

Personality. Is the applicant likable? Has she a personality that is generally pleasing? (She does not need to be the type that will charm a bird off a tree; but, on the other hand, most employers are reluctant to take into their organization an individual whose personality appears to be disagreeable or irritating.) Does the applicant seem to be courteous and considerate of others? Would she be tactful in her dealings with people? Does she appear alert and energetic? Does she seem conceited?

Temperament. Is the applicant calm and confident, or is she shy and nervous? Is she the type that would lose her head in an emergency? Is she reasonably aggressive without being offensively so, or is she the docile, submissive type that will never be able to make her own decisions or to defend them? Does the applicant inspire confidence when she talks about herself? Do her speech and her manner tend to give evidence of directness and honesty or evidence of slyness and excessive shrewdness that might result in her being a liability to the organization?

Knowledge. Does the applicant seem to have clear perception and good comprehension not only of the business but of affairs in general, or does she seem uninformed and ignorant? Does she show an ability to reason out problems and to come up with satisfactory solutions? Does she have the necessary technical skills required by the job? Can she present her ideas without unnecessary hesitation and without being at a loss for the right word?

Mental Attitude. Is the applicant cooperative, or is she argumentative? Is she enthusiastic, or is she indifferent? Does she seem reasonably open-minded and tolerant, or narrow-minded and intolerant? Does she appear to be adaptable to changing conditions? Does she seem optimistic or pessimistic? (A depressed, low-spirited individual is likely to be a difficult person around an office; and an excessively buoyant and over-optimistic person, of course, can be equally objectionable.)

Objectivity. Is the applicant objective? Can she make use of facts in a logical fashion and view them impartially with complete disregard of her own personal interests? (In the light of available data, a person should, within the limits of her own training, be able to make an objective judgment and to disregard her personal interests. This is especially important in business, for office workers are frequently called upon to make judgments in which they represent the firm for which they work. Their personal feelings should always be subdued.)

Self-opinion. What does the applicant think of herself? Is she reasonably self-reliant and self-assured without being objectionable? Or is she excessively timid and shy? Does she seem the bombastic type who is so egotistical, so conceited, and so boastful that she obviously would be a constant irritant to all about her in the office?

Effectiveness with People. Every prospective employer is very much interested in the way in which his employees can deal with people — with fellow workers, with various executives for whom the employee works, and with customers and other businessmen who come into the office. All the qualities previously mentioned have a great bearing on the effectiveness with which the applicant deals with people and are extremely important to the interviewer. The interviewer who has had considerable experience in dealing with applicants will readily detect many of these qualities during a talk with the applicant. As a matter of fact, his questions may be phrased in such a way that he tends to bring out the best and the worst in the applicant in order to make judgments about her ability to deal with people.

Job Interest. Although personal characteristics are of great interest to an interviewer, he will also ask questions about many other things and will endeavor to discern something of the applicant's job interest. Businessmen are interested in employing only those who are keenly interested in doing the job for which they have applied and who are planning to stay on that job for some time, unless, of course, they are making application for a part-time or temporary job.

When a person is applying for a job as a typist, file clerk, or general clerk, the interviewer normally assumes that the applicant is expecting to accept the position and is planning to stay with the firm for a period of

EMPLOYMENT INTERVIEW

Date		AGE	

Considered for

NAME

PRESENT ADDRESS

PERMANENT ADDRESS

TELEPHONE	MARRIED	HEIGHT	WEIGHT

REFERENCES
Name & Address

1.
2.

INTERESTS

1.
2.
3.

HIGH SCHOOL

COURSE

	AVERAGE	RANK IN CLASS	GRADUATED

COLLEGE

	AVERAGE	RANK IN CLASS	GRADUATED

MAJOR   MINOR

OTHER COURSES

ACTIVITIES

	AVERAGE	RANK IN CLASS	

PREVIOUS EMPLOYMENT

Address	From	To	Reason For Leaving
1.			
2.			
3.			
4.			

COMMENTS

Please show latest marks in following subjects:

    English -
    Typing -
    Office Machines -
    Bookkeeping -
    Shorthand -
    Math -

Estimated times absent during current school term -

Upon graduation do you plan to further your education? -
If so, where? -

PERSONAL CHARACTERISTICS INTERVIEW APPRAISAL

NAME (Last)   (First)   (Middle)   DATE OF INTERVIEW

1. *Complete immediately after interview.*

2. *Consider only one factor at a time, separate from all others.*

3. *Base your appraisal only upon observed characteristics; if unable to observe one or more, so state under QUALIFICATION.*

4. *Check the best description; if overlapping, check two; emphasize exceptions; underline or circle those most applicable.*

5. *If, in your opinion, description does not fit, note variation under QUALIFICATION.*

6. *In REMARKS, supplement your check-off with specific illustrations or more information on any characteristic noted as extreme.*

7. *Your RECOMMENDATION may summarize appraisal; if not, explain under REMARKS.*

FACTOR	1.	2.	3.	4.	5.	QUALIFICATION
A. General Appearance	Poor carriage; Slovenly; Disagreeable.	Compares unfavorably with average.	Average in looks; carriage; grooming.	Above average; makes good impression.	Attractive; alert; excellent carriage; sharp; well groomed.	
B. Voice and Speech	Distracting voice; poor use of language.	Dull, monotonous voice; poor enunciation.	Voice and speech average.	Clear, fluent and expressive.	Distinct pleasing voice; excellent word usage.	
C. Fluency	Too talkative; garrulous. No comments; no questions; answers inadequate.	Not offensively talkative but indiscriminate. Difficult to draw out.	Some questions and comments; answers brief but adequate.	Full answers; moderate comments and questions.	Responsive; numerous but intelligent questions and comments; detailed answers and questions. Easy to talk to.	
D. Emotional Stability	Jumpy; flustered; obviously ill-at-ease; belligerent; indignant; resigned.	Casual; blasé; almost smug. Too reserved and stolid.	Some initial constraint but more composed as interview progresses.	Even temperament; steady and calm.	Composed; completely at ease throughout interview; well balanced and cheerful.	
E. Self-evaluation	Conceited; egotistical; boastful; lacks confidence.	Shy; shows little trust in self; over-modest; over-confident.	Normally self-assured but diffident; inclined to be modest.	Intelligent and objective; admits abilities and short-comings.	Completely self-confident but modest. Intelligently rates own value with vocational interest.	
F. Courtesy	Bold; curt; impertinent; flippant; almost rude; not attentive.	Somewhat forward; discourteous; inattentive.	Candid and direct; without being discourteous; attentive.	Frank, open, but smooth; tact and courtesy.	Completely unreserved; very courteous; tactful and attentive.	
G. Convincingness	Arouses considerable doubt; lack of force; evasive; immature.	Not convincing; seems hesitant; lacks motivation.	Reasonably convincing; expresses ideas without difficulty; seems mature.	Logical; tactful; impresses as capable.	Drive and maturity; immediate impression of confidence.	
H. Personality	Flat; irritating; disagreeable.	Does not make impression.	Makes fair or average impression.	Seems pleasant; makes good impression.	Very pleasing; likeable.	

(left margin groupings:)
AUDIO-VISUAL IMPRESSIONS
MENTAL ATTITUDES AND BEHAVIOR

NUMERICAL TOTAL [ ]

REMARKS (Especially noted characteristics - specific)

RECOMMENDATION (Considering only observed characteristics as shown in this interview, do you recommend this applicant (or a position?)

☐ YES, WITHOUT RESERVATION (5)   ☐ STRONGLY (4)   ☐ ROUTINELY (3)   ☐ ONLY IN CASE OF URGENT VACANCY (2)   ☐ NOT AT ALL (1)

BY

An interview appraisal

years. The interviewer will almost invariably ask questions designed to discover the ultimate objectives of the prospective employee. He will expect to get answers that indicate that the applicant is planning to stay with the company, to seek advancement, and to make a career of his job. If a young woman is being interviewed, it is normally assumed that she will probably get married and eventually leave the company. If a young man is making the application, he is generally asked to indicate the kind of promotional opportunity he is looking for. As a rule, office employment can lead to excellent positions for young men. Many men who have been eminently successful in top business and professional positions started out as payroll clerks, mail clerks, cashiers, tellers, and so on.

If an applicant indicates that she really is seeking a career in some entirely different line, such as dancing or dramatics, and is merely applying for an office job to tide her over until the more desirable type of employment is open, she is not likely to be hired. The average firm feels that most employees are worth very little to them during the first six to twelve months of employment; consequently, they do not like to employ people who are not planning to stay at least two or more years. Of course, they always hope that their prospective employees will plan to stay for an unlimited length of time.

Adaptability. In addition to job interest, the adaptability of the applicant to his job is also a very important point of the interview. In coping with adaptability, the interviewer will almost invariably ask questions regarding the applicant's school background, the kind of subjects she studied, the grades she received in those subjects, her interest in doing particular kinds of work, and the extent to which she may have used her clerical or typing skills in connection with the school paper or other student activities. The interviewer will also be looking at any typing tests and clerical aptitude tests that the applicant has taken and may ask certain questions about them. For example, the typewriting test may not be as good as could be expected in the light of the grades the candidate received in school. The candidate may be asked to make some explanation of that. The clerical aptitude test may reveal a very great weakness in clerical background and belie somewhat the school record of the candidate. If grammar, punctuation, spelling, and vocabulary tests have been given, these may indicate points of strength or points of weakness about which the interviewer will want to talk to the candidate. As a result of the discussion, the interviewer will draw certain conclusions regarding the adaptability of the applicant to the particular job for which she is applying.

The Follow-Up. Before you learn the outcome of an interview, you may want to write a letter to the person who granted it to you to thank him for the interview. The letter will also serve as a follow-up to remind him of your availability for the position.

When you are offered a position, all that is left for you to do is to write a letter of acceptance. You will again use your return address in the upper right-hand corner. While you may not have known the company name in the letter of application (if the advertisement gave a box number), you are now fully cognizant of the firm name and address and the person to whom the letter should be addressed. You should clearly restate the title of the position and the salary that you are accepting. You may begin the letter by saying, for example:

> "Thank you for the invitation to join your staff as a general clerk at a salary of $65 a week. I am delighted to accept."

You may then continue:

> "I am looking forward to the opportunity of working in the Personnel Department of Abbott & Company, Inc.
>
> Very truly yours,"

Study Questions

1. How should you dress when you are going for an interview?

2. What are some of the questions you might anticipate in an interview?

3. What will the interviewer's evaluation include?

4. How should you follow up an interview?

What Do You Think?

1. What factors should you keep in mind when answering each of the following questions:

a. "Why do you want to work for this company?"

b. "As a beginning worker, are you more interested in the opportunity to gain experience than you are in the starting salary?"

c. "Why do you want to change from your present position?"

2. If an applicant is given an application blank and told that she may fill it in immediately and leave it, or take it home, fill it in, and mail it, which would be the better thing to do?

Your Personal Qualities

Alice Pickett was asked to appear for an interview at 10:15 a. m. at the office of the Jones Realty Company. She arrived on time, but the interviewer was in a meeting. Alice was required to wait 15 minutes before the interviewer could see her. When she did finally get in, she complained about being required to wait. She remained rather sullen during the entire interview.

Question: What is your evaluation of Alice's behavior?

How's Your English?

Read Appendix C and then indicate which of the following are incorrectly spelled:

accomodate	managing	siezed	dying
superintendent	subdueing	offence	drugist
colateral	milage	improvment	counterfiet
obvius	judgement	vacuum	salaries
		twenty one	cupsful
		sisters-in-law	check book
		by product	

Office Work

1. You may have been interviewed for employment. If so, give a report of the interview.

2. Prepare an appraisal sheet that might be used by an interviewer.

3. Using the appraisal sheet prepared for Exercise 2, rate yourself as you think an interviewer might.

Office Work Assignments

59: Interviewer's Work Sheet

In the particular business where you have applied for a position, the following qualities and characteristics are carefully checked on an appraisal sheet by the interviewer:

Appearance: neat, well-groomed, slovenly, average build, thin, stout, tall, short.

Dress: good taste, worn, careless, flashy, untidy.

Posture: well-balanced, very erect, slightly relaxed, slightly stooped, round-shouldered.

Facial Expression: radiant, happy, thoughtful, solemn, sullen.

Hands and Face: healthy looking, well cared for, physical impairment, heavy makeup, blemished, dirty.

Approach: poised, alert, forward, timid, awkward.

Volume of Voice: too loud, easily audible, too low, pleasant, shrill, monotone.

Enunciation: very clear, clear, passable, indistinct, omits syllables.

Pronunciation: faultless, occasional mistakes, frequent mistakes.

Grammar: faultless, occasional mistakes, frequent mistakes, bad, extremely bad.

Personality: magnetic, animated, pleasant, tactless, conceited, disagreeable.

Temperament: calm, confident, shy, excitable, phlegmatic, sullen.

Knowledge: clear perception, good comprehension, shrewd, understanding, uninformed, ignorant.

Attitude: cooperative, enthusiastic, attentive, indifferent, arbitrary, argumentative.

Self-opinion: modest, confident, timid, self-assured, conceited.

Interest in Position: exceptional, normal, below average.

Standing in Class: first quarter, second quarter, third quarter, fourth quarter.

Summary: superior, above average, average, below average.

Recommend Employment: yes, no.

Comments:

Prepare an appraisal sheet listing all of these items. Interview a fellow student for an office position, and fill in the appraisal sheet.

UNIT 14 | You as an Office Worker

PART 4:

Specialized Clerical Positions

Today's complex office equipment requires the specialized knowledges and operating skills of many trained and experienced clerical employees. Whether the equipment is owned or rented, it is imperative that this expensive equipment be operated by experienced and trained personnel. As a rule, promotions are made from within an organization. Consequently, a competent and alert supervisor is always on the lookout for beginning workers with potential abilities and sound basic skills — new employees who will eventually assume greater responsibilities and perform more demanding tasks after acquiring the necessary experience and training. The demand for specially trained clerical workers is particularly great in electronic data processing, records management, and clerical supervision.

ELECTRONIC DATA PROCESSING (EDP)

Perhaps the greatest unfilled demand for office workers today is in the electronic data processing area, specifically for key-punch operators, tabulating machine operators, and programmers.

Key-Punch Operators. Of the five basic input devices for computers — punched cards, punched paper tape, magnetic tape, optical scanners, and direct keyboard input — the punched cards are the oldest, and still the most widely used, form of computer input. An applicant for a position as a key-punch operator should have a net typing speed of at least 40 words a minute. The typical job description of the position includes "the operating of an alphabetic or numeric key-punch machine to record precoded or readily usable data following generally standardized procedures." The operator may also use a verifying machine to check the accuracy of the card punching of others before the data are fed into the computers. According to a nationwide report on EDP salaries,[1] the average weekly

---

[1]"Eighth Annual Report on EDP Salaries," *Business Automation* (June, 1966), p. 36.

Key-punch operators

salary for key-punch operators in the United States ranges from $77 for a trainee (beginner) to $116 for a senior key-punch operator.

      Tabulating Machine Operators.   This position has four separate classifications: trainee, junior, intermediate, and senior. The job description for a junior tabulating machine operator consists of "setting up and operating the simpler punched-card accounting machines, such as the sorter, reproducer, and the collator, and working from clearly defined instructions or following a repetitive pattern." The tasks of an intermediate tabulating machine operator are more extensive. They involve "the setting up and operating of any type of punched-card accounting machine, including tabulators and multipliers. The operator is required to wire boards from diagrams prepared by others for routine jobs, and to use prewired boards on complex or repetitive jobs." The average nationwide salary[2] is $84 for a trainee, $90 for a junior, $107 for an intermediate, and $126 a week for a senior tabulating machine operator.

      Programmers. The key person in a computer installation is the programmer, the man or woman who puts business and scientific problems

[2]*Ibid.*, p. 45.

in special symbolic languages that the computer can read, or compile, into the binary arithmetic required by the electronic circuits. These are called application programs, and cover computer jobs ranging all the way from payroll to chemical process control.

About half of the business programmers came to their positions with college degrees; the remaining half were promoted to their positions from within the organization. Prospective programmers are usually required to take an aptitude test before they are admitted to the class.

Business Week[3] recently reported that "the supply [of programmers] is far short of the demand, and the gap is widening inexorably. For the foreseeable future, there is literally no possibility that we shall have enough trained people to go around." The average nationwide weekly salaries of programmers reported in the "Eighth Annual Report on EDP Salaries"[4] follows: $140 a week for beginners (Programmer C); $151 for juniors (Programmer B); $179 for intermediates (Programmer A); $211 for Senior Programmers; $229 for assistant supervisors (Lead Programmers); and $247 a week for Managers of Programming.

RECORDS MANAGEMENT

"No physical activity of production or distribution goes on in our modern age without a piece of paper moving along to guide it," said Charles E. Wilson, a former president of the General Motors Corporation. These pieces of paper number in the hundreds of billions annually, and they contain a tremendous variety of vital information. A high percentage of these directives, explanations, forms, letters, memorandums, and reports are filed for future reference. Developing and operating systems and procedures for classifying, sorting, controlling, and retrieving these billions of pieces of paper is truly a monumental task.[5] It requires the services of an ever-increasing number of file clerks, file supervisors, heads of filing departments, and records managers.

All filing systems depend upon alphabetic or numeric sequences, or some combination of the two. Therefore, an office worker must know both sequences, as well as the rules that govern alphabetic and numeric filing systems, to be effective in handling business files. The file clerk's duties are described by the Administrative Management Society as follows:

> Keeps correspondence cards, invoices, receipts or other classified or indexed records arranged systematically in a file according to an established system. Locates and removes material upon request and

---

[3]"Software Gap, a Growing Crisis for Computers," *Business Week* (November 5, 1966), p. 127.

[4]*Business Automation, op. cit.*, p. 45.

[5]Ernest D. Bassett, Peter L. Agnew, and David G. Goodman, *Business Filing and Records Control* (3d ed.; Cincinnati: South-Western Publishing Co., 1964), p. iii.

keeps record of its disposition. May perform other clerical duties which are related but incidental.[6]

In 1966 the national average salary for a file clerk was $66 a week. Salaries were higher in certain urban areas of the United States and Canada and slightly lower in some rural areas.

The supervisor of the filing department must be familiar with all filing systems, equipment, and routines. She must keep up to date on all new developments in the field of records management and control. She must also train her file clerks and develop in them the prime requisites of accuracy in the small details of filing, neatness in the maintenance of records, and orderliness in handling them.

The records manager is responsible for the coordination and supervision of the firm's entire program, which includes the proper storage, retrieval, and disposal of records. His responsibilities often include the maintenance of the central files, the archives, the microfilming division, and in some large installations, the records kept on magnetic tape and discs with an electronic data processing system.

A high school diploma is adequate for a beginning file clerk, but additional courses in such subjects as records management, data processing, systems analysis, and personnel management are recommended for prospective supervisors. Some records managers have been promoted to their present positions from within the company; but because of the tremendous expansion of technical knowledge in recent years, a college degree, preferably in business administration, is rapidly becoming a basic requirement for the position.

CLERICAL SUPERVISION

The purchasing, shipping, receiving, and payroll departments provide excellent opportunities for promotion for ambitious young men and women.

The Purchasing Agent. The head of the purchasing department is usually referred to as the purchasing agent. He and his assistants buy the raw materials, machinery, supplies, and services required by the firm to carry on its operations. This department receives requisitions from the various departments listing and describing needed items. Since purchases can be made from many suppliers, the main task of the department is to select suppliers who offer the best values in the prevailing market. To make the proper selection, the purchasing staff must consider such factors as the exact specifications of the required items, quantity to be purchased, discounts for quantity buying, transportation costs, and delivery date.

[6]*Twentieth Annual Office Salary Survey for the United States and Canada 1966–1967* (Willow Grove, Pennsylvania: Administrative Management Society, 1966), p. 6.

The beginner or trainee in the purchasing department must spend considerable time learning about the firm's operations and purchasing procedures. He may be assigned to the storekeeper's section to learn about such operations as keeping inventory records, filling out forms to initiate purchases of additional stock, or providing proper storage facilities. After an initial training period, the trainee may become a junior buyer of standard catalog items. After he gains experience in the various aspects of purchasing and demonstrates ability to exercise good judgment and accept responsibility, he may be promoted to assistant buyer or assistant purchasing agent, and then to full-fledged purchasing agent.

For a more detailed description of the duties of a purchasing agent, and of shipping and receiving department supervisors which follows, read the *Occupational Outlook Handbook*. A revised edition of the *Handbook* is published every two years by the Bureau of Labor Statistics of the United States Department of Labor.

Shipping and Receiving Department Supervisors. High school graduates are preferred for beginning jobs in shipping and receiving departments. Business arithmetic, typing, clerical practice, and other business subjects are helpful in qualifying for a job. Also, it is very important that the applicant have legible handwriting. Both the shipping and receiving departments offer a young man a first-hand opportunity to learn about a firm's products, policies, and business procedures. Before a shipment is sent out, a shipping clerk checks it to be sure that the order has been filled correctly. He may type or prepare bills of lading and other shipping forms needed, look up freight and postal rates, record the weight and cost of the shipment, and check to see that the shipment is properly addressed. He may also maintain shipping records. A receiving clerk does similar work when the shipment reaches its destination. He makes sure that his employer's order has been correctly filled by comparing the original order with the items received and the accompanying bill of lading or invoice, and he must check to see that all the items have arrived in good condition. He usually maintains records of all incoming shipments.

A beginner often does routine work, such as checking addresses and attaching labels to each shipment, checking the items included, and filing. As he acquires experience, he may be assigned tasks requiring a good deal of independent judgment — for example, tracing lost shipments, or handling problems that arise because of damaged merchandise.

After he has the necessary training, a competent and conscientious employee has opportunities to become a department supervisor, an industrial traffic manager, or a warehouse manager. His chances for advancement are greatly improved if he takes collegiate courses in transportation,

A supervisor instructing a payroll clerk

systems management, personnel management, accounting, and other courses related to his duties.

Payroll Department Supervisors. There are four basic steps in payroll procedures:

1) Obtaining a record of the time worked by employees and their respective pay rates
2) Computing and recording the gross earnings of employees
3) Deducting and recording the tax deductions to find their net earnings
4) Preparing the following records: payroll register, employee's earnings record, and the paycheck

Payroll procedures have progressed through three stages in the last fifty years. Up to that time all employees were paid in cash, and there were no tax deductions. With the introduction of posting machines, the employee's earnings record, the payroll register, and the paycheck were completed with a single simultaneous operation. Payroll records were computed with tabulating machines when card-punch systems were installed. And today, one of the prime uses of computers is to prepare large and complex payrolls.

After a payroll trainee has demonstrated his ability to perform routine payroll tasks, to operate standard payroll office machines, and to work well with his co-workers, he may be considered for a more responsible position as a senior payroll clerk. With additional experience and training, he may earn promotion to head of his unit, then to assistant supervisor, and finally, to supervisor of the payroll department.

OPPORTUNITIES FOR FEDERAL EMPLOYMENT

Civil Service Positions. Since the federal government is the largest single employer of men and women in the United States, providing jobs for over 2.5 million civilians, you should be interested in knowing about the clerical job opportunities it offers. Almost half of the employees of the federal government are office workers, the majority of whom are women. They are engaged in many of the same office positions found in private industry, such as typist, clerk-typist, general clerk, stenographer, office machine operator, and receptionist. They are also engaged in office positions that are unique to federal employment, for example, as postal clerks, as office employees in the Internal Revenue Service, and as foreign service office workers for the Department of State.

After you have successfully completed a four-year high school program, you may qualify for a clerical civil service position without any previous business experience. Equal opportunities are given to all applicants regardless of their race, creed, or color.

Civil Service Tests. Performance tests are given for all branches of civil service for office positions requiring such measurable skills as typewriting, shorthand, transcription, and office machine operation. A minimum typing rate of from 40 to 50 net words a minute on straight copy is usually required for initial employment as a typist. Shorthand dictation is generally given at rates ranging from 80 to 100 words a minute. The notes must be transcribed on a typewriter within a reasonable time at a transcription standard set by the examining board.

Under certain circumstances arrangements may be made with some schools for teachers to issue a certificate (on a Civil Service Commission form) attesting to the required degree of proficiency in typing or stenography. The certificate must show that the applicant, not more than six months previous to the filing of the certificate, demonstrated the required proficiency to a teacher of typing or stenography in a public, parochial, or private four-year high school, or an accredited institution such as a business or commercial school, junior college, or college. The typing or stenography portion of the written tests will not be required of applicants who present a certificate.

The federal office worker

Written tests designed to measure intelligence, aptitudes, and general information possessed by the candidates are administered by the Civil Service Commission. Short-answer questions, which can be scored by machine, are used in preference to essay questions. They are presented in a number of forms: multiple-choice questions, true-false statements, and the matching of related facts. The answers are marked on a separate answer sheet with a special graphite pencil or a stylus.

All candidates must pass the verbal and clerical aptitude tests (including arithmetic computation) given as part of the examination.

Qualifications Requirements. In addition to passing the written tests, one must meet the following qualifications requirements to be eligible for the positions and grade levels included under the examination:

For Position of	The Requirement is
TYPIST GS-2 STENOGRAPHER GS-3	a. Successful completion of a four-year high school course; OR b. Six months of appropriate experience.
TYPIST GS-3	a. Successful completion of one academic year of substantially full-time study in a resident school above the high school level; OR b. One year of appropriate experience.

General Requirements. In addition to educational and experience requirements, there are some general requirements you will have to meet.

Age. There is no maximum age limit for federal civil service employment. The usual minimum age limit is 18, but for most jobs high school graduates may apply at 16. When an examination has a different minimum, the announcement will state it.

Citizenship. Examinations are open only to citizens or to people who owe permanent allegiance to the United States.

Physical Condition. You must be physically able to perform the duties of the position, and you must be emotionally and mentally stable. This does not mean that a physical handicap will disqualify an applicant as long as he can do the work efficiently without being a hazard.

Selection. When an agency wants to hire a new employee, the appointment officer of the agency asks the Civil Service Commission for the names of the persons who are eligible. The Commission then sends the agency the names of the top three persons on the eligibility list. The officer makes a selection from the three. In deciding which candidate to appoint, the officer may ask all three to come in for personal interviews. The names of those who are not selected are retained for future consideration.

Veteran's Preference. Candidates who establish veteran's preference and make passing grades on civil service examinations have five or ten points added to the scores they make in open competition examinations for appointment to jobs in the federal government. Extra points contribute to a higher ranking on eligibility lists.

Pay. A modern position-classification plan is used to determine the salary for each job according to the level of difficulty and responsibility of the work involved. Congress sets nationwide pay scales for 18 pay grades of classified positions. Employees receive periodic within-grade increases for satisfactory service.

Depending upon their qualifications, clerks are classified in grades GS-1 or GS-2; typists and alphabetic key-punch machine operators in grades GS-2 or GS-3; stenographers in grades GS-3 or GS-4; and teletypists in grades GS-3, GS-4, or GS-5.

The following table of salary rates for the first 15 grades of positions in the federal government is in accordance with the general schedule of the Federal Employees Salary Act of 1966. It was issued on July 1, 1966, by the United States Civil Service Commission:

SALARY RATES FOR FEDERAL EMPLOYEES

Grade	Entrance Salary (Step 1)	Maximum Salary (Step 10)
GS-1	$ 3,609	$ 4,711
GS-2	3,925	5,119
GS-3	4,269	5,560
GS-4	4,776	6,220
GS-5	5,331	6,915
GS-6	5,867	7,645
GS-7	6,451	8,368
GS-8	7,068	9,180
GS-9	7,696	10,048
GS-10	8,421	11,014
GS-11	9,221	12,055
GS-12	10,927	14,335
GS-13	12,873	16,901
GS-14	15,106	19,810
GS-15	17,550	23,014

OPPORTUNITIES FOR STATE AND MUNICIPAL EMPLOYMENT

Job Opportunities in State Governments. There are clerical positions available in all of the state government offices for qualified high school and college graduates. There are many opportunities in state government for high school graduates who have had no work experience. Each year many states conduct examinations for clerical jobs with no minimum education or experience requirements. During recent years New York State alone has been hiring 2,000 office workers annually.

The New York State Commission urges candidates who have had any training or experience in stenography or typing to go to the nearest state employment service office and sign up for an immediate examination. If they pass, they may be notified and on the job in a state agency within a week. The Commission reports that there are more than 5,000 stenographers and typists working for the state.

Working Conditions in State Civil Service. While working conditions in state civil service vary slightly from state to state, the following conditions prevail in most states:

1) State employees work a five-day week ranging from 35 to 40 hours, in state office buildings and installations that are noted for their modern, air-conditioned facilities.
2) The states maintain a salary schedule for the different job classifications that is in keeping with the prevailing rates of pay for

comparable jobs in private industry and in federal and municipal civil service systems.

3) Promotions to higher positions in state governments are generally filled from within the state civil service. As a rule, only the highest posts (policy-making and administrative positions or positions requiring highly specialized technical training and experience) are filled from outside the state civil service system. Most states maintain a wide variety of training programs designed to increase employee efficiency and to prepare employees for advancement within the system.

4) State employees usually receive a four-week paid vacation and pay for ten or eleven legal holidays each year, which is more than the average number granted to employees in private industry and in federal civil service.

5) Most state employees are members of a retirement system and are permitted to retire at half pay after 35 years of service. The tendency is to reduce the retirement age — at least one state has an optional plan of retirement at age 55.

Municipal Civil Service. The number of municipal civil service employees in units of the local governments, such as counties, municipalities, towns, school districts, or special districts, varies with the size of the municipality, ranging from fewer than one hundred employees in small communities to over a quarter of a million in some of the larger cities. The employment policies vary with the size of the municipalities. The larger ones tend to follow closely the state civil service policies and practices of their respective states by filling positions through some type of formal civil service tests and making promotions on the basis of merit. Municipal salaries and working conditions for office workers compare favorably with those offered by private industry in the same regions of the United States and Canada.

Study Questions

1. What are some of the reasons for the increased demand for office workers with specialized training as key-punch operators, tabulating machine operators, and programmers?

2. Why is post-high school training recommended for prospective filing supervisors?

3. What two major filing systems and sequences are used in most filing installations?

4. What are some of the major changes that have taken place in payroll procedures in the last fifty years?

5. Where could you find career information and detailed descriptions of the duties of purchasing agents, shipping clerks, and receiving clerks?

6. What are some of the office positions that are available only in civil service employment?

7. Depending upon their experience and previous training, typists and alphabetic key-punch machine operators are employed in two grades in the federal civil service. What are the two grades and what are the annual entrance salaries for these grades? What are the approximate weekly salaries for these grades?

8. What are the minimum shorthand dictation and typewriting speeds required for federal civil service employment?

9. What tests, other than the typewriting performance tests, are usually given for civil service clerical positions?

10. Assuming that you have had no previous office experience, where would you have your greatest opportunities for employment?

What Do You Think?

1. What specialized office positions do you think you would prefer and why?

2. What do you consider to be the advantages and disadvantages of taking an office position with a municipal agency, such as the board of education, the city hospital, or the village treasurer?

3. Assuming that the starting salaries are about the same, why do you think you would prefer to work either in private industry or for the federal government? In deciding upon your preference, consider the following factors:

    a. Your interest in the job and its surroundings.

    b. Your interest in the people you would work for and the people you would work with.

    c. Your relative opportunities for advancement and salary increases.

    d. The relative fringe benefits of private and public employment, including: the workweek; the number of paid holidays; the paid vacation time; the hospitalization, medical, and group insurance benefits; and job security.

4. Why do you think a merit system is desirable in government employment?

Your Personal Qualities

Miss Arlene Martin has had business training in high school and part-time experience in industry. She has decided that she would like to work for the federal government because she believes that the salaries are higher than those paid in private industry and that the fringe benefits are greater. The Civil Service Commission has announced a performance test for *Data Typist*, a new position in the electronic computing field, described as:

"Operates electric typewriter equipped with special keyboard to transcribe coded program instructions or data on magnetic tape."

Arlene prefers typing to machine transcription because she has the ability to type accurately at the rate of 60 words a minute, but she cannot transcribe at rates higher than 20 words a minute. If she passes the performance test, she will be called for an interview. She will also be asked to furnish references as to her education and experience.

Questions: 1. Should Arlene take the performance test for the position of data typist?

2. Should she take the job even though it may mean never using her ability to transcribe from a dictating machine?

How's Your English?

After reading Appendix D on abbreviations, identify the following:

Ala.	B/L	gr.	RSVP	UW
La.	do.	op. cit.	SS	WB
adv.	EOM	prem.	TO	chgs.

Office Work

Interview two office workers: one employed in a civil service position and one employed in private industry.

Ask them questions such as:

1. How did you get your job?

2. What qualifications did you have to have for the job?

3. What are your principal duties?

4. What phase of your work do you like best?

5. What training has been most helpful to you on the job?

6. In what areas do you feel that you should have had more training?

7. What suggestions do you have to offer to prospective office workers?

Prepare a typewritten report of your interviews.

UNIT 14 | *You as an Office Worker*

PART 5:

Your Career and You

A lot depends upon your choice of the right job. But your success on the job and your advancement depend upon yourself, your relationships with others, and your efficiency on the job. Your efficiency and your self-confidence in any new position will be increased if you are given some type of company orientation or preliminary on-the-job training.

Orientation of New Employees. The personnel departments of large companies offer formal orientation programs to all of their new employees. The programs are designed to give them an understanding of the importance of their jobs, the company's personnel policies and procedures, and a broad picture of the role of the company in the business world. An orientation program may cover many topics, but it usually includes:

1) A brief history of the company — its foundation, present organization, and role in the business world.

2) The products made by the company or the services rendered.

3) The type of customers or clients served by the company.

4) Basic salary information — payroll period, computation of pay (including the policy for the payment of overtime), and information on withholding for taxes.

5) The standard payroll deductions for fringe benefits, such as group life insurance, hospitalization, surgical benefits, and employee pension plan.

6) The company's policy with regard to hours in the workweek, paid holidays, and paid vacations.

7) The company's merit rating policy and its rules of conduct.

8) The company's promotion policy.

9) The structure of the specific department to which the new employee has been assigned.

10) The best methods of performing the work in the specific department with a minimum of effort.

The orientation of a new employee in a smaller company is much more informal — it may be given by your immediate supervisor or by a senior office worker. It, too, is designed to give you a better attitude toward your job and to eliminate the mistakes that you would inevitably make if you were left to turn out your work on a trial-and-error basis without supervision.

Your Office Image. First impressions are often lasting; therefore, you should try to create a favorable first impression on your new job. Here are some of the ground rules for creating a favorable office image:

Do

1) Dress the part of an office worker — even on those days when you have a special date after work or during the lunch hour.
2) Watch your grooming. Rain or shine, your hair must look smooth; your nails must be well cared for; your heels can't get run down.
3) Develop a well-modulated voice and keep it that way. Never talk to someone across the room. Go over to his desk.
4) Remember your posture when you are walking, when you are sitting, and especially when you are sitting at your typewriter.
5) Follow the company's regulations with regard to office hours, lunch periods, and coffee breaks.
6) Remember that your ultimate success depends upon the quality and quantity of your work and the attitude with which you do it.

And for avoiding an unfavorable image:

Don't

1) Call your immediate supervisor by his or her first name because some of your co-workers do.
2) Become too friendly too fast. Try to be on good terms with everyone, but do not join a particular office group at once. If you do, you may regret it later.
3) Make personal telephone calls unless they are absolutely necessary.
4) Use the company's time, stationery, and stamps for your personal correspondence.
5) Tell others how to do their jobs — without being asked.
6) Gossip.

Efficiency on the Job. If you are to get off to a good start on your new job, and it is essential that you do, you must work efficiently. Follow these six suggestions to increase the efficiency of your office work:

1) *Follow directions.* Do the job exactly as it was outlined to you. Be sure to listen to the directions carefully and write them down

so that they will not have to be given to you again the next time you do the same type of work.

2) *Ask questions.* If you are not sure how you should go about an assignment, ask your supervisor. Do not rely upon the person working next to you — he or she may not know and may give you incorrect information.

3) *Follow standard office practices.* Check the files to be sure that you are using the form and style that are used in typing letters, reports, interoffice memoranda, and all other previous correspondence. If you think that your method of doing the assignment is better, discuss it with your supervisor before attempting it.

4) *Produce your work on time.* If your employer is waiting for something you are doing, or if there is a specified time limit or deadline, complete the work even if it does take part of your lunch hour or if it keeps you overtime. Remember, when you are starting on a new job, you may not get things done so fast as your more experienced co-workers.

5) *Maintain high standards.* Whatever work you produce, keep your production standards high. No copy should leave your machine until you are absolutely positive that there is not a mistake in it, that corrections are not obvious, and that the paper is smudge free. No matter how tired you are or how pressured you are, don't let letters with poor erasing pass. In fact, find the eraser that works best for you on the paper used in your office.

6) *Check your facts and figures.* Check all facts, figures, titles, names, addresses, and dates at their source whenever it is possible. Remember, you cannot blame errors on someone who gave you the wrong answer to your question.

Your Personal Relationships. Your ability to get along with your supervisor, your co-workers, and the general public, and to work effectively with them, is just as important as your ability to work efficiently. A favorable attitude toward your work and good office habits usually go hand in hand; therefore, you should constantly try to be:

1) *Punctual* — no matter when your employer or your supervisor comes to work, you should be there on time; in fact, a bit early. Otherwise, you will feel rushed at the beginning of the day and may make many needless mistakes. Furthermore, if you are habitually late, you leave yourself open to criticism.

2) *Dependable* — get the work out even if it inconveniences you. Keep your absences to a minimum.

3) *Responsible* — always check your work. Make no snap judgments.

4) *Cooperative* — get one important concept in your mind: As an office worker, you are there to help your employer perform his clerical duties successfully; and your responsibility is to cooperate with your co-workers and your supervisor in turning out the

work assigned to your division. If you ever feel that you are more important than your supervisor or your employer, you cease to be of help to the firm.

5) *Pleasant* — do things with a smile. If your supervisor asks you to do something that will greatly inconvenience you, don't grimace, but agree to do it quickly and cheerfully. You must do it — one way or another.

6) *Sincere* — be as considerate and as courteous to your co-workers and to those who may work for you as you are to your supervisor and your employer.

7) *Loyal* — work for the best interests of your company and your own department. If you feel that something is wrong, discuss it with your immediate supervisor. Do not criticize him or his department to other employees. However, if you are completely dissatisfied and unhappy, change jobs. Always give at least two weeks' notice before quitting.

Your Merit Rating. After you have been employed for a probationary period — three months, six months, or possibly as long as a year — you may receive a merit rating. The purpose of the rating is to tell you how you are getting along on the job or how you "stand." It should reveal your strong points and your weaknesses — and yet afford you time on the job to overcome the latter. A satisfactory or a superior merit rating is a clear indication of your continued employment, possibly with an increase in salary.

If you should work for a small company, your rating may be informal: your supervisor may call you into his office and discuss your ability, your performance on the job, and your probable future with the company. A large company with established personnel policies is more apt to give you a formal merit rating, a rating that you would then discuss with your supervisor during a private interview.

Your Promotion. Eventually you will expect to be considered for promotion — to be given an opportunity for advancement. A promotion always carries with it added prestige, and usually a higher salary, but it also carries with it added responsibilities. It may also require special skills and supplementary knowledge. There is no clearly charted course to promotions — no standard set of procedures that will automatically insure your promotion — only a few suggestions that may be of help to you:

1) Master your present job completely. You cannot be seriously considered for a promotion until you have.

2) Strive to overcome any personality defects. You cannot supervise others if you cannot discipline yourself.

3) Maintain and, if possible, increase your office skills, especially your production rate in typewriting and your efficiency in the

operation of transcribing machines, calculators, duplicators, and other office machines.

4) Continue your general education — in evening courses, in extension courses, in company in-service courses, whenever and whereever you have the opportunity to do so.

5) Display initiative on the job. Think of ways to improve your efficiency, and be willing to take on new and different tasks.

6) Don't make the mistake of being overly ambitious and try to win a promotion at the expense of a better qualified candidate. If you have the qualifications, they will be recognized. Management is constantly seeking qualified employees for higher positions.

Study Questions

1. What are the advantages of an orientation program?
2. What are fringe benefits?
3. When should you be permitted to make personal telephone calls from an office telephone?
4. Why should you be as considerate and as courteous to the people who work for you as you are to your supervisor?

What Do You Think?

1. Discuss the Do's and Don'ts for creating a favorable office image. What are some which you would add to those listed on page 579?
2. Discuss what you would consider to be a good promotion policy.

Your Personal Qualities

Miss Patricia Moore was employed in the collection department of the Continental Book Company for approximately one year — from January 2 until December 31. On December 15, she told her supervisor that she was leaving on December 31 to become a full-time student at a community college. On December 22, every other member of the department who had been employed for a year or more received a Christmas bonus of two weeks' pay. She received none.

Question: Do you think she should or should not have received a Christmas bonus?

APPENDIX A | Grammar

In speaking or in writing, grammar plays a most important part. A command of the rules of grammar is necessary if the office worker is to meet adequately the responsibilities placed upon him.

While it is assumed that you as a student of office practice will have studied grammar, it nevertheless seems wise to review briefly the most bothersome phases of the subject.

Grammar is a study of the words of a language, but particularly a study of the relationship of those words to one another. Words are divided into eight classifications that are known as parts of speech. These classifications are: noun, pronoun, adjective, verb, adverb, preposition, conjunction, and interjection.

Nouns. A noun is a word that is used as the name of a person (Thomas Jefferson), place (Washington, D.C.), thing (desk), quality (goodness), action (fishing), or idea (immortality). A common noun names any of a class of beings or things. Examples of common nouns are: men, trees, tables. A proper noun names a particular being or thing. Examples of proper nouns are: Alexander Graham Bell, New York, Empire State Building. The distinction between the two types of nouns is that a proper noun is always capitalized.

A common noun that names a group is called a collective noun. Examples of collective nouns are: company, committee, crowd, jury, and group. A collective noun may be used to express either unity or plurality.

Pronouns. A pronoun is a word that is used instead of a noun. Most of the office worker's problems with pronouns arise from the use of personal and relative pronouns.

Personal Pronouns and Their Antecedents. A *personal pronoun* is a pronoun that shows by its form whether it represents the speaker (first person), the person spoken to (second person), or the person spoken of (third person). The *antecedent* of a pronoun is the noun for which it stands. The pronoun must be in agreement with its antecedent in person, number, and gender. There are several cases that often are misunderstood:

1. When two or more singular antecedents of a pronoun are connected by *and*, the pronoun must be plural.

> The stenographer and the mail boy have had *their* pay increased.

If, however, the antecedents are merely different names for the same person or thing, the pronoun must be singular.

> The well-known businessman and philanthropist has received *his* award.

2. When two or more singular antecedents of a pronoun are connected by *or* or *nor*, the pronoun must be singular.

> Either Joyce or Linda must bring *her* notebook.

If one of the antecedents is plural, it should be placed last, and the pronoun should be plural.

> Neither the general manager nor his assistants realized that *they* had so little time.

3. If the antecedent of a pronoun is a collective noun that expresses unity, the pronoun must be singular.

> The committee quickly reached *its* decision.

If the collective noun refers to the individuals or parts that make up a group, however, the pronoun of which it is the antecedent must be plural.

> The class brought *their* own lunches.

4. The number of an antecedent is not changed when it is followed by such connectives as *in addition to* and *as well as*.

> The boy, as well as his brothers, did *his* duty.

5. Since there is no third-person, singular-number, common-gender pronoun, the

masculine *he, his,* or *him* is generally used when the antecedent requires such a pronoun.

> Each office worker must do *his* best.

When it is especially desirable to convey accuracy, both masculine and feminine pronouns may be used.

> Every employee should be careful about *his* or *her* personal appearance.

Relative Pronouns. A relative pronoun is one that joins a subordinate clause to its antecedent. *Who, which, what,* and *that* (with their declined forms) are the relative pronouns. For example:

> Secretaries *who* know grammar are valuable.

The compound relatives, which perform the same function as do the single relatives, are *whoever, whosoever, whichever, whichsoever, whatever,* and *whatsoever.*

We face two basic problems in using relative pronouns: using the correct relative with reference to persons and things, and using the correct case form. *Who* refers to persons, and sometimes to highly trained animals; *which* refers to animals or things; *that* refers to persons, animals, or things.

Who, whoever, and *whosoever* are in the nominative case and are the correct forms when a relative pronoun is the subject of a subordinate clause.

> Mr. Johnson is a man *who* can do the job.

Whose is in the possessive case and is used as is any possessive.

> *Whose* hat is this?

Whom, whomever, and *whomsoever* are in the objective case and must be used when a relative pronoun is the object of a verb or preposition.

> Grace is the girl *whom* we are addressing?

The Pronoun after "Be." The same case must be used after the verb be in any of its forms (am, are, is, was, were, be, being, have been) as appears before it. This is usually the nominative case. When the object of a transitive verb, however, precedes the infinitive *to be,* the objective case must follow it. For example:

> It was *she.* (not *her*)
> If I were *he.* (not *him*)
> Did you expect those children to be *them*? (not *they*)

Adjectives. An adjective is a word that is used to modify a noun or a pronoun. There are two types of adjectives: descriptive or qualifying adjectives, and definitive or limiting adjectives. A *descriptive adjective* names some quality of or describes the person or object expressed by the noun or pronoun that it modifies, as: *pretty* girl, *handsome* child, *white* frock. A *definitive adjective* points out or expresses the number or quantity of the object named by the noun or referred to by the pronoun, as: *eight* people, *this* book, *that* desk, *ten* pages.

Proper Adjectives. Proper adjectives are those derived from proper nouns, and they are always capitalized: *French* language or *American* interests.

Comparison of Adjectives. Comparison is the inflection of an adjective to indicate an increasing or decreasing degree of quality, quantity, or manner. These degrees of comparison are positive, comparative, and superlative.

The *positive degree* is expressed by the simple form of the adjective: *light.*

The *comparative degree* is used to compare two objects. The comparative degree of almost all adjectives of one syllable, and of a few of two syllables, is formed by the addition of *r* or *er* to the simple form: *lighter.* The comparative degree of most adjectives of two or more syllables is formed by the placing of *more* or *less* before the simple form of the adjective: *more beautiful* or *less useful.*

The *superlative degree* is used to compare three or more objects. The superlative degree of most adjectives of one syllable, and some of two syllables, is formed by the addition of *est* to the simple form: *lightest.* The superlative degree of most adjectives of two or more syllables is formed by the placing of *most* or *least* before the simple form of the adjective: *most satisfactory* or *least attractive.*

Some adjectives are compared irregularly. The following are a few:

Positive	Comparative	Superlative
good	better	best
much	more	most
little	less	least
far	farther	farthest

Articles. *A, an,* and *the* are called articles. *A* and *an* are indefinite articles as they merely limit the noun to any one in a class: *a* person, *an* application. *The* is called a definite article because it singles out a particular person or thing in a class.

The manager read *the* application.

Verbs. A verb is a word that shows action or state of being of the subject. Verbs are classified as transitive and intransitive.

A *transitive verb* is one that requires an object to complete its meaning. The object may be a noun or a pronoun and it must be in the objective case. The object is used to complete the meaning of the verb.

He *reported* the accident.

To determine the object of a transitive verb, ask "What?" or "Whom?"

An *intransitive verb* does not require an object to complete its meaning.

The light *shines.* The boy *ran.*

Many verbs may be used both as transitive and intransitive verbs. For example, in the sentence "The boy ran," *ran* is an intransitive verb requiring no object. The verb "ran" may, however, be used as a transitive verb.

The boy *ran* a race.

Here *race* becomes the object of the verb *ran,* and the verb becomes transitive.

Some verbs, however, may be used correctly only as intransitive verbs. *Sit, lie,* and *rise* are examples of verbs that are always intransitive as they permit no object, while *set, lay,* and *raise* are examples of verbs that are always transitive because they require an object to complete their meaning. *Sit* and *set, lie* and *lay,* and *rise, arise,* and *raise* are frequently misused.

Voice of Verbs. Voice indicates whether the subject of the verb is the doer of the action or the receiver of the action that is expressed by the verb. A verb in the *active voice* identifies the subject as the doer of the action.

The new stenographer *typed* the letter.

A verb in the *passive voice* identifies the subject as the receiver of the action.

The letter *was typed* by the new stenographer.

Any transitive verb may be used in either the active or the passive voice.

In the independent clauses of a compound sentence or in a series of related statements, verbs of the same voice should be used. This is known as *parallel construction.*

Wrong: The letter *was dictated* by the executive and the secretary *transcribed* it.

Right: The executive *dictated* the letter and the secretary *transcribed* it.

Tense. Tense denotes the time of the action. There are three primary tenses: present, past, and future. The *present tense* of a verb is used to denote the present time. It is used in expressing a general truth or that which is generally customary. The present tense is also used to describe more vividly what took place in past time. This is known as *historical present.*

Washington *crosses* the Delaware and immediately *attacks* Trenton.

The *past tense* denotes past time.

We *shipped* your order yesterday.

The *future tense* denotes that which will take place in the future. The future tense is expressed by the use of *shall* or *will* with the present form of the verb.

I *shall go* early. You *will arrive* on time. She *will come* in at eight o'clock.

Frequent errors are made in the use of *will* and *shall.* The future tense may be used to express simple futurity or to express determination or promise. Simple futurity is denoted by the use of *shall* with the first person, and *will* with the second and the third persons.

I *shall be* happy to see you when you arrive.
He *will be* home early.

If determination or promise is to be expressed, the rule for futurity is reversed. Use *will* with a first-person subject, *shall* with a second- or third-person subject.

I *will be* there without fail.
You *shall* certainly *go.*
They *shall return* tomorrow.

In asking questions, use *shall* when the subject is in the first person (I, we).

Shall we go?

When the subject is in the second or third person, either *shall* or *will* may be used, depending upon which form is expected in the answers, as:

Will you write the letter? (Answer expected: I *will* write the letter.)
Shall you miss your friends when you move? (Answer expected: I *shall* miss my friends.)

In addition to the primary tenses, there are three verb phrases, known as the perfect tenses, that represent completed action or being. They are the present perfect, the past perfect, and the future perfect. The *present perfect* tense denotes an action or an event completed at the present time. It is formed by the placing of *have* or *has* before the perfect participle.

I *have read* several chapters.
He *has studied* his French.

The *past perfect* tense denotes an action or an event completed at or before a stated past time. It is formed by the placing of *had* before the perfect participle.

They *had completed* the picture by the time dinner was served.
I *had assumed* you would come by plane before we received your letter.

The *future perfect* tense denotes that an action or an event will be completed at or before a stated future time. It is formed by the placing of *shall have* or *will have* before the perfect participle.

I *shall have gone* before you arrive.
He *will have reached* his destination before you can get there.

Whether *shall have* or *will have* is used depends upon the basic rule for the use of *shall* or *will*.

Mood. Mood is that property of a verb that indicates the manner in which the action or state of being is expressed. The three moods are indicative, imperative, and subjunctive.

The *indicative mood* is used in asserting something as a fact or in asking a question. The *imperative mood* is used in expressing a command, a request, or an entreaty. The *subjunctive mood* is used in expressing a doubt, a wish, a future contingency, or a supposition contrary to reality. A condition contrary to present reality is expressed with *were*, not *was*.

Wrong: If I *was* tall, I could reach the book.
If Ann *was* going, you could go along.

Right: If I *were* tall, I could reach the book.
If Ann *were* going, you could go along.

A condition contrary to past reality is expressed by *had been*.

If the plane *had been* on time, this might not have happened.

Agreement of Verb and Subject. The agreement of verb and subject sometimes causes trouble. A verb must agree with its subject in person and number. The verb *to be* has person and number forms: *I am, you are, he is, we are, you are,* and *they are; I was, you were, he was, we were, you were,* and *they were.* Other verbs have only one inflection for number and person. When the subject is in the third person, singular number, a verb or an auxiliary in the present or the present perfect tense must end in *s*.

Mr. White *dictates* very slowly.
Miss Stewart *has* been his secretary for a long time.

A very common error is the use of a singular verb with a plural subject.

1. When the verb and the subject are separate in the sentence, you must be careful to see that the verb agrees with its subject. A common error is to make the verb agree with the word near it rather than with the real subject.

Wrong: The *activity* of the board at its meetings *are* always interesting.

Right: The *activity* of the board at its meetings *is* always interesting.

2. If the subject is plural in form but singular in meaning, a singular verb is required.

The news *has* been good.

3. Two or more singular subjects connected by *or* or *nor* require a singular verb.

Neither Kurt nor Bill *is* at the office.

4. When two or more subjects connected by *or* or *nor* differ in number, the plural subject is placed nearest the verb and the verb made plural.

> Neither the office staff nor the executives *are* to have that bulletin.

When two or more subjects connected by *or* or *nor* differ in person, the verb must agree with the subject that is nearest it.

> Either you or I *am* at fault.

It is frequently better to rephrase the sentence so as to use a verb with each subject.

> Either you *are* at fault or I *am*.

5. Two or more singular subjects connected by *and* require a plural verb.

> The typewriter and the adding machine *are* both in need of repair.

6. When the subjects connected by *and* refer to the same person, a singular verb must be used.

> The great novelist and playwright *is* on his way home.

7. When the subjects connected by *and* represent one idea or are closely connected in thought, a singular verb should be used.

> Ice cream and cake *is* a popular dessert.

8. When either or both of the subjects connected by *and* are preceded by *each*, *every*, *many a*, etc., a singular verb is required.

> Each stock boy and foreman *is* expected to work late on the inventory.

9. When one of two subjects is in the affirmative and the other in the negative, the verb agrees with the one in the affirmative.

> The teacher, and not the students, *is* planning to attend.

10. The number of a subject is not affected by words connected to it by *as well as*, *and also*, *in addition to*, etc.

> Mother, as well as the rest of the family, *is* expecting to go.

11. When a collective noun expresses unity, a singular verb is used.

> The jury *is* asking that a point be clarified.

When a collective noun expresses disunity or separate and independent action by the individuals, a plural verb is used.

> The jury *were* out a long time, but they failed to reach a decision.

Contractions. Contractions may be used in letters to people with whom the writer is on an informal plane or to add a more personal tone. In writing contractions, remember that *don't*, the contraction of *do not*, is plural and is used with plural nouns and the pronouns *I*, *we*, *you*, and *they*. *Doesn't*, the contraction of *does not*, is singular and is used with singular nouns and the pronouns *he*, *she*, and *it*.

> It *doesn't* bother me much, but I *don't* like it.

Infinitives. An infinitive is a form of the verb that asserts nothing, but merely names in a general way the action or the state of being. It is characterized by the word *to* placed before the verb: *to be*, *to walk*, *to talk*, *to cry*. The infinitive may be used as a noun, the subject of a sentence, a predicate noun, or the object of a verb. It may also be used as an adjective or an adverb.

The sign of the infinitive is omitted after such verbs as *bid*, *dare*, *feel*, *see*, *need*, *help*, *hear*, *let*, and *make*.

> She saw him *open* the door.

Participles. A participle is a verb form used as an adjective having the double function of verb and adjective. There are three forms of the participle: present, past, and perfect. The *present participle* is formed by the addition of *ing* to the simple form of the verb. It expresses action as being in progress, usually at the same time as some other action. It is used as an adjective and at the same time retains some of the properties of a verb.

> The clerk *counting* the money is new here.

In this sentence *counting* is an adjective modifying the noun *clerk;* it also has the property of a verb in that it takes the object *money*.

The *past participle* expresses action prior to that of the governing verb. It is used as an adjective and is usually formed by the addition of *d* or *ed* to the present tense of the verb.

> The machine *used* by the secretary was defective.
> The teacher, *interrupted* by the students, did not complete her grading.

The *perfect participle* is formed by the combination of *being, having,* or *having been* with some other participle.

> *Having written* the letters, she was free to go.

In the preceding sentence the perfect participle *having written* modifies the subject of the sentence *she.*

A common error is that of putting at the beginning of a sentence a participial phrase that does not modify the subject. This is referred to as a *dangling* participle.

> **Wrong:** Having completed the statement, it was time to file the letters.
>
> **Right:** Having completed the statement, she found it was time to file the letters.

Adverbs. An adverb is a word used to modify a verb, an adjective, or another adverb. An adverb answers the questions *how, when, where, how much?*

> She walked *lightly.*
> He arrived *early.*
> The report is *here.*
> The clerk will file *more.*

Adverbs modify adjectives and other adverbs by expressing degree, answering the questions *how, to what degree?*

> He is used to *very* hard work.
> Julia writes *rather* well.

Comparison of Adverbs. Like adjectives, adverbs are compared to show degree. A few adverbs are compared by the addition of *er* or *est* to the simple form of the adverb: *thin, thinner, thinnest.* A few are compared irregularly: *well, better, best,* or *far, farther, farthest.* Most adverbs, however, are compared by the use of *more* or *most,* or *less* or *least,* with the simple form of the adverb.

Placing the Adverb. Ordinarily an adverb follows the verb it modifies, but it may precede it, especially if the verb is followed by a complement or has other modifiers. Fundamentally it should be placed where its meaning is most clearly shown. *Only, merely,* and *also,* which are sometimes adverbs and sometimes adjectives, give the most trouble in placing, as they may convey very different meanings in different positions in a sentence:

> *Only* I saw him.   I saw *only* him.
> I *only* saw him.   I saw him *only.*

Other Problems with Adverbs. There are a few other errors in the use of adverbs that are commonly made.

1. *Very* or *too* should not be used to modify participles.

> **Wrong:** She was *very* pleased.
>
> **Right:** She was *very* much pleased.

2. *Too,* which is an adverb that means *also* or *more than enough,* should be spelled correctly and not confused with *to* or *two.*

> By *two* o'clock she had *too* much work *to* do.

3. *Well* is usually an adverb. In speaking of health, however, *well* is used as an adjective. Be careful not to use *good* as an adverb in place of *well.*

> **Wrong:** He does his work *good.*
> I don't feel very *good.*
>
> **Right:** He does his work *well.*
> I don't feel very *well.*

4. *Very* is an adverb of degree, while *real* is an adjective of quality. Do not use *real* in place of *very.*

> **Wrong:** He had a *real* beautiful office.
>
> **Right:** He had a *very* beautiful office.

5. Adverbs of manner, those ending in *ly,* are frequently confused with adjectives derived from the same root. Adverbs of manner modify verbs that express action.

> She sings *sweetly.* (Adverb)
> Her singing is *sweet.* (Adjective)

6. Two negatives should not be used to express negation.

> **Wrong:** The clerk will *not* wait for *nobody.*
>
> **Right:** The clerk will *not* wait for *anybody.*
>
> **Right:** The clerk will wait for *nobody.*

Prepositions. A preposition connects a noun or a pronoun with some other element of the sentence and shows the relationship between them. The noun or pronoun that follows the preposition is its object. A group of words made up of a preposition and its object, together with any words used to modify the object, is called a *prepositional phrase*. The object of a preposition may be determined by asking *whom* or *what* after the preposition; what the phrase modifies may be determined by asking *what* or *who* before the preposition.

In order to avoid ambiguity, phrases, like adjectives and adverbs, should be placed as close as possible to the words they modify.

Choice of Prepositions. Many errors are made in the use of prepositions because some words demand certain prepositions: *angry with* is used in reference to persons, and *angry at* is used in reference to things, animals, or situations. There are many situations in which prepositions are misused. Some of the most common follow.

1. *Into* should be used after a verb that indicates the motion of a person or a thing from one place to another. *In* is used after a verb expressing the idea of rest or, in some cases, motion within a certain place.

> The girl went *into* the classroom.
> The clerk is *in* the filing department.

2. *Between* should be used only in reference to two persons or objects. *Among* should be used when referring to three or more persons or objects.

> The two boys divided the work *between* them.
> Gifts were distributed *among* the natives.

3. Prepositions that are not needed should not be used.

> **Wrong:** The wastecan is *in under* the desk. Where is it *at?*
>
> **Right:** The wastecan is *under* the desk. Where is it?

4. Do not omit prepositions that are needed to make sentences grammatically correct. Avoid telegraphic style in letters.

> **Wrong:** Mr. Finley will arrive North Station 11:00 Sunday.
>
> **Right:** Mr. Finley will arrive at the North Station at 11:00 a.m. Sunday.

Conjunctions. A conjunction is a word used to connect words, phrases, or clauses. There are two kinds of conjunctions, coordinate and subordinate. *Coordinate conjunctions* connect words or clauses of the same grammatical relation or construction, neither dependent upon the other for its meaning.

> You *and* I are elected.
> Their father is out of town, *and* their sister is on a vacation.

A *subordinate conjunction* connects a subordinate clause with some word in the principal clause upon which it is dependent for its meaning.

> The man left hurriedly *lest* he be seen.

Correlative conjunctions are conjunctions that are used in pairs; the first introducing, the second connecting the elements. They must be placed just before the elements that they introduce or connect.

> **Wrong:** I will *either* meet you in Boston *or* Washington.
> I will meet you *either* in Boston *or* Washington.
>
> **Right:** I will meet you in *either* Boston *or* Washington.
> I will meet you *either* in Boston *or* in Washington.

Or should always be used with *either; nor*, with *neither*. They are used in reference to two things only.

> **Wrong:** *Either* Bob, Jack, *or* Don will pitch today's game.
> *Neither* the superintendent, the principal, *nor* the teachers agreed with him.
> *Neither* Jack *or* Don will pitch today's game.
>
> **Right:** Bob, Jack, *or* Don will pitch today's game.
> The superintendent, the principal, *and* the teachers disagreed with him.
> None of them — the superintendent, the principal, the teachers — agreed with him.
> *Neither* Jack *nor* Don will pitch today's game.

As . . . as is used when equality is expressed, while *so . . . as* is used for a negative comparison.

> I earn *as* much *as* you do but not *so* much *as* your brother does.

Some things to watch in the use of conjunctions follow.

1. Conjunctions should not be used in place of some other part of speech.

> **Wrong:** Seldom *or* ever should such an example be used.
> You should try *and* improve your speech.
>
> **Right:** Seldom *if* ever should such an example be used.
> You should try *to* improve your speech.

2. A clause, which is a part of a sentence containing a subject and a predicate, having meaning in itself, is connected to the other parts of the sentence by either a conjunction or a relative pronoun. A phrase, which contains no verb and has no meaning in itself, is introduced by a preposition, participle, or infinitive, but not by a conjunction.

> The project cannot be completed *without* your help. (*Without* is a preposition.)
> The project cannot be completed *unless* you help us. (*Unless* is a conjunction.)

3. *Except* and *without* are prepositions and should not be used in place of *unless*, which is a conjunction.

> **Wrong:** You will not master shorthand *except* you concentrate.
>
> **Right:** You will not master shorthand *unless* you concentrate.

4. *Like* is not a conjunction and should never be used in place of the conjunction *as.*

> **Wrong:** She walks *like* you do.
>
> **Right:** She walks *as* you do.

Grammar Reference Books. Although many questions concerning grammar can be answered by using a good dictionary, you should have available a standard reference book on English grammar.

In Appendix G you will find a list of recommended books. A ready reference on grammar will help you produce better letters and reports for your employer.

APPENDIX B | Punctuation

Punctuation is used to make more forceful and to indicate more clearly the relationships of written thoughts. Punctuation is the written substitute for the change in voice, the pause, and the gestures that are used in oral expression.

Generally speaking, the extravagant use of punctuation marks is not considered good form at the present time. Notwithstanding the tendency to simplify punctuation, the importance of an accurate usage of punctuation marks is illustrated daily by the serious errors that may be found in correspondence.

You will be responsible for the correct punctuation of your business writing. Although you are not expected to be an authority on punctuation, you should be familiar with the most important rules. The following rules cover the most common uses of punctuation marks.

Period. The period is used:

1. After complete declarative or imperative sentences.

> Today we shall study the use of the period.

2. After initials in a name.

> R. L. Andrews

3. After most abbreviations. Following are some exceptions approved by several authorities:

> Mme (Madame), Mlle (Mademoiselle); IOU, c/o, OK, SOS, A1, %; chemical symbols, H_2O, Zn, Pb; offices and agencies of the federal government, SEC, FBI, FCC

4. Before decimal fractions, between dollars and cents when expressed in figures, and after the abbreviations *s.* and *d.* for shillings and pence.

> 3.45 $16.13   13s.   7d.

5. For ellipses. Usually three periods or dots are used to indicate the omission from quoted matter of one or more words when the omitted portion does not end with a period. Four periods are used when the omitted portion does end with a period.

> The path was long and narrow . . . the weary boys walked slowly. . . .

Comma. The comma is the most frequently used form of punctuation; therefore, errors in its use are more frequent. The comma is used:

1. To set off a subordinate clause preceding a main clause.

> When the bell rings, you may leave.

2. To set off a nonrestrictive phrase or subordinate clause. (A phrase or a clause is nonrestrictive if the main clause in the sentence expresses a complete thought when the nonrestrictive phrase or clause is omitted.)

> My doctor, who is now on his vacation, will prepare the report next week.

3. To separate long coordinate clauses that are joined by the conjunctions *and, but, for, neither, nor,* and *or.* The comma precedes the conjunction.

> He worked far into the night, for the deadline was noon the next day.

4. To set off phrases or expressions at the beginning of a sentence when they are loosely connected with the rest of the sentence.

> Generally speaking, we feel the way you do about it.

5. To separate words, phrases, or clauses in a series. Note that a comma precedes the last item in the series.

> The group now has no meeting place, no supplies, and no money.

> They told us when they heard it, where they heard it, and from whom they heard it.

6. To separate two or more adjectives if they both precede or follow the noun they modify, provided each adjective modifies the noun alone. If an adjective modifies a combination of a noun and another adjective, however, no comma is used between the two adjectives.

> An old, shaggy, forlorn-looking dog came limping out to greet us.
> Happy young people come here frequently.

7. To set off words and phrases used in apposition.

> My cousin, whose name is Jean, will arrive soon.

8. To set off parenthetical words, clauses, or phrases.

> Tomorrow, on the other hand, business will be much better.

9. To set off words in direct address.

> Finally, children, we must all be ready when the time comes.

10. To set off *yes* or *no* when used in sentences.

> Yes, you may go now.
> Frankly, no, I don't care.

11. To set off the name of a state when it is used with a city.

> They lived in Denver, Colorado, for many years.

12. To separate the day of the month from the year and to set off the year when used with the month.

> The project must be completed by August 20, 1961, at the latest.

13. To set off a mild interjection.

> Ah, he surely enjoyed that story.

14. To set off a participial phrase used as an adjective.

> Smiling pleasantly, she entered the office.

15. To separate unrelated numbers.

> In 1960, 25 new students enrolled.

16. To divide a number of four or more digits into groups of three, counting from right to left.

> 1,567,039

17. To set off phrases that denote residence or position.

> Professor William Smith, of Harvard, will speak.

18. To indicate the omission of a word or words readily understood from the context.

> In June the book sales amounted to $523; in July, to $781.

19. Before a short, informal, direct quotation.

> The employer asked, "Have you transcribed those letters?"

Semicolon. The semicolon is used:

1. In a compound sentence between clauses that are not joined by a conjunction.

> That is good taste; it suggests discretion.

2. Before connectives, when such words introduce sentences, principal clauses, or an abrupt change in thought. (The comma follows the connective when used in this manner only if the connective is to be emphasized.) Some of these connectives are *also, consequently, for, hence, however, if, in fact, in short, nevertheless, that is, therefore, whereas, yet.*

> It is February; therefore we have many holidays.

3. Before such words and abbreviations as *e.g., i.e., viz., for example, namely,* and *to wit* when they introduce a long enumeration or list of items. A comma precedes the enumeration.

> . . . number of points; for example, accuracy, neatness, . . .

Interrogation Point. The interrogation point (question mark) is used after a direct question, but not after an indirect question.

> Are you ready?
> He asked what caused the fire.

A technically interrogative sentence embodying a request but courteously disguised as a question does not need the interrogation point.

> Will you please let us know your decision at once.

Exclamation Point. Like the period, the exclamation point represents a full stop. It is used at the end of a thought expressing strong emotion or command. The thought may be represented by a complete sentence, a phrase, or a word.

> Ha! We caught you this time!

Colon. The colon is used:

1. To introduce formally a word, a list, a statement, or a question; a series of statements or questions; or a long quotation.

> The book had many good points: it contained an interesting story; it contained humor; it was well illustrated.

2. Between hours and minutes when they are expressed in figures.

> 8:30 a.m.   1:45 p.m.

3. After salutations in some styles of business letters:

> Dear Sir: Gentlemen:

Apostrophe. The apostrophe is used:

1. To form the possessive case of nouns.

> corporation's records

2. To show omission or contraction.

> the Class of '67
> don't (for do not)
> it's (for it is)

3. To form some plurals. (See Appendix C for rules for forming plurals.)

4. Followed by a *d* to form the past and past participle of arbitrarily coined verbs.

> OK'd   yes'd   bravo'd

The Possessive Forms of Words. There are several rules that govern the forming of the possessive case of words, depending on the ending letter or syllable of the word and whether the word is singular or plural. A few important rules for the formation of possessives follow:

1. The possessive of singular and plural common and proper nouns not ending in a sibilant (excepting *ce*) is usually formed by the addition of an apostrophe and *s* to the singular form.

> secretary's letter   women's hats
> Dun's Review   Lawrence's mail

2. The possessive of singular and plural common nouns ending in *s* is formed by the addition of only the apostrophe.

> boys' hats   ladies' manners
> committees' reports

3. The possessive of a monosyllabic proper noun ending in a sibilant is generally formed by the addition of an apostrophe and *s*, although in journalism addition of only the apostrophe is frequently seen.

> Burns's poems   Marx's ideas

4. The possessive of proper nouns of more than one syllable ending in a sibilant (excepting *ce*) is formed by the addition of an apostrophe only.

> Essex' papers   Adams' chronicle
> Burroughs' house

5. The possessive of a compound word or expression is formed by the addition of the apostrophe or the apostrophe and *s* (according to Rules, 1, 2, and 3) to its *last* part.

> mother-in-law's visit
> City of Detroit's council
> letter carrier's route
> passers-by's expressions

6. The possessive of a series of names connected by a conjunction denoting joint ownership is indicated by apostrophe or apostrophe *s* to the last name.

> Simon and Walters' garage
> Adams and Anderson's firm

7. If joint ownership does not exist in a series of names, the possessive case is formed by the addition of an apostrophe or apostrophe and *s* to each proper name in the series.

> Macy's and Haynes's stores
> Jack's, Joe's, and Bill's gloves

8. The possessive of abbreviated words is formed by the addition of an apostrophe and *s* to the last letter of the abbreviation.

> YMCA's membership
> the X's function
> the Mr.'s position in the heading
> the OK's presence

9. The apostrophe is not used to form the possessives of pronouns.

Dash. The dash is formed in typewriting by the striking of two hyphens in succession without a space preceding or following them. The dash is used:

1. To denote a change in the sense or the construction of a sentence.

> Hemingway, Wolfe, Greene — these are my favorites.

2. Instead of a comma to emphasize or to guard against obscurity.

> The laborer is worthy of his hire — if his labor is.
> If — and only if — we go, the day will be complete.

3. To indicate an omission of letters.

Mr. K —, of P — Street

4. To precede a reference.

No, the heart that has truly loved never forgets. — Moore.

Parentheses. Parentheses are used:

1. To enclose figures or letters that mark a series of enumerated elements.

She wanted three things: (1) promotion, (2) salary increase, and (3) more responsibility.

2. To enclose figures verifying a written-out number.

twenty (20) dollars
twenty dollars ($20)

3. To enclose material that is indirectly related to the main thought of a sentence.

We shall postpone (at least for the present) a decision.

4. To enclose matter introduced as explanatory material.

The answer (see page 200) is puzzling.

Parentheses with Other Marks of Punctuation. The rules covering the use of other marks of punctuation with parentheses are:

1. If needed in the sentence, a comma or dash that normally precedes a parenthetic element is transferred to follow the closing parenthesis.

He sent a belated, though clever (and somewhat personal), greeting.

2. Punctuation at the end of a parenthetic expression precedes the parenthesis if it applies to the parenthetic material only; it follows the parenthesis if it applies to the sentence as a whole.

When I heard him (he shouted, "Who goes there?"), I was surprised.
(See the discussion on page 78.)
This experiment had interesting results (see Table I).

Quoted Matter. When quoted matter appears within a letter, an article, or a report, it is advisable that it be indicated as a quotation. This may be done in three ways: (1) the material may be indented from the regular margins on the left and right, (2) it may be underscored throughout, or (3) it may be enclosed in quotation marks. Sometimes the matter being quoted is both indented and enclosed in quotation marks. The practice of using quotation marks is the most common.

A long quotation is frequently single-spaced, even though the rest of the copy is double-spaced.

Quotation Marks. Quotation marks are used:

1. To enclose direct quotations. Single quotation marks are used to enclose a quotation within a quotation.

The director said, "I hope you are familiar with this play."
She said, "Unkind as it may be, I can't help saying 'I told you so' to her."

2. To enclose the titles of articles, plays, lectures, reports, etc., and the titles of subdivisions of publications (that is, the titles of parts, chapters, etc.). The titles of books and magazines are not enclosed in quotation marks, but underscored or typed in all capital letters.

Have you seen "My Fair Lady"?
She thought the chapter "Producing Mailable Transcripts" was helpful.

3. To enclose unusual, peculiar, or slang terms.

Her "five o'clocks" were famous.
When they saw us, they "flipped."

4. To enclose words used as words, words used in some special sense, or words to which attention is directed in order to make a meaning clear.

He said "yes," not "guess."
The term "title by possession" is often used.

5. To enclose the names of ships, the titles of pictures, the titles of short poems and songs, and the names of art objects.

"U.S.S. Oregon"
Shelley's "To a Skylark"
Leonardo da Vinci's "Mona Lisa"
the statue of "Winged Victory"

6. When consecutive paragraphs of the same work are quoted, at the beginning of each paragraph but at the end of only the last paragraph.

Quotation Marks with Other Marks of Punctuation. At the end of quoted material, a quotation mark and another mark of punctuation are often used together. The rules governing the order of these marks are not entirely logical; but since they are well established and generally accepted, you should follow them.

1. A period or a comma should precede the quotation mark even though it may not be a part of the quotation.

"I saw you," he said, "when you left."

2. A semicolon or colon should follow the closing quotation mark, even though it may be a part of the quotation.

They visited that "house of antiques"; and the "antiques" were really unusual. There is this to say about his "mission": it is fictitious.

3. Other marks of punctuation should precede the closing quotation mark if they apply to the quotation only, and should follow the mark if they apply to the sentence as a whole and not just to the quotation.

She asked, "Will you go?"
Did you read the article "Better Sales Letters"?

Spacing after Punctuation Marks. One space is left after punctuation marks within a sentence, with the exception of the colon. Two spaces are left after colons and all punctuation marks at the ends of sentences.

Exceptions to the basic rules above are that you do not space after:

1. A period used within an abbreviation written in small letters. (a.m., c.o.d., etc.)

2. A period used as a decimal point within a series of figures. (3.141, 10.5)

3. A comma used to separate a number into groups of three. (1,268,749)

4. An apostrophe written within a word. (don't)

5. The first punctuation mark when two marks are used together. ("Why not?")

Emphasis. A typist can emphasize an important word, phrase, or sentence in typewritten material in several ways. The kind of copy and the purpose for which it is being typed determine to some extent the relative emphasis that should be indicated.

In typewriting, underscoring takes the place of printed italics and is the method most often used to give prominence to a word or group of words. Punctuation marks (except the hyphen in compound words) and the spaces between words are not underscored. Emphasis is also achieved by typing in red in the midst of copy typed in black or blue, and by making characters darker by typing over them several times.

Lists of Itemized Data. A listing of books, items of merchandise, prices, etc., is frequently easier to read as a tabulation. In setting up material of this sort, the typist should set off the tabulation from the rest of the copy by indenting from both margins and by leaving space before and after the tabulation. Care in centering the tabulation will be reflected in the appearance of the work on the page.

Paragraphing. Paragraphing is a mechanical device that separates written matter into parts. It divides a sentence or a group of sentences from the rest of the copy by spacing and indention. In this way the reader's attention is called to only a part of the copy at a time, and he is not confused by too many thoughts given without interruption or pause.

Paragraphing is more than a mechanical means of dividing copy into parts. In well-written work a single paragraph develops one thought or a group of thoughts that can be logically presented together. A paragraph division should, then, guide the reader by indicating that there is at least a slight change in thought.

In a business letter, relatively short paragraphs — shorter than those found in ordinary composition — are usually considered desirable. The reader of business letters is often forced to do this work hurriedly and with many interruptions. Short paragraphs that make the thoughts stand out clearly are therefore helpful to him. Although long paragraphs are to be avoided, a series of paragraphs averaging only two or three lines in length is also undesirable. Overparagraphing not only interrupts the thought but also, by its frequency, fails to provide the distinct break that is needed between parts of a letter.

APPENDIX C | Spelling and Word Choice

Every office worker must have a knowledge of spelling and the meaning of words. It will be your responsibility to spell correctly. Misspelled words, even if they are nothing more than typographical errors, distract the attention of the reader and thus detract from the effectiveness of written material.

The selection of the right word for the occasion requires a true understanding of the meanings of words. The selection is sometimes made difficult by certain peculiarities of the English language, such as the prevalence of words that sound alike but are spelled differently and have different meanings. Poor enunciation by the user furthers confusion many times.

To produce accurate and attractive written material, you must also have a good working knowledge of compound words, plural forms of words, and rules for word division. The habit of consulting a dictionary is a wise one for you to acquire.

Spelling. The only way to learn to spell is to become so familiar with words that you spell correctly without giving special thought to it. You undoubtedly are certain about most words, but there are probably some about which you are never certain. You should always refer to your dictionary when you are in doubt, and you may find it helpful to record such words in a list that you can review from time to time. In this way you will soon master those difficult words and thus get a competence in writing that will be of immeasurable value to you.

Spelling rules are noted for exceptions. There are, however, a number of them that are helpful to those who are attempting to master the words they use.

1. A final *e* is usually dropped before a suffix beginning with a vowel.

hope, hoping	guide, guidance
judge, judging	manage, managing
prove, provable	subdue, subduing
Exceptions:	
shoe, shoeing	dye, dyeing

2. Final *e* is usually retained before a suffix beginning with a consonant.

lone, lonely	hate, hateful
move, movement	pale, paleness
Exception:	
argue, argument	

3. Before the suffix *ing*, *ie* is changed to *y*.

die, dying	lie, lying

4. A final double consonant is retained before a suffix.

will, willful	odd, oddly
ebb, ebbing	

5. Usually the final consonant is doubled in words of one syllable, or words ending in a single consonant preceded by a single vowel with the accent on the last syllable, before a suffix beginning with a vowel.

occur, occurred	refer, referring
begin, beginning	plan, planned
Exceptions:	
fix, fixed	refer, reference

6. Final *y* preceded by a consonant is usually changed to *i* before a suffix not beginning with *i*.

worry, worried	army, armies
Exceptions:	
shy, shyness	beauty, beauteous

7. Final *y* preceded by a vowel is usually retained before any suffix or the letter *s*.

annoy, annoyance	buy, buyer
delay, delayed	pay, payable
journey, journeys	attorney, attorneys

8. Final *l* is always single in words ending in *ful*.

careful	hopeful
doubtful	skillful

9. Only one word ends in *sede — supersede;* only three words end in *ceed — exceed, proceed,* and *succeed;* all other words having this sound end in *cede — concede, intercede, precede, secede.*

10. When *i* or *e* come together in the same syllable, generally *i* is used before *e*,

596

except when they have the sound of long *e* following *c* or when they have the sound of long *a.*

belief	friend
priest	ceiling
conceit	receipt
receive	freight

Exceptions:

either	seize
counterfeit	weird

Words That Are Pronounced Alike. Words that are pronounced alike but are different in meaning are known as *homonyms.* They are much more apt to be confusing than are *antonyms,* words opposite in meaning, or *synonyms,* words that have the same general meaning.

Typical homonyms are:

aloud, allowed	heard, herd
bear, bare	medal, meddle
break, brake	their, there
capital, capitol	through, threw
coarse, course	to, too, two

You should be aware of not only true homonyms, but also words that should not be pronounced alike but often sound much alike. Common words in this group are:

adapt, adept, adopt
addition, edition
affect, effect
all ways, always
assent, ascent
council, counsel
disburse, disperse
instance, instants
patience, patients
test, text

Only by studying words constantly can one avoid the confusion that can be caused by homonyms.

Compound Words. In the regular routine of daily business, one class of words that gives considerable trouble is made up of compound words. Compound words fall into three groups: hyphenated compounds, single-word compounds, and two-word compounds.

There are a few rules that will assist you in becoming familiar with certain groups of compound words that use the hyphen.

1. A hyphen is always used in a compound number.

twenty-one, fifty-eight

2. A hyphen is used between the numerator and the denominator of a fraction written in words, except (a) when one of the elements contains a hyphen and (b) when the fraction is used as a noun.

four-fifths share   forty-one hundredths
two-thirds interest forty one-hundredths
one half of the total
two fifths of the class

3. A hyphen is used between two or more words when the words serve as a single adjective *before* a noun. In applying this rule you must be careful that the words are not a series of independent adjectives. The exception to the rule is that proper nouns made up of two or more words are not hyphened when used as adjectives.

a well-liked boy, *but* a boy well liked
a fresh-water fish, *but* a fish from fresh water
a New England dinner, a New Jersey product
a large black horse; a deep, clear pool

4. Groups of three or more words used as a single word are usually hyphened.

give-and-take, four-in-hand, well-to-do, sister-in-law

5. A hyphen is used after a prefix (a) when the prefix is joined to a proper noun; (b) to prevent confusion between some verbs and a few compounds; and (c) to prevent an awkward piling up of consonants. Ordinarily, however, a prefix is written as a part of the main word.

pro-English, re-form (meaning to form again), re-sign (meaning to sign again), bell-like

When *any, every, no,* and *some* are combined with other words, the compound is a single word: *anything, everyone, nowhere, somehow.* Sometimes, however, the parts of the compound expression are written as separate words: *no one, every one.*

A great many compounds are not covered by these rules. When in doubt consult a good dictionary. The following compounds are in common use and therefore deserve attention:

Hyphened Compounds:

by-line	half-dollar
by-product	interest-bearing
court-martial	looker-on
cross-file	ready-made
cross-question	self-confidence
ex-president	trade-in
follow-up	vice-consul

Single-Word Compounds:

aforesaid	laborsaving
afterthought	layman
already	letterhead
although	makeshift
altogether	makeup
always	meantime
bankbook	middlemen
beforehand	midnight
billboard	misspelling
bimonthly	network
bondholder	nevertheless
bookkeeper	northeast
businesslike	notwithstanding
bylaws	outgoing
cannot	overdue
checkbook	overhead
faraway	payday
forever	payroll
guesswork	percent
handmade	policyholder
handwriting	postcard
headline	postmarked
headquarters	takeoff
henceforth	trademark
hereafter	transatlantic
inasmuch	viewpoint

Two-Word Compounds:

account book	income tax
all right	notary public
assembly room	parcel post
bank note	pay envelope
card index	post office
cash account	price list
civil service	trade name
fire escape	trade union
ice cream	vice versa

The Plural Forms of Words. Some words exist in only the plural form (*annals, news, thanks*), and other words are the same in both the singular and the plural forms (*deer, corps, chassis*). Still other words are irregular in form (*man, men; child, children; foot, feet*). Generally speaking, however, the plural of a word is formed by adding *s* if the plural has the same number of syllables as the singular, or *es* if the plural has an extra syllable. An exception to this rule is found in some words ending in *o* (*motto, mottoes; potato, potatoes*), although other words ending in *o* follow the rule (*piano, pianos; folio, folios*).

You will find the following rules for the forming of plural words helpful:

1. Form the plurals of nouns ending with *y* preceded by a consonant by dropping the *y* and adding *ies*. When the *y* is preceded by a vowel, add *s* only.

> salary, salaries; story, stories; alley, alleys

2. Form the plural of a hyphened compound noun by changing the principal word of the compound from singular to plural. The principal word of a compound is not always the last word.

> sisters-in-law, cross-purposes, passers-by

3. Form the plural of a single-word compound by adding *s* to the end of the word.

> cupfuls, viewpoints, headquarters

4. The plurals of some words of foreign origin are formed in accordance with the rules of the language from which they are taken.

> axis, axes; datum, data; alumnus, alumni; alumna, alumnae

5. A few words of foreign origin have both foreign and English plural forms. In some cases, one form is preferred over the other (*strata* instead of *stratums*), while in other cases both forms are considered equally acceptable (*indexes* and *indices; memorandums* and *memoranda*). Consult a dictionary to see if there is a preferred form for plural words of foreign origin.

6. Two persons bearing the same name and title may be referred to in the following manner: *The Messrs. Haviland, The Misses McKenzie, The Doctors Butler*, or *The Mr. Havilands, The Miss McKenzies, The Doctor Butlers*. In formal and business language, the plural form of the title is preferred.

7. The plurals of figures, letters, noun-coinages, proper nouns of more than one syllable ending in a sibilant, and words used as words only are formed by the addition of an apostrophe and *s* to their singular forms.

> the 1920's
> the &'s
> Her I-don't-care's were . . .
> The Curtis's said . . .

Word Division. Frequently a word must be divided at the end of a line in order to keep the right margin even. Words should be divided only between syllables. In case of doubt, consult a dictionary. The following rules apply to typewritten copy:

1. When a final consonant preceded by a single vowel is doubled before addition of a

suffix, divide the word between the two consonants.

2. A single-letter syllable at the beginning or the end of a word should not be separated from the remainder of the word. (*above* not *a-bove*)

3. A two-letter syllable at the end of a word should not be separated from the rest of the word. (*slowly* not *slow-ly*)

4. A syllable that does not contain a vowel should not be separated from the rest of the word. (*wouldn't* not *would-n't*)

5. Hyphened words should be divided only at the hyphens. (*by-product* not *by-prod-uct*)

6. A four-letter word should not be divided; it is seldom permissible to divide five- or six-letter words. (*into* not *in-to*)

7. When a word containing three or more syllables is to be divided at a one-letter syllable, the one-letter syllable should be written on the first line rather than on the second line. (*maga-zine* not *mag-azine*)

8. When a word is to be divided at a point where two vowels that are pronounced separately come together, these vowels should be divided into separate syllables. (*continu-ation* not *continua-tion*)

9. Compound words should be divided only between the elements of the compound. (*turn-over* not *turno-ver*)

10. Proper names should not be divided, and titles, initials, or degrees should not be separated from names.

11. Avoid dividing words at the end of more than two successive lines, at the end of a page, or at the end of the last complete line of a paragraph.

12. Avoid awkward or misleading divisions that may cause difficulty in reading. (*carry-ing* not *car-rying*)

13. When the single-letter syllable *a*, *i*, or *u* is followed by *ble*, *bly*, *cle*, or *cal*, do not separate the single-letter syllable and the suffix.

14. Avoid the division of figures and abbreviations, the parts of an address or date. If necessary to separate an address, leave together the number and street name.

| 2143 Market | *not* | 2143 |
| Street | | Market Street |

In separating a date, leave the day with the month.

| March 3, | *not* | March |
| 19-- | | 3, 19-- |

Words That Are Obsolete, Archaic, Colloquial, Dialectal, and Slang. Not all the words that are in the dictionary are entirely suitable for business correspondence. The dictionary indicates that some are obsolete, archaic, colloquial, dialectal, or slang. The meanings of these classifications are:

Obsolete: Words no longer in use.

Archaic: Words long out of use in ordinary language.

Colloquial: Words limited in use to distinct districts and to ordinary conversation.

Dialectal: Words used in certain dialects or professional forms of a language.

Slang: Words of a widely current but usually ephemeral nature (especially coined or clipped words) having a forced, fantastic, or grotesque meaning or exhibiting eccentric or extravagant humor or fancy.

All of these groups should be avoided in work that you compose. If such words are dictated, you probably should transcribe them unless you know your employer is willing to have improvements made in his word usage.

In some instances your employer may want slang expressions enclosed in quotation marks to indicate that he is conscious that they are slang. Such quotation marks are necessary only if an expression that is used as slang might not be recognized as such without quotation marks.

Technical Words. Technical words are those that apply to a narrow range of activity. Every activity has its own group of technical words. The *tonsilectomy* of the medical profession, the *tee* of the golf course, the *differential* to be repaired in the garage, and the *dihedral angle* of airplane wings are examples of technical words.

If you are to be employed in a specialized activity, you must learn the technical words and terms used. The ability to use the words accurately and to spell them correctly is essential. In some fields, highly specialized dictionaries or special word lists have been developed. These will undoubtedly be available in the offices of firms in these fields.

Use of the Dictionary. The office employee who wishes to advance does not guess about the spelling or the usage of a word; in cases of doubt, she always consults a dictionary. A single misspelled word or a word inaccurately hyphened is not worth the time saved by not using the dictionary. It may detract seriously from the effectiveness of the writing. If such an error is discovered by your employer, it may alter his opinion of your ability. The employee whose advancement is not to be limited gains confidence in her work by consulting the dictionary and thus knowing that the material she types is entirely accurate.

APPENDIX D | Abbreviations

The use of abbreviations is guided by custom and preference. A general rule for correspondence is to use abbreviations sparingly — for words that are traditionally abbreviated. A more generous use of abbreviations is allowed in the typing of forms, such as invoices and statements, where there are space limitations.

Abbreviations of Proper Names. For proper names there are generally accepted rules that should be followed carefully.

1. A person's family name should never be abbreviated. Given names may be represented by initials, but it is desirable for others to conform to a person's own style of signature. For example, if a person signs his name *Henry R. Grimm*, it is good form for others to write his name that way, rather than *H. R. Grimm*. As a general rule, given names such as Charles or William should not be abbreviated to Chas. or Wm., unless the person himself uses the abbreviations so consistently that it is obvious that it is the spelling he prefers.

2. Names of cities, with the exception of the word "Saint," should not be abbreviated.

3. As a general rule, names of states and territories should be spelled out. For general correspondence, the Post Office Department has no approved abbreviations for Alaska, Idaho, Iowa, Hawaii, Maine, Ohio, and Utah. Other states and territories *may* be abbreviated as follows:

Ala....................Alabama
Ariz...................Arizona
Ark....................Arkansas
Calif..................California
C. Z...................Canal Zone
Colo...................Colorado
Conn...................Connecticut
D. C...................District of Columbia
Del....................Delaware
Fla....................Florida
Ga.....................Georgia
Ill....................Illinois

Ind....................Indiana
Kans...................Kansas
Ky.....................Kentucky
La.....................Louisiana
Md.....................Maryland
Mass...................Massachusetts
Mich...................Michigan
Minn...................Minnesota
Miss...................Mississippi
Mo.....................Missouri
Mont...................Montana
N. H...................New Hampshire
N. J...................New Jersey
N. Mex. (or N. M.).....New Mexico
N. Y...................New York
N. C...................North Carolina
N. Dak. (or N. D.).....North Dakota
Nebr. (or Neb.)........Nebraska
Nev....................Nevada
Okla...................Oklahoma
Oreg. (or Ore.)........Oregon
P. R...................Puerto Rico
Pa. (or Penna. or Penn.)...Pennsylvania
R. I...................Rhode Island
S. C...................South Carolina
S. Dak. (or S. D.).....South Dakota
Tenn...................Tennessee
Tex....................Texas
Vt.....................Vermont
Va.....................Virginia
V. I...................Virgin Islands
Wash...................Washington
W. Va..................West Virginia
Wis. (or Wisc.)........Wisconsin
Wyo....................Wyoming

Although in the past abbreviations have not been advised for envelope addresses, the Post Office Department has now approved a list of two-letter all-capital state abbreviations. They were developed for the convenience of those businesses using automated data processing equipment, but anybody can use them. The only restriction is that they cannot be used unless the ZIP code is also used — if they are, the mail is subject to return.

Alabama...........................AL
Alaska............................AK
Arizona...........................AZ
Arkansas..........................AR
California........................CA
Canal Zone........................CZ
Colorado..........................CO
Connecticut.......................CT

Delaware...........................DE
District of Columbia...................DC
Florida...........................FL
Georgia...........................GA
Guam............................GU
Hawaii............................HI
Idaho...........................ID
Illinois...........................IL
Indiana...........................IN
Iowa.............................IA
Kansas...........................KS
Kentucky.........................KY
Louisiana.........................LA
Maine............................ME
Maryland.........................MD
Massachusetts.....................MA
Michigan..........................MI
Minnesota.........................MN
Mississippi........................MS
Missouri..........................MO
Montana.........................MT
Nebraska.........................NB
Nevada...........................NV
New Hampshire...................NH
New Jersey.......................NJ
New Mexico......................NM
New York........................NY
North Carolina....................NC
North Dakota.....................ND
Ohio.............................OH
Oklahoma........................OK
Oregon..........................OR
Pennsylvania......................PA
Puerto Rico.......................PR
Rhode Island......................RI
South Carolina....................SC
South Dakota.....................SD
Tennessee........................TN
Texas............................TX
Utah.............................UT
Vermont..........................VT
Virginia..........................VA
Virgin Islands.....................VI
Washington.......................WA
West Virginia.....................WV
Wisconsin.........................WI
Wyoming.........................WY

Abbreviations in the Body of a Letter.
The shortening of words in the body of a letter can convey a lack of care and time in presenting an attractive, thoughtful message. One should not write: The adv. can be supplied for your dept. @ 50¢ per p. It would be better to say: The advertisement can be supplied for your department at the rate of 50 cents per page.

Abbreviations may be used in the body of a letter when they have become commonly recognized symbols, such as SEC, FTC, CIO, and YMCA. A letter should be understood rather than made to follow a single practice. If, therefore, a person is writing to someone who may not understand an abbreviation, it is better to spell

it out so that any possible confusion may be avoided. If the term is referred to frequently, it may be spelled out the first time and abbreviated thereafter. For example, the complete title "Securities and Exchange Commission" may be used first; then in subsequent references, the abbreviation SEC may be used if the document being prepared is not a formal document.

A list of abbreviations commonly used in business is given below. Remember, however, that they are used primarily in tabulations and forms, with the exception of a limited number that are in general usage. There is considerable variation among business offices in the use of periods and capitalization, and the forms given here are not the only correct forms but merely those thought to be in most general use.

A

ABA............American Bankers Association, American Bar Association
ac., acct.........account
ad int............in the meantime
adm.............administration, administrative, admiral
admin...........administration
adv.............adverb, advertisement, advertising, advisory
advt............advertisement
AEC.............Atomic Energy Commission
AFL-CIO.......American Federation of Labor and Congress of Industrial Organizations
agcy............agency
agt..............agent
alt...............alternate, altitude
amt.............amount
anon............anonymous
ans..............answer(ed)
a/o.............account of
app.............appendix, apparatus
approx..........approximate(ly)
apt..............apartment
arr..............arranged, arrival, arrive
asgd............assigned
asso., assoc......associate, association
assn............association
asst.............assistant
att., attn.........attention
atty.............attorney
avg.............average
avdp............avoirdupois

B

bal..............balance
bbl..............barrel, barrels
BD.............bank draft
bk..............bank, book
bkg.............banking
bkt.............basket, bracket
BE.............bill of exchange

B/L	bill of lading	dec	deceased, declaration, decrease(d)
bldg	building	deg	degree(s)
blk	black, block, bulk	dep	depart, department, deposit, depot, deputy
BO	bad or back order, branch office, buyer's option	dept., dpt	department
BP	bills payable	dif., diff	difference, different
BR	bills receivable	dis., disc	discount
br	branch, brass, brown	dist	distance, district
bro(s)	brother(s)	distr	distribute, distribution
brt. fwd., B/F	brought forward	div	divided, dividend, division
BS	balance sheet, bill of sale	DL	day letter (telegrams)
bu	bureau, bushel(s)	do	ditto, the same
bull	bulletin	doc	document
bx	box	dol	dollar(s)

C

C	carbon, centigrade, hundred
CA	capital or current account
canc	canceled, cancellation
cap	capacity, capital, capitalized
cat	catalog
CC	carbon copy
CD	certificate of deposit
cert	certificate, certification, certify
cf	compare, confer
CFI	cost, freight, insurance
chap	chapter
chem	chemical, chemist, chemistry
chg(s)	charge(s)
cir., circ	circular
ck	check
cl	claim, class, clause, clearance, close
clk	clerk
cml., coml	commercial
c/o	in care of
co	company, county
COD	cash on delivery, collect on delivery
col	college, color(ed), column
coll	collected, collector
collat	collateral
com	commissioner, committee, common
comm	commission, commonwealth
conf	conference
cong	congress, congressional
cont	containing, contents, continued, control
corp	corporation
cor. sec	corresponding secretary
CPA	Certified Public Accountant
CPS	Certified Professional Secretary
cr	credit
CS	chief of staff, civil service
ct	carat, cent, count, court
cts	cents
cu	cubic
cur	currency, current
cust	customer
CWO	cash with order
cwt	hundredweight

D

DBA, d.b.a	doing business as

doz., dz	dozen(s)
dr	debit, debtor
DS	days after sight
dup	duplicate

E

ea	each
econ	economic(s), economist, economy
ed	edited, edition, editor education
elec	electric, electrical, electricity
enc., encl	enclosure
engr	engineer, engraved, engraving
env	envelope
EOM	end of month
esp	especially
est	established, estate, estimate(d)
et seq	and the following
exc	excellent, except(ed)
exch	exchange(d)
exec	executive
exp	expense, export, express
ext	extension, exterior, external(ly), extra

F

FAS	free alongside
fed	federal, federation
FHA	Federal Housing Administration
fig	figure, figurative(ly)
FOB	free on board
fol	folio, following
FR	full-rate (telegrams and cables)
frt	freight
ft	feet, foot, fort
fut	future
fwd	forward(ed)

G

gal	gallon(s)
gds	goods
gen	general(ly)
gov	governor
govt	government
GPO	Government Printing Office
gr	grain(s), gross, grade
gr. wt	gross weight

H

hd.............head
hf.............half
Hon...........Honorable
hon............honor, honorary
hp.............horsepower
HP.............high pressure
HR.............House of Representatives
hr.............hour(s)
ht.............height

I

ib., ibid.........the same, in the same place, from the same source
IBM...........International Business Machines
ICC............Interstate Commerce Commission
id.............the same
i.e............that is
ill., illus.........illustrated, illustration
imp............imperative, imperfect, import(ed)(er)
in.............inch(es)
inc............incorporated, increase
incl............inclosure, including, inclusive
incr............increase(d)
ind............independent, index, industrial, industry
ins............inspector, insurance
inst............instant, institute, institution, institutional
instr...........instructor, instrument(s), instrumental
int............interest, interior, internal international
introd..........introduction
inv............invoice
i.q............the same as
ital............italic, italicized

J

J..............judge, justice
jct., junc.........junction
jour............journal
JP.............justice of the peace
jr.............junior

K

kc.............kilocycle(s)
kg.............keg., kilogram(s)
kt.............karat
kw.............Kilowatt

L

l..............left, length, line, liter
lab............laboratory
lb(s)...........pound(s)
LC.............letter of credit
LCL............less than carload lot
LH.............left hand
lit............literal(ly), literary
ll.............lines
ltd............limited
lv.............leave

M

M..............Monsieur, thousand
man............manual
manuf...........manufacture(d), manufacturing
mar............maritime
max............maximum
MC............Member of Congress, master of ceremonies
mdse...........merchandise
mech...........mechanical, mechanics
med...........medical, medicine, medium
mem...........member, memoir, memorial
memo...........memorandum
Messrs.........Messieurs, Gentlemen
met............metropolitan
mfg............manufacturing
mfr............manufacture(r)
mgr............manager
mi.............mile(s), mill
min............minimum, mining, minister, minor, minute
misc...........miscellaneous
mkt............market
Mlle............Mademoiselle
mm.............millimeter
Mme............Madame
Mmes...........Mesdames
mo.............month
Mr.............Mister
Mrs............Mistress
MS.............manuscript
Ms.............Miss or Mrs. (when title uncertain)
MSS............manuscripts
mtg., mtge........mortgage
mun............municipal

N

NAM...........National Association of Manufacturers
nat............national, native, natural
natl............national
neg............negative(ly)
NF.............no funds
NG.............no good
NL.............night letter (telegrams)
No.............north, number
non seq..........it does not follow
NP.............notary public
nr.............near
nt. wt...........net weight

O

obj............object, objective
obs............observation, obsolete
OC.............overcharge
OD.............overdraft, overdrawn
o.e............omissions excepted
op. cit..........in the work cited
opp............opposite
ord............order, ordnance
orig............original(ly)
o/s............out of stock
oz.............ounce(s)

P

p. . . . . .page, part, penny, per,
               pint, post
PA. . . . . .power of attorney,
               purchasing agent
pam. . . . . .pamphlet
par. . . . . .paragraph, parallel
pat. . . . . .patent(ed)
payt. . . . . .payment
PBX. . . . . .private branch exchange
PC. . . . . .petty cash
pc(s). . . . . .piece(s)
pct. . . . . .percent
pd. . . . . .paid
per an. . . . . .per annum, by the year
perf. . . . . .perfect, perforated
pert. . . . . .pertaining
pfd. . . . . .preferred
pk. . . . . .park, peak, peck
pkg. . . . . .package
pl. . . . . .place, plate, plural
PO. . . . . .post office, postal or
               purchase order
pop. . . . . .popular, population
PP. . . . . .parcel post
ppd. . . . . .prepaid, postpaid
pr. . . . . .pair, price, printed
pref. . . . . .preface, preference,
               preferred, prefix
prelim. . . . . .preliminary
prem. . . . . .premium
prep. . . . . .preparatory, prepare
pres. . . . . .present, president
prin. . . . . .principal
prod. . . . . .production
pro tem. . . . . .for the time
PS. . . . . .postscript
pt. . . . . .part, payment, pint, point,
               port
publ. . . . . .publication, published

Q

qr. . . . . .quarter, quire
qt. . . . . .quantity, quart
ques. . . . . .question
quot. . . . . .quotation

R

rec. . . . . .receipt, record(ed)(er)
recd. . . . . .received
ref. . . . . .reference, referred,
               reformed, refunding
reg. . . . . .register(ed), registrar,
               regular, regulation
Rep. . . . . .Representative,
               Republic(an)
retd. . . . . .returned
rev. . . . . .revenue, reverse, review(ed),
               revise(d), revision
Rev. . . . . .Reverend
RFD. . . . . .Rural Free Delivery
RH. . . . . .right hand
rpt. . . . . .repeat, report
rm. . . . . .ream, room
RN. . . . . .registered nurse

RR. . . . . .railroad, rural route
RSVP. . . . . .please reply
rt. . . . . .right
rte. . . . . .route
ry. . . . . .railway

S

sc. . . . . .scale, scene, science
sch. . . . . .school
SEC. . . . . .Securities and Exchange
               Commission
sec. . . . . .second(ary), secretary,
               section(s)
sect. . . . . .section
secy. . . . . .secretary
sel. . . . . .select(ed), selection
sen. . . . . .senior
Sen. . . . . .Senate, Senator
ser. . . . . .serial, series
serv. . . . . .service
seq., seqq. . . . . .next, following
sgd. . . . . .signed
sh. . . . . .share
shpt. . . . . .shipment
shtg. . . . . .shortage
sig. . . . . .signal, signature
sld. . . . . .sealed
sp. . . . . .spelling
spec. . . . . .special, specifically
sq. . . . . .square
Sr. . . . . .senior, sister
SS. . . . . .steamship
st. . . . . .street
stet. . . . . .let it stand (printing)
stg., ster. . . . . .sterling
stge. . . . . .storage
stk. . . . . .stock
subj. . . . . .subject
supp., suppl. . . . . . .supplement(ary)
supt. . . . . .superintendent
syn. . . . . .synonymous, synonyms
syst. . . . . .system

T

T., twp. . . . . .Township
TB. . . . . .trial balance
tech. . . . . .technical, technology
tel. . . . . .telegram, telegraph,
               telephone
terr. . . . . .territory
tfr. . . . . .transfer
tk. . . . . .truck
tng. . . . . .training
TO. . . . . .turn over, turnover
tonn. . . . . .tonnage
trans. . . . . .transaction(s), translation,
               transportation
treas. . . . . .treasurer, treasury
TWX. . . . . .teletypewriter exchange

U

ult. . . . . .ultimate(ly)
UN. . . . . .United Nations
univ. . . . . .universal(ly), university
UW. . . . . .underwriter

V

v.	versus, vice, volume
viz.	namely
vol.	volume
VP	Vice-President
vs., v.	against, versus
vv.	vice versa

W

w.	watt
WB.	waybill
whf.	wharf
wk.	week, work
whsle	wholesale
wt.	weight

Y

yd.	yard
yr.	year, younger, your

Periods in Abbreviations. The tendency seems to be to drop the periods from an abbreviation when it is commonly recognized and does not require the period for clarity. For example, NBC, SEC, and FTC are written without periods and without spaces between the letters. The omission of a period in some abbreviations, however, might be confusing. For example, without the periods, in. for "inch" might be mistaken for the preposition; a.m. for "morning" might be confused with the verb form. If, in order to avoid confusion, periods are used with an abbreviation such as a.m., they should also be used in p.m. in order to maintain a consistent style.

Abbreviations with Numbers. The abbreviations *st, d,* and *th* should not follow the day of the month when it is preceded by the name of the month. Correct usage is:

> He was planning to leave on the 21st of August.
> He leaves for London on August 21.
> Mr. Smith went to Los Angeles on the 3d of July.

In enumerations, it is better to write first, second, third, rather than 1st, 2d, 3d.

These abbreviations, *st, d,* and *th,* do not require the use of a period.

Diagonal Lines in Abbreviations. The use of the diagonal signifies the omission of such words as per, of, to, upon. In abbreviated forms including the diagonal, the period is not commonly used, as in B/L. The period is sometimes retained, however, in three- or four-word combinations, as lb./sq. ft.

Plurals of Abbreviations. Most plural forms of abbreviations are formed by adding *s* to the singular form. The singular and the plural forms of some abbreviations, however, are the same.

> (plural) chgs., lbs.; (singular and plural) cwt., deg., ft., in., oz.

Several plural forms of abbreviations are double single letters.

> pp. for pages, JJ. for Justices, ll. for lines.

Plurals of capitalized abbreviations may be formed simply by adding a small *s*. Apostrophe *s* may be added to form the plurals of abbreviations composed of letters (capital and small), signs, and symbols. There is no definite rule, however, that completely governs all of the cases that may arise.

> YMCAs, a.m.s, IOU's, P's, Q's, 6's, f.o.b.'s, O.K.'s, #'s.

Coined Verbs. Often an abbreviation is used as a verb in informal correspondence. To make the necessary change, an apostrophe may be added with *s, d,* or *ing,* to the abbreviation.

> OK'd

Possessives of Abbreviations. Generally, the singular possessive is formed by adding the apostrophe and *s*; as, *Jr's., RR's, Sr's., SOS's.*

The plural possessive is formed by adding an apostrophe to abbreviations whose plural forms end in *s*; as, *Jrs'., Drs'.*

APPENDIX E | Titles, Capitalization, and Numbers

Titles. The use of titles is ruled rather strictly by custom. You must exercise care in using them, especially the titles of the persons to whom you are writing. People are quick to notice and often to resent errors in their titles.

Birthright Titles. Every adult has at least the title of Mr., Miss, or Mrs.

Mr. is used before the name of a man who has no higher title. *Messrs.*, the abbreviation of *Messieurs* (French for *gentlemen*), is the plural of *Mr.*

Mrs. is the title given to married women and usually to widows. A married woman is usually addressed by her husband's name, as *Mrs. John Brown*. A widowed woman may be addressed by her Christian name, such as *Mrs. Helen Brown*, or by her deceased husband's name, such as *Mrs. John Brown*, whichever she prefers. With the names of two or more married women, the title *Mesdames*, or its abbreviation, *Mmes.*, is used, as *Mmes. Clark, Wright*, and *Grant*.

Miss is the correct title for an unmarried girl or woman. If there is doubt as to whether the person is married, it is a good policy to use *Miss* or the abbreviation *Ms. Misses* is the plural of *Miss*, as the *Misses Alice Henderson* and *Dorothy Jones*.

Doctor. *Dr.* is the title of one who holds any one of the various doctors' degrees. It is usually abbreviated. When two doctors are being addressed, the word *Doctors* or the abbreviation *Drs.* may be used. Since there are so many different types of doctors, doctors of medicine and dentistry frequently use the degree letters after their names and no title preceding, as *Frank B. Dana, M.D.* This practice, of course, could be used by anyone possessing a doctor's degree.

Reverend. This title is properly carried by a minister, priest, or rector. The abbreviation *Rev.* is commonly used, although it is considered better usage to write the word in full. Ordinarily when a person with this title is *spoken* of, the word *the* precedes his title and given name or initials. More than one *Reverend* may be addressed as *Reverend Messrs.* or the repetition of the word *Reverend* before each man's name.

Abbreviated Titles Following Personal Names. *Senior* and *Junior*, the distinction between a father and a son of exactly the same name, are written after the name as the abbreviations *Sr.* and *Jr.* The abbreviation is capitalized, followed by a period, and usually separated from the name by a comma. *Second* and *Third*, the distinction between members of the same family or close relatives whose names are the same, are indicated by the abbreviations *2d* and *3d*, or by the Roman numerals *II* or *III*. The former style is now more common. Note that these abbreviations are not followed by a period, but they may be separated from the name by a comma.

The abbreviation *Esq.* is used after a gentleman's name in England. In this country it is rarely used. When it is used, the title *Mr.* is omitted.

Double Titles. A title may be used both before and after a person's name if the two titles have different meanings, but two titles that indicate the same honor or degree should not be used. For example, it is correct to say *Dr. H. C. Samuel, Moderator*, but not *Dr. H. C. Samuel, M.D.*

Titles in Addresses and Salutations. Except for *Mr., Mrs.*, and *Dr.*, all titles used in the addresses and salutations of letters are better written in full. Abbreviations, however, are not uncommon. Whenever you are in doubt, type the title in full. No one will be offended by seeing his title in full.

The correct titles and salutations to be used for federal and state officials, educators, and churchmen are given in Appendix F. Whenever you are unsure of a title or salutation, refer to such a list or an authoritative source.

Capitalization. A good dictionary is an excellent source for determining practices in capitalization that are most acceptable. A person who must refer to the dictionary for the most elementary information of this type, however, consumes much time. An understanding of the purpose for and a knowledge of the principles of capitalization should be a part of the training of an office worker.

One of the purposes of capitalization is to designate the names or titles of specific things, positions, or persons. Overuse of capitalization, however, tends to detract from the effectiveness of the written matter.

The following are the most common rules of capitalization:

1. Every sentence begins with a capital letter.

2. The pronoun *I* and the interjection *O* are always capitalized.

3. The salutation and the complimentary close of a letter begin with capitals.

4. The days of the week, holidays, and the months of the year are capitalized.

5. All important words in the titles of the main agencies of a government begin with capital letters.

6. Direct quotations begin with a capital letter.

Business Titles and Positions. Titles are capitalized when they immediately precede or follow individual names and are directly related to them, or when they refer to specific persons.

> President W. L. Matthews will speak.
> Mr. R. Hubert McGraw, Jr., Vice-President, Investors Corp.
> Mr. Samuel Jones is Executive Secretary and Treasurer of Hammett Co.

Business titles are not capitalized when they do not refer to specific persons.

> Three men have been president of this company.
> A treasurer will be elected at the meeting tomorrow.

Geographic Names. Names of countries, cities, rivers, bays, mountains, islands, commonly recognized names given to regions of countries, and sections of cities are capitalized.

> Ohio River, Pacific Ocean, Union County, Harlem, the Great Plains, the Mississippi Valley.

A geographic term such as *river, ocean, county, city,* and *street* that is not a part of the name but is used before the name, or a geographic term that is used in the plural, should not be capitalized.

> the river Danube
> county of Hamilton
> the city of San Diego
> the Atlantic and the Pacific oceans
> at the corner of Grant and Lee streets

Points of the compass designating specific geographic sections of the country are capitalized.

> the South, the Midwest, the Northwest

The points of the compass that merely indicate direction are not capitalized.

> South Dakota is south of North Dakota.
> The wind is coming from the west.

A noun that refers to the inhabitants of a particular part of the country is capitalized.

> Westerners, a Southerner, a New Englander

Proper names denoting political divisions are always capitalized.

> British Empire, Ward 13, Platt Township, the Papal States

Words before Figures. With the exception of *page, line,* and *verse,* words used in connection with figures in typewritten references are usually capitalized. It is important that one rule be followed consistently. If the word *figure* is capitalized when followed by a number in one place, it should be capitalized in all other places in the material.

> Chapter XV   Division 3
> Figure 8   page iii

Individual Names. Capitalize all names of individuals, except some surname prefixes. *Von, du, van,* or *de,* as a part of a surname might not be capitalized, depending upon how the person uses it himself, unless it begins a sentence or stands alone within a sentence (that is, is not preceded by a given name or title).

Hyphened Words. In general, there are three rules that govern the capitalization of the parts of a hyphened word.

1. If both parts of a hyphened word would ordinarily be capitalized when written alone, then both parts should be capitalized in the hyphened word.

> Senate-House debate
> Spanish-American War

2. In a heading or title, it is permissible to capitalize the parts of a compound word to conform to a general style.

> Forty-Second Street
> Mid-January Sales

3. In straight text material, the manner in which a word is used determines the part of a compound word that should be capitalized.

> Thirty-first Street   anti-Nazi
> mid-January   pro-British
> Treasurer-elect   French-speaking
> ex-President   pre-Pueblo

Headings and Titles of Articles and Reports. Only the first word and important words in headings or titles — nouns, pronouns, verbs, adverbs, and adjectives — are capitalized. Short, unimportant words are not capitalized. Examples of such words are the conjunctions *and*, *but*, and *or*; the articles *a*, *an*, and *the;* and the prepositions *of*, *in*, *to*, and *but*. If the word needs to be stressed, however, it may be capitalized. Frequently, long prepositions such as *between*, *after*, *before*, and *among* are capitalized.

Numbers. Numbers can be written as figures or as words. Although figures are used almost exclusively in business forms, both figures and words are used in letters and other types of transcripts that are written in sentence and paragraph form. If there are two or more ways in which an amount can be expressed, it is usually written in the way that requires the fewest words. A number such as 1,300 is written as *thirteen hundred* rather than *one thousand three hundred*. The following rules specify the proper usage in writing numbers.

Numbers at the Beginning of a Sentence. A number that begins a sentence should be spelled out, even though other numbers are expressed in figures in the same sentence. It is wise, therefore, to avoid beginning a sentence with a large number that is cumbersome in words.

Amounts of Money. Amounts of money, except in legal documents, should be written in figures. Amounts less than one dollar are written in figures with the word *cents* following. In writing even sums of money, the decimal and ciphers are omitted.

> We enclose our check for $21.75.
> He paid 22 cents for the paper.
> He will pay $125 for the painting.

Round Numbers. Round numbers are spelled out, unless such numbers are used with others that cannot be expressed conveniently in words.

> We have fifty employees.
> We have 50 salesmen in our group of 295 employees.

Dates. Except in formal or legal writing, the day of the month and the year are usually written in figures. When a date appears in the body of a letter, the year is customarily omitted if it is the same as that which appears in the date line. It is unnecessary to use *st*, *d*, or *th* in dates, unless the day is written before or is separated from the month.

> the 3d of June
> in July, either the 3d or 4th

Streets. It is considered good form to use words for the names of streets that are numbers that are ten or less; figures should be used for numbers above ten. When the name of a street is a number that is written in figures, it is separated from the number of the building by a dash. If the street name is preceded by one of the words *South*, *North*, *East*, or *West*, that word should not be abbreviated.

> Tenth Street   Fifth Avenue
> 72 — 125 Street   72 Fifth Avenue
> 19 West 115 Street 173 Street
> 22 West 110 Street 1 West 12 Street

Time of day. The abbreviations *p.m.* and *a.m.* may be written in capital or small letters but should be used only with figures. The hour is spelled in full when *o'clock* is used.

> School starts at 8:30 a.m.
> He will leave the office at four o'clock.
> 12 midnight is written 12 p.m. or 12 P.M.
> 12 noon is written 12N. (12M, while correct for 12 noon, can be mistaken for 12 midnight.)

Measurements. Practically all measurements are written in figures.

Fractions and Decimals. Common fractions appearing alone are spelled out in ordinary reading matter. Mixed numbers are written as figures. Decimals are always expressed in figures.

Miscellaneous Usage. Sessions of Congress and the identifying numbers of various military bodies, political divisions, and dynasties are always written in words.

> the Thirty-sixth Congress
> Thirteenth Ward   Sixteenth Infantry

The result of a ballot is written in figures.

> The count was 34 in favor of the motion, 36 against it.

Page, chapter, section, and footnote numbers are always written in figures.

> pp. 45–67   Section 7
> [2]Hawley, J.   Chapter 9

When two numbers immediately follow each other, it is better that the smaller one be spelled out and the larger one be expressed in figures.

> 125 two-cent stamps
> Five 100-dollar bills

Unrelated groups of figures that come together should be separated by commas. Hundreds should be divided from thousands by a comma except in dates, policy numbers, street numbers, telephone numbers, and the like.

> In 1966, 417,296 gallons were sold.

APPENDIX F

Special Forms of Address, Salutations, and Complimentary Closings

This appendix gives the correct forms of address with appropriate salutations and complimentary closings for the following special groups:

United States Government officials
Diplomatic representatives
State and local government officials
Members of the clergy
School officials
Private citizens

The correct forms of address for envelopes and letters are shown at the left. Open punctuation is used in addresses. The appropriate salutations and complimentary closings are given in the order of decreasing formality.

United States Government Officials

Address	Salutation	Complimentary Closing

President of the United States

The President The White House Washington, D.C. 20500	Sir: Mr. President: Dear Mr. President: My dear President Johnson:	Respectfully yours, Very truly yours,
The Honorable Lyndon B. Johnson President of the United States The White House Washington, D.C. 20500		

Vice President of the United States

The Vice President United States Senate Washington, D.C. 20510	Sir: My dear Sir: Dear Sir: Mr. Vice President: My dear Mr. Vice President:	Respectfully yours, Very truly yours, Sincerely yours,
The Honorable Hubert H. Humphrey The Vice President of the United States Washington, D.C. 20510		

Chief Justice of the United States

The Chief Justice The Supreme Court Washington, D.C. 20543	Sir: Mr. Chief Justice: Dear Mr. Chief Justice:	Respectfully yours, Very truly yours, Sincerely yours,
The Honorable Earl Warren Chief Justice of the Supreme Court of the United States Washington, D.C. 20543		

Associate Justice of the Supreme Court

Mr. Justice Potter Stewart
The Supreme Court of the United States
Washington, D.C. 20543

The Honorable Potter Stewart
Associate Justice of the Supreme Court
Washington, D.C. 20543

Sir:
Mr. Justice:
My dear Mr. Justice:
My dear Justice Stewart:
Dear Justice Stewart:

Very truly yours,
Sincerely yours,

Speaker of the House

The Speaker of the
   House of Representatives
Washington, D.C. 20515

The Honorable John W. McCormack
Speaker of the House of Representatives
Washington, D.C. 20515

Sir:
My dear Sir:
Dear Sir:
Mr. Speaker:
My dear Mr. Speaker:
Dear Mr. Speaker:
My dear Mr. McCormack:
Dear Mr. McCormack:

Very truly yours,
Sincerely yours,

Member of the Cabinet

The Secretary of State
Washington, D.C. 20520

The Honorable Dean Rusk
Secretary of State
Washington, D.C. 20520

Sir:
My dear Sir:
Dear Sir:
My dear Mr. Secretary:
Dear Mr. Secretary:

Very truly yours,
Sincerely yours,

Senator (male)

The Honorable Frank J. Lausche
The United States Senate
Washington, D.C. 20510

Senator Frank J. Lausche
The United States Senate
Washington, D.C. 20510

Sir:
My dear Sir:
Dear Sir:
My dear Mr. Senator:
My dear Senator:
Dear Senator:
My dear Senator Lausche:
Dear Senator Lausche:

Very truly yours,
Sincerely yours,

Senator (female)

The Honorable Margaret Chase Smith
The United States Senate
Washington, D.C. 20510

Senator Margaret Chase Smith
The United States Senate
Washington, D.C. 20510

Madam:
My dear Senator Smith:
Dear Madam:
My dear Madam Senator:
Dear Mrs. Smith:

Very truly yours,
Sincerely yours,

Representative (male)

The Honorable Paul A. Fino
The House of Representatives
Washington, D.C. 20515

Representative Paul A. Fino
The House of Representatives
Washington, D.C. 20515

Sir:
My dear Sir:
Dear Sir:
My dear Representative Fino:
My dear Congressman:
Dear Mr. Fino:

Very truly yours,
Sincerely yours,

Representative (female)

The Honorable Florence P. Dwyer
The House of Representatives
Washington, D.C. 20515

Representative Florence P. Dwyer
The House of Representatives
Washington, D.C. 20515

Madam:
My dear Mrs. Dwyer:
Dear Madam:
Dear Representative Dwyer:
Dear Mrs. Dwyer:

Very truly yours,
Sincerely yours,

Head of a Government Bureau

The Honorable Harold Howe II
Commissioner of Education
Department of Health, Education,
   and Welfare
Washington, D.C.   20201

Sir:
My dear Sir:
Dear Sir:
My dear Mr. Commissioner:
My dear Mr. Howe:
Dear Mr. Howe:

Very truly yours,
Sincerely yours,

Diplomatic Representatives

American Ambassador

The Honorable Charles E. Bohlen
American Ambassador
Paris, France

Sir:
My dear Mr. Ambassador:
Dear Mr. Ambassador:

Very truly yours,
Sincerely yours,

American Minister

The Honorable William A. Crawford
American Minister
Bucharest, Rumania

Sir:
My dear Mr. Minister:
Dear Mr. Minister:

Very truly yours,
Sincerely yours,

American Consul General

Charles Gilbert, Esquire
American Consul General
United States Embassy
London
United Kingdom

Sir:
My dear Mr. Gilbert:
Dear Mr. Gilbert:

Very truly yours,
Sincerely yours,

Secretary General of the United Nations

His Excellency U Thant
Secretary General of the United Nations
New York, New York   10017

Excellency:
My dear Mr. Secretary General:
Dear Mr. Secretary General:

Very truly yours,
Sincerely yours,

United States Representative to the United Nations

The Honorable Arthur J. Goldberg
United States Representative
   to the United Nations
New York, New York   10017

Sir:
My dear Mr. Goldberg:
Dear Mr. Goldberg:

Very truly yours,
Sincerely yours,

State and Local Government Officials

Governor

His Excellency
the Governor of New York
The Executive Chamber, Capitol
Albany, New York   12224

The Honorable Nelson A. Rockefeller
Governor of New York
Albany, New York   12224

Sir:
My dear Sir:
Dear Sir:
My dear Governor Rockefeller:
Dear Governor Rockefeller:
Dear Governor:

Respectfully yours,
Very truly yours,
Sincerely yours,

Attorney General

The Honorable Harold M. Mulvey
Attorney General of Connecticut
State Capitol
Hartford, Connecticut   06115

Sir:
My dear Mr. Attorney General:
Dear Mr. Mulvey:

Very truly yours,
Sincerely yours,

State Senator

The Honorable Nelson F. Stamler
State Capitol Building
Trenton, New Jersey 08625

Senator Nelson F. Stamler
State Capitol Building
Trenton, New Jersey 08625

Sir:
My dear Sir:
Dear Sir:
My dear Mr. Senator:
Dear Senator:
My dear Senator Stamler:
Dear Senator Stamler:

Very truly yours,
Sincerely yours,

State Representative

The Honorable Kenneth L. Wilson
The State Assembly
Albany, New York 12224

Representative Kenneth L. Wilson
The State Assembly
Albany, New York 12224

Sir:
My dear Sir:
My dear Representative Wilson:
My dear Mr. Wilson:
Dear Mr. Wilson:

Very truly yours,
Sincerely yours,

Mayor

The Honorable Richard J. Daley
Mayor of the City of Chicago
City Hall
Chicago, Illinois 60602

The Mayor of the City of Chicago
City Hall
Chicago, Illinois 60602

Sir:
My dear Sir:
My dear Mr. Mayor:
Dear Mr. Mayor:
My dear Mayor Daley:
Dear Mayor Daley:

Very truly yours,
Sincerely yours,

Members of the Clergy

Bishop (Protestant Episcopal)

The Right Reverend Horace W. B. Donegan
Bishop of New York
The Bishop's House
Cathedral Heights
New York, New York 10025

Right Reverend and dear Sir:
My dear Bishop Donegan:
Dear Bishop Donegan:

Respectfully yours,
Sincerely yours,
Yours faithfully,

Bishop (Methodist Episcopal)

The Reverend Hazen G. Werner
Bishop of the Ohio Annual Conference
12 North Third Street
Columbus, Ohio 43215

Reverend Sir:
Dear Sir:
My dear Bishop Werner:
Dear Bishop Werner:

Respectfully yours,
Sincerely yours,
Yours faithfully,

Clergyman (Protestant)

The Reverend John W. Meers, D.D.
1841 Euclid Avenue
Cleveland, Ohio 44115

Reverend Sir:
My dear Sir:
Dear Sir:
My dear Dr. Meers:
Dear Dr. Meers:

Respectfully yours,
Sincerely yours,
Yours faithfully,

Pope (Roman Catholic)

His Holiness
Pope Paul VI
Vatican City
Rome, Italy

Your Holiness:
Most Holy Father:

Respectfully yours,
Yours faithfully,

Cardinal (Roman Catholic)

His Eminence, Francis Cardinal Spellman
Archbishop of New York
452 Madison Avenue
New York, New York 10022

Your Eminence:
Dear Cardinal Spellman:

Respectfully yours,
Sincerely yours,
Yours faithfully,

Archbishop and Bishop (Roman Catholic)

The Most Reverend Joseph Bernard Brunini
Auxiliary Bishop of Natchez-Jackson
123 North West Street
Jackson, Mississippi 39201

Your Excellency:
Dear Bishop Brunini:

Respectfully yours,
Sincerely yours,
Yours faithfully,

Monsignor (Roman Catholic)

The Right Reverend William T. Caldwell
Immaculate Heart of Mary Church
8 Carman Road
Scarsdale, New York 10585

Right Reverend and
  dear Monsignor:
Dear Monsignor Caldwell:

Respectfully yours,
Sincerely yours,
Yours faithfully,

Priest (Roman Catholic)

The Reverend Raymond J. O'Sullivan
St. John's Church
1999 Shepard Road
St. Paul, Minnesota 55116

Reverend and dear Sir:
Dear Father O'Sullivan:

Respectfully yours,
Sincerely yours,
Yours faithfully,

Brother (Roman Catholic)

Brother Lucius, O.F.M.
St. Francis Seminary
Louisville, Kentucky 40204

Dear Brother:
Dear Brother Lucius:

Respectfully yours,
Sincerely yours,
Yours faithfully,

Superior of Sister Order (Roman Catholic)

Reverend Mother Mary Eunice
Maryknoll Sisters
Maryknoll, New York 10545

Reverend Mother:
Dear Reverend Mother:

Respectfully yours,
Sincerely yours,
Yours faithfully,

Sister (Roman Catholic)

Sister Marie Judith, O.P.
St. Thomas Aquinas High School
2801 South West 12 Street
Fort Lauderdale, Florida 33312

Dear Sister:
Dear Sister Marie Judith:

Respectfully yours,
Sincerely yours,
Yours faithfully,

Rabbi (Jewish Faith)

The Rabbi of Congregation Shaaray Tefila
160 West 82 Street
New York, New York 10024

Sir:
My dear Dr. Bamberger:
My dear Rabbi:
My dear Rabbi Bamberger:

Respectfully yours,
Sincerely yours,
Yours faithfully,

School Officials

President of a University or College

Dr. Mason W. Gross
President, Rutgers University
New Brunswick, New Jersey 08903

Dear Sir:
Dear President Gross:
Dear Dr. Gross:

Very truly yours,
Sincerely yours,

Dean of a College (male)

Dr. John C. Payne
Dean, School of Education
New York University
Washington Square East
New York, New York 10003

Dear Sir:
Dear Dean Payne:
Dear Dr. Payne:

Very truly yours,
Sincerely yours,

Dean of a College (female)

Dr. Kathryn L. Hopwood
Dean of Students
Hunter College
695 Park Avenue
New York, New York 10021

Dear Madam:
My dear Dean Hopwood:
Dear Dean Hopwood:

Very truly yours,
Sincerely yours,

Professor of a College or University

Dr. T. James Crawford
Professor of Business Administration
Indiana University
Bloomington, Indiana 47403

Dear Sir:
Dear Professor Crawford:
Dear Dr. Crawford:

Very truly yours,
Sincerely yours,

Superintendent of Schools

Superintendent Joseph F. Donovan
Tupper Lake Central Schools
Tupper Lake, New York 12986

Dear Sir:
Dear Mr. Donovan:

Very truly yours,
Sincerely yours,

Principal of a School

Mr. Spencer B. Ames, Principal
Alexander Hamilton High School
Elizabeth, New Jersey 07202

Dear Sir:
Dear Mr. Ames:

Very truly yours,
Sincerely yours,

Private Citizens

One Individual

(Use Mr. when the given name may be that of a man or woman.)
Mr. Carroll Barker
75 South Water Street
Chicago, Illinois 60601

Dear Mr. Barker:

Very truly yours,
Sincerely yours,

One Individual

(Use Miss rather than Mrs., if there is uncertainty about a woman's marital status.)
Miss Virginia L. Morgan
172 State Street
Seaford, New York 11783

Dear Miss Morgan:

Very truly yours,
Sincerely yours,

Two Individuals

Mrs. Thomas E. Brown
Miss Mabel Hastings
70 Margaret Street
Plattsburgh, New York 12901

Dear Mrs. Brown and
Miss Hastings:

Very truly yours,
Sincerely yours,

Three Individuals (male)

Messrs Baker, Weeks, and Smith
One Wall Street
New York, New York 10005

Gentlemen:

Very truly yours,
Sincerely yours,

Three Individuals (female)

(Mesdames is used when addressing two or more married and single women.)

Mesdames Collins, Nolan, and Webster
77 Coach Lane
Newburgh, New York 12552

Mesdames:

Very truly yours,
Sincerely yours,

Physician

Herman G. Hofmann, M.D.
274 Main Street
Springfield, Massachusetts 01105

Dear Dr. Hofmann:

Very truly yours,
Sincerely yours,

Attorney

Mr. Marshall F. Horton
Attorney at Law
60 East 42 Street
New York, New York 10017

Dear Mr. Horton:

Very truly yours,
Sincerely yours,

APPENDIX G | Reference Books

For its clerical and secretarial employees, an office should have at least three reference books available for immediate use: a desk-size dictionary, a secretarial or clerical handbook, and a telephone directory.

Dictionaries. You will find the dictionary indispensable in verifying the spelling, syllabification, and proper usage of words as you prepare and type business papers. It contains not only the realistic pronunciation and derivation of words but also the meanings of foreign expressions and standard abbreviations, the names of places and notable people, and other essential information.

Four of the acceptable desk dictionaries with recent additions to the vocabulary of the language are:

The American College Dictionary. New York: Random House, 1959.

Funk & Wagnalls College Standard Dictionary, 3d ed. New York: Wilfred Funk, Inc., 1965.

Webster's New Collegiate Dictionary, 7th ed. Springfield, Mass.: G. & C. Merriam Company, 1963.

Websters New World Dictionary of the American Language. College Edition. Cleveland, Ohio: The World Publishing Company, 1960.

If a desk-size dictionary is not readily available, you should invest in a paperback pocket-size one. The *Merriam-Webster Pocket Dictionary* is recommended as a transcription tool because it contains definitions for 25,000 words. In addition, it includes guides to correct spelling and pronunciation; lists of synonyms and antonyms; commonly used abbreviations, foreign words and phrases; and population figures for the United States and Canada.

Secretarial Handbooks. The secretary's handbook is a compact, thoroughly indexed reference book encompassing a wide range of secretarial practices and procedures. It is an authoritative source of information on such topics as proper grammatical construction, plural and possessive forms, pronunciation and punctuation, and the correct writing of numbers in letters and reports. It can be of great help in deciding, for example, where to place the *subject line* in a business letter, whether to place the apostrophe before or after the letter *s* in *womens salaries*, and when to capitalize direction in geographic areas such as on the *East Coast* or in *western Montana*.

Some of the outstanding handbooks are:

Beamer, Esther Kihn, J Marshall Hanna, and Estelle L. Popham. *Effective Secretarial Practices*, 4th ed. Cincinnati: South-Western Publishing Company, 1962.

Doris, Lillian, and Besse May Miller. *Complete Secretary's Handbook*, 7th ed. Englewood Cliffs, N.J.: Prentice-Hall, Inc., 1960.

Hutchinson, Lois Irene. *Standard Handbook for Secretaries*, 7th ed. McGraw-Hill Book Company, Inc., 1956.

Larsen, Lenna A., and Apollonia M. Koebele. *Reference Manual for Office Employees*, 4th ed. Cincinnati: South-Western Publishing Company, 1959.

Telephone Directories. The most frequently consulted reference book in any office is the telephone directory. It is used not only to find the telephone number of listed subscribers but also to verify the spelling of their names and the correctness of their addresses. The Yellow Pages, or classified section of a telephone directory, may also serve as a buyer's guide because the names, addresses, and telephone numbers of business subscribers are listed under the appropriate product or service.

A small booklet supplied by the telephone company, designed for use as a personal telephone directory, can save considerable telephoning time. On alphabetically arranged pages it provides spaces for writing the names, addresses, area codes, and telephone numbers of frequently called local and out-of-town telephones.

Writing References

The content and format of all types of business communications can be improved if appropriate reference books are consulted as they are written, revised, and edited for publication.

Business Communications. Two recommended reference books for the writing of business letters and other communications are:

Aurner, Robert R., and Paul S. Burtness. *Effective English for Business*, 5th ed. Cincinnati: South-Western Publishing Company, 1962.

Mayo, Lucy Graves. *Communications Handbook for Secretaries*. New York: McGraw-Hill Book Company, Inc., 1958.

Business Reports. Manuals are available to serve as references on how to present papers and reports in written form. Three outstanding manuals are:

Keithley, Erwin M. *A Manual of Style for the Preparation of Papers and Reports*. Cincinnati: South-Western Publishing Company, 1959.

A Manual of Style, 11th ed. Chicago: The University of Chicago Press, 1949.

United States Government Printing Office Style Manual. Washington, D.C.: Superintendent of Documents, 1959.

Business Speeches. A wide variety of reference books may be consulted to provide the prospective speaker or master of ceremonies at a business function with words, phrases, ideas, and quotations that will enhance and enliven his presentation. They include:

Roget's International Thesaurus of Words and Phrases, 3d ed. New York: Thomas Y. Crowell Company, 1962.

Fernald, James C. *Funk & Wagnalls Standard Handbook of Synonyms, Antonyms, and Prepositions*. New York: Wilfred Funk, Inc., 1947.

Webster's Dictionary of Synonyms. Springfield, Massachusetts: G. & C. Merriam Company, 1942.

Bartlett's Familiar Quotations, 13th ed. Boston: Little, Brown and Company, 1955.

Stevenson's Home Book of Proverbs, Maxims and Familiar Phrases. New York: The Macmillan Company, 1948.

Specific References

Reference books in all fields from many different sources, ranging from the *American Library Association Catalog* to the *Zweng Aviation Dictionary*, are listed and annotated in a single volume, the *Guide to Reference Books*. To determine what, if any, reference books are available on a specific subject, first consult this guide:

Winchell, Constance M. *Guide to Reference Books*, 7th ed. Chicago: American Library Association, 1951.

Another invaluable guide for businessmen, office workers, teachers, and writers containing over 3,900 standard references is *How and Where to Look It Up*. It tells how to get information, where to find it, and how to use and evaluate it. This reference book is:

Murphy, Robert W. *How and Where to Look It Up*. New York: McGraw-Hill Book Company, 1958.

Specific information on business and related subjects may be obtained from many reference books. The information includes statistics on all major industries, directories of all large corporations, biographies of notable people, and factual information on a wide variety of business topics. The examples that follow are arranged alphabetically by subjects.

Accounting. The standard handbook in which leading authorities cover the major divisions of accounting is:

Accountants' Handbook, 4th ed. New York: Ronald Press, 1956.

Almanacs. Published annually, there are three widely used and comprehensive American almanacs of miscellaneous information. They are:

World Almanac and Book of Facts. New York: Newspaper Enterprise Association.
Information Please. New York: Simon and Schuster, Inc.
Reader's Digest Almanac. Pleasantville, New York: Reader's Digest Association, Inc.

Banks. The Bankers Blue Book, one of the leading bank directories published semiannually with monthly supplements, is:

Rand McNally Bankers Directory. Chicago: Rand McNally & Company.

Biographical Information. Revised and reissued every two years, the best-known and generally the most useful biographical dictionary, with full biographical sketches of approximately 60,000 notable American men and women, is:

Who's Who in America. Chicago: The A. N. Marquis Company.

Books. A complete list of all available books, new and old, including hardcovers, paperbacks, trade books, textbooks, adult books, and juvenile books is published annually with full ordering information in:

Books in Print, U.S.A. New York: R. R. Bowker Company.

A world list of books in the English language is published annually with monthly supplements in the following:

Cumulative Book Index. New York: The H. W. Wilson Company.

Business Libraries. A reference book that should be consulted to be sure that the business library is used efficiently and that no available source of business information has been overlooked is:

Johnson, H. Webster. *How to Use the Business Library with Sources of Business Information*, 3d ed. Cincinnati: South-Western Publishing Company, 1964.

City Directories. City directories are compiled, published, and sold commercially for most of the cities of the United States and Canada. Each directory contains the names, the addresses, and the occupations of all individuals residing in a community. It usually contains a street directory and a map of the city.

City Officials. A directory of city officials is usually published annually for each large city. The *City of New York Official Directory*, for example, lists all branches of the city government, the courts, and the state and federal government agencies with offices in New York. It contains an index of the names of all executives listed in the directory. It may be obtained by writing for:

> *The City of New York Official Directory.* Room 2213 Municipal Building, New York, New York 10007.

Colleges. A widely used college guide gives the entrance requirements, accreditation, and other factual information about more than 2,800 American colleges and universities. It also contains related information about junior colleges, community colleges, and technical institutes. The guide is:

> Lovejoy, Clarence I. *Lovejoy's College Guide,* 7th ed. New York: Simon and Schuster, 1964.

Congress. A directory containing the names, addresses, and brief biographies of all congressmen and chief executives of the federal government is issued annually. In it are also listed the members of all congressional committees, the executives of all departments and agencies of the federal government, and all diplomatic representatives. It may be obtained by writing for the:

> *Congressional Directory.* Superintendent of Documents, U.S. Government Printing Office. Washington, D.C. 20402.

Corporations. A complete national directory of executive personnel in approximately 28,000 companies engaged in all branches of business and industry is published in *Poor's Register of Corporations, Directors, and Executives.* Each company listing includes: the names and addresses of all officers, directors, and other executive personnel; the number of employees and the approximate annual sales; and all products and services of the company in the order of their importance.

The register is sold commercially and is not available in most public and school libraries. It may be obtained by writing for:

> *Poor's Register of Corporations, Directors, and Executives.* Standard & Poor's Corporation. New York, New York 10014.

Credit Ratings. Credit ratings and credit reports are distributed for retail, wholesale, and manufacturing companies. The reports are not available to the general public. They may be obtained by annual subscriptions from:

> *Dun & Bradstreet Ratings and Reports.* Dun & Bradstreet, Inc., New York, New York 10007.

Encyclopedias. The value of an encyclopedia is that it provides authoritative information on a great number of subjects in concise and convenient form. Because no other single reference book can offer so extensive a survey of universal knowledge, it is often wise to start an inquiry with an encyclopedia. Two outstanding encyclopedias are:

> *The Encyclopaedia Britannica.* (24 volumes). Chicago: Encyclopaedia Britannica, Inc., 1965.
> *The Encyclopedia Americana.* (30 volumes). New York: Encyclopedia Americana Corporation, 1964.

A compact single-volume general encyclopedia available for instant reference with concise articles on places, persons, and subjects is published in hardcover and paperback editions:

> *Columbia Encyclopedia,* 3d ed. New York: Columbia University Press, 1963.

Etiquette. Business and social etiquette are covered in a number of books on etiquette, but the two most prominent authors are:

> Post, Emily Price. *Etiquette,* 10th ed. New York: Funk & Wagnalls Company, 1960.
> *Amy Vanderbilt's Complete Book of Etiquette,* Rev. ed. Garden City, New York: Doubleday & Company, Inc., 1963.

Geographical Information. Atlases and gazetteers are reference sources for all kinds of geographical information. An atlas is a book of maps with supporting geographical statistics and population figures for each area. Such a book may be an atlas of the world, of a country, of a state, of a county, or of a city. Two of the atlases frequently used in business offices are:

Rand McNally Cosmopolitan World Atlas. Chicago: Rand McNally & Company, 1962.
Hammond Medallion World Atlas, New Perspective Edition. Maplewood, N. J.: Hammond, Inc., 1966.

A gazetteer, on the other hand, is a geographical dictionary giving, in alphabetic order, the names and descriptions of towns, villages, cities, rivers, mountains, and countries with pronunciations and related historical and geographical information. One of the most comprehensive gazetteers with information about all of the world's important places and all of the incorporated cities, towns, and villages in the United States and Canada with populations of 1,500 or more is:

Webster's Geographical Dictionary, Rev. ed. Springfield, Mass.: G. & C. Merriam Company, 1960.

Law. A three-volume law directory, published annually with a complete list of the lawyers in the United States and Canada given in volumes I and II and digests of the laws of the states in the United States and the provinces of Canada in Volume III is:

Martindale-Hubbell Law Directory. Summit, N. J.: Martindale-Hubbell, Inc.

Magazine Articles. Articles in a selected number of periodicals are indexed according to author, title, and subject and listed in an annual publication with monthly supplements which is available in all public libraries. It is:

Reader's Guide to Periodical Literature. New York: The H. W. Wilson Company.

Manufacturers. A list of almost all American manufacturers with a classification of their products, trade names, and brands is published annually as follows:

Thomas' Register of American Manufacturers. (4 volumes). New York: Thomas Publishing Company.

Medicine. A register of legally qualified physicians of the United States and Canada with related medical biographies and a list of approved medical schools and hospitals is published every two years as follows:

American Medical Directory. Chicago: American Medical Association.

Newspaper Articles. All items and reports printed in *The New York Times* are briefly summarized, indexed, and cross-referenced by subject and name. They are listed alphabetically with the date, page, and column of publication in the following:

New York Times Index. New York: The New York Times Company.

Postal Information. A complete listing of the postal services in the United States with detailed regulations and procedures covering these services, together with up-to-date postal rates, is given in the following publication:

Postal Manual. Superintendent of Documents, United States Government Printing Office. Washington, D.C. 20402.

Shipping Information. Shipments are frequently made by means other than parcel post — by rail, truck, bus, ship, and more frequently, by air express. A complete shipper's guide containing rates and routings for parcel post, express, and freight shipments is published in separate editions for different parts of the country. This guide also includes information concerning Canadian and foreign parcel post. It is:

Leonard's Guide. New York: G. R. Leonard & Company, Inc.

A complete list of all post offices, railroad stations, shipping lines, and freight receiving stations is published in:

Bullinger's Postal Shipper's Guide for the United States, Canada, and Newfoundland. Bullinger's Guides, Inc., Westwood, New Jersey.

Information about air express, the newest and swiftest method of door-to-door transportation service, may be obtained by referring to:

Official Air Express Guide. Air Express Division of REA Express, New York.

Travel Information. Travel information is available in many forms of guide books, bulletins, and directories.

Guides. Ratings for approximately 20,000 accommodations and restaurants in the United States are published in the paperback editions of the *Mobil Travel Guides* by Simon and Schuster, Inc., New York. The guides also list the outstanding historical, educational, and scenic points of interest throughout the country. Regional guide books are revised and reprinted annually for: California and the West; the Great Lakes Area; the Middle Atlantic States; the Northwest and Great Plains States; the Northeastern States; the Southeastern States; and the Southwest and South Central Area.

Bulletins. Travel bulletins may be obtained from all travel agencies. Two of the better known agencies with offices in all of the principal cities of the world are *Thomas Cook & Son* and the *American Express Company.*

Directories. Travelers are almost as interested in their accommodations as they are in their means of transportation. The most frequently consulted directory which annually lists hotels and motels approved by the American Hotel Association with their respective rates, accommodations, and plans of operation is:

Hotel & Motel Red Book. New York: American Hotel Association Directory Corporation.

Overseas Guides. A recent innovation is *The Businessman's Guide to Europe*, available at most overseas airlines offices.

One of the most interesting and beneficial businessman's guides for European travel has been written by Paul B. Finney with the assistance of the staff of *Business Week*. It is a handbook of facts, tips, and ideas to help the businessman get around Europe smoothly and efficiently. It contains pertinent facts about the European common market, the leading trade fairs, and the currencies of the different countries. Legitimate travel tax deductions, free ports for buying gifts, and other worthwhile information are also given. The guide provides the traveler with an informative appraisal of golf courses, restaurants, and hotels. It is:

Finney, Paul B. *The Businessman's Guide to Europe.* New York: McGraw-Hill Book Company, 1965.

INDEX